Louis Johnson and the Arming of America

LOUIS JOHNSON
AND THE
ARMING OF AMERICA

The Roosevelt and Truman Years

Keith D. McFarland and David L. Roll

Indiana University Press / *Bloomington and Indianapolis*

This book is a publication of

Indiana University Press
601 North Morton Street
Bloomington, IN 47404-3797 USA

http://iupress.indiana.edu

Telephone orders 800-842-6796
Fax orders 812-855-7931
Orders by e-mail iuporder@indiana.edu

The paper used in this publication meets the minimum requirements of American National Standard for Information Sciences—Permanence of Paper for Printed Library Materials, ANSI Z39.48-1984.

Manufactured in the United States of America

Library of Congress Cataloging-in-Publication Data

McFarland, Keith D., date–
Louis Johnson and the arming of America : the Roosevelt and Truman
years / Keith D. McFarland and David L. Roll.
p. cm.
Includes bibliographical references (p.   ) and index.
ISBN 978-0-253-34626-1 (cloth : alk. paper)
1. Johnson, Louis Arthur, 1891-1966. 2. Cabinet officers—United States—Biography.
3. United States. Dept. of Defense—Biography. 4. Roosevelt, Franklin D. (Franklin
Delano), 1882-1945. 5. Truman, Harry S., 1884-1972. 6. United States—Politics and
government—1933-1945. 7. United States—Politics and government—1945-1953.
8. United States—Military policy. 9. United States—Defenses—History—20th century. I. Roll, David L. 1940- II. Title.
E748.J738M38 2005
355'.0092—dc22

2005001853

3 4 5 6 7   13 12 11 10 09 08

To Carolyn and Dianna

KEITH D. MCFARLAND

To Nancy, together wing to wing; and to the traditions of
excellence and public service that define Steptoe & Johnson

DAVID L. ROLL

CONTENTS

Acknowledgments   ix

Introduction   1

1. Bedford Blood   4
2. Foot in the Door   11
3. Like Feuding Schoolboys   30
4. "Basic Shift in Mobilization Planning"   47
5. Understanding FDR   57
6. Surviving FDR   75
7. "But You Promised Me"   91
8. Personal Representative of the President   111
9. Long Shot Pays Off   133
10. Inside the Pentagon   153
11. Revolt of the Admirals   168
12. "Like a Meatchopper on Roundsteak"   188
13. "My God, the Russians Have the Bomb"   205
14. Entangling Alliance   234
15. "Till the Dust Settles"   250
16. Last Week in June   275
17. "Give Me Two American Divisions and I Can Hold Korea"   303
18. Means of Descent   320

19. "Lou, I've Got to Ask You to Quit"   339
20. "Lest Darkness Come"   352
Conclusion   359

Notes   365
Select Bibliography   427
Index   437

ACKNOWLEDGMENTS

Our FIRST DEBT is to serendipity—the unexpected confluence of individuals and events which made this book possible. Keith McFarland began this project nearly thirty years ago, early in his career as a history faculty member. With two books completed and this project well under way, Keith got sidetracked into university administration, beginning as an assistant dean and eventually becoming president of Texas A&M University-Commerce. As a result, the research notes and initial drafts for this book languished in file drawers for twenty years. Meanwhile, Dave Roll, an antitrust partner with the law firm of Steptoe & Johnson in Washington, D.C., who knew nothing of Keith McFarland and his work but had learned a good deal about Louis Johnson, was beginning his research for a history of Johnson and the law firm he co-founded (Dave's law firm, Steptoe & Johnson). One day in 2001, Dave was talking to Judge Frank Maxwell in Clarksburg, West Virginia, who recalled that "some professor" had been in Clarksburg many years ago and was working on a biography of Louis Johnson. Using the Internet, Dave located Keith and proposed that they join forces to make this study a reality. Keith is convinced that if Dave had not taken that initiative, this book would have never seen the light of day, and he is grateful that Dave rescued the manuscript and turned it into a published work. On his part, Dave will be forever indebted to Keith for allowing him the pure pleasure of researching and writing about the fascinating and controversial career of Louis Johnson and the two great presidents he served.

Together, we wish to acknowledge with gratitude a number of individuals who early in this project provided the encouragement and support to do the research. Keith's department heads, Frank Jackson and John Carrier (who would later be president of Concord College, West Virginia), gave him the time and encouragement to pursue the research and write many of the early drafts. The Organized Research Committee of Texas A&M University-Commerce (then East Texas State University) provided two grants for travel to various research libraries and archives.

No political history study can be completed without the knowledge, skills, insight, and dedication of professional librarians, archivists, and other professional staff at facilities that contain historical documents. Thus, we wish to thank those who labored in the vineyards to assist in the study. Especially helpful were staff members at the Franklin D. Roosevelt Library, Hyde Park, New York; the Harry S. Truman Library, Independence, Missouri; the University of Virginia Library (now Harrison Institute and Small Library), Charlottesville, Virginia; Butler Library, Columbia University, New York, New York; the National Archives, Library of Congress, Office of the Joint Chiefs of Staff and Historical Office, Office of the Secretary of Defense, all in Washington, D.C.; the George Marshall Library, Lexington Virginia; the Douglas MacArthur Library and Archives, Norfolk, Virginia; American Legion Library and Archives, Indianapolis, Indiana; Bedford City/County Museum, Genealogy Library, Bedford, Virginia; the Virginia Room, Roanoke Public Library, Roanoke, Virginia; the Clarksburg-Harrison Public Library, Clarksburg, West Virginia; the Mayflower Hotel archives, Washington, D.C.; and the Kiplinger Research Library, Historical Society of Washington, D.C.

Our utmost appreciation goes to the dozens of family members, friends, associates, law partners, and others who knew Louis Johnson and shared with us their views, opinions, perceptions, insights, and firsthand knowledge of Johnson the man and key events in his life. Most but not all of those individuals are listed in the notes and select bibliography.

Of all those who assisted, none was of more help than the late Ruth Maxwell Johnson. Through numerous conversations and letters, she provided a rich store of information and insights into her husband's thoughts and deeds. She placed no restrictions on the use of any materials and information provided. She also put us in contact with many individuals who knew her husband and who otherwise might not have been willing to share their recollections.

We owe special thanks to Dave Roll's assistant for thirty years, Esperance Biegel, who labored alongside us, patiently inputting constant and confusing changes in the manuscript and footnotes and producing a final manuscript for our publisher. Added thanks go to Marcia Mailey, who worked with Ms. Biegel on the manuscript; to the marvelously cooperative staff at Steptoe & Johnson, including research librarian Elmo Dattalo; and to the Steptoe & Johnson partners who contributed to this project and allowed Dave to pursue his passion.

Above all, we are grateful to our loving wives, both named Nancy, and to our wonderful grown children (Mark, Carolyn, Dianna, Rich, and Molly) for enduring this project with bemused patience and always supporting our respective careers — Keith's in academics and education, and Dave's in law, government, and an Internet startup.

Louis Johnson and the Arming of America

Introduction

WAS IT HAPPENING AGAIN? Louis Johnson, nervously tapping his pipe in the ashtray beside him, could hear what the feisty and fastidious man behind the big desk in the Oval Office was saying, but he had difficulty comprehending the meaning of the words.

As he began to process what was being said, Johnson's mind flashed back ten years to a similar conversation that had taken place in the same room. Back then, in the summer of 1940, it was President Franklin Roosevelt who had delivered the devastating news, breaking what Johnson believed was an ironclad promise to promote him from assistant secretary to secretary of war. Whether or not Roosevelt actually made a promise to his loyal assistant secretary of war, the president had decided, in order to maximize his chances for election to a third term and to unite the nation behind him when war seemed imminent, that he would bring in two highly regarded Republicans to head up the War Department. This meant that Johnson and Secretary of War Woodring would have to resign. Although Johnson was terribly hurt, he had come to understand and respect FDR's political judgment.

Now it was September 1950 and the country was in the third month of the Korean War. Johnson was secretary of defense, one of the most important and controversial individuals in the Truman administration. And the man who was delivering a crushing blow this time, Harry Truman, was an old friend who owed Louis Johnson his presidency. Both Johnson and Truman knew that if Johnson had not stepped forward to raise the money needed to carry on the 1948 campaign, Harry Truman would probably be living back on North Delaware Street in Independence, Missouri.

As these thoughts and memories rushed through his mind, and as President Truman's words slowly began to sink in, big, broad-shouldered Louis Johnson experienced an array of strong emotions—disbelief, denial, anger, bitterness, and betrayal. The president was asking him to resign as secretary of defense or be fired!

At first, Johnson was so overcome with emotion that he could not speak. After regaining his composure and his voice, Johnson begged Truman to reconsider, claiming that the situation in Korea was finally improving and that with the surprise invasion at Inchon only a few days away this was not the time for the president to fire his secretary of defense. Truman was unyielding. "I have made up my mind, Lou, and it has to be this way."[1]

With that statement, Louis Johnson's public career in Washington was over. Except for a few days in the limelight when he testified at the MacArthur Hearings in 1951 and a flurry of news stories in the mid-1950s about a possible run for the U.S. Senate from West Virginia, Johnson became a forgotten man. He never wrote his memoirs, nor did he speak for the record about America's defense establishment or the presidents he served. Historians, biographers, and memoir writers have never critically examined Johnson and his role in the Roosevelt and Truman administrations. Instead, they have left us with only a few sentences, diary entries, and footnotes, much of which is unflattering, some of which is inaccurate, and most of which lacks context.

Moreover, after Dean Acheson wrote in his acclaimed and widely read *Present at the Creation* that Louis Johnson was mentally ill[2]—a malicious and extremely damaging assertion that was completely inaccurate—Johnson was regarded by subsequent writers as "unsuited" for the job of secretary of defense, "possibly the worst appointment Truman ever made."[3] As a consequence, the man has never been objectively assessed.

This book proposes to provide a fair and objective assessment not only because Louis Johnson's place in the history of the Roosevelt and Truman years has never been fully examined but, more important, because his career offers insights into the political and leadership strengths and weaknesses of two of America's greatest, although vastly different, chief executives. Johnson's career as an advocate of military preparedness needs to be objectively examined because the battles he waged to advance the goals of these two presidents have resonated in the same profound disagreements between the national defense establishment, the State Department, and Congress in every subsequent administration.

Colonel Johnson had the distinction of being the only civilian who was influential in shaping the national security and military preparedness policies of both the Roosevelt and the Truman presidencies. He was the only top official used by each of these presidents to confront and carry out extremely unpopular initiatives—massive changes in the size and strength of American military power. And he was the only senior appointee dismissed by both Roosevelt and Truman.

Faced with a public, a Congress, and a secretary of war opposed to U.S. involvement in European wars, President Roosevelt skillfully exploited and manipulated Johnson's ambitions and talents to prepare the nation's military and industrial base for war. This study confirms the view of most historians that FDR was by no means a reluctant noninterventionist who was dragged into war. Rather, he was a sophisticated and steadfast internationalist who was convinced by public opinion to move cautiously, albeit deviously, to prepare the public for war.[4]

With Roosevelt in mind, James MacGregor Burns wrote that great leaders "broaden the environment" in which they operate and "widen the channels in which choices are made."[5] By this standard, President Truman would not be regarded as a great leader. Through the eyes and ears of Louis Johnson, this book provides additional support for the view, already held by Clay Blair and Arnold Offner, that Truman was a parochial nationalist who often lacked an understanding of the nations and cultures he had to deal with.[6]

President Truman enlisted Johnson as his loyal hatchet man to wield a sharp blade and pare down the military. Truman was motivated, however, not by an informed worldview or grand strategy but by an overriding desire to balance the budget, a visceral cynicism toward the military, and a misplaced reliance on America's nuclear monopoly. As David McCullough, Melvyn Leffler, Alonzo Hamby, and other writers have argued, Harry Truman faced greater challenges and more adversity than most of our presidents, but, as this book will suggest, he lacked insight—his choices led to confrontation rather than detente.[7] And Louis Johnson was his instrument of confrontation.

CHAPTER ONE

Bedford Blood

T WENTY-SIX-YEAR-OLD Marcellus Alexander Johnson paced through the dimly lit rooms above the grocery store in the grimy working-class neighborhood. Outside, a cold wind was blowing sleet through the streets, weather which normally would have distressed the young merchant because it was bad for business. However, on that gray morning of January 10, 1891, the storekeeper had more important things on his mind. He was anxiously waiting for his wife, Katherine Leftwich Arthur, to give birth to their first—her third—child. Fortunately, the labor did not last long, and Marcellus soon learned that he was the father of a big healthy boy. As he and Katherine, who everyone called Kate, had previously agreed, the baby was named Louis Arthur.[1]

The boy would bring pleasure and pride to the young couple. He would be hugely successful in law and government, he would be rich, he would befriend presidents, and he would be driven to become president. Yet at the same time he would be overbearing, arrogant, and imperious.

Although he was a child of Marcellus and Kate Johnson who ran a grocery store in Roanoke, Virginia, Louis Johnson's roots lay deep in the soil of Bedford County, Virginia.

Bedford County

Bedford County is a stunningly beautiful piece of the Virginia piedmont. It is bordered on the north by the majestic Peaks of Otter in the Blue Ridge. South from the mountains the rich rolling farmland ripples and unfolds until it reaches the Staunton River. Along the eastern border, north of the old Lynchburg-Salem

Turnpike, Thomas Jefferson built his second architectural masterpiece, the magnificent octagonal retreat called Poplar Forest.[2]

Louis Johnson's mother, born on August 10, 1861, in Bedford County, was the product of two very prominent county families, the Leftwiches and the Arthurs. The Leftwiches trace their ancestors back to the Norman Conquest. Kate's great-grandfather, Thomas Leftwich, the sheriff of Bedford County, was a captain of the Virginia Militia in the Revolutionary War who was later promoted to colonel and commanded the rearguard of General Gates's division at the battle of Camden.[3] In the War of 1812, he was colonel of the 10th Regiment of the Virginia Militia. The Leftwiches settled in the southern part of Bedford County at a home called Mt. Airy near Leesville, where Thomas was buried in 1816.[4]

The Arthurs, the other prominent family from which Kate descended, settled along Goose Creek and Craddock's Creek not far from Leesville. The Arthurs are lineal descendants of Lord William Russell, the Duke of Bedford. Kate's father, James Lewis Arthur, who inherited slaves and landholdings in his early twenties, was first lieutenant and then captain of Company C (the Big Island Greys) of the 58th Virginia Infantry. Under Stonewall Jackson, James Lewis Arthur and the Big Island Greys fought in the Valley and Seven Days' Campaigns of 1862 and at Cedar Run, Second Manassas, Chantilly, Harpers Ferry, and Sharpsburg. On May 12, 1864, Kate's father was wounded at the "Mule Shoe" during the Spotsylvania Court House battle, one of the most savage and legendary engagements of the entire Civil War.[5]

After the war, James Lewis Arthur returned to his family in Bedford County. In addition to his daughter Kate, James and his aptly named wife America raised five sons and six daughters on their family estate. Although the war had devastated the Bedford County economy and his farmlands lay in shambles, James Arthur was able to make his family comparatively comfortable as he tried to pick up the pieces and resume his career as a successful planter. He had plenty of acreage to sell, and the Bedford County land records confirm that he was an active buyer and seller of Bedford County farmland in the years following the Civil War. Captain Arthur entered public life, serving two terms in the Virginia Senate, one term as county treasurer, and ten years as justice of the peace.[6] Louis Johnson always remembered his grandfather telling him that "no man is worth anything unless he is a Democrat."[7]

While Kate was coming of age in Bedford County, Marcellus Johnson, her eventual husband and the father of Louis Johnson, was working on his mother's small family farm near Union Hall in Franklin County not far from the Bedford County line. Marcellus's father had died when he was only three, leaving his mother, Elizabeth Haynes, to raise eleven children.[8]

Although Marcellus Johnson was born in 1865 in Franklin County, he was less than a generation removed from Bedford County; his father, John Wesley Johnson, had been born and raised in southern Bedford County on Craddock's

Creek not far from the estates of the Leftwiches and the Arthurs. And Marcellus's grandfather, Martin Johnson, who owned a small farm on Craddock's
Creek, was married to Sarah Leftwich.[9]

As Kate entered her early twenties, she caught the eye of a son of the distinguished Saunders family who had settled across the Staunton River at Ivy Cliff.
In 1884, she married Edgar Saunders.[10] Within the next two years the couple
moved to Roanoke City, a bustling railroad hub, probably to escape the de-
pressed postwar economy in Bedford County. The parents of the young couple
must have given them a substantial wedding gift because they were able to purchase a frame building and establish a successful grocery business near the
booming Roanoke Machine Works.[11]

The couple settled down and set up housekeeping above the grocery store at
the corner of Wells and 4th Street. Kate gave birth to two sons, Edgar and
Henry.[12] In 1887, Marcellus Johnson arrived in Roanoke and was hired as a clerk
in Saunders's grocery store.[13] Within a year tragedy struck the young family. First
Edgar Saunders died of typhoid, then his eldest son died of measles.[14] These dev-
astating losses left Kate with a four-year-old son, Henry, and the grocery store.
She was a long way from Bedford County and the comfort and security of the
Arthur estate. But she was a strong, proud woman and she would not look back.

Marcellus was four years younger than Kate. In terms of social standing, family lineage, inherited wealth, and manners, he was vastly "beneath" her. Yet before long, probably due to proximity, convenience, and mutual attraction, he
began courting her. Marcellus was a big rawboned man who was strong and
hardworking, and Kate believed he would be a good provider. On January 29,
1889, Marcellus A. Johnson and Katherine Leftwich Arthur were married.[15]

So the yeomanry and the aristocrats of Bedford County were united—the
blood of the Johnsons, the Leftwiches, and the Arthurs was mixed and poured
into the veins of Louis Arthur Johnson. Johnson would be a worker, a fighter,
a gambler, and a roughneck. He would also emerge as a climber and a relentless seeker of wealth, power, and status. This was the legacy of Bedford County,
Virginia.

Magic City

Although Louis Johnson's roots were in the hills and creeks of Bedford County,
he was indelibly shaped by the "Magic City"—the name the promoters gave to
Roanoke, Virginia, in the 1890s. Roanoke in the gay nineties was both magical
and a very rough place.

Only a few years before Louis Johnson was born, the town was called "Big
Lick." Once the decision was made to connect the Shenandoah Valley Railroad with the Norfolk & Western at Big Lick, the boom began as thousands of
workers streamed into town. When the population reached 5,000 in 1884, a

charter was granted and the new city was named Roanoke. The railroads built huge machine shops in the northeast area of the city where the two railroads converged. Streets were laid out and hundreds of identical row houses for the workers were built. Dozens of hotels, saloons, restaurants, boarding houses, and banks and even a few "skyscrapers" sprang up almost overnight.[16]

By 1900, the population of Roanoke had swelled to over 21,000, and by 1910 it had exploded to 39,000. With the influx came promoters, gamblers, prostitutes, saloonkeepers, and all manner of thieves and lawbreakers. Roanoke was a wide-open lusty railroad town.[17]

The Johnson corner grocery store was a two-story frame building in the northeast section of the city surrounded by workers' row houses and not far from the gigantic Roanoke Machine Works, which manufactured freight cars and locomotives and employed thousands.[18] Marcellus and Kate had three more boys and a girl in the thirteen years following Louis's birth. From a very early age, Louis Johnson worked for his parents in the family store, where he learned the rudiments of what became both his expertise and passion in adulthood—how to supply an army.

The Johnson store was situated in the midst of an army of workers. Since there was no refrigeration, the workers were completely dependent upon the Johnson store for their daily grocery needs. The store would be crowded by 6 A.M. every day except Sunday. To accommodate their customers, Marcellus, Kate, Louis, and the other family members of working age had to have the store stocked and ready by a very early hour. Often a predawn trip to the market house across the tracks was made to purchase supplies for the day. This meant harnessing the horses to a grocery wagon to transport supplies. During the day the horse-drawn wagon was used to deliver groceries.

Louis grew up learning about and performing these tasks. He anticipated what was needed, restocked the shelves, harnessed and cared for the horses, drove to market, purchased supplies, and delivered groceries. He learned the fundamentals of logistics and supply. When Louis was in high school, his father opened an account book and began charging him for clothing, school supplies, sports equipment, and other items he wanted or needed. Louis was obligated to repay Marcellus for those goods by hours worked in the store. Since his father assigned him a low hourly rate, Louis usually worked two to three hours before and after school and another twelve to fourteen hours on Saturdays to repay his debts.

During summer vacations when he was in high school, Louis was permitted to secure more lucrative employment in the foundry of the Roanoke Machine Works. Due in no small part to his size, strength, and energy, Louis loved this work. The propensity for hard work that developed in these early years was to stay with Louis for a lifetime, and he worked hard and long at every job he ever had in order to achieve success.[19]

In addition to a rigorous work ethic, Marcellus and Kate did their best to teach their children the value of a spiritual life and the importance of organized religion. The year Louis was born, his father was on the building committee for a new neighborhood Methodist church, the Grace Mission. The church was built on a lot just a few doors from the Johnson store, and when it opened in 1892 it was called Grace Church.[20]

Every Sunday morning and evening and Wednesday night would find the entire Johnson family at Grace Church. At the age of four, Louis was adept at telling Bible stories and quoting scripture. By the age of twelve, he had succeeded in organizing the youth of the city's three Methodist churches into a single youth organization, the Roanoke Epworth League.[21] The importance of religion that was ingrained in Louis in those early years was to remain with him throughout his life, and while he was not what would be called a deeply religious man, he was always an active church member.[22]

Because of the many temptations afoot in the Magic City, youth organizations such as the Epworth League abounded. In Roanoke, a constant war was being waged between the wets and the drys, with religious leaders backing the drys and saloonkeepers making sure the city remained wet. It is not known whether Louis was influenced by the Epworth League, Grace Church, or his parents, but from the time of his high school years until the end of his life he was a teetotaler. He didn't preach about the evils of alcohol, but he was never known to have taken a drink.

A deep respect for education was also a value that was learned in the Johnson home. From his earliest years, Kate taught Louis the importance of reading, especially for the purpose of understanding the scriptures. His superior reading ability enabled him to do very well in public school. He was an outstanding elementary and high school student who enjoyed and excelled in history, literature, public speaking, and debate.[23]

By the time he reached Roanoke High School, Louis, taking after his father, had developed into a large-boned 200-pounder. Along with his size came an agility and strength that helped make him an outstanding football and baseball player. Both in the classroom and on the athletic field Louis exhibited an extreme aggressiveness and competitiveness—characteristics that were to be evident throughout his life.

During his high school years, it became apparent to his parents, teachers, and classmates that Louis had unusual potential and that he needed to continue his education. In particular, his mother, who was such a driving force in his life, continually urged him to go to college, even though she knew that he would have to work to pay his tuition and expenses. In addition, Louis remembered his grandfather Captain James Lewis Arthur talking politics and telling him that the most noble of occupations was that of a lawyer.[24]

So in the spring of 1908, the decision was not difficult. Louis Johnson decided to enroll at the University of Virginia for the purpose of studying law.

The University

On September 8, 1908, Louis stepped off the train at Charlottesville and walked up University Avenue to "the Corner" near the entrance gate to the university, with its poolrooms, barbershops, newsstands, and the old Temperance Hall where students bought their books. Student idlers and loungers, called "Corner loafers," were impressed with Johnson's height and bulk, but they said nothing as he trudged through the "Long Walk" gate.[25]

When he saw the Rotunda and the Pavilions that Thomas Jefferson had helped design for the first time and when he realized he was joining company with distinguished graduates such as Woodrow Wilson and Edgar Allen Poe, he felt a sense of history, pride, and excitement. Although he would never let it show, he was also afraid that he wouldn't measure up in the classroom or that he wouldn't be able to surmount the social barriers.

Joining Johnson in the fall of 1908 were 296 other students who had enrolled in the "College," as they called it. Everyone was required to attend the College for one year before entering one of the university's professional schools or continuing in the study of humanities. Total enrollment that fall was 768.[26] Academically, Louis's first year was anything but a success; for Louis, mathematics and English literature were nearly insurmountable obstacles to further study. Finally, however, the first year ended and he managed to earn grades just high enough to gain entrance into the Department of Law.[27]

If the first year in the College was difficult for Louis, the challenge of law school was even more formidable. The University of Virginia law school in the fall of 1909 was one of the most highly regarded law schools in the nation. It was crammed into the basement of the Rotunda, and the law school faculty was small (there were only four tenured professors), but it included gifted teachers and it produced top-rank legal scholarship. Professor Raleigh Minor wrote critically acclaimed books on conflicts, international law, real property, and federalism. Armistead Dobie, who was to serve with Louis Johnson in the headquarters of the 80th Division in World War I, achieved national renown as a legal scholar, authoring hornbooks on federal procedure and bailments.[28] Louis Johnson met this challenge, and during his three years of law school he compiled an outstanding scholastic record.[29] This was done in spite of his tendency to prepare for examinations by a single reading of his class notes. His ability to perform in the classroom won the respect of his professors, and in his senior year he was selected to serve as an assistant professor in the law department, a position that entailed tutoring other students and administering examinations. When he graduated in the spring of 1912, he ranked tenth in his law class of thirty-one.[30]

Johnson's academic achievements were impressive, but he really excelled as a campus leader, promoter, joiner, and doer. He was president of his law class for three consecutive years. In addition, he was a member of the prestigious Raven

Society; associate editor of the yearbook, *Corks and Curls*; member of the South-west Virginia Club; legal advisor and vice president of the Roanoke Club; vice president of the YMCA; member of the Delta Sigma Rho forensics honorary society; and secretary and treasurer of the Civics Club.[31]

He did not pledge one of the top fraternities. Instead, as vice president of Delta Chi social fraternity, one of the smaller and less-prestigious fraternities, Johnson was responsible for forming an alliance of the second-tier fraternities and independents which succeeded in controlling campus politics. In this endeavor, Louis was able to further perfect the oratorical skills that were to serve him so well in the years ahead. He was so successful in winning campus debates and public-speaking contests that in his senior year he represented the university at both the Virginia and Southern Oratorical Meetings.[32]

Figuratively as well as literally, Johnson was the big man on campus. At 6 foot 2 and still gaining weight, he caught the eye of John Sterling LaRowe, proprietor of a pool hall which was the most popular student hangout at the Corner. LaRowe, an ex-Marine and boxing instructor at the Virginia Military Institute, was not only king of billiards at the Corner, he was also the coach of the university's boxing and wrestling teams. In Johnson, LaRowe saw his next heavyweight champion.[33]

Louis was an eager and excellent pupil, and he trained hard under Coach LaRowe to learn the fundamentals of boxing and wrestling. By his senior year, Louis was the university's heavyweight boxing and wrestling champion and served as president of the Boxing and Wrestling Club.[34]

The opportunity to study law and engage in campus politics and sports at the University did not come free. There were tuition and fees to be paid, books to be purchased, and room and board payments to be made—obligations that Louis had to meet, since his parents were unable to help foot the bills. Desiring to have as much time as possible for his numerous activities during the school year, he worked long and hard during the summers to earn enough money to see him through each year. During his vacations he did everything from working for the Norfolk & Western Railroad to selling Bibles from door to door. One summer he and a friend published a weekly newspaper for summer-school students and were so successful in selling advertising that they both made enough money to pay all their expenses the following year.[35]

Johnson dedicated his brains, his strength, his work ethic, and his burgeoning political skills to the university, and it all paid off when he received his Bachelor of Laws degree in June of 1912. The institution had served him well, academically and socially, and he never forgot that he owed it a great deal in return.[36] Now, however, it was 1912, and the 21-year-old lawyer was ready to go out and make his mark on the world.

CHAPTER TWO

Foot in the Door

THE POWERFUL BALTIMORE & OHIO locomotive chugged its way through the rugged mountains of north central West Virginia toward the city of Clarksburg in Harrison County. The September sun shone brightly on the leaves that were just beginning to turn. On board were two recent graduates of the University of Virginia law school, Louis Johnson and John Strode Rixey. Rixey was the son of a four-term congressman from Culpepper, Virginia.

The young men had become good friends shortly after their arrival on the Charlottesville campus, and during their junior year they had decided to become law partners following graduation. They also agreed that they would not hang out their shingles in the hometown of either one but would scout out a town that would be acceptable to both. Rixey wanted to investigate Birmingham, Alabama, while Johnson wanted to look at Clarksburg, West Virginia. An uncle of Johnson's had told him that Clarksburg was a city of considerable potential, and he had heard that it was a young man's town.[1] The two men decided to go first to Clarksburg, then to Birmingham.

Young Man's Town

They arrived in Clarksburg on the evening of September 15, 1912, and spent the night at the huge and elaborate Waldo Hotel, a one-block-long, Moorish-style six-story building that appeared to be out of place in a small industrial town snuggled in the mountains of one of the poorer states in the nation. The next morning, when they began to walk around the town, they quickly discovered that the place was indeed booming. The population of the city had more than doubled in the past decade and had shot past the 10,000 mark. The population of Harrison County was also skyrocketing; by 1910 it was approaching 50,000.[2]

The basis for the rapid growth was the rich deposits of natural gas, oil, and zinc which served as major attractions to new industry and the coal mines in the mountains and valleys to the north. The town was headquarters for coal and coke companies, foundries, a box factory, graphite companies, chemical companies, sheet and tin mills, twelve glass factories, and a host of other concerns. The prosperity which resulted from the industrial expansion was evident from the town's seven banks, paved streets, six theaters clustered in a "theater district," electric streetcars, two hospitals, a handful of modern hotels, and three tall office buildings, the largest of which was a ten-story building owned by the Union Bank.[3]

In addition to the diverse and growing economy, which was being fueled by northern capital, the young lawyers had heard that Harrison County, whose courthouse, land records, and offices were seated in Clarksburg, was widely known as having a distinguished bar with outstanding legal talent. Lawyers by the name of Harrison, Davis, Haymond, and Maxwell had distinguished themselves in the bar, on the bench, and in politics and business, and they were known for training and mentoring their sons and other promising young lawyers.[4]

Clarksburg in 1912 was a young man's town, it was a young lawyer's town, and it was in the north—a long way from the still-struggling post–Civil War economy of Virginia and its old-fashioned southern ways. It did not take Johnson and Rixey more than a day or two to agree that this was the place where they would establish their practice. In the fall of 1912, in a one-room office in Clarksburg, West Virginia, they opened the law office of Rixey & Johnson.

The life of a young lawyer in a new town was not easy, since clients were not pounding the door down to seek the services of either partner. Fortunately, neither man had a family to support, so it was just a matter of making enough to pay office rent and room and board. Although Louis initially did not have much work to do, he had a great deal to keep him busy because he immediately set out, as he had in college, to make as many acquaintances as he could. He was a natural mixer with a gift for remembering names and making people feel important. He followed his college pattern of joining everything he could in Clarksburg, becoming a member of such organizations as the Masons, Odd Fellows, and Elks. He quickly got to know numerous people throughout the city and began demonstrating even then a knack for getting to know the "right people"—those with money and power.[5]

Birth of a Law Firm

Knowing many people was nice, but it did not pay the bills. To make ends meet, Johnson volunteered to serve as an assistant prosecuting attorney for Harrison County in 1913. In that capacity, he was soon involved in preparing a case against a former deputy sheriff who was charged with embezzlement. Although the defendant was ultimately acquitted, the case was to have a major impact on Johnson's career since it required that he brief and argue an appeal before the West Virginia Supreme Court of Appeals.[6]

In order to learn how to properly handle a matter before the state's highest court, Johnson wisely looked for an experienced mentor and teacher among those in the vaunted Harrison County bar. Johnson could have turned to the Davis firm for help or to any number of other lawyers. However, he chose Philip Pendleton Steptoe, a University of Virginia graduate who had begun practicing law in Harrison County in 1902 and was ten years his senior. Steptoe had a fine reputation as a low-key, methodical, and scholarly attorney. Johnson sought him out not only for those qualities but also because the two of them had something far more important in common—Bedford County. Philip Steptoe's great-grandfather, James C. Steptoe Sr., known as "Jemmie" Steptoe, was one of the most famous citizens of Bedford County, and his name, reputation, and social standing were well known to the Johnsons, Leftwiches, and Arthurs. A close personal friend and college classmate of Thomas Jefferson, who often summered in Bedford County at Poplar Forest, Jemmie Steptoe was clerk of Bedford County for fifty-six years, which in those days meant that he essentially was the CEO of the county.[7]

So it was no accident that Johnson approached Steptoe for guidance on his West Virginia Supreme Court appearance. Steptoe had a "brand name," he had married well, he had an aristocratic background, he was a highly regarded lawyer, and he might be a good fellow to hook up with. During their first meeting, the two men immediately took a personal liking to each other. Steptoe mentored Johnson on the embezzlement appeal, and before long they began talking about forming a law firm. On September 13, 1913, Rixey and Johnson merged their fledgling practice with Steptoe, forming the firm of Steptoe, Rixey, & Johnson. The following year, for reasons which have never been disclosed, John Rixey withdrew from the firm and moved to Norfolk. Thus, in 1914, the firm became known as Steptoe & Johnson—a law firm that was destined to become one of the most prestigious in the country.[8]

From the standpoint of personalities and their respective strengths as lawyers, the new partners were virtual opposites, but they complemented one another perfectly: the reserved, self-effacing, and gifted Steptoe provided the analytic and intellectual firepower, and the outgoing, gregarious, and supremely confident Johnson supplied a knack for public relations and for persuading potential clients that his firm had the expertise to dispose of their legal problems quickly and to their advantage.[9]

Corporations and wealthy individuals flocked to Steptoe & Johnson, and the firm prospered from the moment it opened its doors for business. After 1914,

Louis Johnson never had any financial worries. Although the money and trappings of wealth he derived from his law firm were very important to him, he saw those things merely as a means to achieving what he really wanted—power, status, and respectability.[10] Recalling the teachings of his grandfather, Captain Lewis Arthur, Johnson was convinced that the road to further success and prestige was to be found in politics, so he decided to seek his first elective office—that of mayor of Clarksburg.

Politics

Despite the fact that it was the birthplace of Stonewall Jackson, Clarksburg had long been a Republican stronghold—at the national, state, and local levels. To challenge that entrenched power would have been considered pure folly by most, but not by Louis Johnson. In early 1914, the 23-year-old lawyer, a southerner who had been in town less than two years, announced that he would run for mayor as a Democrat. His chutzpah was breathtaking. One of his friends said, "Lou, you don't have a chance. No one has heard of you." Louis replied, "When the race is over everyone in Clarksburg will know my name."[11]

A city-wide convention of Democrats was held and those present gladly nominated the aggressive young lawyer as the party candidate. In the weeks that followed, Johnson challenged the local Republican establishment as it had never before been challenged. He charged that the incumbent mayor, Will H. Cole, was really the tool of the local GOP bosses, Sherman C. Denham and Virgil L. Highland. Promoting himself as a reform candidate, Johnson pledged to bring good government and promised to restore "political liberty" to the city. With the support of the Democratic *Clarksburg Exponent* and the effective use of his gift for public speaking, the young man garnered more support than anyone had thought possible. However, in the end all came to naught: Cole was reelected by a fifty-vote margin—1,239 to 1,189.[12]

Although he was not victorious in this first attempt to win public office, Johnson served notice that he was a man to be reckoned with in the future. And his enhanced name recognition helped him attract clients to the law firm, a benefit that Johnson surely had in mind when he told his friend that everyone would know his name when the race was over.

During his first few years in Clarksburg, Johnson met two men who were to have a major influence on his life. One was a lawyer, John W. Davis, and the other was a minister, Reverend Josiah T. Carter. Davis, who practiced law with his father in the firm of Davis & Davis, went on to become a congressman, U.S. solicitor general, ambassador to the Court of St. James, president of the American Bar Association, and, in 1924, the unsuccessful Democratic nominee for the president of the United States. Davis is the "Davis" in the famous New York City law firm Davis Polk & Wardwell. The friendship and respect that developed between Johnson and Davis in these early years when they both practiced law in Clarksburg lasted a lifetime.[13]

The other close friend, Reverend Carter, was the rector of Christ Episcopal Church, a plain but beautiful old church on Main Street built in 1853. The two men had first met in a boarding house a few weeks after Johnson arrived in town, and before long the preacher invited him to move into the rectory. The church facilities included an educational building which housed a small gymnasium where they spent many hours boxing, wrestling, and playing basketball. Such activities enabled Johnson to maintain the physical stamina and reflexes that had characterized his college days. The relationship with Carter fostered Johnson's spiritual life as well as his physical well-being. Because of Carter, Johnson joined the Episcopal church and became one of its most active members, eventually becoming a vestryman. Johnson continued this association with Christ Church for the rest of his life; he always maintained an interest in its activities and supported it financially.[14]

Like many powerful and ambitious men, Johnson had hundreds of acquaintances yet only a few intimate friends. As a result of his outgoing, aggressive nature he came to know almost everyone in town, yet his arrogance, ego, and tendency to be overbearing repelled many people. Even those closest to him acknowledged that his forcefulness was both a great strength as well as a major weakness. While he did not make many close friends, he treasured the ones that he had, such as Reverend Carter, and each of them were assured of his lifelong devotion, loyalty, and dependability. As Johnson once put it, "One does not have many true and understanding friends and therefore we value all the more those we do have."[15]

After his political defeat in 1914, Johnson bided his time by drumming up business for the law firm and getting to know more people around town. Then, in 1916, he again decided to seek political office. This time his goal was a seat in the West Virginia House of Delegates. In that contest, eight candidates, four from each party, were seeking the four seats allotted to Harrison County, and as usual the Republicans were expected to capture all the positions. The sweep did not take place, however, because one Democrat, Louis Johnson, succeeded in winning a seat after waging a brief but very aggressive campaign during which he delivered thirty-three public speeches.[16] The victory made it evident that the young lawyer had won many supporters in Clarksburg and throughout the county, even if he was a Democrat.

In January 1917, Johnson traveled to Charleston to undertake his legislative responsibilities. Politically, things were topsy-turvy in the state capital because after decades of Republican domination the Democrats had captured control of the governorship and the House of Delegates. The House of Delegates, with the Democrats now in control, was undergoing a major reorganization, which opened many opportunities for new leadership, and Johnson, opportunist that he was, took advantage of that situation. By personal, persistent politicking, the freshman legislator succeeded in being named chairman of the politically powerful Judiciary Committee and with that post came the position of majority leader of the House.[17]

As the legislature began its various tasks, Johnson quickly emerged as one of its most charismatic and effective members. His generally serious nature and evidence of a good sense of humor put him in good stead with nearly everyone. That he chaired one committee and served on seven more was not as impressive as the fact that he took such an active role in virtually all House activities. In the early months of 1917, he introduced more than a dozen bills and eight resolutions, was responsible for numerous committee reports, and on several occasions presided over the House when the speaker was absent. He was clearly the most active and visible of the 104 House members: he participated in nearly every floor debate, frequently displaying his widely acclaimed oratorical skills. During the regular session, the legislature passed a number of significant pieces of legislation, and in most of them Johnson played a major role.

Johnson made it a point to do something every day to get his name in the House *Journal*, even if it was only a motion to recess or to go into executive session.[18] It did not take long for the press to note that the young lawmaker had won the respect of both parties and thus was "a very available man" for a congressional seat in the next election.[19] There was even talk that he could be gubernatorial material.[20]

Unfortunately, when the West Virginia legislature was forced by a requirement of the constitution to adjourn on February 23, 1917, it had not passed the state appropriations bill. Governor Hatfield, the outgoing Republican governor, immediately called for a special session to convene the following day. Johnson led the House forces as they tried to get the Senate to go along with its more austere appropriations bill, but these efforts were unsuccessful and on March 3 the special session adjourned with the bill still not passed.[21]

The next day, John J. Cornwell, a newspaperman from Romney and a Democrat, assumed the governorship amid all the fanfare that normally surrounds such an event. (Cornwell's grandson, Steve Ailes, was to become a distinguished partner at Steptoe & Johnson and secretary of the army under President Kennedy.) Cornwell had come to know Louis Johnson a few years before, and when Johnson assumed his leadership role in the legislature the two men became very close friends, personally and politically.[22] In the weeks following his inauguration, Cornwell consulted regularly with Johnson about the prospects of getting an appropriations bill passed in another special session, but before a decision on that matter could be made, events in Europe and Washington radically altered the course of things to come throughout the world, including West Virginia.

On February 1, 1917, Germany resumed unrestricted submarine warfare, and by mid-March German torpedoes were sending American vessels to the bottom of the Atlantic on a regular basis. The United States responded on April 6 when Congress honored President Woodrow Wilson's request for a declaration of war. Immediately, the Council for National Defense, which had been created the year before, began asking each of the states to set up Councils of Defense and gave them the authority to deal with problems that arose during prosecution of the war. West Virginia quickly responded to the challenge.

Governor Cornwell called for a special session to convene on May 14 for the purpose of establishing a State Council of Defense and approving an appropriations bill. During that session Cornwell relied heavily on Louis Johnson, as House majority leader, to get the measures he supported passed. The advent of war brought a spirit of cooperativeness not previously evident, and in just twelve days the legislature created a State Council of Defense, approved an appropriations bill, provided special taxes for a war defense fund, passed measures to conserve food, provided punishment for individuals attempting to corner the market in foodstuffs and fuel, and permitted absentee voting for servicemen.[23] After clearly indicating its willingness to do what was necessary to make the world safe for democracy, the legislature adjourned and its members returned home.

The Maxwells

In the early summer of 1917, Louis Johnson began preparing to make his personal contribution to the war effort. From the day the United States entered the war, he had made up his mind that he would join the army—following in the footsteps of Captain James Lewis Arthur and Colonel Thomas Leftwich. He explored the possibility of getting into Officer Training School. However, the nation's efforts to establish a large, well-trained army were just getting under way, and Johnson was informed that with all the chaos that reigned it would be at least August before he would learn if he was accepted. As August approached, he turned his cases and clients over to his partner, Philip Steptoe, and they hired an experienced real estate lawyer, Leo Caulfield (thereafter nicknamed "The Inspector"), to help out with work on oil-, gas-, and coal-leasing work while Louis was away.[24]

On the one hand, Louis was anxious to go into the army and get to where the action was, but on the other hand, he was thankful for the delay because his life was becoming increasingly complicated as a result of his courtship of a young woman, Ruth Frances Maxwell. Given Johnson's drive for status and respectability, it is not surprising that he chose to pursue Ruth Maxwell, who was from one of the richest and most prominent families in Clarksburg. Her father, William Brent Maxwell, whose family had settled in Harrison County in the 1790s, had started out as a farmer and stockraiser in Harrison and Doddridge Counties in the years following the Civil War; in time, he amassed nearly 8,000 acres of the best grazing land in the state. Old-timers used to say that "you can walk from the Potomac to the Ohio River and never leave the Maxwell land."[25] In the late 1890s and early 1900s, both oil and gas were discovered on the land and his fortune grew even larger. Soon Brent Maxwell turned to oil production and banking, and before long he was acknowledged to be one of the wealthiest citizens of Harrison County.

The power and prestige Brent Maxwell commanded in Clarksburg on the eve of World War I was extraordinary. Among other business pursuits, he was founder and president of Union National Bank, the skyscraper in Clarksburg in which Steptoe & Johnson had its offices on the tenth floor. After the death of his first wife Emma, who bore him two children, Brent married Lillian Jarvis and they had four children—the first being Ruth Frances, who was born in 1896. Ruth enjoyed all the privileges and advantages that came with wealth, including a fine education at private schools in New York and summers riding and swimming at the Maxwell summer home at Mountain Park in western Maryland.

Shortly after Louis Johnson arrived in Clarksburg, he met the Maxwells at their huge new house on West Pike Street, but since Ruth was only sixteen years old at the time, neither paid much attention to the other. Two years later, however, they began to date regularly, and three years later, in the summer of 1917, they were engaged to be married.[26] Several weeks after his engagement, Johnson and his good friend Reverend Josiah Carter received word from the West Virginia draft officer that they had passed their mental and physical examinations and had been selected to attend the Second Officer's Reserve Training School at Fort Benjamin Harrison, Indiana.[27] Louis urged Ruth to marry him immediately, but she held firm to an earlier decision not to marry until the conflict in Europe was over.[28]

The Great War

On August 17, 1917, Louis began what was to be, both physically and mentally, one of the most demanding three months of his life as he became a civilian candidate in training for a commission in the U.S. Army. The long days at Fort Harrison were filled with intensive classroom work in such subjects as army organization, tactics, operations, and communications. As hectic as the mental pace was, it was nothing compared to the physical demands. Candidates spent hours running, exercising, engaging in close-order drill, practicing with their bayonets, and firing weapons. While the drop-out rate was high, Johnson was never in danger. His years as a student and lawyer had prepared him well for the mental aspects of the training. Physically, his propensity to stay in shape and maintain the same agility, strength, and stamina that he had possessed as a college wrestler and boxer made it easy for him to meet the challenges. On November 26, his training came to a successful end and as the second-ranked student in a class of 109, he was commissioned as a captain in the infantry.[29]

Captain Louis A. Johnson was immediately ordered to Camp Lee, near Petersburg, Virginia, where he was assigned to the 80th Division. The 80th, one of the original twelve divisions of the National Army, was called the Blue Ridge Division because its personnel were drawn from Virginia, West Virginia, and western Pennsylvania. For the next three months Johnson served with various units of the 80th.[30] Eventually, the army stumbled upon the real talents of the former grocery delivery boy, because on March 15, 1918, he was assigned as adjutant of the Headquarters Detachment, Motor Battalion of the 305th Ammunition Train (AT).[31] During World War I, ammunition trains supplied and transported ammunition of all kinds to field artillery and the front-line troops. Johnson was placed in command of an operation he had grown up with and which he would pursue for the rest of his public life—supplying an army.

On May 26, 1918, the 305th AT departed for France. After arriving in France at Brest, the 80th Division and the 305th AT began training with British and American artillery units at various locations in France, and it was probably at one of these training exercises that Louis Johnson first met and got to know Harry S. Truman.[32]

In mid-September, the 80th Division and Johnson's 305th AT began concentrating with other American units to fight in what they believed would be the greatest military battle of history—the Meuse-Argonne offensive. Ruth Maxwell, telling her mother about letters Louis wrote a few weeks earlier, said "L.A.J. writes the most optimistic letters and seems to think the Boche are in for a good whipping."[33] On the night of September 25–26th, when the offensive was to begin, a touch of frost was in the air, and many who were there remember the huge and brilliant moon which hung over the battlefield. At 2:30 A.M. the artillery supporting the 80th commenced firing. By 4:20 A.M. some 2,700 guns along the front had opened fire with a deafening and unforgettable roar. During forty-eight days of continuous battle, Johnson and his 305th AT supplied and supported the 80th as well as units of the 4th, 5th, and 90th Divisions.[34]

Although Johnson emerged unscathed and his unit received praise and commendation from superior officers for the effective job they had done in supporting the great offensive which ended the war, he was deeply affected and some of his feelings were not positive. He witnessed slaughter and incredible destruction inflicted by combatants who had little or no idea of what they were fighting for. His disgust for the enemy was aimed at the German political leaders rather than the German soldiers; he had first-hand knowledge of instances where the soldiers treated French civilians with a sense of humanity and respect.[35]

On November 11, 1918, the armistice was signed and the fighting in Europe came to an end, but an early return home was not in the offing for Johnson because his unit was assigned to the 90th Division, which was a part of the U.S. Army of Occupation in Germany.[36] To combat boredom and sagging morale, the 90th and other units stationed in Germany near Coblenz staged elaborate athletic events, including boxing matches, and it is probable that Louis Johnson, the former University of Virginia heavyweight, participated.[37] At this time Louis also learned that Theodore Roosevelt Jr., the former president's son, and other top officers of various army divisions were meeting in Paris in February of 1919 to organize an association of veterans, eventually called the American Legion, which would wield tremendous political power in postwar America.

In Germany, Johnson had considerable time to reflect on what he had experienced in the U.S. Army during the course of the war and after. What emerged was a serious concern over American military disorganization and the nation's lack of preparedness. He also developed a firm conviction that the United States had a responsibility to assume a position of world leadership.

Johnson felt strongly that the United States should join the League of Nations. He believed the nation could not afford to turn its back on Europe and the rest of the world. In an early 1919 letter he wrote, "We have unquestionably taken our place among the great nations of the earth, but can we hold it unless we assume the burdens and pay the price?" The purely partisan attacks that many politicians made on Wilson's Covenant were especially disturbing to him.[38] When U.S. membership in the league ultimately went down to its second, and final, defeat in the Senate, Johnson was extremely upset by what he considered to be a major blunder. In the years that followed he never forgot his country's rejection of the league, and he looked forward to the day when the United States would join and take a leadership role in a worldwide peace organization.[39]

Of all the things that bothered him, none was more aggravating than the chaos he witnessed in the American military machine. Because he was an organizer, Johnson was appalled at what he felt was the army's wholesale disorganization. While most soldiers merely whined about the situation they found themselves in, he decided to do something about it. On the return voyage home in May 1919, the 29-year-old captain wrote a 67-page letter to Army Chief of Staff Peyton C. March, telling him exactly what was wrong with the army and how it could be corrected. Johnson expressed his great concern about the waste of material and supplies, inadequate personnel classification, unsatisfactory recreation programs, the undemocratic nature of the Articles of War, and the failure to make soldiers aware of what they were fighting for.[40]

When he returned home, Johnson was sent to Camp Dix, New Jersey, and from there he mailed his long letter to the War Department. The letter was never acknowledged. Shortly thereafter, on June 5, 1919, while his promotion to major was still pending, he was discharged from the service.[41]

Marriage

The citizens of Clarksburg and his friends and law partners welcomed Johnson home in June 1919. Now that he was once again a civilian, he turned his attention to matters of a more personal nature, namely his relationship with his fian-cée, Ruth Maxwell. During his time in the army he had written steadily to the girl he left behind who had been living with her half-sister Sue and her family in Georgetown. Louis expected to marry Ruth in the late summer or fall of 1919. However, Ruth put him off and expressed misgivings about marrying him. The ever-confident Louis was devastated. Eventually, however, Ruth came around, and by January of 1920 she was in New York City shopping for her wedding and apologizing to her mother for spending so much money.[42]

At 9 P.M. on Saturday, February 7, 1920, in the big Maxwell house on West Pike Street, Ruth and Louis were married by Louis's longtime friend, Reverend Josiah Carter. Although there was an orchestra and the downstairs rooms in the mansion were beautifully decorated with flowers, it was a small family wedding. Unfortunately, Kate and Marcellus, Louis's parents, could not attend "owing to illness of several members of our family," as Kate wrote to Mrs. Maxwell.[43]

The planned honeymoon in Florida got off to a rough start. Writing to his new mother-in-law from the Willard Hotel in Washington, D.C., four days after the wedding, Louis said that Ruth was "so much better" and had now "agreed" to make the trip to Florida. Once the couple arrived in Florida, Ruth's spirits were sky high as she told her parents that "Louis is so wonderful to me" and that "my only objec-tion to him as a husband is that he wants me to eat more than I really can."[44]

After the newlyweds returned from their honeymoon, they resided for a time at the Maxwell mansion. With characteristic energy, enthusiasm, and stamina, Louis plunged back into the practice of law at Steptoe & Johnson and became increasingly active in the American Legion and Democratic Party politics. He also became a regular tennis player and an avid golfer. His size, agility, and strength, combined with his ferocious competitiveness, helped him become an excellent golfer and a sought-after partner at the Clarksburg Country Club.[45]

Ruth, quiet, reserved, and cultured, settled down into the life of young ma-tron, the wife of a rising and successful lawyer. In November 1920, their first daughter, Lillian, was born. Three years later, shortly after their second daugh-ter, Ruth Katherine, was born, Ruth suffered some kind of a mental breakdown. It must have been very serious, because for the entire seven months between December 1923 and June of 1924, Ruth was confined at Johns Hopkins Hospital in Baltimore.[46] The Maxwells helped Louis cope at home with the two babies, but it plainly was a difficult and distressing time for the young couple. It is not known whether Ruth's mental health was responsible, but Louis and Ruth never had another child.

The Rise of Steptoe & Johnson

By the fall of 1924, Ruth had returned to Clarksburg and Louis had purchased a house for the family on Main Street, a block or two from his partner, Philip

Steptoe, and not far from Ruth's parents.[47] Even after she was back from Baltimore and living in her own house, Ruth saw less of Louis than did his colleagues at Steptoe & Johnson.

It seemed as if Louis was always working. Except for a delightful second honeymoon—a trip to Bermuda in 1925 when Ruth wrote that Louis was "having a jolly time playing golf and tennis and dancing almost every night"—the bulk of his time was spent practicing law and developing the clients and reputation of Steptoe & Johnson.[48] He had the physical stamina to work from early morning to late at night, day after day, week after week. Few men have been able to get more out of a 24-hour day than did Louis Johnson. He coupled his willingness to work with his first-rate mind and developed into an excellent lawyer. It was not unusual for him to quickly study a legal brief prepared by someone else and then walk into a courtroom and argue it most convincingly.[49] However, what he enjoyed more than the legal work was the opportunity to attract profitable new business for the firm and recruit outstanding lawyers to handle that business. Specializing in corporate law, natural resources law, and trials, Steptoe & Johnson gained a reputation as the top law firm in the state during the 1920s.

But without Philip Steptoe, it is unlikely that Steptoe & Johnson would have achieved that reputation. In 1919, while Louis Johnson was still overseas, Steptoe drafted a statute for Governor Cornwell known as the Steptoe Gas Bill. The measure was designed to prevent West Virginia natural gas from being transported beyond the borders of the state (where it fetched higher prices) until the needs of West Virginia consumers and businesses had first been satisfied. Knowing the bill was fraught with constitutional issues, Steptoe's draftsmanship was clever and highly sophisticated. The Steptoe Gas Bill was enacted into law in 1919 and it was immediately challenged by Ohio and Pennsylvania.[50]

By the time Louis Johnson returned to the firm, the case challenging the constitutionality of the Steptoe Gas Bill was headed to the U.S. Supreme Court and Steptoe & Johnson was representing the State of West Virginia. Louis Johnson and a new associate in the firm worked on the briefs. This was one of the most important and celebrated natural resources cases ever presented to the Supreme Court, and the little firm of Steptoe & Johnson from the mountains of West Virginia was moving into the big time.

The high-stakes case was argued before the Supreme Court not once but twice. Philip Steptoe presented the arguments for West Virginia; his opponent was Johnson's friend John W. Davis, the former U.S. solicitor general from Clarksburg who was then practicing in New York City. Steptoe persuaded Justices Holmes and Brandeis that the law he wrote was constitutional, but he eventually lost the case by a split vote.[51] Nevertheless, Steptoe & Johnson demonstrated that it had the brains and the muscle to duke it out with the best lawyers in the country. Steptoe & Johnson had arrived. It was on the map.

Despite its location, Steptoe & Johnson stayed on the map primarily because of the business Johnson brought in and the high-quality lawyers he was able to recruit. Almost every spring, he and Philip Steptoe would make the rounds of the top law schools and identify the two or three best students and then try, usually successfully, to get them to come to Clarksburg. With the superior talent that they brought into the firm in the early years, success followed, and as the group's reputation grew, so did its business.[52] As one member of the firm put it, "Johnson made the lawyers of the firm feel like they were competent and respected and was able to persuade his clients that he had the best lawyers in the world to handle and look after their affairs."[53] The list of companies and individuals the firm served continued to grow, and in 1928, it opened offices in Charleston, the state capital.

With the legal success that came in the 1920s also came considerable financial success, and from that time on Johnson enjoyed an economic independence that made it possible for him to pursue goals of a less-tangible nature. While he always remained close to the legal profession, he increasingly involved himself in ventures that offered power, prestige, and service to others. These motives led him to plunge once more into numerous community activities. As a member and usually the leader of the Chamber of Commerce, the Rotary Club, the Elks, the Masons, the Odd Fellows, the Harrison County Bar Association, and Christ Episcopal Church, he made hundreds of valuable contacts that he could call on for support at a later date.[54] It was about this time that he was promoted to lieutenant colonel in the Infantry Reserve and many of his friends as well as all of his subordinates began to address him as "Colonel Johnson" and refer to him as "The Colonel"—a title which he encouraged and which was to remain with him for the rest of his life.

During the 1920s, Johnson stepped up his involvement in Democratic Party political activities. In early 1924, he began seeking support for the presidential nomination of his old friend and fellow Clarksburger, John W. Davis.[55] That summer, Johnson was a delegate to the Democratic National Convention at Madison Square Garden, the first Democratic convention covered by radio. The high point was Franklin Roosevelt's return to national politics following his bout with polio and his courageous speech nominating Al Smith, the "Happy Warrior," for president. After nine days of balloting and on the 103rd ballot, the discordant Democrats nominated Davis as the standard-bearer.[56]

Johnson returned to Clarksburg and headed the Local Notification Committee for the Davis homecoming, at which Davis would be formally notified and then would accept the nomination. When Davis arrived at the Clarksburg train station on August 9, 1924, Louis Johnson was the first one to shake his hand as he stepped onto the platform.[57] In the months that followed, he worked hard for Davis's election, but his friend conducted a lackluster campaign and went down to defeat at the hand of the incumbent president, Calvin Coolidge. Johnson, however, personally benefited from Davis's candidacy by making many valuable contacts in state and national Democratic circles.

The Legion

Of all the endeavors that Johnson engaged in during the 1920s, none was to pay bigger dividends than his activities as a member of the American Legion. While serving with the Army of Occupation in Coblenz during the winter of 1918–1919, Captain Johnson, always the organizer, understood the future political potential that could be wielded by the more than 2 million members of the Allied Expeditionary Force, and he knew that a group of like-minded officers was meeting in Paris to lay the foundation for the American Legion. The organization could not be formalized until chartered by Congress, but in the meantime the plans went forward for making the Legion a viable active organization of all World War I veterans dedicated to promoting national defense, patriotism, and fellowship.[58]

Shortly after Johnson was discharged from the army in June 1919, he was chosen to serve as chairman of the West Virginia delegation to the first Legion convention in Minneapolis in November. For Louis, being selected to participate in that event marked the beginning of a 47-year association with the patriotic organization. That summer, he met with a group of his veteran friends in Clarksburg to form the Roy E. Parrish Post No. 13 of the American Legion. During that period, he helped lay plans for the West Virginia department of the legion. In the fall he attended the convention in Minneapolis, which adopted a constitution and set up the state organization. There, he was elected to a two-year term on the National Executive Committee.[59]

Throughout the 1920s Johnson played an active role at the state and national level. He rarely missed an opportunity to attend a legion function and renew old acquaintances and make new ones. At the Kansas City convention in 1921, Johnson renewed his friendship with Harry Truman, who was in charge of decorations at that raucous drunken affair.[60] In all of these gatherings, the barrel-chested, hand-shaking, and loquacious Louis Johnson was always one of the most visible participants. Some individuals considered him pushy, but most saw him as merely an extremely outgoing person.

Johnson's politicking and extensive work on behalf of the legion led to his selection as head of the state delegation to the 1927 convention in Paris. Accompanied by Jim Guiher, his Steptoe & Johnson partner, and his friend, physician, and golfing pal, Dr. Frank Langfitt, Johnson sailed to Europe with fellow veterans of the Great War on the SS *Pennland*. They toured the battlefields, including the dugout from which Jim Guiher had been machine-gunned, and then they, along with 20,000 other veterans and their families, converged on Paris for an emotional and sentimental reunion in the country where they had witnessed so much death and destruction. At the convention Johnson was awarded the French Legion of Honor Medal, but the highlight of the Paris trip was the huge parade from the Arc de Triomphe down the Champs Elysées. An old sepia-toned photograph shows Louis Johnson in a straw hat marching down the avenue with a group of former doughboys.[61]

After the Paris convention, Colonel Johnson continued his rise within the American Legion organization. He was named West Virginia department judge advocate and chairman of the National Legislative Committee. Then, in September 1930, he was elected state commander of the 10,000-man West Virginia department. Many of the previous state commanders had viewed the office as primarily a ceremonial one, but not Louis Johnson. In his year in the position he devoted more than 25 percent of his time to the organization's affairs and traveled more than 30,000 miles, visiting every post in the state.[62]

By the time Johnson came to head the West Virginia Department of the American Legion, the national body, with its 10,760 posts and nearly 1 million members, was clearly "the most widely organized [and] probably the most effectively organized" pressure group in the United States.[63] Johnson recognized that heading the national organization would not only be personally satisfying but could also open doors to further power and prominence. Thus, he set out to capture the big prize—becoming national commander of the American Legion.

In 1931 at the national convention in Detroit, Johnson made an unsuccessful run for the top spot. At the Portland, Oregon, convention held at the Hotel Multnomah in September 1932, Johnson came prepared with a formidable campaign organization. Under the leadership of Phil Conley of Charleston and Ed Blake of Roncaverte, thirty-eight West Virginians worked night and day to convince the state caucuses to elect Louis Johnson as national commander. His friend Paul Griffith, who would later work with Johnson at the War Department and the Defense Department, headed the largest state delegation, Pennsylvania, and he threw his support to Johnson. In a crowded field of candidates, Louis Johnson won the election on the first ballot.[64]

Looking back, it is difficult to understand and appreciate the prestige and significance of being national commander of the million-man veterans' lobbying group in 1932. It was truly a very big deal. Because of the number of votes he could either deliver or influence, politicians of all stripes, from the president of the United States down to county commissioners, would court the national commander and pay close attention to his views.

Immediately following his election, Johnson was welcomed back to Clarksburg as West Virginia's favorite son. His homecoming on September 26 was marked by the longest parade (four miles), the largest crowd, and the "greatest pomp ever accorded a public figure in mountain state history."[65]

As head of the large and influential veterans' group, Johnson had the opportunity to gain considerable national exposure, and he took full advantage of it. Invitations to speak before civic, veterans', patriotic, business, and educational organizations poured in from across the country, and the dynamic West Virginian rarely turned one down. Many of his addresses, such as the November 11,

1932, dedication speech at the Tomb of the Unknown Soldier in Arlington National Cemetery, were carried on national radio. In all of his appearances Johnson used his well-honed public-speaking skills to drive home the need for adequate defense preparedness and the obligation to provide sufficient benefits for the nation's veterans. Although his message was nearly always the same, the effectiveness of his delivery never failed to move his audiences.[66]

Inside the White House

Of all the doors the position of national commander opened for Johnson, none was more important than the one to the White House. Almost immediately, Johnson was inside the White House with Herbert Hoover during his final weeks as president to explain the legion's new position on bonus payments and other legislative initiatives adopted at the Portland convention. Less than two months after Johnson's election, Franklin D. Roosevelt was elected president of the United States, a development that was to be of profound consequence to the lawyer from Clarksburg.

In 1932–1933, the national commander of the American Legion had ready access to the White House because he represented approximately 1 million disgruntled and disillusioned World War I veterans and their families. Their economic plight at the outset of the Great Depression had become an explosive political issue, which played a significant role in the defeat of Herbert Hoover and the election of Franklin Roosevelt, the first Democratic president since Woodrow Wilson. During the summer of 1932, President Hoover called up U.S. army troops, under the overall command of Army Chief of Staff Douglas MacArthur, to drive the Bonus Army out of Washington. Hoover was held responsible for the excessive force used by MacArthur's troops, and he was branded as insensitive to the plight of the unemployed.[67]

In contrast to the Veterans of Foreign Wars (VFW), the other veterans' organization which was much smaller (about 200,000 members) and more radical, the American Legion stood on the sidelines and did not launch a serious protest against the violence which so outraged the American people. This was because the conservative leadership of the Legionnaires believed that many in the Bonus Army were extremists and had been infiltrated by communist "agitators." Moreover, the legion was committed by resolution adopted the year before at its convention in Detroit to support President Hoover in his effort to prevent early payment of veterans' bonuses on the ground that the huge payouts would worsen the Depression.[68] However, at its contentious convention in Portland in September 1932, the legion, supported by Louis Johnson's West Virginians, completely reversed its position and, by a vote of 1,169 to 109, adopted a resolution in favor of legislation to require "full and immediate payment" of the bonuses.[69]

As national commander, Johnson did not push very hard for full and immediate bonus payments because he was certain that Congress and the new president would not enact such legislation in 1933. He also knew that he would need help from the White House to fend off anticipated efforts to cut back on existing veterans' disability benefits. Therefore, with a keen sense of the politics likely to affect both veterans' bonuses and disability payments and with an eye to his own political future, the new national commander immediately took up the banner as supporter and defender of the new chief executive and his policies. On Roosevelt's first day in office, Johnson publicly urged all veterans to stand by the new president as he attempted to meet the daunting problems facing the depression-racked nation.[70]

The veterans, however, quickly found such support hard to give because on March 10, 1933, Roosevelt sent to Congress an Economy Act which, among other things, would confer broad discretion on the president to promulgate regulations reducing veterans' disability payments. A number of Legionnaires reacted bitterly against the bill, and some of their lobbyists attacked it as well as the president who advocated it. Commander Johnson, however, stood by his pledge to support the president, and he successfully urged most Legion members to keep their powder dry because they would be needing the president's good will. As Johnson had expected, the Economy Act was quickly and overwhelmingly adopted by Congress.[71]

Johnson's political judgment was further questioned when, on April 1, the White House issued new regulations pursuant to the Economy Act which included drastic cuts in disability benefits. Many veterans were greatly upset, including one group in California which considered another march on Washington.[72]

As soon as he had analyzed the new regulations, Commander Johnson wrote to Roosevelt criticizing the cuts, but he did so in a constructive manner and he offered his services to help make them more equitable. Publicly, he continued to support the president's economy program, and he urged the legion to oppose any marches on Washington.[73] In taking this stand, Johnson was bucking most of the legion hierarchy and thus, as one contemporary described it, "we had, in the spring of 1933 the curious spectacle of the National Commander of the American Legion reiterating before the public the Legion's pledge to the President and, simultaneously, the Legislative Committee bringing every sort of pressure upon departments, posts and individual members to oppose him."[74]

Johnson's political judgment paid off. His decision to refrain from attacking the president and to keep the White House door open to the American Legion was the smart thing to do. On May 10, FDR invited the Colonel to meet with him at the White House to discuss and alleviate the concerns of the veterans. At that meeting, Johnson convinced FDR that the cuts in disability benefits were deeper than they should be and that a complete reassessment was needed. Following the meeting, the president announced he was ordering a "review so as to effect more equitable levels of payment."[75]

During the next month, Johnson consulted with Roosevelt and his advisors on all aspects of veterans' disability benefits, and ultimately the chief executive went along with proposals which limited reductions for war-disabled veterans to a maximum of 25 percent—a move which ultimately restored $170 million in disability benefits to veterans. On June 6, 1933, Roosevelt issued amendments to his regulations.[76]

Louis Johnson fared quite well in all of the turmoil over bonus and disability payments. A number of Legionnaires and many other veterans were in his debt for helping bring about restoration of many of the cuts, and the president was in his debt for calming the disgruntled veterans. It was also in the course of this affair that the man from Clarksburg came to know Stephen Early, Roosevelt's press secretary, who had grown up in a small town near Charlottesville. Having served together in the Blue Ridge Division, the two men immediately hit it off and developed a very close personal relationship based on admiration and respect that was to continue for two decades.[77]

No sooner had the problem of disability benefits been handled than Johnson again worked his way into the president's good graces, for the third time in six months, when he helped rally legion support for the National Recovery Act, which was designed to foster industrial growth. On August 3, 1933, Johnson sent "battle orders" to the more than 10,000 American Legion posts throughout the country, calling upon them "to offer their loyal cooperation and services to the officials of the National Recovery Administration . . . and to cooperate in achieving its objective." The support called for was forthcoming, and Roosevelt appreciated the help.[78] Being the politician that he was, FDR never forgot when someone did something for him, and by the fall of 1933, Johnson had done him several favors. The time for repayment would eventually arrive, and Johnson knew it.

As the summer of 1933 neared an end, Louis Johnson was busy making plans for the legion's national convention that would open in Chicago on October 2. To enhance his stature and make a big splash, Johnson endeavored to secure a convention speaker that no one would forget—the president of the United States. While FDR had earlier indicated he might attend the convention, he and his advisors had concluded that because of the problems with veterans it would be best to stay clear of the national gathering. Thus, on September 18 the president informed Johnson that he "must finally and definitely abandon the idea of attending."[79] When he received the rejection Johnson immediately traveled to Washington, where he used his persuasive skills to convince Roosevelt to reverse his decision. Two weeks later, the president went to Chicago, where he addressed the convention and received an extremely enthusiastic reception. That appearance did a great deal to solidify support among veterans for the president.[80] Both Johnson and Roosevelt benefited from the Chicago visit.

The 1933 Chicago convention marked the end of Johnson's term as national commander of the American Legion. However, his ties with Roosevelt were just beginning. He had gotten his size-thirteen foot in the White House door and was not about to back out.

For the next few years, Johnson kept in touch with the president with occasional personal visits and letters and through their mutual friend, presidential press secretary Steve Early. Johnson's service as civilian aide to the secretary of war for the state of West Virginia and his appointment to the Federal Advisory Council of the U.S. Employment Service gave him plenty of excuses for communicating with President Roosevelt and key members of his administration.[81]

In 1934, Johnson announced that he would seek the Democratic nomination for the U.S. Senate. However, fearing what a loss might do to his "political future," he dropped the idea and never filed.[82] Johnson continued to maintain a position of prominence and prestige in the legion and to use his stature within the organization to show his support for the president and his policies.

In early 1936 Johnson organized and headed the Veterans Committee of the Democratic National Committee, a group whose major goal was to win widespread support among veterans for the president's reelection. Combining legal skills with keen political judgment, Johnson prepared a brilliant memorandum for Roosevelt's campaign staff which, according to an exhaustive history of the bonus army, turned Roosevelt's overridden veto of a veterans' bonus into a "political asset."[83] By the summer of 1936 Johnson was completely immersed in the reelection campaign.[84] Little did he realize that the events that were about to unfold would have such an impact on his life.

Ready for Prime Time

The Louis Johnson who had emerged by 1936 was a man who was aggressive, willing to take risks, shrewd, street-smart, a good organizer, and, above all else, political. Whether it was as a grocery delivery boy, college student, lawyer, army supply officer, state legislator, or Legionnaire, he was always working, maneuvering, and manipulating people and events in such a way as to further his own career or cause. At age forty-five, Johnson was about to enter an arena where he would be able to play politics with many of the most important men in America for the next fourteen years. The game he was to be involved in was that of providing for the military defense of the United States. His venture in the politics of defense was about to begin.

CHAPTER THREE

Like Feuding Schoolboys

F ROM THE FRONT PORCH of his home on Main Street, Louis Johnson picked up the morning newspaper to give it the usual scan before going to the office. As his eyes raced over the front page on that August 28, 1936, morning, he saw an item that riveted his attention. The evening before, Secretary of War George H. Dern had died, following a lengthy illness, in a Washington hospital.[1]

While Johnson regretted the death of the former Utah governor who had come to head the War Department in 1933, the opening of the cabinet position interested him greatly.[2] In fact, there was no position in government that Johnson would rather have than that of secretary of war because it played to his interests—the U.S. Army and national defense—and it would call upon his strengths—organization, command, and politics.

The former grocery clerk, army supply officer, and American Legion commander foresaw an enormous opportunity. If he could figure out a way to persuade President Roosevelt to appoint him as secretary of war, Johnson could become a powerful player in the Roosevelt administration and the door would be opened to the charmed political and social circles of the nation's capital.[3] The Clarksburg lawyer had never been one to sit back and wait for opportunity to knock, and this time would be no different. He knew what he wanted, and he set out to attain his goal.

The Top Spot—Almost

Secretary Dern had not yet been laid to rest when political observers began speculating about who would be filling his position. Those mentioned most frequently were Indiana governor Paul McNutt, New York City mayor Fiorello

LaGuardia, Commissioner of the Philippine Islands Frank Murphy, and President Roosevelt's press secretary, Steve Early. Johnson was not included in the initial speculation, nor was Assistant Secretary of War Harry H. Woodring, who since 1933 had been filling the number-two spot in the department and serving as acting secretary during Dern's long illness.[4]

If it had not been an election year, the appointment process would have gone ahead and Johnson probably would not have been in the running. However, in the summer and fall of 1936, President Roosevelt was in the midst of a political campaign for reelection. His first priority was the defeat of his opponent, Alf Landon of Kansas, and the president decided in late August to indefinitely postpone his decision on filling Dern's post.[5]

Louis Johnson likewise had matters of immediate concern, specifically his responsibility of heading the Veterans Committee of the Democratic National Committee. The West Virginian knew that if his hope of gaining the war post were to have any chance of becoming reality, two things were necessary: first, Roosevelt would have to be reelected; and second, the veteran vote would have to be overwhelmingly for the incumbent. Johnson worked long and hard throughout the fall of 1936 for a Roosevelt victory.[6]

The president was also working hard as he carried his campaign across the nation. The strain would have been great on any man, and it was especially telling on the man whose ability to walk had been swept away by infantile paralysis a decade and a half before. In late September, Roosevelt journeyed to his home at Hyde Park for a few days' rest. On the 25th he received an urgent letter from Attorney General Homer S. Cummings stating that it would be necessary to appoint a secretary of war by the following day because the law did not permit a cabinet position to be vacant for more than thirty days.[7] Caught off guard and faced with the necessity of filling the post immediately, the president responded in the only manner he felt feasible—he named Acting Secretary Harry Woodring to the position, and since Congress was not in session, it was a "recess appointment." In the telegram informing Woodring of the action taken and the press release issued from Hyde Park, the president stated that the recess appointment was temporary. The statement led the press to conclude that the chief executive would wait until after the election before naming a permanent secretary of war.[8]

On November 3, 1936, the American people overwhelmingly reelected President Roosevelt. While millions of citizens were overjoyed with the election's outcome, few were as pleased as Louis Johnson. Not only had his candidate won, but the large veteran vote had been delivered to the president just as he had promised. It had taken all of Johnson's political and organizational skills to mold the Veterans Committee into a group that could win such massive support for a man who had not been considered a friend of the veteran early in his administration and had vetoed bonus legislation as late as January 1936.[9] Johnson felt confident that he was in line for an appropriate political reward. He did not want just any position—he wanted to be named the next secretary of war.

The election results were barely in when Johnson began to openly promote himself as a candidate for the secretary of war position. At Johnson's urging, Democratic National Committee chairman James A. Farley, Press Secretary Steve Early, and Assistant Secretary of Commerce J. Monroe Johnson (no relation to Louis) suggested that the president appoint Johnson. In addition, Johnson encouraged many of his friends in the American Legion to send letters to the White House urging that he be named to the post. He also sought and received political support from the six Democratic congressmen from West Virginia, who jointly sent a letter to FDR requesting that he put the Clarksburg lawyer in charge of the War Department.[10]

The impact of this pressure on FDR is unclear, but it was well known that when he selected top advisors, especially cabinet members, he always remained fiercely independent. The president made it clear to those around him that while he would listen to their recommendations on appointees, all selections would be his and his alone.[11]

As 1937 dawned, Johnson was confident that the war post would be his. That optimism was based in part upon the steady flow of press reports which stated that Roosevelt would probably not reappoint Woodring. Furthermore, inside sources such as Farley, Early, presidential advisor Harry Hopkins, and Secretary of the Interior Harold Ickes likewise confirmed signs emanating from the Oval Office indicating that the president would probably not retain his war secretary during his second term.[12]

However, as the early months of 1937 slipped by and Roosevelt failed to take action, the delay strengthened the position of the temporary secretary. Woodring, a genial and sociable former governor of Kansas with an attractive and equally social wife, had been on the Washington scene for nearly four years and during that time had made many friends in the army, veterans' organizations, and Congress. Those supporters and the groups they represented championed him as the permanent secretary. Army Chief of Staff Malin Craig and many members of the general staff voiced strong support for Woodring because he was a personable man with a firm understanding of the army and its problems. Key military publications, such as the *Army and Navy Journal*, the *Army-Navy Register*, *Army Ordinance*, and *The Reserve Officer*, also took stands in favor of Woodring's reappointment.[13]

In spite of pressure from various quarters to name a new secretary, Roosevelt continued to procrastinate. Things were running smoothly at the War Department; Woodring was cautiously but competently carrying out the responsibilities of both secretary and assistant secretary. The president would have been content to let the situation ride, but he could not do so because Woodring was a recess appointment. Under the law, if Woodring was not approved by the Senate or a new nominee was not sent forward and confirmed by the end of the congressional session, the position would become vacant. This legal requirement made it essential that the president make a decision before Congress adjourned that spring.[14]

In the early months of 1937, Johnson was approached on several occasions by Jim Farley and by West Virginia senator Matthew M. Neely about whether he would be interested in being named assistant secretary of war. Each time, he rejected the idea and indicated that his only interest was in the position of secretary. On April 19, Roosevelt discussed the position with Jim Farley, who had been appointed postmaster general, and said that although it would be an unpleasant task, he was going to remove Woodring. The conversation then turned to Louis Johnson. The president asked if the West Virginian would be interested in the assistant secretary position, to which Farley replied that he was interested only in the top spot. The president told Farley that he would put Johnson in Woodring's place but it would only be for a short time. He told Farley to talk to both Woodring and Johnson about the upcoming change. The report of the discussion in the press raised Johnson's hope that he would be appointed.[15]

Those hopes were dashed, however, just one week later, on April 26, when Roosevelt shocked everyone by announcing that he was reappointing Woodring and immediately sending his name to the Senate for confirmation. Approval was quickly forthcoming from the Senate Military Affairs Committee, and on May 6 the entire body gave its assent. Just why the president changed his mind will probably never be known. One explanation is that he did not want to hurt the feelings of Woodring or his young wife Helen (daughter of Senator Marcus Coolidge of Massachusetts), of whom FDR was apparently quite fond. A more likely reason is that Roosevelt was impressed by the fact that things were going quite well in the War Department with Woodring at the helm and he did not wish to disrupt that state of affairs.[16]

Johnson was jolted by the Woodring appointment. He had known that two other former national commanders of the American Legion, Paul McNutt and J. Ray Murphy, were quietly campaigning for the position, and he had resigned himself to the possibility that one of them would get it—but not Woodring.[17] In the weeks following Woodring's appointment, Johnson was approached by Farley on several occasions and asked if he would reconsider and take the position of assistant secretary of war. On each visit, Johnson rejected the offer.[18] Convinced that Johnson would not change his mind, the president decided to begin searching for a businessman to fill the spot. Attention soon focused on a Sears & Roebuck vice-president, William I. Westervelt, and on June 9, Roosevelt sent a note to Woodring asking for his assessment of the Sears executive.

Four days later, before going to the regularly scheduled Friday cabinet meeting, Woodring sent a memo to Roosevelt endorsing Westervelt.[19] However, following the meeting the president called the secretary aside and told him that Johnson had changed his mind and would accept the number two position. Woodring returned to his office and wrote a letter to the president recommending Johnson for the position.[20] At that point Woodring and Johnson had never met. The following Monday, Roosevelt formally announced the Johnson appointment and submitted his name to the Senate for confirmation. Approval was quickly forthcoming.

Just what happened between June 9 and 13 to cause Louis Johnson to change his mind about accepting the assistant secretaryship is not certain, but it is apparent that there was considerable confusion about what was, or was not, promised. That confusion was to have considerable impact on war department operations for the next several years.

According to Johnson, he changed his mind and accepted the assistant secretary position because Jim Farley promised that if he took the job he would be named secretary after a short period of time.[21] This claim is substantiated by Senator Neely (D-West Virginia), who maintained that Farley asked him to urge Johnson to accept the position. According to Neely, Farley said to him, "You can tell Louis I think within three or four months he will be made Secretary if he will take the post."[22] Farley always denied that his statements to Johnson and Neely amounted to a promise, and Roosevelt claimed that he had never authorized such a deal.[23]

Whether Johnson was actually promised the top spot will probably never be known for certain, but what is more important is that he acted as if the promise had been made. For the next three years, Johnson was to say on countless occasions that Farley, on Roosevelt's behalf and with his knowledge, had promised him the secretaryship. As one reporter put it, "Almost in the same breath with which he took office . . . [Johnson] informed intimates that he had been appointed for the express purpose of replacing Woodring in a few months."[24]

Colonel Johnson Arrives

In mid-June of 1937, Louis Johnson said farewell to the seventeen lawyers at Steptoe & Johnson and boarded the midnight train for Washington. After arriving at Union Station, Johnson hailed a taxi which took him and his luggage up Pennsylvania Avenue, past the marble temples of government gleaming white and green in the morning sun. When Johnson climbed out of the cab, the staff of the Mayflower greeted him by name as he had his suitcases and trunks taken up to his apartment in the annex of the famous hotel on Connecticut Avenue. For the next thirty years, Louis Johnson and his family would be members of the Mayflower's "permanent colony," the fortunate residents who had air-cooled rooms, working fireplaces, complete kitchens, and access to servants. Johnson would be joining more than twenty members of Congress and dozens of other prominent people in government and politics who resided at "Washington's Second Best Address."[25]

On June 28, 1937, with his wife and two daughters at his side, Johnson was sworn in as assistant secretary of war. His guests featured Postmaster General Jim Farley, Publicity Director Charles Michelson of the Democratic National Committee, Press Secretary Steve Early, and Senator Neely of West Virginia. Given Johnson's guest list, the ceremony was more like a political powwow than a national defense gathering.[26]

In the summer of 1937 the War Department had jurisdiction over the army and the army air corps (there was no separate air force) but not the navy and the marines. The War Department, along with the Navy and State Departments, was housed in what is today called the Old Executive Office Building next to the West Wing of the White House. The secretary of war's office was a few doors down the hall from the smaller assistant secretary's office. The Oval Office was just a few steps away across a courtyard. The close proximity of these decision makers should have made for a congenial working relationship. However, the relations between Johnson and Secretary Woodring were to be anything but congenial.

Woodring and Johnson were emblematic of ideologies within the American mainstream which were soon to come into sharp and acrimonious conflict. The cautious Harry Woodring was an isolationist but, as he liked to say, only in the sense that he was committed to keeping the nation isolated from war. Woodring was a strong advocate of military preparedness to keep the United States out of foreign wars, but he was an even stronger proponent of carefully limiting military expenditures in accordance with the nation's ability to pay. His conservative views were shared by the vast majority of the Congress and American public.[27]

By contrast, the bold and decisive Louis Johnson, while not an interventionist, was certainly an internationalist, and he seemed much more concerned than Woodring about the growing threats to the national security Germany and Japan posed. Johnson was passionately committed to building the strength and capability of the U.S. Army without much regard for cost.[28] In the summer of 1937, very few Americans shared Johnson's views and his position on the urgent need for military preparedness.

In addition to ideological differences, the assistant secretary had statutory responsibilities that were bound to put him in conflict with the secretary. Under the National Defense Act of 1920, the assistant secretary was given explicit — Johnson would say exclusive — authority and responsibility for procurement of all military supplies, both during peacetime and wartime, and for providing the means whereby American industry could gear up to produce all the material needed to fight a major war. To put it another way, Johnson was authorized by law to plan for industrial mobilization in case of war.[29]

In light of these express statutory powers, it is easy to see how an aggressive assistant secretary like Louis Johnson could clash with a secretary who was charged under the same statute with the job of raising, training, and equipping the army and of supervising the work of the assistant secretary. Sharp disagreements and turf battles were inevitable.

But without FDR, the squabbles and turf battles between Johnson and Woodring would never have reached center stage. Virtually every American president has had squabbling within the inner circle that surrounds him. However, the infighting, backbiting, and feuding among top aides was especially prevalent under Franklin Roosevelt. Roosevelt not only tolerated such widespread bickering among his subordinates, he frequently engineered and encouraged it.[30]

While there is abundant evidence about the number and nature of the feuds promulgated by FDR, it is not clear why he encouraged such behavior so frequently. Nevertheless, an effort must be made to understand Roosevelt's behavior because, as Roosevelt speechwriter Robert Sherwood would later write: "History will achieve no complete understanding of FDR's administration without knowledge of the intramural feuds which so frequently beset it. I do not believe that even history will be able to understand why he tolerated them to the extent that he did."[31]

The explanation for why Roosevelt created and condoned infighting was probably his belief that such situations served to enhance his own political power. It is well known that Roosevelt preferred to run nearly every facet of his administration rather than have subordinates do so. To make sure that no one person or any single view could gain too much influence, the president continually played departments and individuals against one another.[32]

The same motive was behind Roosevelt's practice of playing opposites against one another. By placing individuals whose thinking, philosophies, and personalities were quite different into top positions in a particular department or agency, the president was able to assure that the decision makers frequently would not be able to come to agreement on key policy decisions; thus, it would be necessary that they run to the chief executive to get the matter resolved. This practice not only enabled Roosevelt to make the decisions, it also made it possible for him to know what was going on in the departments because officials would tend to rat on each other.[33]

There is little doubt that Roosevelt knew exactly what he was doing when he chose the people he did to fill the key positions in his administration. When such maneuvering did not give FDR the control he desired, he would frequently delegate authority for a particular task to a personal representative or someone else outside the normal chain of command, and the person so appointed could always be counted on to see the job was done the way the president wanted.[34]

When Roosevelt agreed to appoint Johnson as assistant secretary of war he was well aware that the bold and decisive lawyer would be a good counterweight to the cautious, methodical Woodring, a former banker. And he probably knew that Johnson would be more aggressive, more cooperative, and more decisive on rearmament and mobilization issues than Woodring would. The president's decision to appoint Johnson was consistent with his practice of selecting top officials who would offset each other. However, FDR could not have realized that his choice of Johnson would ultimately have such a devastating impact upon the operations of the War Department on the eve of the greatest conflict the nation had ever experienced.

The War Within

As Johnson settled into his job in the summer of 1937, he did so with the same aggressiveness that he had attacked every other job he had ever undertaken. He had always been a take-charge person, and this time was to be no different. In a matter of weeks, he was openly talking and acting as if he was in charge of the department. According to one news account, "Assistant Secretary Johnson set himself to running the War Department acting very much like a No. 2 man who had been made No. 1 in all but title."[35]

Johnson warned war department officials, both civilian and military, who challenged him that they were talking to the person who was about to be named secretary and that crossing him would not be wise.[36] On numerous occasions in the next three years, Johnson was to inform newsmen, war department personnel, and friends that on a certain date he would be named secretary; however, the day would come and go and no announcement would be forthcoming. Such pronouncements were especially upsetting to officers of the general staff because they had to wonder if Johnson was, in fact, about to become their boss.[37]

As might be expected, Johnson's bold pronouncements became increasingly upsetting to Secretary Woodring, who was soon convinced that his assistant was spending "most of his waking hours in trying to replace me as Secretary of War."[38] The situation was made even worse by Johnson's failure to hide his feeling that Woodring was not the man to be heading the department.[39] With each passing day, the two men became increasingly alienated from one another. When Johnson began making public statements on defense policy without conferring with the secretary, Woodring attempted to call him to task for actions which he felt bordered on insubordination. To that criticism Johnson would respond sharply, claiming that on matters of procurement and industrial mobilization, the subjects he usually spoke on, he was responsible by statute to the president and the Congress, not the secretary.

During Johnson's first year in the War Department, he and Woodring argued primarily over major policies and problems, but thereafter they increasingly fought over matters of less and less significance. Eventually, the situation degenerated to a point where they would disagree so violently and so often that they would not even speak to one another for weeks on end.[40] This made for a very strained relationship at the War Council meeting, a weekly session in which the secretary, assistant secretary, and the chief of staff and their aides met to discuss departmental matters.

When Johnson and Woodring were forced to discuss crucial matters, they tended to act like feuding schoolboys rather than top government officials. Such was the case in a meeting that was held in early 1938 over the number of B-17 bombers that would be procured in the next fiscal year. The program, which had been developed by ground-oriented Chief of Staff General Malin Craig and approved by the cost-conscious secretary, called for only twelve B-17s. When the presentation was complete, Woodring proclaimed with finality, "That will be the plan." "Wait a minute, Mr. Secretary," shot back Johnson. "Oh, we all know you're opposed to it," replied an irritated Woodring. "Yes, I am opposed to it and I want General Andrews [commanding general, general headquarters, air force] to be heard," growled the assistant secretary. As his anger began to get the better of him, Woodring tried to end the conversation, saying, "I don't want to hear General Andrews."

At this point, General Craig jumped in as the peacemaker and persuaded the secretary to let Andrews address the group. Following the general's plea for more bombers, Woodring, his anger under control, calmly pointed to the original proposal and announced with all the authority he could muster, "This is still the plan." Johnson, his lips hardly moving and in an icy and barely audible voice said, "With all due respect to your office, there is a statutory responsibility involved. This is not the program until the commander-in-chief approves it."

After a few moments of awkward silence the meeting broke up. Then Johnson, based on his conviction that he had direct access and responsibility to the president on procurement matters, took the bomber issue to the White House, where he pleaded for a stepped-up program of bomber procurement. Roosevelt, however, was unwilling to engage in such a costly program, and Woodring's plan was ultimately adopted.[41]

Roosevelt's decision on this and subsequent occasions to thwart Johnson's persistent efforts to acquire a larger fleet of B-17s for the army air corps had profound implications. Years later, Army Chief of Staff George Marshall remarked that "Germany would never have gotten off the ground if America had had the full complement of B-17's which [Louis] Johnson had requested before the war."[42]

In early 1938, another dispute occurred that provides insight into the ongoing feud between Johnson and Woodring and shows how the friction could and did impact war department decisions. In January, the State Department, as a means of furthering its Good Neighbor Policy with South America, sent a request to the War Department asking that six of the new B-17 bombers be sent on a flight to Buenos Aires to mark the inauguration of Argentina's new president, Robert M. Ortiz. Secretary Woodring, who was always watching dollars, rejected the proposal on the grounds that it was too costly. That decision was disappointing to many people, especially a number of army air corps officers, who saw in the flight the possibility of a great propaganda tool.

One person who was upset by the Woodring decision was newsman William A. Wieland of the Associated Press, an advocate of the flight to Argentina. Knowing how things worked in the War Department, Wieland went around Woodring and approached Johnson directly. Johnson pledged his support and, with the aid of his friend Steve Early and Undersecretary of State Sumner Welles, put the idea before the president. Roosevelt, knowing full well that his secretary of war opposed the flight, ordered that it be made, and a reluctant Woodring had no alternative but to carry out the directive.[43]

In February of 1938, six B-17 Flying Fortresses under the command of Lieutenant Colonel Robert C. Olds made a historic 12,000-mile flight to and from Buenos Aires without serious mishap, thus proving the reliability of the strategic aircraft that was to be the backbone of the air corps during World War II. When the planes and crews returned to Washington, they were greeted by Secretary Woodring and Chief of Staff Craig. The following day Woodring accompanied Olds to the White House for a special visit with the chief executive, and a month later, Secretary Woodring presented the coveted Mackay Trophy to the Second Bombardment Wing for its aviation achievement.[44] Throughout all the publicity and hoopla that surrounded the flight and its aftermath, Secretary Woodring was hailed again and again for ordering the flight while Louis Johnson, the war department official most responsible for the flight, stewed in silence.[45]

Usually Johnson's feuds with Woodring resulted in nothing more than bruised egos, but there were times when their consequences were far more serious. Such was the case in early 1938, when Johnson left town for a few days on a speaking engagement and in his absence Woodring ordered the revision of procurement procedures for certain aircraft parts. When Johnson returned and learned what had happened, he became furious because he considered the secretary's action to be blatant interference in an area that was clearly his domain. The assistant secretary ordered a halt to the procurement of all the parts in question until the problem could be worked out. For the next several weeks Johnson and Woodring sparred over the language of the contracts until they finally reached a settlement. Shortly thereafter, procurement of the parts resumed, but in the meantime valuable time had been lost.[46]

A similar battle of wills ultimately resulted in a six-month delay in crucial construction projects to fortify the Panama Canal. This fiasco began in the spring of 1939, when Congress appropriated more than $30 million for new airbases, harbor defenses, and anti-aircraft guns for the Canal Zone. These construction projects were normally under the jurisdiction of the assistant secretary, who would award contracts based on competitive bidding. Woodring intervened, however, pointing to a rarely used law that gave to the secretary the authority to issue contracts on a cost-plus basis to a firm of his choice when he felt there was a possibility that military secrets could be revealed.

For weeks the two men bickered over whether the Canal Zone contracts should be granted on a competitive or cost-plus basis. Finally, Johnson persuaded the army quartermaster, Major General Henry Gibbons, to write a memo backing his position. He enlisted Steve Early's aid, and Early got the memo to the president, who agreed with Johnson and ordered that the contracts be issued after competitive bidding. In December 1939, five months after Congress provided the funds, the bids were opened, and in February 1940 Johnson signed the contracts. Again, valuable time had been lost.[47]

In practically every squabble between Johnson and Woodring, there was one individual who got caught in the middle—the chief of staff. The first chief to suffer was General Craig. The general, being a true professional, gave his first allegiance to the man at the top—Secretary Woodring. He was annoyed and upset by Johnson's usurpations and pushiness. Craig clearly viewed many of Johnson's actions as rank insubordination.[48]

When the flight of the B-17s to Buenos Aires was under consideration, Craig was put in a terribly awkward position. After Woodring had rejected the proposal, Johnson informed Craig that he was taking the matter directly to the president and then added, "Don't tell the secretary." Craig refused, pointing out that the secretary was his superior and that it was his duty to keep him informed. Continuing, he asked Johnson, "What would you think about subordinates who did things behind your back or did not share information with you?" Johnson turned and walked away.[49]

General Craig's difficult plight was aptly described by Katherine Marshall, wife of Craig's successor, General George Marshall, who probably understood the situation as few others could. As she described it, Craig "was sitting on the fence between these two gentlemen. If he followed the Secretary's instructions he would be in bad odor with the Assistant Secretary, who was quite powerful. If he followed the lead of Mr. Johnson, Mr. Woodring would have called him to account. It was an impossible and tragic situation." Mrs. Craig put it more bluntly. "[T]hey have crucified my husband," she said.[50]

New Chief of Staff: General Marshall

The difficulties that Chief of Staff Craig had in operating in such a tension-filled atmosphere can be seen in the circumstances surrounding the selection of his successor, General George Marshall. The choice of Marshall for the chief's position was one of the rare instances in which Johnson and Woodring were in agreement, yet the nature of their personal feud jeopardized Marshall's chances.

Johnson first met George Marshall in January 1938, when he was on an inspection tour at Vancouver Barracks, Washington. On that visit, Marshall, then a rising but still quite junior brigadier general, made a deep and highly favorable impression on the assistant secretary. That summer Marshall was ordered to Washington to head the War Plans Division.

In his new position, Marshall came into frequent contact with Johnson, and in a very short period of time the assistant secretary was convinced that he had found the man to replace Craig. He began to aggressively promote Marshall for the chief of staff position even though several generals were ahead of him in seniority. In his typical outspoken fashion, Johnson made pronouncements that Marshall would soon be made deputy and ultimately chief of staff. Marshall found such statements upsetting because he feared that since they came from Johnson, they would anger Woodring and Craig and cost him their support.[51]

While Johnson did a great deal of talking about Marshall, he also acted on his convictions. Indeed, it was Louis Johnson who appointed Marshall as deputy chief of staff, thus exposing him to Roosevelt and those around him so they could witness firsthand his extraordinary abilities and begin to appreciate his potential.

The Marshall appointment came while Woodring was out of town campaigning for Democratic congressmen at Roosevelt's request. As usual, Johnson became acting secretary in the Woodring's absence and had complete authority in all areas. One morning in mid-October 1938, when members of the general staff were gathering for a War Council meeting which Johnson had called, he startled General Craig by asking, "What about a deputy chief of staff?" He asked the question because the former deputy, Stanley Embrick, had just departed for a new assignment and no replacement had been named. Craig, not wanting to act until Woodring returned, replied vaguely, "We'll work that out." Johnson, realizing that delay would enable Woodring to take credit for the appointment, quickly popped the question, "What about George Marshall?" Then, in a menacing tone, he said, "There is not going to be any War Council meeting until that thing is worked out." Craig, knowing that Johnson was dead serious and would not back down, left the room and returned a short time later to announce, "The orders have been issued."[52] Johnson had carried the day. His stubborn insistence that Marshall be appointed deputy chief of staff greatly increased the odds that Roosevelt would soon make him chief of staff.

During that fall of 1938 and in the early months of 1939, there was considerable maneuvering in top army circles for the post of chief of staff. Although Johnson and Woodring both favored Marshall, they knew how Roosevelt operated and they were afraid to push him for fear that it would prejudice his chances. They were fully aware that in 1935 Roosevelt had bypassed the front runner for the chief's position, General Hugh Drum. Instead, the president had turned to Craig, a man who had made no effort to gain the post.[53] As the time for appointment neared, the president made it quite clear that the chief of staff was his personal advisor and that he alone would make the selection.[54]

Marshall was aware that both Johnson and Woodring supported him, but, knowing how each frequently revised their stand on an issue when he learned where the other stood, he was not anxious for either to openly publicize their support. According to Marshall, "Johnson wanted me for Chief of Staff, but I didn't want Woodring to know he was for me. Craig was for me, but I wanted it kept from the President. Woodring was for me, but I didn't want the others to know."[55]

Once again, General Hugh Drum, one of thirty-three generals who outranked Marshall, was considered to be the front runner for the chief of staff post, and he was actively campaigning for the top spot.[56] By contrast, Marshall was quietly trying to discourage outspoken supporters such as Johnson and Woodring from actively campaigning on his behalf. But there was one supporter whose opinions mattered most to Roosevelt, and that was Harry Hopkins. Hopkins was profoundly impressed with Marshall and he let the president know how he felt.[57]

Finally, at a private meeting in the White House on Sunday, April 23, 1939, amid the clutter of his stamp albums and dealers' catalogues, Roosevelt selected George Catlett Marshall as Craig's replacement, effective at the end of Craig's tour on September 1. After a conversation during which FDR agreed that Marshall would be free to speak his mind, Marshall stood up and said, "I feel deeply honored, sir, and I will give you the best that I have."[58] Four days later the White House announced the appointment, and on July 1 Marshall became acting chief when Craig went on extended leave pending his retirement.[59]

It did not take the new chief of staff long to feel the impact of his superiors' feud. As he later recalled, "I had to be chief of staff to a Secretary . . . and his First Assistant who weren't speaking to each other. They not only didn't make any secret of how they hated each other, they ran to the President behind each other's back." It is no wonder that Marshall later indicated that working under Johnson and Woodring was "the most miserable experience of my life."[60]

Morale Suffers

Marshall considered Johnson a very able person with a great deal to offer but felt that he scuttled his opportunity for greatness in that period by not confining himself to his job.[61] Johnson's aggressiveness not only had a negative impact on the chief of staff, it also began to play havoc with the efficiency and morale of the entire War Department. In addition, confusion persisted over who was, and who would be, running the department. Roosevelt's tendency to ignore Woodring for several months and work with Johnson on key defense matters (especially relating to production and procurement) and his refusal to confirm or deny stories that he would soon appoint Johnson as secretary of war seriously undercut Woodring's credibility. Then, when the president would turn against

Johnson and toward Woodring, as he invariably would, Woodring's prestige would rise.[62]

Roosevelt's compulsively devious pattern of turning to Johnson and then Woodring, then back again, created major problems for the members of the general staff. The officers did not know whether to openly support Secretary Woodring, who often seemed to be out of favor with the White House, or to support Johnson, who frequently appeared to be on good terms with the chief executive and repeatedly announced he would soon become secretary. As a result of the confusion about who was truly in charge, "Johnson men" and "Woodring men" began to appear within the War Department.[63] An officer's alignment with one camp or the other was dependent upon whom he felt was really running the department and how he stood on the question of the role of air power in the army. Generally speaking, younger officers and those who championed a strong air arm were Johnson supporters, while older officers and those favoring ground forces were in the Woodring camp.[64]

Of the two factions, the one favoring Woodring was much larger because of the preponderance of infantry and cavalry officers (as opposed to the smaller number of air corps officers) and a widespread conviction that Johnson's aggressive actions were clear-cut cases of insubordination and disloyalty—both considered cardinal sins to the professional soldier. Furthermore, Johnson did not win many friends among high-ranking officers when he sharply curtailed their use of "dog-robbers"—enlisted men who served as yardmen and houseboys. The consequence of all this was that Johnson's standing at the War Department was never very high.[65]

While staff officers inwardly tended to side with one man or the other, they usually attempted to be outwardly neutral. They did this primarily to protect their careers, for they realized that casting their lot with the wrong man could be fatal. Consequently, many fine officers were reluctant to make their views on defense matters known for fear of reprisals. Free, open discussion of problems and possible solutions was stifled. It did not take officers in the nation's capital long to realize that when in the presence of Johnson or Woodring, the safest course of action was to agree with whatever was said or remain noncommittal. When in the presence of both, the latter alternative was the best option because to side with one of the men was to invite instant disapproval from the other. The resulting atmosphere of fear proved to be detrimental to the efficiency of the War Department in the critical years immediately preceding World War II.[66]

The Feud Becomes Public

As the feud between Johnson and Woodring emerged in the fall of 1937 and grew in intensity through mid-1940, its impact began to be felt beyond the confines of the War Department. Eventually the press, the White House staff, cabinet members, and members of Congress were drawn into the conflict.

The first news stories of the arguments between the two war department officials appeared in early 1938. In the following year, political columnists and analysts began to write about the infighting and frequently came to favor one man over the other. In the battle for press support, Johnson's gift for cultivating newsmen paid major dividends as national columnists such as Walter Winchell, Robert Kintner, Joseph Alsop, Henry Ehrlich, and Robert Allen came to favor him. His strongest supporter, however, was Drew Pearson, at that time the most widely read syndicated columnist in the United States.[67]

With the declaration of war by Britain and France against Germany in September 1939, the nature of the newspaper coverage of the feud began to change radically. Prior to this time the trouble was seen merely as a harmless Washington feud like those that have gone on among presidential advisors since 1792. It was good gossip and good copy. However, as the likelihood of U.S. involvement in Europe increased, the press came to portray the feud as a very disruptive situation which was seriously hampering American defense efforts.[68] Typical of the new view was an assessment in the October 9, 1939, issue of *Time:* "With war abroad, rearmament a-swing, and the Army in expensive expansion, the case of Woodring vs. Johnson is now a stench in Washington."[69] Such evaluations were increasingly accompanied by calls for corrective action. For example, an editorial in the September 28 edition of the *Washington Daily News* deplored the "silly and dangerous feud" and recommended to the president that "a very good way to clean up a very bad mess" was "to demand two resignations."[70] Similar stories and editorials proliferated in late 1939 and early 1940.

White House staff members also found events at the War Department increasingly worrisome. Among the staff there was a small faction led by Johnson's friend Steve Early that tried to get the president to remove Woodring and put Johnson in the top spot. Early was aided in his efforts by Roosevelt's military aide, General Edwin M. "Pa" Watson, and presidential assistant Marvin McIntyre.[71]

Among cabinet members, it was Secretary of Interior Harold Ickes, motivated primarily by a dislike of Woodring, who led a concerted effort to bring about a major cabinet reshuffle which would make Johnson secretary of war and then, a short time later, send him to the Philippines as the high commissioner. On numerous occasions Ickes talked to the president about how the Woodring-Johnson fiasco had degenerated into a public scandal that was discrediting the administration. He urged Roosevelt to end the "holy show" by removing Woodring.

Ickes, who noted that Johnson was "so anxious to be Secretary of War that he can hardly stand it," sympathized with the assistant secretary because he realized how frustrating the situation was when the president kept dangling the position in front of him. Through the summer of 1939, Johnson, aware that Ickes was working on his behalf, would call him and reveal his frustrations over not receiving the job he had so long expected. Following such calls Ickes would again take the matter up with the president, but to no avail.[72]

After war broke out in Europe in September 1939, Ickes came to the conclusion that it would be in the best interest of national defense preparation if the president would remove both the secretary and assistant secretary. From that time until mid-1940 he worked more vigorously than ever for the removal of Woodring but did not champion Johnson as his replacement.[73] To further his anti-Woodring plan, Ickes at one time or another enlisted the support of Secretary of Treasury Henry Morgenthau Jr., Secretary of Commerce Harry Hopkins, Undersecretary of State Sumner Welles, presidential advisor Thomas Corcoran, and the head of the Works Progress Administration (WPA), Aubrey Williams. Most of these men were not necessarily Johnson supporters, but they felt that he would be much better than Woodring.[74] Of the efforts to get Roosevelt to make these cabinet changes, Ickes indicated that he doubted if "any comparable pressure has ever been put on the President in a personnel matter."[75]

The man most responsible for persuading Johnson to accept the assistant secretary position, James Farley, vacillated in his support of Johnson for the secretaryship. As postmaster general, Democratic National Committee chairman, and presidential advisor, Farley was able to exert considerable influence on Roosevelt. For a time in late 1937 Farley supported Johnson for secretary because of his conviction that Woodring was not providing the strong leadership that was needed. However, after a December 1938 meeting in which Roosevelt told him he "wouldn't name Louis under any circumstance" to the post, Farley abandoned his active support for the appointment.[76]

In the early stages of the war department feud, members of Congress took little interest in the affair, viewing it not unlike dozens of others they had witnessed in Washington over the years. But as the situation deteriorated in late 1938 and early 1939 and the negative impact upon defense preparedness became increasingly apparent, some members became concerned and interjected themselves into the dispute. Johnson's aggressiveness and arrogance had not done much to endear himself to members of the legislative branch, and several of them tended to be critical of him and supportive of Woodring. Johnson's severest critics in the Senate were Bennett Champ Clark (D-Missouri), Henry Styles Bridges (R-New Hampshire), and Edwin Johnson (D-Colorado). Representatives Andrew May (D-Kentucky) and Charles S. Faddis (D-Pennsylvania) were his leading detractors in the House. Johnson did have a few supporters in the House, such as Leslie C. Arends (R-Illinois) and Dow Harter (D-Ohio).[77] Most senators and representatives, however, stood on the sidelines and hoped that the president would soon move to clear up the mess in the War Department.

Although Roosevelt, like everyone else in Washington, was well aware of the situation, he moved with the speed of a turtle to correct it because he was prone to put off anything that was distasteful. As early as January 1939 he was privately acknowledging that something needed to be done but he could not bring himself to ask Woodring, a good personal friend, for his resignation.

FDR resorted to his time-honored practice of offering to "promote" a trouble-some appointee to another position rather than fire him. Offers of an ambas-sadorship to Canada, Ireland, and Italy were rejected by Woodring, who en-joyed the social life of Washington too much to exchange it for life in a foreign capital.[78] With the secretary unwilling to step aside and the president reluc-tant to remove him, Johnson's chances to advance to the top spot in the War Department were stymied, and his frustrations grew.

There is no doubt that the vast ideological and temperamental differences between Woodring and Johnson and Roosevelt's toleration of, if not encourage-ment of, infighting between the two disrupted and delayed defense activities in the War Department from the fall of 1937 through mid-1940. It is a tribute to Johnson's strength and commitment, however, that he was able to accomplish so much in those three critical years to prepare America for what would be her greatest military challenge. In fact, his contributions in that period were to earn him not only the plaudits of many prominent political and military leaders, in-cluding George Marshall, but ultimately the coveted Medal For Merit, which President Truman presented to him in 1947. He earned that honor for his lead-ership and success in the realm of planning for wartime procurement and in-dustrial mobilization.

CHAPTER FOUR

"Basic Shift in Mobilization Planning"

T HE DEBATE ABOUT FDR's policies and politics on the eve of World War II, when Louis Johnson was responsible for wartime mobilization planning, continues to rage among historians. Was the president essentially an isolationist who was driven by events to finally take sides in Europe's wars?[1] Was he, as James MacGregor Burns has suggested, beguiled by public opinion, opting to wait on events rather than provide clear leadership?[2] Or was he, as some historians have argued, an internationalist at heart who was forced by the isolationist mood of the country in the 1930s to hide his true motives until public opinion was transformed by events in the summer of 1940?[3]

One way historians have approached and enlarged this debate is by focusing not on Roosevelt alone but on some of his key advisors and their bureaucracies. Here, the debate is augmented by examining Louis Johnson's most important contribution to the Roosevelt administration prior to World War II—his leadership of the War Department in establishing workable and successful plans for wartime procurement and industrial mobilization. Whether Johnson did this at FDR's explicit direction or whether he merely received the president's approval and encouragement as he went about his business is not always known. But the large and important point remains: beginning in the summer of 1937, the Roosevelt administration, acting through Louis Johnson, worked day and night to prepare the nation's industrial base for war.

Roosevelt was cautious, and he did not move and probably could not have moved very far ahead of prevailing public opinion and congressional sentiment in those days. However, his approval of Louis Johnson's ambitious planning activities strongly suggests that FDR had advanced beyond "hemispherism," that he had developed and was willing to practice a broad geopolitical view of national security, and that he either was, or was fast becoming, a genuine internationalist.

Learning from the Master

From the time Louis Johnson entered the army during World War I until he became the assistant secretary of war twenty years later, he was an outspoken critic of the failure of the United States to be prepared for that war. At last he had the power to do something to assure that such a lack of preparedness would not occur again when or if America went to war. His despair over the virtual absence of military preparations and planning had been heightened in the early 1930s by the demise of the army and navy which was brought about by the economic cutbacks resulting from the Depression. In the mid-1930s he followed with growing concern the military activities of Germany, Italy, and Japan. By the time he entered his war department post in the summer of 1937, Johnson was convinced that war in Europe was inevitable, and while he hoped the United States could avoid involvement, he was not optimistic about its chances of doing so.

Once he was in a position to make a difference, Johnson decided to do as much as he could to prepare the nation for the worst by pushing vigorously for adequate defense preparations.[4] He fully realized how difficult his task would be; in 1937 neither the Congress nor the public were inclined to do anything that smacked of militarism. When the president merely tested the waters with his famous "quarantine speech" in Chicago in October 1937, the reaction was quick and vehement. Members of Congress raged and shouted, and some called for impeachment. Roosevelt was targeted as a warmonger and was forced to back off, saying he was just expressing an attitude about containing aggressors and that he did not have a program for dealing with them.[5] The mood in America was clearly isolationist, and the military policy was definitely defensive. It was within those confines that Johnson had to operate.

In addition to isolationism and the years of depression which debilitated the armed forces, Johnson knew he faced a number of unique obstacles to carrying out his responsibility to plan for wartime industrial mobilization. Chief among these was the fact that because the United States was a peaceful nonaggressive nation, it could not plan when and where it would go to war and had to be ready for any type of conflict at any time.[6] Johnson had to be prepared to provide the goods of war for a mobilized force of anywhere from 400,000 to more than 4 million men. He could not afford to underestimate the requirements for material and manpower because to do so could ultimately lead to the destruction of the nation.

Another problem was the fact that during the New Deal era, mobilization planning was regarded as pro-business; some even claimed it bore a striking likeness to fascism. These reactions made for tough going at the White House, where the liberal New Dealers that surrounded the president had become increasingly anti-business and pro-labor. Because of Johnson's advocacy of industrial planning and his relationships with the defense establishment, New Dealers had no fondness for him, and they sought to embarrass him whenever they could.[7]

On the other hand, Johnson had some distinct advantages in achieving his goal of putting into place new plans for wartime industrial mobilization. First and foremost, he had direct access to the president, who was generally sympathetic. Provided Johnson's plans did not require the president to ask Congress for substantial funds, and as long as the planning process did not appear to the public as if the administration was pushing to intervene in foreign wars, FDR was happy to let him proceed. In addition, Johnson had the advantage of express statutory authority to plan for industrial mobilization, which he interpreted very broadly.[8] Fortunately, Secretary Woodring did not challenge or interfere with Johnson on mobilization planning, thus giving the assistant secretary a free hand.

The other advantage Johnson had was the friendship and constant advice of Bernard Baruch. In one of his wisest moves as assistant secretary, Johnson, knowing he had a great deal to learn, sought out and befriended Baruch, the one person in the United States who knew more about wartime mobilization than anyone else.[9] During World War I it had been Baruch, an extremely wealthy Wall Street banker, who, as head of the War Industries Board, had become a virtual economic dictator of America and successfully mobilized the nation's industry for war. After the war, Baruch continued to study mobilization issues, and in the 1930s he emerged as the leading critic of the army's mobilization plans. Baruch, who was confidently predicting war with Germany and was always trying to arouse the nation, found a kindred spirit in Louis Johnson. From his mansion in Manhattan or from Hobcaw, his vast plantation in the South Carolina lowlands, Baruch would frequently travel to Washington to confer with Johnson and other Washington officials. After checking into the $1,000-per-month suite that he maintained at the Carlton, Baruch would take meetings with the assistant secretary of war and dispense advice on getting ready for the coming war.

At their first meeting, Johnson and Baruch hit it off extremely well, a fact that resulted in part from personality but even more from the similarity of their attitudes on mobilization. Both believed that in America's next war it would be necessary to mobilize the entire nation and that total mobilization would require a superagency, led by a strong head, that would have the power and authority to get the job done. Throughout Johnson's tenure at the War Department, Baruch provided invaluable advice on mobilizing the economy for war and streamlining the supply and procurement processes.[10]

Allocations and Educational Orders

Of Johnson's many contributions to preparedness planning, none received more public acclaim than his accomplishments in factory allocations and educational orders. Under the War Department's old allocation system, specific manufacturers were assigned (i.e., "allocated") production obligations that they would be expected to fill in wartime. The plants were selected based on production capacity, strategic location, available labor force, and management's willingness to cooperate. Prior to 1937, allocations were primarily paper transactions whereby a certain manufacturer indicated a willingness to supply certain items in certain quantities when and if war came; they were not enforceable contractual commitments.[11] These loose arrangements were frequently handled completely through correspondence.

Realizing that the road to hell was paved with good intentions, Johnson decided that in the event of war, more was needed to assure adequate production than a pledge.[12] He undertook a series of steps to transform the War Department's factory allocation system into a program that would ensure that the military would receive all of the supplies and equipment that would be needed if and when war came. His program included: 1) selling the need for firm and realistic production commitments to industry; 2) surveying the industries that would be affected; 3) assigning realistic production goals; and 4) where possible, issuing educational orders, or government-funded trial runs to enable manufacturers to learn how to efficiently produce high-quality military items.[13]

In order to convince American industry of the need for realistic and enforceable production quotas in the event of war, Johnson set out to sell his program. To this end he traveled from coast to coast giving as many as 100 speeches a year to members of the business community. He also granted frequent press interviews, made radio speeches, and wrote journal articles explaining the program and asking for support and cooperation. Speaking against the tide of noninterventionist public opinion and without getting himself into trouble with Roosevelt or Congress, Johnson used his well-honed public-speaking and persuasive skills to promote and articulate a patriotic appeal for cooperation.[14] When word of a recalcitrant industry representative reached Johnson, he would pick up the phone and call the person or, as he did on many occasions, travel to the representative's plant to ask for cooperation and a firm commitment. In this aspect of the program Johnson was at his best, and he enjoyed it immensely. Under his leadership, more than 20,000 American plants committed to do their part.

The factory allocation program also entailed personal on-site surveys by army officers from the assistant secretary's office and volunteer consultants from business and academia. The resulting inspection and survey reports provided detailed information on which an informed decision on allocation could be made. When a particular plant was chosen, the assistant secretary would send a team of officers there with plans, drawings, specifications, and, if possible, samples of the item or items. Consultation would follow and a realistic production schedule would be agreed upon. Ultimately, agreements were worked out with more than 10,000 plants and an elaborate directory system spelling out their availability and capabilities was developed.[15]

Johnson's factory allocation program worked well with manufacturers that would be producing essentially the same items in wartime that they were already producing in peacetime, such as clothing, boots, and kitchen equipment. However, for those manufacturers that would be expected to produce distinctly military items that they had no experience producing in peacetime, such as anti-aircraft guns and bombsights, Johnson instituted a system of educational orders whereby the War Department would place orders for limited quantities of certain military items. The purpose of such orders would be to educate the manufacturers, enabling them to make or purchase the necessary machine tools and train their personnel to produce the item. Thus, when war came they would have the machinery and know-how to go into immediate production.[16]

Since the end of World War I, the War Department had acknowledged the need for educational orders. However, a program of educational orders required congressional approval and appropriations. Despite numerous attempts, the War Department and the U.S. Army could never convince Congress of the wisdom and necessity of such a program. However, in 1937, the supersalesman from West Virginia burst onto the scene and devoted his energy and political skills to the job of persuading Congress to authorize and fund an educational orders program. He first sold the idea to Roosevelt. Then, with the support of the president, he turned his attention to the legislative branch. Frequent trips to Capitol Hill and letters to army friends in the House and Senate soon paid off. In June 1938, a bill was passed which authorized $2 million worth of educational orders for each of the next five years.[17] Johnson immediately implemented the educational orders system by providing for peacetime production of six items, including M1 .30 caliber semi-automatic rifles, gas masks, and 75mm shell casings.[18]

Initial reaction to the program was so favorable by both the War Department and industry that in November 1938 Johnson appealed directly to the president, asking that he request of Congress an additional $32 million over the next three years. Roosevelt enthusiastically complied, and in April of the following year the funds were provided. New educational orders were then placed with 109 manufacturers for the production of fifty-five essential military items. Furthermore, production studies and detailed plans for plant expansion and construction were drawn up so that manufacturers could convert more quickly if war broke out.[19]

While the scope and cost of the educational orders program of 1938–1940 was rather trivial in light of the actual World War II experience, it was vitally important on at least two counts. First, it was significant that by 1940 nearly sixty essential military items that otherwise would not have been in production were being produced. It was later estimated that educational orders on those products saved between four and twelve months of the time it ultimately took to get the plants into full production. Second, it is clear that many American industries were much better prepared to meet their responsibilities when war came in 1941 than they would have been without the educational orders program.

There is no question that the educational orders program spearheaded by Johnson and actively supported by FDR saved lives because it accelerated the production of wartime material.[20] Due to Johnson's skill and determination, army procurement procedures and planning were better in 1940 than at any time since World War I. The fact that his efforts came to fruition on the eve of World War II was fortunate for the United States.

Mobilization

As important as procurement planning was, it was still just part of the planning picture; the other side was planning for industrial mobilization. The term industrial mobilization is actually a misnomer; the concept encompasses much more than just industry. According to Johnson, it meant "organizing, directing, and controlling the entire economic resources of the nation so as to contribute most effectively to a speedy victory." By 1938, Johnson not only believed that the United States was headed for war, he envisioned war on a massive scale in which "the blood of the soldier on the front line . . . would be mixed with three parts of the sweat of the man in the factory."[21]

Prior to Johnson's arrival at the War Department, industrial mobilization planning was of interest and concern only to those members of the assistant secretary's office directly involved and a few concerned citizens such as Bernard Baruch. Virtually no one in Congress or the executive branch really cared what was being planned for industry in the next war. Johnson changed that state of affairs. According to one scholar of that period, the West Virginian's appointment "signaled a basic shift in mobilization planning" because under him, "mobilization policy became an issue for the Cabinet, the President and other civilians."[22] What had previously been buried in the war department bureaucracy was to become a highly visible political issue.

Four months after he became assistant secretary, Johnson went to President Roosevelt and urged him to appoint an advisory board, headed by Bernard Baruch, to analyze and make recommendations concerning the department's Industrial Mobilization Plan. Johnson argued the need for thorough examination and updating of plans for wartime mobilization. The president agreed in principle, but because he knew that Baruch would propose that a "strong man" (namely himself) should head up war mobilization, he postponed indefinitely any decision on the establishment of a board.[23] The president was also concerned that if he went public in late 1937 with an advisory board headed by Bernard Baruch to study industrial mobilization plans for war, isolationists and many New Dealers would be alarmed.

Johnson, realizing that he could expect no public support from Roosevelt for his proposal, proceeded in early 1938 to appoint a board of officers from the department's Planning Branch to analyze the current mobilization plan and recommend changes. In the year that followed, Johnson continually prodded the board and provided considerable input on the revisions. The plan that finally emerged, the Industrial Mobilization Plan of 1939, reflected Johnson's influence. The plan was only twenty pages long (with an appendix of more than 500 pages), but it was a potent piece of political and military advocacy.

The proposed Mobilization Plan of 1939 contained a number of significant and innovative changes. The major change was the expansion of power given to a wartime government superagency called the War Resources Administration. Under the plan, the new superagency would handle all matters related to facilities, commodities, power, fuel, and transportation and it would coordinate with other agencies on labor, trade, and price controls. Furthermore, the new plan called for the president to delegate enormous power to the head of the War Resources Administration, a provision highly desirable to Johnson and Baruch.[24]

With no objection from the president, the 1939 plan was released for public scrutiny in May 1939. It immediately fomented considerable controversy. This was the first time an industrial mobilization plan had been given such wide publicity, and it was done so at Johnson's insistence (and with FDR's tacit approval) because he believed the American people should know what would be expected of them if war came.

Many Americans did not like what the 1939 plan expected of them, and criticism came from many quarters. Some abhorred the "economic fascism" it would impose on the nation. Labor leaders were upset by the call for wartime suspension of legislation they considered essential for the protection of workers. One irate congressman lambasted the plan because it would give "full and complete dictatorial powers" to the president and suspend the constitutional rights of every American. From the other side came opposition because the plan did not go far enough, and those critics called for even more government controls in order to mobilize successfully. Still other constituencies, such as agriculture, complained because they had been virtually ignored.[25]

Johnson, the principal architect of the Industrial Mobilization Plan of 1939, now became its primary defender. He set out to sell the plan just as he had sold factory allocations to the business community and educational orders to Congress in 1937 and 1938. Through speeches, interviews, radio broadcasts, and magazine articles he forcefully explained and justified the plan's provisions. He drove home the idea that the sacrifices that might be called for were not desirable but would be necessary if the nation were to survive a major war. While many Americans might not have liked what the assistant secretary said, Johnson performed a great public service by educating the citizens about their future wartime responsibilities. Less than three years later, tens of millions of Americans were making the commitments the plan had called for.

Battling Bottlenecks

Throughout the interwar years, war department planners did not consider military and industrial manpower to be a particularly daunting problem. They believed that the country possessed enough people to fight a war and produce all that was necessary to achieve victory. While Johnson accepted this basic premise regarding numbers of people, he was concerned about when and how to raise a large standing army and how to get the right kinds of people in the right jobs. Convinced by his World War I experience that combat forces could be raised in time of war only by a draft, he supported a selective service measure. That he should favor such action was not unusual, but the fact that he urged passage of such legislation in April 1938 when the nation was at peace was both highly unusual and politically risky. He did not advocate peacetime conscription but called for a selective service law to be passed so it would be on the books and ready to go when war came. This was in line with his penchant for having things ready before they were actually needed.[26] The concept he pushed was eventually embodied in the Burke-Wadsworth Selective Service Act, enacted in September 1940.

As for industrial manpower, Johnson believed that such labor would be voluntary, but he was worried about availability of skilled workers, specifically mechanics and tool- and diemakers. He exerted constant pressure on the president, the secretary of interior, and the director of the Civilian Conversation Corps to establish various vocational training programs.[27] Johnson's goal was to use government programs to train upward of 200,000 men to make machine tools, dies, jigs, and other essential manufacturing equipment which would be needed if war came.

Ever since World War I, war planners had recommended that certain strategic materials such as manganese, rubber, tin, chrome, and tungsten be stockpiled for wartime needs. It was an idea that everyone acknowledged needed to be implemented, but no action was ever taken. As the war clouds darkened, Johnson, working primarily through the Army-Navy Munitions Board, and with the encouragement of the president, began pushing for funds to make such purchases. In June 1939, Congress passed the Strategic War Materials Act, which authorized the stockpiling of $100 million worth of materials, but it only appropriated

$10 million. The legislation was significant because it acknowledged acceptance of the concept, but it was passed too late to do any good prior to America's entrance into the war.[28]

Having factories and people to run them were extremely important, but if they lacked the power to run them they were of no value. Following up on this point, Johnson became concerned that power, especially electric power, be available where needed when war came. To achieve that end he urged, and the president agreed in May of 1938, to conduct a survey on the adequacy of electric power for national defense and ways to facilitate coordination of existing power transmission facilities—the first such study ever conducted in the United States.[29] In September, again primarily because of Johnson's request, Roosevelt created the National Defense Power Committee, with Johnson as chairman, the purpose of which was to make recommendations about increasing the capacity of power plants, standardizing the production of turbine generators, and developing a national power transmission grid. In launching the project, Johnson explained his objective. "What we are trying to do is to eliminate what I call 'power bottlenecks.'"[30]

Attacking the electric power problem with his usual fervor, Johnson set up direct negotiations between himself and top utilities executives, including Victor Emanuel, who would become closely associated with Johnson during the war years and thereafter. He urged the electric utilities to voluntarily commit to increase their capacity, standardize turbine production, and provide the necessary connecting links. The same patriotic appeals that he had used so successfully in the past were modestly successful and some progress was made, much to the dismay of New Dealers such as Harold Ickes who detested cooperation between business and government.[31]

Johnson wrestled with another big bottleneck in procurement planning—the lack of military specifications for many key items that would be needed in wartime. When Johnson arrived at the War Department, he found that the army's supply services were hesitant to submit final specifications on certain items out of a fear that improvements in design or performance would soon be forthcoming. While understanding their reluctance, Johnson also realized that when mobilization began it would be necessary to have final specs on hand immediately, not several weeks or months later. Consequently, the assistant secretary put continual pressure on the supply services to finalize and distribute specifications. As a result, the number of military items for which specifications were not approved was reduced from more than 2,500 when Johnson took over to about 700 when he departed three years later.[32]

Recognizing the importance of Alaska to the nation's defense, Johnson "urged and pioneered" the idea of a highway to Alaska that would stretch from the United States to Fairbanks and provide ground access to the air bases he thought should be built in Alaska. With his friend from Clarksburg, Dr. Frank Langfitt, he made a personal air survey in August of 1938 of possible routes from the U.S. border to Dawson Creek or Whitehorse in Canada and from there through the Yukon Territory to Fairbanks.[33]

Johnson's vision of a highway to Alaska was highly controversial and slightly ahead of its time, but it made sense because, as the United States found out when the Japanese attacked Pearl Harbor, Alaska was strategically significant and the air bases to be located there would need a guaranteed way to keep them supplied. In addition, the Alcan Highway would be used to supply the U.S. pilots who were to fly lend-lease aircraft to Soviet crews at Fairbanks throughout the war. In early 1942, the U.S. Army Corps of Engineers began work on the Alcan Highway, thus validating Johnson's foresight.[34]

Accomplishments

While Louis Johnson had many critics in his lifetime, no responsible person, given the realities of America on the eve of World War II, has found fault with the prewar preparations that he advocated, fought for, and instituted. Whether it was a president of the United States such as Harry Truman, a professional soldier such as George Marshall, a statesman such as Cordell Hull, an economist such as Eliot Janeway, or a public servant such as Bernard Baruch, the message is the same — Johnson performed invaluable service in getting the nation ready for war.[35]

Under Johnson's guidance, functional and effective factory allocation and educational orders programs were instituted, the old mobilization plan was substantially revised and the new Industrial Mobilization Plan of 1939 was unveiled, plans were made for manpower mobilization, stockpiling of essential strategic materials was begun, progress was made in establishing a national power grid, a bottleneck in military specifications was substantially resolved, and the idea for the Alcan Highway gained credibility. These accomplishments took place at the same time the assistant secretary was overseeing normal peacetime procurement activities and leading a major fight for an American air rearmament program.

That he could accomplish so much in the midst of the infighting in the War Department was due in part to his effectiveness as an organizer, motivator, and leader and in part because Secretary Woodring did not interfere. But his success was also due to the fact that for the most part he had the support and encouragement—sometimes express, often tacit—of the commander in chief.

Except for instances when Johnson pressed to give too much authority to the War Resources Administration or to suggest that Bernard Baruch and his big ideas might become associated with the Roosevelt administration, Roosevelt collaborated closely with Johnson in preparing the nation both for hemispheric defense and for war on a much broader scale. Roosevelt was cautious and calculating, but as he quietly supported Johnson's industrial mobilization planning in 1937 and 1938, he evidenced a sophisticated global perspective on the growing threat to what he perceived as the national security.

CHAPTER FIVE

Understanding FDR

On a cold weekend in January 1938, French senator Amaury de la Grange, President Roosevelt's old friend from World War I days, was a guest at the White House. A distraught La Grange gave a dismal appraisal of the situation in Europe, expressing alarm over the extent of German air strength and the complete lack of French air power.[1] Throughout the spring and into the summer, similar reports, primarily from the State Department, reached the Oval Office.

To test the validity of such reports, the president encouraged private American manufacturers to visit Europe and form their independent assessments of German air power.[2] One person who undertook such a trip was Johnson's good friend Glenn L. Martin, a major producer of military aircraft. Martin, who had taken advantage of numerous personal contacts to gain an accurate picture of the situation, reported to Johnson that Germany was producing 9,000 planes per year. Their speed and quality, he warned, "compared favorably with the best that others are producing." He concluded that "Germany is greatly superior to England and France insofar as air power is concerned and that superiority is rapidly increasing."[3]

On June 23, Johnson forwarded Martin's assessment to Roosevelt, telling him that Martin agreed with the pessimistic reports from other American manufacturers.[4] Those reports came from such respected men as Lawrence D. Bell of Bell Aircraft and Burdett Wright of the Curtis-Wright Corporation.[5] Then on July 3, 1938, the president received a frightening letter from the American ambassador to Germany, Hugh R. Wilson, which concluded that without question Germany had "an air arm second to none in number and quality of first-line fighting planes."[6]

The worst fears that such reports could conjure in the president's mind were borne out by the Munich crisis in September 1938, when Hitler secured the Sudeten area of Czechoslovakia because England and France were unwilling or unable to stand up to Germany. As information on the Munich deal filtered into the White House in late September and early October, it became increasingly clear to the president that the Allies had capitulated because they could not come close to matching Hitler's air power.

At Roosevelt's request, the U.S. ambassador to France, William C. Bullitt, came back from Paris to brief the president in person on October 13. Bullitt's firsthand observations helped FDR understand that negotiating with Hitler would be impossible. In addition, by conveying to the president that the Luftwaffe was an instrument of terror and that the fear of destruction by air which gripped Europe's capitals had led to the Munich capitulation, Bullitt convinced him that the United States needed to substantially increase its production of military aircraft.[7] It needed to do this, Roosevelt believed, not only to defend against possible attack but, far more important, so that American airplanes could be sold or otherwise conveyed to the Allies, thus altering the balance of air power in Europe in the interests of American security.

By mid-October of 1938, President Roosevelt had come to the conclusion that it would be necessary "to build the one type of armed force with which he could henceforth influence European affairs: air power."[8] FDR knew that he was bucking prevailing American public opinion and that he would be criticized by the noninterventionists and isolationists. Nevertheless, once his decision was made, there was no doubt in his mind that Louis Johnson was the man at the War Department who should lead the air rearmament program.

The assistant secretary had all the prerequisites to undertake air rearmament. First, he was in charge of all procurement for the army air corps; the task he would be undertaking would essentially be one of procuring aircraft. Second, he was an outspoken advocate and longtime champion of air power, especially heavy bombers. Third, he had the enthusiasm, dynamism, and aggressiveness to get things done. Fourth, he was a supersalesman who could convince Congress and the American people of the need for massive air rearmament.

How Many Planes?

Louis Johnson's direct involvement in the air rearmament program actually began on September 11, 1938, a month before Bullitt's meeting with the president. On that day the assistant secretary sent a memorandum to FDR calling attention to the fact that the nation's aircraft production was near its capacity and therefore incapable of further expansion.[9] The following day, Roosevelt, frequently the doubting Thomas, asked one of his closest advisors, Harry Hopkins, who was then director of the WPA, to travel secretly to the West Coast,

study the production capacity of the aircraft industry, and make recommendations on aircraft plant construction under a program which the WPA could
implement.[10]

In the ensuing weeks Roosevelt began formulating plans for aircraft expansion, but he did so by consulting only a few of his very close civilian advisors;
during September, no advice was sought from anyone at the War Department.
Before he could deal directly with Louis Johnson and others in the department,
he had to find a way to work around Secretary Woodring. Roosevelt fully expected Woodring to oppose a vast expansion of the air corps and to favor a balanced increase in ground and air forces.

Roosevelt came up with a devious scheme to bypass the war secretary. Since
midterm elections would take place in early November, he asked Woodring,
who was an effective administration spokesman, to hit the campaign trail on behalf of Democratic members of Congress who were New Deal supporters. Woodring readily agreed, and during most of October he was out of Washington. With
Woodring safely out of the way, the president was free to deal with the acting
secretary of war, Louis Johnson.[11]

On October 14, the day after FDR met with Ambassador Bullitt, he summoned Johnson to the White House, where he revealed his decision to greatly
expand American aircraft production. Whether FDR disclosed the possibility
of selling U.S. planes to the Allies and whether specific production goals were
discussed is not entirely certain, but in all likelihood a figure of 15,000 to 20,000
planes per year was mentioned. In view of the fact that total aircraft production
in the United States was about 3,000 per year, of which only 900 were military
aircraft, this would be a major expansion indeed. The meeting closed with
Roosevelt assigning Johnson the formidable task of determining U.S. requirements and production capabilities for aircraft and then recommending ways to
bring about the hoped-for expansion.[12]

Shortly after Johnson's departure, the president held a news conference at
which he announced that political and military developments abroad were
making necessary "a complete restudy of American national defense," including an examination of mass production of airplanes. When asked if any centralized or interdepartmental body was studying expansion of aircraft production,
Roosevelt curtly replied, "No, I am doing it."[13] What the president was not dis-
closing was that one of his major motivations behind the increased production
was a desire to provide new military aircraft to France and possibly Britain.

Johnson's October 14 meeting with Roosevelt ushered in a 60-day period during which the two men worked very closely with one another in an attempt to
launch a major air rearmament program. During those weeks the president and
the acting secretary were in daily contact, either through memoranda or personal visits. All memos on expansion were directed to Johnson rather than Woodring because the president made it clear that he was treating the air program as

strictly a procurement matter and therefore would be dealing directly with Johnson. Johnson instructed the military staff that all coordination would be through him.

Johnson was definitely in and Woodring was clearly out. This was apparent on October 29, when Johnson and General Hap Arnold, the new chief of the army air corps, took the president to Bolling Field in Washington and personally showed him virtually every type of aircraft the army possessed. The press quickly picked up on the new relationship and began touting Johnson as the "fair-haired boy" of the administration—a tag that he thoroughly enjoyed.[14] Johnson took no small pride in the fact that he, rather than Woodring, was being called upon by the president to head such an important undertaking as the air expansion program.

Johnson's first action after meeting with the president on the 14th was to order Chief of Staff Malin Craig to "seriously" review the entire air program and then "establish our objectives as to air strength we need, not only on M-Day [Mobilization Day] but also by months thereafter for at least two years . . . [and] perfect plans for dependable production . . . to meet such requirements."[15] Based on this directive, it appears that Johnson had no idea that the president's real motive for the air expansion program was his desire to supply U.S. aircraft to European allies.

General Craig responded to Johnson's request within twenty-four hours by citing the air power requirements set forth in the existing Protective Mobilization Plan and stating that the study Johnson called for would take considerable time. The tenor of Craig's memorandum was that the 2,320 aircraft already authorized by the current mobilization plan was adequate.[16]

Given the fact that FDR's true motive for air expansion remained undisclosed, it is not surprising that in this period the military leaders, including air corps officers, were thinking about air strength on a much smaller scale than the civilian advisors working closely with the president. Typical of the military reaction was that of General Craig when Secretary Morgenthau informed him on October 20 that the president was thinking about 15,000 planes per year. "What are we going to do with 15,000 planes? What are you going to fight, what are you going to do with them, with three thousand miles of ocean?" asked the obviously irritated chief.[17] Not only was Craig upset at the prospect but he believed such a production goal was impossible.

Because the president still did not appear to have the size of his air program firmly in mind, Johnson prepared a range of plans—the least ambitious proposing a 10,000-plane air corps in two years, the boldest calling for a production capacity of 40,000 aircraft per year.[18] On October 25, Roosevelt summoned Johnson; Charles Edison, assistant secretary of the navy; and Aubrey Williams, deputy administrator of the WPA, to the Oval Office, where he directed them to develop plans for increasing aircraft production within three years to a total of 31,000 planes.

Since Johnson already had his staff working on similar plans, it was possible for the group to report back to the president in three days. That report made recommendations about the training of aviation mechanics, the establishment of research-and-development facilities, and the expansion of aircraft production, but it was clearly the latter that was most significant to the president. The plan called for a two-year program whereby the existing aircraft industry could produce 11,000 planes and sixteen new government-built plants would produce 20,000, thus meeting the president's goal of 31,000 planes within three years. That the three procurement experts felt this could be done was undoubtedly pleasing to the president, but the bad news was the cost. The price tag of the entire program was a whopping $3.68 billion with a first-year cost of $855 million.[19] These figures were staggering to the president, who had envisioned a program costing no more than $500 million. He thanked the men for the report and told them he would give their recommendations further consideration. What the president's ultimate program would be was still anyone's guess.

From mid-October on, the press began speculating that the president would soon unveil plans for a large air corps and a vast increase in aircraft production capacity. Roosevelt's refusal to affirm or deny the 5,000-, 10,000-, or 20,000-plane figures being batted around merely drove the figures up and increased public concern.[20] This was probably his way of testing public reaction to the various figures mentioned.

General Craig and the general staff sensed a mood in the White House for military expansion, and they saw what they considered a golden opportunity for expansion of *all* army forces rather than just the air corps. Consequently, plans were initiated for overall military expansion.

As the autumn days of late October 1938 passed in Washington, army planners were gathering data, reformulating manpower and equipment needs, speculating on the nature and extent of the president's program, and wondering what the reaction of Congress and the public to the various plans might be.[21] The War Department was turned into a sea of confusion by rumors, proliferation of new war plans, and endless speculation. Although there was a frenzy of activity, not much was being accomplished because no one knew for sure what the president really wanted.

On November 10, General Arnold sent Johnson still another in a series of proposals. In this latest version of the numbers game, the chief of the air corps called for a force of 7,000 planes and an annual production level of 10,000 aircraft. By this time, Arnold was tiring of the games his planners were being forced to play, and he sent a memo to Johnson saying there was a definite need for the president to convene a meeting of army, navy, State Department, and industry officials "to determine the size of each force."[22] Perhaps that suggestion led Roosevelt to take some action. Whatever the precipitating factor was, four weeks of playing cat and mouse were about to come to an end as the president called Johnson, Hopkins, and treasury secretary Morgenthau to a rare Saturday-morning conference.

New Foreign Policy

As his chauffeured limousine pulled up to the White House entrance on the nippy morning of November 12, 1938, Johnson wondered if the president had decided on the magnitude of his air program. In the past four weeks he had visited the president half a dozen times, and in each instance the chief executive had mentioned different figures. That Saturday morning, however, was different. In the Oval Office, the president told Johnson, Hopkins, and Morgenthau exactly what he wanted. Having concluded that his previous goal of 31,000 planes was too ambitious and too costly, Roosevelt informed the three leaders that he would support a yearly production capacity of 10,000 planes to be produced in current plants plus eight to ten new plants, which would be constructed with WPA funds and justified primarily on the grounds that they were a means of fighting unemployment. As to air corps size, Roosevelt tentatively approved General Arnold's latest recommendation of a 7,000-plane force.[23] After discussing the ways that figure could be reached as quickly as possible, the president announced that he would be calling a major meeting on this matter for the following Monday morning.

The November 14th White House conference was one of the most important in U.S. military annals. According to General Arnold, at that meeting the air corps received its magna carta. Present were Johnson, as acting secretary of war; his executive assistant, Colonel James Burns; Generals Craig and Arnold; Deputy Chief of Staff General George Marshall; Secretary Morgenthau; Herman Oliphant, general counsel of the Treasury Department; Harry Hopkins; Solicitor General Robert Jackson; and Pa Watson and Captain Daniel Gallahan, the president's military and naval aides, respectively. Although Secretary Woodring was on vacation, he was at his residence just ten minutes away. He was not notified of the session because in all likelihood the president was afraid he would object to what was about to be said and decided.

The meeting was not a typical Roosevelt session because at this one he did virtually all the talking—an approach he would use when he had made up his mind on a matter and did not desire any further discussion. As the attendees took their seats in the Cabinet Room, Roosevelt was wheeled in. He took a Camel from his tarnished silver cigarette case, inserted it in his long ivory cigarette holder, and lit it with his old silver lighter. He then launched directly into the subject by stating that the only weapons that stood any chance of deterring Hitler's territorial ambitions were airplanes, not land forces. Elaborating on this point, the president said:

Had we had this summer 5,000 planes and the capacity immediately to produce 10,000 per year, even though I might have had to ask Congress for authority to *sell or lend* them to the countries in Europe, Hitler would not have
dared to take the stand he did.[24]

The president went on to say that he had decided that the United States must
greatly expand its capacity to produce warplanes to deter further aggression. To
accomplish this aim, Roosevelt declared that he was prepared to ask Congress
for authority to build 10,000 planes immediately plus a capacity to produce
20,000 planes per year at a cost of approximately $500 million. Achieving this
goal in two years would require maximum production by current facilities and
construction of seven new government plants, two of which would become operational while the other five would be equipped but held in reserve.

At that point, Johnson interrupted by asking what the breakdown of aircraft
would be. The president replied that 2,500 training planes, 3,750 combat aircraft, and 3,750 in reserve would be proper. Continuing, he said he would ask
Congress to provide the funds for 5,000 planes in the upcoming fiscal year.
Then, almost as an afterthought, he stated with breezy self-confidence that he
was working on a $2 billion program for national defense. That rather astonish-
ing comment was duly noted by the military leaders present. After his presentation was completed, the president turned to Johnson and asked how soon he
could prepare a plan to carry out the proposals. "By Saturday!" shot back the
ever-confident acting secretary.[25]

As the president continued around the room seeking support for his proposals, the attendees were in agreement and had very little to add. At last, FDR
came to General Marshall, who everyone knew was a strong candidate to become army chief of staff, and the president said, "Don't you think so,
George?" Marshall, offended at the use of his first name, replied, "I am sorry,
Mr. President, but I don't agree with that at all." The president gave Marshall
a startled look and then, to forestall the general's explanation of the need for a
balanced military force, Roosevelt concluded the meeting by saying he was
announcing a program, not formulating one. When the meeting adjourned,
Marshall believed his tour in Washington was over. He and the rest of the war
department planners hurried back to their offices to begin work on detailed
plans.[26]

The president's statements during this top-secret meeting were highly
significant because they revealed his new reliance on air power as a diplomatic
tool to avoid war in Europe and they forecast the possibility that he might ask
Congress for authority to sell or lend planes to certain European nations.
Whether those present fully understood it or not, the president had disclosed
an entirely new direction in U.S. foreign policy—the United States was no
longer going to remain neutral, and it would look to expanded air power to tip
the balance toward its allies in Europe.

As it turned out, Johnson was one of those who apparently did not fully understand what the president meant. When he returned to his office after the November 14 meeting, he began to formulate recommendations that would ultimately ingratiate him with war planners but seriously diminish his influence with the president. Although the president had said at the meeting that he viewed a large air force as an alternative to a huge army and that it was politically out of the question to send a large army abroad, Johnson incorrectly read into that morning's conference an indication that Roosevelt was ready to move toward all-out preparedness—a course Johnson strongly believed in. Consequently, he decided that the army should take this opportunity to ask for much more than airplanes. On November 15, he sent a memorandum to the chief of staff requesting not only a detailed plan for the president's air program but also the costs of supplies needed to support the Protective Mobilization Plan and to significantly increase the educational orders program.[27] It was soon apparent that such a large and expanded set of plans could not be developed overnight. On November 19, Johnson sent a progress report to the president and informed him that the detailed plans promised five days earlier would soon be forthcoming. He did not mention the much wider scope of the plans he was preparing.[28]

The vast military expansion plan that emerged under Johnson's direction in late November was directed primarily by General Marshall, since General Craig was protesting the fact that so much of the defense planning and decision-making was being done by civilians rather than the military. Craig had indeed been snubbed by the White House because of his advocacy of a balanced program and the fact that he was so closely tied with Woodring. The secretary of war was likewise upset at being ignored. However, if the president chose to ignore him, there was nothing he could do but resign, and that he was unwilling to do.[29] President Roosevelt's treatment of Craig and Woodring during this period was a classic example of his tendency to work around people he disagreed with rather than confront or remove them.

On December 1, Johnson submitted the War Department's plans for expansion to the president. Roosevelt was expecting a plan to increase aircraft production in line with the program he had set forth on November 14, but what he received went much farther. Whereas Roosevelt had requested planes only, the War Department requested pilots, crews and maintenance personnel, air bases, and training facilities—all items that were necessary to build a real air corps. The plan Johnson endorsed called for an increase in the number of army air corps officers from 1,300 to 7,900 and an increase in enlisted strength from 18,000 to 73,000. Rather than the 5,000 aircraft that the president had wanted in the next year, the plan asked for 8,030 planes with a heavier emphasis on combat aircraft.

The total cost of Johnson's proposed air program was $1.29 billion, but the plan went beyond air power. He requested funds amounting to $421 million for the equipment, munitions, and supplies necessary to upgrade the army ground forces. The plan also contained a request for $122 million to step up the educational orders program and a call for a 58,000-man increase in ground forces as well as 35,000 additional national guardsmen, both to be provided over two years. When everything was added together the total cost was $2.1 billion, or more than four times greater than what the president had requested.[30]

Although Roosevelt was both baffled and irritated by the army's program, he agreed to consider it; ten days later, however, he called Johnson in and directed him to completely rework the plan and prepare a full justification for all requests. Apparently, the president felt that his directive would lead to a major downward revision in the scope of the army's proposals, but Johnson, optimistic that the whole program would be supported, did not take the hint.[31] By December 17, the chief of staff, as directed by Johnson, produced a more thorough justification of each previous request without making any substantive changes in the plan. The plan was then forwarded to the White House.[32]

Within hours, Johnson, Colonel Burns, and Generals Craig and Marshall were summoned by a very irate chief executive to come immediately to the Oval Office. When they arrived, the usually affable and mild-mannered FDR jumped all over them for not following his instructions. "I sought $500 million worth of airplanes and I am being offered everything except airplanes," he exclaimed. Congress could not be asked for more than $500 million, and he wanted all that to go to the production of aircraft. Furthermore, he complained, all the talk of army expansion had filtered over to the Navy Department, which was now requesting an additional $100 million. At that point the discussion became rather heated; the war department officials argued in favor of their augmentation plan on the grounds of military necessity and the president attempted to educate them about the political realities of congressional appropriations. In the end, the president would not budge from his $500 million limit: the army's program would have to be drastically cut and therefore rethought and reworked.[33]

Woodring Ascends

As the days of December 1938 faded, so did President Roosevelt's enthusiasm for his air rearmament program and with that his confidence in Louis Johnson. The primary reason behind the president's loss of fervor was the failure of his proposal to gain real traction in any quarter. Powerful isolationist members of Congress such as Senators Gerald Nye, Bennett Clark, and George Norris and representatives such as Andrew May and Charles Faddis expressed bitter opposition to the size of his proposed increases.[34] Newspaper reaction was also quite negative; numerous editorials attacked Roosevelt and Johnson and their plans for a large air force.[35]

In addition, the private aviation sector did not support the plan. Johnson had called aircraft manufacturing representatives to a secret meeting in Washington on November 23 to explain the program and secure their pledges of support. However, they objected to the construction of government plants, which they viewed as competition, and would not grant the endorsement that Johnson expected.[36]

Public reaction appeared to be the same as that of Congress, the press, and the aircraft industry. Those groups were united in their belief that the president's program was too ambitious. By contrast, some war department officials did not support the proposed program because they felt it was too modest and put too much emphasis on aircraft and not enough on a balanced force.[37] The military was one quarter from which the president had not anticipated resistance.

Besieged from all directions, the president began to back away from his program in late December. One of the first indications of his strategic retreat was his gradual turning away from Johnson and toward Woodring. The move was dictated by the popular image Johnson had developed as the nation's leading advocate of air rearmament—a posture which was completely consistent with the president's position at the November 14 meeting.[38] That fall, the press had focused attention on Johnson's numerous preparedness speeches, especially those that called for a large air corps. In his annual report, released in early December, Johnson had completely reversed his position of a year before when he had said the army had "the best and most efficient aircraft in the world" and was now maintaining that foreign powers had overcome American technical superiority and that the nation's ability to produce aircraft in wartime was grossly inadequate.[39] Such reporting served to strengthen Johnson's public image as the champion of military air power. Although the president had coveted this image earlier, now he wanted to put some distance between Johnson and himself.[40]

Throughout the days of wild expansion talk in October, November, and early December, Secretary Woodring had been calling for a moderate expansion to 6,000 planes, and by mid-December that middle-of-the-road approach was gaining wide acceptance. Not surprisingly, FDR, ever the skillful politician, began bearing in that direction. As Christmas approached, Woodring's visits to the White House began to increase while Johnson's decreased. This trend picked up in early January as the president finalized his budget message.[41]

Perhaps the best assessment of what happened to Johnson at this time was made by *Army and Navy Journal* publisher John C. O'Laughlin, who wrote in a December 17 letter to General John Pershing:

> Johnson killed himself by the speeches he made advocating a vast National Defense. What Johnson said was with the approval of the President. If Johnson's program had been met with public favor, he would have continued to be the fair-haired boy of the White House. But the opposition to excessive armaments has become so strong that a sacrifice is necessary and Johnson is the sacrifice.[42]

On January 11, 1939, Secretary Woodring, after more than two weeks of steady consultation with the president and his chief of staff, recommended the establishment of a 6,000-plane air corps. Two days later, Roosevelt went before Congress with his annual budget message and in addition to the regular army appropriations asked for supplementary funds for $200 million worth of "non-air armaments," $120 million for air bases and equipment, and $180 million to purchase 3,000 additional aircraft. Within three months, Congress responded by approving all the amounts requested and passing the so-called Woodring Plan, which would increase the size of the air corps from 2,320 to 6,000.[43] In terms of percent, the expansion was considerable, but it was a far cry from the program envisioned by Roosevelt and championed by Johnson in the previous fall. Using Johnson as a stalking horse, Roosevelt had gotten a little too far out in front. It was apparent that America was not yet ready to rearm.

As 1939 dawned, Johnson was clearly out at the White House. In the next eighteen months, Johnson's influence would rise and fall like a roller coaster as the president pursued his practice of turning from his secretary to his assistant secretary of war and back again. The one who could do FDR the most good at a particular time determined who was in favor.

"Secret" Sales to the Allies

While the president and the War Department wrestled with rearmament questions, a series of events began to unfold in late 1938 that were to eventually arouse as much controversy as the issue of air power expansion. The controversy swirled around the sale of American-built military aircraft to the Allies. Ultimately, the matter became so important that many war department officials, Johnson included, and top leaders in the Treasury Department were called before a congressional committee to explain what was going on.

The controversy stemmed from French efforts to purchase war planes in the United States. The genesis of this pursuit had begun in January 1938, when Amaury de la Grange asked the president if his government could purchase a thousand planes like those being used by the army air corps. After cautioning his friend about the restrictions that neutrality legislation imposed on such purchases, the president proceeded to pledge his full support. A month later, Ambassador William Bullitt and French financier Jean Monnet also visited the White House. Roosevelt again said he would help and even indicated ways they could get around the Neutrality Act in the event that war came and he was unable to get Congress to repeal or modify it.[44]

At this time the War Department was cooperating with friendly foreign governments under a policy on sales of foreign aircraft that had been developed by Secretary Woodring and personally approved by President Roosevelt in 1936. That policy, designed to preserve American air superiority, prohibited any American aircraft firm that was providing the army with a particular model aircraft from selling that aircraft to a foreign government until one year after the initial delivery of the plane to the army. Only then could the War Department approve a request for sale to a foreign government, provided that the sale would not interfere with deliveries to the air corps.[45]

In late February 1938, La Grange returned to the United States and began a search for military aircraft the French could buy. As he toured production facilities around the nation, he was disappointed by what he found available. A number of models could be purchased under the current release policy, but the French considered those aircraft unacceptable. They were, however, impressed by the alleged capabilities of the new P-36 but wanted to know more about it firsthand. The French, therefore, requested permission to have one of their leading pilot-engineers, Michael Detroyat, test-fly the plane. Secretary Woodring rejected the request because it violated established policy; his military advisors, especially General Arnold, supported his position. The French mission, remembering Roosevelt's pledge of support, asked Ambassador Bullitt to appeal to the White House for permission to make the test flight.

On March 10, the president ordered the chief of staff to permit Detroyat to test-fly the P-36. Roosevelt stipulated that anything of a confidential nature should be removed, that the flight should be limited to twenty minutes, and that it should be made from an outlying field and "with utmost secrecy." Detroyat made the flight and was favorably impressed. In April, the French placed an order for 100 export models—a P-36 minus secret instruments and retractable landing gear, with the name changed to Hawk 75-A.[46]

As the French were attempting to work out a deal on the P-36, a British air mission arrived to shop for American planes. The British experience was similar to that of the French except that they wanted to test-fly the still-classified Douglas B-18 bomber. The War Department, as it had with the French, refused permission, and again the president intervened and ordered the flight. The British were not overly impressed with the B-18 and did not place an order. However, they continued to look for planes, and in June they purchased 200 light bombers and 200 pursuit planes, both models that were no longer classified. Within four months of placing those orders, the Munich crisis occurred. Thereafter, British interest in American aircraft waned because they did not want to become dependent upon America for planes and then have that source of supply cut off by the Neutrality Act if war came.[47]

Although Assistant Secretary Johnson was undoubtedly aware of these French and British air missions, there is nothing in the record that indicates he was involved with them and the surrounding events, nor is his position on the issue available. What his stand would have been at that time is difficult to determine; although he was pro-Ally and supported action which would help the American aircraft industry, he was also a firm believer in the principle that the air corps should be assured that it had the finest-quality planes available and in the quantity it needed.

After the British and French capitulation at Munich, the French were even more eager to secure American aircraft because they knew there was no way for their own industry to meet their needs. In late October 1938, Jean Monnet and Ambassador Bullitt again traveled to Washington to meet with President Roosevelt and discuss further French purchases. The president invited Secretary of Treasury Henry Morgenthau to attend the meeting not only because of the fiscal implications of a large purchase agreement but also because of Morgenthau's pro-French, pro-British attitude.

At the meeting an optimistic Roosevelt told the three men that the American aircraft industry could soon supply France with 1,000 bombers and a like number of pursuit planes. Greatly encouraged, Monnet quickly returned to Paris and discussed the possibility of such a purchase with French premier Edouard Daladier. Several days later Daladier decided to send Monnet and three aviation experts on a secret mission to the United States to purchase 1,000 of the latest American-built war planes.[48]

When Monnet's mission arrived in Washington on December 16, 1938, it went, at Roosevelt's direction, not to the War Department but to the Treasury Department, where it was to work through Morgenthau.[49] Roosevelt had been annoyed by the earlier opposition of Secretary Woodring and Generals Craig and Arnold to French and British examination of classified aircraft, so he decided to circumvent the War Department and work through the more-cooperative Treasury Department. Although Roosevelt's ostensible reason for directing the French to Treasury was that its Procurement Division was better prepared to oversee such sales, his real thinking was that if the War Department would not help promote the sales he favored, he would find a department that would.[50]

It was not until December 20, or four days after the French mission arrived, that anyone in the War Department knew of its presence. Information about the French mission was passed on to Secretary Woodring, who lingered after a December 21 cabinet meeting to discuss the matter with the president and Morgenthau. The treasury secretary opened the discussion by requesting that French engineers and pilots be permitted to inspect the Curtis P-40, a fighter, and the Martin 166 and the Douglas B-12, both twin-engine bombers. Woodring protested, but the president sided with Morgenthau. He made it clear that for "reasons of state," the French mission should be permitted to inspect and purchase the planes.[51] At that point, the secretary of war reluctantly agreed, but when he summoned Generals Craig and Arnold to his office later that day and told them what they were expected to do, they balked. As they forcefully made their arguments, Woodring's courage to resist grew. Finally, by December 30, they had reached what they considered a reasonable compromise—they would agree to release the P-40 and Martin 166 but not the Douglas B-12 bomber.

While all of this was going on, Assistant Secretary Johnson was completely out of the loop. Normally, such ignorance would be incomprehensible, but not so in the War Department during the Roosevelt administration. Secretary Woodring had been left in the dark in recent months about the air expansion program, so he did not mind in the least leaving his archenemy in the dark over the French matter. On December 29, Woodring finally told Johnson what had transpired up to that point, and the assistant secretary agreed that the B-12 needed to be protected. The news of what had been taking place was unsettling to Johnson, but not because of the issues involved in the possible sale. What angered him was that the president had completely ignored him and, beyond that, was bypassing the War Department by turning to the Treasury Department.

In early January 1939, the French mission made a tentative decision to purchase 100 Curtis pursuit planes and 60 Martin bombers, but they still were not able to get access to the plane they wanted most to examine—the Douglas B-12 bomber. When Secretary Morgenthau returned from two weeks' vacation in mid-month, he was distressed to learn that in spite of the president's December 21 directive, the army was still dragging its feet about access to the Douglas B-12. A sharp protest to Roosevelt by Morgenthau led to a pledge to correct the situation immediately and Roosevelt called for a White House conference of key civilians in the War, Navy, and Treasury Departments to take place on January 16.

Back in the loop, Johnson rode with Woodring to the Monday-morning conference at the White House, and they speculated about what might happen at the meeting with the president. When they saw Morgenthau and Ambassador Bullitt arrive for the meeting, they knew what was coming. Both sides advanced the same arguments they had in the past, although Woodring, for the first time, emphasized the domestic political considerations, pointing out that release of the Douglas bomber could "prove very embarrassing to the president." In the course of the meeting, Roosevelt implied, suggested, and inferred that he favored the release of the B-12 to the French. Finally, Johnson, tiring of the president's cat-and-mouse game, looked him in the eye and asked, "Do you mean sir, that you wish the Douglas light bomber released to the French government?" Without hesitation the chief executive responded, "I mean exactly that."[52]

There was no longer any question about what the War Department had to do, and Woodring told Johnson to handle it because it was basically a procurement matter at that point. One thing Johnson had learned early in life was that you should do everything possible to please the person who is clearly your boss and has the right to hire and fire you. The president had said he wanted something done and Johnson, even though he apparently did not approve of the decision, intended to carry it out.

On January 19, Johnson met with General Arnold and Captain Harry Collins, who as head of the treasury's Procurement Division had been given the responsibility of assisting the French mission. Johnson stated that the War Department was "willing to cooperate 100 percent with the president's wishes" and would grant permission to the French to visit the Douglas plant, examine the light bomber, and, if desired, place a purchase order for the planes. After making clear that the bombsight was secret and therefore not available for inspection or sale, he asked that all matters pertaining to contracts be cleared through him. He then closed by giving reassurances that there would be no further delays and that he would "cooperate in every way."[53]

Based on the January 19 conference, General Arnold telegraphed a message to the army representative at the Douglas plant and informed him of the pending arrival of three members of the French mission, including one of France's outstanding pilots, Captain Paul Chemidlin. The message went on to say, "They are authorized to inspect [Douglas] attack-bomber secret accessories, fly in it, and negotiate [with Douglas] for purchase."[54]

"On January 23 all hell broke loose," General Arnold was to write later, and for good reason.[55] On that morning the still-secret bomber, with Douglas pilot John Cable and Chemidlin aboard, crashed in a parking lot near the Los Angeles Airport. Cable was killed when his parachute failed to open, but miraculously Chemidlin survived; he was pulled from the burning wreckage with only a broken leg and lacerations. The Frenchman was taken to a local hospital, where Douglas officials, hoping to keep his true identity secret, identified him as one of their mechanics by the name of Smith. Newsmen, however, quickly learned who he was, and before noon the Associated Press put out a rush story that identified the survivor as "Paul Chemidlin of Paris, representative of the French Air Ministry."[56]

As soon as the crash occurred, Douglas officials called the War Department and told them what happened. Johnson had been "quite mad and very sarcastic" that morning even before receiving the news from the coast.[57] His edginess stemmed from his anger and frustration over the way the Douglas inspection had been forced on the War Department by the president and the treasury. Once he learned of the crash, he was even more upset because now he faced the prospect of explaining what a French test pilot was doing on the still-classified American-built bomber.

The day after the crash, the *Washington Star* carried a story which said, "Chemidlin's purpose on the flight was particularly puzzling because of Federal regulations forbidding the export of any military-type plane until it has been in service in this country for a year, or has been rejected for national defense use."[58] In fact, the plane had not yet been submitted to the military for consideration and was therefore still a private aircraft. However, to Congress and the public, this was a mere technicality; as far as they were concerned, the spirit of the law had been broken, and they wanted to know why the Frenchman was allowed to fly in the "secret aircraft." That question set off an inquiry by isolationists and Republicans in Congress, who saw an excellent opportunity to embarrass the administration by showing that Roosevelt was breaking his neutrality commitment and secretly aiding the Allies.[59]

The opening shots of the inquiry came two days after the crash, on January 25, when General Arnold was before the Senate Military Affairs Committee answering routine questions about budget requests for the upcoming fiscal year. In the midst of these questions, Senator Bennett Clark (D-Missouri), who was frequently a thorn in the administration's side, asked General Arnold what the Frenchman was doing on the Douglas plane. Arnold replied nervously, "He was there under the direction of the Treasury Department, with a view of looking into possible purchase of airplanes by the French mission."[60] That statement opened a can of worms that could not be closed for some time.

In the days that followed, the Senate committee delved into every aspect of the French mission and the series of events leading up to the crash. Secretaries Woodring and Morgenthau, Generals Craig and Arnold, and Assistant Secretary Johnson were among those called to testify. Much of the testimony in the secret sessions was off the record in the hope that leaks to the press could be prevented. Such efforts were futile, however; news reporters succeeded in finding out what was being said and were able to publish a fairly accurate record of the proceedings.[61]

After trying unsuccessfully to gloss over the whole affair, both Woodring and Morgenthau revealed that the orders had come from the president—a fact that was not really surprising but was nevertheless unsettling to several senators. In a desire to get the whole story, the committee, in a most unusual procedure, went en masse on January 31 to the White House to talk to President Roosevelt. Four days prior to their visit, however, Roosevelt had moved to steal some of the isolationists' thunder by stating disingenuously that he supported the French sales because they would be good for the American aircraft industry. He also said that the War Department had not objected to his order allowing the French to examine the Douglas plane because it was a "manufacturer's plane which the Air Corps might or might not select."[62]

In spite of such statements, some of the senators were shocked at what Roosevelt told them at the January 31 meeting. He readily admitted that he had approved the French inspection of the Douglas bomber and candidly acknowledged that such action was indeed not neutral. He told the group that France and England could not be permitted to fall, for if they did Germany would then turn its attention on the rest of the world. Refreshingly honest and straightforward, FDR closed by saying that he hoped the Allies could get the best planes available in America and get them fast because their doing so "might mean the saving of our civilization."[63]

It was no surprise that the president's remarks were especially alarming to the isolationists, who feared that such a policy might well draw the nation into a European conflict. For the next two weeks, they continued their official probe into the Douglas incident and did so in a way calculated to embarrass the administration as much as possible. While Woodring and Morgenthau took turns passing the buck before throwing it to the president, Johnson, taking his cue from Roosevelt, attempted to explain away the approval by claiming that the B-12 was an experimental plane owned by Douglas and therefore not under government jurisdiction.[64]

The upshot of the hearings was that Woodring and General Arnold emerged as the reluctant leaders who had been forced to go along with the president, while Johnson clearly came out as the loyal lieutenant who was carrying out the chief executive's orders.

While the debate and discussion over the French mission continued in Congress and the news media, the Frenchmen continued to go about their business, and in late February and early March they placed orders for 555 aircraft, including 100 of the controversial Douglas bombers. Shortly thereafter, the mission returned home and the controversy over aircraft sales to France dissipated.[65] The question of aid to France would lie dormant for nine months and then rear its head once again.

Misreading FDR

As the spring of 1939 came to Washington, Louis Johnson's standing and influence in the White House had diminished, just as the president's ability to persuade Congress of the need to provide arms to France and Britain had waned following the return of a significant bloc of Republicans to the House as a result of the 1938 midterm elections. Johnson may not have realized it at the time, but the fall of 1938 marked a crucial turning point in the president's foreign policy. After Munich and his meeting with Ambassador Bullitt, Roosevelt began talking privately about immediate and massive production of warplanes to give him clout in international diplomacy. At the secret meeting in the White House on November 14, the president disclosed that he wanted to use U.S. air power as a tool to tip the balance of power in Europe in favor of the French and British. By January of 1939, FDR was readily admitting to several senators that the United States could not remain neutral and that it was his policy to provide the Allies with America's latest and best warplanes.

Johnson stuck his thick neck way out for the president on air rearmament. As the leading scholar of aircraft procurement said, "Again and again when opportunity offered, the Assistant Secretary seized the initiative to drive the air rearmament program with vigor. The aggressive leadership of Johnson brought results."[66]

But Johnson either failed to understand, or could not bring himself to agree with, the president's view that air power can and should be used both as a tool to achieve diplomatic objectives and as an alternative to raising and equipping ground troops. He overreached by trying to use FDR's enthusiasm for air rearmament as justification for support for ground troops, and he stood by while Woodring and his generals resisted the French mission. Consequently, Johnson helped put himself and the entire War Department in FDR's doghouse.[67] In a very real sense, the War Department, at least in this episode, was as much a barrier to Roosevelt's policy of "biased neutrality" as the isolationists in Congress were.

CHAPTER SIX

Surviving FDR

ALTHOUGH THE EARLY summer heat was as stifling as ever in the nation's capital, officials there were breathing much easier than they had been several months earlier—not because of the weather, but because of the political situation. It was June 1939, and the tension that followed the Munich crisis the previous fall was quickly dissipating. The war clouds that had seemed so ominous just months before appeared to be breaking—perhaps Hitler had at last seized control of all the territory he coveted. Even President Roosevelt was indicating to close friends his belief that the prospects for war were fading.[1]

What was past was past, and most Americans did not look back; the Depression was something they wanted to forget. Fortunately, things appeared to be looking up—the economy registered its greatest strength in nearly ten years. Of immediate interest was the visit of the king and queen of England to America. George VI was the first British monarch to set foot in the United States while ruling, and he received all the pomp and ceremony official Washington could muster. The hope of the future seemed to be exemplified by the World's Fair which opened in New York City. The fair focused on a world of tomorrow with its promise of less work and more leisure made possible in large part by technological advances. The mood in America was upbeat.

Not everyone, however, embraced the new mood of optimism, and one who clearly did not was Louis Johnson. The assistant secretary of war still believed that Europe was headed for war. He feared that the United States would be drawn into the conflict without being militarily prepared. He was convinced that the president's rejection of his $2.1 billion air and ground rearmament proposals six months before was a major national blunder; he felt that Hitler would again flex his muscles and that the rest of the world would have nothing with which to stop or even slow down his thirst for conquest.[2]

Despite the fact that Johnson had lost his privileged position at the White House, he continued to strive for the military preparedness which he considered critical to the survival of the nation. He labored long and hard to complete the revision of the proposed 1939 Industrial Mobilization Plan, he expanded the educational orders program, he laid the foundation for a program to stockpile strategic materials, he continued to publicly advocate air rearmament, and he spent hundreds of hours on Capitol Hill trying to convince Congress to support legislation beneficial to the army and defense programs in general.[3] By mid-spring of 1939, the assistant secretary had ingratiated himself once more with FDR.

While Johnson's star was once again rising with the president, the bureaucrats responsible for juggling competing demands for office space in Washington sent Johnson a mixed message. In the summer of 1939, they decreed that Johnson and the War Department would have to move down to the old Munitions Building on the Constitution Avenue side of the Mall near the Lincoln Memorial. On the one hand, the order to move meant that Johnson was beginning to build an empire that would soon colonize not only the Munitions Building but also some twenty other buildings in the Washington area. On the other hand, Johnson would no longer occupy his geographically privileged office only a few footsteps from the president. He would be moving to a crumbling and sagging World War I–era "temporary" wooden building with squeaky floors and water-stained walls and ceilings.[4]

Rise and Fall of the War Resources Board

As Johnson's ability to assert himself with the president grew and as the revision of the Industrial Mobilization Plan neared completion, he began a push to establish the superagency that he felt was absolutely essential to the nation's success in the coming armed conflict—a War Resources Administration. From mid-1937 through 1938, he had urged the establishment of a civilian advisory board to study the Mobilization Plan and make recommendations about how it could be improved and carried out. He hoped that the group could address the question of just how American industry could provide for the nation's defense in time of all-out war.

Roosevelt, fearing anything along the lines of the powerful War Industries Board headed by Baruch during World War I, had stymied creation of such an advisory group by inaction.[5] In March and again in April 1939 Johnson suggested to the president that world events made it "both sound and desirable" to "create a council to study the long-range problems of national defense."[6] As in the past, Roosevelt did nothing, but Johnson was not discouraged because he felt that if he could keep the matter alive, its time would ultimately arrive.

As Roosevelt drifted back toward working more closely with Johnson in the spring of 1939, he began looking for ways that he could more readily bypass his increasingly recalcitrant secretary of war. His solution was a July 5 executive order which placed the Joint Army and Navy Munitions Board directly under his control. This meant that Johnson and his navy counterpart, Assistant Secretary of Navy Charles Edison, had direct access to the president on all munitions matters, which could easily be interpreted as covering all defense matters. The order gave the army chief of staff and the chief of naval operations direct contact with the commander in chief.[7] All this meant that Johnson and General Marshall, who began serving as acting chief of staff on July 1, could now legally bypass Woodring and go straight to the president. As a practical matter, the new executive order was merely symbolic, since Johnson had been going directly to the president for at least two years. Nevertheless, the July 5 action was a clear signal to Woodring that he was out once more.

As usual, Johnson read much more into FDR's action than was probably intended. He felt that the executive order gave him the green light to proceed with the establishment of a War Resources Board, the first step in the creation of a powerful War Resources Administration as called for in the 1939 Industrial Mobilization Plan. The decision to push his idea to fruition was probably made in mid-July; all he had to do was wait for the proper moment when Woodring, who was flatly opposed to such a board, was out of town.[8] The anxious assistant secretary did not have to wait long; on August 3, Secretary Woodring and his family set off on a two-week vacation to Panama.

The day after the secretary's departure, Johnson attended the weekly cabinet meeting in his place. At that time he asked for and received from the president authority to establish a War Resources Board.[9] That body, which was to be composed of six civilians, was to review the just-completed Industrial Mobilization Plan and make recommendations to the assistant secretary about what improvements should be made. It was agreed that the announcement of the creation of the board would be delayed several days until its members were chosen.

While Johnson wanted Bernard Baruch to head the group, Roosevelt found him unacceptable and refused to include him at all, instead suggesting Edward R. Stettinius Jr., chairman of the board of US Steel. That choice was acceptable to Johnson, and on August 8 the president gave his formal approval. The next day Johnson met with Stettinius, Assistant Secretary of Navy Edison, Chief of Staff Marshall, Colonel Burns, and Colonel Harry Rutherford, director of the War Planning Branch, to select the members of the new board. After culling names from two lists prepared by the army and Stettinius, the group came up with five names: John Pratt, a director of General Motors; Walter S. Gifford, president of AT&T; General Robert E. Wood, head of Sears Roebuck and a leader of the America First movement; Harold Moulton, president of Brookings Institute; and Karl T. Compton, president of the Massachusetts Institute of

Technology.[10] Later that day, the president, along with Johnson and Edison, announced the creation and membership of the War Resources Board to the press.[11]

Although the president had approved only the creation of a *board* to review war mobilization plans, it quickly became apparent that Johnson had much more in mind. In his August 9 announcement concerning the board's creation, Johnson stated that it would not only review and perfect industrial mobilization plans but would in time of emergency "become an executive agency of the Government with broad powers similar to those of the old War Industries Board."[12] He clearly envisioned the War Resources *Board* as the vehicle for bringing about the War Resources *Administration*.

Johnson felt that such a move was not only logical but necessary because he fully expected that Europe would be plunged into war at any time, that American involvement would inevitably follow, and that the United States would need the machinery necessary to harness the nation's industrial might for the war effort. To accomplish that awesome task would require a skilled executive armed with real authority to get the job done. He believed that in a national emergency the president would have too many things to do and the coordination of industry would require a full-time commitment. This is why Johnson wanted the president to delegate his economic war powers to a War Resources Administration.[13]

Johnson opened the first meeting of the War Resources Board in the old Munitions Building on August 17, 1939. Again he stressed his firm belief that the Board "would become the War Resources Administration visualized in the document called the Industrial Mobilization Plan."[14] The board members assumed that since Johnson and the president were on such intimate terms the assistant secretary was stating the views of the chief executive.

For the next twelve days the newly appointed board worked around the clock studying plans, reading reports, and meeting with mobilization experts such as Bernard Baruch and General John Pershing. The work took on a real sense of urgency when the board members learned of the German-Soviet Non-Aggression Pact, which they assumed would lead to a Nazi attack on Poland. Although the board stated that the president had the responsibility and authority to carry out all mobilization activities, it gave its endorsement to the 1939 Mobilization Plan and its pyramidal organization that peaked with a War Resources Administration. That proposed agency would have final say on all matters regarding economic mobilization.

The group examined other areas of concern such as price controls, production capabilities and bottlenecks, strategic materials, skilled workers, and personnel to fill various positions in the War Resources Administration. As the end of August approached, the members felt optimistic about the progress they were making, and they looked forward to their first meeting with the president, a session scheduled for August 30.[15]

The War Resources Board's first gathering with Roosevelt was unlike any-thing its members had anticipated. Although the board members had expected to have an opportunity to make their case about the best way to mobilize indus-try, the president, who knew what they would be advocating, did all the talking. In what amounted to a stern 15-minute lecture, he rejected the idea of a War Resources Administration and proposed a reactivation of the old World War I Advisory Commission of the Council of National Defense, whereby six or seven civilian advisors would report to him. He then asked the board members to write a revised job description of their duties and responsibilities. Once that was done, he would decide if additional funds would be granted for the group to continue its work. With that, the president dismissed the stunned participants and they numbly left the White House.[16]

Without directly attacking the Industrial Mobilization Plan, Roosevelt had made it clear to the War Resources Board that he did not accept the plan, since its most important feature was the creation of a War Resources Administration. Board members had mistakenly assumed from the beginning that the president had approved the plan, at least in principle. After all, that was the impression that Johnson had given them through his private and public utterances. Now, however, the president had shot all that down and sent the group back to the drawing board. But while the August 30 meeting was upsetting to the Board members, so was the news they received less than forty-eight hours later: Ger-many had attacked Poland. It was September 1, 1939, and Europe was at war.

The president's rebuff of the War Resources Board, and by implication of the Mobilization Plan, bothered but did not dissuade Johnson; he merely con-cluded that he would have to press harder to get what he wanted. Since he be-lieved that the concepts of mobilization put forth in the plan were fundamen-tally sound, he continued to push for them within the War Resources Board. The description of the board's duties and responsibilities that emerged in early September was essentially the same as the one the president had rejected on August 30.

The board's "revised" job description was forwarded to the president via a September 6 memorandum from Johnson and Edison.[17] When FDR read the memorandum on the afternoon of the 6th, he became very irritated. Notwith-standing the invasion of Poland and the declaration of war by both France and Britain, nothing had occurred to change the president's mind, and he refused to approve the memorandum. Later that afternoon he expressed his disgust for the document, its content, and Johnson, saying that the board would have no authority or direct access to the president and that such an utter disregard of his directions was leading him to consider a cabinet shuffle that would, among other things, take both Johnson and Woodring out of the War Department.[18] Johnson did not then realize it, but after September 6, 1939, the days of his War Resources Board were numbered.

At his September 7 cabinet meeting, the president criticized the War Resources Board's perceptions of its responsibilities. He was contemptuous of the fact that the group "was prepared to take over all the functions of government," and he made it clear that he "had no intention of permitting this." Not surprisingly, Woodring used that opening to voice his displeasure about the creation of the board and the fact that it was done in his absence and without his knowledge.[19]

In the days that followed, the president let Johnson know how he felt about the War Resources Board. Sometimes he was subtle and sometimes he was not. He began by cutting by more than half Johnson's request for funds to cover the board's operating expenses. Next, he told the assistant secretary that he had learned the board was discussing who might be the coordinator of railroads and that they should stop wasting their time on such a matter since "it was none of their affair."[20] "The question of transportation," FDR wrote Johnson, is "wholly outside the scope" of the board's responsibilities.[21] On September 14, the president reiterated his thinking in a face-to-face meeting, but this time he did so more strongly than ever before. After this meeting Johnson and the board slowly began to come around to an organization plan along the lines desired by the president—but by then it was too late.

By mid-September the president had tired of the obstinacy of his assistant secretary of war on the board issue, and he began looking for the right time to discredit Johnson and bring Woodring back to the forefront. His opportunity came on the 26th of September, when Johnson was in Chicago attending the national convention of the American Legion. During the cabinet meeting that day, Secretary of Labor Frances Perkins called to the president's attention a new book entitled *Adjusting Your Business to War*, by Leo M. Cherne, which examined the issue of industrial mobilization and told businessmen what they might expect in terms of government controls during time of war. Miss Perkins's concern was in part due to the "economic fascism" called for, especially in regard to labor, but what was most unsettling to her was the fact that the foreword to the book was written by Louis Johnson, thereby making the book appear to be sanctioned by Roosevelt's War Department. Johnson had not said anything that he had not previously said publicly, but in authoring the foreword it appeared as if he was supporting all the views expressed in the book.[22]

Woodring, who had first been asked to write the foreword but refused, happily jumped at the opportunity to discredit his nemesis. At that time the president said nothing, but in the news conference that followed he let fly with two salvos at Johnson. The first shot came in response to a question, apparently planted by Perkins, about whether or not the Cherne book represented the views of the administration. The president replied quite firmly that no book on any defense policy or mobilization topic had the sanction of his administration. Continuing, he said that 90 percent of the books written on such issues were written by people who knew practically nothing about the subject.

Then came the second slap at Johnson. Without forewarning Johnson, Roosevelt announced that the War Resources Board would issue a report in about ten days and that its work would then be finished. Although he did not mention him by name, the president had clipped Johnson's wings. When the president left, Secretary Woodring, who had remained for the press conference, completed the spanking by telling a reporter, "The War Department is not setting up any permanent war boards and war machinery and I hope we never will."[23]

The news media took it from there, and in the next two weeks nearly every major newspaper and news magazine recounted the events of the press conference and explained what it meant in terms of Johnson's influence. One newspaper in his home state reported, "Louis Johnson is in the biggest doghouse in Washington." Some sources even suggested that the assistant secretary do the decent thing and resign.[24]

The events of September 26, 1939, surprised and hurt Johnson, who wrote to his friend Steve Early on October 1 that he was "worried" and "confused" by the recent developments. "Since '31 I have loyally backed the President and if he doubts that . . . there is nothing I can do about it." As to his future course of action he stated, "I haven't said anything and do not intend to do so."[25] He realized that hasty words at this time could permanently alienate him from the president, so he eased off, as in the past, and waited for his star to rise again.

In November, the War Resources Board submitted its final report, which would remain secret until after World War II. In it, the members endorsed the superagency concept, which they had originally supported, and a program through which several agencies would be coordinated by the president, which was more in line with Roosevelt's views. When he received the report, the president thanked the members for their work and said that the board would continue to serve in an advisory capacity. He then locked up the report and never called upon that body again.[26]

Why Did They Do It?

At this juncture, two questions beg consideration. First, why did Johnson continue to push for the War Resources Board as he envisioned it, even after the president had made his opposition clear? Second, why did Roosevelt approve the creation of the board and then turn around and kill it?

To the first question there is no clear-cut answer. Johnson's supporters would point out that because he firmly believed that a strong centralized control mechanism was essential to effective wartime economic mobilization, he did everything he could to convince the president that such an entity should be established. To them, he was a man of great principle who went all out for what he considered to be right. Johnson's advocates have the backing of history on their side when they cite the War Industries Board under Bernard

Baruch in World War I and the War Production Board under Donald Nelson during World War II as successful examples of the ideas Johnson advocated.[27]

To Johnson's critics, his continual pushing for the board as he perceived it, especially in light of the president's clear opposition, was an example of either political naiveté or bullheadedness that stemmed from his arrogance. Those who claim he was naive contend that Johnson had no real understanding of the congressional and public pressures which faced the president and that he failed to comprehend Roosevelt's insistence on running his own show and his reluctance to delegate real authority to another individual.[28] Johnson's severest critics saw him as an extremely arrogant man who thought he knew all the answers and was unwilling to make any accommodation. They maintain that when the president expressed views different from his, whether on the authority of the War Resources Board or on the necessity of air rearmament, Johnson's sense that he knew best led him to ignore what Roosevelt said and advance his own ideas once more.[29]

Somewhere between these extremes lies the real Louis Johnson. It was probably a combination of deeply held conviction, failure to fully understand FDR, and his own arrogance that led him to push so hard for the organizational principles embodied in the War Resources Board.

Roosevelt's motives and methods in first creating, then abolishing the War Resources Board were equally complex. Why did he approve its creation? One explanation is that he could not bring himself to say no. Ever since Johnson had come to the War Department, he had been pestering the president to establish such a group. The president probably came to the conclusion that the way to quiet him and at the same time send up a trial balloon was to give in on the idea of the War Resources Board. Furthermore, the president really had no sound argument as to why an evaluation of the government's mobilization plans should not be made.

As to why Roosevelt quickly abolished the board there appear to be several explanations. First, he was unwilling to relinquish his emergency war powers and he felt that that is what the 1939 Industrial Mobilization Plan and the War Resources Board would have caused him to do. As he explained to one close advisor, "If I were to set up a scheme such as recommended by this report, turning over the sole administration of the economy of the country . . . to a single war administrator . . . even though he were appointed by me — I would simply be abdicating the presidency to some other person."[30] Second, he felt that the board was too representative of Wall Street. From the time the membership was revealed, there was considerable criticism of its pro-business makeup. Labor, agriculture, and the New Dealers surrounding the president let their anti-business views be known. This criticism, along with Roosevelt's own disdain for the business sector, led him to terminate the board. Finally, by abolishing a "war" board FDR hoped to allay some of the growing public fear over the possibility of being drawn into the war under way in Europe.[31]

For these various reasons, FDR killed the War Resources Board. In retrospect that decision appears to have been a wrong one. If Johnson's recommendations had been implemented in 1939, the United States would have been much better prepared when it ultimately entered World War II.

Biased Neutrality

While the War Resources Board issue consumed the bulk of Johnson's time and energy in August and September of 1939, that was not his only preoccupation. On August 17, he was summoned to the State Department by Acting Secretary of State Sumner Welles, where he learned that Hitler had pulled off the impossible by negotiating a non-aggression pact with the Soviet Union—a fact that was not publicly announced until four days later. Welles pessimistically pointed out that a German attack on Poland now appeared imminent, and he concluded that "we ought to be ready for the worst."[32] Johnson, apprehensive that his long-held fears of a world at war might soon come true, hurried back to the War Department and directed General Marshall to prepare detailed plans of actions to be taken when war came.[33] While those plans were being formulated, Johnson became heavily involved in efforts to secure changes in the neutrality laws so that aid could be extended to the Allies.

As early as 1938, President Roosevelt had made known in private that if war came to Europe he would work for repeal or modification of the Neutrality Act so that the victims of Nazi aggression would be able to secure arms from America. Attempts to bring about such changes had failed in early 1939, but the events of August led the president to the decision that he had to renew the battle.

Before going public with Congress and the American people, FDR decided to send up a trial balloon. He called Johnson to the White House and asked him to make several speeches calling for revision of the neutrality legislation. Johnson agreed, and in late August of 1939 he began to test the political waters for the president, just as he had the year before with the air rearmament program. He gave two speeches, the first on the 26th in his hometown of Roanoke and the second before the national convention of the Veterans of Foreign Wars in Boston two days later. In both speeches he strongly criticized the arms embargo provision, claiming that it actually encouraged war. He also attacked those senators who had blocked revision of that provision in the previous session of Congress, stating that "however honorable may have been their intentions they have much to answer for. They played politics when peace was in the balance, and men may die as a result."[34]

The morning after Johnson's Boston speech to the VFW, Roosevelt was asked at a presidential news conference if he agreed with Johnson's statements about the need to revise the neutrality legislation. The president said he did not intend to be "as specific as Johnson," but he expressed his general concurrence.[35]

Johnson's speeches and Roosevelt's official reaction to them enabled the president to lay the groundwork for his renewed battle for neutrality revision.

The responses to Johnson's speeches, which were carried on the front pages of most major newspapers, ranged from overwhelming endorsement by British newspapers and the ambassador to England, Joseph P. Kennedy, to the extreme negativism of Arthur Krock of the *New York Times*, who wrote that Roosevelt should "curb subordinates—notably such obsequious courtiers as Mr. Johnson—from injecting partisan and personal politics into their public utterances in such a time."[36]

War in Europe

At 3:30 A.M. on September 1, 1939, the phone rang in the Johnsons' apartment in the Mayflower annex. On the other end was Colonel Burns with word that Germany's expected attack on Poland was taking place. As he rode through the darkened streets of Washington on the way to his office, Johnson must have worried what the future held. By the time Johnson arrived at the Munitions Building, Woodring, Marshall, and most of the staff were already in their offices and news of the attack and readiness directions were being sent to military installations across the nation and around the world. Woodring indicated that he and Marshall had things under control at the War Department but cited the need for liaison with the State Department and sent Johnson there.

For the next several days, Johnson spent most of his time at the State Department working with Secretary of State Hull, Undersecretary Welles, and Assistant Secretary Adolf Berle, Jr., who had helped Johnson draft his speeches on neutrality. The group made several trips to the White House in those critical days, including a visit on Sunday, September 3, when they met with the president in the Lincoln Study to iron out the president's speech to be made to the American people that night. In that address, Roosevelt stated that the United States would "remain a neutral nation, but I cannot ask that every American remain neutral in thought as well."[37] A few days later he called Congress into special session for the purpose of eliminating the embargo on the export of arms and munitions.

From late September until November 3, when the Neutrality Act was amended to eliminate the embargo and was replaced with a cash-and-carry provision, Johnson spent considerable time on Capitol Hill trying to sell recalcitrant members of Congress on the need to revise the nation's policy of neutrality.[38] He had been an active lobbyist for the War Department that spring, and the contacts he had made then were useful in this latest congressional battle. But just as that problem was coming to a satisfactory conclusion, an issue resurfaced that was to be every bit as controversial as anything Johnson faced as assistant secretary of war—the looming question of a large-scale sale of American-built military airplanes to the Allies.

Sales to the Allies Redux

When Congress finally gave its approval for the sale of arms and munitions to belligerents abroad, the significance of that action meant different things to different people. President Roosevelt envisioned it not only as a means by which the United States could provide Britain and France with the war goods they needed to halt the Nazi menace but also as a foreign policy tool to tip the balance of power in Europe. Secretary Woodring saw it first and foremost as a way to greatly expand the nation's war production facilities, primarily those for aircraft, and to provide for the defense of the Western hemisphere.

The differences in the views of FDR and Woodring were closely related to their perceptions of the German threat and how it should be met. Roosevelt believed that Hitler could be stopped by Britain and France if they were properly armed and supplied. He was committed to a policy that gave priority to aiding the Allies and accorded secondary importance to rearming American forces. Woodring was strongly opposed to such thinking; he worried about what would happen if the nation frittered away its scarce war materials by sending them to Britain and France and those nations fell to Hitler.[39] Johnson tended to be in the middle of these two very different viewpoints, although if he leaned to one side or the other it was generally in the direction of Woodring's thinking. The assistant secretary believed that American defense resources could be divided in a manner that would benefit both sides. He advocated aiding the Allies as much as possible but not to the extent that it would hinder the rearmament of the U.S. Army and Air Corps. This balanced approach was why he sided with the president on some occasions and with the secretary on others.

As the need for administrative machinery to handle the large foreign orders became increasingly clear, the president gave considerable thought to which government department would be most effective in supplying the Allies. Remembering the hassle the War Department had given the French air mission just eleven months before and increasingly aware of the growing chaos being wrought by the Woodring-Johnson feud, the president decided to circumvent the War Department and turn to the Treasury Department's Procurement Division under Secretary Henry Morgenthau. There was no doubt about Morgenthau's capabilities, his dedication to the Allied cause, and his loyalty to the president. On December 6, Roosevelt announced the creation of a special three-person Liaison Committee charged with the responsibility of coordinating foreign sales so that they did not hinder the U.S. rearmament program.[40]

The president did not want to be too blatant in the way he was working around Woodring and Johnson, so he did not place Morgenthau on the Liaison Committee, but he did appoint as chairman Captain Harry E. Collins, director of procurement for the treasury (the same man Morgenthau brought in to assist the French air mission at the time of the Douglas crash). By naming Collins to head the group, the president gave Morgenthau virtual control. The committee's other two members were the quartermaster general of the army and the paymaster general of the navy.[41]

In one of those rare instances of agreement, both Woodring and Johnson criticized the president's decision to establish the Liaison Committee. Woodring even went so far as to say that the Army and Navy Munitions Board, headed by Johnson, was the body best qualified to do the job. Johnson sent a memorandum to the president protesting the removal of foreign sales coordination from the Munitions Board and claiming that it was much better prepared to carry out the task. An obviously irritated Roosevelt fired back a hotly worded reply which said, "I think you fail to realize that the greater part of such purchases is not munitions. . . . With all due deference to the Army and Navy Munitions Board, it is not as experienced in making purchases as the Procurement Division."[42] All the protests were to no avail, and in mid-December the president's Liaison Committee began functioning.

Near Christmas 1939, Arthur Purvis, head of the newly created Anglo-French Purchasing Commission, informed Morgenthau that a very large aircraft order would be forthcoming in a few months but that in the meantime the joint commission wanted to acquire some pursuit planes. That request was not as simple as it appeared because the American aircraft industry had committed nearly all of its resources to producing aircraft under contract to the army air corps.[43] To Morgenthau, the solution was to turn over the planes being built for the air corps to the Allies. In early January 1940, he suggested to the president that every other pursuit plane produced should be sold to the Anglo-French Purchasing Commission. Roosevelt considered that course too extreme, but he did agree to give the Allies twenty-five of the first eighty-one P-40s scheduled for delivery to the army that spring. Woodring, Johnson, Marshall, and Arnold strongly opposed that decision on two grounds: first, the deliveries to the Allies would prevent the air corps from receiving its planes on schedule; and second, it would mean that foreign powers would be receiving aircraft that were superior to those being used by the United States. Johnson, although readily acknowledging his sympathies for Britain and France, made it clear that he opposed any sidetracking of army aircraft deliveries.[44]

The War Department's arguments against and continued criticism of the Liaison Committee led Roosevelt to call top war department officials to the White House in mid-January to stress the importance of cooperation and the need to expedite deliveries to the Allies. Despite Roosevelt's call for cooperation, Johnson continued to criticize the Liaison Committee and Morgenthau's control of it. As a result, the White House was forced to release an endorsement of the committee and the job it was doing on January 23.[45]

In early March 1940, Purvis formally presented the large purchase order of the Allies, which called for 5,000 planes, 10,000 engines, and a large number of superchargers to enhance the power of the engines. All of this was desired by July 1941. In light of the fact that total American aircraft production, both military and civilian, was a little under 200 planes per month, it is not surprising that the army was shocked by the size of the order and upset that in each case the Allies requested the latest and most sophisticated aircraft.[46]

With Woodring, Johnson, Marshall, and Arnold all concurring, release of the latest aircraft and superchargers was denied on the grounds they were still classified as secret and therefore ineligible for export. Twice in 1939 the War Department had eased up on its release policy in response to pressure from the president by reducing the time period between production and release. By the beginning of 1940, war department officials felt they had gone as far as they could go and still assure superior aircraft for U.S. forces, but they were now being asked to go even farther.[47]

On March 12, 1940, word of Roosevelt's decision to release the twenty-five P-40s and revelations that the War Department was opposed to filling foreign orders because they would interfere with Air Corps deliveries reached the press.[48] Although they could not substantiate it, Roosevelt and Morgenthau were convinced that the leak had come from Johnson and Arnold.[49] As a result of these newspaper accounts, Representative Dow Harter, who headed the House Military Affairs Committee's Aviation Subcommittee, called for a hearing to look into the department's aircraft release policy. Some senators also called for an inquiry, but the Senate decided to wait and see what the House learned.[50]

The president, upset about the army's refusal to release the planes, the airing of dirty linen in public, and the potential for damaging hearings on the Hill, immediately summoned Johnson, Arnold, Woodring, and Marshall to the White House, where he read them the riot act. He sternly warned Johnson and Arnold that there were to be no more leaks to the press and he indicated to all of them that he was sick and tired of resistance to his policies and that he fully expected them to cooperate from then on. Looking directly at General Hap Arnold, the president said that officers who failed to do as they were told could always end up on assignment in Guam. He then bore in on Johnson once more, this time chiding him for continued criticism of the Liaison Committee and telling him that henceforth he expected him to say nothing but positive things about its performance and the leadership Captain Collins and Morgenthau were providing.[51] With that scolding, the president made his position crystal clear. From that time on, Johnson was ready and willing to play ball. Some of the others in the War Department were not.

The next day, the Military Affairs Committee asked Secretary Woodring to appear before it in one week and explain what was going on with regard to aircraft release. That gave the secretary and his advisors only a short time to devise a release policy that would be acceptable to them, the president, and the Congress. For the next few days, Woodring, Marshall, and Arnold worked on a new policy. Johnson was not included, probably at the secretary's insistence. During this time, General Marshall came up with a new idea called a "change order" or "delay order." Under this concept, the army would permit planes that were destined for its reserves to be sold to the Allies, and in return the manufacturer would deliver to the air corps later, more-refined models of the aircraft. In this way operational aircraft levels would not be affected, the Allies could receive the best aircraft currently available, and the air corps would ultimately receive planes that were better than originally contracted for.

Since the "change order" was a new concept and needed to be fully vetted, Woodring asked Generals Marshall and Arnold to carefully consider the new policy at a meeting on March 19 and meet back at his office at 7 o'clock that evening so they could finalize the policy and get it approved by the president before he presented it to the House Military Affairs Committee the following morning. Acknowledging that the new policy was basically a procurement matter and that Johnson would ultimately have to defend it, Woodring directed him to attend the session.

That evening as Johnson and the others headed for the War Department, Fulton Lewis was reporting in his evening newscast that at a press conference earlier in the day the president had said that all American-built military aircraft would be released for sale. The sketchiness of the report made it difficult to determine what exactly had been said and meant, but the report implied that the president was saying that there was no such thing as a secret aircraft and that therefore the United States would be willing to sell any model being produced. The impression was that the president was willing to sell with no strings attached. However, the army wanted some strings.

When they arrived for the evening meeting, the participants began speculating about what FDR had actually said and what impact it would have on their decision. Woodring maintained that since the president had made his intentions known to them there was no need to examine what he had put forth for public consumption that afternoon. Johnson challenged him, saying that the president's statement should be clarified before they proceeded. He went to a telephone and called White House stenographer Henry Kannee and asked that the verbatim account of the press conference be sent over to the meeting immediately.

While meeting participants were going over the notes, a call for Secretary Woodring came through from the White House. The president, who had been informed of the move to get the stenographic notes, spoke harshly. He reminded Woodring that his views on foreign sales had been made quite clear and that he expected the policy they came up with to reflect those views. The president then reiterated his "play ball" speech of the week before, adding that those unable to do so should get out. He also gave notice that individuals who appeared before congressional committees would "be considered on trial . . . insofar as any statements were concerned."

After hanging up, a rather stunned Woodring informed the group of the president's message. Realizing that an order had been given by the commander in chief, the officials finally sat down and hammered out a policy that permitted export sales of every military aircraft approved by the president but prevented the release of secret devices, such as the latest bombsight, and provided for change orders. Since it was then the early hours of the morning, Woodring called House Military Affairs Chairman Andrew May and asked if his appearance could be delayed one week, until the 27th. May agreed.[52]

On March 25, 1940, Woodring, Johnson, and Marshall went to the White House and received the president's formal approval of the new release policy. None of the war department officials were happy with the new guidelines, but their commander had spoken and they had reluctantly agreed. For the next several weeks, Woodring and Johnson, along with the top military leaders, appeared before the House and Senate Military Affairs Committees to explain the new policy. Not surprisingly, the testimony was consistent; all war department witnesses attested to the soundness of the new policy. When asked about reports of opposition, they stated that all viewpoints had been advocated and discussed in the course of the policy decision. Both legislative committees expressed satisfaction with the new release policy.[53]

Johnson Goes to the President

Following his March 12 tongue-lashing by the president for opposing his policies regarding aircraft release, Johnson fell into line and began trying to implement them, even though he was not in full agreement. On the 13th he even called a special off-the-record news conference to report that he and the War Department supported the president's position.[54]

Johnson's efforts to comply with the president's order were complicated by continued resistance on the part of Secretary Woodring and General Arnold. In late March, when the Anglo-French Purchasing Commission requested release of General Electric superchargers, Johnson urged release, noting that even if the superchargers fell into enemy hands it would take at least two years for the enemy to begin production. Woodring, strongly influenced by Arnold, would not budge. The story was the same with requests for aircraft. The secretary refused to sign authorizations releasing the latest aircraft in spite of the fact that he had defended the new policy in public and had promised the president and Congress that he would carry it out.[55]

In early April, Woodring was still blocking the way to an aircraft deal with the Allies, and Secretary Morgenthau began pelting Johnson with requests to get the necessary authorizations from Woodring. The purchasing commission was ready and the contracts were drawn up—all that was needed was Woodring's signature. Johnson knew that he was the last person in Washington who could convince the secretary of anything, so he ruled out talking to him. If the secretary were to leave town, thereby making him acting secretary, the problem could be overcome, but for obvious reasons Woodring stayed close to the office.

As his frustrations grew, Johnson came to the conclusion that his only alternative was to go to the president. When Roosevelt returned from a short vacation at Hyde Park on April 9, Johnson told him what had been happening or, more accurately, what had not been happening. After confirming the report with Morgenthau, the president called Woodring and ordered him to grant approval for release immediately. Later that afternoon Woodring complied, and the next morning representatives from the Anglo-French Purchasing Commission met in Secretary Morgenthau's office with representatives of the president's Liaison Committee and signed orders for 2,440 fighters and 2,160 bombers.[56] The War Department's obstinacy was slowly being overcome.

On the day Secretary Woodring finally granted approval for release, Germany simultaneously attacked Denmark and Norway. The hope that the phony war might go on indefinitely and that Hitler was at last satisfied now that he had Poland were crushed that April morning. The war entered a new, more deadly phase—one that would dramatically escalate calls for American aid to the Allies. That new threat and the president's response to it led to even greater problems for Johnson and Woodring and ultimately to their departure from the Washington political scene.

CHAPTER SEVEN

"But You Promised Me"

T HE SPRING OF 1940 was as hectic for Louis Johnson as any period since his arrival at the War Department. In addition to the normal procurement and planning problems and countless meetings with the army chief of staff and the general staff, the assistant secretary found himself heavily involved in lobbying for the appropriations bill, an expansion in the number of aircraft plants, and plans to increase the size of the army. Johnson was working ten to thirteen hours a day at the office and another three or four hours at home. What had previously been a very limited social life for him and Ruth came to a virtual halt.[1]

As April arrived, Johnson could look back over a rather discouraging previous seven months as far as real defense preparation was concerned. After war broke out in Europe the previous September, the assistant secretary thought that the military preparedness he had been advocating for the past two years would translate into concrete actions. However, the response he had expected had not been forthcoming.

Johnson's first big disappointment came when President Roosevelt ignored the War Department's recommendation that the regular army should be increased from 210,000 to 280,000; on September 8, he called for only a 17,000-man expansion.[2] In October 1939, Johnson had worked day and night on ambitious preparedness proposals which called for $879 million in supplemental funds to be used primarily to provide supplies needed to meet the requirements of the Protective Mobilization Plan. Despite Johnson's efforts, Roosevelt did not feel that Congress or the public was ready to accept such a large rearmament program, and he cut the supplemental request to $120 million, or only 14 percent of what the army requested.[3]

By the end of October, disappointed war department officials began turning their attention to preparation of the appropriations bill the president would recommend to Congress in his January 1940 budget message. What emerged from the department was a vast program similar to the one Johnson had urged upon the president early in 1938 and again later that year. It called for $1.5 billion to be used for normal operations plus increased manpower, additional training, and substantial amounts of arms, ammunition and other combat equipment. Roosevelt, still reluctant to stir up isolationist fervor, was willing to ask the lawmakers for only 55 percent of the army's request, which amounted to $853 million for all army expenditures.

FDR was probably right in judging congressional sentiment because in the early spring of 1940, at the tail end of the "phony war," an unsympathetic House Appropriations Committee gave military witnesses a difficult time, and on April 4 the House slashed the president's request to $785 million and sent it to the Senate. The Senate appeared to be headed in the same direction, but before it could act, events across the Atlantic fundamentally altered the situation.[4]

Blitzkrieg

Germany's April 9 attack on Norway and Denmark brought a sudden and drastic change in the attitudes of Congress and the American public. At last, as the victims of aggression were quickly overrun by the Nazis, Roosevelt was willing to ask the keepers of the purse for the large appropriations that Johnson had been urging for two years. When the Senate opened its appropriations hearings in late April, the new mood was expressed rather well by Senator Henry Cabot Lodge Jr.: "I think everyone recognizes that it is the feeling of Congress, and as far as I can gather, among public opinion throughout the country, to provide all the money necessary for the National Defense, and so all you have to do is ask for it."[5]

While the Senate and the president were both wrestling with the question of how much was needed, more bad news arrived from Europe on May 10 when Germany struck Belgium, Holland, and then France. As the Germans pushed the Allied forces toward the English Channel, Roosevelt was at last confident that he had the support of the American people and Congress. In a major defense address on May 16, the president asked Congress for $546 million above what he had requested in January for the upcoming fiscal year. The bulk of the new amount was for munitions and supplies for a 750,000-man protective mobilization force.

Two weeks later, even before Congress could act on his May 16 proposal, FDR asked for still another $700 million. An aroused and alarmed Congress responded with even more than was requested by passing a $1.5 billion appropriations bill on June 13 and an $821 million supplemental measure on June 25.

Included in those bills were funds to provide 3,000 planes and to dramatically expand aircraft production facilities.[6] Those provisions were very important to Johnson because they were program initiatives he had been championing since the fall of 1938.

Throughout the frantic expansion period of April, May, and June 1940, the burden of leadership in the War Department was carried primarily by Chief of Staff Marshall. While Assistant Secretary Johnson provided considerable input and played a role in the presentation of departmental recommendations to the commander in chief, FDR virtually ignored Secretary Woodring.[7] Marshall's emergence as the leading figure in this stage of the rearmament movement was due to several factors, including his competence, the confidence the president had in him, and the fact that the long Woodring-Johnson feud had so weakened their effectiveness that neither could provide the leadership necessary either within or outside the War Department.

During this period of intense activity, Johnson, by now sounding like a broken record, continued to urge the army general staff, the president, and Congress to provide money for more and more material and manpower. As had so often been the case, he found himself asking for even more than professional military men were requesting.[8] Johnson also continued to promote greater air power, especially the need for large bombers. He had been a champion of the B-17 four-engine Flying Fortress since he came to the War Department, and in January 1940 he appealed to the president, albeit unsuccessfully, to stop the Bureau of the Budget from responding to a cost overrun by eliminating forty-two of the big bombers. In his plea Johnson claimed that the aircraft were of "prime importance in all long-range operations and especially in hemisphere defense." He went on to conclude, "We need more of this type instead of less."[9] Although that plea was unsuccessful, he was not one to give up, and on May 10 he sent a memorandum to the president in which he said, "While there are many defense needs of great importance, it is my humble opinion that there is none of more importance . . . than to secure for the United States Army a large additional number of Flying Fortresses." Noting that only 178 were on hand or on order, he called for another 400.[10] About half that number were provided for in the June appropriations.

The strongest case that Johnson made for greater air strength came in a memorandum entitled "Program for Creation of Air Power," which he sent to the president on May 15, 1940. In the opening paragraph he boldly asserted that "this country must accept the fact that air power is not simply an auxiliary to land and sea forces. It has become a paramount factor in national defense."[11] Johnson's program sought authority to order an additional 3,000 planes so that a 6,000-plane level could be reached by January 1, 1942; to construct eight new government aircraft factories to boost production from 9,000 to 19,000 planes per year; and to train 19,000 pilots annually. The cost of implementing his program was slightly more than $1 billion.[12]

In his defense message on May 16, the day after Johnson's appeal, the president called for an aircraft production capacity of 50,000 planes and plans for a 50,000-plane military force. However, he did not include Johnson's specific recommendations concerning aircraft production, nor did he request funds for that program.[13] The massive program Johnson advocated was just around the corner, but by the time it came, he had left Washington.

As the prospects for vast military expenditures mushroomed in April and May, so did Johnson's excitement; he eagerly anticipated the opportunity to begin turning his dreams for military preparedness, which emphasized industrial mobilization and air rearmament, into reality. His expectations were not to be realized, however, for the president, who had already taken coordination of foreign aircraft sales from him, was about to deprive him of even more responsibility.

The day after the May 16 speech, President Roosevelt called in Secretary Morgenthau and asked him to expedite the entire military production program, especially production of aircraft engines. Seven days later, and at Morgenthau's insistence, the president sent the War Department a directive that shocked and upset Woodring, Johnson, and Marshall.[14] It read, "It is of utmost importance that no contracts be entered into from now on either for planes or engines . . . without coordinating these with the general program as a rule. For the time being, until the final machinery is set up, this coordination will be cleared through the Secretary of Treasury to me as Commander-in-Chief. Please see that this is carried out in toto."[15]

The erosion of the War Department's control over aircraft contracts, production, and procurement was now complete. Johnson was extremely disturbed, not only because the president had directed Morgenthau to step in but also because the law vested in him, as the assistant secretary of war, the authority to control all such contracts. Johnson and Arnold went to the president and vigorously protested the transfer of authority and urged him to return it to the War Department, but the chief executive would not back down.[16] Although Johnson did not realize it, at the very time he was lodging his protest, Roosevelt was already making plans to move Morgenthau out of the war contracts business; however, he was not going to hand that authority back to the army. He had other plans.

On May 28, the president announced that he was reactivating the old World War I National Defense Advisory Commission (NDAC), a seven-member body whose commissioners each reported directly to the chief executive on a specific substantive area.[17] The establishment of this body, whose functions were in many ways similar to those of Johnson's abortive War Resources Board, was an admission by Roosevelt that he needed assistance from the private sector in coordinating defense efforts. It also validated Johnson's many attempts to persuade Roosevelt that he needed outside help. However, by using a strictly advisory group that was handpicked and that did not have a chairman, the president was able to maintain complete control over the defense program. His fear of abdicating power to an industrial war czar was all too apparent.[18]

The commission member whose area of responsibility was of most concern to Johnson and the War Department was William S. Knudsen, president of General Motors, who had been made accountable for industrial production. The Danish-born Knudsen was a highly talented executive who in a matter of days created the machinery necessary for investigating, researching, and coordinating the nation's industrial production for war purposes. Acting on Morgenthau's recommendation, the president issued an order on June 6 that gave Knudsen authority to review all army and navy contracts over $500,000.[19] Two weeks later, the president appointed Donald Nelson, executive vice-president of Sears, Roebuck & Company, as the eighth member of the NDAC and made him coordinator of national defense purchases. From that time on, Knudsen cleared all hard goods contracts for items such as aircraft, vehicles, and ordinance and Nelson handled contracts for all quartermaster-type items, or soft goods.[20]

This entire arrangement was formalized on June 26, when Congress authorized the War and Navy Departments to spend certain procurement funds only upon the recommendation of the NDAC and with the approval of the president. Not surprisingly, War Department officials considered this new arrangement to be an infringement upon their contracting rights, and within a year the attorney general sided with the War Department.[21] In the meantime, however, the president's actions curtailing Johnson's contracting authority seriously weakened the army's ability to procure desperately needed military supplies. The necessity of clearing all large contracts through Knudsen and Nelson's offices added bureaucratic obstacles that complicated and delayed military contracting at a time when it should have been simplified and expedited.[22]

While the transfer of contracting authority from the assistant secretary's office to the NDAC had serious negative consequences, it put Johnson and Woodring on better terms with each other than they had ever been. The fact that the new responsibilities of Morgenthau, Knudsen, and Nelson were robbing the War Department of controls which the secretary and assistant secretary felt were vital to its functioning led the two former adversaries into a much more cooperative working relationship as they joined forces to beat back the "enemy" that was attacking from without. The chilly relationship between the two men thawed and policy planning sessions in May and June 1940 took on a new and positive atmosphere. This even extended to their social lives; the two men and their wives occasionally got together for dinner and a relaxing evening.

By early June it appeared as if the hatchet had been buried and that the Woodring-Johnson feud might be nearing an end.[23] However, the attempts to repair the damage done by almost three years of bickering came too late. The feud was in fact about to end, but not in a way that either expected.

Dagger at His Back

While things at the War Department had not been going well for Johnson in the spring of 1940, they had been going even worse for Woodring. The flap over the aircraft release policy in March had again put him out of favor at the White House, and just as that problem was being resolved he began having difficulties with the president over the issue of providing surplus military property to the Allies.

In the early 1930s, disposition of army surplus was not much of a problem because the tight military budgets of those years made shortages, not surpluses, the problem. There were, however, occasions when certain supplies and equipment, usually World War I–vintage arms and ammunition or obsolete aircraft, were declared surplus and sold to foreign governments, usually in Latin America. By and large such disposition was very rare under Secretary Woodring because of his belief that in the event of war every rifle, mortar, and artillery piece, regardless of age, would be of value.[24]

In February 1940, when Finland came under attack from the Soviet Union, Roosevelt began searching for ways to assist the Finns. Barred by neutrality laws from selling directly to Finland because it was at war, FDR came up with the idea of selling government-surplus war materials to neutral nations so they could sell them to the Finnish government. Against the advice of Secretary Woodring and Secretary of State Hull, the president decided on this course of action, but before the transaction could be completed Finland was overrun.[25] Between April and June, the president also considered sales of surplus military supplies to assist Norway, Denmark, Holland, Belgium, and France, but the speed with which they fell to Germany made such transactions impossible.

In mid-May, with all of Europe succumbing to Hitler's war machine and the British Expeditionary Force retreating to the coast of France, the new British prime minister, Winston Churchill, asked Roosevelt to "help us with everything short of actually engaging armed forces." He then specifically requested older ships, modern aircraft, anti-aircraft guns, and ammunition.[26] Roosevelt called on "Mr. Reliable," Henry Morgenthau, to help accommodate the British.[27]

Morgenthau, who had long ago tired of trying to work through Woodring and Johnson, ignored those two and worked directly with General Marshall. The treasury chief pressured for the release of 100 pursuit planes about to be delivered to the air corps and surplus ordinance equipment and ammunition. Marshall, with strong backing from General Arnold, refused to give in on the aircraft request but was more accommodating on the other request.[28] Because of the president's strong indication that he wanted to make arms and ammunition available to the British, General Marshall ordered a survey to determine exactly how much surplus could be released "without endangering the national defense." The study came up with 500,000 Enfield rifles, 100 million rounds of .30 caliber ammunition, 35,000 machine guns, 500 mortar and an equal number of 75 mm. guns, and a number of other items.

The president directed that those items be provided to Britain, but Woodring resisted vigorously. Only after Roosevelt had the attorney general hand down an opinion on the legality of a scheme whereby the surplus would be turned back to the manufacturers who would then sell it to the British did Woodring agree to do what the president wanted.[29] The war secretary's resistance on the surplus issue, coming on top of his opposition to the aircraft release policy, pushed Roosevelt in a direction that he had been thinking about, but trying to avoid, for some time—removal of his secretary of war.

Pressure for Woodring's removal had been coming from within the administration for years; Steve Early and Pa Watson led the movement among the White House staff and Harold Ickes and Morgenthau did so from within the Cabinet. They were joined in the latter half of 1939 by suggestions from numerous columnists and newspaper editors who called upon the president to clean up the disruptive mess in the War Department.

In late 1939, Roosevelt, thinking of the year ahead and the possibility of a third term, began to seriously consider the possibility of forming a coalition cabinet by adding prominent Republicans such as 1936 presidential and vice-presidential candidates Alf Landon and Frank Knox, but those plans were shelved.[30] Throughout early 1940, the calls for a shake-up at the War Department were stepped up, and in June *Life* magazine and the *New York Times*, both great molders of public opinion, joined the chorus.[31] About that time, the leading Republican hopeful for the presidential nomination, Thomas Dewey of New York, also called for Woodring's dismissal.[32]

It was probably during the last week in May of 1940 that Roosevelt, realizing that the miraculous escape of the British army from Dunkirk would increase the pressure to provide aid to England, came to the conclusion that while it would be awkward and unpleasant, he would have to let Woodring go. The secretary of war was no longer just an obstacle to his policies, he was increasingly becoming a political liability. Before the president could act, however, he needed someone to take his place and a "reason" to fire Woodring.

The solution to the first problem came at a June 3 private luncheon with Roosevelt's good friend Supreme Court Justice Felix Frankfurter. Acting at the behest of Grenville Clark, a public-spirited New York lawyer, Frankfurter strongly urged FDR to appoint Republican Henry L. Stimson, a well-known former secretary of war and secretary of state whose foreign policy views were similar to those of the president, as his new secretary of war. And since Stimson was getting to be an old man at seventy-two, Frankfurter further recommended that Stimson's former law partner, Robert P. Patterson, then a judge on the Second Circuit and a much younger man, should become Stimson's assistant secretary. Patterson would supply the energy and youth that Stimson lacked.[33]

Roosevelt was keen on Frankfurter's proposal but he expressed reservations about Stimson's age and health. Within two weeks, Clark, unbeknown to Stimson, extracted a positive report from Stimson's family physician and Frankfurter relayed the doctor's report to the White House.[34] The president was ready to move on Frankfurter's plan.

The president then turned to the problem of when and how to dismiss Woodring and move Johnson aside. That was not going to be an easy task because Roosevelt's good-heartedness made it impossible for him to merely call a person in and fire him. He wanted to do it at the right time and in the kindest way possible.

FDR, knowing better than most that in politics timing is everything, decided to wait for a few days before acting to relieve Woodring and Johnson. The pressures and demands on Roosevelt in early June of 1940 as German troops occupied much of Europe and moved toward Paris were enormous. While the president was thinking about how to gently let his old friends go, he was being bombarded by editorials in leading college newspapers and petitions from college students, including future leaders such as Gerald Ford and Sargent Shriver, begging him not to provide supplies to the Allies and to avoid involvement at all costs.[35]

On the afternoon of June 10, 1940, as FDR and Mrs. Roosevelt boarded the president's special train and headed south to Charlottesville, where the president was to address the University of Virginia graduates on the gathering threats to national security, he received confirmation that Italy had entered the war. This event caused him to insert the famous stab-in-the-back metaphor into his speech, and it was the catalyst for another turning point in the president's foreign policy.

That afternoon, at the university Johnson knew and loved so much, the president at last issued a call to arms. Castigating Italy for plunging a dagger into the back of its neighbor, the president put America clearly on the side of the Allies and announced that the United States would "extend the material resources of the nation" to those fighting the Nazis. He concluded by saying that "signs and signals call for full speed—full speed ahead."[36] The words might just as well have been spoken by Louis Johnson.

Apparently, Secretary Woodring didn't appreciate the essence of the president's message, because a little more than a week later he gave FDR a perfect reason to dismiss him. On June 17, 1940, the day France capitulated to Germany, Secretary Morgenthau, after first getting the go-ahead from the president, moved to obtain the release of twelve B-17s so they could be turned over to the desperate British.[37] General Marshall, noting that the army air corps only had fifty-two of the large bombers, recommended against release. Woodring concurred and sent a memorandum to that effect to the president on June 19.

This was what Roosevelt was waiting for. When he received Woodring's memorandum, the president wrote a personal letter in longhand asking for his secretary of war's resignation, at the same time offering him the job of governor of Puerto Rico.[38] It was not a task that Roosevelt enjoyed. This was the only time in the thirteen years that he served in the presidency that he actually asked a cabinet member to resign.[39]

After dispatching the letter to Woodring, the president picked up the phone, called Stimson at his New York law office, and asked him to take the job as secretary of war. Stimson inquired whether the president had considered his age, and Roosevelt, having already received a positive health report on Stimson, said that it made no difference. Although it was not to be known for several weeks, Roosevelt agreed that if Stimson accepted he would be able to appoint Robert Patterson as his assistant secretary. The elder statesman then asked for a few hours to consult with some colleagues and his wife before giving a firm reply. That evening he called back and accepted.[40]

That same evening, Woodring, unaware of who would replace him, sat down with his wife and wrote his letter of resignation, which included rejection of the Puerto Rico offer. The following morning, after dating the letter June 20 and giving it to a courier for delivery to the White House, Woodring called Johnson and told him he had just submitted his resignation and that the assistant secretary should "take the necessary steps to protect yourself."[41]

Hope Is Eternal

For years, Johnson had hoped and waited for this to happen. At last, the job he had coveted was about to be his. However, what was probably one of the happiest moments of his life was to last only two or three minutes before it was shattered by a phone call from Steve Early. The press secretary told him that he was preparing to release an announcement naming Stimson as secretary of war, and he wanted to make sure Johnson knew about it before hearing it from a reporter. Early went on to say that the president was very pleased with the job he had done as assistant secretary and wanted him to stay on. That was followed by a request that he attend that afternoon's cabinet meeting as acting secretary. Johnson, shocked and hurt because he had not been named secretary, declined, saying he had nothing to bring to the attention of the Cabinet and that he had important work to do at the office. When word of the conversation was relayed to the president, he requested that Johnson come to see him immediately.[42]

As soon as the still-stunned assistant secretary arrived at the White House he was ushered into the Oval Office, where his good friend Bernard Baruch was meeting with the president. He sat in "flushed and indignant silence" as Roosevelt tried to explain why he had found it necessary to put Stimson in the top war department post rather than him. "But you promised me not once but many times," said Johnson in an unsteady voice. FDR acknowledged that he had intended all along to make him secretary of war but that current developments now made that impossible. When it appeared that Johnson was about ready to say something he would later regret, Baruch reached over and gave him "a gentle kick to tell him to shut up," and he did.[43] Regaining his composure, Johnson offered his resignation, but the president refused to accept it, claiming he needed him where he was and adding that he could not educate a new assistant secretary. The conversation ended, and a very dejected Louis Johnson departed. That afternoon he did return for the cabinet meeting.[44]

Although the president had asked him to stay on as the assistant secretary, Johnson knew that his days at the War Department were numbered. His years in Washington, along with Steve Early's statements, convinced him that a man of Stimson's experience would not come to the War Department without authority to name his top assistant. Knowing that, and as wounded as he was, why didn't Johnson simply tender his resignation and leave Washington that unforgettable June day? The answer is rather astonishing and reveals Johnson's hubris and ambition. Johnson did not walk out on the president in the summer of 1940 because he believed the chances were good that he would be the next vice president of the United States.

Ever since he had come to Washington in mid-1937, Johnson had been mentioned as a possible candidate for some prominent political office. Between 1937 and 1939, speculation had centered on the possibility that he might run for the Senate or the governorship of West Virginia, but as 1940 neared, support for him as a Democratic presidential or vice presidential candidate began to emerge and grow. Members of the American Legion and fellow Clarksburgers tagged him as a man who had his eye on the White House or, if that was not possible, the vice presidency.[45] As early as 1938, several state Democratic Party leaders were convinced that Johnson "had ambitions to be number two on the forty ticket."[46] Johnson discouraged proposals that groundwork be laid for his candidacy for the top or runner-up spot two years hence by saying that he did not have the time or inclination to engage in such a venture.[47]

Nevertheless, the stories continued. The December 24, 1938, issue of *Business Week* mentioned Johnson's higher political aspirations and said that Johnson expected "to lead the administration's drive for national defense and counts on this to make him an outstanding contender for the nomination to succeed Roosevelt." Throughout 1939, sporadic proposals to promote him as a candidate for president or vice president were made and then spurned by Johnson, but the newspapers continued to mention the possibilities.[48]

As the presidential election year of 1940 unfolded, talk of Johnson as a vice presidential candidate accelerated. Support came primarily from West Virginians and individuals throughout the nation who were in agreement with his views on the need to beef up the nation's defense and readiness for war. His skills on the stump and in the hustings were regarded as campaign assets as well as his phenomenal physical stamina and his love of mixing with crowds. Furthermore, he was well versed on matters of domestic and foreign policy.

Those assets, however, were countered by serious liabilities, which included his reputation for being a warmonger, a recognition factor based to a large degree on his feud with Woodring, his arrogance, and his raw ambition. However, his biggest obstacle to becoming a Democratic candidate for any office was his unacceptability to New Dealers, who were worried about his ties with business and industry. Politically, his liabilities appeared to greatly outweigh his assets, but apparently he did not see it that way. His optimism set him up for a major disappointment.

Green Light

Any presidential election year is bound to be politically strange, and 1940 was no exception, especially for the Democrats. As the months rolled by, President Roosevelt gave no indication about whether he would be a candidate for a third term. By refusing to declare his intentions, he prevented any other Democratic hopeful from launching a bid for the nomination. While the rank and file of the party seemed to favor a "draft" for a third term, party leaders as well as many of the president's closest friends were divided on the issue. No Democrat was willing to declare his candidacy for fear the president would then throw his hat in the ring and leave him politically naked, and no formidable candidate appeared.[49] As a consequence of this odd turn of events, speculation focused on the second spot on the ticket, and more than a dozen possibilities were mentioned consistently, among them Louis Johnson.[50]

Serious attention was focused on the assistant secretary of war in late March, when leaders in Oregon urged him to run in that state's presidential primary. Johnson, who was by this time convinced that Roosevelt would seek a third term, rejected that offer.[51] Several weeks later, top American Legion officials held a secret meeting in Washington. They wanted a veteran in the White House and had decided to promote the former national commander's candidacy for either the number-one or number-two spot.[52] This meeting took place with Johnson's knowledge but not with his endorsement.

In June, at about the time the Republicans were meeting in Philadelphia to nominate Wendell Wilkie and his running mate Senator Charles McNary, the Oregon delegation to the Democratic National Convention gathered for its organizational meeting. Opposed to a third term for Roosevelt, the Oregon delegation voted to support Johnson as the presidential nominee. A few days later, similar support was forthcoming from the Alabama delegation.[53]

As the July 15 opening date for the Democratic National Convention neared, national political observers increasingly mentioned Johnson as a possibility for vice president. For example, on July 10, Ernest Lindley mentioned him in his nationally syndicated column, and three days later political columnist Ray Tucker wrote that it was "generally admitted he would make a formidable candidate."[54] Such columns, along with the actions of the Oregon delegation and American Legion leaders, no doubt fed Johnson's ego and led him to believe that he had a good chance of receiving the nod for the second post. Then there were Roosevelt's words and actions which made him even more optimistic about his chances.

By the first of July, with the convention just two weeks away, and with the Royal Air Force battling the Luftwaffe for air supremacy over England, the president was still refusing to declare his intentions, but it now seemed quite obvious that he intended to be drafted by the convention. Since he had not indicated whether he would seek or accept the nomination, he could not very well name his choice for a running mate, and he was able to hold the "vice-presidential prize open as bait" down to the very end.[55] While nearly every president and presidential hopeful has used the lure of the second spot on the ticket for personal or political gain, none did so more effectively than Franklin Roosevelt. Using his well-known charm that made it possible for every person to leave his office with the feeling that he completely supported their viewpoint, he was able to convince no less than half a dozen individuals, including Jesse Jones, William Bankhead, Harold Ickes, Paul McNutt, James Byrnes, and even Louis Johnson, that they would be on the ticket with him.[56]

Before leaving for the Democratic convention in Chicago, Johnson visited the president to discuss his future. The assistant secretary again offered to resign his post, but FDR urged him to stay on. The conversation turned to the nominating convention and possible candidates for the second spot. Roosevelt began ticking off Johnson's political attributes and then assured him that he "would be eminently acceptable as the Vice-Presidential nominee."[57] With that word of encouragement, Johnson departed for Chicago, very optimistic about his chances of being chosen.

When the convention was called to order on Monday, July 15, Roosevelt was in Washington, still refusing to say anything that would put him in or take him out of consideration. Tuesday was expected to be a slow day, since the nominating process was not to begin until Wednesday. On that day, Johnson boarded a plane and flew back to Washington to meet with Roosevelt. After a short visit with FDR, the West Virginian left the White House with the excitement and enthusiasm of a young schoolboy because, according to him, the president had given him the green light for the vice-presidential slot.[58] That evening on the convention floor, a spontaneous demonstration for Roosevelt occurred that made it apparent he would be drafted; it was now just a matter of going through the formalities on the following day.

On Wednesday, Johnson, just back from his quick trip to the capital, returned to the convention floor to search for delegate support by reporting that the president had given him the green light. The delegates were not impressed. As Harry

Truman later recalled, Jonathan Daniels, then a Roosevelt staffer, reacted by say-ing, "Louie you won't get but one vote and that will be your own."[59] Another dele-gate said, "Oh, hell Louis, this convention hall is full of candidates with green lights."[60] And indeed it was, with at least a dozen "serious" self-proclaimed candi-dates and another dozen waiting in the wings and hoping that fate might hand them the brass ring. The delegates were unwilling to make commitments; they were going to wait and see what happened.

They did not have to wait long. On Wednesday evening, Roosevelt and four others, including James Farley and Cordell Hull, were placed in nomination, and on the first ballot FDR gained 946 votes while the other men divided the remaining 147. Shortly thereafter, Roosevelt was nominated by acclamation.

With his selection out of the way, the president sent word that his choice for a running mate was Henry Wallace, his secretary of agriculture. The selection of the politically inept and extremely liberal former Republican surprised nearly everyone at the convention, but no one was more shocked than Johnson.[61] Even stronger was a sense of hurt. For the second time in a month the president had let him down. In the next few hours, as Johnson learned of others who had been led to believe that they would get the vice-presidential spot, he felt as if he had been duped.[62]

Stunned by Roosevelt's announcement, Johnson hardly noticed the bitter fight that followed over the second position between Wallace and Senator Wil-liam Bankhead with Wallace winning by a rather close vote (627 of 1,100). The convention closed with the usual displays of party unity, and the Democrats headed back home to begin work on the upcoming presidential campaign. While most of those departing Chicago did so full of enthusiasm, Johnson was not one of them. He was determined to leave the administration before the campaign even got under way.

Abrupt Departure

When he returned to the War Department the Monday after the convention, Johnson was informed that Secretary Stimson, who had been sworn in two weeks before, wanted to see him. Entering the secretary's office, he felt a little uneasy, but the elderly, gray-haired Stimson exhibited tact and class as he explained to Johnson that he intended to bring his friend Robert Patterson, in whom he had great confidence, into the department to assist him in the difficult task that lay ahead. Since Stimson's intentions were clear, he did not need to ask for a resig-nation.[63] After an exchange of a few pleasantries the assistant secretary departed.

The visit with Stimson was not upsetting to Johnson because he had expected all along that the new secretary would want to and should be given the oppor-tunity to bring in his own assistant secretary. If that had been done in the past, he thought, many departments such as State and War would not be in the mess they were in. In addition, Johnson had already made up his mind that he would leave the administration. The president's refusal to appoint him as secretary had come as a real setback and had hurt him deeply. Furthermore, to have led him on over the vice presidential matter and then drop him, had been the crowning blow.[64] It was time to get out.

On July 24, after several revisions, Johnson wrote the following letter to Roosevelt:

My dear Mr. President:

I offered my resignation as the Assistant Secretary of War immediately upon your advising me of your intention to appoint another as Secretary of War. I then understood you desired that I remain. I have therefore so continued. I am now informed that Mr. Stimson had already made different plans.

For three long years, I have given my energy and effort exclusively to the problems of adequate national preparedness. Today I presented our program to Congress and, while there is much to be done, on the whole, that for which we have striven seems on the way. It is with keen regret, therefore, that I tender my resignation—again I have no alternative.

To you, as my Commander-in-Chief and longtime friend, I desire—although I know it is unnecessary—to give assurance of my heartfelt appreciation of the opportunity to serve which has been mine as a result of the confidence you repose in me. The task we found was monumental—the obstacles to overcome were many and great. But the work was rendered less arduous by the consciousness that in all essential principles of the national defense program you and I saw eye to eye.[65]

Always, I shall be gratefully indebted: to the officers of the Army who tolerated me and my efforts for a year, and then so loyally supported me; to the business men of America who have cooperated and made possible the progress on the industrial and supply front; and the understanding friends, particularly my comrades of the World War, who have helped in our efforts to get the American people to agree that the road of adequate preparedness is the only safe road to peace for America.

Returning to my law firm, I shall still carry on for National Defense as best I may.

I am leaving Washington immediately for a very necessary, even if not earned, rest—my first holiday in these thirty-seven months.

This, my resignation, may be made effective on any date you determine.

> With great respect, Sir, I am
> Obediently yours,
> LOUIS A. JOHNSON[66]

Whereas Secretary Woodring had left Washington after his resignation in a polite and graceful fashion, lingering to pay courtesy visits to the president and others he had worked with, Johnson departed in an abrupt and carefully choreographed manner—a method calculated to cause FDR to try to make amends. After he finished his letter, the assistant secretary called for an army limousine to take him to nearby Bolling Field, where he had made arrangements to catch a military flight headed to Hamilton Field, California. When he arrived at Bolling he handed a sealed envelope to the chauffeur and asked that he deliver it to the White House. By the time it was opened an hour later, Johnson was high over the Alleghenies on his way to the West Coast. When the plane made a refueling stop at Albuquerque, he was given a message to call the White House, but he did not respond.[67]

When he reached California, Johnson returned a call from Steve Early, who said that he personally regretted the resignation but that FDR was offering him a job as an administrative assistant to the president on defense matters. Johnson told Early he was not interested.[68] He then departed for Bohemian Grove, the beautiful redwood-covered campsite of San Francisco's male-only Bohemian Club, where he hoped to get some rest. The following morning an army courier arrived with a telegram from President Roosevelt. It read:

Dear Louis,

In acknowledging your letter of resignation of July twenty fourth, I must emphasize that although you have severed the formal ties that make you a member of my official family, there are closer bonds of friendship and affection which will but grow stronger as time passes. I do want you to know how deeply grateful I am for the splendid services you have rendered to the cause of national defense and to government. Your countrymen everywhere will share in this gratitude for all that you have accomplished to safeguard your country and to make secure our democratic way of life.

Regretfully, therefore I accept your resignation as the Assistant Secretary of War, as of this date, because the Secretary of War has asked me to send to the Senate the nomination of Mr. Robert Porter Patterson as your successor. In order that the nation may continue to have the benefit of your outstanding ability and varied experience, I confidently expect and hope that you will soon return to government service. I would like you to serve as an Administrative Assistant to the President. In this position you will be with me in the White House, becoming my eyes and ears and serving by reporting to me on the continuing progress of the entire national defense program, with every phase of which you have become so familiar.

FRANKLIN D. ROOSEVELT[69]

The White House tried to smooth the resignation over as best it could, but the abruptness of Johnson's departure made that impossible. Press reaction was mild because this was anticlimactic after the firing of Woodring and appointment of Stimson. Johnson's departure had been expected. The news media was kind to the departing assistant secretary, acknowledging his contributions to the national defense program and citing his valuable service to the War Department.[70]

Cabinet officials were generally pleased to see him go because his actions were felt to have caused chaos at the War Department and embarrassment to the administration. Secretary of Treasury Morgenthau was especially pleased. Morgenthau distrusted Johnson, so much so that long after Johnson had left the administration the treasury secretary prevailed upon the FBI to investigate Johnson's loyalty to the president based on remarks Johnson allegedly made in a speech to a group of businessmen a few days after the attack on Pearl Harbor. FBI director J. Edgar Hoover reported back to Morgenthau that the bureau found nothing to support the charges, and FDR, who apparently knew of the charges and perhaps the investigation as well, instructed Morgenthau to write Johnson a "nice line telling him that the whole episode is forgotten."[71]

Within the military, Johnson's departure brought a sense of relief to General Marshall and most members of the general staff who had been caught up in the years of bickering. But there were a few top military officers, such as General Arnold, who hated to lose a friend of the air corps. At the White House, only Steve Early was genuinely sorry to see him go. Members of Congress, out of deference to the newly appointed secretary and his right to appoint his own assistant secretary, said nothing.[72]

While Johnson schmoozed with the rich and powerful at the Mandalay Camp in Bohemian Grove, Roosevelt dispatched New Deal lawyer Tommy Corcoran and Steve Early to California to try to convince him to stay with the administration. Whether Roosevelt really wanted him to stay or was just doing the polite thing will never be known. Corcoran told Johnson he was being "childish" because he was "hurt and peeved" and that he was "old enough to know that political promises were made to be broken." To that Johnson reacted bitterly, saying that was not the way he operated.

When Early came to see him, the two old friends had a great visit, after which Johnson told him that while he had been "unfairly treated" he was "not going to bolt the party or do those things that could be interpreted as dictated by a sour-grape attitude." He also indicated that he would not accept any job of lesser importance than assistant secretary of war and since the post the president was creating was of lesser significance he would not accept that offer. Early argued that he could accept Roosevelt's offer "without loss of prestige or the feeling that he was let down." To refuse, he claimed, would be wrong. Johnson argued that to remain would be wrong, but he did agree to stop in and see the president when he returned to Washington in a couple of weeks.[73]

In mid-August Johnson walked into the Oval Office just as he had dozens of times before, only this time he was doing so as a private citizen. As would be expected with Franklin Roosevelt, the visit was a most amiable one. The charming and affable president offered him the position of undersecretary of commerce. When Johnson turned down that offer, Roosevelt once again played to Johnson's ambition—he indicated that Harry Hopkins would soon be leaving as secretary of commerce and that perhaps something could be worked out there. If that were to happen, Johnson said, he "would insist on tying on the string that when the War Office became vacant, I was to be made Secretary of War."[74]

The president was unwilling and unable to make such a commitment. Roosevelt concluded that Johnson, who was indicating that he wanted to return to Clarksburg and the practice of law, really was anxious to return to private life. With Steve Early's September announcement that the West Virginian would not be accepting the undersecretary of commerce position, Johnson's remaining in the Roosevelt administration became a dead issue.[75]

When Johnson returned to Clarksburg in August of 1940 he took with him a complicated mixture of strong emotions that included relief, sadness, pride, and frustration. His sense of relief came from no longer being involved in the pressure-packed atmosphere of the department and a respite from his continual bickering with Woodring. His sadness came from the "unfair" way he had been treated by the president. However, in spite of this feeling, he never, as long as he lived, was to utter a direct criticism or unkind remark about his former chief—his loyalty was unshakable.

Johnson's pride came from knowing that he had made significant progress in strengthening the nation's defense and preparing it for the conflict he was certain was coming. He was particularly pleased that President Roosevelt had put before Congress during that summer of 1940 a defense program which he had helped shape that called for equipment to supply an army of 1.2 million (and reserve stocks for an additional 800,000), an air force of 20,000 planes, and the greatest naval expansion in history.

His frustrations, which were considerable, came in part from his concern that he had not been more successful in leading America down the path of rearmament and in part from having to deal with an isolationist secretary of war and an elusive president who tolerated and perhaps encouraged a dysfunctional War Department. But his deepest resentment came from being denied what he wanted more than anything—to be secretary of war.

From the day Johnson left his position in July 1940, he longed for vindication from the charges that he had disrupted the activities of the War Department. He felt that true vindication could come only when he was named secretary of war some time in the future. That would show to him and the world that those in authority had made a mistake in not giving him the job he so justly deserved.[76] Although it was nearly a decade down the road, that vindication would come.

Fault Lines

When reflecting on the Woodring-Johnson feud and the unfortunate consequences it had on the War Department at such a crucial period in U.S. history, it is only natural to ask who should bear the bulk of the responsibility for the state of affairs. Since Woodring, Johnson, and Roosevelt were the three central figures involved, each should be evaluated in an attempt to determine the extent of blame that should be placed on him.[77]

What about Harry Woodring? The cautious secretary of war has some critics, most of whom argue that since he was the man responsible for the activities of the War Department he should be held accountable for its failure to run smoothly. When the feud erupted, they claim, he should have gone directly to the president and sought clarification on Johnson's role. If he had done so, the dispute could have been cleared up immediately.

While there is some logic behind this position, it ignores several considerations, one of which is why Woodring did not take such action. By alternately embracing and then spurning him, the president kept Woodring from knowing exactly where he stood with him. If the war secretary had asked for a clarification of who was in charge, Roosevelt, depending how he felt that particular day, could well have sided with Johnson. Woodring was unwilling to take that very real risk. Furthermore, the war secretary knew that the president was aware of the turmoil in the department and could have ended it at any time, but since he did not, Woodring concluded that for some reason he wished it to remain as it was.

Faced with this awkward situation, Woodring had two alternatives: resign or make the best of a poor situation. He enjoyed being secretary of war too much to voluntarily give it up, so he was left with the latter option. Complicating the situation was the fact that Roosevelt rarely criticized and frequently praised his running of the department. That was interpreted as a vote of confidence. For these reasons Woodring should receive minimum blame for the feud.

Should Louis Johnson receive most of the blame? From the time word of the dispute first reached the press in early 1938 until the present, Johnson has usually been in the villain's role. His critics, and there are and have been many, point out that things were going quite well until he came charging into the department hell-bent on running it as if he were in fact the secretary. If he had behaved as an assistant secretary was supposed to, none of the turmoil would have occurred.

In defense of Johnson, it should be noted that the president overtly and covertly encouraged his actions. When Johnson informed the press that he was about to be named secretary or when he bypassed Woodring and went directly to the White House, Roosevelt said or did nothing. On other occasions, such as in the case of the air rearmament program, the president had him completely ignore the secretary. Johnson, being the driver that he was, was bound to go as far and as fast as he could before he was told to halt, and perhaps for that he can be criticized. However, Roosevelt rarely told him to halt. Johnson's major "crime" appears to be that he wore his enormous ambition on his sleeve—that he was simply too obvious, too transparent. If this is correct, it hardly seems that he should receive as much blame for the feud as he has received.

What about President Roosevelt? Contemporaries and historians have tended to leave Roosevelt out of consideration when looking at the great war department feud, and that is most unfortunate because he is the man who should receive the bulk of the blame for the situation. The burden of responsibility should be placed on him because he created the situation leading to the feud and was aware of it and its consequences, yet he did not move to correct it. He created the problem when he knowingly placed a person of Johnson's personality and temperament into the War Department in order to offset Woodring's known shortcomings. That he was well aware of the situation is evident from the numerous times that he discussed it with various advisors. The most unfortunate aspect of the whole affair is that while he was aware of the problem, he ignored it and let it rip the department apart for three years when he could have solved it in five minutes by calling the two men in and telling them to shape up or be fired.

In retrospect the solution appears too simple, but for Roosevelt it was not, and for several reasons. First, had he clarified each man's authority, it would have made it difficult, if not impossible, to play one off against the other, because they would have known who was in charge, and the president would have lost his ability to in effect be his own secretary of war. Second, to draw clear lines of authority was not his way of operating. For years, FDR's modus operandi had been to play subordinates off against one another by dividing authority, working around them, or ignoring them, and he had done so effectively. He was not about to change. Finally, his deep sensitivity made him fear and shy away from any action that would hurt people, and that made it virtually impossible to bring himself to fire anyone, no matter what the reason. According to Jim Farley, the president was "one who was forever putting off anything distasteful," but columnist Drew Pearson put it more bluntly and accurately when he wrote, "Firing someone is not one of the President's strong points."[78]

While Roosevelt can be defended for placing men of different viewpoints into a department to stimulate policy alternatives and avoid a body of yes-men, he cannot be defended for letting those differences become so great that they became totally disruptive. For over thirty months he let that situation fester. There can be no excuse or justification for such inaction. Franklin Roosevelt must bear the major responsibility for the chaos in the War Department in those crucial years just prior to World War II.

And what were Louis Johnson's contributions amid all that turmoil? Surprisingly, they were quite substantial, and that causes one to wonder what they might have been had harmony prevailed in the department. That he was able to accomplish so much under such dire circumstances tells us something of his raw talents, and yet his failure to do more, which stemmed from a situation that he helped create, tells us something of his shortcomings.

When Johnson left office in July of 1940, the overall significance of his contributions could not be appreciated. It was only when history conspired to bring about the greatest military conflict the world has ever seen that his contributions became apparent. To say that he was a voice crying in the wilderness for American defense preparedness is to perhaps rely too much on a cliché, but the events of 1941 do reveal him to be a prophet. If war had not come to America in the 1940s, Johnson would have been a minor footnote in some administrative history. But war did come, and as a result of his efforts, the nation, while still deficient, was much better prepared than it otherwise might have been.[79] It seems most appropriate that when President Truman awarded Johnson the Medal for Merit in 1947, he cited Johnson's accomplishments in industrial mobilization, procurement, and air power advocacy, declaring that he "was a major factor in the success of the allied war effort."[80]

Standing Together

The focus on Louis Johnson and his years in the Roosevelt administration has shed additional light on and added evidence to the strands of historical debate that still swirl around Roosevelt's prewar years. Perhaps the most significant insight is that while Roosevelt rejected or distanced himself from many of Johnson's strident public views on the imminence of war and his ambitious and expensive preparedness proposals, Roosevelt agreed with Johnson in a very basic and fundamental way. He wasn't always consistent, and he was very careful to avoid being too far ahead of public opinion, but Roosevelt believed, like Johnson, that the world had shrunk, that the oceans could no longer protect America, and that distant wars in Europe and Asia threatened the national security of the United States.

Johnson stood for a brief time in Roosevelt's enormous shadow. Neither realized it at the time, but they stood in those years at the fulcrum of the twentieth century. To the dismay of the New Dealers, the military-industrial complex was born under Johnson's stormy stewardship and with Roosevelt's knowing acquiescence. As Johnson departed the Roosevelt administration in July 1940, the Europe-centered world order was crumbling and America was beginning to arise and show signs that she would lead the Allied coalition and emerge as a global superpower.

CHAPTER EIGHT

Personal Representative
of the President

ALTHOUGH IT WAS light, the September sun had not yet risen over the mountains surrounding Clarksburg. "Good morning, Colonel Johnson," said the elevator operator as the large, trim, balding man stepped on. Not another word was spoken as they rode to the tenth floor of the Union Bank Building, the floor entirely occupied by the firm of Steptoe & Johnson. It was six o'clock, and as usual Louis Johnson was the first one at work. Within two hours the office would be alive with activity as the firm's two dozen lawyers arrived to work on a variety of complex legal problems and litigation for some of the largest corporations in America.

In the meantime, however, Johnson would have time to himself in his large office in the northwest corner. After lighting his first cigar of the day, he finished the job of reading the morning newspapers—a task generally started at the breakfast table. He had always devoured newspapers and news magazines, but since leaving government service he did so even more closely as he followed events and people in the nation's capital that he knew so well. That particular September 1940 morning he felt a sense of pride as he read that Congress had just passed the Burke-Wadsworth Selective Service Act—a measure he had advocated two years before.[1]

Johnson was also pleased to read that morning that Wendell Wilkie, the Republican who was running against FDR, was not going to object to the destroyers-for-bases deal that had just been announced by the White House and that fifty of the desperately needed warships would be on their way to England just as the Luftwaffe was commencing massive bombing raids on London. As a lawyer and a recent insider, Johnson had to admire the brilliant legal work of his future nemesis, Dean Acheson, who with his co-author Ben Cohen arranged to publish in the *New York Times* a legal analysis which gave the president a way to bypass Congress on the destroyer deal.[2]

Putting aside his newspapers, Johnson began his daily review of the cases, transactions, and matters they were currently working on. Frequently, he would call one of the lawyers in to discuss strategy or potential problems on a particular case. Since Philip Steptoe had retired to his farm in 1934, Johnson had become completely responsible for the growing group of lawyers he had assembled. Fortunately, when he went to the War Department in 1937 he was able to call on partners like James Guiher and Stanley Morris to step in and oversee operations, but even when he served in government Johnson was kept well aware of what was going on and he retained final say on significant issues affecting the firm, including who was or was not hired. As in the past, Johnson did not do the legal work. He brought in virtually all of the business and tended to the care and feeding of the firm's clients.

Heading the prestigious law firm was financially rewarding and a task which Johnson thoroughly enjoyed, but something seemed to be missing.[3] Johnson had had three solid years of daily interaction with powerful people such as the president of the United States; the secretaries of state, treasury, and war; and the army chief of staff and chief of the air corps. He had appeared before House and Senate committees, made speeches before large and influential groups, and inspected military bases and production facilities throughout the nation. He still spent a great deal of time in Washington and New York developing business for the firm, but no matter how pleasant his life in Clarksburg was, there was bound to be a letdown, especially to a man with a tremendous ego and enormous ambition.

Keeping in Touch

By early October Johnson was becoming restless. He could not forget what he had left behind in the nation's capital. He kept in close contact with what was happening in the White House through Steve Early, in the State Department through Adolf Berle and Sumner Welles, and in the War Department through Colonel James Burns. He also kept in touch with Generals Marshall and Arnold but primarily on a social basis, and it was to his credit that he made no attempt to offer advice on war department activities.[4] The only special consideration he asked of his former colleagues was when the West Virginia Military Area asked how long it would take him to get things in order before he was called to active duty. He had remained in the Officer Reserve Corps and mobilization of troops was under way, which made it highly likely that the 49-year-old lieutenant colonel would be called back into the army. Perhaps it was his age or a feeling that his varied experience could be better utilized in another capacity that led him to ask General Marshall to grant a delay. "I want no waiver or exemption—but with three years of 'service,' I do want a little time free from official duties," said Johnson. Marshall responded by sending a directive to waive action in his case "for the present."[5] With that matter out of the way, Johnson was able to turn his attention to helping Roosevelt in his bid for reelection and championing administration policies.

That fall Johnson contributed $5,500 of his own funds to the president's reelection effort and he worked closely with the Veterans Advisory Committee of the Democratic National Committee to rally veteran support for FDR's third term.[6] Since Johnson had helped form that group in 1936 and chaired it from its inception until 1937, he was well equipped to aid it in planning and implementing campaign strategy.

Johnson also did what he could to help the president break down the walls of American isolationism. On October 15, after Charles Lindbergh had delivered a strong isolationist speech that was particularly upsetting to Roosevelt, Steve Early suggested that Johnson be utilized to repudiate it. The president agreed, and with the help of Adolf Berle, Johnson prepared a major speech that he delivered to a nationwide radio audience. In that address, he criticized the aviation hero for stepping out of his area of expertise and showing his naiveté by suggesting appeasement of the Axis. By advocating such a stance, "Colonel Lindbergh displays alike his ignorance of the United States, of its state of preparedness, and most of all, of its iron will," charged Johnson. After the speech, Johnson stopped by Adolph Berle's office at the State Department and was ebullient about the favorable reception. Johnson's address was greatly appreciated by an administration that was growing increasingly concerned about Lindbergh's pronouncements.[7]

With a little more than two weeks to go before the election, it certainly helped the president to have a former assistant secretary of war that he had let go championing the cause of his former chief. Roosevelt was kept aware of the support Johnson was giving him and on at least one occasion expressed his appreciation for his loyal backing.[8]

When Americans went to the polls in November 1940 and gave Roosevelt an unprecedented third term, Johnson was overjoyed. The president, still basking in victory, sent a telegram saying, "I want you to know how much I appreciate your loyalty and cooperation."[9] Seven weeks later they exchanged Christmas pleasantries.[10] In spite of all that had happened in that hectic year of 1940, the two men respected one another and were still on good terms personally.

That the president was not just going through niceties was apparent in early 1941 when he sent Pa Watson to see Senator Matthew Neely, who was the governor-elect of West Virginia, to urge him to appoint Johnson to the Senate seat that Neely was vacating two years early. Watson argued vigorously for Johnson's selection, but Neely, who liked and respected the Clarksburg lawyer,

had already made a commitment to Dr. Joseph Rosier, president of Fairmont
State Teachers College.[11] Although the effort was unsuccessful, the fact that it
was attempted indicated that Roosevelt was looking for a place for Johnson.

After the election, Johnson again focused his attentions on his law firm and
his family. His oldest daughter, Lillian, who had attended the Emma Willard
School in Connecticut and Finch College in New York City, had just turned
twenty-one. She was a beautiful young woman who had attended balls at the
Mayflower, receptions at the White House, and Army-Navy games with her parents. Some time after her trip to Europe in 1939 she became psychotic. She was
eventually diagnosed as a schizophrenic, and the Johnsons had her admitted to
Chestnut Lodge, a private mental hospital in Rockville, Maryland, that was
later celebrated in the novel *I Never Promised You a Rose Garden*.[12] In 1941, Lillian was at Chestnut Lodge undergoing psychoanalysis, and she would reside
there for several years.[13] Obviously Lillian's situation brought trauma, heartbreak, and stress to the Johnson family. Lillian had shown great promise as a
young woman, but now her parents' hopes and dreams for her would never be
realized. Ruth Johnson and her housekeeper traveled frequently to Chestnut
Lodge to visit Lillian.[14] Louis Johnson rarely spoke of her.

The Johnson's younger daughter, Kay, had attended the Madeira School in
McLean, Virginia, while the Johnsons were living as a family at the Mayflower,
but because of a shadow on her lung she was sent to a school in New Mexico. In
1941, when Kay returned to Clarksburg, she fell desperately in love with a local
boy, Ronald Moist, who was described as a bit of a blade. Louis and Ruth tried
to discourage the relationship. Nevertheless, despite Johnson's particularly
strong objections, 19-year-old Kay and Ronald Moist eloped. Kay was to divorce
him before the end of the war, but severe and permanent damage was done to
the relationship between her and her father.[15]

Despite the stresses and dashed expectations brought on by their daughters,
Ruth and Louis seemed to maintain strong emotional attachments with one another even though they lived apart much of the time due to Louis's travels to
Washington, New York, and countless other places.[16] In 1941, they purchased one
of the largest and most prestigious old homes in Clarksburg, the Harrison House
on Buckhannon Avenue just across the street from Johnson's friend and partner,
Jimmy Guiher. Built in 1860 by Thomas W. Harrison, one of Clarksburg's most
distinguished lawyers, the Harrison house was a three-story stately residence made
of handmade bricks kilned on the property and surrounded by ancient oak trees.[17]

Johnson threw his energies into overseeing the landscaping of the spacious
Harrison property and began raising orchids, a passion that lasted for the rest
of his life. During those years, he lavished his love and affection on a sheepdog
named Jeff that was the size of a small bear. In addition, he played golf and gin
rummy with his pals Jimmy Guiher and Dr. Frank Langfitt, and he pursued
with enthusiasm his interests in photography and art collecting.[18]

All of these things seemed to keep Johnson busy but far from satisfied. On July 25, 1941, he sent a message to Steve Early saying, "One year ago today I was ousted from the government. For me it has been an unhappy year. In some respects personally and otherwise a tragic year." He proceeded to reaffirm his loyalty by expressing hope that Roosevelt knew "that I have been a good soldier," as if to say he was available to serve.[19]

During that fateful year he made a number of speeches before national organizations, but he refrained from talking about defense matters, choosing instead to focus on the dangers of isolationism. In one instance he went to Fargo, North Dakota, to deliver a speech attacking the isolationist sentiments associated so closely with that state's junior senator, Gerald P. Nye. His address was well received, and he confidently wired back to the White House, "Fargo meeting eminently successful. North Dakota not isolationist. Nye has no friends there and state wants to repudiate . . . all he stands for."[20] By the fall of 1941, he felt that progress was clearly being made. In a letter to Early in which he mentioned his activities, he proclaimed, "We are going to put the isolationists to complete rout. They are definitely on the run now."[21] Little did he realize that within two months, events abroad would bring a crashing halt to American isolationism.

Like millions of other Americans, Johnson was home that first Sunday afternoon in December 1941 when news arrived of the Japanese attack on Pearl Harbor. He sat in stunned silence as the first reports of death and destruction came over the radio. He had expected for some time that the United States would ultimately be drawn into the war against the Axis, but never in this fashion.[22] After a minute or two he walked over to the desk in the dining room, grabbed a notepad, and wrote a telegram to President Roosevelt:

> Since my release from the War Department . . . I have given everything I had speaking and working for national unity. That is not necessary now. The country will back your farsighted leadership without question. You know I will help in every way I can in this serious hour.[23]

That afternoon and in the days that followed the president received thousands of such telegrams. Some of those volunteering their services were serious, while others did so because it seemed to be the thing to do—they never expected to be taken up on their offers. Louis Johnson was serious. On December 16, he wrote to Roosevelt, "May I again say how *anxious* I am to be of help in any way possible in this serious hour."[24] That was followed six weeks later by a telegram stating, "Again . . . I tender my services to my commander-in-chief."[25] In each case Johnson routed his messages through Steve Early to make sure they got to the president. The consequence of these appeals was that Johnson's name was kept before Roosevelt at a time when, because of wartime exigencies, there were many important posts to be filled. It was just a matter of finding the right spot for him.

It wasn't long before Roosevelt found a way to make use of Johnson's talents and experience. The assignment was to take Johnson on a mission halfway around the world to, of all places, India. Although he was initially unfamiliar with that country, its heritage, and its problems, he was soon to become well acquainted with that distant nation.

India and Independence

By the late eighteenth century, Great Britain had established India as its most important and most modern colony. The Crown permitted the princes of the hundreds of provinces or native states to exercise autonomous rights in their domains, while the mother country controlled national defense, external affairs, fiscal and trade policies, and the transportation network through the viceroy. Under this system, as with most colonial schemes, the British profited handsomely while the Indians gained little.

Not surprisingly, a nationalistic movement began to emerge in the 1880s, but it made little headway prior to World War I. During the war the British succumbed to pressures for independence, pledging "gradual development of self-governing institutions."[26] However, very little was done in the postwar years, and nationalistic movements gained strength. With growth came factionalism, and by the mid-1930s the movement had split into two key groups: the Hindu-dominated Indian National Congress, under the leadership of Mahatma Gandhi and Jawaharlal Nehru; and the rival Muslim League, headed by Mohammad Ali Jinnah.

In 1935 the British Parliament, in spite of opposition from imperialists such as Winston Churchill, passed a Government of India Act that provided a new constitution similar to those of other British dominions, which meant that India was to be structured as a federation of British provinces and Indian nation-states. The act was not acceptable to the Indian Congress, which by this time was demanding outright independence. The new federation could not become a reality, and friction between the various groups continued.[27]

When war broke out in Europe in September 1939 and the British viceroy, Lord Linlithgow, announced that India was at war against Germany, the Indian Congress voiced its disapproval and said it could not support a war that was declared without popular consent. Although the Muslim League pledged support for the war, the Congress, feeling it had been ignored by the government of India, made its opposition felt by ordering all its provincial ministers to resign, which they did. Undaunted, the British government stated that its aim of dominion status for India remained the same but that the war made any immediate move for independence impossible.[28]

In the summer of 1941, Indian hopes for independence soared when Churchill and Roosevelt included in the Atlantic Charter a provision for "the right of all peoples to choose the form of government under which they will live." A few weeks later those hopes were dashed when Churchill announced that the Atlantic Charter did not apply to India. By this time the Muslim League, which was growing increasingly fearful that it would not be adequately protected under a government controlled by the Hindus, was calling for the creation of a separate Muslim nation of Pakistan when Britain relinquished control.[29]

In 1940 and 1941, American interest in India grew, and it became increasingly evident to officials in Washington that they were handicapped in formulating policy for that area because all their information came through the British—no official U.S. representative was permitted because of India's status as a colony. To correct that problem, Assistant Secretary of State Adolf Berle succeeded in convincing President Roosevelt and Secretary of State Hull to pressure Britain into permitting the United States to send a state department representative to India and having an Indian agent-general assigned to the British Embassy in Washington. This unique arrangement served to facilitate the exchange of information and permit the resolution of nonpolitical problems between the United States and British India. Because India was a colony, the mother country was not willing to permit her to receive a minister; thus, it was agreed that the United States representative would be called a commissioner.

In July 1941 the arrangements were completed and Thomas Wilson, a career diplomat, was appointed U.S. commissioner to India, posted in New Delhi, and Sir Girja Shankar Bajpai became India's agent-general, posted in Washington. Even though the United States had adopted a rather unusual arrangement to establish limited diplomatic relations with India, it had no desire to get involved in British-Indian internal affairs.[30]

The Mission

In the weeks immediately following the attack on Pearl Harbor, U.S. interests in India changed significantly. As Guam, Wake Island, and Hong Kong fell and with the Philippines and Singapore under attack, the Roosevelt administration began searching frantically for ways to halt Japanese expansion. India took on a new importance, which led to the president's January 1942 directive ordering a study on the issue of extending military assistance to that nation. About that same time, Agent-General Bajpai was urging that an American mission be sent to his country to study and recommend what technical aid would be required to significantly expand industrial production and thereby permit expansion of the Indian army from 275,000 (mostly Muslims loyal to the Muslim League) to 1 million men by the end of the year. Assistant Secretary of State Berle realized that because the American priority was the war in Europe, the only hope of supplying the Indian army in a manner that could enable her to resist a possible

Japanese attack was to turn to resources within the country. He pushed the idea of the mission; the president agreed and told him to proceed with the necessary plans.[31]

Since the matter was in Adolf Berle's hands, he had the responsibility of recommending to the president who would head the mission and who would serve on it. Berle realized that the person heading the group needed a good grasp of military supply. Despite strong objections from Vice President Wallace, Berle believed that Louis Johnson was best suited for the job.[32] Berle had worked closely with Johnson when he had been in the War Department and had continued to work with him on several speeches after he had left. The two men respected one another and shared similar views on foreign policy.[33] When Berle recommended Johnson for the mission, the president, who had been looking for a spot for Johnson, readily agreed, and in mid-February 1942 Johnson was offered the assignment. Without hesitation, Johnson, who was anxious to make a significant contribution to the war effort, responded in the affirmative. In the weeks that followed he and Berle worked to assemble the team that was to make the trip.

After a number of frustrating delays, the White House finally announced on March 9, 1942, that Johnson would head an advisory mission that "will go to India to assist in the war effort." The primary function "would be to assist in the development of India for the production of war materials."[34] Joining Johnson were Henry F. Grady, a former assistant secretary of state, who was to concentrate on economic surveys; Arthur W. Harrington, a longtime Johnson friend and president of the Society of Automotive Engineers, who was to examine vehicle and automotive production; Harry E. Beyster, an engineer who would concern himself with plant organization; Dirk Dekker, a personnel expert from the Illinois Steel Corporation who was going to look at ways to train skilled and semi-skilled workers; and Lieutenant Colonel Paul Griffith, an old Johnson protégé from the early American Legion days, who was to serve as Johnson's aide. Rounding out the group were another half-dozen engineers and stenographers.[35]

At the time Johnson's appointment was announced, it appeared that he would be going to India for what was essentially a technical fact-finding mission so that recommendations for increasing the nation's industrial war production capability could be made to the president. This was not to be the case, however, because of a serendipitous mixture of political and military considerations.

In mid-February, at about the time Berle first contacted Johnson about the technical mission, the Japanese captured Singapore, opening the door for possible attacks on Burma and India. Berle convinced Roosevelt that pressure needed to be brought on Britain to adopt a new approach to the Indian question—one that would persuade the Indian Congress, which had gone on record as willing to support the war in return for immediate independence, to give full and enthusiastic support to the war effort.[36]

Roosevelt and top state department officials felt that the desired Indian military support could be gained only through a satisfactory solution to India's fundamental political problem — its relationship with Great Britain and its eventual independence. Hence, from this time on, the military hopes for India were invariably tied to political considerations. That the two were intertwined, thus complicating both military and political decisions, can be seen in Roosevelt's late February message to the U.S. ambassador to England, John G. Winant, in which he expressed the quandary he was in by saying, "I hate to send [Churchill] a message [concerning eventual independence for India] because in a strict sense it is not our business. It is, however, of great interest to us from the point of view of the conduct of the war."[37] Roosevelt's envoys and Roosevelt himself had raised the matter of India's independence with Churchill on several occasions, but Churchill had always stuck to his earlier position of denying immediate independence.[38] Roosevelt and Churchill were able to sit down and intelligently discuss the issues and come up with an acceptable compromise with most problems relating to the conduct of the war, but matters relating to India were entirely different.[39]

Finally, in March, Roosevelt's gentle pressure, along with the fall of Rangoon and growing American public support for Indian independence, led Churchill to announce that he was sending a member of his War Cabinet, Sir Stafford Cripps, on a mission to India to attempt an amicable political settlement.[40] The selection of Cripps, an ascetic vegetarian and left-leaning Labour Party member who was sympathetic to Indian independence and a friend of Gandhi and Nehru, was well received in India and the United States. Roosevelt's pleasure with the announcement of the Cripps mission was tempered by his knowledge of the way Churchill had privately reacted to the issue of independence. Nevertheless, he was highly desirous of seeing Cripps succeed and he wanted to do all he could to see that he did. Toward that end he decided to send Johnson to India not for the purpose of heading the industrial preparedness mission but to do what he could to assure the success of the Cripps negotiations. To put him in a position where he could achieve that task, Berle, with Roosevelt's concurrence, decided that Johnson should replace Thomas Wilson as the U.S. commissioner to India.[41]

The day after Churchill made the Cripps announcement, Johnson was called to the State Department, where he was offered the position of commissioner and was vaguely told what his real responsibilities would be. He immediately agreed to undertake the task but protested the title of commissioner, claiming that where he came from that term connoted "a conspicuously unsuccessful lawyer"; he said that as a lawyer he could not accept that title. After Johnson and Berle consulted with several officials it was finally agreed that Johnson would be called the "personal representative of the president" with the rank of minister.[42]

On March 16, the White House indicated that Johnson would be going to India as a minister, and on the 24th the State Department issued a formal announcement of his new status. However, except for Berle's admonition that Johnson should "foster friendly relations" between the United States and India, nothing more was said about the nature of his duties or the aim of his mission.[43] In his cable to the viceroy, Lord Linlithgow, FDR merely introduced Colonel Johnson as a person "with broad experience with problems relating to military supply" who was "specially qualified to further the mutual interests" of India and the United States.[44] Roosevelt did not provide any specifics because he knew that the issue of Indian independence was explosive and that the British, especially Churchill, would resent U.S. meddling. He also did not further define Johnson's mission to the viceroy because the president and his State Department were not clear about exactly what they wanted their personal representative to do.

At his State Department briefing, Berle told Johnson that his duties as personal representative would take precedence over his technical mission activities. Furthermore, in a nebulous and indirect way he was informed by Berle that he was to try to facilitate a settlement between Cripps and the Indian Congress and that he was to act "with the utmost care." Johnson complained that he "had not been given any very positive information about anything" and that he was unable to obtain clarification about what was expected of him. Although he was the president's personal representative, he never consulted with the chief executive or the secretary of state on his assignment. Adolf Berle, an assistant secretary of state, was the highest-ranking official he came into contact with before his departure.[45] Perhaps Roosevelt or Adolf Berle had in mind what they wanted Johnson to accomplish, but if they did, they certainly did not convey it to Johnson, to Churchill in London, or to the viceroy in New Delhi.

While the failure to define Johnson's mission may seem strange, it was typical of Roosevelt's unusual way of operating. In all likelihood it was a well-calculated and shrewd move by the president rather than an administrative foul-up. By early March it was evident that Roosevelt considered a satisfactory solution of the Indian independence issue to be of sufficient importance to urge the British to make concessions to the nationalists. But Roosevelt needed someone else to do it so that if things did not work out he could distance himself without jeopardizing his relationship with Churchill. FDR's desire to press the British while giving himself political cover and deniability led him to approve Berle's choice of Johnson for the diplomatic mission. Roosevelt needed someone who was loyal, aggressive, and outgoing; someone who would not need specific instructions and would take the initiative to get involved in the negotiations and bring the two sides together.

The traits FDR was looking for were all embodied in Johnson. As one expert on Indian affairs put it, "If Roosevelt had intended to withdraw from the Indian problem, he would have sent someone other than Johnson."[46] The fact that the directives were so vague gave Johnson the opportunity to pursue a solution to the issue of Indian independence on whatever grounds he chose. Furthermore, although his new title technically brought with it the same authority given to the commissioner, it was much more impressive because it carried the connotation that he spoke for the president, and that gave him an entrée he would otherwise not have had.

While Johnson was preparing to leave for his assignment, Sir Cripps arrived in New Delhi, and on March 29 he released the British proposal for India, which called for independent dominion status, a new constitution to be drawn up at war's end by an Indian body, an opt-out provision for any province that wished to stay out of the new union, and a treaty with the new government assuring protection of religious and social minorities. Although Cripps urged all Indian political groups to support the war effort, he also made it clear that no major changes, including control over national defense, would be possible during the war.[47]

The Cripps proposal was accepted by nearly every group, both inside and outside of India, except the Indian Congress, which was unhappy with British retention of control of national defense and the proviso permitting provinces to opt out of the union—a move that would encourage the establishment of a separate Muslim state. On April 2, the Working Committee of the Congress rejected the Cripps proposal but vowed to continue negotiations.[48]

The Johnson Formula

On April 3, Johnson arrived in New Delhi after a long and dangerous flight.[49] The next morning he aggressively threw himself directly into the negotiations. He first met with Cripps and then with General Archibald Wavell, commander in chief of British and Indian armed forces in India. From them he learned that the big issue with the Indian Congress was the defense issue; both sides wanted to control military operations. After considerable discussion, the three men concluded that the only hope for a settlement lay in British agreement to cede control of the Defense Ministry to India but with the stipulation that no action could run counter to imperial war policy as determined by the commander in chief in India.

After those discussions, Johnson cabled Roosevelt, via the secretary of state, strongly urging him to "intercede with Churchill" and recommending acceptance of the concession the three men had just worked out. If that was not done, Johnson maintained, then "it would seem that Cripps' efforts are doomed to failure."[50] Less than eighteen hours later, Acting Secretary of State Sumner Welles replied that the president did not consider it "desirable or expedient" to take the requested action at that time.[51]

Undeterred, Johnson doggedly pursued his goal. For the next five days he traveled around Delhi meeting day and night with Cripps, Wavell, Linlithgow, Nehru, and Maulana Abul Kalam Azad, president of the Indian Congress, as he attempted to bring the sides to agreement. Johnson's efforts at compromise centered on a means for dividing defense authority between the British and the Indians—the issue that remained the major stumbling block.[52]

As a result of continued shuttling and hard negotiations, Johnson's efforts and his persistence paid off. By April 8, he had secured agreement from Cripps, Wavell, Nehru, and Azad for a plan, known to the principals as the "Johnson formula," that would divide military control.[53] Johnson cabled the secretary of state, "The magic name over here is Roosevelt . . . the land, the people would follow and love, America."[54] Optimism prevailed in the Indian capital, and even Nehru later admitted that there was about a 75 percent chance of agreement at that time.[55] Johnson tingled with excitement at the prospect that in his debut as a diplomat he had done the impossible and brought the factions together.

Late on the evening of April 9, Cripps called Johnson, Nehru, and Azad to come and see him. When they arrived, he shocked them by announcing that the agreement of the previous day based on the Johnson formula was unacceptable to the British War Cabinet in London and that he was being directed to resubmit his original defense proposal—which they all knew would not be accepted by the Indian Congress. The three visitors did not argue because it was evident that the decision had not been made by Cripps and could not be changed by him.[56] Two days later the Congress formally rejected the British proposals and the chances for settlement disappeared.

Johnson was furious that the compromise he had so arduously put together had been rejected. He had no doubt about where the responsibility for failure to reach agreement lay. "London wanted a Congress refusal," he cabled back to Roosevelt. In explaining what had happened he made it clear that the problem was not in India, for in referring to Cripps Johnson said, "He is sincere . . . he and Nehru could solve it in 5 minutes if Cripps had any freedom or authority." Of Nehru he reported, "He has been magnificent in his cooperation with me . . . he is our hope here. I trust him."[57] Although Winston Churchill's name was not mentioned, it was clear that Johnson put the blame squarely on his shoulders.

While Johnson's efforts to negotiate a settlement were greatly appreciated and later praised by all of the parties in New Delhi, they had caused great alarm in London. On the morning of April 9, *before* Cripps had been ordered by the British Cabinet to reject the Johnson formula, Harry Hopkins, Roosevelt's closest advisor, who was in London to discuss military matters, was grilled by an obviously angry Churchill about how, why, and by what authority Johnson had inserted himself into the negotiations between Cripps and the Indian Congress. The Johnson formula had just arrived in London, and the War Cabinet was going to take it up at a noon meeting. The prime minister made it clear to Hopkins that he did not appreciate the meddling in British foreign affairs by Roosevelt's personal representative.

To diffuse Churchill's anger, Harry Hopkins did something that in retrospect seems brutally unfair, but he and the president may have planned it in advance. Hopkins completely undercut Johnson by telling Churchill that Johnson was not the president's representative on anything other than "Indian munitions," that Johnson was not authorized by FDR to become involved in matters involving Indian independence, and that Roosevelt was "entirely opposed to . . . intervention or mediation" of issues involving Indian independence.[58]

Almost immediately, Churchill cabled the viceroy in New Delhi and reiterated what Hopkins had told him—namely, that Johnson was acting on his own and that President Roosevelt opposed any efforts by Johnson to help mediate political issues in India.[59] Churchill then proceeded to the cabinet meeting, where it was decided to reject the Johnson formula and stick with the original defense offer.[60]

After the meeting with the prime minister, Hopkins sent a message to the president decrying Johnson's actions and urging that his activities be downplayed.[61] If Hopkins was trying to alarm the president and cause him to recall Johnson, he apparently did not succeed because Roosevelt never did or said anything that would discourage his representative in India from acting as he saw fit. Nor is there any record that the president criticized Hopkins for what he did to Johnson.

It is impossible to know for sure what advance understandings Hopkins and the president might have had about the Johnson mission, but it would seem that if the president was upset with anyone, it should have been with Hopkins, whose comments to Churchill completely doomed Johnson's chances of negotiating a settlement. As long as it was felt that Johnson was carrying out Roosevelt's instructions, his words wielded great influence, but when Hopkins told Churchill that Johnson was acting on his own he took the mediator's power away. Had Hopkins not undercut Johnson, Churchill may not have been so willing to reject the compromise worked out in New Delhi. The formula the Cabinet rejected had only marginal differences from the one originally proposed by Cripps and could have removed the most serious stumbling block to agreement, clearing the way for a broad settlement.[62]

On April 11, two days after the British rejection, President Roosevelt, largely at Johnson's insistence, sent an uncharacteristically presumptuous message to Churchill on the Indian independence issue. By then he had received both the prime minister's and Johnson's accounts of why the negotiations had failed and had had time to reflect on where things stood. He began with an appeal that the negotiations be kept open in the hope that a settlement would be forthcoming. Continuing on, he said:

> The feeling is almost universally held that the deadlock has been caused by
> the unwillingness of the British Government to concede to the Indians the

right of self-government, notwithstanding the willingness of the Indians to
entrust . . . defense control to . . . British authorities. . . . I read that an
agreement seemed very near last Thursday night. If [Cripps] could . . . resume negotiations . . . with the understanding that minor concessions
would be made on both sides, it seems to me that an agreement might yet
be found.[63]

Roosevelt's blunt message, received by Churchill at Chequers at 3:00 A.M.
while he was still wide awake and talking with a weary Harry Hopkins, clearly
reveals that FDR accepted Johnson's interpretation of what had happened
rather than Churchill's. Furthermore, it discloses a strong desire to reach a settlement and helps explain why he never expressed dissatisfaction with the method
or substance of Johnson's efforts to mediate a resolution. Although Roosevelt's
April 11 criticism of Churchill's position was bold and unprecedented, it came
too late, because by the time it was received in London, Cripps had already left
for home and Churchill was not willing to send him back.[64]

Churchill's rejection of Roosevelt's request to keep the negotiations open was
couched in mild terms; he told FDR that "anything like a serious difference
between you and me would break my heart."[65] However, the prime minister was
completely outraged, and he fumed over FDR's interference in a matter which
he felt the president did not understand or appreciate. He even indicated to
Hopkins that he was ready to resign over the issue.[66]

Throughout the rest of April Johnson continued to try to broker a settlement.
At his urging, Nehru sent a letter to Roosevelt suggesting that further pressure be
brought on Britain to resume negotiations.[67] By this time, however, the president
was convinced that to push the issue farther would endanger his overall good relationship with Churchill, so he left the matter in abeyance. Johnson suggested
to Nehru that they fly to Washington together to discuss the desire of the Indian
Congress to negotiate a settlement. This proposal stemmed from his belief that
Nehru's charm and sincerity could persuade the president in a way that messages
could not. However, Nehru rejected this idea; he feared that such apparent close
cooperation with the United States would weaken him in his own party.[68]

By mid-April the personal representative of the president, while still hoping
that negotiations might be reopened, turned his attention to another matter of
diplomatic significance. The All-India Congress was scheduled to meet on
April 29 and was going to consider adoption of a resolution sponsored by Gandhi that would call for nonviolent resistance to Japanese aggression. Nehru favored armed resistance and was opposed to the Gandhi resolution. So was
Johnson, and he set out to do what he could to strengthen Nehru's hand. That
could be done, he felt, only by convincing the Indians that America would use
its influence over Britain to force a settlement that would be favorable to them.

Johnson's attempt to convince the Indian public began at a special reception held by the Indian Press Association on April 22, where he made a rather

straightforward announcement that American troops were in India and that more would be coming. He then went a bit overboard, at least as far as the State Department and the British were concerned, affirming American interest, both the president's and the public's, in India and the well-being of its people. He said essentially the same things the next day in a speech delivered over All-India Radio.[69] The implication of this speech was that Roosevelt would help bring about a settlement of the issue of independence from Britain. The broadcast was well received in India but was upsetting to state department observers, who feared it would lead to unrealistic expectations in India and would deeply offend the British.[70]

In another move to strengthen Nehru's hand before the upcoming Congress, Johnson proposed that the United States, Britain, and China join in issuing "Pacific War Aims" that would include a statement pledging freedom for India and a determination to defend it from aggression. That request was rebuffed by Secretary of State Hull on the grounds that there was not time to prepare such "aims" before Congress met. At the same time Johnson received a stern warning from Hull "not to identify yourself too closely with any particular group or groups in Indian national life."[71] Apparently, the secretary of state felt that Johnson was getting too close to Nehru. Nevertheless, Johnson's efforts to support Nehru and encourage armed resistance were to no avail; when the All-India Congress met, it adopted Gandhi's call for nonviolent resistance to Japan and Nehru was forced to go along in order to preserve his position in the party.[72]

On May 4, Johnson made one final plea to the press for a British-India settlement, but by that time, officials in Washington had come to see India's problems in strictly military terms, and they rejected Johnson's attempt.[73] With that rejection, Johnson came to the conclusion that there was nothing more he could do to accomplish the goal for which he believed he had been sent to India—to help bring about a settlement of the independence issue between the British and the political factions in India.

Similarly, there was not much left to do regarding Johnson's secondary duties—those related to the industrial preparedness mission. Johnson had already spent a great deal of time meeting with numerous Indian industrialists, visiting factories, and developing definite ideas on what could be done to expand the country's war production. In early May, when he checked with Henry Grady, who had taken charge of the technical mission, he found that the group was completing its survey and would be returning home before the end of the month.[74]

On May 9, shortly after receiving a call from Secretary of State Hull thanking him for his efforts, saying that the situation was now "largely military" and that further attempts to solve the problem would "further alienate the Indian leaders and parties from the British," Johnson requested permission to return home, citing a serious sinus infection that had hospitalized him as the reason.

The president, fearing that Johnson's abrupt departure at that time might be interpreted as an abandonment of India by the United States, coaxed him into staying a little longer.[75]

In the next few days, however, Johnson's sinus condition worsened and he was operated on by U.S. Air Force surgeons. In a letter dated May 14, the chief surgeon of the 10th Air Force in India urged Johnson to return to the United States "by the next available transport plane."[76] On May 26, after six weeks of frantic diplomacy, Johnson left India.[77] When he arrived in the United States he went straight to the White House for lunch and a discussion of his mission, after which he was flown to the Mayo Clinic, where he underwent additional treatment for his nasal condition.[78] By the first of June he was back in Clarksburg recuperating from the ills of his foray into the world of international diplomacy; it took him most of the summer to recover.

Not content to rely on Johnson's ill health to deter him from returning to facilitate Indian independence, senior British officials moved to ensure that Johnson stayed home. On May 29, the British secretary of state for India, Lord Amery, cabled Churchill with the following very British suggestion: "This fellow Johnson is rather too much of a good thing. Is it at all possible to prevent his return to India?"[79]

Blame for Failure

In the year that followed Johnson's mission to India, he regretted his failure to bring about a satisfactory British-Indian settlement.[80] However, the fault was clearly not his; in fact, he did everything possible to bring one about. Leaders on both sides of the issue who worked with him in New Delhi lauded his efforts. From the floor of the House of Commons, Sir Stafford Cripps praised Johnson by giving thanks for "the personal help of a very able and pleasant American citizen" who negotiated with all parties and was "a great help in clarifying the situation."[81] Nehru, who had become a good personal friend, made public pronouncements of praise for his assistance in the negotiations.[82] Johnson, Cripps, and Nehru had done their best, but that had not been good enough.

Who to blame for failure of the Cripps mission has been and will continue to be the subject of debate, but Johnson always felt that Churchill alone was to blame.[83] He was convinced that the prime minister dispatched the Cripps mission for show and that he never had the slightest intention of working out a settlement. For that reason, Johnson never held Churchill in the esteem that most other Americans did.[84]

Johnson probably never saw the cables between Churchill and Harry Hopkins, but if he did he would have placed at least some blame for his failure at the feet of FDR's special advisor. Hopkins told Churchill repeatedly that Johnson was not authorized by the president to act as a mediator in the settlement of issues concerning Indian independence.[85] In a message to the viceroy, Churchill said, "Mr. Hopkins expressed himself in scathing terms about Johnson who carries no special weight with the President."[86] Because of Hopkins's close relationship with FDR, Churchill asked him to tell President Roosevelt that "We [the British] do not at all relish the prospect of Johnson's return to India."[87]

Three months after Johnson left India, the All-India Congress, at Gandhi's urging, launched a "Quit India" movement designed to disrupt British control of the country. This led to open rebellion throughout the colony. In an attempt to put down the disorder, the British imprisoned Gandhi, Nehru, and thousands of Congress supporters. Robbed of leadership, the movement for independence languished through the war years.

Fortunately, although the Japanese navy shelled the capital of Ceylon (now Sri Lanka) and menaced Indian shipping, they never invaded the country, and, in spite of the stand of the Congress to the contrary, India supported the Allied war effort industrially and with a 2-million-man army. At the end of the war, nationalistic pressures reemerged and on August 15, 1947, Britain gave up India and recognized the existence of two independent states, India and Pakistan. When that day arrived, no American was happier than Louis Johnson.[88]

Alien Property

While Johnson was still convalescing at his home, he was contacted by Leo Crowley, the alien property custodian, who was also chairman of the Federal Deposit Insurance Corporation and head of the Office of Economic Welfare. Crowley was a controversial and allegedly corrupt Democratic Party supporter who had played a major role in delivering the state of Wisconsin to Roosevelt in the 1940 election. As alien property custodian, Crowley's job was to oversee the operations and eventual dispositions of the companies and assets of the Axis powers which had been seized by the government.[89]

The largest and most important companies that Crowley had within his grasp in 1942 were General Aniline and Film Company (GAF) and its sister company, General Dyestuff, each of which was an affiliate of I. G. Farben, the huge German chemical cartel that produced the cyanide that exterminated millions of European Jews and (many say) financed and sustained the German war machine. GAF manufactured a number of products which were essential to the war effort, including photographic equipment, a critical resin, a quinine substitute called Atabrine, high-quality dyes, and other key chemical products. It owned thousands of patents and had assets of over $60 million. General Dyestuff was the exclusive sales agent in the United States and Latin America for GAF.[90]

Leo Crowley called Louis Johnson that June day of 1942 to ask him to serve as president, general manager, and a member of the board of directors of General

Dyestuff at a salary of $50,000 per year.[91] This post would be critical to the war effort, but it was also a political plum and a financial windfall. Given Crowley's memo to the president dated July 6, 1942, confirming the offer to Johnson and telling FDR that "Louis will therefore have an opportunity to be of real service," it is likely that the president himself suggested that Crowley give the job to Johnson.[92] Even if the president was not directly involved, there is no doubt that the president and his friends, most likely Steve Early, were watching out for and taking care of Louis Johnson. Outwardly, his service as assistant secretary of war and personal representative may have seemed thankless, but Roosevelt had a not-so-subtle way of saying thanks.

After discussing the offer with the president to make sure that he did not have any other plans for him, Johnson accepted, and in July he began a high-profile and financially lucrative job that was to last for the next five years. Since General Dyestuff was headquartered in New York City, Johnson leased another apartment there in addition to his apartment at the Mayflower, which he maintained throughout the war years. From July 1942 until he resigned as president in 1947, Johnson spent three to four days per week in New York City directing the operations of General Dyestuff and two to three days per week running Steptoe & Johnson and developing legal business in New York, Washington, Clarksburg, and Charleston.[93]

In the spring of 1943, Leo Crowley forced out the president of GAF because of his problems cooperating with the management of General Dyestuff and laid plans for appointing a new board of directors. By July 13, 1943, his plans had matured and a new board, which included Louis Johnson, was elected.[94] Using his GAF board membership, Johnson eventually arranged for one of Steptoe & Johnson's rising young stars, Henry Ikenberry, to move to New York to work in the general counsel's office of GAF, the second-largest manufacturer of photographic equipment and supplies in America.[95]

Through his dealings with Leo Crowley, Johnson became much closer to one of Crowley's business associates, Victor Emanuel, whom Johnson had met when he was chairman of the National Defense Power Committee. In 1942, Victor Emanuel controlled several major corporations, one of which was Consolidated Vultee Aircraft Corporation, known as Convair. During the war, Convair, one of the largest U.S. makers of airplanes, accounted for nearly 13 percent of total U.S. output of airplanes and almost 60 percent of the deliveries of large four-engine bombers. Because of Johnson's contacts with the Roosevelt administration, his experience in government, and his knowledge of the aircraft industry, Emanuel's management team asked him to join the board of directors of Convair. With assurance from Steve Early that service on Convair's board would be "in accordance with the President's desires," Johnson accepted the invitation.[96] Thus, Johnson began a long and at times controversial relationship with Convair which would later haunt him when he became secretary of defense.[97]

In addition to his work for the alien property custodian, his service on the board of Convair, and his law practice, the American Legion continued to be an important part of Johnson's life; he remained especially active at the national level. Every fall, following the organization's national convention, an event at which he was always conspicuous, Johnson would take the newly elected national commander to the White House to meet the president.[98] He also served on various committees, chairing the important Commission on Postwar America, whose report was approved at the 1944 convention.[99] The American Legion had always been good to him, and he in turn continued to be good to it. It was not unusual in those days for officers of state organizations to learn, several days before their state gathering, that the former national commander would be joining them. In these ways and others, Johnson remained prominent in the veterans' organization that had one and a half million members by 1945 and was destined to grow much larger in the postwar period.

Postwar Vision

In October 1944, Philip Pendleton Steptoe, Louis Johnson's mentor and cofounder of Steptoe & Johnson, died quietly at Falling Spring, his farm outside Shepherdstown, West Virginia, near the Potomac River, where he had lived since retiring ten years before. When Johnson arrived for the funeral services that bright October day in his chauffeur-driven black Lincoln, he was at the height of his physical and mental powers. Big beefy Louis Johnson strode into the living room of the antebellum Greek revival mansion, paid his respects, and chatted with the Steptoe & Johnson lawyers and other mourners. Johnson was in complete command.[100]

It was perhaps on this day that Johnson, having chaired the American Legion's Commission on Postwar America, began thinking seriously about how he could position and lead his law firm to greater prominence in the postwar era. His friend John W. Davis, who had a distinguished background in government, was leading a great law firm on Wall Street which would become Davis Polk & Wardwell. Elihu Root Jr., son of the lawyer-statesman who was Johnson's role model, was heading the powerhouse New York firm Root Ballantine, which would one day become Dewey Ballantine. Other prominent lawyers making their mark in top government positions, such as Henry Stimson, Robert Patterson, and John J. McCloy, would be assembling large high-quality law firms with national reputations.

Johnson, never lacking confidence in himself and predicting a postwar boom in America, decided that he could compete with these great lawyer-statesmen and their law firms. However, he would position his firm not in New York City but in Washington, where he believed the growth in postwar government regulation would generate an enormous amount of high-value legal business.

So it was that Johnson, long before other law firms, envisioned that he could establish a successful branch office of his firm in the nation's capital which would specialize in government regulation. To make his plan work, Johnson, always the organizer, knew that he would have to be ready to open and staff an office in Washington shortly after the war was over. To assure that his plan would succeed, Johnson would have to become even more involved in Democratic politics so that he could gain the support and the clout to be invited to join Roosevelt's or a subsequent president's Cabinet or even, like his friend John Davis, run for president. Johnson was convinced that the stature and visibility that would come to him with these high-level government positions would also benefit his law firm and enable him to attract clients.

President Truman

Johnson never gave up hope that he might be called upon to again assume a position of prominence in the Roosevelt administration. His desire for vindication of the events of 1940 not only remained but grew stronger. In late 1944, after Roosevelt had captured an unprecedented fourth term in office, Johnson wrote a personal letter to him asking for an opportunity to serve "in the direct war effort in association with you." As a result of that request, FDR directed Steve Early to try to come up with an appropriate job for Johnson. It was then that Johnson suggested to his old friend that perhaps he might return to the War Department as secretary or assistant secretary.[101] Early and the president were still looking for the right spot for the West Virginian on April 12, 1945, when Roosevelt died unexpectedly at his retreat in Warm Springs, Georgia.[102] The president's death hurt Johnson, as it did practically all Americans, but in more ways than one; he not only lost a dear personal friend but also a chance to find vindication under him.

Into the presidency came Vice President Harry Truman, a man whom Johnson had met briefly in 1918 in World War I and again in 1921 at the American Legion convention but did not get to know until Johnson arrived at the War Department in 1937 when Truman was the junior senator from Missouri. Although the two men were not close, Truman's respect for the former assistant secretary of war grew rapidly during the war when the Senate Special Committee to Investigate the National Defense Program, which he headed, investigated war production and he was able to appreciate the value of the contributions that Johnson made in the prewar years.[103] Truman regarded Johnson as an excellent administrator and for that reason considered, but did not act upon, naming him secretary of war in 1945 and head of the Veteran's Bureau in 1947.[104]

Within a month of Truman's ascent to the presidency, the war in Europe ended, and three months after that the war in the Pacific came to a halt. A few months later than he had planned, Johnson and his longtime administrative assistant, Ruth Nutter, assembled a staff and made arrangements for space so that Steptoe & Johnson could open its doors for business in Washington, which it did on November 1, 1945, in the Shoreham Building. The resident lawyers in Washington included Johnson, of course; Bill "Smokey" Miller, a partner who moved over from Clarksburg; and Guy Farmer, a former Rhodes scholar who had been associate general counsel of the National Labor Relations Board.[105]

With the end of World War II and the establishment of the United Nations, American optimism about a world of peace blossomed, only to wilt with the growth of hostility between the United States and the Soviet Union. What started out as misunderstandings and concerns in 1945–1946 quickly evolved into the Cold War of 1947–1948 with its Truman Doctrine, Marshall Plan, and Berlin Airlift to halt communist expansion. The emergence of the Cold War confronted Truman with more key foreign policy decisions in a shorter period of time than any other American president.

While Louis Johnson tried to keep abreast of major foreign relations issues, he was keenly interested in legislation moving through Congress in the spring of 1947 that was designed to create a powerful new cabinet-level position in government called secretary of defense. On July 26 of that year, a day known to Missouri farmers as Turnip Day because it was the day to sow turnips, President Truman signed the National Security Act, which abolished the War and Navy Departments and sought to unify the army, navy, and air force, each with its own secretary, under a single secretary of defense and within a nebulous new entity, the National Military Establishment. The first secretary of defense was James Forrestal, who had headed the Navy Department during the war years. In 1949, the National Security Act was amended to create the Defense Department (and eliminate the National Military Establishment) and to strengthen the secretary's power and authority over the three military services.

In addition to the numerous foreign affairs problems and civil defense reorganization challenges that were thrust upon him, Truman also found himself faced with a myriad of thorny domestic issues such as rampant inflation, demobilization, labor difficulties, the beginnings of the civil rights movement, and the transition to a peacetime economy. Although the man in the White House was not responsible for the many ills facing the nation, Americans, as always, tended to place the blame at the president's feet. As the election year of 1948 approached, Truman was in very big trouble; a Republican-controlled Congress criticized him at every turn and the public ridiculed his lack of leadership. The president's popularity slipped to an all-time low. Almost everyone thought the salty old politician would be sent home to retirement in Missouri. During the summer of 1948, Republicans began counting the days until they reentered the White House, while the Democrats waited for the inevitable.

What lay ahead for the nation was the most unusual and astounding presidential campaign and election in the nation's history. In that bizarre piece of American history, Louis Johnson was to play a critically important role. In fact, so significant was his role that he was able to parlay it into the vindication he so desperately longed for. And when it came, it appeared in the form of a position more powerful and important than he had ever expected—secretary of defense.

CHAPTER NINE

Long Shot Pays Off

J EAN KEARNEY WAS an attractive, fun-loving, and irreverent young woman when she worked for the Democratic National Committee (DNC) during the summer and fall of 1948. Remembering Louis Johnson in those days, Ms. Kearney said, "He was a gambler." "Colonel Johnson," she went on, "got into the business of raising money for the 1948 campaign in a cold-blooded, calculating way—he gambled that Truman might win and if he raised money for him it would advance his standing as a Washington lawyer and a national figure."[1]

The Odds

In the early months of 1948, any chance that Harry S. Truman might have had of being elected president of the United States in his own right seemed to pass into oblivion as he committed blunder after blunder. January was marked by a lackluster State of the Union Address that even loyal Democrats found hard to defend. Later that month he dismissed two prominent New Dealers—Marriner Eccles, chairman of the Federal Reserve Board, and James Landis, head of the Civil Aeronautics Board—moves that greatly upset party liberals.[2]

Things were just beginning to warm up, however, for in February the president incited the wrath of the southerners when he sent to Congress a message calling for a broad civil rights program. Then in March he alienated Jewish voters when he suddenly withdrew support for a plan calling for a partitioning of Palestine and urged creation of a United Nations trusteeship. By early spring, the incumbent president was witnessing a widespread flight of supporters from his party and political analysts were echoing the sentiments of Democratic senator John Sparkman of Alabama, who said that in the upcoming election, "the Democratic Party will be cut to ribbons."[3]

As the president's political fortunes began to collapse in early 1948, his military aide and confidant, Major General Harry Vaughn, who realized that the road to victory would be an extremely difficult one, saw the need for Truman to build political support among the large body of veterans found in every state in the union. Vaughn first tried to sell his idea to the DNC, but that group, disheartened by the president's slide in popularity and financially strapped, was unwilling or unable to support the endeavor, and in early February Vaughn acted on his own to ask Louis Johnson to help carry out the plan.[4]

That Vaughn should approach Johnson was not surprising. The fine job that the West Virginia lawyer had done in organizing and directing support among veterans for President Roosevelt's reelection in 1936 was common knowledge in Democratic circles, and when Johnson contacted Truman in December 1947 and offered to discuss some off-the-record remarks made by Republican hopeful Thomas Dewey, General Vaughn detected a willingness to help the president.[5] The general requested Johnson's aid, and Johnson responded in his usual enthusiastic manner.

From February through May, Johnson contacted many of his wealthy associates in the American Legion and other veterans' organizations and convinced them to make contributions to the nearly depleted coffers of the Democratic Party and pledge their political support to the president.[6] During that period, Senator J. Howard McGrath, the new DNC chairman, who was on the lookout for effective fund-raisers, noticed Johnson's skill at raising money.

Johnson and McGrath eventually developed a close working relationship, but their first meeting was not promising. That encounter took place in May 1948, when Johnson visited the chairman's office to discuss what role he could play in the upcoming presidential campaign. When Johnson arrived, McGrath was on the phone. He was informed of Johnson's presence but accepted another call before receiving his visitor. Unaccustomed to being kept waiting, Johnson exploded, "Young man, I didn't come here to cool my heels waiting for you. I have more important things to do. I came here to help the Democratic Party. I have nothing further to say to you. Good-by."

As Johnson stormed toward the door, McGrath intercepted him, told him of the importance of the calls, and pointed out that they shared the goal of helping the Democratic Party. Johnson calmed down and after further discussion agreed to use his spare time to raise funds for the party.[7] Johnson immediately began beating the bushes for money, but his task became increasingly difficult because as the summer wore on the prospects for a strong Democratic showing seemed increasingly remote.

By June, President Truman had used his patronage power to greatly increase the chances that he would be nominated at the upcoming national convention, and he set off on a nationwide tour to rally bipartisan support. As he traveled to California by train, he stopped and made seventy-five off-the-cuff speeches in the 18-day sojourn. While in Spokane, the president finally touched upon a chord that the lackluster trip needed when he criticized the Republican-dominated 80th Congress as being the worst ever.[8] The crowds responded with shouts of "pour it on, Harry."

Nevertheless, Truman's popularity remained about the same, and when the Republicans opened their convention in Philadelphia in late June, they were convinced that they were about to select the next president of the United States. Congresswoman Clare Booth Luce kicked off the convention and set the celebratory tone when she told the cheering delegates that Truman was a "gone goose."[9] Although there were several qualified contenders for the top spot on the Republican ticket, including Robert Taft, Arthur Vandenberg, and Harold Stassen, New York governor Thomas Dewey, who almost beat Roosevelt in 1944, led from the beginning and secured the nomination on the third ballot. Joining Dewey on the ticket was a California liberal, Governor Earl Warren.

As the convention closed, the Republicans felt better than ever. They had a formidable candidate, a ticket of young and talented governors from the two largest states, a progressive platform, and a sound, well financed organization. Furthermore, with a country racked by inflation and labor difficulties and a Democratic president under attack from all quarters, the GOP was confident that it was about to break the opposition's 16-year control of the White House.[10]

While the Republicans seemed to have their house in perfect order, the Democrats were in deep trouble. Serious feuding had split the party. Truman's "conservativeness" had alienated the liberal New Deal wing of the party, and in late 1947 that group, led by Henry Wallace, Roosevelt's former secretary of agriculture and vice president, bolted the party after a dispute with Truman and formed the Progressive Party with Wallace as its presidential candidate. Then, in early 1948, Truman's advocacy of a strong civil rights program cost him the support of southern Democrats. Those factors plus the chief executive's low standing in popularity polls led to a movement from within the party to convince General Dwight D. Eisenhower to be the standard-bearer. Based on a diary discovered in 2004, it appears that President Truman himself, despairing of his chances, asked General Eisenhower to announce that he would be willing to run as the Democratic candidate for president; Truman said that he would be glad to serve as Ike's vice president.[11]

However, on Friday, July 9, on the eve of the Democratic convention, Eisenhower made a statement that he would not run and it became clear that Harry Truman, the incumbent president, would be the nominee. Meanwhile, Truman was almost begging William O. Douglas, a member of the Supreme Court and a card-carrying New Dealer, to be his running mate. But Douglas turned him down, reportedly telling friends that he "didn't want to be number two man to a number two man."[12]

The 1948 Democratic National Convention opened on July 12 at Convention Hall in Philadelphia, where the Republicans had nominated Dewey only weeks before. Delegates would later remember the heat and humidity along with and the lights and paraphernalia that went with television coverage. Louis Johnson was on the floor shuttling between the West Virginia delegation, the DNC hierarchy, and the American Legion leadership.

After a made-for-television keynote speech by Senator Alben Barkley of Kentucky that roused the sweat-soaked delegates out of their seats, the delegates rather unenthusiastically nominated Truman and chose Barkley as his running mate. Truman had more anger about Douglas's refusal to become the vice presidential nominee than enthusiasm about the choice of Barkley, a 71-year-old politician who would bring no geographic diversity to the ticket.

The real excitement of the 1948 convention came when a floor fight broke out over the civil rights plank in the party platform. On July 14, young mayor Hubert Humphrey of Minneapolis electrified the convention and the nation when he courageously told the delegates, "The time has arrived for the Democratic Party to get out of the shadow of states' rights and walk forthrightly into the bright sunshine of human rights."[13] Although Truman favored the civil rights platform, he was terribly distressed by Humphrey's speech because he felt the firebrand Humphrey was almost daring southerners to leave the party. In fact, that is what happened. In the glare of the TV lights, the southerners walked out of the convention and formed the States' Rights Party, nominating Governor Strom Thurmond of South Carolina as their candidate and Governor Fielding Wright of Mississippi for the second spot on the Dixiecrat ticket.[14]

With the party badly fractured and the convention in complete disarray, Harry Truman stepped up to the podium at 2 A.M. on July 15, long after the television audience was asleep, to deliver his acceptance speech, a speech which brought the exhausted delegates to their feet and showed them the measure of the man who would lead them against all odds. With his chin out and his voice strong, he began by saying, "Senator Barkley and I will win this election and make these Republicans like it—don't you forget that."[15] The delegates roared and stamped their feet with genuine affection and admiration for the courage of the feisty little man in the spotless white linen suit.

Notwithstanding Truman's gutsy speech and his political masterstroke of calling the Republican-dominated Congress back into special session on "Turnip Day," July 26, and daring them to make good on their platform promises, the fact remained that the Democratic Party was caught in a three-way split. President Truman's chances for victory seemed to be practically nil—a view widely predicted by political analysts and "confirmed" by public opinion polls.

As the hot summer days of August passed, it became increasingly apparent that come January, Thomas Dewey would be entering the White House.[16]

Money Man

While the summer faded, Truman continued to express great optimism over his chances of winning the election. However, his apparent confidence was not shared by the public or even his own party leaders. Because of the prospect of "certain defeat" in the upcoming presidential election, the DNC found raising money for Truman's candidacy next to impossible, and as the real campaign season prepared to open in early September the party was broke. After all, no one wanted to pour their money down a rat hole.[17]

Truman realized that to win the election it would take much more than enthusiasm—it would take money too. Trains, radio time, newspaper advertising, and professional staff all cost a great deal of money, and without it there could be no campaign. With this in mind, on August 19, the president asked Bernard Baruch, who had just turned seventy-eight, to join the DNC finance committee and perhaps become its chair. A week later, Baruch responded pleasantly that he had a policy of never serving on any party committee, which was true.

Harry Truman was outraged that this self-styled advisor to presidents would turn him down in his hour of need. On August 31, the president wrote Baruch, "A great many honors have been passed your way, both to you and to your family, and it seems that when the going gets rough it is a one-way street. I am sorry that this is so."[18] Bernard Baruch would not enter the White House again during the Truman presidency.

On September 1, with the election only two months away, the Democratic Party did not even have a chairman for its finance committee. During the first week in September the president invited nearly eighty well-to-do party members, including Louis Johnson, to the White House to discuss campaign finances. At that gathering, which was attended by only fifty of those receiving invitations, Truman optimistically predicted he would be victorious, but only if he had the necessary funds. He then appealed to the group for a volunteer to head the finance committee. Not surprisingly, no one stepped forward.[19] According to one party insider, "Nobody wanted the tough job of going out and asking people to put up money on somebody that was going to lose."[20] During the course of the meeting, several individuals suggested that Johnson, who had been exhorting them for not coming to the aid of the party, undertake the job, but he declined, and the gathering ended with the position still unfilled.[21]

The following morning the president called Johnson and privately explained his plight. He needed an effective finance chairman—and he needed one fast. The opening leg of the campaign was a week away and the party was broke. Would Johnson take the job? After a brief discussion of what would be required,

Johnson replied, "Yes."[22] A few days later, on September 14, just three days before the president started out on a nationwide whistlestop campaign, Howard
McGrath officially announced that Johnson would serve as the DNC's finance
chairman.[23]

Johnson's motives for accepting the post were and continue to be the subject of
conjecture. According to the West Virginian, he undertook the job out of loyalty
to the Democratic Party and out of friendship with Harry Truman.[24] Many of
Johnson's detractors, as well as some of his advisors and friends, such as Jean Kearney, considered his explanation to be nonsense. They contended that he was willing to gamble that Truman might pull off the impossible; if that happened, the
finance chairman would be in line for a substantial political appointment.

Other critics saw Johnson as even more calculating, maintaining that he envisioned from the beginning that he could parlay his position as fund-raiser
into an appointment as secretary of defense. The motive, they contended, was
to gain the vindication he had been looking for ever since Roosevelt had
forced him out of the War Department eight years before.[25] According to gossip in the capital, Johnson accepted the position only after Truman promised
him the defense post if he was victorious. Both Truman and Johnson steadfastly denied any such agreement, and no evidence has ever been discovered
to substantiate such a pact.[26] Nevertheless, no one who knew Johnson was
naive enough to think that he was not well aware of the fact that if he accepted
the job and Truman won, he would be appropriately rewarded.

While Johnson's enemies, admirers, and friends had different views about
why he accepted the finance post, they could not argue about how well he performed the job. In less than two months, he almost single-handedly raised what
at that time was the very sizeable amount of almost $2 million. Shortly after the
election, the president noted that before Johnson got involved, the campaign
was "strapped" and "couldn't buy radio time" or pay for tours, but after he became the fund-raiser "we were able to make the necessary tours and get some
. . . radio time."[27] The assessment of Jack Redding, the DNC's publicity director, was that "Johnson had a tremendous impact on the campaign. If it had not
been for his truly gargantuan fund-raising efforts, the whole thing would have
collapsed."[28] The president's daughter, Margaret, later noted that Johnson
"took on the thankless job and proceeded to accomplish miracles."[29] Another
close observer of the 1948 campaign assessed his contribution by noting that
"without his efforts there would have been disaster."[30]

Campaign Finance

With the DNC treasury empty when he was appointed finance chair in mid-
September, Johnson sprang into action. The first thing he did was sign a personal note for $100,000 which provided cash to pay off debts and keep the

wolves from the door. By putting his own assets and name on the line, Johnson signaled his confidence in Truman, which enabled him to persuade others to make similar financial commitments.

After paying off the most persistent creditors, Johnson's next challenge was to quickly raise the cash needed to pay for the campaign train, which was scheduled to leave Union Station on September 17—the beginning of the legendary whistlestop campaign. He called around Washington and invited a number of wealthy friends and clients to the White House. At that gathering in the Red Room, Truman got up on a chair and appealed for financial support—noting that if $25,000 was not forthcoming the Truman Special would not get beyond Pennsylvania. Two of Johnson's friends pledged $10,000 each. Several others chipped in, and the Truman Special departed on schedule.[31]

Having solved the most immediate problem, Johnson got organized. Because he lacked confidence in the DNC and didn't completely trust many of its people, he moved most of the fund-raising operations into his own offices at Steptoe & Johnson. He also established an office at the Biltmore Hotel in New York City and persuaded Manhattan plastics manufacturer Nathan Lichtblau to become his chief deputy. Together, they quickly drew up a plan and set out in search of substantial funds. Although some help was forthcoming from party workers, Johnson and Lichtblau did most of the fund-raising.[32]

According to Johnson, he "worked like hell" and "telephoned everybody." By "everybody" he meant exactly that. He contacted all cabinet members, high-ranking bureaucrats, ambassadors, and Democratic senators and representatives. Most of those contacted made some contribution, but a few, such as Secretary of Defense James Forrestal, refused. Johnson had just picked up a check from treasury secretary John Snyder when he ran into Forrestal in Snyder's waiting room. Johnson put his arm on Forrestal's shoulder and said, "Jim, I'm glad to see you. I just picked up $10,000 from John and his wife for the campaign. I'll be over to see you in a few days." Forrestal replied, "Don't come to see me. I'm not going to give a dime to the campaign."[33]

Forrestal's refusal was bad news for the campaign, but it was the best possible news for Louis Johnson and his ambition to become the next secretary of defense. Johnson made sure that Truman and practically everyone else knew that Forrestal had refused to help the president in his hour of need.

Johnson called on countless business and labor leaders and pressured them to contribute. Floyd Odlum, who had taken over control of Convair (on whose board Johnson continued to serve), contributed $3,000 and raised another $20,000 from his wealthy friends and business associates. Cornelius Vanderbilt Whitney, a devoted Democrat who had helped finance and found Pan American Airways, was a key "angel," as was Robert Butler, a St. Paul shipbuilder, banker, and ambassador to Cuba. Carrol Cone, a vice president of Pan American Airways and a Democrat from Arkansas, raised more than $300,000 from

Democrats as well as Dixiecrats and Republicans. Edwin Pauley, a California oilman and grain speculator, squeezed large sums out of his West Coast oil buddies. Tom Evans from Kansas City raised more than $100,000 in the Midwest. William Helis, who had become rich in the oil business and was known in New Orleans as the golden Greek, made large personal contributions and helped Johnson raise money, just as he had for Huey Long. Finally, David Dubinsky, president of the International Ladies Garment Workers' Union, succumbed to Johnson's persuasive powers and ended up raising a great deal of money for Truman; he also paid for several radio broadcasts.[34]

The survival of Israel rested in the hands of the next president, and Johnson and Lichtblau raised a bundle of money from the Jewish community. Jacob Blaustein, a multimillionaire who was president of the American Jewish Committee, became a major contributor, as did Milton Kronheim, who controlled the wholesale liquor business in Washington, D.C. Albert Greenfield, one of the biggest hotel, theater, department store, and real estate operators in the country, was instrumental in helping Johnson and Lichtblau pump money into Truman's whistlestop tours and radio broadcasts.[35]

Johnson did not limit his fund-raising efforts to Democrats. He followed what he called the "two-party system"; he visited individuals who had contributed to Dewey's campaign and urged them to take out "insurance" by contributing to Truman's cause — just in case the president won. Of the first $300,000 raised, $200,000 was gathered from such an appeal.[36]

Johnson also used his ties with Legionnaires throughout the country to good advantage. When he contacted such acquaintances, he would use his powers of persuasion and charm to secure support. If that did not work, he would use his physical size and overbearing nature to gain his ends. In either case, people found him a very difficult man to say no to, and his appeals brought hundreds of thousands of dollars into the party coffers.[37]

In spite of such herculean efforts, money for many campaign activities frequently was not available, and in numerous instances Johnson used personal funds to meet expenses. Although he was ultimately reimbursed for funds he advanced, he had no real assurance he would ever get his money back. Meeting day-to-day expenses was usually a nightmare, and he was forced to use all the ingenuity he could muster to meet the challenge. Frequently, this meant writing a check on Saturday for funds not yet received, then raising the money over the weekend and depositing it on Monday before the check cleared.

Another tactic had to be developed when NBC and CBS demanded payment for radio broadcasts in advance; they would cut off broadcasts exactly when the time purchased was up. On several occasions this resulted in the president being cut off in mid-sentence. At first the finance chairman was appalled at such "insulting treatment of the President," but then he saw it as a positive factor because he believed that such actions would annoy other Americans just as it did him and project the image of a man waging an uphill battle against all fronts. One day, in the middle of one of Truman's speeches, a broadcast executive called Johnson and said, "We'll have to cut him off in a minute unless you agree to put up $25,000." Johnson replied, "Go ahead, that will mean another million votes." Eventually, Johnson had Truman's broadcasts intentionally cut off early to dramatize the shortage of campaign funds.[38]

Because of the desperate need for funds, the temptation to skirt the $5,000 limit on individual contributions was great. On one occasion Johnson told DNC counsel Wellburn Mayock to return a $30,000 check by a single individual because "30 is more than 5." Mayock arranged to have the $30,000 given to the DNC in the form of several smaller contributions by individuals and institutions. In his own words, "I got rid of the $30,000 and got it where it was supposed to go."[39]

Whether Johnson knew of this and similar efforts to avoid the spirit of the campaign finance laws during the 1948 campaign is not known. What is known is that the laws were loosely written, that Johnson was a good lawyer who purported to comply, and that there is no evidence that Johnson knowingly participated in violations of campaign finance laws.

While Johnson was working night and day to raise money, President Truman was engaged in the most strenuous and exhausting campaign ever conducted by an incumbent president. Traveling over 31,000 miles by train, he made 356 whistlestop speeches in mid-sized and small towns across the country. An estimated 12 to 15 million Americans came out to see him.

Choosing to ignore the renegades from his own party and not wishing to meet the formidable Governor Dewey head on, Truman decided to attack the "do nothing" Republican-controlled Congress for failing to pass measures he had advocated even after he had given them another chance by calling a special session of Congress on Turnip Day following the convention. As he put it, he was going "to give them hell" — and he did. But he also advocated his own programs, which called for strong civil rights legislation, higher price supports for agriculture, expansion of Social Security, and repeal of the Taft-Hartley Act.

The size of the crowds that mobbed Truman on that famous whistlestop campaign surprised and astounded the pundits, pollsters, and reporters. The president was consistently outdrawing Dewey, and "give 'em hell Harry" was connecting with the crowds. Yet the pollsters still predicted a Dewey victory, and reporters overwhelmingly concurred.[40]

In late October, with the help of Louis Johnson, the American Legion paid Truman's expenses to address its convention in Miami. A crowd of 200,000 greeted the president as he drove through Miami. Just before the president arrived at Roney Plaza, Johnson was called to the presidential suite, which was jammed with Legionnaires and politicians. Johnson asked Truman's advance man, "Is there anything I can do?" The reply came back, "Yeah, get these people out of the suite. This is for the president and Mrs. Truman and Margaret." So 240-pound Louis Johnson began pushing people out of the suite, and *Life* magazine featured a photo of him doing it. Among the people he shoved out was Strom Thurmond, who was running on the Dixiecrat ticket against Truman.[41]

Truman delivered one of his few foreign policy speeches of the campaign to the Legion delegates gathered at Dinner Key, an unbearably hot barn with a galvanized-iron roof. There, he made clear his desire to promote greater understanding with the Soviet Union. This was an effort to diffuse the storm of criticism he had received a few weeks before when it became known that he had authorized and then canceled a special mission by Chief Justice Vinson to negotiate peace with Joseph Stalin. The aborted peace mission by a Supreme Court Justice with no foreign policy experience was regarded as a desperate election-year stunt and an insult to the secretary of state, George Marshall.[42]

As the dramatic campaign of 1948 entered its final stages, Johnson continued his all-out efforts. Less than a week before the election, the Democrats felt that they had a chance of carrying New York, but only if they could raise an additional $50,000 for advertising and a radio broadcast by Eleanor Roosevelt. Fund-raisers were not optimistic that the money could be found, but Johnson promised to come up with the funds, and in several days he succeeded. Thanks to Louis Johnson, Mrs. Roosevelt delivered a very expensive ($25,721) six-minute short-wave broadcast from Paris.[43] In addition, the DNC was able to pay for and disseminate comic books on the life of Truman. During the last few days of the campaign, Johnson helped Hollywood distribute a film on Truman which was shown in movie theaters across the country.[44]

In spite of the efforts of Truman, his talented staff, the New Dealers who were returning to the fold, and his principal fund-raisers, the outlook on election day did not appear bright. Even many of Truman's closest friends and most ardent supporters were not optimistic, and the political polls confirmed that Dewey would be victorious.[45] All the gloomy talk did not discourage Johnson, and he remained optimistic about the outcome, at least outwardly. When his friends suggested that he had probably bet on the wrong horse, he was not bothered because he knew that when one bets on a long shot and wins, the rewards are substantial.[46]

The campaign came to an end on November 2, when more than 46 million Americans voted. The following morning Truman and his supporters learned that they had won. It was the political upset of the century. For Johnson, who had been up most of the night, the morning of November 3 brought forth a new burst of activity. When he was sure that Truman had won, he called Jean Kearney from his apartment at the Mayflower and said, "Miss Kearney, do you recall that I gave you a list of seventy-five names and I dictated a letter? Type up that letter and send it to those seventy-five people *now*." Kearney protested, "I've been up all night and I think I'm getting pneumonia." Showing no mercy, Johnson said, "I didn't ask you how you felt, I told you to do it now."[47]

So Jean Kearney hustled back to the DNC offices and typed up and sent out the seventy-five letters to wealthy individuals who had declined to contribute during the campaign or who might like to give more now that Truman had won. Johnson's letters indicated that President Truman would greatly appreciate contributions to pay off campaign debts, and the letters inferred that those who contributed immediately would be treated as pre-election supporters of the president.

While Kearney was rushing to the DNC, an imposing-looking gentleman was waiting outside the darkened offices of Steptoe & Johnson on the tenth floor of the Shoreham Building. Henry Ikenberry, the first lawyer to arrive that morning, recognized the man in the shadows immediately. "Mr. Harriman," said Ikenberry, "how can I help you?" Averell Harriman, dressed in a hand-stitched cashmere topcoat and smoking a cigarette, said in a low, cultured voice, "I would like to see Colonel Johnson." Ikenberry let the fabulously wealthy Harriman into the Steptoe offices, made him comfortable, and told him the Colonel would be in very soon. When Johnson arrived a few minutes later, the two of them went into Johnson's inner sanctum and closed the door.[48]

There is no record of what Averell Harriman and Louis Johnson discussed that morning. Harriman, famously parsimonious, had only given $500 during the election campaign.[49] In light of the timing of his visit to Johnson's office and in view of Harriman's vast wealth and ambition to continue in government service, it is very likely that he made a substantial additional contribution to the campaign and that he asked Johnson to back him in his bid to persuade Truman to appoint him as secretary of state.

Later that day—the day after the election—Louis Rosenthal, the CEO of Schenley Liquors, who had contributed $25,000 to the Dewey campaign and would become a client of Steptoe & Johnson, arrived at Johnson's office with a check for the DNC. Johnson called Matt Connelly, one of Truman's aides, and asked what he should do with the check. Connelly said, "You have to pay your bills, take it. Just make a little notation [that it was late]."[50]

With men like Harriman and Rosenthal courting him and acknowledging his newfound influence and access to Truman, Louis Johnson was exactly where he wanted to be. He had worked incredibly hard and a stunning success had been achieved. That the president appreciated the job Johnson had done was evident from the telegram he sent him, which said, "It was a glorious victory in the achievement of which you made such an outstanding contribution. A less valiant spirit would have fallen before the obstacles which you overcame. My eternal gratitude is yours."[51] Johnson appreciated the gratitude, but he was hoping for something a little more tangible for his efforts.

Several days after the election, the president, at his doctor's insistence, headed to Key West for a much-needed vacation. When he arrived, he telephoned Johnson and invited him down for some relaxation himself. Johnson declined on the ground that he was still heavily involved in fund-raising activities—and indeed he was.[52] Beginning the day after the election, Johnson received the first of thousands of backdated checks from individuals who had "just discovered" that their secretaries or wives had "forgotten" to send in their contributions. These belated efforts to show "Harry" they were behind him "all the way" brought in several hundred thousand dollars. As Margaret Truman later revealed, when the Trumans returned to Washington after the election, they found "our money man," Louis Johnson, "sitting under a blizzard of back-dated checks—some $750,000 worth, attributable to the . . . get-on-the-bandwagon set."[53]

The cascade of additional funds was used to pay off the remaining expenses, and what was left was put aside for future party activities. When Johnson ultimately gave up his finance job in January 1949, he left the Democratic National Committee in extremely good financial shape.[54]

Much has been written to explain and analyze the election of 1948. Most of those accounts either explain how Dewey and the Republicans lost it or how Truman single-handedly won it. Certainly the president and his top campaign advisors, especially Clark Clifford, did a masterful job. But a large share of the credit is also due to the man who took the job of raising the money necessary to carry on the campaign when no one else was willing to step forward. Truman was not wealthy and neither were his friends, and money had to be raised from outside sources. When Truman found the DNC broke just one week before he was to begin his campaign in earnest, it was Johnson who stepped in and performed his miraculous money-raising act.

Many students of the election fail to realize a factor pointed out by Truman's publicity director, Jack Redding. Redding noted that without Johnson, "There would have been no money for which to pay for the president's campaign train, there'd have been no money for radio, no money for printing, no money for any of the multitude of items which require cash to be transformed into action."[55] That Johnson's contribution was significant was beyond question.

Payoff?

In the latter days of December and early January, Johnson was heavily involved in planning the inauguration ceremonies with Perle Mesta, the stout, opinionated, and very rich widow who ruled Washington society mainly because she was a friend of the president and an even closer friend of First Lady Bess Truman. On several occasions Johnson and Mrs. Mesta conferred with the president in the White House on such things as the parade, the inaugural ball, and the reception.[56] Throughout this period the press consistently speculated that Johnson would receive a political plum, and the position of defense secretary was frequently mentioned.[57]

At last all of the planning came to fruition, and on Inauguration Day, January 20, the nation's capital celebrated the beginning of Truman's first full term as president. That evening, as Louis and Ruth traveled to the National Guard Armory for the inaugural ball, he realized that they were witnessing the beginning of an important new chapter in the nation's history. In that chapter he hoped to play a major role.

The events that led to Johnson's nomination as secretary of defense are not entirely clear, not because information on that subject is lacking but because there are so many conflicting stories from those involved. Perhaps somewhere in the maze of facts lies the truth. According to Johnson, the appointment was completely unsolicited. He maintained that shortly after the election he told the president that in taking the finance chairmanship he had disqualified himself from any federal position and that he "neither wanted nor would accept any appointment." He also made this position clear to Ruth in the weeks prior to the inauguration.[58]

Johnson claimed it was a complete surprise when Truman summoned him to the White House on January 28, where the chief executive informed him that Secretary of Defense James Forrestal wished to speak to him. A few minutes later he met with Forrestal in the vacant office of appointments secretary Matthew Connely. According to Johnson, Forrestal told him that with the president's approval he was asking him "to take over his job as secretary of defense because he thought I was the best-qualified man in America to succeed him." The conversation then turned to discussion of rumors that each had been trying to undercut the other, and both denied that they had engaged in any such activity.

As Johnson recalled, the two men then went down the hall to visit with Truman, who "insisted" that Johnson accept the defense position. In trying to persuade him to take the job, Truman stated that both General Eisenhower and General Marshall had indicated that Johnson was the "logical successor" to the post. "I had no choice under the circumstances. I accepted the position—tough as I knew it was going to be," Johnson later said. Discussion then turned to the transition; they decided that the change of command would take place on May 1 and that in the interim the two men would work together to make the change as smooth as possible.[59]

Johnson gave this account of what transpired several weeks after his appointment and stuck with it until his dying day. Ten years later, he was to say, "I have had so many inquiries about this appointment that it is disgusting."[60] He then reiterated his original story—an account approved by Truman before Johnson ever gave it.[61] In essence, Truman was later to substantiate Johnson's account by recalling that Forrestal "left because of failing health" and that "he, himself, recommended Louis Johnson as his successor."[62]

Although Johnson's and Truman's stories appear to be in general agreement and there are no reports of Forrestal's version, probably due to his mental illness and subsequent suicide, there are a number of reasons to question if events really occurred as reported. In a secret memorandum written in 1950, Truman recalled,

> When I saw Jim Forrestal was cracking up under the pressures of reorgani-
> zation of the defense departments [*sic*], I looked around for a successor.
> Louis Johnson had been known to me since 1918. He had been . . . Assistant
> Secretary in the old War Department . . . and had helped me to win the
> election of 1948. I came to the conclusion that he could relieve Forrestal
> and do the unification job that needed to be done.[63]

In this account, given eighteen months after the events, the president states that he, not Forrestal, had come up with the possibility of Johnson. This is in sharp contrast to his much later recollection that Forrestal suggested Johnson.

Likewise, the president's comments to his aides during the period prior to the inauguration lend credence to the conclusion that it was Truman, not Forrestal, who originated the idea that Johnson should replace Forrestal. One day in January, Truman asked his naval aide, Captain Robert Dennison, "Do you know who the Secretary of Defense is?" Dennison, not knowing for sure whether the president was joking, said, "Yes, sir. It's James Forrestal." "You're wrong," said Truman. "I'm the Secretary of Defense. Jim [Forrestal] calls me ten times a day to ask me to make decisions that are completely within his competence, and it's getting more burdensome all the time."[64]

Johnson's story is also suspect because of his claims that Generals Eisenhower and Marshall had supported him as the "logical successor" to Forrestal. According to Eisenhower, it was in early March when Forrestal "told me that his place was to be taken by Louis Johnson."[65] Eisenhower's surprise at the news suggests that he was not an active supporter of the nomination before it was announced. Then there is Marshall, and it appears unlikely, in light of his unpleasant and difficult dealings with Johnson in 1939 and 1940, that he would have promoted him for the position.[66] Moreover, both of the generals had been on the Washington scene far too long to risk going out on a political limb by actively pushing a person for the secretaryship.

Finally, Washington columnist Drew Pearson, who was frequently fed information by Johnson, reported that Truman brought up the secretary of defense position and the possible departure of Forrestal on January 13, before the inauguration.[67] Pearson's diary says that after Truman called Forrestal a "God-damn Wall Street bastard" and brought up the secretary of defense job to Johnson, Johnson said, "I don't want to talk about that or anything else. You don't owe me anything. I just want to tell you some time how Forrestal tried to cut your throat during the campaign."[68]

Whether there was ever an agreement before election day, stated or implied, that Johnson would be rewarded with a political position if Truman won is unknown because both men vehemently denied it and no evidence of such an understanding has ever surfaced.[69] There was, however, a widespread feeling among defense officials, reporters, and columnists that such was the case. Marx Leva, a Washington lawyer who served under Forrestal and later as assistant secretary of defense under Johnson, stated, "It was my impression that as the leading fund-raiser he had his choice of jobs. This [secretary of defense] is the one he wanted."[70] Typical of the attitude held by many news analysts were those of Doris Fleeson, Marquis Childs, and Joseph C. Harsch, all of whom contended that Johnson was being given the post as payment for the job he did in raising campaign funds.[71] Even Johnson's good friend Senator Harley Kilgore believed that Johnson received "a promise of a Cabinet post from Truman, in exchange for raising campaign money."[72]

Press reports that Johnson might replace Forrestal surfaced shortly after Truman's November victory. There seemed to be a growing consensus that Forrestal's problems surrounding unification of the armed forces, his differences with the president over policy in Palestine, his close ties with Wall Street, and his refusal to support Truman in the recent campaign, both verbally and financially, had sealed his fate at the Pentagon. Although several possible replacements were mentioned, Johnson's name came up most frequently. Such speculation subsided for a time in mid-January, when Forrestal indicated he would stay on and the president told the press that he would.[73] As a result of those statements some observers felt that as Inauguration Day arrived, Forrestal had ridden out the storm.

But the political winds buffeting Forrestal did not subside. Even though they admit there is no direct evidence, Forrestal's biographers, Townsend Hoopes and Douglas Brinkley, believe that Truman told Forrestal in a private talk on January 11 that he was going to nominate Johnson as his new defense secretary.[74] The circumstantial evidence indicates that Truman and Johnson probably agreed during an off-the-record meeting on January 17 that Johnson would replace Forrestal but that they decided to say nothing until after the inauguration.

Although Forrestal later contended that it was not until March 1 that he learned of the change in command, the evidence does not lend persuasive support for that view. In February, Johnson and Forrestal and their respective offices were in frequent contact—an unlikely alliance if the change had not already been discussed.[75] Moreover, Brigadier General Louis Renfrow was detached from the White House and sent by Johnson to the Pentagon to act as liaison between himself and Forrestal.[76] On February 4, Forrestal went to Johnson's office for a two-hour visit, a rather long time for a social chat. Three days later Johnson accompanied Truman to Key West, and in the days that followed he requested that Forrestal send numerous reports and information to him. The material was taken to Johnson's office at Steptoe & Johnson and then forwarded to him.[77] It was at this time that unification and economization of the armed forces were identified as the president's major concerns. The fact that

Forrestal did not accompany the others indicates his low standing with the chief executive at that time.

The primary reason for the delay in naming Johnson was a pending request by the air force to purchase an additional three dozen B-36 bombers. The delay stemmed from the fact that the planes were built by Convair, the company controlled by Floyd Odlum, and Johnson was a member of its board of directors. He needed time to cut his ties with that corporation and he wanted Forrestal to make any decision on the aircraft so that he could not be accused of conflict of interest.[78] In late February, the air force request was getting near the secretary's desk, but before it did, President Truman felt that time for the anticipated change of command could not be put off any longer.

On March 1, Forrestal was summoned to the White House. The president minced no words as he told him that circumstances were such that he found it necessary to request his resignation immediately. A shaken Forrestal returned to his office not really sure what had happened or why.[79] More than a year later, Truman claimed that he was forced to act because Forrestal "was cracking up under the pressures of reorganization."[80] Whether that was his real reason or whether subsequent events were to make that a plausible explanation is unclear. Perhaps he felt that he could not delay attending to the pressing problems of unification.

That evening, Forrestal returned to Prospect House, his eighteenth-century mansion in Georgetown overlooking the Potomac River. Working alone in his study, with his mentally ill and alcohol-addicted wife Josephine upstairs, Forrestal began drafting his letter of resignation, speaking several times to his close friend Ferdinand Eberstadt in New York.[81] The next morning, Forrestal submitted his resignation, effective March 31, and Truman immediately accepted it. The following day the president announced Forrestal's resignation and Johnson's nomination at a White House press conference.[82]

The capital was abuzz. At a fashion show, Perle Mesta blurted to reporters, "Did you hear the news? That stinker Forrestal is out. My man Johnson is in."[83] Press reaction to the official announcement that Johnson would move to the Pentagon was mixed. Some sources, such as the *Army and Navy Journal*, praised the selection, citing Johnson's training and experience as well as his "character, ability, extraordinary vigor and determination." Others followed the lead of the *New York Times*; editorial writers remained cautiously neutral by indicating they would take a wait-and-see attitude before making a judgment. Although most news analysts saw Johnson's appointment as a blatant form of political payoff, they were willing to give him a chance to prove himself.[84]

That the selection of Johnson was in part politically motivated cannot be denied. However, to draw the conclusion that he was chosen only to pay a political debt ignores the fact that Johnson had a number of professional and personal qualifications which made him a logical if not obvious choice for the defense post. First, he was very experienced in defense matters. His military background in supply and logistics and his service with the American Legion and the War Department had prepared him for the job of secretary of defense, and he had an outstanding record in each of these areas. Even his severest critics acknowledged his enthusiasm, administrative ability, and overall competency. Second, he was a dynamic, hard-charging person who was not afraid to knock heads when necessary.[85]

By mid-1948 Truman felt that Forrestal accommodated his service secretaries and military leaders too much,[86] and Johnson's strengths seemed quite attractive. Then there was the West Virginian's propensity for personal loyalty. One characteristic that Johnson had displayed during his years in the War Department and after was a fierce loyalty to the chief executive, and if there was anything Truman tended toward in his cabinet appointments it was a person who would be loyal.[87] In short, the president was looking for an experienced defense executive who could be hard-nosed with subordinates and would be completely loyal to his superior. Harry Truman thought Louis Johnson fit that bill perfectly.

Vindication

In the days following the announcement, Johnson moved swiftly so he could hit the ground running when Forrestal's resignation became effective. He dispatched General Renfrow to the Pentagon to evaluate the second-tier talent and establish working relationships with key personnel. Johnson's first instinct was to fire all of Forrestal's people and replace them with his own, but Renfrow said he could not run the Pentagon without at least two of Forrestal's aides—Marx Leva and Wilfred McNeil. As Renfrow told Johnson, "Leva knows the law; McNeil knows the money and you've got to keep them there." Fortunately, Johnson did not fire these people, and he was to tell Renfrow only a few weeks later that "I couldn't run this shop without them."[88]

Renfrow carried out other changes. Forrestal had been squirreled away in a small unpretentious office on the Mall side of the Pentagon. Renfrow decided that the secretary of the army's much-larger office on the river side would be far more appropriate for the new secretary of defense, so he told the outgoing army secretary, Kenneth Royall, that he would have to vacate his office a little early. In addition, he turned the adjoining chief of staff's office into a dining room for the secretary and moved several pieces of antique furniture, including a beautifully finished table and large highboy which Forrestal had donated to the Pentagon, into the new dining room.

To furnish the secretary's new office, Renfrow found a magnificent 48-drawer desk which had belonged to a secretary of the navy from Vermont in the 1840s in the Pentagon's fourth subbasement and had it refinished and moved upstairs. (This desk would soon be replaced by an even grander desk—

the nine-by-five-foot walnut desk used by General John "Black Jack" Pershing.) He also secured a large table which had been used as General George McClellan's desk when he commanded the Army of the Potomac during the Civil War. Behind the secretary's desk and above the McClellan table he hung a large portrait of George Rogers Clark, the solder-explorer after whom Clarksburg was named.[89]

While Renfrow evaluated talent and set up offices, Johnson himself continued, as he had throughout February, to be in frequent contact with Forrestal as he attempted to learn as much as he could about the position. Those meetings were not very productive because the outgoing secretary became increasingly nervous and distracted. In retrospect, those around Forrestal could see the beginnings of a nervous breakdown, but at the time they thought it was merely overwork. Johnson told Drew Pearson that he first became aware that Forrestal was mentally ill when the two of them met together in the Goldfish Room following a meeting with the president. Johnson said that Forrestal's eyes "bulged" and he displayed some of the same symptoms he saw in his own daughter Lillian who, he told Pearson, was an "incurable mental case."[90]

Whatever the cause, it is clear that during March Forrestal sent mixed signals about his reaction to Johnson as his successor. On March 17, the secretary digressed from a prepared speech to say, "I could hardly leave my job in better hands. By experience, training and temperament, Colonel Johnson is admirably qualified to head our National Military Establishment."[91] Yet a week later he called his special advisor, General Eisenhower, and said, "I simply can't turn the job over to Louis Johnson. He knows nothing about the problems involved and things will go to pot."[92] The latter statement is probably more indicative of his true feeling.

Although Forrestal probably did not believe Johnson was up to the job, and despite the mental illness which led to his suicide, Forrestal sat down two days before he left office and dictated, without benefit of notes, several lengthy memoranda for Johnson and his people on every single defense project. Forrestal told General Renfrow, "I'm going to have these girls put that in a little black book that I want you to give to Johnson, because this will tell him the whole story of the Defense Department around the world." Thus, Forrestal left Johnson with a primer on all of the issues and programs he would soon be dealing with.[93]

While all this was going on, Johnson was busy putting his personal affairs in order so he could assume his new post. He formally terminated his association with all businesses, including Convair, General Dyestuff, GAF, and Steptoe & Johnson. However, he remained on the board of the Union National Bank of Clarksburg, the bank founded by his father-in-law,[94] and he continued to preside at annual meetings of Steptoe & Johnson lawyers, although at Johnson's insistence the firm adopted a policy of not accepting any defense-related legal business during his service as secretary of defense.[95] Having formally divested himself from any venture which might appear to create a conflict of interest, he was ready for scrutiny by the Senate.

In light of the controversy that had surrounded his earlier career in Washington, Johnson expected to be subjected to a thorough and possibly hostile and contentious inquiry by the Senate Armed Services Committee before his name was sent to the floor of the Senate for confirmation. Surprisingly, however, no real problems developed. Only one witness objected, eccentric inventor Lester Barlow, who had been rebuffed by Assistant Secretary of War Johnson in the late 1930s. On the positive side came accolades from representatives of the aircraft industry such as Glenn Martin, founder of Martin Aircraft.

The only topic that seemed to be of vital concern to the committee members was whether Johnson had severed all business associations in which the government was involved, particularly his relationships with Convair and Victor Emanuel. When he gave the group a written statement to that effect, the committee voted unanimously to recommend confirmation. A few days later, on March 23, the committee chairman, Senator Millard Tydings (D-Maryland), presented Johnson's name to the full Senate.[96] In a somewhat unusual development, three Republican senators, Kenneth Wherry of Nebraska, Chan Gurney of South Dakota, and George Malone of Nevada, proceeded to praise Johnson and express confidence in his ability to handle the defense job. Afterward, the nomination was confirmed without objection.[97]

Johnson's swearing in was scheduled to take place at noon on March 28. That morning, the president received a call in the Oval Office. With his aide Captain Dennison, standing next to his desk, Truman listened for a few minutes and then said, "Yes, Jim, that's the way I want it." After hanging up, the president said to Dennison, "That was Forrestal. He wanted me to tell him whether I really wanted him to be relieved by Louis Johnson today."[98]

The swearing in of Colonel Louis Arthur Johnson as the nation's second secretary of defense went forward as scheduled at a ceremony in the center courtyard of the Pentagon so elaborate and so well attended that wags called it "the inaugural."[99] With military bands playing, precision drill teams marching, flags waving, and a thundering flyover of air force fighters and bombers, more than 11,000 people were witnesses as Johnson placed his hand on a Bible given him by a Sunday school teacher when he was a boy in Roanoke and took the oath of office administered by Chief Justice Fred Vinson.

Louis Johnson looked terrific that day. He had just taken off thirty-five pounds through diet and the stress of the campaign, and he appeared trim and powerful in his hand-tailored midnight-blue double-breasted suit.[100] His wife Ruth was by his side, and his friends and law partners from Clarksburg were there. His parents, however, were too old and frail to attend and his daughters were absent—Lillian was still confined at Chestnut Lodge and Kay was no longer on speaking terms with her father, having defied him once again by marrying a man he did not approve of.

Johnson was ebullient—he savored every second of the carefully staged but brief ceremony. At last he had been vindicated! He was the secretary of defense. Nearly a decade earlier the top war department post had been snatched from him, causing him heartbreak and embarrassment. At last the wrong had been righted—to him this moment of glory both acknowledged that what happened in 1940 had been a mistake and marked an opportunity for him to gain a place in history as the head of the National Military Establishment. March 28, 1949, was a big day in his life—it marked an end to years of frustration and the beginning of a great new challenge.

As soon as the swearing-in ceremony was completed, the new secretary issued a statement which set forth his major areas of challenge—economization and unification. He pledged to carry out a defense policy that would provide "the maximum of strength within the limits of our economy" and unite the army, navy, and air force "as one in the service of the nation."[101] At the time, no one realized just how much those two goals were to dominate his service as secretary.

Johnson and Forrestal then proceeded to the White House, where the president had arranged a surprise party for the outgoing secretary, the highlight of which was the presentation of the Distinguished Service Medal. Little did anyone present at that gathering realize the tragic sequence of events that were about to overtake Forrestal in the form of a complete mental breakdown and, within months, the taking of his own life.

That evening the president held a gala dinner in the White House to honor his new defense chief. From Truman, his cabinet members, members of Congress, and generals came praise for the incoming secretary of defense—a situation undoubtedly satisfying to a man with an ego the size of Louis Johnson's. It was an enjoyable evening—a true celebration—a kind of last hurrah before the fun stopped and the real work began.[102] As Johnson basked in the limelight that spring night and thought over the events of the day—probably the greatest day of his life—he understood the magnitude of the task facing him. He knew the job would be "the toughest I have yet tackled."[103]

CHAPTER TEN

Inside the Pentagon

"I AM THE RESURRECTION and the life. . . . Death is swallowed up in victory," intoned the white-robed Episcopal priest. Thus began the burial service for the first U.S. secretary of defense in the marble-columned Arlington amphitheater. As the marine corps honor guard fired three sharp volleys and a bugler sounded taps, James Forrestal finally found peace in a sailor's grave beneath a plain white marker.

Big bald Louis Johnson, Forrestal's successor, walked down the hill, hat in hand, amid the crowd of departing mourners. Only a few days before, on May 22, 1949, Forrestal had shocked the nation when he either leaped or tried to hang himself and then fell to his death from the top floor of Bethesda Naval Hospital, where he had been hospitalized for severe mental illness. Louis Johnson had visited with him for half an hour on April 27 and told reporters that Forrestal "looked fine" and was "making good progress."[1] But everyone knew he was deeply disturbed. Moments before his death, he was copying Sophocles' poem "The Chorus from Ajax," in which Ajax, forlorn and "worn by the waste of time," contemplated suicide.[2]

Many in the capital were saying that the enormous pressures of managing America's defense establishment drove Forrestal to commit suicide. At the funeral and memorial services, they said the job was simply too difficult for one man to handle without losing his sanity. Johnson knew this wasn't true. He had seen the face of mental illness in his daughter Lillian. He believed that Forrestal's paranoia and increasingly erratic behavior were due to some inherent mental defect, not to the stresses of the defense job, no matter how difficult it was.

Johnson seemed to be immune from stress. When Carl Vinson, chairman of the House Armed Services Committee, told him, "You hold the most important,

most controversial, most thankless and most fateful post in the city of Washington," Johnson could not have been happier. Unlike Forrestal and subsequent
secretaries of defense who heard similar words, Johnson felt no sense of dread,
no sense that the weight of the free world rested on his shoulders. He cherished
Vinson's words, particularly the phrase "most important."[3]

As head of the National Military Establishment (as it was called before August
1949, when it became the Department of Defense), Johnson was in charge of an
organization that was the largest employer and biggest single spender, public or
private, in the nation. The department employed 1.6 million uniformed personnel
and several hundred thousand civilian workers. It had an annual budget of $15 bil-
lion, more than one-third of the entire federal budget.[4] The management of such
an enormous operation would have been a staggering task, but to add to that the
handling such thorny problems as unification, economization, equal opportunity,
selective service, and the Soviet threat in a manner pleasing to the president, Congress, the armed services, and the public made the job close to impossible.

Yet Johnson reveled in the opportunity to tackle it. The reasons for the thrill
of the challenge were complex, but they went to the essence of the man. In addition to vindication, there was an opportunity to put his own stamp on the
American military establishment; a chance to achieve lasting fame; and the possibility that the position could serve as a stepping-stone to even bigger and better
things—namely the presidency of the United States.

The defense post offered a perfect opportunity for Johnson's massive ego to
be stroked. Whether Johnson ever seriously considered parlaying the position
into a presidential nomination in 1952 will never be known, but a number of
Pentagon officials, numerous political observers, some close associates, and
most of the people back in Clarksburg steadfastly believed that the ambitious
lawyer had his eyes on the White House. Johnson, however, consistently denied
he had any such aspirations.[5] The only elected office that he ever acknowledged
any interest in was U.S. senator, but he never seriously pursued that idea.[6]

Colossus

The Pentagon was perfect for a man with Johnson's raw ambition and thirst for
power. It was the biggest building in the world—a colossus which symbolized
America's preeminence as a military superpower. It was also the corporate
headquarters for by far the largest business organization the world has ever seen.

From its inception, the Pentagon was highly controversial. It was the subject
of months of debate in Congress on the eve of World War II, when isolationists
had been bitterly opposed to the Pentagon project, most in Congress had objected to its cost, many (including Roosevelt) had fought over its location, and
almost everyone thought it would be a vacant "white elephant" when the war
ended. One remarkably prescient congressman stated, "They want these big

buildings so we can police the world when the war is over." Finally, the deadlock was broken when Congress decided that the building should be designed so that it could be turned into a veteran's hospital after "peace is restored and the Army no longer needs the room."[7]

Construction began five months before Pearl Harbor on a swamp and automobile graveyard across the Potomac River called Hell's Bottom and was completed sixteen months later in January 1943. The building was large enough to house over 27,000 people and had three times the floor space of the Empire State Building, but by the time it opened it was already too small. The five-sided Pentagon was five stories high with several subbasements. It was made up of five separate concentric buildings, labeled the A, B, C, D, and E rings. The five buildings contained eighty-three acres of offices and public spaces, including a shopping center, and seventeen and a half miles of corridors.[8]

At 6:30 A.M. on March 29, 1949, his first day as secretary, Louis Johnson stepped into his office in Room 3E880 on the third floor of the outer ring on the Potomac River side of the Pentagon. The walls had been freshly painted pale blue. It took several long strides for him to walk from the inner door of his office to the huge Pershing desk. Behind his desk, on the McClellan table, he could see three colored phones—a white phone with a direct line to the White House, a red phone that would link him to military commands across the world, and a blue phone that would connect him with his inner circle of aides.[9]

On that first day, virtually all of the 27,000 government workers throughout the cavernous building felt the power of the new secretary because more than half of them were engaged in a "gigantic game of musical chairs." Johnson had implemented a vast and intricate office-shifting plan in order to put an end to the separation of services within the Pentagon and to force generals to rub shoulders with admirals.[10] He also announced that he was abolishing almost 100 advisory committees, groups, and agencies which Forrestal had set up in order to arrive at decisions by consensus rather than by fiat. Snorting that "there are too damn many committees for efficiency's sake," he signaled his intention to grab hold of the Pentagon, quickly make the tough decisions that had to be made, and see that orders were carried out with no second-guessing.[11]

Working with Johnson

After an opening-day press conference which was regarded as a disaster because Johnson hadn't been properly briefed, he retreated to his enormous office, closed the doors, and began to educate himself about the daunting job that lay ahead.[12] Beginning with the detailed memoranda left behind by Forrestal, Johnson immersed himself in briefing materials and issue papers. His powers of concentration were legendary and, as always, he was a very quick study.

Attacking the defense job with the same vigor he gave to every other assignment meant arriving at Room 3E880 by 6:30 A.M. and frequently not departing until 9 or 10 at night. Once he became secretary he rarely socialized, opting instead to remain at home poring over reports and studies. When he had extra time, he read recently published biographies or other works of history that provided insights which would help him in his job.[13]

Not only did Johnson work long and hard, he was extraordinarily efficient. On an average day the secretary would receive thirty-five visitors, attend several meetings, take more than fifty phone calls, make dozens of decisions on administrative and policy matters, and read, approve, and sign countless letters and reports. During his frequent travels, often to address veterans' or business groups (he gave more than fifty speeches during his tenure as secretary), he rarely relaxed, choosing instead to use the opportunity to get caught up on reports and recommendations.[14]

Johnson demanded much of himself and he expected a great deal from those who worked under him. Working for the secretary of defense was not one of the more pleasant pastimes to be found in the nation's capital in 1949 and 1950. While he asked for major commitments in terms of time and energy, it was not so much those demands that created problems as it was his manner of dealing with people. He required accuracy, clarity, and conciseness of himself, and he simply could not tolerate it if he did not receive the same from others.[15] Furthermore, he frequently found it difficult to be civil to those who disagreed or openly challenged him. He could be, and in fact frequently was, arrogant, condescending, and often outright rude.[16] Sometimes it would only be a caustic remark, such as the time he interrupted a briefing officer who was reading from a flip chart and said, "Say what you have to say. I can already read!" Other times he was brutal. Once when a general was making a presentation on projected costs, the secretary, believing the figures were out of line, barked out, "General, you're a liar. Come back tomorrow and apologize. You only missed it by $300 million."[17]

Many subordinates were afraid of him—no one enjoyed being browbeaten. Even his peers considered him difficult to work with. Some leaders, such as Secretary of State Dean Acheson, felt his outbursts reflected mental instability.[18] Others were embarrassed by his actions, such as the time when Major General James Burns cried after Johnson exploded and walked out of a meeting with Dean Acheson and other officials from the State Department.[19] Even a corporate lawyer as tactful as Air Force Secretary Thomas Finletter was forced to admit that "Mr. Johnson was not a very easy man . . . to negotiate with about the problems where there was possible differences of viewpoint."[20]

Service Secretaries

Johnson inherited three civilian service secretaries: Secretary of the Army Kenneth Royall, Secretary of the Navy John Sullivan, and Secretary of the Air Force Stuart Symington. Each headed up branches of the military which were to be unified and subordinated to the Secretary of Defense as military departments in August of 1949 when amendments to the National Security Act went into effect. Under that legislation, Johnson was to acquire unqualified authority and control over the secretaries and their military departments—powers that Forrestal never had.

Secretary of the Army Kenneth Royall, a southerner who had led the fight to block or delay implementation of Truman's July 26, 1948, executive order to racially integrate the army,[21] had already decided to resign by the time Johnson arrived. (Royall would eventually head a distinguished New York City law firm, Rogers & Wells, which was merged into Clifford Chance, a London-based global megafirm.) Commenting on Royall's departure, Johnson said "I'm glad he's gone."[22] Weeks before he was sworn in, Johnson began looking for strong candidates who would support the administration's policy on equal opportunity if not full integration. His first choice to replace Royall as army secretary was Curtis Calder, a utility executive who held controlling interests in Convair and had business ties to Victor Emanuel and Floyd Odlum. Johnson disingenuously tried to convince columnist Drew Pearson and others that the controversial Calder was Truman's pick, not his.[23]

While Johnson was trying to recruit Calder, Gordon Gray, a lawyer and newspaper publisher from North Carolina who was serving temporarily as acting secretary of the army, was being recruited as dean of the University of North Carolina Business School. Early on the morning after Gray accepted the deanship, Johnson telephoned him at home and said, "I can't get Calder to take the job [as secretary of the army]. What do you think about my recommending you to the President?" Gray replied, "Louis, I don't want it. The President knows I want to return to North Carolina and please do not suggest my name because I'm honestly not a candidate."

Gray went off that day to West Point to deliver the commencement address, and while he was gone, Johnson met with President Truman and told him he wanted him to nominate Gray for secretary of the army. Added Johnson, "He wants it so bad he can taste it." Truman was "delighted" and immediately sent Gray's nomination to the Senate without checking with Gray. When Gray returned and learned what had happened, he was outraged. He immediately went to the White House to explain to Truman that he did not want and could not take the job because he was already committed to UNC. After listening to Gray, Truman thought for a minute and then said, "Well, I'll take the rap. I'll just have to send a message up to the Senate and say I made a mistake."

As Gray recalled later, "Suddenly it dawned on me that you don't do that kind of thing to the President of the United States." Gray told Truman he would figure out a way to withdraw from the deanship and would serve as army secretary for a "respectable time." Truman, visibly relieved, said he was "grateful."[24]

There is no record of what either Gray or the president said about Johnson when they met that day, but it is likely that Johnson's handling of the Gray appointment did not sit well with Truman. Despite this rocky start and with the notable exception of his views on integration, Gray went on to serve with distinction under Johnson as secretary of the army. In the spring of 1950, Gray was elected president of the University of North Carolina, and he left government service later that year.[25]

Within a month after Johnson was sworn in, Navy Secretary John Sullivan, another Forrestal holdover, resigned in protest over Johnson's highly controversial cancellation of the Navy supercarrier USS *United States.* This incident led to the "revolt of the admirals" (the subject of the next chapter). Sullivan was replaced by Francis P. Matthews, a lawyer-banker from Omaha who had worked with Johnson as a fund-raiser in the 1948 campaign. Known as the "rowboat secretary" because of his lack of experience with the navy and the ways of Washington, Matthews candidly admitted during confirmation hearings that he had "little prior training or preparation."[26]

The third Forrestal holdover, Air Force Secretary Stuart Symington, a former president of Emerson Electric who would later become a respected senator from Missouri, was increasingly at odds with Johnson over his cost-cutting policies and the way Johnson treated him, but he stayed on for more than a year before resigning. Symington was described as "very nervous," the kind of guy who "thought that the way to get along with the big boss was to be in his office every hour on the hour."[27] Johnson wouldn't put up with Symington's nervous ubiquity. At that time, a special elevator gave Symington direct access to Johnson's office without going through his gatekeepers. He was able to pop into Johnson's presence at any time day or night, and he did so frequently. Johnson used to say, "Now Stu, let me tell you something. When I want you, I'll send for you. But I don't want you to come down here bothering me every hour on the hour. I've got a lot of things to do." Symington persisted. Finally Johnson said, "Now, look, do I have to put a lock on that elevator? You stay out of here until I send for you, and I don't want you in here until I do."[28]

Johnson also suspected that Symington was leaking unfavorable information about him to Stewart and Joe Alsop, the widely read columnists who in early 1950 declared war on Truman's defense policies and on Johnson in particular. One day Stewart Alsop was meeting with Symington in his Pentagon office when Johnson burst in "and stood there, saying nothing, nodding his huge bald head up and down with the air of a virtuous husband who has at last caught his erring wife in flagrante delictu [*sic*]."[29]

The relationship between Johnson and Symington continued to deteriorate until Symington was either asked to resign or simply decided he could not continue to work with Johnson. On April 24, 1950, after ceremonies honoring him, Stuart Symington, flanked by Louis Johnson and Air Force General Hoyt Vandenburg, marched down the front steps of the Pentagon on the river side and got into a waiting car.[30] He was replaced by Thomas Finletter, a well-known Philadelphia lawyer and air power advocate who was Truman's choice rather than Johnson's. In the brief time they worked with one another, just over four months, Johnson and Finletter did not get along.[31]

Secretary Johnson got along much better with top military leaders than he did with the civilian leadership. This undoubtedly stemmed from the fact that an officer could not survive the rise to the top echelons of the military without learning how to work successfully with cantankerous civilians. This is especially true of chiefs of staff and chiefs of the services, including General Dwight Eisenhower. According to Eisenhower, when Johnson asked him to stay on as temporary head of the Joint Chiefs, "I agreed readily, not only because Mr. Johnson was a friend but because I was extremely anxious to see the Defense Department so organized that we could minimize the service rivalries that plagued it."[32]

Johnson also had fine working relationships with Air Force Chief of Staff General Hoyt Vandenburg and Army Chief of Staff General Omar Bradley. However, Johnson never developed a very successful rapport with Bradley's replacement, General J. Lawton "Lightning Joe" Collins.[33] For reasons that will become apparent, Johnson's relationship with Chief of Naval Operations Admiral Louis Denfeld began to deteriorate from the outset and he had virtually no other supporters among navy brass. Nevertheless, the secretary respected all of his top military advisors and almost always listened carefully to what they had to say—a situation that did not hold for his civilian secretaries.

Inner Circles

When Johnson sought advice on difficult and sensitive defense matters he generally looked to a handful of men in the Pentagon. That group, which contained individuals of greatly varying abilities, was comprised of both inherited staff and appointed personnel. From Forrestal's staff, Johnson inherited three top-flight lawyers and civilians whom he came to trust and rely on: Wilfred J. McNeil, a financial wizard who ultimately became comptroller of the Defense Department; Marx Leva, a brilliant Alabama-born troubleshooter who later became Johnson's assistant secretary of defense for legal and legislative affairs; and John M. Ohly, a special assistant who left in November 1949 to become director of the Mutual Defense Assistance Program in the State Department.[34] Johnson worked closely and effectively with these men and although each developed respect for Johnson and regarded him as a very effective secretary of defense, none became his close friend.[35]

The real insiders consisted of a group of longtime friends and associates that Johnson brought with him to the Pentagon. By far the most visible was Steve Early, who had a well-deserved reputation as one of the most skillful and successful public-relations executives in the nation and had been earning $50,000 a year working for the Pullman Company.[36] Although Early knew little about defense issues, Johnson put his old friend and supporter from the Blue Ridge Division into the number-two slot, the newly created position of undersecretary (which became deputy secretary after August 1949).

Washington politicos and pundits whispered that the Early appointment was a shrewd move by Johnson to burnish his image and position himself for a presidential run in 1952. In fact, however, there is evidence that Early was not Johnson's first choice for the undersecretary job and that Truman rejected his preferred choices, John J. McCloy, president of the World Bank, and John Franklin, CEO of United Steamship Lines, because they were too close to Thomas Dewey. Drew Pearson wrote that it was the president himself who suggested Steve Early and that he may have done it because he knew Johnson would need an experienced and trusted friend to help control his temper and smooth his rough edges.[37]

Regardless of who was responsible for bringing Early to the Pentagon, the question of whether he was the right person for the deputy secretary job continues to be debated. Early was certainly loyal to Johnson, and he was one of the few people who could and did openly challenge him. Drew Pearson recalled a time when Early, knowing that Johnson had told him that Curtis Calder was Truman's choice to be secretary of the army and not his own, said, "Louis, you've got to quit lying. You can't lie and get away with it."[38] Early was excellent at public relations and dealing with the press. But he knew nothing about defense issues during a very critical period when Johnson needed someone who was better versed on such matters. Early was a good man—Johnson just had him in the wrong position.[39]

Two other insiders who lacked relevant qualifications and had far less stature than Steve Early were held in mild contempt by the decorated combat veterans who populated the Pentagon in those days, and their presence led to charges of cronyism.[40] A longtime American Legion pal, Paul Griffith, who was in reality Johnson's alter ego in the Defense Department, was made special assistant and later assistant secretary of defense for administrative and public affairs. Griffith, a native of Uniontown, Pennsylvania, had helped Johnson get elected national commander of the Legion and had run the Legion's office in Washington before World War II. During the war, he worked in the War Department, accompanied Johnson to India, and somehow managed to achieve the rank of brigadier general. Griffith drafted all of Johnson's correspondence, operated as a gatekeeper, and was Johnson's liaison with the White House through Truman's military advisor, General Harry H. Vaughn, another American Legion friend who had achieved a high rank in the military while scarcely leaving a Washington desk.[41]

The other insider regarded as a Johnson crony was Brigadier General Louis Renfrow, yet another armchair general, who had been a close friend of Harry Truman and Harry Vaughn since 1919. A dentist in St. Louis and an active

Legionnaire bigwig until he came to Washington in 1941, Renfrow was assigned to the White House shortly after Truman became president. When Johnson asked Truman in January of 1949 if he could take Renfrow with him to the Pentagon, Truman said, "Louie, you can have anybody you want in the White House but me." Renfrow, in good humor, responded, "Mr. President, I know exactly how a galley slave feels when he's sold down the river."[42] Renfrow became a special assistant to Johnson and essentially served as a political troubleshooter. From his first days as a liaison to Forrestal until Johnson's final day in office, Renfrow was completely devoted and loyal to Johnson. But he and Griffith were always looked upon as Johnson gauletiers.[43]

Two other members of Johnson's inner circle were excellent appointments. The day after he took office, Johnson, in one of his smartest moves, named General Joseph T. McNarney, an active-duty air force general, as his special personnel and management expert and charged him with the responsibility of finding ways to cut costs and increase efficiency. Johnson quickly developed a liking for McNarney, and he leaned heavily on him for advice. Eventually Johnson made him chairman of a specially created Management Committee that was to implement his economy program.[44]

Finally, Johnson brought Major General James Burns out of retirement. Burns, who had worked with Johnson when he was assistant secretary of war, was bright, highly respected, and regular army. He understood defense issues as well as the moods and thinking of service personnel. His portfolio was political-military affairs, and eventually his office became responsible for relations with the State Department, the National Security Council, and the North Atlantic Treaty Organization. Because of a heart condition, Burns rarely spent a full day in the Pentagon and relied on his two principal deputies—Najeeb Halaby (who would be CEO of PanAm and father of Queen Noor of Jordan) and Major General Lyman Lemnitzer. Despite his heart condition, Burns was regarded as "a balance wheel" in the secretary's office, which meant that he wasn't afraid to speak openly and candidly to Johnson. As a result, Johnson, even though he had great respect for Burns, often directed his explosive anger and frustration at him, and in some quarters Burns was described as "Johnson's whipping boy."[45]

Those who worked for or around Louis Johnson had strong feelings about him one way or the other. They either liked or despised the man; the attitude was rarely neutral. Supporters pictured him as an open, personable, sincere, and dedicated public servant who knew virtually everything that was going on at the Pentagon. While they may have conceded that at times he was a little rough on people, the important thing was that he got things done. His detractors saw him as an arrogant, ambitious politico who thought he knew everything but actually knew very little. What was being accomplished, they claimed, was being done in spite of the secretary rather than because of him.[46]

Perhaps the major reason Johnson created controversy when he became secretary was that people compared him to his predecessor, James Forrestal. From the standpoint of personality and leadership style, the two men could not have been more different. The big, outgoing, gruff, and gregarious Johnson came across rather strong when compared to the slight, quiet, cerebral, and at times shy Forrestal. The main difference, however, was in decision making. Forrestal tended to thoroughly examine, analyze, study, and discuss with his staff a problem facing him. He would try to forge a consensus, and only then, almost reluctantly, would he arrive at a decision. This deliberate style was in marked contrast to Johnson's style, which was to quickly, almost intuitively, assess a situation and then announce his decision. To many staff members, Johnson's brand of decision making was an attempt to rule by fiat, and that was not appreciated.[47]

The Hill

The same sort of controversy that surrounded Johnson at the Pentagon was also present in his relations with Congress. There was scarcely a single senator or representative that did not have strong feelings, positive or negative, about Secretary of Defense Louis Johnson. Some lawmakers were generally supportive because they agreed with what he was trying to do; advocates of economy in government and balanced budgets applauded his rhetoric and decisions, as did those who favored his stands on such matters as unification, selective service, and racial integration. Since many of the programs he advocated were supported by members of both parties, Johnson was able to find advocates in both camps. In the Senate, Republicans Kenneth Wherry of Nebraska and Chan Gurney of South Dakota were among his strongest supporters, as were Democrats Millard Tydings of Maryland and John Sparkman of Alabama. In the House, Armed Services Committee chairman Carl Vinson of Georgia and Overton Brooks of Louisiana, both Democrats, and Dewey Short of Missouri and Leslie C. Arends of Illinois, staunch Republicans, could be counted upon to defend him.[48]

The number of detractors was far larger. Johnson's enemies were not a cohesive group, though, because they disliked him for a variety of reasons. For some, the hostility was based simply on personality; they considered him haughty, cocky, or completely self-serving. Some disliked him because of his alleged political ambitions. The vast majority, however, were at odds with him because of policy stands. Some felt he was anti-navy and some believed he was doing too much for the air force, while others felt he was not doing enough.[49] A story circulated the halls of Congress that shortly after his appointment Johnson told Admiral Richard Connally, "There's no reason for having a Navy and a Marine Corps. . . . We'll never have any more amphibious operations. That does away with the Marine Corps. And the Air Force can do anything the Navy can do, so that does away with the Navy."[50]

Whether true or not, stories like this took on lives of their own and brought out strong feelings among members of Congress. Because Johnson was under orders from President Truman to drastically cut the defense budget and unify the services, it was easy to make enemies on the Hill. Johnson gave a high priority to the establishment of a "closer working relationship with the Congress." He believed that under Forrestal the Defense Department had failed to keep the legislative branch, specifically the House and Senate Armed Services Committees, informed of what it intended to do and why. He felt that the initiative to assure "maximum possible cooperation" between the armed services and Congress had to come from the secretary of defense.[51] Because of his desire to keep Congress fully informed, Johnson and numerous Pentagon officials made frequent trips to Capitol Hill to testify on defense issues. Johnson thoroughly enjoyed the give-and-take that characterized appearances before congressional committees. However, unlike Forrestal, Johnson's appearances before Congress were sometimes greeted with skepticism. In fact, military witnesses often had more credibility with the lawmakers than did Johnson. As Assistant Secretary Marx Leva put it, the legislators "were constantly suspicious of Johnson" and he had a kind of wheeler-dealer air about him that made even his supporters scrutinize his testimony very closely.[52]

The Press

Although the secretary would not have won a popularity contest at the Pentagon or on the Hill, there was one group where he might have done so — the members of the Washington press corps. Reporters liked him because he made good copy and he was accessible. With the assistance of Steve Early, he came to know all the reporters on a first-name basis, he treated them well, and he always gave them something newsworthy. The secretary was prone to give reporters frequent off-the-record interviews; they could attribute the information he gave them to a "high-ranking official." With this practice, the reporters got considerable inside information to share with their readers and Johnson had the advantage of being able to deny any information attributed to him. This served him well on numerous occasions, but in some instances, such as when he suggested that all or parts of the marine corps might be eliminated or incorporated in the navy or air force, it got him into hot water.[53]

In addition to the beat reporters at the Pentagon, Johnson fed information to numerous Washington news columnists. He would frequently spend time with Drew Pearson, Robert Allen, and Stewart Alsop to share information with them that they could include in their columns. As he did in the late 1930s, he invariably slanted the information to make him look good or an adversary look bad.[54]

By and large, Johnson used the press to his advantage, but he did so by keeping it at a proper distance. For example, he rarely held formal news conferences because his tendency to shoot from the hip would get him into trouble. The few formal news conferences he had as secretary of defense were near-disasters because he dispensed inaccurate information or said virtually nothing. For the same reason, he shied away from radio programs that followed a question-and-answer format. Lawrence Spivak of *Meet the Press* tried throughout Johnson's tenure to get him on the famous program, but Johnson kept putting him off. Eleanor Roosevelt tried unsuccessfully to get him on her radio "talk" show.[55]

That Secretary of Defense Louis Johnson was controversial was certainly an understatement. In Washington, where there is rarely agreement on anything, there was general recognition in 1949 and 1950 that "Johnson is one of the Capital's most controversial big shots and he likes it."[56] From his years in Washington Johnson knew that even though he was highly controversial and stepped on many toes, to keep his job the only person he really needed to please was Harry S. Truman, and that is what he intended to do.[57]

Racial Justice

When Louis Johnson arrived at the Pentagon at the end of March 1949, he knew he would be stepping into an explosive civil rights issue: the integration of the nation's armed forces. In 1948, impatient with Forrestal's halting attempts to change the racial practices of the armed forces through gradualism, pressed by civil rights leaders, and faced with a need to win the allegiance of minority voters, President Truman issued Executive Order No. 9981, which promised equality of opportunity in the armed forces. The president also appointed a citizens' committee, called the Fahy Committee (named after Charles Fahy, former solicitor general and future federal judge), to see that his directive was carried out.

Whatever his personal beliefs, Johnson knew that as Forrestal's successor he would have to take bold and decisive action to demonstrate, at least publicly, his commitment to the goals announced in the president's executive order and to forestall the Fahy Committee from undermining his authority as head of the Department of Defense.[58] Fortunately, when Johnson arrived at his office on his first day, a plan had already been developed by an internal Personnel Policy Board which enabled him to seize the initiative. On April 6, 1949, with great fanfare and maximum press coverage, Johnson issued a public directive to the nation's armed services which ordered them to accord equal treatment and opportunity to all persons and to submit detailed plans to him describing new programs for carrying out his directive.[59]

But Johnson hit a brick wall of resistance, excuses, delay, and half-hearted attempts to comply. Eventually, the air force and the navy came up with acceptable changes, but the army, by far the largest service, remained resistant to change, a situation exacerbated by Secretary of the Army Gordon Gray, who continued to believe that "separate but equal" segregation would give black soldiers the best chance of developing leadership skills. As a result, the Fahy Committee continued to press the army for change, and Johnson's strategy of seizing the initiative and neutralizing the Fahy Committee began to falter.

During the summer and fall of 1949, criticism from the press and liberal members of Congress over the protracted negotiations between the army and the Fahy Committee intensified. The president sided with the Fahy Committee, urging it to continue to press the army for solutions and implicitly renouncing Johnson's efforts to gloss over the army's truculence. It did not take long for Johnson to conclude that the whole issue had become a political liability for him. As a consequence, the secretary of defense simply retired from the controversy and left Gordon Gray with the task of dealing with the recalcitrant army bureaucracy.[60]

Looking back at Louis Johnson's less-than-successful experience with racial justice in the armed forces, it is not clear whether he had any personal commitment to the principle of racial integration. Obviously he saw the political benefits of aligning himself with the president's executive order. As long as Johnson could make headlines by advocating equal opportunity in the armed services, which at least created the illusion of forward movement, he would do so. But when the army dug in and the Fahy Committee began to garner the headlines, Johnson adopted a hands-off policy on integration. Morris MacGregor wrote of both Johnson and his successor George Marshall that they "were not social reformers. Whatever their personal attitudes, they were content to let the services set the pace of racial reform."[61]

The Boss

The relationship between Louis Johnson and "the Boss," as President Truman's close advisors referred to him, was not based on genuine friendship or affection. The two men had known each other since World War I and of course their paths had crossed often as each rose to positions of power and prominence. During the 1948 campaign, they were in frequent contact, but even then they never developed a warm and comfortable regard for each other. Perhaps because Johnson didn't drink or possibly because Truman thought he was pompous and arrogant or maybe because of both, Johnson was never invited into Truman's poker games or his excursions down the Potomac on the *Williamsburg* with Chief Justice Vinson and Truman's other pals. Instead, their meetings, including their regularly scheduled session every Tuesday at noon, tended to be formal and very businesslike, with little joking and no frivolity.[62]

Theirs was a marriage of mutual advantage and obligation which was consummated during their private White House meetings in January 1949 when Truman first laid out his agenda for the new defense chief and Johnson agreed to take the job. There is no known written record of Truman's private instructions to Johnson at these meetings. However, it is virtually certain that Truman saw in Johnson someone who was tough enough and mean enough to help him force through a strategy and a budget that would drastically reduce defense costs, tip the balance in favor of the air force (and against the navy), and bash heads at the Pentagon to achieve unification of the armed forces. Given Truman's well-known contempt for the intelligence of professional military officers, it is probable that he laced his instructions to Johnson with statements he later made public such as "No military man knows anything at all about money. All they know is how to spend it and they don't give a damn whether they're getting their money's worth or not."[63]

Johnson, recalling his experiences as a supply officer in World War I and his years as assistant secretary of war, was able to appreciate the president's disdain for the generals and the admirals and might have even agreed with him. But it doesn't really matter whether he sincerely shared Truman's contempt and his cost-cutting zeal in these private meetings or not, because Johnson saw in President Truman the man who could give him the one thing he wanted more than anything in his life—the position of secretary of defense.

The irony is that Johnson had built his reputation as a crusader for military preparedness. In order to get the job he most coveted, he had begun his relationship with the Boss by committing to cut the defense budget to the bone, a policy that could very well come into direct conflict with principles he had stood for all of his life.

Given the growing Soviet threat and the spread of communism early in 1949, it can be argued that Johnson's ambitions overrode his principles or that the only guiding principle he ever had was political survival. This is a judgment perhaps too harsh for the man and the times. It is far more likely that both Truman, and to a greater extent Johnson, having no real grasp of grand strategy and the use of military power and believing that the United States had exclusive possession of the atomic bomb for the foreseeable future, sincerely believed that they could cut the defense budget without diminishing military preparedness.

Even if Johnson's guiding principle was political survival, it is important to remember that his tendency to support the commander in chief's wishes to the hilt also had a great deal of merit. Perhaps Secretary Johnson, as a result of his experiences in France during World War I, realized that just as the working of a smooth military machine depends on a host of men loyally carrying out the tasks assigned them, so must the top military and civilian leaders loyally and efficiently carry out the orders of the top decision maker—the president. Without discipline from top to bottom, the system would fail.

President Truman carefully selected cabinet members to run his executive departments. They were expected to carry out his policies, and they served at his pleasure and his alone. Louis Johnson had longed for the job as secretary, and he wanted to keep it. It is difficult to fault him for trying to retain his job by being a good soldier for the president of the United States. In March 1949, what the president of the United States wanted for the National Military Establishment was true unification of the armed services and real economy while keeping the nation's defense sound. Whether he was motivated by pragmatism or principle, Louis Johnson threw all of his considerable energies and talents into the achievement of those two goals.

CHAPTER ELEVEN

Revolt of the Admirals

I N STEPPING INTO the secretary of defense position in early 1949, Louis Johnson acknowledged, as did his friends and enemies, that he was assuming what was clearly, next to the presidency itself, the most difficult job in Washington.[1] The scope and complexity of the tasks facing him were beyond the comprehension of most experienced administrators. Both at the Pentagon and on Capitol Hill there were many who were convinced that no single executive could handle such a large and diverse organization. However, Johnson was convinced that he could do the job and do it as it should be done.

From the outset, the principal problem Johnson faced centered on unification of the armed forces. Under the National Security Act of 1947, the nation was attempting for the first time to unify its land, naval, and air forces. While some progress had been made under Secretary Forrestal, a great deal remained to be done. The multitude of problems stemming from unification would have been challenging in and of themselves, but they were exacerbated by the fact that the president was demanding deep cuts in defense spending. Viewed separately, unification and economization were extremely explosive issues. The combination made the political-military situation in the nation's capital about as stable as nitroglycerin.

Secretary Johnson was fully committed to both challenges. Johnson understood that opposition would come not only from outside the military—from Congress, the public, and the press—but even more so from within the military establishment. What he did not realize was that his initial efforts would lead to the most flagrant challenge ever hurled by top-ranking American military men at the civilian leadership of the United States. That rebellion, by an elite group of battle-hardened admirals who had devoted their lives to serving their country, was known as the "revolt of the admirals."

Seeds of Discontent

The 1949 revolt was a flare-up of an old feud between the advocates of land-based airpower and those of sea-based airpower. Throughout the years of this conflict, both sides were convinced that their particular arm provided the soundest platform on which to build the nation's defense. In the 1920s, the dispute was between General Billy Mitchell and the admirals, while in the 1930s the two groups battled for the few dollars the Depression-racked nation could provide.

While it would seem that the unity of purpose during the war years of the 1940s might have worked to reduce interservice rivalry, in fact the war actually increased tensions as the navy, army, and army air corps continually bickered over missions, roles, and responsibilities. These disputes gave rise to a feeling in Washington that unification of all services under one cabinet department would be desirable, but there also was a consensus that any drastic change in the command setup would have to await the conclusion of the war.[2]

That unification would not fade away in the postwar period became certain on April 12, 1945, when President Roosevelt died and was succeeded by Harry Truman. Although the new chief executive did not hold rigid views on many topics, he was firmly resolved from the outset of his presidency to achieve unification of all of the armed services. Just one week after assuming office he directed his service secretaries to prepare a proposal for a single department of defense.[3] With this impetus from the top, both services moved to finalize their respective plans.

The army, which accepted as a foregone conclusion that the air corps would emerge as a separate entity, favored a true merger of the armed forces with control exercised by a single cabinet secretary. Secretary of War Robert Patterson spoke out strongly for the plan, as did army generals Dwight Eisenhower, George Marshall, Hap Arnold, and Douglas MacArthur.

The navy, on the other hand, accepted only very reluctantly the idea of a separate air force and vigorously opposed a merger with the army, opting instead for a plan to "coordinate" the separate services. Backed by a study headed by his longtime friend Ferdinand Eberstadt, Secretary of the Navy James Forrestal adamantly opposed the army plan. He was especially critical because he felt that administering a department which encompassed both the army and navy was "beyond the capacity of any one man." Similar statements, although in most cases much stronger, were made by such leading naval figures as Admiral William Leahy and Fleet Admiral Ernest King.[4]

The interservice battle raged on throughout the fall of 1945. The president listened to both sides and in mid-December sent Congress his unification plan, a scheme closely aligned with the army's ideas.[5] Instead of calming the situation, however, Truman's proposal thoroughly alarmed the navy. When a bill based on the chief executive's recommendations came before House and Senate committees, naval officials were so critical that the president was forced to insist that they stop discussing the plan publicly.[6]

While the navy attack probably irritated Truman, it seemed to make him more conciliatory because in May he directed Patterson and Forrestal to work out their differences and present him a compromise they could live with. In the negotiations that followed, Forrestal won many concessions. The president then resolved those issues that Forrestal and Patterson could not agree on.[7] Finally, by the spring of 1947 the administration and both services had a plan they could live with. After lengthy congressional hearings, the National Security Act of 1947 was passed and signed into law.[8]

What the 1947 act provided for was not a unified command or a single department but a coordinated National Military Establishment which was made up of three equal executive departments—army, navy, and air force—each headed by a secretary with cabinet status. Military input was to be provided by a Joint Chiefs of Staff (JCS), consisting of the army and air force chiefs of staff and the chief of naval operations. The act provided for a secretary of defense, but the position was weakened because the secretary's authority was limited to coordination and general supervision.[9] Clearly, the navy view of a coordinated rather than a unified command had prevailed.[10]

President Truman's choice for the first secretary of defense was Secretary of War Patterson, who refused the post on the ground that he needed to reenter the private sector in order to support his family. In reality, Patterson rejected the position because he did not feel it provided the power and authority needed to carry out its assigned responsibilities.[11] Next, the president offered the job to Secretary of the Navy Forrestal, the man primarily responsible for the structure of the new National Military Establishment, and he accepted.

As the new secretary attempted to implement the provisions of the National Security Act, he was hampered by the fact that in 1947 and 1948 the challenges of the Cold War in Greece, Turkey, Czechoslovakia, Germany, and China placed great pressures on the American military. At the same time, the president was pressing for major reductions in the defense budget. The president's commitment to a balanced budget, coupled with his contemptuous conviction that military leaders "seldom had any idea of the value of money," that they "squandered billions of dollars," and that all of the services "made excessive demands," led him to continually push for reduced defense expenditures.[12] And, with a decreasing defense pie, competition among the services for the limited dollars became increasingly intense. The three civilian secretaries and their top military advisors began fighting over the missions and responsibilities they felt were needed to assure the well-being of their respective services.[13]

When Truman signed the National Security Act he also issued Executive Order No. 9877, setting forth the roles and missions of each military service. Because that document was vague on a number of points, Forrestal had to work with the three service secretaries to clarify responsibilities. There were two serious efforts to resolve service differences in 1948, the first coming in March at a conference in Key West, and the second in Newport, Rhode Island, in August. Although some progress was made at those sessions, substantial differences remained.[14] According to the navy, the air force wanted control of "anything that flew," while the air force contended that the navy wanted to retain a second air force by disingenuously labeling it "tactical air power." Both services felt they should have strategic bombing capabilities, which meant the ability to deliver atomic bombs. The army wanted control over anything that walked or moved over land—a goal that worried the navy because it might lead to the loss of the marines.[15] As the debates continued, the navy became increasingly paranoid, convinced that the air force wanted to take away its aviation capability and that the army wanted to deprive it of its amphibious responsibilities.

In late 1947 and early 1948, the air force began a unilateral lobbying campaign to build and maintain a force of seventy air groups (which called for 6,869 aircraft, including 988 heavy bombers, of which a majority would be B-36s), as opposed to the fifty-five groups the president advocated. Air advocates successfully exploited the recommendations of a Truman-appointed Air Policy Committee, headed by Thomas K. Finletter, and a Joint Congressional Aviation Policy Board, both of which stressed the need for more air power and called for seventy air groups.[16] Such views appeared to reflect a growing conviction among the American public and members of Congress that the air force was the first line of American defense.

Forrestal indirectly opposed the air force campaign, urging a balanced-force concept by which funds would be divided evenly among the three services. However, the long-standing practice of allocating equal shares stopped working when it was discovered how small the shares were to be. Before long, representatives of each branch of the military were publicly demanding a greater portion of the defense funds, despite Forrestal's request that they not air their differences in public. Forrestal's lack of control over the civilian and military leaders of the various services increasingly concerned the president, who felt he was too lenient in dealing with his subordinates.[17] Furthermore, Truman believed that Forrestal's leniency was delaying unification and making it difficult for the services to adhere to the fiscal restraints that he, as commander in chief, was calling for.

Before the National Security Act was passed Truman had said that he would appoint "the hardest, meanest so and so" he could find to be secretary of defense.[18] Obviously he had not found him in Forrestal. When Forrestal chose not to take part in the 1948 campaign, refusing even to provide financial support,

Truman quietly made up his mind that if he was returned to office, the defense secretary would have to go. At private sessions with Johnson in January 1949 after his surprise election victory, Truman found in Johnson that "hard, mean so and so" who could bring about unification and economy.

Johnson's Broadside

Although Johnson's appointment was generally well accepted in army and air force circles, high-ranking navy personnel were not happy. Losing a pro-navy secretary of defense was alarming enough, but now their man Forrestal was being replaced by an ambitious politico who was known for his pro–air force stance. It had been nine years since Johnson had made any pronouncements on the role of the various armed services, but navy officials had no reason to believe that time had changed his views. The admirals were already jumpy because on February 11 General Eisenhower replaced Admiral William D. Leahy as primary military advisor to the secretary of defense and the president, an action that removed another naval advocate from the administration's top circle of advisors.[19]

By the time Johnson was sworn in as secretary at the end of March 1949, he had made it clear that he intended to bring real unification and economization to the defense establishment, but just how soon he would act or how far he would go was still uncertain.[20] The answer, however, was soon revealed. On April 7, the day after Army Day, he announced that from that day forward all such observances by the individual services would be eliminated. The purpose was to get the services to think of themselves as one defense establishment rather than three.

A week later he took a much bolder step when he issued Consolidation Directive No. 1, which set forth new public information policies, including a provision that a newly created review branch located in the office of the secretary of defense would handle all security reviews of statements by active-duty and retired personnel. Heretofore, any written or oral information supplied by military sources was to be reviewed not just for security reasons but also for "propriety." Outspoken naval officials interpreted this as an attempt on Johnson's part to "gag" them and keep them from speaking their minds.[21]

In mid-April, Johnson also recommended and the president approved an earlier air force request to cancel procurement of a number of fighters and medium bombers and to purchase thirty-six of the highly controversial B-36 heavy bombers instead.[22] This action seemed to fit into the navy's preconception that Johnson would move to strengthen the strategic bombing capabilities of the air force. It also provided the navy with an explosive political issue because Johnson had served on the board of directors of Convair, the company which manufactured the B-36s. It was beside the point that the proposal had originated months before Johnson arrived on the scene and that Forrestal and Symington had approved the transaction before Johnson was sworn in.[23] The navy saw what it wanted to see—Johnson as a villain.

As alarming as the new secretary's actions were during his first three weeks on the job, they were merely firecrackers compared to the blast he was about to set off. On April 23, less than a month after taking office, Johnson took a step that was to ignite the revolt of the admirals—he canceled construction of the gigantic new navy aircraft carrier, the USS *United States*, a warship that symbolized the navy and its future as guardian of the free world. Johnson's decision to cancel was as demoralizing to the navy as almost anything he could have done.

Navy plans for a large flush-deck carrier capable of launching planes that could deliver atomic bombs had started shortly after the war, and in early 1948 Secretary of the Navy Sullivan unilaterally announced plans to build a 1,090-foot, 65,000-ton supercarrier. To cover the $189 million cost, the navy agreed to halt construction of thirteen ships and the conversion of many others. Since the responsibility for strategic bombing was still unresolved, the navy believed that its new prototype vessel would gain a share of that responsibility and a greater share of the shrinking defense pie. In the months that followed, plans were finalized, contracts were let, and, finally, on April 18, 1949, the keel was laid in Newport News, Virginia.[24] These plans to design and build the carrier had proceeded amid great controversy because the air force believed the navy was attempting to move in on its strategic bombing responsibility.

Since the keel had not yet been laid when Johnson came to office, he had a duty to study the issue and make a decision about whether to proceed with the project.[25] At Johnson's very first meeting with General Eisenhower (then serving as temporary chief of the JCS as well as president of Columbia University) and the Joint Chiefs, the supercarrier was discussed, but very briefly, and no recommendations were made. Four days later, however, Johnson asked Eisenhower and the Joint Chiefs to present their individual views on the advisability of continuing construction of the carrier. The chiefs quickly made their positions, and the reasons behind them, known to Johnson. Both Army Chief of Staff Omar Bradley and Air Force Chief of Staff Hoyt Vandenberg opposed construction while Chief of Naval Operations Admiral Louis Denfeld supported it. Eisenhower expressed his opposition by telephone.[26]

Secretary Johnson briefed the president on the issue on at least half a dozen occasions, primarily to report what was happening rather than to seek advice, for Truman saw this as a Johnson decision.[27] Believing that the problem was strictly a military matter on which the Joint Chiefs had full input, the secretary chose not to discuss it with any of his service secretaries, even though Secretary Sullivan had requested an opportunity to do so.[28]

By the evening of April 22, after reading the final drafts of the written recommendations the Joint Chiefs would present, Johnson had made up his mind to cancel. Before informing the president he sounded out the chairmen of the House and Senate Armed Service Committees, Representative Carl Vinson (D-Georgia) and Senator Millard E. Tydings (D-Maryland), both of whom supported the decision.

The following morning, Saturday, April 23, five days after the keel of the supercarrier had been laid, Johnson called the president and told him of his decision to cancel—a determination with which Truman fully concurred. Johnson then directed that the order be prepared, but not released, until Admiral Denfeld, acting in Eisenhower's absence, brought him the written opinions of the three chiefs. When Denfeld delivered the documents and Johnson noted that nothing new had been added to the earlier drafts, he issued the order to Secretary Sullivan that construction of the carrier be halted immediately. The order was simultaneously released to the press.[29]

Secretary of the Navy Sullivan, a prominent New Hampshire Democrat and a Harvard-educated lawyer, was in Corpus Christi for a speaking engagement when he learned of the decision. He was outraged and embarrassed that Johnson had not told him, let alone consulted him, before making and then publicly releasing his decision to cancel. Sullivan immediately returned to Washington brandishing a scathing letter of resignation but was persuaded by the White House staff to deliver a short, courteous letter of resignation to Truman, which was immediately accepted. Sullivan then changed the name on the emotionally charged letter he had originally brought over to the White House and addressed it to Secretary Johnson. By handling it this way, Sullivan preserved his relationship with Truman while focusing his full fury on Johnson.[30]

When Sullivan entered Johnson's office in the Pentagon and handed him the letter, the Colonel scanned the document, looked up, and said, "John, you didn't write this letter. Some admiral wrote this for you." Sullivan said, "No, Mr. Secretary, I signed it." Johnson responded, "Well, you may have signed it, but you didn't write it. You wouldn't write me a letter like that."[31] Johnson, a golfing buddy and friend of Sullivan's, refused to believe that Sullivan was the actual author of the letter, and perhaps he wasn't.

Nevertheless, Sullivan's angry letter to Johnson appeared in newspapers around the country. The main thrust of the letter and his primary criticism was "the unprecedented action on the part of the secretary of defense in so drastically and arbitrarily changing and restricting the operations plans of an armed service without consultation with that service." The consequences of Johnson's action, Sullivan warned, would be "far-reaching and can be tragic." He revealed just how far the navy's fear of Johnson went when he wrote, "The conviction that this will result in a renewed effort to abolish the Marine Corps . . . adds to my anxiety."[32] The prospect that Johnson might try to eliminate the marines was based in part on an infamous off-the-record conversation he had with reporters on April 27.[33]

Neither the criticism from Sullivan nor the uproar caused by his decision to cancel the carrier bothered Johnson. In truth, he actually relished the controversy. To him the carrier decision provided an opportunity to advance his two major goals—unification and economy—in one fell swoop. Progress toward unification would result from halting an earlier unilateral decision by the navy to proceed with the carrier project and forcing all the services, through the Joint Chiefs, to evaluate and make a recommendation on it. Economy would be effected through saving nearly $200 million.[34] It also demonstrated to the generals and admirals in all services that he was in control and that he was not afraid to make hard decisions. Johnson was going to be a real secretary of defense. As he later put it, "The President put me over there at the Pentagon to take charge, and I did."[35]

Sullivan's resignation immediately became a cause célèbre for navy brass. He was hailed as a man of principle who was willing to sacrifice his career for a just and noble purpose. While the admirals were holding a quiet farewell ceremony for Sullivan on the day he was to leave the Pentagon, Johnson seized the arm of one of his senior aides, Brigadier General Louis Renfrow, and said, "Come on, we're going over there." Renfrow was shocked. "Mr. Secretary, you can't do that. When Al Capone kills them in Chicago, he sends them flowers, but he doesn't go to their funeral." Johnson replied, "John [Sullivan] and I are good friends. We're both members out at Burning Tree [an exclusive all-male golf club]. He understands." With Renfrow in tow, Johnson barged into the ceremony. Said Renfrow later, "These admirals, they looked daggers at him."[36]

Johnson didn't care what the admirals said or thought about him. He was convinced that his decision to cancel the supercarrier, which had the unqualified backing of the president, was in the national interest. Nevertheless, nothing could mask the fact that the navy had suffered a stunning setback and the air force had gained a major victory in the ongoing battle between the two services over the issue of strategic bombing responsibilities.[37] Johnson's cancellation order seemed to confirm the navy's fears that the new secretary of defense was indeed the enemy it fully expected him to be.

While the navy was critical of the cancellation, it stood alone in its disapproval. As would be expected, the army and air force lauded the action as most reasonable. Although there was some criticism in the press because the secretary of the navy was not consulted, there was general support for halting construction. Typical was a *New York Times* editorial criticizing Johnson's "unnecessary brusqueness" but concluding, "the Joint Chiefs of Staff is the body charged with passing on questions of top military strategy and a majority of the Joint Chiefs last week voted against the carrier. This advisory opinion formed the basis of Mr. Johnson's decision."[38]

Naval advocates in Congress such as Republican senator Kenneth Wherry and Democratic congressman Harry Sheppard were critical of the decision, but much more typical was the statement on the House floor by Armed Services chairman Carl Vinson, a longtime navy supporter, who said that Johnson "made a courageous and momentous decision . . . and is to be commended both for the nature of his decision and for moving promptly to resolve this important matter."[39]

Submarine Attack

Career navy officers were frustrated and extremely angry in the aftermath of the cancellation. Many top-ranking naval aviators concluded that the very existence of the U.S. Navy was as stake. According to one naval scholar, "the anxiety of the officer corps hit a peak higher than at any time in its history."[40]

In this charged atmosphere, senior navy officers began mobilizing for a battle they perceived as essential to save their service from a crippling blow at best and extinction at worst. They identified their three major enemies: 1) President Truman, whose insistence on a total military budget of under $15 billion for fiscal years 1949 and 1950 was making all the squeezing necessary; 2) Secretary of Defense Johnson, who was determined to build up the air force at the expense of the navy and who, by claiming he could cut defense expenditures by another billion dollars a year, was taking the economy drive even farther than Truman was calling for; and 3) the U.S. Air Force, which was misrepresenting what airpower could do and the navy could not do in providing for the nation's defense.

With the "enemies" identified, the questions became which ones to attack and how. For patriotic and political reasons, the president had to be ruled out, leaving Johnson and the air force as prime targets. The method of attack was propaganda, both positive, which would build up the navy, and negative, which would launch a full-scale assault on the defense secretary and the air force.[41]

Early in 1949, Cedric R. Worth, a former naval commander who was serving as a special assistant to Undersecretary of the Navy Dan A. Kimball, began compiling all the negative information he could gather against Johnson and the air force. Utilizing rumors, half-truths, and a sprinkling of accurate information, and with the help of a defense contractor who had lost out to Convair, probably Northrop, Worth prepared an "anonymous" dossier which cited fifty-five allegations of wrongdoing against Secretary Johnson, Secretary of the Air Force Stuart Symington, and the air force's B-36 program.

The essence of Worth's charges was that the controversial eight-engine B-36 bomber was an ineffective and vulnerable weapon that could not live up to expectations and that Johnson and Symington still went ahead with procurement even though they were aware of the bomber's problems. The dossier alleged that the two officials had approved purchase because they were friends of Floyd Odlum, head of the corporation that controlled Convair, the supplier of the plane, and because Johnson had been a director of Convair until he resigned to take the defense post. Furthermore, they claimed that Odlum had pumped nearly $6 million into the president's 1948 campaign.[42] As the underground document circulated in Washington in May 1949, its author remained unknown.

Not surprisingly, especially to those used to the ways of Washington, Worth's document quickly found its way into the hands of Congressman James E. Van Zandt (R-Pennsylvania), a reserve naval officer who was a member of the House Armed Services Committee. On May 26, Van Zandt gave an impassioned speech in which he revealed the charges and called for a congressional investigation.[43] The allegations were so sensational and received so much publicity that Carl Vinson, the Georgia congressman who was chairman of the House Armed Services Committee, had no choice but to have his committee look into the matter. On June 9, Vinson's committee voted to investigate the charges, assess the capabilities of the B-36, examine the roles and missions of the services, and determine whether the decision to cancel the supercarrier had been sound.[44]

Carl Vinson, a powerful autocrat who controlled the purse strings of national defense, was a legend on the Hill. Known as the "Swamp Fox of Georgia," and sometimes more affectionately as "Uncle Carl," Vinson was a tobacco-chewing backwoods lawyer from Milledgeville. There is a story that Truman once sent an aide to the Capitol to ask the Swamp Fox to be secretary of defense. Vinson said, "Aw, shucks, I'd rather run the Pentagon from here."[45]

Vinson divided the upcoming hearings into two phases, the first to start in August and the second in October. During June and July both services worked hard to prepare their cases for the committee. The navy hoped that by discrediting the air force's procurement program, and the men responsible for implementing it, it could reassert itself by gaining congressional and then public support for its program. The air force merely intended to defend its evaluation and procurement procedures. Until the hearings began, the normally outspoken Johnson, who loved to speak to the members of the press off the record, stepped completely out of character by refusing to comment on the charges against him.

Round One for Johnson

The revolt of the admirals, which initially consisted of behind-the-scenes grumbling about the carrier cancellation, came out into the open for the first time in the August hearings before Vinson's House Armed Services Committee. That first phase of the investigation, which was formally called the "Investigation of the B-36 Bomber Program," lasted eleven days, beginning on August 9 and concluding on August 25.

Led by Secretary Symington, the air force went first and presented a thorough review of the history of the procurement, performance, and evaluation of the B-36. Most of the anonymous charges were discredited as a result of the detail and precision of the air force's testimony.[46] By contrast, the testimony by the navy witnesses lacked focus and often amounted to nothing more than handwringing about low morale and the shortcomings of the B-36, which they labeled "the billion dollar blunder." They contradicted one another, and one even challenged the destructive power of the atomic bomb, the weapon the navy so desperately wanted to get its hands on. A young navy commander actually told the committee, "You could stand in the open at one end of the north-south runway at the Washington National Airport, with no more protection than the clothes you now have on, and have an atom bomb explode at the other end of the runway without serious injury to you." "Uncle Carl" Vinson pushed his glasses down so he could get a better look at the witness, expectorated into the spittoon behind the dais and then drawled, "Well, if it is going to drop that close, I want to be in Georgia."[47] The hearing room exploded with laughter.

As the committee turned to an examination of the charges of political and personal favoritism in the awarding of defense contracts, Secretary Johnson strode into the packed hearing room. He opened by decrying "terroristic accusations of those opposing unification in an attempt to scare me away" and branded the charges against him as "lies." He described his seven-year relationship with Convair and testified that he had incurred an $85,000 loss by selling stocks, including his Convair holdings, in order to avoid any possible charges of conflict of interest. He destroyed the "fantastic and utterly false" claims that Floyd Odlum gave more than $6 million to the president's campaign (an amount three times greater than all funds raised) and he explained that his April 14, 1949, approval of the purchase of additional B-36s was merely a "rubber-stamp" reaffirmation of a decision that Forrestal had previously made following normal Pentagon review procedures. Johnson's testimony was credible and convincing. After General Counsel Joseph B. Kennan finished interrogating him, no one, including Representative Van Zandt, had questions.

On August 24, the day after the secretary's appearance, the veracity of Johnson's statements was corroborated by a surprise witness, Cedric Worth. In two days of testimony, Worth "confessed" that the "anonymous" document containing the charges was a spurious piece of work he had concocted for narrowly partisan reasons.[48] Some observers were convinced that Worth had "taken a dive" to protect navy officers and civilians up the line. Nevertheless, with the author of Van Zandt's charges now identified and the allegations of irregularities in procurement now discredited, phase one of the hearings came to a close and the committee recessed until October 5. The air force had come out well by demonstrating the thoroughness of its evaluation of the B-36 and the integrity of its procurement procedures. As for Johnson and Symington, Chairman Vinson put it best on the last day of the August hearings when he said they had "come through the inquiry without the slightest blemish and that these men continue to merit the confidence of the American people."[49] The navy's first attempt to revolt against Johnson and the air force had not fared well. It had been caught and embarrassed, but it was not ready to give up the cause.

Johnson's Hand Is Strengthened

By the end of August, Secretary Johnson was in a stronger position than he had been since taking on the new post. This was true in part because of the way he had emerged from the first phase of the House hearings but also because of two other developments that took place between May and August: the appointment of Francis Matthews as the new secretary of the navy and the passage of the 1949 amendments to the National Security Act.

Following Secretary Sullivan's departure in April, Johnson prevailed upon the president to nominate Francis Matthews to the position. Matthews, a land-locked Nebraskan who admitted that his knowledge of naval matters was limited to what he knew about a "rowboat at my summer home," was chosen primarily because he had been an important fund-raiser for Truman in the 1948 campaign, which earned him Johnson's friendship and trust. The White House also wanted him because he was a prominent Catholic layman with outspoken anti-communist views.[50]

Matthews moved into his new position in May, heavily indebted to Johnson and sadly lacking in knowledge of the navy's pride, traditions, organization, and weapons. Unlike Secretary Sullivan, Matthews was beholden to Johnson, had no reason to support the navy admirals, and, in any case, knew so little about the navy that it would take years to educate him. While the appointment of Matthews might have been bad for the navy, it was good for Johnson.[51]

Johnson's position was strengthened to an even greater extent in August with the passage of the 1949 amendments to the National Security Act. In June and July, he had appeared before both the House and Senate Armed Services Committees to forcefully advocate strengthening the powers of the secretary. He candidly asked the congressmen "to give me the authority to do what the country wants without going to the President."[52] When members of Congress expressed fear that too much power would lead to a "military dictatorship," Johnson said that such a possibility was preposterous.

During the hours Johnson spent before the committees arguing for greater power, he was at his very best, exhibiting strength when necessary and understanding where appropriate. Several encounters between Johnson and the Swamp Fox of Georgia were classics in confrontations between Congress and presidential appointees. In the end, Johnson's ideas for strengthening the authority of the secretary of defense prevailed over those advocated by several members of Congress.[53] On August 10, the National Security Act Amendments of 1949 became law, giving Johnson the power to bring about true unification of the armed services and achieve vast economic savings.

Continued Cost-Cutting

Johnson's newly conferred powers did not worry the navy nearly as much as several other of his decisions in the summer of 1949. Although in June he made a pro-navy decision by approving modification of two Essex-class carriers, navy brass felt that move was like an island in a sea of anti-navy moves.[54] They felt that his other actions were more indicative of his true feelings. For example, they were very uneasy about Johnson's revocation and then reinstatement of Consolidation Directive No. 1, the order which curbed public statements by senior military officials. Navy officers felt that he was playing games with their right to speak their minds on procurement, unification, and economy issues.[55] When he attempted, although unsuccessfully, to keep a pro-navy article by Rear Admiral Dan Gallery from appearing in *The Saturday Evening Post,* they believed he was really showing his bias.[56] When he began making well-publicized speeches in which he took navy "partisans" to task for conducting "a campaign of terror against unification," they knew for sure he was biased.[57]

Nothing bothered the navy more, however, than Johnson's continuing efforts to cut costs. In a mid-July conference held at the Greenbrier, a posh spa in West Virginia, the secretary informed the service chiefs that the budget for fiscal 1951 would be even more austere than those of the past two years, a mere $13 billion, and would not be divided evenly; the navy would be receiving less than the air force and army. A few weeks later he was more specific; he indicated that he would advocate cuts of all navy programs, especially carriers, carrier groups, and marine aviation, which was targeted for a 50 percent cut.[58]

On August 19, the day the 1949 amendments were passed, Johnson, armed with expanded authority, appointed a National Defense Management Committee, headed by General Joseph McNarney, whose purpose was to recommend economy moves that would result in substantial savings for the Department of Defense. Johnson believed that eliminating waste, duplication, and unessential programs would save a billion dollars a year, and he expected the committee to identify exactly where and how the cuts could be made and the savings achieved. On September 8, after gaining approval from Johnson, McNarney informed the services that the secretary would not be waiting for fiscal 1951 to make substantial cuts but would do so in fiscal 1950. The cuts amounted to $929 million: the air force lost $196 million, the army $357 million, and the navy $376 million.[59] This time the navy was convinced that Johnson had gone too far. First the carrier cancellation, then the series of anti-navy moves and statements, and now a major cut from what had already been a bare-bones budget—where would it all end? Naval leaders felt they had no choice but to fight; if they did not, Johnson would sink the navy and knock its air arm out of the sky more effectively than any enemy force could. The allegations about the B-36 during the August hearings had been kid stuff. Now they were ready to really rebel.

Open Warfare

On September 10, the revolt entered a new phase, one in which press leaks, innuendos, and challenges to the administration's defense policies became even more rampant. On that date Captain John G. Crommelin, a prominent naval aviator serving on the staff of the Joint Chiefs, stepped onto the Washington flight deck. Crommelin, a Naval Academy graduate who lost two brothers during the war, had narrowly escaped death himself when he was blown off the deck of a carrier.

Crommelin had expected to be called as a witness before a naval court of inquiry which had been convened to investigate charges made during the Armed Services Committee hearings. When the court recessed without calling him, Crommelin was incensed. Without informing his superiors, he called in the press and issued a statement claiming that the navy was being systematically and intentionally "nibbled to death" by Secretary of Defense Johnson and the Joint Chiefs. He told the reporters that he knew he was throwing away his 33-year career but that he had to speak out because his beloved navy "was going to pot."[60]

The next day the nation's newspapers trumpeted Crommelin's charges. Immediately, both active and retired navy men came to Crommelin's defense. Fleet Admiral William W. "Bull" Halsey, popular wartime commander in the South Pacific, issued a statement of support, saying Crommelin had "shown wonderful courage."[61] Chief of Naval Operations (CNO) Denfeld and Undersecretary Kimball not only moved to protect him but attempted to reward him with a favorable reassignment which would put him in line for a promotion.

Seven hours later, navy secretary Matthews intervened, reversed the admirals, and ordered Captain Crommelin to a new and less-desirable post.[62] At a press conference, Truman said he supported Matthews's decision.[63] With the backing of both the president and Secretary Johnson, it is apparent that Matthews removed Crommelin from the Pentagon and publicly criticized his judgment because he wanted to demonstrate that he would not tolerate such behavior by other officers and that he did not want them to air their criticisms publicly. By this time, Matthews was also opposed to the proposed budget cuts, but he felt that he and his subordinates should take up the matter with Johnson privately. He directed that all complaints related to the proposed cuts be sent to him through channels, after which he would turn them over to Captain Arleigh Burke, who, as chief of the Organizational Policy and Research Division (called Op 23), was in charge of preparing the navy's case for the upcoming phase of the House Armed Services Committee investigation.

During the first week in October, Johnson assured Matthews that the navy could present its budget concerns to him and that he would listen. Hoping he could persuade the defense chief to restore some of the cuts, Matthews wanted to postpone the House Armed Services Committee hearings until January.

Postponement, he argued, would provide an opportunity to solve the problems in house. The navy secretary persuaded CNO Denfeld of the merits of delay and appeared to have won Chairman Vinson over when dynamic Admiral Arthur W. Radford, an outspoken former vice chief of naval operations and commander in chief of the Pacific Fleet, returned to Washington to lead the admirals in revolt. Citing a confidential letter from Vice-Admiral Gerald P. Bogan that claimed that morale in the navy was at an all-time low, Radford convinced Vinson to proceed with the inquiry.[64]

At about the same time, Captain Crommelin surreptitiously dropped off copies of the Bogan letter, with endorsements by Radford and Denfeld, to the United Press and the Associated Press in the National Press Building. Publication of these confidential letters, in which the navy's top admirals said that morale was lower than it had ever been, created a sensation. Secretary Matthews was greatly embarrassed, and it didn't take him long to find out that Crommelin had once again gone to the press. Matthews suspended the headstrong captain and ordered him to remain in Washington pending a court-martial.[65]

Bradley Scores a Direct Hit

When the House Armed Services Committee reconvened on October 5, it formally ended the August probe of Van Zandt's charges and moved ahead to the second phase of its inquiry, called "The National Defense Program—Unification and Strategy." The revelations concerning low morale throughout the navy made the areas of examination—the soundness of the B-36, the cancellation of the supercarrier, and the roles of the respective services—more important than ever.

Chairman Vinson opened the hearings by vowing, "We are going to the bottom of this unrest and concern in the Navy." He said he wanted the witnesses to speak openly and candidly without fear of reprisals, and he ordered Secretary Matthews and Admirals Denfeld, Radford, and Bogan to be present.[66]

The first witness was Secretary of the Navy Matthews, who blithely stated that "the general morale of the Navy is good."[67] Without mentioning names, he criticized those naval officers who chose to go public with their grievances rather than work within the system. He drew jeers from the audience when he said he knew of no reason why naval officers should not feel free to voice their opinions during these hearings.

After Matthews stepped down, the navy officer corps took over. The men in blue set out to show that unification, as implemented by Johnson and the Joint Chiefs, was not working and in fact was tearing the navy apart. The first eight days of the probe belonged to the navy as it paraded before the committee such prominent and distinguished war heroes as Admirals Bull Halsey, Thomas C. Kinkaid, Chester W. Nimitz, and Raymond Spruance; Fleet Admiral Ernest J. King; and a number of others. The essence of their case was that the air force had sold the nation a bill of goods in the form of the atomic blitz theory of warfare and that the instrument of that policy, the B-36, was an ineffective "billion-dollar blunder."

The navy witnesses also testified that unification was not working because Secretary Johnson and the Joint Chiefs were making decisions that properly belonged to the navy, the unsound carrier cancellation being the best example. They took Secretary Johnson to task for undermining congressional will by implementing an economy program that prevented hundreds of millions of appropriated dollars from being spent on the navy. They also expressed their fear that under the present regime the marines might lose their amphibious responsibilities to the army.[68]

When Admiral Radford was called to the witness table, he attacked the B-36 and atomic blitz theory of warfare on moral grounds. Radford said that if the American people knew that the B-36 lacked precision-bombing capability and would be used to annihilate civilian populations, they would consider it "morally reprehensible."[69] Asked if the top naval officers lacked confidence in the office of the secretary of defense, Radford, risking his career, responded, "I think so."[70]

While Admiral Radford had been coordinating and leading the attack, Admiral Denfeld, the CNO, had tried to remain aloof to avoid antagonizing his civilian chiefs. It was a dramatic moment, therefore, when Denfeld opened his testimony on October 13 by declaring, "As the senior military spokesman for the navy, I want to state forthwith that I fully support the broad conclusions presented to this committee by the naval and marine officers . . . who preceded me."[71] Denfeld went on to criticize what he called arbitrary reductions in funds allocated to the navy and arbitrary decisions made in the Pentagon. He said there was a steady campaign at the Pentagon to "relegate" the navy to "convoy and antisubmarine service" and that the unification process being forced on the navy was not "in accord with the spirit or concept of unification." In making these claims, the CNO was unmistakably criticizing Secretary Johnson and Secretary Matthews and, by implication, President Truman.[72] When Denfeld finished, he was praised by Vinson and several members of the committee and navy and marine officers crowded around him to congratulate him. Secretary Matthews, having been attacked by his own outfit, "abruptly rose" and stormed "red-faced" out of the hearing room.[73]

Following the navy's presentation, the air force had its opportunity to fight back. Secretary Symington and General Vandenberg essentially denied everything the navy had said. Symington suggested that the admirals were trying to deprive the civilian leadership in the Pentagon of their authority to make military decisions.

The most effective response to the allegations by the navy, however, was not made by anyone associated with the air force but by 56-year-old Army General

Omar Bradley, the recently appointed chairman of the Joint Chiefs of Staff. Known to the public as modest, shy, and rather colorless, Bradley electrified the crowd in the hearing room as he proceeded to blast the navy in what was the most forceful presentation of the hearings. He criticized the navy for being too preoccupied with the past and failing to foresee a need for fresh military strategies. Bradley noted how the navy had opposed unification from the beginning and had never stopped resisting it. Beyond that, he claimed, on numerous occasions naval leaders had deliberately made false accusations against Louis Johnson and the Joint Chiefs simply because they did not get their way.[74] He concluded by deploring the navy's "open rebellion against the civilian control," and he accused the "overzealous enthusiasts" and "self-appointed martyrs" of being "fancy Dans who won't hit the line with all they have on every play, unless they can call the signals."[75]

The next day newspapers from coast to coast carried stories on the "fancy Dans" in the navy. Omar Bradley, who was known to the world as the GI's general because he cared about the lot of common soldier, almost single-handedly deflated the rebellion of the admirals.[76]

On the last day of the hearings, Secretary Johnson again came up to the Hill to explain his side of the story. Johnson accused the navy witnesses of presenting an "erroneous picture" of what was taking place. "A straw man was built for you by those who would have you believe that we expect to win a war by push-button tactics and atomic blitz," he told the committee members. National defense would be conducted in the interest of "the American people," not in the interest of "professional seamen, professional airmen, or professional soldiers."[77]

Johnson then told his side of the decision to cancel the supercarrier, making clear that he received input from all the chiefs, including the navy CNO, before making his decision. He also went to great lengths to justify his economy moves and emphasized that all services, not just the navy, were being forced to make cuts. He noted, however, that while all three services were unhappy with the reductions, only two, the army and air force, had made their views known through Pentagon channels. He further acknowledged that cries of anguish were bound to be heard when economies were imposed, but that the strains and stresses on the national economy made it "impossible . . . for any service to get all that it wants."

The secretary concluded on a conciliatory note by saying that "[t]his country needs, and will have, a strong Army, a strong Navy, and a strong Air Force," thus emphasizing his firm belief that there would be "an essential and honorable role for each of the armed forces." He closed with a call for increased understanding among each of the services so that true unification could be achieved.[78]

The hearing's final witness was former president Herbert Hoover, who stressed the need for unification and praised Secretary Johnson for what he was doing to bring efficiency and economy to the Pentagon. With that, the hearings came to a close on October 21, 1949.[79] Although for all intents and purposes the revolt of the admirals had been put down that day, the ending was not apparent until later.

Casualties

That the revolt had failed became apparent in a series of events which began shortly after the hearings concluded. The first casualty was Admiral Denfeld. At a press conference on October 27, President Truman began by announcing, "I have received a request from the Secretary of the Navy to transfer Admiral Denfeld to another post, and I have given him permission to do it."[80] Thus, less than a week after the hearings and three months after being given a two-year reappointment as CNO, Denfeld was ousted. This move was initiated by Secretary Matthews and approved by Johnson.[81] Denfeld's position was filled by Admiral Forrest H. Sherman, the current commander of the Mediterranean fleet, who had chosen not to involve himself in the revolt.

Denfeld maintained that the action taken against him was for the purpose of showing other naval officials what would happen to those who would "outspokenly oppose the wishes of Secretary Johnson and Secretary Matthews."[82] Denfeld added, "For thirty-odd years I've been sticking to my guns, and if they want to kick me out, I'm still sticking to my guns."[83] Congressional and public reaction was by and large sympathetic to Denfeld and critical of Johnson rather than Matthews or the president. Johnson had pledged during the hearings that there would be no reprisals against military personnel who chose to testify, and many felt that he had violated that pledge. Johnson lamely responded that Denfeld was removed not as a reprisal but because he lacked the qualifications for his position. He did not explain, however, how or why a man he and Matthews had praised and recommended for two more years on the job just three months earlier was no longer qualified.[84] President Truman was much more direct. He said the change was necessary "to restore discipline in the Navy."[85]

In the months that followed, Captain John Crommelin was purged and two of the testifying admirals, Blandy and Bogan, were forced into retirement. However, an attempt by Matthews and Johnson to punish one of the wayward officers went awry. They tried in December to block the promotion of Captain Arleigh Burke, head of Op 23 and primary architect of the navy's presentations in the hearings. Truman's intervention thwarted their effort, and Burke was promoted.[86] Neither Burke's nor Admiral Radford's actions during the revolt had lasting effects on their careers; they both went on to distinguish themselves, Burke as CNO (1955–1961) and Radford as chairman of the Joint Chiefs of Staff (1953–1957).

Two months after the hearings, the House Armed Services Committee issued the first report on its inquiry which dealt with the initial phase of the hearings—the B-36 procurement charges. Vinson's committee praised the air force and its handling of the B-36 program. The committee's report cleared

Secretary Johnson and Secretary Symington of any wrongdoing and expressed complete confidence in both of them.[87]

On March 1, 1950, the committee issued its second report, on unification and strategy. Its thirty-three findings and conclusions pointed out the complexities of unification and called for more cooperation, consultation, and education to make true unification a reality. The report criticized Secretary Johnson for the manner in which the supercarrier was canceled, but it upheld the cancellation itself. It also criticized him for thwarting the will of Congress by refusing to spend appropriated funds. The strongest criticism of Johnson, however, was not in relation to any facts brought out in the hearings but was aimed at the subsequent reprisal against Admiral Denfeld—an action the committee denounced because "it violated promises made" and therefore "tends to intimidate witnesses and hence discourages . . . free and honest testimony to the Congress."[88]

Notwithstanding these criticisms, the committee's two reports provided no solace to the navy. Offering sympathy for the plight of the navy but nothing else, the reports wrote the last official word on what by that time had become apparent: the revolt of the admirals had failed.

Fallout

While the committee reports and the removal of Admiral Denfeld were indications that the revolt of the admirals had not succeeded, more evidence of its failure can be seen when one asks the question, "What did the admirals achieve?" The answer is very little. There were no discernible changes in the military budget for fiscal 1950 or 1951 either in terms of total amount or percentage of distribution. The atomic blitz theory continued to hold sway throughout the nation and B-36 procurement continued unabated.[89] Strategic bombing remained the primary responsibility of the air force, and construction of the supercarrier was not resumed. Moreover, unification of the services under a single secretary of defense was achieved. None of the things that the navy had set out to change had been accomplished.

For Secretary of Defense Johnson, the impact of the revolt was not clear cut, for he emerged as both a winner and a loser. On the positive side, there were several considerations: he established himself among the armed services, Congress, and the public as a bold, forceful individual who fully intended to make unification work regardless of opposition. More important for the nation, he made unification work through sheer force of personality and determination. He also educated Congress and the public about the very difficult nature of his job and the need for unification and the elimination of waste and inefficiency.

As Johnson was later to recall, the supercarrier and B-36 controversy was "the issue that gave me the chance to run the department. The secretary didn't have control before. This was the thing that gave me control."[90] Therein lies the major significance of Johnson's handling of the revolt—in acting boldly and decisively, he significantly transformed the position of secretary of defense. After the revolt, it was clear that the secretary of defense was in charge. The old cooperative and consensus-driven style of Forrestal was out, and the strong-forceful-leader approach that has prevailed until the present was in. Johnson used the conflict between the services to significantly strengthen his own position and consequently the position of secretary.[91]

Whether Johnson strengthened his position with the Boss is open to question. On the one hand, Truman completely supported, if not encouraged, Johnson's decision that led to the revolt—the cancellation of the supercarrier—and he supported Johnson's approval of Matthews's decision to oust Admiral Denfeld. Given his years in the House and his experience chairing investigations of the military, Truman also had to have admired and respected the way Johnson handled himself in the grueling hearings before Vinson's Armed Services Committee. Moreover, Truman must have understood the terribly difficult position he had put Johnson in. From early 1949, Truman and his budget people exerted unrelenting pressure on Johnson to reduce defense costs. The revolt of the admirals was a direct result of Truman's own initiatives.

Yet Truman began to have misgivings about Johnson's brusque way of handling people. Truman liked Secretary Sullivan, and he believed that if Johnson had shown some consideration for him, his public outrage and messy resignation could have been avoided. Truman confided to White House aide Eben Ayers that "he did not greatly blame Sullivan" for quitting.[92]

Furthermore, as the public spectacle dragged on and the witnesses debated whether the best way to destroy the Soviet Union was through atomic bombs delivered by B-36s, Truman became increasingly concerned about the foreign relations impact of the hearings. It is not known whether the president blamed Johnson for letting things get out of control, but, fairly or not, Truman may have placed at least some of the blame on Johnson's broad shoulders.

The revolt and the resulting congressional hearings probably also diminished Johnson in the eyes of some members of Congress, the press, and the public who felt his handling of defense issues and his demeanor revealed a man who was too arrogant and insensitive to really make unification work. Moreover, it brought about complete and irreparable alienation between him and the navy, and his stature in the other two services began to deteriorate. This would ultimately loom large in problems he was to encounter with the president in the summer of 1950; with the coming of war in Korea, the secretary of defense would need the complete confidence and support of all the military services, and that he did not have. It is ironic that some of the seeds of Johnson's ultimate downfall were planted during what he regarded as his finest hour—the defeat of the revolt.

CHAPTER TWELVE

"Like a Meatchopper on Roundsteak"

Louis Johnson's accomplishments in gaining control over all of the armed services and making unification work were the successes as secretary of defense that he would have most liked to have been remembered for. Unfortunately, he is most identified with a scorched-earth economy program that ended up weakening the military strength of the United States.

That Johnson's successes in unification should go largely unnoticed while his cost-cutting receives the lion's share of attention is due primarily to the fact that the Korean War began fifteen months into his tenure as secretary. When that conflict erupted in the summer of 1950, the American people, Congress, and the president focused on who to blame for the predicament the country found itself in. The understrength, poorly equipped army became the target of a storm of criticism. As usual, the nation began searching for someone to condemn for the military's failures. It did not take long for a scapegoat to be found, and Secretary Johnson was put on the sacrificial altar. He was put there by the president, and politicians and the public generally applauded the offering.

What is richly ironic about the fate that Johnson was to suffer is that the economy measures he so successfully instituted in the armed services were done at the insistence and encouragement of President Truman and with widespread support from Congress, the public, and the press. One well-known observer of the Defense Department summed it up best when he wrote, "Economy in Defense Department spending was blamed then for permitting that surprise attack [on Korea], and Johnson, the image of military frugality, became a scapegoat, actually for having carried out Truman's policy so well."[1]

Budget Imperatives

From the day Johnson took over the Defense Department, he made it clear that economy would be the hallmark of his administration. In his very first statement to the press he signaled his intention to provide the nation with "the maximum of strength within the limits of economy," but what those limits would be he was not yet willing to say.[2] In the weeks that followed, he made it clear that he supported the president's austere $14.2 billion military budget for the upcoming fiscal year, and in the year that followed he proved to be more committed to economy than anyone had expected.

Johnson's reasons for championing the cause of defense austerity were motivated by sincere economic concerns, loyalty to President Truman, his instinct for political survival, and, probably, by his presidential ambitions. His commitment to lean defense budgets stemmed in large part from a conviction that excessive defense spending would bankrupt the U.S. government, thereby leading to its ultimate destruction. To him, it was not the military threat facing the nation that presented the biggest challenge of the Cold War, it was the danger of economic ruin. If extravagant defense spending was not curbed, he warned members of Congress, the result would be exactly "what the Russians want: wreck the economy of America."[3] Later he elaborated on that idea by remarking that the Soviet leader, Joseph Stalin, "doesn't look to a clash of arms, [but] he expects America to spend itself into bankruptcy."[4] Such beliefs led him to conclude that if severe limitations were not imposed on American defense spending it would surely lead to the country's economic ruin, after which the Soviet Union would take over America.

In holding such economic views, Johnson was in company with a large number of Americans, including many in Congress, who believed "that the economy was already at the limit, if not over it, of what it could spend on defense."[5] Many lawmakers maintained that one of the major reasons for passing the National Security Act of 1947 was the expectation that it would bring about substantial savings in defense expenditures. Johnson's desire to cut back on defense outlays was by no means unique, but he was in a better position than most people in Washington to do something about it.

While economic motives were essential to Johnson's economy program, loyalty and political considerations were not far behind. Johnson's cabinet job could be retained only as long as he remained loyal to and pleased the Boss. If he could continue to do that, the position he had so long coveted would belong to him, but if he failed to please Truman he would be gone. Commenting on Johnson's motives, Secretary of State Dean Acheson said, "The zeal with which [Johnson] undertook to impose . . . [economy] upon the uniformed services came more from loyalty to the President and the zest of battle than from belief in it on its merits."[6]

What would Johnson need to do to keep the Boss happy? From the beginning, when Johnson and Truman met privately in January 1949, the president had made it clear that he wanted unification and economy brought to the National Military Establishment and that while he desired both, economy was most important. If Johnson was to keep his job he had to bring about real savings in defense expenditures. As Johnson himself was to say in later years, "The President gave me a job to do and I intended to do it."[7]

Beyond an obvious desire to please the president, Johnson may have had more subtle political motives. There was considerable speculation that the real motive behind his economy drive was political; that is, to earn a reputation as a fiscal conservative that would set him apart from other more liberal Democrats and pave the way for a presidential nomination in 1952. While Johnson always denied such conjecture, even his close friends were forced to admit that such a possibility had probably not escaped him.[8]

Although Johnson's own beliefs and political goals were important, they were not as significant as President Truman's views on defense spending; in the final analysis, he was the person who called the shots. The Boss held firm ideas on a number of issues, but his views about balancing the federal budget were rigid and dogmatic. Two principles dominated his thinking: first, that the preparation and oversight of the budget was a solemn obligation which required his personal attention; second, that it was essential that the budget at least be balanced and if possible show a surplus to hold down inflation and reduce the nation's debt. It was no idle boast when Truman said, "I have always taken an intense interest in all stages of the preparation of the budget and devoted considerable time to its details."[9] The president was convinced that the health of the nation was dependent on economic prosperity which could be reattained only if the federal government ran in the black. Truman was successful in this endeavor; in FY 1947 and 1948 there were budget surpluses, which increased to $4 billion for the period July 1, 1946, to June 1, 1950. Only the Korean War kept that trend from continuing.[10]

The president's determination to balance the budget guided his every decision on government expenditures. This meant that it frequently fell on his shoulders to say no to an agency or department that was requesting more funds. Although Congress and the United States at large generally shared the president's views on a balanced budget, most members of executive departments did not, especially those of the armed services. The military establishment felt that the man from Missouri was too stingy in providing funds for national defense. The nation's military leaders always felt it was better to be overprepared rather than underprepared, and the military was continually asking for more and more funds.

In later years, the president recalled that "many pressures were brought to get me to approve larger appropriations. This was particularly true of the military. All of them [army, navy, and air force] made excessive demands."[11] Truman repeatedly refused to give in to such pressures. To guide him in determining how much money should be spent on defense, he used what he delighted in calling the "remainder method." He would take the anticipated revenues for a fiscal year, then subtract the amount needed to fund all civilian programs; the remainder was the ceiling of defense expenditures.[12] This approach seemed "ass backward" to most military men, who felt defense expenditures should be calculated first and that the other programs should be funded out of what was left over.[13]

To provide sophistication and credibility to his "remainder method" of arriving at the defense budget, the president relied heavily on Director of the Bureau of the Budget James E. Webb and his successor Frank Pace; Secretary of Treasury John Snyder; presidential assistant John Steelman; and Chairman of the Council of Economic Advisors Edwin G. Nourse. These four men shared Truman's views on defense spending and a balanced budget and believed that if the line were not held the result would be new taxes or inflation.[14]

With an unshakeable commitment to a balanced budget, President Truman held the line on defense spending. The depth of his determination to adhere to his budget ceilings was made quite evident to Secretary of Defense James Forrestal, who, after failing to get the president to increase the defense budget in 1948, noted that he had experienced "in the person of Harry Truman . . . the most rocklike example of civilian control the world has ever witnessed."[15]

Turning Fat into Muscle

On March 4, the day after announcing Johnson's nomination, Truman called Johnson and all three service secretaries to the White House. As always, the Boss was impeccably dressed, he was freshly shaven, and he looked like he was just starting his day. Mirroring the purpose of the meeting—a harsh, no-nonsense order to support severe cuts in the defense budget—the president's desk was bare and the Oval Office was brightly lit.[16]

The president informed Johnson and his service secretaries that while Congress wanted to increase his FY 1950 defense budget of $14.2 billion, it was "highly essential that you and your staffs continue support of the 1950 budget so that we can maintain a proper balance within the military and between the military and other essential programs. . . . I want you to impress this necessity on your staff."[17] He added that in the following year, FY 1951, he would expect them to support a ceiling on defense expenditures that would be around $13 billion. Johnson broke the ensuing silence by saying, "Can we argue?" Truman curtly replied, "No."[18] If Johnson had not previously gotten the message, he had now.

In later years, Johnson was frequently criticized for going much farther in his economy moves than President Truman had ever intended. Such charges seem unwarranted when one examines Truman's statements, both public and private. Over and over Truman stated that he considered $14 billion a year for defense to be excessive and that he looked forward to an annual outlay in the range of $5 billion to $7 billion. One thing is certain: if Johnson had not been following the president's directives, he would have heard about it because Truman was not one to hide his feelings. Truman never indicated to Johnson that he was bringing "too much economy" to the Defense Department.

Although Johnson had missed consideration of the FY 1950 appropriations bill by the House of Representatives, he arrived in time to make his presence felt when the Senate began work on the bill in late spring of 1949. On June 16, when he went before the Senate Appropriations Committee, he stunned the senators by declaring, "I think we can save about a billion dollars by cutting out wastage, duplication and by cutting down unnecessary civilian employment."[19] When the senators pressed him on the billion-dollar figure, Johnson confidently predicted that he could institute changes that would bring such savings by year's end. His billion-dollar savings pledge got the senators' attention, and they invited him back to an executive session the following week to explain how he could effect such savings. At that session the secretary informed the lawmakers that his planned economies would take more than a year to implement but that half a billion dollars could be cut from the 1950 budget.

Johnson's testimony was persuasive. The Senate agreed to cut appropriations by $434 million and to permit the cuts to be made at the discretion of the secretary—an unprecedented idea Johnson himself suggested. He persuaded the senators that if he had this discretion he would use it to implement cutbacks that would not diminish the military's fighting capability. According to its report, the committee gave Johnson broad authority because the senators were pleased with the Secretary's moves to cut defense spending. He also impressed them with his arguments to eliminate $800 million from the budget by reducing the number of air groups in the air force from fifty-eight to forty-eight. Johnson's thinking was clearly evident when the Senate passed an appropriations bill in August which was more than $1 billion less than the $14.2 billion originally proposed and allowed Johnson to make discretionary cuts.[20]

It took weeks for the Conference Committee to work out the $1.1 billion difference in the House and Senate versions of the bill. However, in the end the cuts approved by the Senate were restored. When it was finally passed by both houses, the FY 1950 defense budget was $14.3 billion, which was divided fairly evenly among the three services.[21] Although the discretionary cuts Johnson had desired were not a part of the final bill, his commitment to budget reduction had made a deep impression on Congress. When the president refused to spend $800 million of additional funds appropriated for the air force, the budget was actually less than the $14.2 billion target that Truman had originally set. What had looked to the administration like an extremely difficult budgetary task at the beginning of the year had become reality by the fall of 1949.

Throughout the summer and fall of 1949, Johnson continued to preach the virtues of austerity, pointing out how he was already saving American taxpayers millions of dollars and that even greater savings would be forthcoming. In late June, testifying before the House Armed Services Committee in support of amendments to the National Security Act, Johnson claimed that true unification of the services would bring about considerable savings by eliminating waste, duplication, and extravagance. On numerous occasions Johnson even talked of a $1.5 billion rate of savings within eighteen months. He assured Vinson's committee that this could be accomplished by reorganization and management reform and without diminishing the fighting capabilities of the military.[22] As a consequence of Johnson's proselytizing on the Hill and his off-the-record talks with the press, he soon became known as the "Secretary of Economy."[23]

While Johnson was in the midst of trying to convince the Senate to accept the administration's FY 1950 budget, he was working hard on the FY 1951 defense budget. On the afternoon of July 1, 1949, the president summoned Johnson, the service secretaries, the Joint Chiefs of Staff, Secretary of State Dean Acheson, and the president's budget team to the White House. The Boss walked into the meeting and after a few pleasantries began reading from a prepared text. He summarized the economic problems facing the nation and the dangers of running a budget deficit and announced that he would establish lower ceilings for all major government departments for the remainder of FY 1950 and for FY 1951 with the objective of achieving the best balance between national security and a sound economy.

When Johnson asked what the Defense Department ceiling would be for the coming fiscal year, Truman declared that the absolute ceiling on defense expenditures for FY 1951 would be $13 billion. Johnson, not taken by surprise at all, informed Truman that the tentative number the Pentagon was prepared to propose was actually somewhat lower than $13 billion.[24] Truman polled the service secretaries by asking if $13 billion would be satisfactory to them. Each nodded affirmatively, but one veteran numbers-cruncher later said that "none of them realized what the hell it would do to each one of them."[25] Secretary of State Dean Acheson, the person in the administration most responsible for understanding the potential threats to the national security from abroad, expressed no misgivings about the president's lean $13 billion ceiling.[26]

Louis Johnson accepted the $13 billion ceiling for FY 1951 without reservation. The FY 1951 budget would be his first effort at preparing a defense budget from scratch, and he fully intended to exert strong leadership and produce a final proposal that would be in line with the president's directive. Keenly aware of Forrestal's problems in preparing the 1950 budget, Johnson was determined to avoid any show of weakness. In his budget sessions with his civilian and military advisors he made it abundantly clear that the president's guidelines would be followed, and he never deviated from that position. Good soldiers marched when ordered to do so, Johnson frequently reminded his listeners, and they had been given their marching orders.[27]

During July the three services made their cases for why they should not suffer the contemplated cuts to no avail. By mid-August Johnson had sketched the basic outline of the FY 1951 budget. The bulk of the reductions would be borne by the navy and to a lesser extent, the army, with support for the air force remaining near current levels.[28] The Joint Chiefs, sensing Johnson's determination, had to play ball because they had no real alternative other than resignation.[29] By such dictatorial means the 1951 budget was rammed through the Pentagon.

When Johnson presented the Defense Department's $13 billion FY 1951 budget to the president in December 1949, Truman was delighted, and with good reason. It was within the fiscal limits he had set forth; it had the endorsement, if not the enthusiastic support, of the civilian secretaries and Joint Chiefs; and it had been accomplished in house without stirring up a controversy in the Congress or the press.[30] These accomplishments stood in sharp contrast to the problems that had been encountered in the preparation of the previous defense budget when Forrestal was secretary—a fact not lost on the president. It was nice to have a man at the Pentagon he could count on.

On January 9, 1950, President Truman presented his FY 1951 budget to Congress, which sought $13 billion for defense. The next day Louis Johnson held one of his rare press conferences to explain and discuss the departmental budget. He acknowledged that the services had originally wanted $20 billion but that when they were asked to pare the figure down to the president's ceiling they had done so. When pressed by reporters, Johnson indicated that the force levels to be supported were not as great as the Joint Chiefs wanted, but he added, "It is my opinion that this country cannot, in time of peace, afford to support a military establishment of the size that military considerations . . . might call for." He assured reporters that "we are securing the most effective defense possible."[31]

A short time later, Johnson issued his first semi-annual report as secretary of defense, which reiterated his theme of economic austerity. In that document he noted that his major goal was to provide a "maximum of national security at a minimum cost." He pointed out how the reforms he had instituted toward that end were well on the way to saving $1 billion in the current year and would save $1.5 billion the following year. Included in the report was a statement that would come back to embarrass him in later years. He likened the armed forces to a fat man who needed to get into good shape to run a race and thus had to transform his fat into muscle.[32] The press picked up on the phrase. Henceforth, Johnson would be known as the man who was trimming the defense "fat" and transforming what was left into "muscle."[33]

In the spring of 1950, the secretary was deeply involved in selling his and the president's lean defense budget to the Congress. Johnson defended the reduced funding before the House Appropriations and Armed Services Committees. Some lawmakers expressed concern that the cuts were too deep, but the defense secretary and the Joint Chiefs gave assurances that an adequate peacetime defense was being provided for. That the Joint Chiefs were so supportive was surprising even to a seasoned observer such as Albert J. Engel (R-Michigan), who said he had never before "seen the Army, the Navy and the Air Force rather weakly accept the cutting of costs."[34] The show of unity was no accident—it was a carefully orchestrated performance, directed if not dictated by Johnson. He made it clear to his service secretaries and military advisors that he would not tolerate the kind of public backbiting that had occurred the year before under Forrestal.[35]

One may ask why the military leaders would go along with the cuts in light of their serious reservations about the effect of the reductions on the nation's military readiness. Why didn't they openly protest or resign to show their dissatisfaction? It is likely that General Bradley's answer to that question captured the thinking of all of them:

> I do not think that is the proper role for a military advisor. In fact, if men of any organization, civilian or military, should feel it necessary to resign every time their superiors made a decision with which they did not wholly agree, there would be constant upheavals and resignations. . . . I do not think that such a pseudodramatic act would have had the slightest effect during the economy drive that was sweeping Congress and people in the spring of 1950.[36]

Years later, Bradley wrote in his autobiography that his agreement to go along "was perhaps the greatest mistake I made in my postwar years in Washington" and that the $13 billion budget for FY 1951 was "perhaps the greatest [mistake] of Truman's presidency."[37]

As the House hammered out the defense budget that spring, Johnson was bitterly criticized by members who felt that his desire for economy was going too far. Armed Services Committee chairman Carl Vinson, who frequently was supportive of Johnson, attacked the secretary because his "economy scalpel not only carved away some service fat but cut deeply in some areas—into the sinews and muscles of the armed forces."[38] Another detractor, Representative Charles Plumley, likened Johnson's economies to those of a "man who cuts his wife's throat to stop her nosebleed."[39]

Such criticism, however, was in the minority, because the cost-cutting mood clearly dominated. On May 10, 1950, the House passed a bill which provided for $12.8 billion in defense expenditures for FY 1951. Again, Johnson and Truman could look with satisfaction at what had emerged—they were after economy and that is exactly what they were getting.

In late April 1950, while discussion of the FY 1951 budget was nearing conclusion in the House, the Senate took up the measure. Johnson had reworked the speeches he had given to the House and was beginning to serve them up to the Senate. However, before the Senate could act, war had broken out in Korea, and the proposed budget was dead in the water.

Flair for Drama

Hammering out a defense budget inside the Pentagon to meet the president's ceiling was a remarkable achievement, and selling it to Congress and the American public was no small task either. However, actually implementing the cutbacks involved rock-hard determination, superb administrative skills, and a herculean effort.

From his first weeks in office, Johnson's record of actually achieving savings in defense outlays was impressive. The main tool for implementing the cutbacks was the National Defense Management Committee, headed by General Joseph McNarney, which Johnson established shortly after he took office. Johnson was counting on the McNarney group because the $13 billion limit on the 1951 budget had already been announced by Truman and Johnson wanted to "bleed down" to that figure by the end of FY 1950 so that a drastic and demoralizing cut would not have to be made all at once when FY 1951 arrived.[40]

Although expecting great things from the McNarney Committee, Johnson knew that its proposals were weeks, if not months, away. He needed to act quickly to cut costs. On August 23, 1949, Johnson unveiled a plan, the presentation of which was probably staged by Steve Early, that was bold, dramatic, and unprecedented in the nation's capital. That afternoon more than 100 senators and representatives received telegrams from Secretary Johnson inviting them to attend a special briefing to be held at the Pentagon at 9:00 A.M. the following morning. This highly unusual invitation was both frustrating and irritating to the members of Congress; frustrating because they could not find out the nature of the upcoming briefing and irritating because they were used to having defense officials come to see them.[41] At 9:15 the next morning, Secretary Johnson stepped to a podium in the Pentagon theater before a crowd of unruly members of Congress and dozens of newsmen and coolly announced the dismissal of 135,000 civilian employees, the release of more than 12,000 reserve officers from active duty, the closing of 51 military installations, and the inactivation of 18 air force squadrons. The resulting savings of more than $200 million per year, he announced, was only the beginning of an extensive economy program.

During his brief remarks, Johnson made it clear that the decisions were made by the civilian rather than the military leadership in the Pentagon and that the motive was to provide adequate defense within the nation's economic means. He then proclaimed, "So long as I am Secretary of Defense we want a dollar's defense for each dollar you give us, and I personally will tolerate no WPA in the administration of the Defense Department."

When the secretary finished, an obviously angry Senator Charles W. Tobey (R-New Hampshire) asked, "Is this a *fait accompli*? Has the oracle spoken and the colors fallen? Is it accomplished as of noon today?" Johnson replied, "I don't like the word 'oracle.' It is the result of an impartial and fair study . . . and will be in effect today." After another short but heated exchange, Senator Tobey pointed out all the suffering the layoffs would cause. The secretary expressed sympathy for those affected and added that he hated to fire anyone but that "circumstances make it necessary."[42]

As the session ended, the grim-faced members of Congress filed out of the room buzzing like hornets. They had been invited to the meeting because they represented districts and states that would be impacted by the cuts. Most were angry, many were insulted, and almost all of them complained. Of course they were all for economy in government—but not in their district. Representative John Rooney (D-New York), in whose district the hard-hit Brooklyn Naval Yard was located, was indignant about the decision, which he claimed would do nothing but create unemployment. Senator Claude Pepper of Florida, another hard-hit state, lamented the fact that local merchants would suffer from the harsh decision to close facilities. Another obviously outraged congressman, Representative August Anderson (R-Minnesota), noted that spending nearly $1,000 in telegrams to "summon Congressmen to today's wake" opened to question the secretary's commitment to saving money.[43]

While Johnson's dramatic and headline-grabbing cutback decisions may have gained him some enemies, it won him many friends on the Hill, in the media, and among the public. Bipartisan support was forthcoming from members of both houses of Congress. Senator Harry F. Byrd (D-Virginia) praised the secretary's move, calling it "the first honest-to-goodness effort that has been made toward reduction in government personnel" in a decade.[44] Senator Arthur H. Vandenburg (R-Michigan) wrote a personal note to Johnson saying, "At least one member of Congress enjoys, applauds and glories in your economy 'gut.'"[45] In the House of Representatives, Frank W. Boykins (D-Alabama) and Albert J. Engel (R-Michigan) led the chorus of praise.[46]

On the evening of the secretary's announcement, Americans from coast to coast heard radio news commentator Morgan Beatty open his nightly program in this fashion:

> And the news tonight is the tornado that walks like a man, the tornado that has struck Washington and seems to stick around, kicking anything that gets in its way. It's a tornado by the name of Louis Johnson, Secretary of Defense. A big wing of Congress got in the way today and the tornado, named Johnson, started to work on the Hill like a meatchopper on roundsteak. The Secretary of Defense actually called the congressmen to his own bailiwick at the Pentagon and he told them in effect: You've been yelling for economy for a long time. Now you are going to get it.[47]

Similar support, but articulated in more sophisticated language, was forthcoming from many leading newspapers. Typical of editorial reaction was that of the New York Times, which commended Johnson for his move "to see to it that the nation gets value received for its outlay." It noted that the government had been talking a lot about saving but had done nothing and that now at last something positive was being done.[48] The *Washington Post* found it "encouraging that Secretary Johnson, in face of considerable pressure to delay, has had the resolution to start housecleaning without waiting for the consummation of this long overdue budgetary reform."[49] Scores of other prominent newspapers throughout the nation carried editorials expressing the same views. The overwhelmingly positive press reports, along with an avalanche of letters from citizens praising the secretary's actions, evidence the depth of support for his economy move.[50]

During the August briefing, Johnson indicated that the cutbacks were just the beginning, and it soon became apparent he had not been kidding. Nearly every month he announced additional economy measures. One year after taking office Johnson had implemented real savings that totaled nearly $750 million that year; the next year the savings was more than $1 billion.[51]

Wielding the Knife

As Johnson had forecast in his dramatic Pentagon briefing, the bulk of his cost savings came through personnel cutbacks, both civilian and military. By March 28, 1950, a year after taking office, civilian workers had been reduced by 163,000, resulting in an actual savings of $200 million for that year and projected savings in excess of $500 million in the following year. That same time period also witnessed substantial reductions in military personnel: total armed forces strength fell nearly 160,000, from 1,649,800 to 1,490,300—a far cry from the 12 million force level in existence less than five years before. Of all the services, the army was the target of the largest personnel cutbacks, although the navy and marine corps also suffered substantial reductions. These manpower reductions saved $79 million by March 28, 1950, and would have saved $277 million the following fiscal year.[52]

Going hand in hand with personnel reductions was the closing of fifty-one military installations, which saved $169 million. Thirteen army facilities were affected, including major installations such as Camp Kilmer, New Jersey; Fort Smith, Arkansas; and Fort Jackson, South Carolina. Eighteen air force bases were closed down. The navy experienced the greatest number of closings with twenty bases affected, including ordnance plants, supply depots, and air stations. Most of the civilian worker cutbacks came from the closing of these bases.[53]

In addition, drastic cost reductions were achieved by canceling and delaying construction of new facilities. These projects included barracks, runways, docks, and hangars. These cutbacks saved $80 million in FY 1950 and were expected to save $240 million the following year.[54]

Johnson also spearheaded cuts in procurement costs. Backed by Truman's cynical views on military waste and based on his years of experience with the army, Johnson was well aware of the military's tendency to ask for and obtain more than it really needed. In Johnson's words, the armed services were "still suffering from costly war-born spending habits."[55] Both he and Truman were convinced that the services had hundreds of millions of dollars' worth of material sitting in warehouses that was just rusting away.[56] Acting on his convictions, Johnson cut procurement costs by over $400 million for FY 1951.[57]

The personnel cutbacks, base closings, construction cancellations, and procurement reductions were the big savings areas, but as Johnson indicated to a friend, he was "determined to eliminate, as a matter of public duty . . . waste, duplication, inefficiency, obsolescent procedures and needless projects" wherever he found them.[58] He searched high and low for areas in which savings could be realized—and he found many. For example, he saved $60 million per year by eliminating flight status for thousands of administrative personnel who flew only to get extra pay. By insisting that the National Guard and Organized Reserves use World War II surpluses instead of purchasing new equipment, the Defense Department saved $56 million.[59]

After a year in office, Johnson was well on his way to accomplishing his billion-dollar-plus defense savings, but he did not let up. Throughout the spring of 1950 he continually admonished his service secretaries and his military advisors, complaining that "there had not been a sufficient reduction of personnel in the Washington area." He felt there were still "too many people at the Pentagon and still too much loafing."[60] At a meeting in mid-April of 1950 he expressed concern over a growing public feeling that the department was relaxing its economy program.[61] He then proceeded to make it clear that just the opposite was true, that they were "tightening up" and the job was "just starting." The past had been easy, he said, because it "was easy to use a butcher's knife; in the future it will take the scalpel of a surgeon." But reductions would be made.[62]

Several weeks later on May 12, Johnson directed McNarney's Defense Management Committee to initiate "new programs which will contribute to efficiency and cost reductions."[63] When war came to Korea in June 1950, Secretary Johnson's drive for defense economy was going as strong as ever and seemed well on its way to saving $1.5 billion per year.

As Johnson's economy moves were announced, they were greeted with varying degrees of moans and groans from some professional military men and a few members of Congress, but they were adhered to. However, on one occasion the secretary met his match, and that was over the issue of hospital closings. On February 1, 1950, after analyzing recommendations about how to reduce hospital costs without consulting the senior medical officer in the Pentagon, Rear Admiral Joe J. Boone, Johnson announced the closings of eighteen military hospitals at a savings of $25 million per year. Negative congressional reaction to this announcement was both immediate and broad-based. Pressure mounted, and in early March Admiral Boone told a House Armed Services Subcommittee

that the closings were premature and "shortsighted." As a result of Boone's testimony and pressure from constituents, Chairman Vinson asked Johnson to suspend his order pending further congressional scrutiny. In early April, as criticism mounted, Johnson reluctantly agreed to "take another look" at his closing
orders. Several weeks later, realizing he had made a political blunder, Johnson
revised his earlier order by closing only three hospitals and transferring two to
the Veterans Administration.[64]

Although most officers and enlisted men in each of the military services were
adversely affected one way or another by the cutbacks emanating from the
Johnson austerity program, they tended, in general, to look favorably upon him
because he championed three things that were near and dear to their hearts: a
pay raise, increased medical care for dependents, and better military housing.
While Johnson frequently feuded with top brass and held many of them in contempt for their laziness or stupidity, he always had great respect and admiration
for the officers and men on the line, and he always looked out for their welfare.[65]
One of the first things Johnson advocated when he came to office was legislation for a military pay raise, and he began vigorously lobbying the House and
Senate Appropriations and Armed Services Committees. His primary argument for the raise was that it would enable the military to retain many highly
skilled personnel who were being lost to the private sector. When the Career
Compensation Act was ultimately passed on October 12, 1949, no one was more
pleased than the secretary of defense. Under this legislation, which was the first
major revision in four decades, officers' pay increased approximately 25 percent
while that of noncommissioned officers rose about 20 percent.[66] The Compensation Act did more than any other military-related legislation passed in the
postwar years to elevate service morale.

No sooner had the pay raise gone into effect, however, than the new director
of the budget, Frank Pace, proposed eliminating medical care for dependents
of military personnel. Johnson, who had not been consulted, immediately sided
with the military and protested vigorously to Pace and President Truman. The
effect of taking away one of the major fringe benefits of military service, he argued, would do untold damage to service morale. Members of Congress, veterans' organizations, and large segments of the public likewise protested, and the
controversial proposal was dropped.[67]

The absence of housing on or near military bases for dependents was another
factor that diminished morale in the armed services. Realizing the magnitude
of the problem, the secretary created a departmental Housing Commission to
report to him on ways to provide adequate housing for military personnel and
their families. Armed with the data that group provided, Johnson pushed vigorously and successfully for passage of the Wherry-Spence Act, which provided
for construction of family quarters overseas, especially in Okinawa and Alaska,
and gave financial incentives to encourage construction of rental properties

near military installations. When Johnson left the Defense Department, considerable progress had been made in housing, but even he acknowledged that "the problem is still serious."[68]

Thus, while Johnson earned, and deservingly so, a reputation as a penny-pincher, he never directed his knife at the welfare of military personnel. On the contrary, by promoting a pay raise, defending medical care for dependents, upgrading housing, and continually telling the nation how competent and dedicated military personnel were, he made it difficult for men and women in uniform and their families to fault him.

Throughout his tenure as secretary of defense, Louis Johnson maintained that "our watchword is and must be economy in every activity."[69] He never lost sight of that goal. He was continually preaching to everyone — members of Congress, cabinet members, military personnel, and the American public — how he had already saved money and how he was going to save even more. He used public speeches, radio broadcasts (one radio executive claimed that "if the Secretary received all the free time he requested he would be on the air more than Arthur Godfrey"), appearances before congressional committee, letters to members of Congress, and statements to the press to report how successful he was in simultaneously saving money and strengthening the nation's military forces.

In the spring of 1950, Secretary Johnson announced that the nation's defenses were in better shape then they had been since World War II. Then, in a statement that prompted hilarity throughout the Pentagon, Johnson bragged that "[i]f Joe Stalin starts something at 4:00 A.M., the fighting power of the U.S., spearheaded by the Air Force, will be on the job at 5:00 A.M." It is not surprising that many people considered him "the biggest pop-off in Washington."[70]

While it is true that Johnson was a self-promoting "pop off," there is also no question that his economy program resulted in very substantial savings in defense outlays. The exact amount is difficult to determine with precision, but by any objective assessment it is safe to conclude that he was responsible for saving approximately $750 million during his first year in office. This was no small accomplishment.[71]

Cutting into Muscle

Johnson saved money and would have saved more had it not been for the Korean War, but the key question is whether the economy drive initiated by Truman and carried out by Johnson significantly reduced America's military capability. Johnson always maintained that his cost cutbacks did not reduce U.S. military strength. The facts point to a much different conclusion. The defense cuts not only removed the fat but in many cases penetrated well into the muscle and in some cases clear to the bone.

The impact of Johnson's military manpower reductions is quite evident. When he assumed office in late March 1949, overall military strength stood at 1,646,711. From that point it dropped steadily until June 1950, when it reached 1,461,352, a decrease of 11 percent. Reductions hit all services, but the army, which lost 98,300 men, was hardest hit. From a previously authorized strength of 677,000, the army actually numbered only 591,000 in June 1950. Of these, 360,000 were in the United States and only 108,500 were stationed in the Far East. During the same period, the navy lost almost 76,000 officers and enlisted men, while the marine corps experienced a decline of 11,500 as it dipped from 88,000 to 75,000. Even the air force, which was at the height of its glory, experienced a slight reduction as it dropped from 417,000 to 411,200.[72] Although Johnson claimed that despite the cutbacks more personnel were in combat units, everyone in the military, from the chief of staff down to the private, knew that combat effectiveness was not being maintained.

Johnson's austerity knife also cut into the acquisition of many vital weapons. The number of the navy's major combat vessels dropped from 271 in June 1949 to 237 one year later; most of the reductions consisted of destroyers and submarines. Naval aircraft were also drastically reduced by 1,300, dropping from 5,600 when Johnson took office to 4,300 in June 1950. During this same period, air force strength declined from sixty-six to forty-eight air groups, a number that Johnson and Truman considered adequate. Johnson explained away this reduction by noting that under the recent reorganization some groups had more aircraft than they had previously and that new aircraft were more efficient than earlier models. These claims were in fact true, but what Johnson failed to point out was that in his first fifteen months in office the number of operable aircraft dropped by 1,100, going from 9,900 to 8,800.[73]

The combat readiness of the army and marine corps likewise suffered. In the postwar years virtually no changes were made in the weapons used by ground forces. Whenever funds were requested for new, up-to-date equipment, Congress would point to the huge surpluses left over from World War II and claim they were sufficient to meet any conventional war emergency. As a result, the army was equipped with World War II weapons: M-1 rifles, Browning automatic rifles, .30 and .50 caliber machine guns, 105mm howitzers, and Sherman tanks. In June 1950, the army had only 310 of the new Patton tanks, and all were in the United States. The World War II antitank bazooka had been replaced by a 3.5-inch bazooka, but there were only a few on hand and none in the Far East.

In June 1950, the army consisted of ten tactical divisions and nine regimental combat teams, most of which were operating at greatly reduced strength and with poorly trained soldiers who relied on weapons and ammunition produced during the last war.[74] The marines suffered the same equipment problems as the army and experienced serious reductions in their aviation capability. As General Matthew Ridgway later put it, "We were, in short, in a state of shameful unreadiness."[75]

It is evident that Johnson's economy programs seriously weakened the effectiveness of America's fighting forces—a situation for which a heavy price would eventually be paid. Obviously, Johnson did not foresee the consequences of his actions. He was a fiercely patriotic American who believed that what he was doing was in the national interest. Had there been no Korean War, Johnson might well have been praised as the man responsible for helping Truman balance the budget, halt inflation, bring true unification to the armed services, and end the orgy of wasteful spending on defense. He could even have been a contender for the presidency in 1952.

Tunnel Vision

With the benefit of hindsight, it is difficult to understand why Johnson, let alone Truman, did not foresee the consequences of the draconian cuts in the nation's defense budget. After all, world communism was on the rise. Cold War challenges had already been hurled at the United States in Greece, Turkey, Berlin, China, and other hot spots. The Soviets had three times more combat aircraft and an army four times larger than the United States, but that did not seem to alarm Johnson. As secretary of defense, Johnson, perhaps more than any American, should have been working to at least maintain conventional ground strength.

Instead, Johnson continued to cut funds and rely on the atomic bomb. He thought that the United States would have a monopoly over the atomic bomb until at least 1952 and that it would take other nations several more years to develop an effective delivery system. Like many others at the time, Johnson believed that if war ever came to America again it would be in the form of an all-out conflagration in which victory would be achieved by air force delivery of atomic bombs. Convinced that that was the only real contingency to prepare for, Johnson supported the air force and its nuclear weapons capability and discounted the importance of conventional ground forces.

Johnson simply could not imagine that moral and humane considerations would impose limits on the use of nuclear weapons and that the United States would need conventional forces as a deterrent to communist aggression and for deployment in limited regional conflicts. This lack of vision stemmed not only from overreliance on the atomic bomb but also from his belief that military and foreign policy issues should be compartmentalized—he never came to understand how a thorough assessment of the real threats to the national security could be used to fashion a defense policy and a budget to support it.[76] Consequently, he did not believe that his major responsibility was to work seamlessly with others to implement an integrated national security strategy; rather he felt his chief duty was to achieve large defense savings that would keep the American economy healthy and at the same time please his boss, Congress, and the

American public. Unfortunately, that goal, which at one time seemed so laudable, "turned sour," said noted military historian Walter Millis, "leaving him, when emergency arose, under savage criticism for not having provided the armaments which the people and their political representatives had been unwilling to pay for."[77]

The piquant irony is that the enormous amount of criticism that was ultimately to come Johnson's way was due to the fact that he had been so successful in fighting his battle for economy. While Johnson must share considerable responsibility for the deterioration of the armed forces that took place when he was secretary, several extenuating circumstances need to be kept in mind. In the first place, his economy program had widespread support. It is clear that congressional and public opinion was overwhelmingly in agreement with his view that the nation needed to economize in the realm of defense expenditures. Moreover, he was following President Truman's orders. The president had let Johnson's predecessor go in part because of an inability to gain the support of the armed services for his budget ceiling. Johnson realized that if he could not put into effect the cuts desired by the president, he too would be gone.

More fundamentally, the Truman administration lacked a comprehensive and well-conceived strategic defense policy, which meant that Johnson and his top advisors had no real direction to guide their strategic thinking and actions. While they understood the reality of the Cold War, they did not understand what it meant in terms of the appropriate level of defense preparedness in 1949. The administration did not come to grips with the need to think through and adopt a national security strategy until the spring of 1950, when Assistant Secretary of State Paul Nitze and his team developed NSC 68, a document that outlined a strategy for defending the nation against threats posed by the Soviet Union and called for dramatic increases in the manpower, weaponry, and composition of forces needed to implement that strategy.

Finally, even with a strategy in place, no one—certainly not Johnson or any other secretary of defense—knew how much should be spent on the armed forces during peacetime. Representative George Mahon (D-Texas), chairman of the House Appropriations Committee's Subcommittee on Armed Services, put it best when, in 1949, he said, "If war comes soon, we are appropriating too little. If we have miscalculated the dangers, if the threat of war is just a deceptive mirage on the horizon, we are appropriating too much."[78]

The amount spent on defense was and continues to be a value judgment based on the degree of calculated risk a nation and its leaders are willing to take. Only the future will reveal whether an amount spent is too much, too little, or just right. History shows that Johnson believed in too little.

CHAPTER THIRTEEN

"My God, the Russians Have the Bomb"

Louis Johnson's ability to fight so successfully for austerity in the defense budget, especially during his first six months in office, was due to the fact that in the tension-filled conflict with the Soviet Union the United States held the trump card: it had the atomic bomb. In early 1949, even the most pessimistic U.S. officials were predicting that the USSR would not be able to detonate an atomic weapon before 1952. Dr. Vannevar Bush, the renowned scientist who headed the Office of Research and Development during World War II, claimed that America would have a monopoly on nuclear weapons until 1956, and many senior military officials believed the monopoly would last until 1960. This meant that in the late 1940s, America's national security and foreign policies were premised on the assumption that no other nation possessed or would soon possess the bomb.[1]

Control of the Nuclear Arsenal

In the weeks immediately following the surrender of Japan, President Truman, sensing the awesome responsibility that possession of atomic weapons placed upon him and the nation, considered approaching the Soviet Union about an agreement to forestall a dangerous and expensive arms race. This bilateral approach was soon abandoned and it was decided to turn information concerning nuclear fission over to the newly formed United Nations and provide through it the machinery for international control of atomic energy.

During the period 1946 through 1948, the United States and the USSR frequently sparred before the UN Atomic Energy Commission over questions of international control of nuclear weapons. The United States insisted that it had to retain its stockpile of atomic weapons until the UN machinery for safeguarding America's security was in place. The Soviets demanded that the United States destroy all atomic weapons and halt production before they would even discuss the issue of international control. They were also opposed to on-site inspections, a requirement the United States considered absolutely essential. By early 1949, no real progress had been made. President Truman had all but given up hope that international control would become a reality.[2]

While consideration of UN control of atomic energy was under way, the United States began to develop the machinery to control it domestically. The mechanism that emerged reflected President Truman's conviction that control of atomic energy must be under civilian rather than military jurisdiction. His tenacious stand ultimately resulted in the Atomic Energy Act of 1946, which conferred control of the entire program on a five-member Atomic Energy Commission (AEC), made up of civilians who were appointed by the president and confirmed by the Senate. The commission would exercise control over atomic research and development as well as production of all atomic weapons.[3]

As a sop to Pentagon officials and congressional supporters of military control, the legislation provided for a Military Liaison Committee to the AEC. This body, composed of two representatives from each of the military services and chaired by either a civilian or military person, all appointed by the secretary of defense, could advise and consult with the AEC on all military applications of atomic energy. It also had the authority to make requests to the AEC on military weapons production; if the two disagreed, the secretary of defense could take the issue to the president for a final decision.

Nevertheless, the Atomic Energy Act made crystal clear that the civilian-controlled AEC would determine the kinds of weapons to be developed, where they would be located, and, most important, when and under what conditions they would be used.[4] January 1, 1947, was a sad day for the military because on that date the AEC assumed control of all of the nation's atomic energy programs. The president warned the commission members that the army would continue to fight to regain control of the program, and it did so during the remainder of his administration.[5]

Security Blanket

While the Pentagon, the White House, and Congress feuded over the question of control of nuclear weapons, the American public ignored the controversy because it felt secure behind its atomic shield. A barrage of media accounts about the annihilation of Hiroshima and Nagasaki and newsreels of the 1946 nuclear tests in the South Pacific vividly demonstrated the destructive capability of the new weapon. Knowing the power inherent in their atomic arsenal and realizing that no other nation possessed such a weapon, Americans concluded that no nation, including the Soviet Union, would dare challenge U.S. military hegemony.

During those postwar years, Americans did not realize how thin the security blanket of the atomic bomb was. The public assumed, as did U.S. allies and enemies, that America was armed to the teeth with thousands of atomic bombs that could be delivered without much difficulty to prime targets anywhere in the world. If the U.S. public had known the true strength of the arsenal, it would have been shocked and horrified.[6] If America's enemies had known, they would probably have been more aggressive.

For obvious reasons, one of the U.S. government's best-kept secrets was the number of atomic bombs it possessed. The figures were considered to be so important to national security that they were never put in documents; instead, the information was placed on separate pieces of paper or conveyed verbally to the members of the AEC and other top officials who needed to know.[7] In April 1947, just three months after the AEC assumed its responsibilities, the commission's chairman, David E. Lilienthal, delivered a written report to the president which said, "The present supply of atomic bombs is very small. The actual number for which all parts are available is   ." When Lilienthal told the president in person what the real number was, Truman appeared shocked. The information that followed was even more bleak, for the chairman revealed that "none of those bombs is assembled" and that the teams necessary to carry out that difficult task were not yet available.[8]

How many bombs were they actually talking about in early 1947? Probably about a dozen. While that figure would be significantly increased in the following year, the number was probably no more than fifty when the Berlin Crisis began in the spring of 1948.[9]

1948 was a key year in the development of the American nuclear arsenal. That summer the B-36, the first true intercontinental bomber, was delivered, greatly improving U.S. nuclear strike capability.[10] Also of great importance was a technological breakthrough in the production of nuclear cores, which significantly reduced the amount of fissionable material needed for each bomb. This new process enabled the AEC to step up its production schedule; the agency predicted that it would have 400 completed bombs by January 1, 1951—two years ahead of its previous prediction.[11]

Another important development came in September, when President Truman, for the first time, indicated privately that if absolutely necessary he would order a nuclear attack. This was significant because while the president's advisors and the American public believed that Truman would order a nuclear strike, as he had done to end World War II, this was the first time the president, the only one who could order such a strike, had said that he would do it again if necessary.[12]

While the AEC was addressing the problems of weapons production and control, the Pentagon and the White House were moving toward a nuclear arms policy. In the aftermath of World War II, the United States demobilized with unprecedented haste, going from 10 million personnel in 1945 to 1.4 million in 1947. While the Soviet Union also demobilized, it still had a force of between 3 and 4 million in this period.[13] Because of this disparity, American military planners knew that the nation would not be able to confront and defeat the Soviets by deploying conventional forces and they therefore focused on the concept of a strategic air offensive, using the destructive power of the atomic bomb, as the primary initial thrust in a conflict with the USSR. In 1948, Truman endorsed this military strategy, privately pledging to use the bomb if necessary and approving NSC 30, a document which recognized that the military "must be ready to utilize promptly and effectively all appropriate means available, including atomic weapons" in a future war.[14]

The atomic weapons strategy that emerged in 1947 and early 1948 was solidified in the summer of 1948 when President Truman made his decision to limit the defense budget to $15 billion or less in the year ahead. This fiscal limitation ended any hope the military had of developing adequate conventional forces and compelled the United States to rely on the atomic bomb as its primary means of providing adequate defense.

It was this reliance on the air force and its nuclear capability that so upset the navy and led to the 1949 revolt of the admirals. But if the navy doubted the wisdom of this strategy, the air advocates did not. By 1949 the air force was convinced that an atomic blitz of any enemy would achieve total victory.[15] This view was widely shared in Congress, where many politicians agreed with Senator Brien McMahon (D-Connecticut), chairman of the Joint Congressional Committee on Atomic Energy, who maintained that strategic bombing with atomic weapons was the "keystone of our military policy."[16] Various Gallup Polls conducted during those years revealed that a large majority of Americans agreed.[17]

Atomic Blitz Theory

By the time Louis Johnson arrived at the Pentagon in the spring of 1949 the air advocates were clearly in control—a situation which was pleasing to the new defense secretary. His long-standing advocacy of air power as the ultimate military weapon made him supportive of a policy in which the air force was the dominant armed service. His plans for bringing economy to the defense establishment could best be achieved with the atomic blitz concept because while the production and delivery of nuclear weapons would be expensive, they were not nearly as costly as providing conventional forces sufficient to meet the Soviet challenge. Even if Johnson had been sympathetic to a balanced force, it would have been impossible to make any progress in that direction in view of the president's limitations on defense spending. Whether by conviction or fear of losing his job, Johnson came to the defense post committed to a program that was heavily dependent on the acquisition of atomic bombs and their delivery systems—long-range bombers.[18]

Because the AEC controlled the development and procurement of atomic weaponry, Johnson worked frequently with its chairman, David Lilienthal. Unfortunately, the two men never got along. The friction resulted not only from personality factors (the soft-spoken, humble Lilienthal was turned off by Johnson's boastfulness) but also from philosophical differences. Johnson's view was that the AEC should serve essentially as "munitions-makers, who accepted requisitions from the military and asked no questions," but Lilienthal's firm belief was that Congress, at Truman's insistence, had put the civilian sector and not the military in control of atomic energy, including weapons. Beginning with their very first meeting, Johnson made it clear that he wanted and expected to secure large numbers of atomic bombs for the military.[19]

Johnson also believed that the government should make clear its willingness to use such weapons. Only if potential enemies knew the United States would use the atomic bomb could it have the deterrent value that he considered so important. The new secretary pressed the president on this matter, and on April 6, 1949, Truman publicly announced for the first time that if necessary he would use the atomic bomb again.[20] Just how influential Johnson was in that decision is not clear, but he nevertheless was pleased with it.

The unity of thought which the president and his new defense secretary appeared to display on the vastly expanded role of atomic bombs in future warfare, which implied a large air force capable of delivering such weapons, soon began to alarm some of the men surrounding the president. Newly appointed budget director Frank Pace expressed to Truman his concern that the administration was moving toward a situation in which it would be committed to unrestricted atomic warfare in any future conflict. Truman's naval aide, Rear Admiral Robert L. Dennison, also urged the president to examine what appeared to be too great a reliance on a nuclear air offensive.[21]

As a result of these concerns and recommendations, Truman requested and received a briefing on April 29 from Air Force Chief of Staff Vandenburg on what would happen if war broke out with the Soviet Union. The following day the president directed Johnson to expedite two studies initiated under Forrestal, the first to determine the ability of the air force to deliver atomic bombs to their assigned targets in the Soviet Union and the second to analyze the impact if all the bombs reached their targets. Johnson told Truman that the studies would be given top priority but warned that they would take considerable time.[22] The first study moved very slowly and was not completed until January 1950.[23] The second study was ready by mid-May. This analysis was performed by a seven-person task force known as the Harmon Board, named after its chairman, Air

Force Lieutenant General Hubert R. Harmon. The board's report was upsetting to the air force because it found that massive bombing would not "per se,
bring about capitulation," nor would it seriously impair the ability of the Soviet
army to advance into neighboring nations. Nevertheless, in light of the president's views on the defense budget, the board saw no alternative and concluded
that "every reasonable effort should be devoted to providing the means to be
prepared for prompt and effective delivery of the maximum number of atomic
bombs to appropriate targets."[24]

Air Force Chief of Staff Vandenburg disagreed with the Harmon Report because he felt that it greatly underestimated the air force's capabilities. Several
heated discussions about the report took place among the JCS, but with the support of General Bradley and Admiral Denfeld the document was submitted, virtually unchanged, to Secretary Johnson on July 28, 1949. Accompanying the report was a letter from Vandenburg that expressed serious reservations about its
conclusions but not its recommendations.[25]

When Johnson received the Harmon Report from the JCS, he was no more
pleased with it than the air force had been. The reasons for his displeasure are
not known, but it is evident that Johnson was reluctant to share the Harmon Report with the president. He did not discuss it with Truman until mid-October,
some three months after he received it, and the report itself was never made
available to the president. Johnson's rationale for not submitting the Harmon
Report to the Boss was his belief that it was of no real value without the first study,
which would indicate how many bombers would actually get through to their
targets.[26] As that study proceeded in the latter half of 1949, Johnson was immersed in other nuclear weapons issues.

Sharing Secrets

Although Johnson entered the Truman administration seeing eye to eye with
the president on the importance of airpower and atomic weapons, the two
men did not agree when it came to sharing atomic energy information with
Britain and Canada. During World War II, the United States had cooperated
closely with the British and Canadians because of their access to raw uranium
in the Belgian Congo. When the war ended, however, the British wanted the
precious element for their own nuclear program. Negotiations with the
United States moved in fits and starts, and in January 1948 the three nations
reached a temporary agreement whereby virtually all uranium produced in
the Congo in 1948 and 1949 would go to the United States in return for information about nuclear energy in all fields except that of weapons development.
That agreement went into effect on an optimistic note, but by the summer of
1948 the British were demanding information on plutonium weapons development and production.[27]

Senior military and AEC officials were divided over whether this sensitive information should be provided to the British. The military argued that Britain, as America's closest ally and possessor of airbases within range of Moscow, should be given the information. On the opposite side were those who believed the information was so vital to the national security that it should not be shared. Since both views had strong advocates, the president had appointed a special committee in February 1949 comprised of his new secretary of state, Dean Acheson; Secretary Forrestal; and AEC chairman David Lilienthal to examine the issue and make a recommendation.[28]

On March 2, 1949, the day Forrestal submitted his resignation, the group proposed an agreement with Britain and Canada whereby the United States would collaborate and share its nuclear information with them in return for 90 percent of the Congo's uranium. Although the specifics of the sharing obligation were ambiguous, the president accepted the proposal. But before he proceeded, he decided to apprise the Joint Congressional Committee on Atomic Energy of his intentions.[29]

By the time Johnson arrived at the Pentagon in late March of 1949, the proposal to collaborate with Britain and Canada appeared to be a fait accompli. Because of more pressing problems the proposal lay dormant until mid-June, when the president met with Johnson and Acheson to make plans to gain congressional support for the plan. While Truman and Acheson did not doubt the merits of the proposal to share, Johnson was not so sure. The new defense secretary was receiving mixed signals from his advisors. The JCS mildly embraced the idea of close collaboration, but many other advisors were still cautioning Johnson of the danger of "giving away secrets."[30]

The president's first task was to convince the chairman of the Joint Congressional Committee, Senator McMahon, of the merits of collaboration with Britain and Canada on nuclear information, and he asked Dean Acheson to spearhead the effort. On the afternoon of July 6, Johnson went to Secretary Acheson's office, where the two men were joined by AEC Commissioner Sumner T. Pike (representing Lilienthal) and Senator McMahon. The defense chief listened while Acheson and Pike advanced the administration's proposal. If the presenters had expected enthusiastic support, they were certainly disappointed; McMahon not only expressed his own concerns but he also predicted that the idea would meet considerable opposition in his committee. While Johnson may have shared many of the senator's reservations, he realized that as a good soldier he could not openly oppose the administration. So he remained silent, and his silence may have implied support for the plan. Before the meeting adjourned, it was agreed that selected members of the Joint Congressional Committee should meet secretly with the president to discuss the proposal.[31]

At eight o'clock on the evening of July 14, an impressive array of administration and congressional figures arrived during a violent thunderstorm at Blair

House, the president's temporary residence while the White House was undergoing renovation. Among those representing the administration were the president, Vice President Barkley, Acheson, Johnson, Lilienthal, Pike, General
Eisenhower, and the newly appointed undersecretary of state, James Webb.
Representing the Joint Committee were Senators McMahon, Bourke Hickenlooper (R-Iowa), Arthur Vandenberg (R-Michigan), Tom Connally (D-Texas),
and Millard Tydings (D-Maryland), and Representative Carl Durham (D-
North Carolina), who was vice chairman of the Joint Committee. As was usual
when the president met with an important congressional delegation, Speaker
of the House Sam Rayburn was also present.

President Truman opened the meeting with a statement which recalled the
close cooperation between the United States, Britain, and Canada in developing the atomic bomb and stressed the need to assure adequate raw materials if
the nation's atomic energy needs were to be met. Acheson presented the administration's sharing proposal and its rationale and Lilienthal emphasized the
need for such an agreement if the AEC was to have the uranium necessary to
meet the weapons goals of the Joint Chiefs. The president then called on
Johnson, who was uncharacteristically brief in expressing his concurrence with
Acheson's analysis. Johnson quickly turned the floor over to Eisenhower, who
said that from a military point of view cooperation with Britain was desirable.

The administration's hopes for quick support from members of Congress
were immediately dashed. Senators Vandenberg and Hickenlooper voiced
strong opposition while Chairman McMahon questioned the legality of the
proposal and expressed skepticism about how his committee would react. After
more than two hours of intense discussion, the group, pledging silence to the
press, departed, having agreed only that the proposal would be presented to the
Joint Committee six days later.[32]

On the afternoon of July 20, Johnson and General Eisenhower went to Room
48G in the Capitol Building, where they were joined by Acheson and Lilienthal
and the entire membership of the Joint Congressional Committee. Acheson,
who was in charge of the meeting, made an opening statement but did not set
forth the administration's proposal. As he had done at the Blair House conference, he first called on Lilienthal for his statement of support before calling on
Johnson.

The defense chief stunned his colleagues in the administration by merely
turning the microphone over to General Eisenhower and asking him to present
the military viewpoint. Some of the hostile congressmen noted Johnson's obvious refusal to personally endorse the administration's proposal, and they
quickly jumped on Eisenhower with questions the general had great difficulty
in answering. Sensing a breakdown within the ranks of the administration, the
opponents of the plan attacked. Senators Hickenlooper, Eugene (R-Colorado),
and Knowland (R-California) made it clear that they did not want Britain to

have U.S. atomic secrets. By this time it was evident that Acheson had lost control of the meeting.[33]

Then, just as both sides appeared to be going for the jugular vein of the other, Louis Johnson stepped in as peacemaker. He told the irate senators that if they would not publicly attack the proposal he "would see to it that the Defense Establishment reviewed its entire position in the light of what had been said at the meeting" and perhaps they could come up with some new ideas.[34]

Johnson's suggestion, which Lilienthal referred to as "a neat rug-pulling job on Dean," and which Acheson described as the point "when Johnson neatly separated himself from me," had the effect of calming the irate congressmen but had the greater consequence of dooming the administration's proposal.[35] By indicating a willingness to reexamine the scheme and possibly make modifications, Johnson sent a signal to the Joint Congressional Committee that the administration's position was fluid.[36] Johnson, who by this time had decided that the government should not share any atomic secrets with Britain, had marked time until he saw an opportunity to undercut what he had come to believe was an unwise course.

Five days later, on July 25, Johnson, citing extreme congressional hostility, urged the president to back down on the issue of sharing nuclear information. When Truman insisted that he had the constitutional authority to take the desired action without congressional approval, a position supported by Acheson and Lilienthal, Johnson disagreed and claimed that sharing was not legally permissible under the Atomic Energy Act.[37] The president rejected Johnson's legal arguments, but he agreed with Johnson and Acheson's recommendation to "fall back and regroup."[38] Two days later the two secretaries went before the Joint Congressional Committee to deliver the administration's decision to discuss areas of mutual concern but not to develop a new agreement or extend the areas of collaboration.[39] For the time being at least, the administration was backing down.

In the weeks that followed, the State Department prepared for the negotiations with Britain and Canada on collaboration and sharing. While Johnson publicly endorsed the extension of the current "temporary" agreement, he privately believed that even it went too far in sharing valuable information. Behind the scenes, he attempted to undermine the upcoming talks by claiming that sharing nuclear information was illegal and that the AEC wanted to "give away the secret" of the atomic bomb.[40]

Nevertheless, the talks with Britain and Canada got under way and were still going on in February 1950 when British scientist Klaus Fuchs, who had worked on the Manhattan Project, was arrested in London for passing atomic secrets to the Soviets. The public and congressional uproar that followed led to a suspension of the talks, and Johnson blocked efforts to resume them as long as he remained in office.[41] Although Johnson's stated objections to the sharing of atomic information were based on legal grounds, his opposition was in fact premised on his belief that protection of atomic secrets was essential to national security and that sharing top-secret nuclear information with any nation, including England and Canada, would increase the possibility of that information falling into Soviet hands.

Alarming Discovery

While Johnson was in the midst of the nuclear collaboration issue and was trying to work with Acheson and Lilienthal on a study of whether to expand the nation's atomic weapons program, events abroad radically altered the U.S. defense picture, especially as it related to atomic weapons.

On Saturday, September 3, 1949, the Air Force Long Range Detection System in Washington received a report from a weather reconnaissance plane that was en route from Japan to Alaska indicating above-average concentrations of radioactivity in the area. Since the detection system, which had only been in operation about a year, still had some bugs to be worked out, the report did not cause much concern. However, during the next few days aircraft sent to the area confirmed the earlier reports so conclusively that by Wednesday, September 7, it was evident that nuclear fission had taken place. The question was whether it came from a bomb or a nuclear accident.[42]

The detection reports forwarded to the Pentagon went first to William Webster, chairman of the Military Liaison Committee to the AEC, who was in effect Johnson's deputy on atomic energy issues. On September 7, Webster presented the reports to Johnson, who refused to believe that the source of the radioactivity was a bomb. While there were a few in the military who had informed him that the Russians would have an atomic bomb within a year, he was more inclined to accept the assurances of men such as Lilienthal and top Pentagon intelligence personnel that such a development, while inevitable, would not occur until 1952 or later.[43] Nevertheless, he agreed that the matter needed to be investigated and approved Webster's suggestion to ask the AEC to create a special committee to interpret the information being gathered.

The AEC panel of experts, which was headed by Dr. Vannevar Bush and included the father of the atomic bomb, Dr. Robert J. Oppenheimer, began work immediately. By September 14, most members of the Bush panel and other officials who reviewed the evidence tended to believe that the Soviets had indeed detonated a bomb. Two important skeptics remained: Johnson and Truman. Webster pointed out to Johnson that the analysts were 95 percent sure that it was a bomb, but the secretary chose to focus on the 5 percent chance that it was a laboratory accident. He did not favor making any public announcement about what had allegedly taken place. He wanted more solid data.[44] The other doubter, President Truman, called Dr. Oppenheimer to Blair House to discuss the evidence. Oppenheimer stated that in his opinion a bomb blast had oc-curred, but the president did not believe him.[45]

The Bush panel continued its deliberations. On the morning of the 19th, the group came to the conclusion that the fission products found in the atmo-sphere came from a Soviet atomic bomb detonated on August 29.[46] They called the bomb "Joe I" after Premier Joseph Stalin.

The Bush report, along with Air Force Chief of Staff Vandenberg's concur-rence, convinced Johnson of what he had earlier refused to accept—the Rus-sians had the atomic bomb. The secretary immediately concluded that the news, as alarming as it was, should be announced to the American people as quickly as possible. Believing the matter to be urgent, Johnson made an ap-pointment to visit the president with Deputy Secretary Early and the new chair-man of the JCS, General Omar Bradley. At the meeting in Blair House, Johnson pressed Truman to make an immediate announcement, but Truman demurred. First, he was still not convinced the Russians had the bomb. Beyond that, he felt that the international situation—Britain had devalued the pound the day before—was too volatile to make an announcement at that time.

Johnson understood Truman's reluctance to go public, but he pointed out that if the American people learned the information from another source it would seriously undermine the administration's credibility. There were already some 300 people aware of the situation, and the lid of secrecy could not be held down much longer. Backed by his staff, Johnson argued that by personally mak-ing the announcement, Truman would show the American people that the U.S. intelligence agencies were well aware of what was going on in the USSR and that the president was not unduly alarmed by the new development. Those two factors would do much to alleviate the nation's fears.

Johnson's arguments appeared to get nowhere, however, and when he and his entourage departed, Truman seemed determined not only to delay any pub-lic announcement but also to put off any disclosure to the Joint Congressional Committee on Atomic Energy.[47] Johnson, feeling that the president was mak-ing a grievous error, returned to his apartment at the Mayflower a dejected man, convinced he had failed to protect his president.

The following day Johnson again pushed the issue, but Truman seemed wedded to his earlier decision not to make an announcement, in spite of a visit from Lilienthal, who pressed home the same points that Johnson had. Appar-ently, however, those arguments were beginning to have some effect, because that evening the president requested that Johnson and the Joint Chiefs come to see him the next morning.

At that September 21 meeting, the president reviewed with Johnson and the Joint Chiefs the evidence relative to the bomb and obtained assurances from them that there had, in fact, been an explosion. Although still skeptical, the president decided to invite the chairman of the Joint Congressional Committee,

Senator McMahon, and the ranking Republican, Senator Hickenlooper, to the White House to discuss the opinions of Johnson and the others. Since Senator Hickenlooper was out of town, Senator McMahon came alone to the September 22 meeting at the White House. Truman shared with him the report of the Bush panel and informed him of his intention to disclose the information to the Cabinet and then release a statement to the press.[48] A shaken McMahon returned to his office and called an emergency meeting of the Joint Congressional Committee for the following morning.

On Friday morning, September 23, as McMahon was convening the Joint Congressional Committee on Capitol Hill, the president was opening his regular weekly cabinet meeting. While those two groups were receiving information on the Soviet detonation of an atomic bomb, Press Secretary Charlie Ross called the press corps into the Blair House briefing room and distributed a mimeographed statement from the president. As the reporters' eyes raced over the sheet, the words that jumped out were, "We have evidence that within recent weeks an atomic explosion occurred in the U.S.S.R."[49] Although Truman still refused to use the word "bomb," what the 217-word statement boiled down to was put succinctly by United Press White House correspondent Merriman Smith, who exclaimed, "My God, the Russians have the Bomb!"[50]

While the reporters scurried to phone in their stories about what *Newsweek* called "the biggest news since the close of the Second World War," the cabinet meeting ended and the members slipped away before reporters could question them. That is, all except Louis Johnson, who was caught as he was about to step into his limousine for the return trip to the Pentagon. Never one to decline to answer questions from the press, the secretary told the group that the president had told the Cabinet "everything," but he would not elaborate. He went on, however, to say that Soviet possession of the atomic bomb would bring no major change in America's military policy. He suggested that the reporters not get too excited. "Let's keep calm about this," he urged. "Don't overplay the story."[51] Nevertheless, in the ensuing months, the blast and the nature of America's response to it were constantly discussed and debated in the press, the Congress, and the highest echelons of the executive branch.

The president's September 23 announcement relieved Johnson's fear that the news would come from another source. However, that problem paled in comparison with the challenge of fashioning a strategic response to the new Soviet threat. Although Johnson told the press that the blast was nothing to get excited about and would result in no real change in policy, he and the other leaders of the administration knew better. After all, the monopoly on the most awesome weapon yet developed by humankind, the weapon which had enabled him to cut way back on conventional ground and naval forces, had vanished.

As head of the Defense Department, it was Johnson's responsibility to play a central role in formulating the administration's response to the new reality, and in the months that followed he spent nearly every waking hour doing just that. Johnson focused most of his attention and energy on expansion of the nation's atomic weapons stockpile and development of a new "super bomb," the so-called hydrogen bomb.

Expanding the Atomic Arsenal

That Johnson was to have a major say on whether the United States should significantly expand its nuclear stockpile had been decided on July 26, more than a month before the Soviet detonation, when the President appointed a special committee of the National Security Council (NSC), consisting of Johnson, Acheson, and Lilienthal, to advise him on expansion.[52]

As the three men met in August and September to plan their report to the president, they did so in a stilted and strained atmosphere. Neither Lilienthal or Acheson had any great fondness for Johnson, nor he for them.[53] In addition to a personality clash, Lilienthal was upset by Johnson's contention that he did not intend to let the AEC determine weapons needs and that the decision would be made in the Defense Department.[54] Acheson was resentful of Johnson's undercutting of the administration's proposal to collaborate with the British and Canadians and his continual barbs about how Acheson was running the State Department.

In the special committee discussions, Johnson pushed vigorously for adoption of the JCS recommendation to significantly expand the atomic arsenal. While his two cohorts were less than enthusiastic, they were able to offer no viable alternative, particularly after it became apparent that the Soviets had the bomb. The committee report that was submitted to the president on October 10 clearly reflected Johnson's views. The conclusion reached was that the "proposed acceleration of the atomic energy program is necessary in the interest of national security."[55] The report maintained that its decisions were not influenced by the recent Soviet detonation but were based on previous plans— a view which Lilienthal privately called "bunk."[56]

Given the significance of the special committee's recommendations, it is probable that Truman discussed the report with Acheson and Johnson during their regularly scheduled visits. Johnson had every reason to believe that the president would endorse the report because it had the support of the JCS, the State Department, and the AEC. Furthermore, he had been encouraged by Truman's private statement that he felt the chances of UN control of atomic energy were nil, and "since we can't obtain international control we must be strongest in atomic weapons."[57]

It was apparently such thinking that caused the president to authorize a significant expansion of the nation's nuclear arsenal on October 17 that was to cost an initial $319 million and $60 million per year in operating funds.[58] The actual extent of the expansion remains classified, but it is likely that the proposal contemplated doubling the JCS goal from 400 to 800 atomic bombs.

The following day Truman discussed the details of the expansion plan before directing Lilienthal to initiate the necessary construction program. Amazingly, with all the people involved in the nuclear expansion question—the JCS, the AEC, the State Department, the Pentagon, and the White House—the matter still remained a secret. The press either did not get wind of it or decided not publish it; in either case, it says a great deal for the integrity of those involved.[59]

Super Bomb

While the deliberations leading to atomic weapons expansion did not leak into the public domain, such was not the case with the hydrogen bomb. During World War II, while working on the atomic bomb, one of the Manhattan Project's most prominent physicists, Dr. Edward Teller, began to explore the possibility of a much more powerful weapon of mass destruction. He envisioned a weapon which would unleash its force not by nuclear fission—as in the case of the atomic bomb—but through fusion of the nuclei of hydrogen. However, because of technological, financial, material, and manpower limitations, the idea of a hydrogen bomb, or "super bomb," as it came to be called, had to be put on the shelf until the atomic bomb was developed.[60]

In the postwar period, Teller attempted to rally support for development of the super bomb but was thwarted at every turn by Robert Oppenheimer. In 1946, largely at Oppenheimer's insistence, the government halted research into fusion weapons. Teller left government service and accepted a position at the University of Chicago. However, he continued to advocate construction of the hydrogen bomb, which he claimed would be more than a thousand times more powerful than the one dropped on Hiroshima. Oppenheimer blocked serious consideration of the project; in 1947, he assumed the influential position of chairman of the General Advisory Committee (GAC) to the AEC.[61] There the matter of the fusion bomb rested at the time the Soviets detonated Joe I.

One of the immediate consequences of the Soviet blast was the resurrection of the super bomb idea. Among the officials most enthusiastic about the potential new weapon was AEC member Lewis Strauss, a former navy admiral and businessman who had long been the "great dissenter" on the commission. Strauss had stood alone on many issues such as collaboration with Britain and Canada, exporting atomic bombs to Britain, and sharing other scientific information with Britain. The frustrations of being continually outvoted 4 to 1 caused him to seriously consider resigning, but he stayed on.[62] He did have one top administration official who seemed to share the same views on these controversial matters—Secretary of Defense Louis Johnson—but as yet their paths had not crossed.

In the days following the announcement of the explosion of Joe I, Strauss turned over in his mind the impact of that event on the national security of the United States. He crystallized his ideas in an October 5, 1949, memorandum, which he sent to the other commissioners and to Senator McMahon. In that document he claimed that in view of recent events, "the time has now come for a quantum jump . . . [and] we should now make an intensive effort to get ahead with the super [bomb]." He then called for "a commitment in talent and money comparable . . . to that which produced the first atomic weapon."[63] He concluded by recommending that the AEC and the Joint Congressional Committee on Atomic Energy call upon the GAC to present its views on how to proceed.

Senator McMahon received Strauss's call for action enthusiastically, and he immediately set out to attract support for the idea in the Joint Congressional Committee. However, reaction ranged from cool to red-hot opposition.[64] Although some scientists such as Teller and Dr. Earnest O. Lawrence and Dr. Luis Alvarez of the Berkeley Radiation Laboratory supported development of the super bomb, the bulk of the scientific community was opposed on moral and practical grounds.[65] In late October, the GAC followed the lead of Chairman Oppenheimer and unanimously renounced development of the weapon.[66] On November 9, the AEC, in a 3-to-2 decision, with Strauss and Gordon Dean dissenting, recommended against development of the H-bomb.[67]

Meanwhile, in early October, while the members of the AEC, the GAC, and the Joint Congressional Committee were busy debating the super bomb, Strauss had been working to gain support from another source—Secretary Louis Johnson. With the assistance of his old friend Marx Leva, Strauss engineered an opportunity to meet with the secretary. During a session that started in the afternoon and supposedly lasted until after dark, Strauss posed the question, "Mr. Secretary, isn't it an American tradition that we will never accept the idea that we will be less armed than our enemies?" Johnson agreed that it was and pledged his full support for developing the weapon.[68]

The following morning Johnson met with Steve Early, General Bradley, General Burns, and Robert LeBaron, newly appointed chairman of the Military Liaison Committee to the AEC. The super bomb, Johnson told the group, was essential to the nation's defense, and its development was of the highest priority. Early and Burns expressed their agreement, but Bradley was ambivalent. The chairman of the JCS maintained that current atomic weapons had sufficient destructive power to level Moscow and that the new weapon would have limited application. On the other hand, he believed that the super bomb could become an important psychological weapon.[69]

Like Bradley, the JCS were initially skeptical. They also feared that a crash program on the super bomb would take funds away from production of the atomic bomb and from conventional fighting forces. In view of the extremely limited defense funds available, this was a major concern, but by mid-October, primarily under the influence of Johnson and Chief of Staff Vandenberg, the JCS and the Military Liaison Committee had come to support development of the H-bomb.[70]

Johnson's efforts on behalf of the H-bomb were not directed solely at military officials. Realizing that the bulk of the opposition came from the scientific community, he enlisted the support of Dr. Karl Compton, former president of MIT, chairman of the Defense Department Research and Development Board, and a leading physicist with considerable government experience. Compton not only lined up support for the super bomb from several scientist friends, he also appealed directly to the president.[71]

By mid-November, President Truman was being pressured from all sides on the H-bomb controversy. On behalf of the GAC, Oppenheimer was voicing his implacable opposition to its development, but Senator McMahon and the Defense Department were urging a crash program. The AEC was divided on the issue, but individual commissioners forcefully advocated their views.

In light of such sharply divided counsel, the president appointed a special NSC committee, called the Z Committee, on November 19 composed of Acheson, Johnson, and Lilienthal (the same group he had called upon several months before to evaluate expansion of the atomic weapons arsenal) to wade through the mass of conflicting information and formulate a recommendation on the H-bomb. To assist the Z Committee, a working group headed by NSC executive secretary Sidney Souers and composed of three members from the AEC and State Department and four members from Defense, was established.[72]

Because of the personality conflict between Johnson and Lilienthal, the bulk of the deliberations of the Z Committee were conducted by the working group. Through his emissaries on the working group, Johnson, with the backing of the JCS and the Military Liaison Committee, argued for immediate development of the super bomb. Lilienthal, through his spokespersons, pushed for delay, calling for a complete and thorough examination of U.S. foreign and defense policies before making a decision on whether to proceed. Acheson followed a middle course; he sympathized with Lilienthal's views but found Johnson's to be more realistic.

The three members of the Z Committee did not meet until December 22. In that session, Johnson indicated that the only development that could dissuade the Defense Department from pursuing the super bomb was Soviet acceptance of international control—a likelihood that no one held out as a real possibility. He explained that the military viewed the decision as a very technical one because the major question was whether it was technically and economically feasible to build the bomb. Lilienthal immediately rose to the bait, saying that such a position ignored broader philosophical questions such as whether reliance on larger and larger weapons might not "close the door to any other course."

Johnson, displaying the acerbity that so annoyed Lilienthal, countered by saying that there was no place for morality and philosophy in this kind of decision—a contention the AEC chairman regarded as appalling.[73] Acheson, who later described the December 22 meeting as "a head-on confrontation between Louis Johnson and David Lilienthal . . . [that] produced nothing either new or helpful to the President," stayed above the fray by saying very little.[74] The meeting ended with no agreement other than to let the working group continue its work.

While the working group of the Z Committee continued its deliberations, public and congressional pressure was building in favor of the H-bomb.[75] On November 1, Senator Edwin Johnson (R-Colorado), a member of the Joint Congressional Committee, appeared on a television show in New York City and revealed that scientists had been working on a super bomb that would be at least a thousand times more powerful than the one dropped on Nagasaki. Initially, the statement was ignored, but several weeks later the *Washington Post* picked it up and made it a nationwide story.[76] Interest quickly turned from Senator Johnson's security "blunder" to debate on whether or not the bomb should be developed. News analysts frantically worked their sources as they tried to give their readers inside accounts of the debate going on within the administration.[77]

Concern in Congress about the H-bomb went hand in hand with the rise of public interest. Congress had recessed until after the first of the year, but a barrage of questions on the H-bomb kept the issue before them. After a visit to AEC facilities and conversations with numerous officials, Senator McMahon returned to Washington to write a 5,000-word letter to President Truman urging immediate development of the bomb. When Congress reconvened in January, the Joint Congressional Committee announced it would hold closed hearings before making a recommendation to the president. Secretary Johnson welcomed such pressures on the White House. In early January of 1950, he made the substance of a soon-to-be-released JCS position paper on the H-bomb available to McMahon so the information could be shared with the committee. He also shared his personal views with McMahon.[78]

On January 13, 1950, the JCS formally submitted to Johnson a memorandum that addressed technical, political, and moral objections to developing the bomb. The Joint Chiefs dismissed the moral issue, contending it was spurious to argue that one weapon was more immoral than another. They went on to say there was no need for a crash program but agreed that determining the feasibility of the super bomb should be a top priority. They concluded by declaring that while the decision on production could await further developments, unilateral possession of the weapon by the Soviet Union would be intolerable to the United States and there was no alternative but to proceed with the necessary research.[79] While Johnson was probably not pleased with all the points made, he certainly agreed with its major recommendation and decided he would use it to push for the bomb.

Up until this time the various reports from the AEC, the State Department, and the Defense Department had gone to the Z Committee working group for study. The procedure was designed to keep the president from being bombarded with documents that would cloud the picture before the final recommendation was made. In the case of the January 13 memorandum from the JCS to Johnson, however, this procedure was not followed. Johnson bypassed the working group and the Z Committee and sent the JCS memo directly to the president.[80] While the ethics of Johnson's actions can be questioned, the impact it had cannot, because on January 19, after reading the document, Truman remarked to Sidney Souers that it "made a lot of sense and he was inclined to think that was what we should do."[81] Some observers believed it was at this time that Truman made up his mind.

Super bomb advocates received another boost on January 23 when Lieutenant General John Hull briefed President Truman, the three service secretaries, and others in the Cabinet on the long-awaited report concerning the number of bombers that could be expected to reach their targets in the event of war with the Soviet Union. While it was indicated that between 70 and 85 percent of the bombers would reach their targets, they could succeed in damaging beyond repair only between one-half and two-thirds of the Soviet industrial facilities. The pessimistic tone of the report appeared to shake Truman and the others.[82] What was implied from the analysis was that super bombs, if available and used, could inflict much heavier damage on the targets than conventional atomic bombs.

By the last week in January it had become clear to Acheson, Johnson, and Lilienthal that they had to get their recommendations to the president in short order. The Joint Congressional Committee was nearing the end of its hearings, after which it would send its recommendations to the president. If that happened, it would appear as if Congress would be telling the administration what to do instead of the administration deciding what should be done.[83]

Consequently, the Z Committee met for the second and final time on Tuesday, January 31 in Admiral Souers's office in Room 216 of the old state department building next door to the White House. Acheson opened by stating that a great deal of staff work had been done and that now it was time for the committee to formulate its recommendations. He distributed proposed recommendations that called on the president to: 1) order the AEC to determine the technical feasibility of constructing the H-bomb; 2) defer any decision on production until feasibility was established; and 3) direct the State and Defense Departments to undertake a complete reexamination of the nation's foreign and military policies in light of the actual and potential threats posed by Soviet nuclear and conventional weapon capabilities. He also included a proposed presidential statement to be released when Truman approved the recommendations.[84]

Johnson immediately moved that the second recommendation be deleted, which would open the way for the president to make the production decision as soon as he felt it was time to begin. That is exactly what Lilienthal wanted to avoid. Acheson, having consulted with Lilienthal prior to the meeting, seemed to favor the idea of deferring the production decision, but now, feeling that "nothing could prevent" such presidential action, he reversed himself and concurred with Johnson's position.[85]

Johnson then proposed revisions of the president's statement, which was further modified and approved. Lilienthal, whose resignation from the AEC had been accepted and was just two weeks away, made an impassioned, last-ditch appeal for delaying the development and production of the super bomb and urged reconsideration of a defense policy that relied on simply producing larger and more powerful weapons. He also contended that efforts to develop the H-bomb would delay and hinder the development of other weapons and would therefore be a mistake.

While Acheson was moved by Lilienthal's appeal, he felt that it did not deal with two realities: the Soviet Union would proceed to develop the super bomb regardless of what the United States did, and the American public, fearing for its national security, would not tolerate such a delay. The secretary of state also indicated that he was mindful of the congressional pressure that was building. Johnson concurred, adding, "We must protect the President."[86]

Seeing no real alternative to what Johnson was advocating, Acheson sided with him. Surprisingly, in spite of the views he had just expressed, Lilienthal signed the document. It was now shortly after noon and Johnson, who had a 12:30 P.M. meeting with the president, suggested that the three of them walk over to the White House to see the president.[87] At 12:35 P.M. the men were shown into the Oval Office. No time was wasted as Acheson presented the Z Committee's two recommendations and the proposed press release and indicated that Lilienthal wanted to make a statement. The AEC chairman began by telling the president that he considered the decision about to be made to be unwise and felt that another approach was possible. At that point Truman, who had already made up his mind, interrupted him. Referring to the H-bomb, the president asked, "Can the Russians get it?" Lilienthal responded, "They could." Everyone else nodded their agreement. Admiral Souers said, "We don't have much time." "In that case," Truman said, "we have no choice. . . . We'll go ahead." As if to justify his quick decision, the president added that public and congressional pressure had become so great that he really did not have other options. Having politely cut Lilienthal off, the president approved the Z Committee's recommendations and signed his name to the statement to be released to the press. It was 12:42 — the meeting had lasted seven minutes.[88]

To say that Louis Johnson was the most persuasive force leading to the president's far-reaching decision to develop the H-bomb would be to ignore numerous other forces — political, strategic, and historical — that came into play. However, no top-ranking administration official championed the development of the super bomb as aggressively as Johnson, who was labeled by one contemporary as a "missionary for the H-bomb."[89] Although he initially faced opposition from Acheson and Lilienthal, two highly respected and independent-minded members of the Z Committee, Johnson ultimately persuaded both men to support his position. In addition, the way in which he orchestrated the views of the JCS and other Pentagon groups and the Joint Congressional Committee to accomplish his goal displayed a high degree of political sophistication. Although Truman's decision might well have been made even without Johnson's advocacy, there can be no question that Johnson made it much easier for him to make it.[90]

Events in the months and years that followed the president's January 31 decision indicate that from the U.S. point of view President Truman made the right decision and that he did so just in time. Less than a month later, Secretary Johnson, spurred on by a JCS recommendation, asked the president to immediately implement a program "of all-out development of Hydrogen Bombs and their production and delivery."[91] Once more, Truman called on the Special Committee of the NSC, which now consisted of Acheson, Johnson, and AEC member Henry Smyth, who had replaced Lilienthal. Johnson's skill, preparation, and aggressiveness again convinced the group to recommend approval, and on March 10 the president approved the committee's recommendation that the H-bomb program be declared "a matter of highest urgency."[92]

The AEC began its work under these mandates and in May 1951 achieved a fusion reaction. On November 1, 1952, the first thermonuclear bomb was detonated on the Eniwetok Atoll in the South Pacific, a blast that was 150 times more powerful than the Hiroshima explosion. Only ten months later, in August 1953, the Russians detonated their first H-bomb. The following year the United States had a deliverable H-bomb, which was soon put into production. Such accomplishments were quickly duplicated by the Soviet Union, and by 1955 the two superpowers not only had the ability to destroy each other but all humankind as well.[93]

During those critical months in the winter of 1949–1950, there was no attempt to achieve a diplomatic solution. Neither the United States nor the Soviet Union approached the other to discuss a ban on thermonuclear weapons.

NSC 68

Within several hours of President Truman's January 31 meeting with the Z Committee, he acted upon the second of its two major recommendations and sent Secretary Acheson and Secretary Johnson a directive asking that they "undertake a reexamination of our objectives in peace and war and of the effect of these objectives on our strategic plans, in light of the probable fusion bomb capability and possible thermonuclear bomb capability of the Soviet Union."[94]

From that directive emerged one of the most vitally important documents of the Cold War era—NSC 68.

Although the National Security Council had been established in 1947 for the primary purpose of helping develop and implement a unified foreign, military, and budgetary policy, it was still in its infancy, and in spite of the great strides it was making, an integrated national policy was still not a reality. There was cooperation between the State and Defense Departments in many areas, but there was also underlying friction. The reasons were ideological, budgetary, and personal.

Ideologically, the Defense and State Departments were divided by the age-old tendency of military personnel to see force as the answer to all or most international challenges and the inclination of the diplomat to see persuasion, logic, and compromise as the means to settle disputes. This ideological chasm has been a fundamental source of tension between strong-willed secretaries of defense and state over the years, and it persists today.

The budgetary friction between State and Defense stemmed from the fierce competition for the limited funds the administration was willing to provide for national security. State officials were fearful that a major increase in defense expenditures would draw funds away from foreign aid programs while at the Pentagon the concern was that expanded foreign aid would lead to more reductions in the military budget. Since the president seemed so adamant about his budget limitations, officials in both departments were convinced that additional funding would not be forthcoming and that it would be necessary to gain funding from existing programs.[95]

Cooperation between the State and Defense Departments was further complicated by the strained personal relationship between Secretaries Johnson and Acheson. The fact that the two leaders had no admiration or respect for one another, and made no attempt to hide the fact, did little to foster a feeling of goodwill or cooperation between their respective departments.[96]

It is impossible to pinpoint what precipitated the deepening rift between Johnson and Acheson. Almost as soon as he was sworn in as secretary, Johnson began trying to undercut Acheson as the most influential member of Truman's Cabinet. In turn, Acheson's friends in the capital gossiped and schemed in an effort to deflate Johnson's power and influence. Johnson believed, as many defense secretaries have, that the secretary of state was meddling in Pentagon business. Acheson was convinced that Johnson was doing the same thing to him— and he was. In background, temperament, and appearance, the two men could not have been more different. Educated at Groton, Yale, and Harvard, Acheson, who dressed like a British diplomat, was witty and well mannered, but he came across to many, including Louis Johnson, as condescending, patronizing, snobbish, and a bit of a phony. In turn, Acheson regarded Johnson as a political hack, a lightweight lout whose ambition was too obvious, too transparent.[97]

The friction between his two most powerful advisors did not escape Truman.

One day in the fall of 1949, he took Undersecretary of State James Webb aside and said, "Acheson is a gentleman. He won't descend to a row. Johnson is a rough customer, gets his way by rowing. When he takes out after you, give it right back to him."[98]

As if these difficulties between State and Defense were not enough to complicate the attainment of an integrated national security policy, other developments in late 1949 added to the problems: the fall of China to the communists, the establishment of the North Atlantic Treaty Organization (NATO), questions surrounding the Mutual Defense Assistance Bill, the Soviet detonation of an atomic bomb, and the revolt of the admirals.[99] It was in this atmosphere of bureaucratic friction, international tension, and personal animosity between the secretaries of defense and state that President Truman issued his January 31 directive to Acheson and Johnson to reexamine and reevaluate the administration's Cold War foreign and defense policies.

Secretary Johnson did not welcome President Truman's call for a major policy reappraisal for several reasons. First and foremost, such an examination could possibly serve as "an invitation to cause trouble with the economy program" that Johnson had so vehemently championed at the behest of the president.[100] Second, it was bad timing. In March, the secretary was to go to the NATO Defense Committee meeting in Brussels; he would be completely involved in preparing for that conference and would not have time to take an active role in the reassessment process. Finally, it forced the Defense Department to cooperate on a working level with the State Department, a situation Johnson opposed because he felt it undercut his authority and that of the JCS.

Johnson's concern—some would characterize it as an obsession—with maintaining the authority, independence, and stature of the Defense Department was extraordinary. Shortly after he became secretary, he issued, with Truman's concurrence, a directive indicating that no official communication could take place between defense and state department officials except through General Burns. Johnson's directive was motivated by a desire to be kept informed, to prevent subordinates from making decisions or commitments that needed to be decided at a higher level, and to assure that the Pentagon was able to speak with a united voice to the State Department. However, the idea of funneling all information between two such large bureaucracies through one person was unrealistic and unworkable. Burns quickly realized there was no way he could keep abreast of all the matters being discussed by Pentagon officials and their counterparts across the river, so he solved the problem by authorizing "consultative arrangements" in which he did not personally have to be involved.[101]

Johnson delegated the responsibility for implementation of Truman's directive for a complete reappraisal of all foreign and defense policies to General Burns. Realizing the far-reaching impact the study could have on the JCS, Burns approached Chairman Bradley and requested a representative from that body to serve on the study group. Following the JCS tradition of not letting anyone represent them in such a group for fear it could commit them to a certain position, Bradley refused. He agreed, however, that the Joint Strategic Survey Committee (JSSC), a relatively independent interservice group that advised the JCS on national security matters and strategic planning, could be used. He made it clear that the positions the JSSC members took would in no way be binding on the Joint Chiefs or the secretary.

Air Force Major General Truman H. Landon, Army Major General Ray T. Maddocks, and Rear Admiral Thomas H. Robbins were selected to represent the JSSC on the study group. Although Burns formally headed the Pentagon delegation, his heart condition, which limited his work schedule to half days, forced him to place the burden on Landon, who immediately emerged as the key defense spokesperson. Also included in the group were Burns's assistant, Najeeb E. Halaby, and Robert LeBaron.

Paul Nitze, who had recently succeeded George Kennan as director of the Policy Planning Staff at the State Department, chaired the State-Defense study group and headed the state department delegation. Unlike Kennan, Nitze was neither scholarly nor brilliantly intuitive, but he was powerful in his argumentation and his command of the facts. Nitze, who had achieved considerable wealth as an investment banker with Dillon Read in New York, had become deeply distrustful of the Soviets, and by 1950 he was convinced that they were in a position as never before to act aggressively against the West.[102] Assisting Nitze at state were several members of his staff, including Robert Tufts, John Davies, and Robert Houser. Rounding out the group was the new executive secretary of the National Security Council, James Loy, and his assistant, Everett Gleason. The latter two were primarily observers, serving as liaison with the NSC.[103]

As the high-powered study group began its deliberations in mid-February of 1950, the lines of communication to the respective secretaries were radically different and had unpleasant consequences. At the State Department, Nitze, who had the complete confidence of Secretary Acheson, reported daily on the group's activities. No such communication took place in the Defense Department, and as a result Johnson was completely unaware of what was transpiring. That the defense chief was kept in the dark about the work of this vitally important study group was no accident. General Burns felt that if the study was to provide a fresh new look at the nation's strategic situation it would be necessary that the evaluators think as independently as possible. He had known Johnson for a long time, and he realized that if the secretary knew what was being discussed he would use his influence to move the group in the direction he felt it should go. Consequently, Burns gave Landon the freedom and independence to take the study in the direction he felt it should go.

General Landon initially had misgivings about joining the group because he envisioned it as just another exercise to justify the lean budgets that were being mandated by the White House. However, in the early sessions, when it became evident that Nitze's group was really thinking along lines of what would be needed to make the nation secure rather than what was politically feasible, he became enthusiastic because he saw an opportunity to break away from the cost-cutting mentality that had prevailed since Johnson's arrival.[104]

The ideas, policies, and programs that began to emerge from the group were indeed vastly different from those the administration had been pursuing. From the outset, the group adopted Nitze's premise that "the USSR has already committed itself to the defeat of the United States." Recognizing the grave threat the Soviets posed to the United States and the entire free world, the group drafted a policy statement which maintained that the United States "must lead in building a successful functioning political and economic system in the free world."[105] Toward that end, the draft statement called for development of a strong alliance system, expansion of the atomic weapons arsenal, and, perhaps most significant, substantial strengthening of conventional air, ground, and sea forces.[106] This was a radical departure from the world of Truman's low ceilings for defense budgets and Johnson's severe austerity policies. The new policy statement was to be known as NSC 68 because it would be the 68th position statement issued by the National Security Council.

By mid-March Nitze's group concluded it was time for Secretary Johnson to be briefed on the direction it was headed. General Burns arranged for Johnson to meet with the group and Secretary Acheson at 3:00 P.M. on March 22. The draft policy statement, together with a two-page summary, was forwarded to Johnson more than a week before the meeting, but Johnson, who was working feverishly to prepare for the NATO Defense Committee conference in Brussels, apparently did not read it.[107]

At about 3:15 P.M. on March 22, 1950, Johnson, General Bradley, and General Burns arrived at Nitze's planning staff room next door to Acheson's office at the State Department for their scheduled meeting. The initial mood seemed relaxed as the defense chief shook hands with Acheson, the members of the study group (all of whom were present), and Admiral Souers, who had recently been appointed by Truman as his national security advisor. But as soon as the participants had taken their seats, Johnson announced that neither he nor General Bradley had read the paper, which he claimed had just been made available to him, and that he did not intend to approve anything he had not read. According to the official account, Johnson then said that he "did not like being called to conferences without having had the opportunity to read the material, that this was the fourth time the State Department had done this to him, and that he didn't want any more of it." Sitting next to Johnson was a very embarrassed General Burns, who had arranged the session. Acheson offered to postpone the meeting until Johnson could study the paper, but Johnson refused, saying that since he was there, they should proceed.[108]

Acheson then called on Nitze to present the salient points of the draft document, and as he began talking Johnson leaned back in his chair and scanned the report. Suddenly, the defense chief surged forward in his chair, his feet struck the floor, and his fist hit the table with arresting force. As Acheson recalled later, he was "scared out of his shoes." "No one," Johnson shouted, as he rose to his feet, is "going to make arrangements for [me] to meet with another Cabinet officer and a roomful of people and be told what [I am] going to report to the President." The stunned assemblage sat motionless as Johnson demanded, "Who authorized these meetings contrary to [my] orders? What was this paper which [I have] never seen?"

Before General Burns could reply, Acheson stepped in to say that he had called the meeting and that the paper had been sent a week before. Whether Johnson heard the reply is questionable because by that time he had broken into a tirade against the proposal and the way he had learned about it. With a final pronouncement that he would not be "bullied around by subordinates," he announced that the meeting was over and stormed out of the room he had entered less than fifteen minutes before.[109] Those who remained in the room stared at each other in shock and disbelief. General Burns, both humiliated and deeply hurt, put his face in his hands and wept. According to Nitze, Burns said, "I'm going to have to resign," but Nitze implored him to stay on, saying, "You're the essential link between the two departments. You've got to stay; otherwise this report will never be finished."[110]

A few minutes later, Acheson's aide reported that Johnson was waiting in Acheson's office to see him. As Acheson entered his own office, Johnson resumed where he had left off a few minutes before, angrily complaining that he had been insulted by this "outrageous thing." By this time Acheson had had all he could take, and he asked Johnson to leave, but not before indicating that the State Department "would complete the report alone and explain why."[111]

Within an hour, President Truman, who had been informed of Johnson's outbursts by Admiral Souers, called Acheson to express his unhappiness with Johnson's actions and to say that he wanted him to carry on the project. The president also indicated that he should be notified immediately of "the slightest sign of obstructionism or foot-dragging in the Pentagon."[112]

Armed with the president's mandate to proceed, Nitze's group worked out the remaining minor points of contention and began finalizing NSC 68. What finally emerged in late March was a 60-page document that provided a penetrating and brutally honest assessment of where the United States stood in the international scene, articulated its foreign policy and military objectives, and explained how those objectives could be secured. As Acheson explained later, the purpose of NSC 68 was "to so bludgeon the mass mind of 'top government' that not only could the President make a decision but . . . the decision could be carried out."[113]

Focusing more on the capabilities of the Soviets than their actual intentions, the report asserted that they had a strong desire to dynamically extend their authority and ultimately to eliminate any effective opposition to that authority. According to NSC 68, the Kremlin saw the United States as "the principal enemy whose integrity and vitality must be subverted or destroyed by one means or another."[114] After ponderously setting forth the Soviet threat, the report examined the ability of the United States to meet the challenge and concluded that it was in no real position to do so. As for the nation's defense capability, it claimed, "When our military strength is related to the world situation and balanced against the likely exigencies of such a situation, it is clear that our military strength is becoming dangerously inadequate."[115] While acknowledging the need to keep the door to negotiations with the USSR open, it concluded that not much could be accomplished in that realm in the foreseeable future.

In light of the Soviet threat and the dim prospects of a negotiated settlement, the report concluded that "a more rapid build-up of political, economic and military strength and thereby of confidence in the free world than is now contemplated is the only course which is consistent with progress toward achieving our fundamental purpose."[116] The military buildup called for in NSC 68 included conventional air, ground, and sea forces as well as atomic weapons, but the document did not say what those force levels should be. Nor were there any specifics on the costs of the proposed buildup; the respective estimates by state and defense officials were vastly different. Military planners were thinking in terms of a cost of $18 billion per year (or $5 billion more than the current defense budget), whereas state department planners were looking at $35 to $50 billion per year.[117]

By March 27, the report was ready for analysis and evaluation by officials outside the study group. Within the State Department, its circulation was limited, perhaps to attract as little criticism as possible. Nevertheless, two of the department's foremost Soviet experts, George Kennan and Charles "Chip" Bohlen, were very critical of the draft report which became NSC 68—Kennan because he believed it failed to correctly assess Soviet intentions as opposed to capabilities and Bohlen because he felt the report overstated Soviet ambitions to expand.[118]

In the Defense Department, the draft report was widely circulated by General Burns, who encouraged reactions to it. That such widespread distribution occurred was possible because Johnson was out of the country from March 28 to April 3 attending the NATO conference. The JCS, who had been briefed on the document by those members of their service on the study group, approved the document on April 4. The following day, the report, accompanied by the endorsement of the JCS, the three service secretaries, and the chairman of the Military Liaison Committee, was presented to Secretary Johnson, who had returned from Europe two days earlier.[119]

That Johnson was displeased with the report would be an understatement.

The most upsetting aspect of the document was that it called for the nation to move the defense establishment in the opposite direction that Truman and Johnson had been leading it. Johnson had built his reputation by preaching and teaching the merits of economy and by assuring Congress and the public that the current fleet of B-36s armed with atomic bombs could adequately meet any Soviet military challenge. Now he was being asked to approve a report that claimed that the U.S. military posture was inadequate and recommended a far-reaching expansion of all the armed forces.

The program called for in NSC 68 was in essence a fundamental rejection of the defense policy of Johnson and Truman.[120] For these reasons, plus Johnson's violent reaction to the proposed document at the March 22 meeting, Acheson and most of the framers of the document did not expect him to approve it. However, Johnson surprised everyone and signed it on April 7. Acheson affixed his signature the same day and it was forwarded to the White House.

Truman did not immediately approve the sweeping changes proposed in the signed document. Instead, he equivocated. On April 12, the president referred the report to the NSC and requested "a clearer indication of the programs which are envisaged . . . including estimate of the probable cost of such programs."[121] When it was referred to the National Security Council, the document was given its now-famous file number—NSC 68.

Although NSC 68 was regarded as a turning point in American foreign policy, in fact it was never fully implemented and it was not officially approved by President Truman until September of 1950, long after the beginning of the Korean War. The cost estimate for full implementation was about $40 billion per year, expenditures that Truman and his administration would not seriously consider. Nevertheless, NSC 68 had a profound effect on the way Truman, Johnson, and other top aides viewed the Soviet threat and responded to North Korea's attack on South Korea.

Why Johnson Signed

Why Secretary Johnson signed NSC 68 is uncertain, but there were several factors that undoubtedly influenced him. First, the document had such widespread support within the Pentagon that to reject it would put him in the position of going against the advice of nearly all of his military and civilian advisors. From the time he assumed the defense post, Johnson had privately maintained that "a unanimous military judgment of the Joint Chiefs is something the President has to follow."[122] If that held true for the president, it would most certainly hold true for the secretary of defense. Second, there was the dilemma of how a secretary of defense could oppose any responsible proposal that defined a threat to the nation's security and called for a substantial strengthening of the armed forces. For Johnson to have done so would have cost him the support of the military and called into question, in congressional circles and vast segments of the public, his commitment to a strong national defense.

Thus, it is likely that Johnson signed NSC 68 because he had little choice. But perhaps there is a more complicated explanation. Johnson may well have signed NSC 68 because it would give him the greatest degree of latitude in future political and military decision making. If sentiment for the measures called for in NSC 68 grew within the administration and Congress, he could point to his support from the beginning. On the other hand, if the president rejected NSC 68 or accepted only parts of it, Johnson would have a basis for saying that he reluctantly signed on to its broad proposals but he could still speak out against specific aspects, claiming they were not originally spelled out.[123] In the final analysis, to sign seemed not just the only way to go but, logically and politically, the best way to go.

Since NSC 68 called for a strengthening first of the United States, then of its allies, implementation of the new policy would mean that detailed planning and cost estimates for the military buildup would be done by the Department of Defense. Johnson, who had patched up things with General Burns, gave him the responsibility for planning the details of the expansion. It was evident that Johnson did not accord the highest priority to the military buildup called for in NSC 68 because he directed Burns to handle the project through normal channels and told him that initial force and cost estimates would not be due until November 1. The JCS were still gathering information for the force and cost estimates on June 25, 1950, when the North Koreans attacked.[124]

Between the time the president referred the Nitze study to the NSC and the outbreak of war in Korea, Secretary Johnson found himself in an extremely awkward and uncomfortable position. He had, at the president's insistence, wielded the economy knife and thus became the symbol of the administration's "economy in government" movement. In doing so, he had instituted cuts in all the services, especially the army and navy. Now the president seemed to be toying with the idea of completely reversing his field and moving to strengthen the nation's defenses. Throughout that spring Truman seemed to equivocate—one day he talked as if he was about to implement NSC 68 and the next day as if he was wedded to his previous budget limitations.

As the president hedged, so did Johnson; he wanted to be able to move in whichever direction the commander in chief wanted to go. This desire for political flexibility explains the inconsistencies in Johnson's statements on defense spending during that period.[125] For example, following an April 20 meeting with the president, Johnson privately indicated that his "economy program was dead, and that he had shaken hands with the president on it."[126] A week later he appeared before House and Senate appropriations subcommittees to request that an additional $550 million be put into the defense budget, yet at the same time he assured the lawmakers that his economy program was more essential than ever before.[127] With such conflicting signals, it is difficult to know just where Johnson stood.

Events in Asia would soon make the expansionist defense policies called for in NSC 68 a necessity, and the document would achieve a prominent place in Cold War history. In the meantime, however, there was little congressional or public support for the huge military buildup contemplated by NSC 68. Even if Truman had been persuaded by the document, he was not about to expend political capital trying to marshal support for such a drastic change. Similarly, Johnson, who was uninvolved in the preparation of NSC 68 and was angered when he learned of it, was not interested in advocating a reversal of his economy program. Johnson's lack of involvement was due in large part to his intense focus on a less expensive way of meeting the Soviet challenge—implementing a military alliance with the Europeans to deter Soviet aggression.

CHAPTER FOURTEEN

Entangling Alliance

T HE MILITARY TRANSPORT PLANE carrying Secretary of Defense Louis Johnson touched down at Washington's National Airport at about 4:45 P.M. on April 4, 1949. The flight from Philadelphia, where just several hours earlier the secretary had commissioned the cruiser USS *Roanoke*, had taken nearly an hour. After threading his way through rush-hour traffic, Johnson's driver dropped him off at the Commerce Department auditorium on Constitution Avenue just in time to witness a historic ceremony in the blue-and-gold splendor of the crowded hall. On the flag-bedecked stage stood the new secretary of state, Dean Acheson, flanked by President Truman and Vice President Barkley, and eleven other foreign ministers from Europe and Canada. Johnson watched intently as Acheson and the representatives of the member nations solemnly affixed their signatures to a treaty which would join them together in a collective security arrangement known as the North Atlantic Treaty Organization, or NATO.[1] There was no doubt that the ratification and implementation of the new defensive agreement, which was the West's answer to the Soviet military threat, would stir considerable controversy in the days ahead.

Although Johnson had assumed office only one week before the treaty was signed, he was briefed sufficiently on its ramifications to realize that the United States was stepping out in a bold new direction as it prepared to depart from Thomas Jefferson's famous admonition that the nation should avoid entangling alliances.[2] Under the NATO treaty, the signatories pledged "to unite their efforts for collective defense" in order to provide for the stability and well-being of the North Atlantic area. The treaty called for peaceful settlement of disputes among members, but the heart of the agreement and the most controversial part was Article 5, which provided "that an attack against one or more of them

. . . shall be considered an attack against them all." Most significant, Article 5
also said that in the event of an attack, each nation "will assist" by taking "such
action as it deems necessary, including the use of armed force, to restore and
maintain the security of the North Atlantic area."[3]

At a state dinner that evening at the Carlton Hotel, President Truman toasted
the foreign ministers who had signed the new North Atlantic Treaty, saying,
"we have really passed a milestone in history today."[4] For the United States his
words were particularly apt; America had never before agreed to a permanent
alliance during peacetime.

The initiative for the North Atlantic Treaty had not come from Truman or
the State Department but from Ernest Bevin, Britain's foreign minister. Early
in 1948, Bevin proposed the idea of a mutual defense treaty as a way to contain
new threats of aggression from the Soviet Union, and his concept was endorsed
by Secretary of State George Marshall and Undersecretary Robert A. Lovett.
Lovett and Republican senator Arthur Vandenberg had played the leading roles
in bringing the United States into an alliance with the nations of Europe.[5] Together, the two drafted what became known as the Vandenberg Resolution, a
sense-of-the-Senate resolution which was passed on June 11, 1948. It was vaguely
worded but it constituted a radical transformation of American foreign policy,
moving the nation away from unilateralism toward multilateralism and effectively committing the United States to an alliance with the nations of Europe.
The Vandenberg Resolution or, as Chip Bohlen called it, the Vandenberg-
Lovett Resolution, was formalized a year later in the North Atlantic Treaty.[6]

Although Truman was neither an initiator nor a particularly ardent proponent of the North Atlantic Treaty, he looked upon it with favor in part because
it would allow the United States to reduce its military presence in Europe and
thus save money. He knew that by signing the treaty the United States would
have to provide substantial monetary assistance to the Europeans, but he believed that this would be cheaper than maintaining a huge number of ground
troops in Europe for the foreseeable future.[7]

Notwithstanding his economy-driven motives, the April 4, 1949, signing ceremony turned out to be a triumphant occasion for President Truman. However, as Woodrow Wilson's experience of three decades earlier had shown, a
treaty means nothing if it is not ratified. With that thought in mind, Truman
asked Lovett to quietly continue to work with Senator Vandenberg and others
to prepare for the two big battles ahead—Senate ratification of the treaty and
congressional funding of a mutual assistance program which would enable
NATO to become an effective deterrent force.

Truman put his top foreign affairs and military advisors to work selling the
treaty to the Senate.[8] Since NATO was basically diplomatic in intent but military in implementation, the secretary of defense would become one of the administration's principal advocates. The senators would want to know what

military aid they would be called upon to provide and the consequences such commitments would have on the nation's defense. It was only natural that they should seek input from Colonel Johnson.[9]

The DAR Speech

Just how Louis Johnson really felt about NATO is difficult to ascertain because the ideas he expressed after he joined the administration were different from those he expressed before that time. Prior to 1949 he was a strong advocate of the UN and felt that because of its peacekeeping machinery there was no need for the United States to enter into military alliances.[10] Even in later years, when many Americans lost confidence in the UN, Johnson never doubted the advisability of relying on it to deal successfully with problems of international aggression.[11]

When the Cold War heated up in 1947 and 1948, he became even more supportive of the UN because he felt that it was the most effective means of meeting the Soviet challenge. By early 1948, he was convinced that the USSR was a major threat to the American way of life, and he condemned the nation's close World War II ally for establishing "a form of totalitarianism . . . which differs from the swastika in name only." Johnson believed that if the Soviets expanded into Western Europe, war between the USSR and the United States was inevitable because, as the 1930s had shown, "appeasement would only lead to war." He became an advocate of containment but initially was hopeful that the UN could do the containing.[12]

As it became apparent to the Truman administration that the veto power of the USSR in the UN Security Council was destined to frustrate efforts to halt Soviet expansion, the U.S. began to use unilateral efforts to stop or slow down the Soviets, as exemplified by the Truman Doctrine and the Marshall Plan. Johnson's reaction to this unilateral approach was mixed. He was pleased because someone was standing up to the Soviets, but he would have preferred that it be the UN.

In light of his strong confidence in the UN, it was not surprising that in 1948 Johnson publicly set forth his opposition to suggestions that the United States should join collective security agreements to protect Europe against Soviet aggression. Speaking to the national convention of the Daughters of the American Revolution at Constitution Hall in 1948 before he became secretary, he acknowledged that a defensive alliance called the Brussels Pact, a direct precursor to NATO, would probably benefit the signatory nations and was permitted under the UN Charter. He then made a statement that ultimately proved very embarrassing:

> It is now proposed that the United States should join that military alliance.
> I am not in favor of this. Military alliances are not in the tradition of the

United States. We cannot give to any foreign nation or groups of nations the power to say when the United States should go to war. . . .

Our job is to try to see that peace is kept through the United Nations. . . . We should not be talking the language of military alliance but the language of international law.[13]

Before giving his speech, Johnson forwarded a copy to Truman along with a note saying he had given it a great deal of thought and was confident that the proposed speech "is about the way you have been thinking and I believe it is right."[14] Johnson's statements in the spring of 1948 were consistent with Truman's previous public pronouncements on the role of the UN.[15] However, after the Berlin Crisis, Truman increasingly became an advocate of U.S. adherence to a European regional defense pact.

The inconsistency between Johnson's DAR speech and the administration's growing support of the North Atlantic Treaty became painfully apparent to Johnson when he was being briefed on the NATO talks by James Forrestal and General Lyman Lemnitzer before being sworn in as secretary of defense. As Lemnitzer began to tell Johnson about the status of the talks, Johnson's "large face suddenly darkened and he held up his hand" to interrupt. "General," the Colonel said, "what is this talk about an alliance?" He then angrily reminded Lemnitzer and Forrestal of his DAR speech. Lemnitzer, who would later become NATO commander, calmly informed Johnson that the treaty was a done deal and that he would shortly be called before the Senate Foreign Relations Committee "to urge ratification of the alliance treaty." As General Lemnitzer would recall years later, "Johnson got to his feet and glared" at him. "The meeting was over."[16]

Ratification

On April 12, President Truman submitted the treaty to the Senate with a request for ratification. Shortly thereafter, the new secretary of defense was called to testify before the Senate Foreign Relations Committee as an advocate of NATO. Realizing that his DAR speech of the previous year was bound to come up in his Senate appearance and knowing how embarrassing it could be to him and the administration, Johnson assigned his closest advisors the task of coming up with an "explanation" of what he had "really" said to the ladies of the DAR.[17]

The Senate hearings on the NATO Treaty opened on April 27 with Secretary of State Acheson, who emphasized that the security of the United States was inseparable from that of the North Atlantic nations. He also made it clear that if the treaty was ratified, the administration would commit to a $1.1 billion military assistance program for the pact's members. For nearly a full day Acheson was aggressively questioned, mainly by senators hostile to the pact. The following morning, the U.S. ambassador to the United Nations, Warren Austin, took up the cause by explaining that the treaty was consistent with the UN Charter.[18]

On the afternoon of the second day Johnson made his appearance before the Senate Foreign Relations Committee. In spite of the fact that he had been in office less than a month and was making his first visit to the Hill as secretary of defense, he was his usual confident, if not cocky, self; he noted that he was new to the job but assured his distinguished inquisitors that he had done his homework and was prepared for his first appearance.

In his opening statement, he immediately moved to "explain" his DAR speech. The treaty under consideration, he maintained, was not a "foreign military alliance in the customary sense" but a defensive arrangement similar to the Monroe Doctrine. Therefore, he claimed, the North Atlantic Treaty was consistent with the policy of seeking international security through the United Nations, and it did "not give to any foreign nation or group of nations the power to say when the United States should go to war." Following this dubious explanation, he noted that when he had made the DAR speech he was a private citizen and did not have access to the information that was later made public.[19]

Johnson hoped that he had stolen the thunder of his critics, and he proceeded to advocate ratification of the NATO treaty. From a military standpoint, he contended, the organization would help deter war or, if war came, "attain maximum military effectiveness." He warned the senators that mere political adherence to the treaty would not be enough to deter Soviet expansion; it would also be necessary to provide substantial support in arms and equipment to America's NATO allies. Such commitments, political and military, would enhance the security of the United States and the world.[20]

The opening statement was the easy part of Johnson's first appearance on the Hill. For the next two hours and fifteen minutes, inquisitive and at times rude senators grilled the new boy on the block. They pressed him for further explanations and clarifications on such matters as the DAR speech, his counterintuitive contention that the treaty was not a "military alliance," the need for collective security, and the importance of the $1.1 billion military assistance program for NATO.

The questioning also led to many issues not covered in the statement. When asked what the billion-dollar-plus assistance program would translate into in terms of numbers of planes, tanks, and other military equipment that would be shipped abroad, the secretary did not know but assured those present he would supply them with the information. Two senators, Brien McMahon and H. Alexander Smith (R-New Jersey), pressed the idea that the assistance program should be funded out of the $15 billion military appropriations budget. But even the cost-conscious Johnson stood fast in opposing that idea. He made it clear that the assistance program would have to be above and beyond national defense needs.[21]

Throughout the questioning Johnson proved to be well informed about his subject. While most of the exchanges were cordial, there were times when tempers rose. For example, Johnson told Senator Hickenlooper that he was tired of "disagreeing on Tweedledee and Tweedledum" and said he was not going to "argue with you further" about minor points.[22]

A major confrontation occurred between Johnson and extreme NATO critic Forrest Donnell (R-Missouri), who was not a committee member but had been given approval to sit in on the hearing.[23] Donnell's cantankerousness had become evident when he bombarded the committee's first witness, Secretary Acheson, with such penetrating questions as "Why is it that this document is called the 'North Atlantic Treaty'?" Acheson replied brilliantly, "It has to do with the defense of the North Atlantic area."[24] Senator Donnell proved to be just as irritating to Johnson as he peppered him with questions on such things as how many divisions Stalin used on the Eastern Front and how many U.S. divisions were sent abroad during World War II. On one occasion, Johnson, fighting back his anger, calmly told Donnell, "Your question is wrong."[25] On another, Johnson managed to maintain control of his temper when Donnell asked, "Do you know approximately how many troops in each of those two wars [WWI and II] that Belgium placed in the field?"[26]

Notwithstanding such petty harassment, Johnson's appearance before the Senate Foreign Relations Committee went well as he fielded the legitimate questions in a convincing, clear, and concise manner. Generally, the press reported his defense of the treaty in positive terms and did not mention the obvious inconsistency between his current stand and the one he had expressed in the DAR speech.[27]

In ably championing the NATO treaty Johnson displayed two characteristics that were evident throughout his public career. First, he had a remarkable ability to take a firm stand on an issue and then confidently explain away an earlier, totally inconsistent position. Second, he had no difficulty abandoning one position and embracing another for political advantage. These traits were especially apparent during the debate on the NATO Treaty. To Johnson's critics his "explanations" were considered wishy-washy, unethical, or politically inspired. They saw him as a man of no real principles, a political animal whose only real desire was to further his own career. To his supporters, Johnson's traits were marks of flexibility, open-mindedness, and political acuity. But the most accurate assessment rendered by contemporaries, including personal friends and those who examined his career later, is that Johnson was simply a good self-serving politician.[28]

Whether Johnson's testimony had any influence on the ratification vote is almost impossible to assess because there were ninety-six witnesses who testified and most senators appeared to have had their minds made up even before the hearings opened. In any event, the administration ultimately prevailed. The committee unanimously reported the treaty to the Senate floor and after lengthy debate in the old Supreme Court chamber of the Capitol (the Senate chamber was being renovated), the treaty was ratified on July 21, 1949, by a vote of 82 to 13.[29]

Military Assistance to NATO

Senate ratification meant that one obstacle had been surmounted, but that merely cleared the way for a larger one—passage of the Mutual Defense Assistance Program, or, as it came to be called, the Military Assistance Program (MAP). President Truman, Secretaries Acheson and Johnson, and their advisors realized that without the passage of the MAP, with its massive financial outlays for military supplies and equipment, NATO would remain a paper tiger.[30] As Johnson told the members of the Foreign Relations Committee during the hearings, "the ratification of the treaty cannot, in itself and without further action, safely be relied upon to accomplish the objectives of the treaty." What would be needed, he said, was to "go further and supply our friends with some of their deficiencies in arms and equipment and help them help themselves." The $1.1 billion for the NATO nations, plus another $300 million for five non-NATO countries, would be but a "beginning, to make those people keep the frontier against possible aggression over there, instead of it being on the Atlantic seaboard."[31]

Johnson was under no illusion about the magnitude of the battle yet to come; many of the treaty's supporters had already made it clear that they felt that the administration's plan of implementation was entirely too costly. A fight was brewing, but Johnson did not really mind—he had been there before.

While the MAP was essentially military in nature, the president turned responsibility for its passage over to Secretary Acheson because he saw it as an extension of the North Atlantic Treaty and therefore as a foreign policy matter. Acheson had guided the treaty through the Senate with a great deal of finesse and Truman was pleased with that performance. If Johnson was upset that he was not charged with the leading role in coordinating passage of the MAP, he never indicated he was nor did his actions suggest he was displeased.

But Johnson was destined to become a central figure in the fight for the MAP fight because the program primarily involved the extension of military aid. While Acheson could articulate the need for the program, the members of Congress wanted more specific information about the kinds and extent of military aid and the impact it would have on the nation's defense structure, and they wanted to question those who were best qualified to supply it—the secretary of defense and the Joint Chiefs of Staff. As Senate Foreign Relations Committee chairman Tom Connally of Texas told his committee members, he wanted to talk to defense officials because those in the State Department "don't know much more about it than we do."[32]

During the treaty ratification fight only one part of Congress had to be won over, but for the MAP both the House and Senate had to be sold. That the task would be difficult became evident on the day the president introduced the plan to Congress; immediately howls of protest went up from both sides of the Capitol Building. Especially vocal in their criticisms were Republican senators Arthur Vandenberg of Michigan and John Foster Dulles of New York,[33] both of whom complained about the failure of the administration to seek congressional participation in formulating the program, the inclusion of a "blank check" to the president to help any country he thought to be in need of assistance, the absence of a well-conceived and coordinated strategic defense plan, and the open-ended nature of the program.

On the basis of these concerns, Senate Republicans urged passage of a stop-gap measure pending an in-depth examination of the program. Both Acheson and Johnson vigorously opposed such a move because it would delay assistance to the needy nations and could lead to long, drawn-out hearings on the whole range of U.S. foreign and defense policies.[34] They worked for immediate passage of the measure as introduced.

Although the hostility expressed in the Senate attracted the most publicity, the House too had its critics, and since it was that body that first opened hearings on the MAP, it was there that the most interesting battles were fought. On July 29, Johnson appeared before the House Foreign Affairs Committee to urge passage. In the confident, forceful manner which characterized nearly all his presentations before Congress, Johnson warned of the "impending danger of [Soviet] aggression" and urged immediate passage of the MAP because it offered "the only way that we can start to make our allies strong enough so that they can make a material contribution to our security as well as to their own." The president's program, he contended, was by no means excessive, as charged by some critics, but was a bare minimum to start the signatories "on the road to military self sufficiency." The defense chief also defended the broad discretionary powers granted to the president and assured the committee that the extension of "surplus" and "reserve" arms would not appreciably weaken U.S. forces and that no American troops, other than a few technicians, would be sent abroad.[35]

In the examination that followed, the secretary fielded numerous questions, many of them hostile, about such matters as the powers to be conferred on the president, whether such a program marked an abandonment of the UN goal of disarmament, and the nature of the defense plans worked out with NATO. In the sparring that went on, the apparent lack of adequate strategic defense planning proved to be the most salient point made by representatives opposed to the plan. The cold hard fact was that the funds requested by the administration for the MAP "bore no relationship to any strategic concept."[36] Nevertheless, Johnson's job was to convince the committee that there was a coordinated plan that would justify large outlays of taxpayer dollars. He did a most creditable job.

At this juncture a question emerged that, strange as it may seem, had not been asked of an administration spokesman: How long was the program expected to last? Johnson replied, "Personally, I think the program will require 4 or 5 years."[37] Of all the things Johnson said that day, it was that prediction that received most of the attention in the press.

Army Chief of Staff General Omar Bradley followed Johnson before the House panel. Picking up on the issue of lack of planning, the general told the congressmen that a clearly defined strategy of defense was already in place. In case of an attack against a NATO nation, the strategy was for the United States "to deliver the atomic bomb" and help "keep the sea lanes clear"; the European nations would provide "the hard core of the ground power."[38]

The Monday after his House appearance Johnson returned to Capitol Hill, this time to testify before a joint hearing of the Senate Foreign Relations and Armed Services Committees. On the first day of the inquiry, August 2, Acheson and Johnson, in executive session, were informed in no uncertain terms that the Senate would not go along with the president's Military Assistance Program. According to Senator Vandenberg, "I gave 'em an ultimatum—write a new and reasonable bill or you will get no bill and it will be your fault."[39] Vandenberg and other senators were critical of the excessive powers given to the president, the implied movement away from the UN as the primary peacekeeping force, and the failure to consult Congress in preparing the program.[40] Vandenberg was not exaggerating a great deal when he wrote to his wife that after their encounter with the committee, Acheson and Johnson "went downtown to write a new bill."[41] In fact, the two secretaries did go "downtown" to the White House, where they informed the president of their chilly reception.

Given the hostility of the senior lawmakers and realizing that rigidity could easily lead to postponement if not a major reduction of the MAP program, the president agreed to relinquish the broad discretionary powers that had been conferred on him. Immediately, state and defense department officials began reworking the measure and Truman publicly announced that he was gladly giving up the "blank check" powers.[42]

On August 5, Acheson and Johnson returned with a much more concise bill which limited the president's discretion to allocate aid among various countries but carried the same price tag as the original plan. In the hearings that followed, Acheson made it clear that the administration was unwilling to accept any dollar figure that was less than requested.[43] Shortly thereafter, however, Johnson ignited a controversy that for a time appeared to undercut the administration's position and seriously endanger the assistance program.

While most of the committee hearings were in secret session, some were public, and this was the case on August 9 when Johnson testified. After a dynamic opening statement in support of the request, Senator Vandenberg, whose health was failing and who would die of lung cancer the following March, asked

Johnson why Congress could not provide half the total funds requested during the present year and substitute contract authorizations for the remaining half during the following year. Without hesitating, Johnson replied, "Senator, I do not care how you do it . . . we will not disagree."

Sensing the unexpected advantage that had come his way, Vandenberg continued by asking if he was not correct in assuming that everything being sought could be provided by "a reduction of 50 percent in the appropriation for fiscal 1950 and the substitution of contract authorization for the balance with respect to fiscal 1951." Johnson, moving right along with the senator, agreed that "the general approach to that is correct and all I seek—and I speak for no one else—is the money and the authorization, if you want to couple it that way."[44]

In the questioning that followed Johnson made no attempt to back away from Vandenberg's proposal. The next day, however, he probably realized his blunder because he backtracked on his stand by saying what would be needed was "60% funding and 40% contract authorization."[45] By then, however, it was too late.

What Johnson had unwittingly done was compromise the administration's firm position that it wanted and needed the funds for the MAP as requested. In agreeing to receive funds for half the amount one year and contract authorizations for the other half in the following year, the defense secretary had in reality agreed to a 50 percent reduction in what was being asked for the first year; furthermore, when a request would be made to fund the contracts for the second year of the program, Congress could reject the request.

Johnson had opened the door just a crack, but Vandenberg now pushed it wide open, because on August 15 he came out with a new proposal that a small amount, in the vicinity of $100 million, would be authorized immediately, with more funds released when the president approved plans for "an integrated defense of the North Atlantic area"; half the funds would be in the form of contract authorizations for 1951. The impact of Johnson's testimony was quite evident in this new plan, which Acheson described as being "wholly without merit." Nevertheless, with the Vandenberg proposal, "the tide of battle," said Acheson, "moved in such a sudden and unexpected direction that the administration rose above ideology to the best compromise possible."[46]

Just how or why Johnson let himself get suckered in by the senator from Michigan is not clear.[47] Perhaps it was merely an off-the-cuff exchange during which what was being said at the time seemed to be sound but in retrospect was not. Maybe it was the result of fatigue, because while the MAP hearings were taking place, so was the "revolt of the admirals" investigation, and Johnson was making almost daily visits to the Hill to testify. Whatever the reason, Johnson's mistake was inexcusable.

There is no direct evidence that the president and Acheson were unhappy about Johnson's mistake. However, it is difficult to imagine how they were not, since his comments ran counter to all their public statements indicating they would not accept anything less than what they requested.[48] It is likely that the administration would ultimately have had to compromise, but its position would have been much stronger had Johnson not blundered.

Just how much jeopardy the MAP was in became evident on August 15, less than a week after Johnson erred, when the House Foreign Affairs Committee came within one vote of recommending a 50 percent slash in the funds for NATO nations. A few days later, when the bill came to the floor of the House, the critics carried the day by engineering passage of a 50 percent cut in the administration's request by a vote of 123 to 73. Even an impassioned speech by the powerful speaker of the house, Sam Rayburn, could not rescue the administration.[49] While there is no proof that Johnson's weakening of the administration's position was responsible for the House action, it could not have failed but to have had some influence.

Throughout August and well into September as the Senate committees continued to work on the MAP, Johnson remained conspicuously and uncharacteristically silent about the whole matter of military aid. Whether this silence was imposed by Acheson or the president is not known, but during this period the administration's cause was almost entirely championed by the Joint Chiefs of Staff, who had returned from their recent European trip enthusiastic about the prospect of an integrated defense plan. Their testimony, especially that of General Bradley, was well received by the senators.[50]

In mid-September, both Senate committees reported the MAP bill to the floor, and the measure was approved on September 22. It called for a total authorization of $1.3 billion, with $314 million going to non-NATO nations and the remaining $1 billion to NATO signatories. There were some strings attached to the $1 billion: first, half the amount was in cash and the remainder was in contract authorizations; and second, only $100 million could be spent pending presidential approval of the NATO Defense Committee's integrated defense plan. Except for the contract authorization feature, the administration was pleased with the Senate bill. However, the program's future was still very much up in the air when it was sent to a conference committee to work out the major differences between the Senate and House versions.[51]

Within twenty-four hours of the MAP's submission to the conference committee, President Truman made his shocking announcement that the Soviets had detonated an atomic explosion. That event, more than anything the administration could have done, created an atmosphere favorable to a strong Military Assistance Program. The conference committee quickly agreed to the Senate version, and on September 28 both houses gave overwhelming approval to the measure officially called the Mutual Defense Assistance Act of 1949.[52] The Military Assistance Program was finally signed into law by President Truman on October 6.

Except for his error in responding to Senator Vandenberg, Secretary Johnson's dealings with Congress on NATO ratification and the subsequent

Louis Johnson's mother, Katherine ("Kate") Leftwich Arthur Johnson, in her early twenties. She and her father, Captain James Lewis Arthur, who fought under Stonewall Jackson in the Civil War, stoked Louis's drive to succeed in politics and law. COURTESY NANCY J. ZOLLMAN FAMILY COLLECTION.

Marcellus Alexander Johnson, Louis Johnson's father. With help from Kate and his children, he ran a grocery store near the Roanoke Machine Works for forty years. He was also Roanoke's first Central Registrar, member of the Roanoke City Council, and a founder of Grace Methodist Church. COURTESY NANCY J. ZOLLMAN FAMILY COLLECTION.

Louis Arthur Johnson at about age four. COURTESY NANCY J. ZOLLMAN FAMILY COLLECTION.

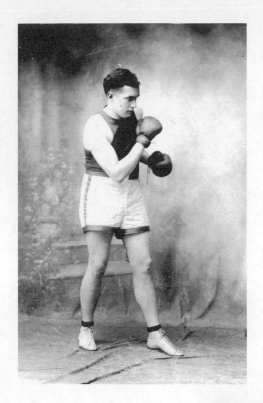

University of Virginia heavyweight champion, 1912. As Harry Truman confided to an associate, "Johnson is a rough customer, gets his way by rowing. When he takes out after you, give it right back to him." COURTESY HOLSINGER STUDIO COLLECTION (#9862), SPECIAL COLLECTIONS, UNIVERSITY OF VIRGINIA LIBRARY.

Big, rawboned Louis Johnson on the front steps of his parents' house in Roanoke with his brothers and sisters, about 1916. Louis is in the front row with his sister Helen. In the second row from left to right sits Gordon, Marcellus Jr., and Henry (Louis's half-brother). In the back row Paul is sitting on the left with Kate and Marcellus standing behind him. COURTESY NANCY J. ZOLLMAN FAMILY COLLECTION.

Louis and Ruth on their "second honeymoon" in Bermuda, 1925. Ruth wrote that "Louis was having a jolly time playing golf and tennis and dancing almost every night." COURTESY NANCY J. ZOLLMAN FAMILY COLLECTION.

Johnson being sworn in as assistant secretary of war on June 28, 1937. Left to right: Senator Matthew M. Neely of West Virginia; Johnson; General Malin Craig, army chief of staff; and Frank Hoadley, assistant chief clerk, War Department. COURTESY LOUIS JOHNSON PAPERS (#8476), SPECIAL COLLECTIONS, UNIVERSITY OF VIRGINIA LIBRARY.

Johnson (right) and Major General Oscar Westover, chief of the army air corps, inspecting the army's new four-engine "experimental" B-17 bomber at Bolling Field in Anacostia on April 2, 1938. After World War II, Army Chief of Staff George Marshall remarked to Bernard Baruch, "Germany would never have gotten off the ground if America had had the full complement of B-17's which [Louis] Johnson had requested before the war." COURTESY LOUIS JOHNSON PAPERS (#8476), SPECIAL COLLECTIONS, UNIVERSITY OF VIRGINIA LIBRARY.

On February 16, 1939, Johnson and others were called to Capitol Hill to explain why a French test pilot was found aboard the still-classified Douglas B-12 attack bomber when it crashed in a Los Angeles parking lot. Emerging from the hearing room, left to right are: Secretary of Treasury Henry Morgenthau; Representative Andrew J. May, Chairman of the House Military Affairs Committee; Undersecretary of the Treasury John W. Hanes; Secretary of War Harry Woodring; and Assistant Secretary of War Johnson. COURTESY LOUIS JOHNSON PAPERS (#8476), SPECIAL COLLECTIONS, UNIVERSITY OF VIRGINIA LIBRARY.

When President Franklin Roosevelt cut short his vacation at Hyde Park because the Germans had overrun Denmark and were invading Norway, Johnson was at Union Station to greet him on April 10, 1940. Left to right: Roosevelt, Secretary of State Cordell Hull, Johnson, and Assistant Secretary of State Sumner Welles (with situation maps in hand). Courtesy Louis Johnson Papers (#8476), Special Collections, University of Virginia Library.

At Bolling Field in April 1940, Johnson shows President Roosevelt the latest American warplanes. General Hap Arnold, who succeeded General Westover as chief of the army air corps, is in the middle. Courtesy Louis Johnson Papers (#8476), Special Collections, University of Virginia Library.

Johnson's home on Buckhannon Avenue in Clarksburg, West Virginia. Known as "the Harrison house," the stately residence was built in 1860 by Thomas Willoughby Harrison, a prominent attorney and judge. Louis and Ruth purchased the house in 1941, and although Louis usually worked and lived on weekdays in Washington and New York, he almost always returned on weekends to preside at Steptoe & Johnson, play golf, and tend his orchids. Photo by David L. Roll.

Louis Johnson, the personal representative of the president, arriving in India on April 3, 1942, via Air Transport Command. COURTESY LOUIS JOHNSON PAPERS (#8476), SPECIAL COLLECTIONS, UNIVERSITY OF VIRGINIA LIBRARY.

Vindication! On March 28, 1949, almost a decade after being let go by FDR, Johnson is sworn in as President Truman's second secretary of defense by Chief Justice Fred Vinson (right). A gaunt James Forrestal, who would within two months take his own life, is in the center reluctantly joining hands with Johnson and Vinson. COURTESY LOUIS JOHNSON PAPERS (#8476), SPECIAL COLLECTIONS, UNIVERSITY OF VIRGINIA LIBRARY.

With the secretary of defense leaning on his desk and a host of congressmen and military personnel looking on, President Harry Truman signs the 1949 Amendments to the National Security Act in the Oval Office on August 10, 1949. This law gave Johnson the power and authority to unify the armed services and achieve vast economic savings. COURTESY LOUIS JOHNSON PAPERS (#8476), SPECIAL COLLECTIONS, UNIVERSITY OF VIRGINIA LIBRARY.

In high spirits at the American Legion National Convention in Philadelphia, August 29, 1949. Truman, American Legion National Commander Perry Brown (center), and Johnson (right), former national commander of the Legion. COURTESY LOUIS JOHNSON PAPERS (#8476), SPECIAL COLLECTIONS, UNIVERSITY OF VIRGINIA LIBRARY.

During a break in the hearings on the B-36 investigation in August 1949, Johnson chats with Carl Vinson (right), the powerful chairman of the House Committee on Armed Services, known as the "Swamp Fox of Georgia." According to Johnson, the controversy which sparked these hearings and led to the crushing of "the revolt of the admirals," was "the issue that gave me the chance to run the department . . . the thing that gave me control." COURTESY LOUIS JOHNSON PAPERS (#8476), SPECIAL COLLECTIONS, UNIVERSITY OF VIRGINIA LIBRARY.

On the flight deck of the aircraft carrier *Franklin Roosevelt*, September 29, 1949. Left to right: General Omar Bradley, chairman of the Joint Chiefs of Staff; General Hoyt Vandenburg, air force chief of staff; Johnson; Admiral Louis Denfield, chief of naval operations; General J. Lawton ("Lightning Joe") Collins, army chief of staff. Courtesy Louis Johnson Papers (#8476), Special Collections, University of Virginia Library.

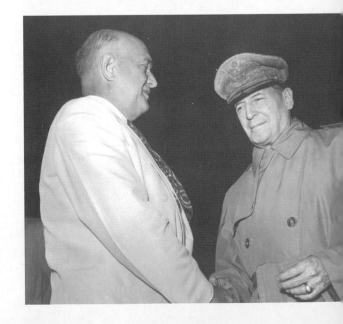

General Douglas MacArthur greeting Johnson when Johnson arrived in Tokyo on June 18, 1950, to confer with MacArthur on the Japanese peace treaty and the defense of Formosa. Johnson regarded MacArthur as "one of the greatest, if not the greatest, generals of our generation." Courtesy Louis Johnson Papers (#8476), Special Collections, University of Virginia Library.

Johnson (left) and Secretary of State Dean Acheson (right) greet a worried President Truman at National Airport on Sunday, June 25, 1950, following Truman's trip back from his home in Independence, Missouri, to Washington to deal with the surprise invasion of South Korea. Truman was in a "grim mood" and after this photo was taken he snapped, "That's enough! We've got a job to do." COURTESY LOUIS JOHNSON PAPERS (#8476), SPECIAL COLLECTIONS, UNIVERSITY OF VIRGINIA LIBRARY.

Following a meeting with congressional leaders in the White House on Tuesday, June 27, 1950, during which President Truman announced that he had "ordered United States air and sea forces to give the [South] Korean Government troops cover and support," Truman, Johnson (right), and Attorney General J. Howard McGrath (left) walk over to the president's temporary residence at Blair House to join the rest of the Cabinet for lunch. On the two previous nights, Truman, Johnson, and twelve other key advisors had met at Blair House, where they made fateful decisions leading to U.S. military support of the South Koreans and the defense of Taiwan (Formosa). COURTESY AP/WIDE WORLD PHOTOS.

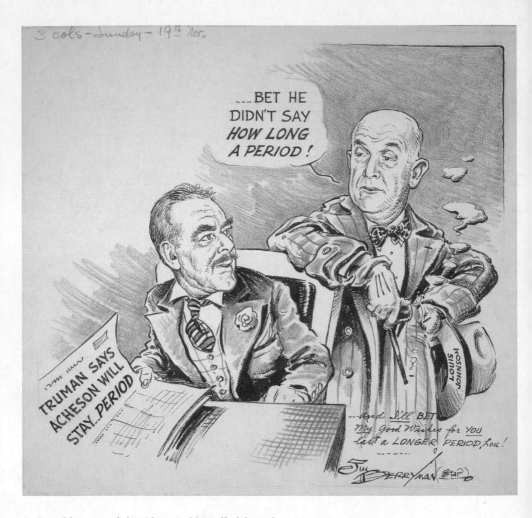

As Republicans and the China Lobby called for Acheson's resignation, it was no secret in Washington that Johnson, who disagreed violently with Acheson on Far Eastern policy and intensely disliked the man, wanted him removed from the Truman administration. Courtesy Louis Johnson Papers (#8476), Special Collections, University of Virginia Library.

On September 1, 1950, the day President Truman said he made up his mind to fire his secretary of defense, Johnson, believing he had weathered the summer storm of criticism, gathered the entire defense establishment at the Pentagon for an "informal luncheon." Seated around the table, left to right: Johnson; Ambassador to the Court of St. James Lewis W. Douglas; Secretary of the Air Force Thomas K. Finletter; General J. Lawton Collins, army chief of staff; Admiral Forrest P. Sherman, chief of naval operations; Hubert Howard, chairman of the Munitions Board; Secretary of the Navy Francis P. Matthews; U.S. High Commissioner for Germany John J. McCloy; Deputy Secretary of Defense Stephen Early; Averell Harriman, special assistant for foreign affairs to the president; General Hoyt Vandenberg, air force chief of staff; General James H. Burns (Ret.), assistant to the secretary of defense; General Omar Bradley, chairman of the Joint Chiefs of Staff; Secretary of the Army Frank Pace; and Secretary of State Dean Acheson. COURTESY LOUIS JOHNSON PAPERS (#8476), SPECIAL COLLECTIONS, UNIVERSITY OF VIRGINIA LIBRARY.

THROWN TO THE WOLVES

After prevaricating for more than a week, President Truman finally summoned the courage to tell his old friend Louis Johnson—the man who had raised the money to enable him to win the presidency in 1948—that he had to go. At a private meeting in the Oval Office on September 11, 1950, Truman said, "Lou, I've got to ask you to quit." As this cartoonist saw it, Truman and Acheson threw Johnson to the wolves in order to stanch administration criticism. COURTESY LOUIS JOHNSON PAPERS (#8476), SPECIAL COLLECTIONS, UNIVERSITY OF VIRGINIA LIBRARY.

Military Assistance Program had been almost flawless. To say that he was largely responsible for their passage would be an overstatement in view of the numerous factors that influenced the actions of Congress. However, for the most part he performed admirably before the various legislative groups, and the fact that congressional leaders expressed their confidence in his abilities certainly helped the administration's case.[53]

Diplomacy

After ratification of the North Atlantic Treaty by the twelve signatory nations, the treaty went into effect on August 24, 1949. From that day forward it was officially possible for operational organization and planning to begin, which happened on September 17 when the implementing body of NATO, the North Atlantic Council, consisting of the foreign ministers of each NATO nation, met in Washington. In accordance with the treaty, the North Atlantic Council set up a Defense Committee composed of the defense ministers of the member nations and gave that committee the responsibility of developing broad coordinated defense plans for the entire North Atlantic area.

Since the council directed that the chairmanship of the Defense Committee should be on a one-year rotating basis, starting with the United States, Louis Johnson became that body's first chairman. Johnson had to get his committee functioning quickly and effectively because of the congressional stipulation that no more than $100 million of the military aid funds could be spent until the president had approved the Defense Committee's integrated defense plans. Accordingly, Johnson summoned his committee to meet in Washington on October 5.

At the opening session of the NATO Defense Committee held in the Pentagon, Johnson used the opportunity to sound a warning to the Soviet Union that the NATO nations were determined to resist aggression "with all our combined might." Although this was his first meeting as chairman of an international negotiating body, Johnson had learned a great deal about how to lead such a multinational group during his time in India in 1942. Drawing on that experience, Johnson's performance was impressive as he moved the committee through a crowded agenda in an efficient and expeditious manner.

Originally, the Defense Committee had planned on a three-day conference. However, Johnson kept them in a six-hour marathon session during which all matters were disposed of in a single day. In the course of this one meeting, the committee agreed to the principle of an integrated defense system, set up the Military Committee with General Bradley as its chairman and provided it with guidelines to be used in drawing up regional defense plans, and directed that a newly appointed Military Production and Supply Board meet in London in December to begin allocating military production responsibilities to the various NATO nations. When the committee adjourned, its members were committed to the idea of pressuring their staffs to produce the detailed defense plans that were urgently needed.[54]

In the weeks that followed, the military and diplomatic staffs of the various nations developed strategic defense plans, and in early November the State Department submitted to the member nations a draft of a bilateral agreement which spelled out what aid would be extended to each of the signatory nations. Shortly thereafter, defense and state department officials traveled to the respective countries to work out differences. When those tentative agreements had been reached, Johnson called the committee back into session. Throughout the negotiating process, indeed throughout the entire defense planning process, Secretaries Acheson and Johnson and their department personnel worked closely and harmoniously together. When differences did appear they were quickly resolved.[55]

The second NATO Defense Committee meeting was held in Paris on December 1. When Johnson arrived, he quickly learned that the harmony that characterized the earlier conference was in danger of disintegrating and that a walkout of some of the ministers was a real possibility. The main problem came from the Danish Cabinet, which found unacceptable a statement that one of NATO's objectives was to "insure the ability to carry out strategic bombing including prompt delivery of the atomic bomb." When Johnson was informed by the Norwegian defense minister that failure to eliminate the phrase about the atomic bomb might cause "a serious contretemps," he took it seriously. In private negotiations, the secretary agreed to eliminate the language, but when the matter came up before the entire body, the Belgian, Italian, and Dutch representatives objected to dropping the phrase because they felt that "fear of the A-bomb was one of the greatest contributing factors to preventing a Russian attack." Johnson solved the dilemma by negotiating a compromise whereby the reference to the atomic bomb would be dropped from the official statement, but the minutes of the meeting would carry a strong statement on strategic bombing including the use of the atomic bomb.[56]

Another problem Johnson faced was a proposal the French representative intended to present which called for France to have primary responsibility for NATO military communications in the Mediterranean—a matter of great concern to U.S. naval officials because it raised questions of who would be in command of the sea in that area if war broke out. To head off this possibility, Johnson enlisted the aid of the British defense minister, Albert Alexander, and together they convinced the French to delay consideration of the matter until the next meeting, pending a complete examination of the issue.

The third major concern was the request of the Norwegians that the guidelines for regional planning, which were being drawn up by a subcommittee, be distributed and discussed by all members. State and defense department advisors opposed the move because of the considerable delay such action might bring. Notwithstanding these objections, Johnson went along with the Norwegians to maintain a spirit of cooperation and harmony among the member nations.[57]

In spite of these problems, the Paris meeting was, according to one inside observer, "one of harmony with a . . . greater solidarity among the Defense Ministers than in the first meeting."[58] The major accomplishments included a unanimous agreement on "strategic concepts for the integrated defense of the North Atlantic area," an understanding on production of military supplies, coordination of regional defense plans, and cooperation in intelligence gathering, training exercises, base construction, and equipment standardization. While the details of the strategic concepts were not made public, it was known that they ran along the lines previously described by Chief of Staff Bradley, with strategic bombing and sea power commitments falling heavily on the United States and ground force responsibilities being shouldered by the European nations.[59]

That the meeting was so productive was due to the efforts of many individuals, but there is no question that Chairman Johnson's adroit handling of potentially explosive issues, both in the sessions and behind the scenes, and his overall leadership contributed immeasurably to its success. It was a masterful job of international diplomacy.[60]

Five weeks later, the North Atlantic Council readily approved the recommendations of the NATO Defense Committee, thus paving the way for President Truman's approval and authorization to spend additional military assistance funds. On January 27, 1950, the day he signed bilateral aid agreements with eight of the NATO nations, the president publicly announced his acceptance of the proposed integrated defense plan.[61] The congressional stipulation that such a plan be in place before the bulk of the military assistance funds could be expended had been fulfilled, and the way was at last open to begin the aid program.

Launching such a massive program required considerable coordination between state and defense department officials and their European counterparts, and it was not until mid-March 1950 that the first aircraft and other armaments began to flow to the recipient nations. In late spring, the machinery of procurement and distribution began to function more smoothly, and by the end of June 1950, all of the aircraft and 134,000 tons of rifles, combat vehicles, anti-aircraft guns, artillery, and other war matériel had reached their destinations.[62]

As the MAP got under way in early 1950, Secretary Johnson continued to carry on the battle to strengthen NATO through his leadership of the Defense Committee and by working with Secretary Acheson on the aid program to be presented to Congress for the following year, fiscal 1951. On April 1, the NATO Defense Committee held its third meeting in Brussels, and it was Johnson's preparation for this meeting that diverted him from focusing on NSC 68. When he arrived for the Brussels meeting Johnson made a public statement that indicated that the objective of his committee was "to deter aggression . . . to defend ourselves and finally to defeat an aggressor if he forced war upon us." At that gathering, the affairs of the Defense Committee ran very smoothly, thanks again to Johnson's efficiency and skill as chairman. That things went well was due in part to the fact that Johnson visited privately with each defense minister to find out where he stood on various issues.[63] His one-on-one meetings did much to lessen tensions and put the group at ease.

When the third meeting of NATO defense ministers concluded—it was another six-hour session—the committee announced that it had agreed to an integrated strategic plan for the entire North Atlantic area. Johnson acknowledged that a great deal more needed to be done, but he hailed the steps taken because they moved NATO from a planning mode to real defense preparation.[64] Slowly but surely progress was being made to meet and contain the Soviet threat.

Throughout this period Johnson and the Joint Chiefs were deeply involved in formalizing plans for the second year of the MAP. On June 1, 1950, President Truman presented the program, which carried a $1 billion price tag.[65] Immediately, Acheson and Johnson stepped forward to lead the administration's offensive to push the MAP through Congress. On June 2, the secretary of state went before joint sessions of the Senate Foreign Relations and Armed Forces Committees. In strongly urging continuation of the program, Acheson predicted that the cost of military assistance to foreign nations would become even higher in the future.

Several days later, on June 5, Johnson told the same group the exact opposite, maintaining that the cost of military assistance to NATO would probably get smaller each year rather than larger. His reasoning was that as economic recovery by the European allies continued, they would be able to carry a heavier share of the defense burden.[66] When asked to explain his disagreement with Secretary Acheson, Johnson claimed that there were "no disagreements" but said, "I think I have been living a little more closely to the field of military expenditures than he." Johnson's testimony was embarrassing to Acheson and the administration—to the former because it made him appear as if he did not know what he was talking about and to the latter because it made it appear as if the left hand did not know what the right hand was doing.

The congressional floor fights that were expected on the administration's MAP proposal never developed, not because Johnson and Acheson were such persuasive witnesses but rather because several weeks after their appearance, on June 25, war broke out in Korea which resulted in a new American awareness of the communist threat. The fresh sense of urgency soon led to nearly unanimous passage of the bill by both houses exactly as it was presented.[67] That passage was to mark the beginning of a major congressional commitment to NATO.

Reason to Be Proud

While there may have been some doubt about Louis Johnson's commitment to collective security for Western Europe before he became secretary of defense, there is no question that from the time he became secretary until he departed the post he was a strong supporter of NATO and the programs designed to make it an effective organization. After serving as an able spokesman for NATO in the ratification process, he went on to play a key role in the administration's battle to secure passage of the MAP and in setting up the machinery to provide the military hardware to the recipient nations. As chairman of the NATO Defense Committee, Johnson was instrumental in formulating the strategic plans for the defense of the entire North Atlantic area.

Louis Johnson was proud of his role in establishing NATO as a key fixture of U.S. foreign and defense policy, and his pride was justified. Throughout the battles on Capitol Hill and with U.S. allies in Europe, Johnson's performance for the most part was outstanding. Of particular and remarkable significance was the fact that he and Dean Acheson actually worked well together on NATO-related issues. In contrast to the acrimony and infighting that characterized most of their dealings with one another, Johnson and Acheson generally saw eye to eye on the role and responsibilities of the United States in helping her allies in Western Europe meet their defense needs.

On only one major issue in the European defense picture did Johnson disagree with Acheson and that was the question of rearming and ultimately admitting West Germany into NATO. Johnson and President Truman held the widely accepted view of their fellow Americans, and most Western Europeans, that rearming Germany was out of the question. According to Johnson, the United States had "no intentions of rearming Germany" and on that policy there was "no hedging and no dodging."[68] Acheson, on the other hand, believed that a rearmed but closely controlled Germany, with its enormous political, military, and industrial potential, was absolutely essential to the establishment of stability in Europe.[69] Prior to mid-1950, Acheson's view could not, for political reasons, be openly expressed. However, events in the Far East, specifically Korea, were to change that and many other positions of the Truman administration.

CHAPTER FIFTEEN

"Till the Dust Settles"

IT WAS MID-AFTERNOON ON December 22, 1949. Laidler Mackall, who had been a World War II bomber pilot and was then a young associate at Steptoe & Johnson, had "borrowed" a military DC-3 transport from the Air National Guard at Andrews Air Force Base and was flying a handful of Steptoe associates to the firm's conference in Clarksburg.

As he was landing at the small airport nestled in the mountains, Mackall could see that another olive-drab DC-3 had landed just ahead of him so he knew that "the Colonel," who would preside over the firm's conference, had already arrived. Mackall quickly taxied up to the tiny airport terminal and the young lawyers piled out of the DC-3 to greet the secretary of defense, who stood on the tarmac chatting with his pilot and Mrs. Johnson.[1]

One of the Steptoe associates, Dick Whiting, fresh out of the army and Yale Law School, good looking, cocky, and full of mischief, was eager to meet the Colonel. He walked up to him, thrust out his hand and said, "Hi, Colonel Johnson. I'm Dick Whiting, your replacement at the firm." The Colonel's face darkened, the muscles of his jaw tightened, and he fixed a cold stare at Whiting. Louis Johnson saw no humor in the young lawyer's flippant remark.[2]

Whiting and the rest of the associates had no reason to know it, but Johnson was not in a good mood. Just a few hours before, he had had lunch with President Truman at Blair House. For months, Johnson had been battling with the secretary of state and others over the issue of providing military assistance to the Nationalist Chinese who had been defeated on the mainland and were holding out against the Red Chinese on the island of Formosa (now called Taiwan). At lunch that day, Truman told his secretary of defense that he had lost his battle. The president said that he was siding with Johnson's nemesis,

Dean Acheson, and that there would be no support for the beleaguered Nationalists.[3]

This was a setback for Johnson, but there would be other battles to fight and he knew he would bounce back. More than anything, he was disheartened by the president's lack of an overall policy—a thoughtful vision—for dealing proactively with the rapidly changing strategic situation in the Far East. And he believed that the president, who admittedly knew little about the history, politics, and culture of Asia, was not being served well by his secretary of state.

Policy Vacuum

While the United States had a readily understood and widely supported European defense policy which the Truman administration had formulated with great care and then sold to Congress and the American public, this was not the case when it came to Asia. As 1949 dawned and President Truman turned to pressing foreign and military affairs problems, he did so with a new secretary of state, Dean Acheson, and a new secretary of defense, Louis Johnson, and virtually no guidelines about national goals or objectives in Asia and the Western Pacific. As one qualified observer of the political scene put it, "That the United States lacked a 'policy' for the Far East was a favorite commonplace of American political conversation during 1949, uttered with every shade of cynicism, exasperation and concern."[4]

The complete absence of a Far Eastern policy in the late 1940s was due to several factors, of which remoteness from America was one. Because of sheer distance and huge cultural differences, U.S. public and policymakers had a difficult time relating to the Far East. The Orient continued to be a kind of mystic, exotic land that seemed to exist more in the mind than in the real world. The problems of Europe, on the other hand, always seemed closer and more real to Americans.[5]

Another obstacle to the development of a comprehensive and coordinated policy was the limited funds available for foreign and military aid. As Congress and the executive branch moved to meet the domestic and foreign affairs problems in the Cold War era, they came face to face with the reality that they could not afford to do everything they wanted to. It was a matter of priorities and it was the consensus of the Truman administration that long-standing domestic government services, a host of Fair Deal programs, the Marshall Plan, and support for NATO were more important than aid and military assistance to Asian nations.[6]

A third very important reason for the policy vacuum related to the multitude of problems that emerged in that section of the world with the collapse of the Japanese empire at the end of World War II. No sooner had the fighting stopped than the same East-West conflict that had emerged in Europe began to arise in the Far East as the USSR and the United States struggled for hegemony in China, Indochina, Japan, and Korea.[7]

There was also widespread division, dissension, and disagreement within the executive and legislative branches and the public about what policies the United States should pursue in those distant corners of the world. Probably no American was more concerned about the chaos of the nation's Asian policy than Secretary Johnson. Less than three months after assuming his new position he made his frustrations known to the members of the National Security Council. In a bold and highly significant memorandum to his NSC colleagues on June 10, 1949, he was extremely critical of the "day-to-day, country-by-country approach" to Asian problems that had characterized U.S. foreign policy in the postwar era. This piecemeal approach, he contended, was no longer acceptable in view of the danger of Communist expansion in that part of the world, especially China. What was needed was a "carefully considered and comprehensive plan" that would contain the spread of communism.

Johnson therefore requested the NSC staff (not the State Department) to reconsider U.S. policies toward individual countries and devote resources to the development of an overall plan for Asia. Johnson's memorandum helped stimulate the NSC to action. Six months later, as will be seen, a comprehensive foreign policy plan became a reality.[8]

Why Johnson, a West Virginia lawyer, would choose to insert himself into the policy vacuum and call for a full-scale review of Asian and Far Eastern policy is a question that is difficult to answer. Most likely, he was driven by opportunity, politics, and his intellectual interests. Johnson had a lifelong fascination with the history, culture, and art of Asia. As a boy in Sunday school in Roanoke, he loved the tales of the missionaries in China. When he matured, Johnson maintained his interest and became a collector of Asian art, a student of Asian history, and an expert on Japanese landscaping and gardens. In preparing for his wartime mission to India, he further immersed himself in the history and politics of Asia and came to understand and appreciate the emergence of nationalism among the nations of Asia that would have a profound influence on the strategic interests of the United States.

During his mission to India in 1942, Johnson established a friendship with Jawaharlal Nehru, who would become India's postwar prime minister, and the two had carried on a lively correspondence since that time. It is probable that Nehru impressed the secretary with his views on the relationship between the rise of nationalism in Asian nations and the spread of communism. And it is likely that Johnson's relationship with the great Indian leader factored into his decision to demand a review of U.S. policy toward Asia.[9]

When he decided to inject himself into the foreign policy arena by calling for a review of U.S. policy toward Asia, Johnson also injected himself into Nehru's first state visit to the United States, which took place during the last two weeks of October. Following state dinners, ceremonial meetings, and a private talk with Acheson, during which Nehru advised him to recognize Red

China and not get involved in Vietnam, the prime minister was Johnson's guest at a dinner he hosted on October 29, 1949, at The Greenbrier.[10] Like Acheson, who thought many of Nehru's ideas were "specious," Johnson almost certainly disagreed with Nehru's advice on China and Vietnam, but at least the two key cabinet members in Truman's administration had the benefit of the nuanced views of a wise and learned Asian leader, advice that in retrospect perhaps should have been taken to heart.

Fall of China

As the spring of 1949 approached, Johnson and the rest of the Truman administration did not have the luxury of waiting for the NSC to come up with a comprehensive policy for the Far East. Events in China forced the administration to confront difficult and controversial political realities and led to the opening salvos in what became a bitter battle between Secretary of State Dean Acheson and Secretary of Defense Louis Johnson.

When World War II came to an end in the Pacific, American policymakers hoped that a free united China would emerge as a stabilizing force in that sector of the world. They realized that the longtime conflict between the pro-American Nationalist government of Chiang Kai-shek and the Communist forces under Mao Tse-tung would need to be resolved. Thus, in late 1945 President Truman sent former army chief of staff General George Marshall to China as his personal representative to settle the differences between the warring factions. Neither side was willing to make concessions, the mission failed, and in 1946 full-scale civil war erupted again.[11]

Although disillusioned and disappointed by Chiang's refusal to institute monetary and land reforms and by the corruption among his top officials, the Truman administration chose to support Chiang's "democratic" regime against the forces of the "godless" Communists. Between 1945 and 1949, the United States extended some $2.8 billion in foreign assistance and military aid to Chiang, including the $400 million appropriated in the China Aid Act of 1948.[12]

Under General Marshall's stewardship, the Truman administration approved a program to send military advisors to train Nationalist forces in the immediate postwar years. However, Truman rejected a 1947 request from army general Albert C. Wedemeyer for a massive material assistance program and a commitment of 10,000 military and technical advisors.[13] By this time, the administration had come to the conclusion that nothing it could do would save Chiang's regime. While it was questionable whether the Communists could have been halted with substantial U.S. aid, it was a foregone conclusion that they could not be stopped without it.

The maladministration, corruption, and resistance to reform of the Nationalists led to a further breakdown of the civil and military machinery, morale of fighting forces, and popular support that any government needs to survive. The Communists, encouraged by their successes in the field and the growing defections among the opposition, drove south from their northern strongholds in late 1947 and 1948. In September of 1948, they proclaimed a North China People's Government and in the months that followed they moved south of the Yangtze River and ever closer to the Nationalist capital at Nanking.

Then, on January 21, 1949, the day after Truman's inauguration, Chiang "retired." He had lost more than half his army, primarily due to defections, and had let more than 80 percent of the American-supplied equipment fall into Communist hands. Chiang turned the government over to General Li Tsung-jen and left the mainland for the island province of Formosa, where he began to prepare a sanctuary for his regime. From this island redoubt, located 100 miles from the mainland, Chiang intended to keep his government and his army intact until he could liberate his vast homeland from the Communist aggressors.[14]

With Chiang's departure from the mainland, the Truman administration, at Acheson's insistence, prepared to disengage itself from the supposedly doomed Nationalist government, but members of Congress vigorously objected. The ardent pro-Chiang, anti-Communist advocacy that took place in the halls of Congress came from the so-called China Lobby, a largely right-wing group of legislators led by Senators William Knowland of California (known as "the Senator from Formosa"), Alexander Smith (R-New Jersey), Styles Bridges (R-New Hampshire), and Pat McCarran (D-Nevada), and Representative Walter H. Judd (R-Minnesota), a former medical missionary to China. Those congressmen and their powerful cohorts, with the help of the New York Times, Luce Publications, the Scripps-Howard chain, the Manchester Union Leader, and Senator Knowland's Oakland Tribune, successfully rallied widespread public support for Chiang and convinced a significant segment of the American public that the man in the White House and his advisors were "selling out China and the free enterprise system to communists."[15]

In early February 1949, when the president attempted to halt shipments of military supplies destined for China under the 1948 China Aid Act on the grounds that the goods would fall into Communist hands, the China Lobby in Washington raised such a fuss that the president rescinded his order. Later that month, Senator McCarran introduced a bill calling for $1.5 billion in loans to the Nationalist government and authorizing U.S. army officers to take command of Nationalist army units. Although the bill did not pass, the fact that so many members of Congress voiced support for it signaled to the administration that Chiang had many influential friends on the Hill.[16]

On February 24, 1949, Dean Acheson met with thirty-five congressmen, many of whom were members of the China Lobby and had been vilifying the Truman administration for the "loss of China." During this meeting, Acheson, who later wrote that he personally favored recognition of the new Communist government, tried to explain that a new policy toward China could not be developed until the dust and smoke of the Chinese civil war had settled.[17]

After this supposedly private meeting, some of the congressmen leaked a report to the press suggesting that Acheson had characterized U.S. policy toward China as "waiting till the dust settles." The phrase became a Republican slogan and was used against the Truman administration and the State Department to demonstrate that they had no policy other than to await a complete Communist takeover of China.[18]

Louis Johnson took delight in Acheson's "wait till the dust settles" predicament. He went around Washington saying, "I'll keep asking what our China policy is until I find out."[19]

Protect Formosa?

As the Communist forces under Mao Tse-tung swept southward and captured Nanking in the spring of 1949, it was only a matter of time before Mao conquered the entire Chinese mainland. The question facing Johnson and Acheson and their respective departments became what U.S. policy should be regarding the large and strategically situated Chinese island of Formosa (MacArthur likened it to "an unsinkable aircraft carrier") that was occupied and ruled by Chiang and his Nationalist government?[20]

The Joint Chiefs, who had been studying the Formosa issue in 1948 and had already concluded that its fall to the Communists would be "seriously unfavorable" from a strategic viewpoint, had previously recommended that measures should be taken to keep it in friendly hands. The navy had even gone so far as to propose that it establish a foothold there until a UN plebiscite could be held. The State Department also felt it was desirable to keep Formosa out of Communist control but did not want to actively support Chiang's regime until the dust settled and it became clear what policy should be pursued. In National Security Council paper 37/2, which was approved by the president on February 3, 1949, the state department view was accepted as official U.S. policy.

A few days after NSC 37/2 was approved, Acheson requested that the JCS again assess the strategic importance of Formosa and address the need for military action to save it from Communist takeover.[21] When this report came forward from the JCS in late March 1949, Johnson encountered his first Far Eastern issue as secretary of defense.

After studying the recommendations of the JCS, Johnson accepted their general views that "the strategic importance of Formosa [does not justify] overt military action at this time." The secretary left the door open to possible intervention, however, by noting that "future circumstances" might make "overt military action eventually advisable."[22] Since Johnson had been in office for only a few days when this issue came up, he really had no alternative but to go along with the JCS position, but the fact that he left the door open to a possible change in policy was significant.

In April 1949, Acheson initiated a project, popularly known as the China White Paper, which was to trigger his first major league conflict with Johnson. Designed to answer the criticisms by the China Lobby and others that were overwhelming the administration, the soon-to-be-famous white paper, written by experts in the State Department, turned into a 1,054-page tome filled with official documents which, in Acheson's words, demonstrated "the unfortunate but inescapable fact . . . that the ominous result of the civil war in China was beyond the control of the government of the United States." The only alternative, he concluded, would have been "full-scale intervention" by American troops, a decision which "would have been condemned by the American people."[23] The paper went even farther when, in light of very little evidence, it tied the Communist regimes of China and the Soviet Union closely together.[24]

In a florid cover letter to the white paper, Acheson observed that the Nationalist government had lost its fighting spirit, was riddled with corruption, and had lost the confidence of the Chinese people. In addition, he said Chiang's government could not be resurrected by military, economic, or technical assistance programs.[25]

As the white paper neared completion, Louis Johnson actively urged that it not be released to the public. In mid-summer he told Acheson in no uncertain terms that it should never be released in its current form because, as he later recalled, "I didn't think it was accurate and thought it was politically unwise."[26] When its accuracy was questioned, Acheson sent a representative to the Pentagon to see if some of the discrepancies between State and Defense could be clarified. As a result of those visits, some changes were made, but not enough to satisfy Johnson and his top advisors.

Johnson's political reason for opposing release of the China White Paper was based on his strong feeling that the Nationalist government, even with its many shortcomings, was the last best hope for keeping Formosa out of Communist hands and that nothing should be done to weaken it. He believed the white paper, with its disparaging assessments of Chiang's government, would seriously undermine the only prospect for stability in China. All the defense secretary wanted to know was "What purpose was to be served . . . by the issuance of such a document which had as its one seeming object to destroy a government [in Formosa] that was established and which offered the only hope?"[27]

Even after Acheson and Truman had agreed that the white paper would be disclosed to the public, Johnson, with the backing of the JCS, made two last-ditch efforts in late July to discourage release. First, in a July 21 memorandum to Acheson, Johnson started off with a bit of sarcasm, saying he was "very glad to have [Acheson's] assurance" that the Defense Department had nothing to do with the preparation or publication of the white paper. He closed with an ominous warning that "you [Acheson] and the President should carefully consider whether the usefulness of this Paper . . . is greater than the [political] risks inherent in the disclosures which are made."[28] Second, he invited Acheson to fly out with him to the annual encampment at Bohemian Grove, where he could persuade him not to release the China White Paper to the public and perhaps reach "an agreement on a new China policy."[29] Acheson must have turned Johnson's offer down because he was not at the Grove that summer.

Despite Johnson's efforts to change Acheson's mind and his warning that release would do political damage to the president, Acheson and Truman apparently concluded that release was worth the risk because on August 5, 1949, the China White Paper was published. The reaction it caused probably led them to wish that for once they had listened to Johnson because the uproar in Congress and the press was much greater than they had ever anticipated.[30] Members of the China Lobby were joined by members of the House and Senate from both parties in vehemently condemning the white paper and the thesis it presented. The so-called defeatist views espoused in the document fueled the already raging fires set by Senator Joseph McCarthy, who purported to have a "list" of more than 200 members of the Communist Party "still working and shaping policy in the State Department."[31] Many other prominent Americans from all walks of life and influential news columnists such as Walter Lippmann joined in the criticism of "Acheson's claim that our China policy was essentially right and that [the loss of China] was beyond our control."[32]

Charges that Truman and the State Department had sold out to the Communists were soon being hurled from coast to coast. The release of the white paper was a political and public-relations disaster, which Acheson later reluctantly admitted.[33]

Johnson Takes a Stand

While the white paper controversy was boiling, the JCS were once again examining their policy concerning the defense of Formosa. In an August 17 memorandum to Secretary Johnson, the Joint Chiefs reiterated their earlier position that stressed Formosa's strategic importance to the United States but claimed, as they had in February, that military intervention to defend it was not justified. Again they did not rule out a future military commitment to protect the island.[34]

This was the last time the Joint Chiefs would side with Acheson and Truman on the defense of Formosa. After August 17, the attitude of the Defense Department on Formosa began to increasingly reflect the view of Secretary Johnson—a view which was much more sympathetic and supportive of the Nationalist Chinese cause.[35]

From the time Johnson entered the Defense Department, if not before, he was concerned about what he considered to be the "political domination of

Defense in many ways by State."[36] He believed that in too many instances defense department officials, including the JCS, were unduly influenced by the thinking of state department officials. In no case, he felt, had the influence of the State Department over the Pentagon been more evident than on the Formosa issue, and he hoped to lead the Pentagon in making a fresh assessment free of political pressure from the State Department.[37]

Johnson firmly believed that in the hands of the Chinese Communists, Formosa would be a serious threat because it would enable them to strike U.S. defense installations at Okinawa and the Philippines, control sea routes from Japan to Malaysia, and neutralize Japan's value to the United States in the event of war.[38] For these strategic reasons, and with the solid support of General MacArthur, Johnson felt it was absolutely in the national interest to keep Formosa free, and he felt that the Nationalist government could do that with proper assistance.[39]

While legitimate questions have been raised about whether Johnson's public statements on the defense budget and NATO were based more on political expediency than sincerity, there can be no question that his views on the need to protect and defend Formosa were deeply and sincerely felt. Whether Johnson's ideas were developed through his own study and understanding of Asian history and politics or whether he was heavily influenced by leaders of the Nationalist government, General MacArthur, and/or leading Republicans is much less clear.

Some scholars have said that Chiang's ubiquitous ambassador to the United States, Wellington Koo, met frequently, often in secret, with Johnson and Assistant Secretary of Defense Paul Griffith in an effort to influence administration policy toward Formosa and devise ways to exert pressure on Acheson.[40] There is nothing in the papers of Johnson or Griffith which support these assertions. However, the Wellington Koo papers provide a wealth of evidence that Koo was in frequent contact with General Griffith (including Saturday lunches at Griffith's country house in Potomac, Maryland) and a mysterious defense department operative known as "Colonel" Victor O'Kelliher and that Koo used the two of them to influence Johnson. Koo's detailed diaries and his oral history indicate that Griffith and O'Kelliher, almost certainly with express authorization from Johnson, constantly told him that Johnson was a friend of Nationalist China and would do everything he could to help protect and defend Formosa and that Acheson might be forced to step down as secretary of state.[41] They repeatedly told Koo that Johnson had to be circumspect in his relationships with the Nationalist government because he would be running for president in 1952.[42]

Koo's papers reveal that Tommy Corcoran, former Roosevelt aide and Washington lobbyist who was representing the military procurement arm of the Nationalist government, arranged a private dinner between Madame Chiang and Secretary Johnson which took place on October 22, 1949, at Madame's residence in Riverdale, New York.[43] Through conversations at this dinner and messages relayed via Griffith and O'Kelliher, there is little doubt that Johnson provided assurances to the Nationalist government that he would fight to change Acheson's opposition to military assistance for Formosa.

State department officials suspected that O'Kelliher was conducting a backdoor operation for Johnson with Chiang's government but Johnson covered his tracks.[44] If President Truman, who had already warned Johnson to stay out of the China problem, had known that Johnson was using Griffith and O'Kelliher to undermine administration policy as well as his nemesis Dean Acheson, Johnson's career in public service likely would have ended much sooner than it did.

Setting aside questions of who influenced him and who he or his aides may have secretly met with, Johnson acted on his strongly held views about the need to defend Formosa. As the first step in his attempt to change U.S. policy toward Formosa, Johnson, adopting an idea advocated by Tommy Corcoran,[45] urged the JCS in September 1949 to send a military mission to Formosa to determine the true situation "because our information and the State Department information did not agree."[46] In response, the Joint Chiefs concluded that military assistance to Chiang's government "was desirable," but since no funds were available for such assistance there was no reason to send a fact-finding mission.[47] Although dismayed by the JCS stand, Johnson was not about to give up.

Another opportunity to push his position came in late October, when a top-secret CIA report concluded that Formosa would fall to Mao's forces in 1950 "unless the United States chooses to hold it with military forces." At the instigation of Army Chief of Staff Collins, whom Johnson was pressing to look at the issue "from a purely military point of view," the CIA report caused the JCS to begin to rethink their earlier stand against overt military assistance and intervention.[48] The Joint Chiefs were still in the process of finalizing their latest recommendations when the Nationalist government and its exhausted army fled to Formosa on December 10. The Communist People's Republic of China, which had formally been proclaimed on October 1, was now in complete control of the mainland.

Spurred on by events in China and Johnson's admonitions, the Joint Chiefs recommended on December 18 that "a modest, well-directed, and closely supervised program of military aid to the anti-Communist government in Formosa would be in the interest of the United States." The Joint Chiefs recommended sending a military mission to determine what assistance would be required to defend Formosa against an attack.[49]

Armed with the backing of the Joint Chiefs, Johnson began actively lobbying for the military mission. However, Acheson bitterly resisted his proposal on the grounds that such action would constitute a reversal of the U.S. policy of disengagement from Chiang and that even if the aid were sent it offered virtually no chance of saving the regime.[50]

As Acheson pushed for maintenance of the current policy, Johnson pushed even harder for its reversal, and he went to the president on at least three occasions in December to urge that the mission to Formosa be sent. On each visit, Johnson made it clear that he was not calling for a commitment but for a fact-finding mission so that a sound decision on whether to send aid could be made.[51]

Johnson also expressed his views in a December 15 memorandum to the president in which he maintained that it was not in the national interest to place "the American flag on Formosa" but that "efforts should be continued and perhaps increased to deny Formosa to the Communists" by providing "military advice and assistance short of overt military action."[52] Attached to Johnson's memorandum was a letter from Senator Homer Ferguson (R-Michigan), who had just returned from Formosa and who expressed great concern over the fate of the strategically located island. Another attachment was a note from Tracy Vorhees, undersecretary of the army, who had met the previous week with General MacArthur in Tokyo and relayed the views of the general, including a position paper in which MacArthur argued that the United States was bound by the Potsdam agreement of 1945 to protect Formosa pending a determination of its legal status and conclusion of a Japanese peace treaty. MacArthur contended that the fall of Formosa to the Communists would be "fatal" to the U.S. defense position in the Far East.[53]

There can be little doubt that Johnson's highly visible stand on Formosa was aggravating to Truman and Acheson; it challenged a foreign policy position they clearly agreed upon and his stand put him in the camp of a group of Republican senators, led by Alexander Smith and William Knowland, who were calling for military support to keep Chiang's army from collapsing.[54] It also aligned Johnson with General MacArthur, whom Truman distrusted and disliked; he referred to him in his diary as "Mr. Prima Donna, Brass Hat, Five Star MacArthur."[55]

Nevertheless, Johnson persisted. On December 20, he met President Truman, who was returning from his vacation in Key West, at the airport so he could use the time on the trip to the White House to press his stand on Formosa.[56] Two days later, he took advantage of his regularly scheduled private lunch with the president at Blair House to make a final effort to win him over. All his appeals were for naught, however, as Truman told him that he would not support military assistance to help defend Formosa. As Johnson recalled during his testimony at the MacArthur hearings in 1951, "I was told, without quoting [Truman] directly, that he wasn't going to argue with me about the military considerations but that on political grounds he would side with the State Department." When Johnson left the president that afternoon, he knew "I had lost my fight on Formosa."[57]

Johnson was aware that there would be a meeting of the National Security Council on December 29 to consider U.S. policy on Formosa. However, since it was apparent that the president would not reverse himself, Johnson asked and received permission to get away from Washington for a few days' vacation during the Christmas holidays.[58]

After flying to Clarksburg on the afternoon of December 22 to preside over Steptoe & Johnson's annual firm conference and relax at home, Johnson and his wife flew to Hobe Sound in Florida for a few days in the sun. While there, he received a call from Steve Early about a meeting Acheson had called to iron out their differences on the Formosan issue before the NSC met on December 29. An irate Johnson stated that since the "matter was already decided, there was 'no point' in his being there and unless the President specifically wanted him to attend the meetings he would not do so."[59] That the president did not urge him to come is not surprising.

Since Johnson did not attend the meeting with Acheson and his advisors on the 29th, the responsibility for advocating the Defense Department's new position for extending aid to Chiang fell on General Bradley. He noted that in the fall the JCS had concluded that aid was "desirable" but that since no funds were available the idea had been dropped. Now, however, Bradley expressed hope that the $75 million provided for the "general area of China" in the October Mutual Defense Assistance Act could be used. He also noted that the October CIA report predicting the early fall of Chiang was being revised to indicate that he could hold out much longer than had been expected. The JCS made it clear that they had no intention of sending combat troops to Formosa but expected that retired U.S. officers would be hired by the Nationalists as advisors.

When Bradley finished his presentation, Acheson countered with a strong rebuttal which accused the Defense Department of prejudgment because it was requesting military aid and a fact-finding mission at the same time. The meeting closed with Acheson stating that unless the Joint Chiefs could come up with strategic reasons beyond those presented, he was of the mind that the "political price for sending the mission was too high to pay."[60]

Later that day, the NSC recommended, and the following day President Truman approved, the State Department's hands-off policy toward Formosa and the Chinese Nationalists. After the president made his decision, neither the Joint Chiefs nor Secretary Johnson felt that they could or should speak out. They had had their opportunity to make their position known and the commander in chief had decided against them.[61] The hands-off policy lasted until June 25, 1950, when the North Koreans attacked South Korea. On that date, the entire strategic situation in the Far East was drastically altered and all prior policies were candidates for reconsideration.[62]

New Policy for Asia

While the decisions of the NSC and the president on Formosa marked a major defeat for Secretary Johnson, not all was lost; at the NSC meeting on December

29 the staff distributed a document which became known as NSC 48/2 once it was approved by the president. This document, entitled "The Position of the United States with Respect to Asia," contained the integrated and comprehensive statement of U.S. military and foreign policy in Asia that Johnson had called for in his prescient June 10 memorandum.[63]

Although Johnson disagreed with specific recommendations in NSC 48/2 regarding aid to Formosa, he supported the document's overall objectives and was pleased that the United States was finally on the way to having an integrated policy in Asia and the Far East. The new policy set forth in NSC 48/2 would apply the doctrine of containment to the Far East. Its goal was to halt the encroachment of communism and reduce the power and influence of the USSR in that region. As far as specific countries were concerned, NSC 48/2 would recognize but not provide military aid to the Nationalist regime; give economic aid and military advice to the Republic of Korea (South Korea); "strengthen the over-all U.S. position with respect to the Philippines, the Ryukyus [Okinawa] and Japan"; and take certain unspecified actions to enable "non-Communist nationalist leaders" to win "support of the Vietnamese."[64]

Originally, Truman and Acheson had hoped to have time to consult with the Senate and House Foreign Affairs Committees before publicly setting forth their new Far Eastern policy, especially as it related to Formosa; however, events forced them to do otherwise. Beginning in late November, Republican critics of the president's China policy began to exploit the acrimonious split that had developed between Acheson and Johnson over the issue of military aid to Formosa. As Congress prepared to reconvene in January 1950, the danger that the disagreement between the State and Defense Departments would be exploited even more alarmed the president.[65] The day after the December 29 NSC meeting, while Johnson was still in Florida, newspapers carried stories that the NSC was bitterly divided over aid to Formosa. Drew Pearson attributed the split to the Johnson-Acheson feud and suggested that Steptoe & Johnson had represented Chiang's brothers-in-law and the Soong dynasty. The China Lobby launched a torrent of criticism against Truman and Acheson.[66]

The fact that the NSC, Acheson, and the president had adopted an overall foreign and military policy for Asia became lost in all the clamor. All attention was focused on the defense of Formosa. In an attempt to lower the noise level, the president released a statement on January 5 that the United States "has no desire . . . to establish military bases on Formosa at this time. Nor does it have any intention of utilizing its armed forces to interfere . . . in the civil conflict in China." He added that "the United States Government will not provide military aid or advice to Chinese forces on Formosa."[67]

Before issuing his statement, Truman permitted Johnson and Omar Bradley to insert last-minute revisions which would enable the United States to retreat from its "hands-off policy." At Johnson's suggestion, Bradley persuaded the president to add the phrase "at this time" so that in the event of war with the Soviets, the United States could seize Formosa for use as a large military base. Johnson convinced Truman to remove a clause in the president's original draft which would have precluded the United States from using its armed forces to "detach" Formosa from mainland China.[68]

In the days that followed, the president abandoned the field to Acheson, who was given the tasks of defending past China policy, promoting the new policy espoused in NSC 48/2, and justifying the decision not to provide more military aid to Chiang. The secretary of state relied on moral and legal arguments in his defense of the administration's new foreign policy in the Far East.[69] He did not try to use a strategic justification for abandoning the Nationalist government because he did not want the differences between the Defense and State Departments over that issue to emerge. He vividly recalled the December 29 meeting when General Bradley stated that from a "military point of view" the JCS "had always considered Formosa important."[70]

On January 12, with the controversy over Far Eastern policy at its height, Acheson decided to use a speech to the prestigious National Press Club of Washington as a vehicle to explain and justify the administration's new policy. In what he characterized as "one of the most brilliant as well as the most controversial [speeches] he ever made," Acheson discussed the nature of the Soviet threat to East Asia and the Western Pacific and concluded that since nationalism rather than communism was the dominant fact in contemporary Asia, the United States would be the best friend of those nations.[71]

Acheson's self-described brilliant pronouncements were soon to be forgotten because what was remembered was his statement that the "defensive perimeter" of the United States in the Pacific region ran from the Aleutian Islands to Japan and the Ryukyus and down to the Philippines. Although he noted American economic responsibilities to areas west of the line, he clearly did *not* include Formosa, Vietnam, or Korea within the defensive perimeter.[72]

In the months and years following his speech, Republicans used it to lambaste Acheson, the Truman administration, and future Democratic presidents. By excluding Korea from the U.S. defensive perimeter, Acheson would be accused of giving the green light to Kim Il Sung's plan to attack South Korea, which he executed five months later. By excluding Formosa, Acheson gave additional ammunition to the China Lobby, Senators McCarthy and Taft, and Republicans in general who would charge for years that Acheson and the Democrats "lost China" and were "soft on Communism." Finally, by excluding Vietnam, Acheson was accused of giving encouragement to Mao Tse-tung, who recognized Ho Chi Minh's government in North Vietnam on January 17, and to Joseph Stalin, who granted recognition to Ho Chi Minh on January 31.[73]

Acheson would be blamed as the dominoes began to fall. And Johnson saw to it that the blame for the spread of communism would remain focused on

Acheson. "At a closed committee hearing," Senator Harley Kilgore recalled, "Johnson stared over at a man from the State Department and inquired, 'Is everyone here cleared for security?'"[74]

Vietnam: Beginning of U.S. Involvement

The adoption of the new policy for Asia, together with the recognition of North Vietnam in January 1950 by the Soviet Union and China, led the NSC to undertake an assessment of what was then called "Indochina"—Cambodia, Laos, and Vietnam. In March, the Joint Chiefs were asked by the NSC to provide a strategic assessment of Southeast Asia and recommendations about what military measures "might be taken to prevent Communist expansion into Southeast Asia."[75] The Joint Chiefs' report was forwarded to Johnson, who wrote a cover memorandum to Acheson on April 14 in which he voiced support for the JCS call for "military, political and economic aid" to halt Communist expansion in Southeast Asia. Included in that memorandum was a request for $15 million in military aid "at the earliest practicable date" and the sending of a U.S. military aid group. Johnson also suggested the initiation of "a program of special covert operations designed to interfere with Communist activities in Southeast Asia."[76]

Johnson's memo was sent to the NSC and was basically embodied in NSC 64, which set forth the U.S. position with respect to Indochina. That document, which Truman approved on April 24, maintained that "Indochina is a key area of Southeast Asia and is under immediate threat." It was therefore considered important to the nation's security that action "be taken to prevent further communist expansion" in that area. Toward that end, the NSC asked the State and Defense Departments to develop a program "to protect United States security interests in Indochina."[77]

Acting on Johnson's April 14 memorandum, Acheson prepared a request to President Truman for $23 million in economic aid and $15 million for military aid to Indochina.[78] On May 1, the president allocated $13 million to the Defense Department "for furnishing supplies and equipment from United States military stocks to friendly forces in Indo-China." This amount, according to Truman, would be but a start in halting the Communists in that area, and he called on Johnson and Acheson to "submit to me an estimate of the scope, character and timing of economic and military assistance which may be required to accomplish our objectives in . . . Indo-China."[79]

After Truman's directive, Johnson turned the matter of military aid to Indochina over to General Lemnitzer of the Office of Military Assistance. Lemnitzer began working through the Mutual Defense Assistance Program and the wheels were put in motion to get the aid on its way. In mid-June, the first arms shipments were made and ships left West Coast cities headed for Saigon.[80] The extent of the aid program would be drastically affected by the outbreak of war in Korea, but by

June of 1950 American aid was being extended to the French in Vietnam in the hope that their efforts to halt Communist expansion would be successful.

As American military aid began to flow into Vietnam in the late spring of 1950, Louis Johnson was pleased to see the United States standing up to the Communists in that part of the world. Little did he or anyone else in the administration realize that the small aid program would mark the beginning of U.S. involvement in a conflict which would eventually become one of the longest, costliest, and most divisive wars the nation was ever to experience.

Korea: "Of Little Strategic Value"

Although Acheson's exclusion of Korea from the U.S. defensive perimeter in his January 12, 1950, speech prompted a storm of criticism after the North Koreans attacked in June, at the time of his speech, his statements about Korea were hardly controversial and they attracted little attention in the press. In fact, Acheson's statements were nothing more than a restatement of established administration policy toward Korea which had been codified in NSC 48/2 and approved by President Truman.

Before Acheson's speech in January 1950, there was no convincing reason for the Truman administration to have anticipated that Korea would become the place where the Cold War would turn into a shooting war. At the end of World War II, the USSR and the United States had agreed, for occupation purposes, to a temporary division of Korea at the 38th parallel; the Soviets controlled the area north of the line and the United States controlled the south. The intention, as provided in the 1943 Cairo Declaration, was that Korea should "in due course" become an independent country under a single government.[81]

The temporary division of Korea was expected to prevail until national elections were held. However, that "temporary" situation soon developed into a more permanent one when extensive Soviet-U.S. negotiations failed to reach an agreement that would provide a government acceptable to both. Each country feared a settlement which would result in a unified Korea going into the opposition's camp. During this period of political sparring, both powers administered their sector through military governments.

By 1947, the United States, not wanting to remain in Korea yet also not wanting it to fall into the hands of the Communists, submitted the problem to the UN with a suggestion that a trusteeship be established. However, when the Soviets remained obstinate, the UN created a Temporary Commission on Korea, which supervised elections and the establishment of an independent Republic of Korea (ROK) in the south with Syngman Rhee as its president.

Later that year, the Soviets helped create the North Korean Democratic People's Republic, headed by a former anti-Japanese guerilla leader, Kim Il Sung. The Soviets then withdrew all their troops from the north, but the United

States, at the urging of President Rhee, agreed to delay departure of its troops from the south until 1949, when it was felt the South Korean government would be more secure. While Rhee was an ally, defense department and other U.S. officials were fearful that he might attempt to unite Korea by force. When the last American troops departed South Korea in June 1949, they left behind only defensive weapons and a 500-man Korean Military Advisory Group commanded by Brigadier General W. Lynn Roberts that was to assist in training the ROK Army.[82] When U.S. occupation forces withdrew, all responsibility and authority in Korea were relinquished by the military and turned over to the State Department. This meant that General Roberts reported not to General MacArthur but to Ambassador John Muccio, a young man who understood the byzantine world of South Korea politics but little about military issues.[83]

Throughout the period from 1945 through 1949 there was unanimity in U.S. military circles that extradition from Korea was desirable. In 1947, when the Joint Chiefs provided their first assessment of the situation, they concluded that the United States "had little strategic interest in maintaining the present troops and bases in Korea" and that their withdrawal would not endanger the nation's military position in the Far East. The following year the Joint Chiefs reaffirmed that position and urged withdrawal of troops at the "earliest practicable date."[84]

The same view was echoed by General MacArthur in a January 1949 assessment which concluded that South Korea would not be able to halt a North Korean invasion and that adequate U.S. assistance could not be extended to enable it to do so. He concluded that there was no military reason to prolong occupation and that withdrawal should be completed as quickly as possible.[85]

The ideas expressed by the Joint Chiefs and MacArthur, along with state department proposals to provide political, technical, and military assistance to Rhee's government, were incorporated in NSC 8/2, which the president approved on March 23, 1949—a week before Johnson became secretary.[86] This meant that the key decisions on Korea had already been made and the machinery for final troop withdrawal was functioning by the time Johnson took over. The only role he played in the departure process came that spring when he approved a state department request for a slight delay in the scheduled withdrawal of a regimental combat team and later refused a request to extend the delay beyond the June 30, 1949, deadline.[87] His rigidity on the deadline did little to endear him to people at the State Department.

Following the military withdrawal and the shift of all responsibility for Korea to the State Department, the military establishment virtually ceased to have anything to do with the country and the State Department was not inclined to ask for any advice or assistance.[88] In light of this transfer of responsibility and the Truman administration's unified view that Korea was "of little strategic value" and would not be defended, there was no reason for the Department of Defense to prepare war plans, and it did not do so.[89]

While the Pentagon seemed content to cede responsibility for Korea to the State Department, General MacArthur was uneasy. Shortly before the conflict began in Korea, the general lamented to Johnson that "as far as Korea is concerned, it is in the hands of the State Department. Undoubtedly, if we have some trouble out here, I will be asked as the commander of our forces in the Far East to take the responsibility, but I don't have the policy making in these areas or any voice in it."[90]

In retrospect, General MacArthur's concerns were warranted. Although the CIA and MacArthur's intelligence chief were reporting that war between North and South Korea was unlikely that summer, tensions ran very high along the 38th parallel as hundreds of "border incidents" and probes by both sides were reported.[91] And despite efforts by General Roberts and Ambassador Muccio to create the impression that the ROK troops could readily repel any attack from the north, those troops were in fact badly equipped and poorly led by the ROK officer corps.[92]

As with most "surprise" attacks, there were signs, warnings, and intelligence reports which when pieced together would later show that an attack was likely. But virtually no one in Washington in the spring of 1950, including Louis Johnson, believed that war would break out in Korea that summer.

Peace Treaty with Japan

While Truman, Acheson, and Johnson generally agreed that Korea would not likely pose a significant foreign relations or military problem in 1950, a serious policy dispute emerged over the question of when the United States should negotiate a peace treaty with Japan. As with Formosa, Johnson's disagreements with Acheson over the Japanese treaty issue were bitter, acrimonious, and personal. And once again, he found himself aligned with the Joint Chiefs and against Truman.

Following the collapse of Japan in 1945, the United States moved unilaterally to rule the country. Under General Douglas MacArthur, who served as commander in chief of U.S. forces in the Far East as well as Supreme Commander for the Allied Powers (SCAP), a dual policy of punishment and reform was instituted. The former included punishing war criminals, disarming the military, dismantling war industries, and purging the society of militaristic elements. In the realm of reform, MacArthur instituted changes designed to make the country a political and economic democracy.

To implement these policies, the United States relied on a large military occupation force. Surprisingly, the Japanese people came to readily accept MacArthur and the changes he wrought, and in time he came to accept a greater sense of responsibility for their well-being.[93] In the spring of 1947 he publicly called on the U.S. government to immediately negotiate a moderate nonpunitive peace treaty. A peace treaty, he contended, was timely and essential because the purposes of occupation had been achieved and Japanese economic recovery could not take place until an agreement was concluded.

Although MacArthur's views were not shared by army officials in Washington who favored a punitive treaty with military guarantees, the economy-minded Congress supported MacArthur's position because an early treaty would bring an end to the costly occupation. The State Department likewise concluded that an early treaty was desirable, but efforts to convene a preliminary conference on the issue that year were squelched because of Soviet and Chinese opposition.[94]

By the spring of 1949, events abroad had created the need to reevaluate the Japanese treaty issue. Of greatest concern was the military progress being made by Mao Tse-tung's forces in China. That, plus the need to have a strong counter to Soviet pressure in the Far East, made it extremely important for the United States to have a stalwart yet friendly Japan as its ally. Increased pressure from American allies who were fearful that the USSR might initiate a treaty in order to gain the goodwill of the Japanese made it essential that the United States at least examine its treaty position. On May 23, the State Department initiated a reevaluation.

At the Defense Department, Johnson immediately forwarded the State Department's request for a strategic evaluation of Japan to the JCS. The Chiefs, citing the key geographic location of Japan as well as its manpower and industrial potential, pointed out that if the country fell under Soviet domination, U.S. bases and interests in that part of the world would be endangered. The JCS concluded that "from the military point of view a peace treaty would, at the present time, be premature."[95] The Joint Chiefs also insisted that if there was to be a treaty with Japan, the USSR and China would have to be parties. Although this stipulation was allegedly based on the need to meet wartime commitments, it is more likely that it was a delaying tactic since it was known that the USSR and China would not agree.[96]

That Johnson held the same views on the treaty was quite evident, but what is not clear is to what extent he was reflecting the JCS position and to what extent they were reflecting his. General Collins maintained that the Joint Chiefs had arrived at their position independently;[97] however, General MacArthur believed that the Joint Chiefs were "expressing the view of Secretary Johnson."[98] Nevertheless, the Defense Department stood united in its opposition to an early treaty with Japan.

Across the river at the State Department there was also unity by mid-1949, but it was in favor of an early treaty. At the urging of Secretary Acheson, who believed that Japan should be developed as a bulwark against Far Eastern Communist expansion, the State Department had reversed its earlier position and stood with General MacArthur in support of a treaty.[99] Throughout the fall of 1949, Acheson continued to push for an immediate treaty in several ways, one of which was to openly call for an agreement. That tactic was annoying to Johnson because he felt it unduly "raised great hopes in Japan."[100] Acheson also attempted to exploit the differences between Johnson and the JCS on one hand and General MacArthur on the other. In early January of 1950, Ambassador-at-Large Philip C. Jessup met with MacArthur in Japan and discussed the treaty issue. MacArthur was critical of the JCS, saying that they lacked familiarity with East Asian problems and "certainly did not express the view of SCAP." He felt that the treaty "was not a decision which should be left to the JCS" and that they could and should be overruled on the matter. The general expressed in strong terms his feeling that the JCS position "did not reflect a military judgment but General Bradley is merely speaking for Secretary Johnson."[101]

Three weeks after Jessup departed, the JCS arrived in Tokyo to meet Mac-Arthur. Apparently, the general was not so outspoken on that occasion because he left the Joint Chiefs with the impression that he did not consider an immediate treaty that important; they returned home convinced that they should stick with their current position.[102] By this time Johnson and his advisors were increasingly resisting the treaty on legal grounds, claiming that the surrender terms called for the departure of U.S. troops when occupation ended—a position that could not be tolerated at that time.[103]

In April 1950, Acheson's Far Eastern experts, believing there was a "wider area of agreement between the JCS and the [State] Department than appears," urged a meeting with Johnson and his military advisors.[104] On April 24, Johnson and Bradley traveled to Foggy Bottom to explore their respective positions.[105] By this time the acrimony and tension between Acheson and Johnson, triggered by controversies over Formosa, the China White Paper, and NSC 68, were at an extremely high level. Acheson opened the meeting by noting that in view of the Defense Department's insistence that American military forces remain in Japan and that the USSR and China be parties to the treaty, their contention "that a peace treaty was 'premature' was a masterpiece of understatement" since these requirements would make the conclusion of a peace treaty impossible.[106] He then reiterated the political considerations which he felt made a nonpunitive treaty an urgent necessity.[107]

When Acheson paused for Johnson to respond, the defense chief jumped in and began castigating state department officials. He loudly proclaimed that he was "gravely disturbed" by the information about the treaty that was being leaked by the State Department. He demanded assurances that no leaks of this meeting would come from state and pledged that none would come from defense. He then turned the floor over to General Bradley, who reiterated the earlier stand of the JCS that a treaty was premature. Bradley also contended that General MacArthur saw a treaty proposal as only a propaganda move and feared a peace treaty because it would mean "U.S. forces in Japan would be reduced to a mere token force."[108] (The confusion over MacArthur's true feeling stemmed from his tendency to tell State one thing and Defense another.)

Johnson interjected that "the only propaganda for a peace treaty was that which came out of the Department of State," and he forcefully stated his full support of the JCS position that "there should be no treaty." He continued his attack on state department officials by noting the "wide disparity between the views of General MacArthur as reported by the Joint Chiefs and other officials." He concluded by announcing that in order to clarify those discrepancies, he and General Bradley were personally going to Japan on June 12 to ascertain MacArthur's true views.[109]

After expressing surprise at Johnson's announcement that he and Bradley would be visiting MacArthur, Acheson set forth his position that changing conditions in Japan and the entire Far East made a treaty a necessity but that his advisors were not proposing any reductions of U.S. forces in Japan. Force reductions, he contended, were and would remain a defense department decision. Personally, he said, he could not accept the Pentagon's position that a peace treaty was premature. Johnson, sensing no movement by the State Department, proposed that in light of his upcoming Far Eastern trip further consideration of the treaty be delayed until July 1, and his proposal was accepted.[110]

Two days later, on April 26, Acheson appointed John Foster Dulles, former New York senator and a leading Republican foreign affairs expert, as a consultant to the secretary of state. The appointment of such a prominent Republican was distasteful to Truman and Acheson, but it was done to placate Senator Vandenberg and other administration critics. Dulles's initial job was to write a paper seeking presidential authority to prepare and negotiate a peace treaty.[111] Dulles quickly obtained authority from the president, and on May 18 he was placed in charge of a team to draft a Japanese peace treaty. That same day, President Truman announced that negotiations for a treaty would begin "when the time is propitious . . . and I hope that won't be too far off."[112]

Encouraged by Truman's announcement, state department advisors pressed forward on the treaty issue, but in view of the position of Johnson and the JCS, they decided to avoid them and work instead with General MacArthur. They assigned their top man in Tokyo, Ambassador William J. Sebald, to obtain the real views of the SCAP commander.[113]

At a May 25 meeting with Sebald, General MacArthur expressed "wonderment at the apparently small differences between the two Departments." He searched for a compromise and came up with an outline of a treaty which would provide specific bases for the United States and would go into effect only if a national plebiscite approved it. This new approach, which made base rights a part of the treaty rather than a separate bilateral agreement, was alarming to Sebald because it represented "a very sharp veering from his previous views" which had been "fully in accord with our own." (MacArthur had earlier favored a separate bilateral agreement to handle base sites and troop movements.)

MacArthur told Sebald that he would not convey his position to Secretary

Johnson unless specifically requested to do so.[114] However, Johnson learned of the conversations and protested vigorously to Acheson about what he called Sebald's "offside play" in discussing essentially military matters with MacArthur and demanded that the practice be halted. The secretary of state, now convinced that the treaty problem "was only a part of the larger problem of Louis Johnson," ignored the request and the contacts between Sebald and MacArthur continued.[115]

Meeting with MacArthur

Johnson regarded MacArthur as "one of the greatest, if not the greatest, generals of our generation." Johnson hoped that his June meeting with MacArthur would solidify and strengthen defense department thinking on the two thorniest problems in the Far East—aid to Formosa and the Japanese peace treaty.[116] Johnson also hoped to turn it into a sort of working vacation in which he and Bradley, accompanied by their wives, would visit a number of Far Eastern military installations.

On Sunday, June 11, General Bradley, his wife Mary, Ruth Johnson, and a number of top advisors left Washington for St. Louis, Missouri, where they picked up Secretary Johnson, who, along with President Truman, had attended a reunion of the 35th Division.[117] The group proceeded to San Francisco and then to Hickham Field in the Hawaiian Islands, where they were entertained and briefed by Admiral Radford, Commander in Chief Pacific (CINCPAC). From Hawaii, the party flew on to Guam and Clark Field in the Philippines before arriving in Tokyo on Sunday, June 18.[118]

Several hours before Johnson arrived, John Foster Dulles, who had been sent by Acheson on a fact-finding mission to the Far East regarding the Japanese peace treaty, had stopped at Tokyo to meet with Sebald and MacArthur before proceeding to Korea. While Dulles was to return to Japan several days later when Johnson was still in the country, the two groups seemed to go out of their way to make sure they did not meet. That they did not see each other may have been coincidental but in all likelihood was a deliberate attempt to demonstrate the major differences between State and Defense over the treaty. Supposedly Johnson was there to assess military matters while Dulles was to evaluate political, social, and economic factors.[119]

On the Sunday morning of their arrival, Johnson and Bradley were ushered into MacArthur's headquarters at the Dai Ichi Building in Tokyo, where they were to receive a briefing from Ambassador Sebald and other SCAP officials. But before the briefing got under way, Johnson shocked those present with a 15-minute "harangue" in which he roasted "the State Department crowd" for its early treaty stance and criticized department officials in Japan who had been making statements which encouraged "the withdrawal of all United States troops from Japan." He then "characterized Dulles as an impractical man who approached the world's problems with a religious, moral, and pacifistic attitude."

According to Sebald, the secretary's tirade was "a particularly unpleasant and . . . completely unjustified episode."[120] This explosion over the actions of people in the State Department was similar to his outburst of two months before over the drafting of NSC 68 and reveals the level of frustration Johnson was feeling about Secretary Acheson and his advisors. It was obvious that by this time the defense chief was personalizing his policy differences with Acheson.

After venting his frustrations, Johnson explained to Sebald that he and the JCS were convinced that Japan's defense was essential to U.S. interests and that the only way to assure its defense was for America to have the authority, as it currently did, to have as many troops as it wanted in Japan and to be able to locate them whenever and wherever needed.[121] Only the status quo, Johnson maintained, could adequately provide for the security of both nations.

In the briefing by Sebald that followed, Johnson was disappointed to learn that MacArthur was siding with the State Department. The general's views were set forth in a 10-page memorandum which he had prepared especially for Johnson on June 14. In that paper, MacArthur deplored the publicity about the differences between Defense and State and noted that, except for Defense demands that the USSR and China be signatories, there were no insurmountable difficulties. He then proposed an immediate call for a peace conference and suggested that a basis for compromise between feuding U.S. policymakers be "a normal treaty . . . embodying a security reservation" which would continue to give the United States its present garrison rights but at the invitation of the Japanese people rather than by treaty edict.[122]

Johnson was not only upset to read MacArthur's views in the June 14 memorandum, he also felt the general was wrong. He could not conceive that the Japanese people might voluntarily agree to the retention of American forces in their country.[123]

That afternoon MacArthur hosted a luncheon for his visitors, but the gathering was strictly a social occasion. The next morning, however, the general met with Johnson and Bradley to discuss substance. MacArthur's memorandum put the Washington visitors on the defensive because they had to open the talks by trying to beat back the general's pro-treaty stance. Johnson did all he could to convince MacArthur to reverse his stance and support the position of delay which he and the JCS advocated. However, the general would not budge.

Johnson then put forward two defense department counterproposals: one was that a collective security arrangement for Japan be initiated but that U.S. base sites be retained—a proposal which MacArthur rejected as a move toward colonization; second, that Japan be given sovereignty in everything except security, which the United States would control—an idea which MacArthur rejected as being "worse than the Occupation."

The secretary gave it all he had, but came away empty-handed. He went to Japan searching for an ally in his fight with Acheson over the Japanese peace treaty; however, he found MacArthur in the enemy camp.[124]

But if Johnson lost one in Japan, he also won one on the question of aid to Formosa. On the same day he set forth his views on a Japanese peace treaty, General MacArthur prepared a five-page memorandum on Formosa, and on this issue he saw eye to eye with Johnson. Again using the analogy of the unsinkable aircraft carrier, MacArthur declared that "the strategic interest of the United States will be in serious jeopardy if Formosa is allowed to be dominated" by a hostile power and thus it should not be permitted to fall. The administration "should initiate measures to prevent the domination of Formosa by a communist power." The first step in accomplishing that goal, the general maintained, was a military mission to Formosa to determine the extent of military assistance needed to keep the country out of hostile hands.[125]

MacArthur's position on Formosa was exactly what Johnson had been calling for during the past nine months, but the president and State Department had rejected his proposal for political reasons. Johnson now had some ammunition to resume his battle when he returned to Washington.[126]

After the June 19 meeting with MacArthur, which the press noted was conducted in an atmosphere of secrecy, Johnson spent three days visiting U.S. bases in Japan and Okinawa and trying out their golf courses.[127] Bradley stayed in Tokyo for a private off-the-record meeting on June 20 with General Lynn Roberts, an old West Point friend who was commander of the Korean Military Advisory Group. Bradley had been hearing disturbing reports that the North Koreans were on the verge of invading South Korea and wanted to know "from the horse's mouth" whether the ROK troops could repel an attack. Roberts assured Bradley that "the ROK Army could meet any test the North Koreans imposed on it." Because of his confidence in Roberts's judgment and professionalism, Bradley felt "greatly relieved that we had no cause for concern in Korea."[128]

Naturally, Bradley would have shared what Roberts told him with Johnson. When they were questioned much later about why the invasion was so surprising and so successful, the secretary of defense and the chairman of the JCS were able to say that they had consulted the American commander on the ground in Seoul on June 20 and that he had assured them that there was no reason to be concerned about war in Korea.

Before leaving Tokyo for Washington on June 23, Johnson and Bradley again met with MacArthur, who presented Johnson with yet another memorandum — this one dealing with U.S. forces and Japanese security. It recommended that the United States pay Japan $300 million annually to maintain security forces in the country and called for Japanese approval regarding the disposition of U.S. armed forces in Japan. While these proposals were not pleasing to Johnson, there was a stipulation that in case of a threat to Japanese security there would be "unrestricted freedom for the United States . . . to take such strategic dispositions as may be necessary" to meet the threat. This stipulation, which was a very large loophole, provided substantial solace to the defense secretary and allowed him to leave Tokyo with at least some concession on Japan from MacArthur.[129]

Carrying the three memos MacArthur had prepared for him, Johnson and his party boarded their flight to Alaska and on to the nation's capital. The secretary had visited nearly all major military installations in the Pacific; however, he had not visited two of the countries left outside of what Acheson had described as the U.S. defensive perimeter—Formosa and Korea. In the case of Formosa, Johnson probably wished to avoid antagonizing Truman and Acheson by making a trip which might imply support for the Nationalist regime. Furthermore, he did not wish to give false hope to Chiang and his leaders.

As for Korea, Johnson had personally been invited to visit by South Korean president Syngman Rhee, who had hosted Dulles from June 17 through 19.[130] But Johnson and his advisors chose not to go. That decision, which greatly distressed President Rhee,[131] was probably made both because there was no military installation in the country and because responsibility for Korea was under the State Department. With the difficulty between State and Defense, Johnson probably thought it would be best if he did not go nosing around in Acheson's territory.

Besides, the private meeting between Bradley and General Roberts, the highest-ranking American officer in Korea, had given Johnson what he thought he needed to know about Korea. Based on Roberts's assurance, it is doubtful that Johnson gave any more thought to Korea on his Far Eastern trip. After all, the JCS had written off the nation in terms of strategic importance to the United States, it was the State Department's responsibility, and the American commander on the ground had assured General Bradley that there was no reason why the Department of Defense should be concerned about the situation there.

The Johnson-Bradley party arrived back in Washington at 11:00 A.M. on Saturday, June 24, 1950. After taking Mrs. Johnson back to their apartment at the Mayflower, the secretary went to the office, where he worked for several hours—part of which was spent preparing a speech he was scheduled to give the next afternoon in Norfolk, Virginia.

About 4:15 P.M. Johnson left the Pentagon and headed home for the first relaxing evening he had had in weeks.[132] The anticipated evening of leisure was not to come that night. While Johnson had been at the office that Saturday afternoon, North Korean army troops had crossed the 38th parallel in a savage attack on South Korea.

CHAPTER SIXTEEN

Last Week in June

Shortly after 10 p.m. on Saturday, June 24, 1950, the phone rang in Louis Johnson's Mayflower apartment. It was a United Press International reporter who had questions about a dispatch just received from correspondent Jack James in Seoul reporting that North Korean troops had launched a broad-based early morning attack against South Korea all along the 38th parallel.[1] The secretary, surprised and embarrassed by his lack of information, said he had received no such report and thus could not comment. Johnson doubted the accuracy of the dispatch. He knew that there had been hundreds of border incidents along the 38th parallel. However, he had to discount the possibility of a full-scale invasion since he had just returned hours earlier from his two-week Far Eastern trip and there had been no suggestion that such an invasion was expected in any of his numerous briefings.[2]

The implausibility of a full-scale invasion was still racing through his mind when the telephone rang again. It was the Pentagon duty officer calling to inform him of an unconfirmed report of a major North Korean attack. The secretary, completely exhausted from his long flight back from Tokyo, directed that any more reports on the matter be forwarded to recently appointed Secretary of the Army Frank Pace Jr.[3]

No sooner had Johnson hung up when the phone rang a third time. It was Frank Pace, who had been at an elegant dinner party at Joe Alsop's house in Georgetown with Assistant Secretary of State for Far Eastern Affairs Dean Rusk when Rusk had received word of the attack from the state department duty officer.[4] Pace, thinking Johnson was still not back from his Far Eastern trip, had immediately hurried over to the Pentagon where he learned Johnson was, in fact, home and called him. According to Pace, a cable had been received from

Ambassador John Muccio in Seoul reporting an all-out offensive, but not much more was known.

Johnson told the 37-year-old Pace, a rising star in the Truman administration, that he was temporarily delegating to him authority to act on behalf of the Defense Department. He justified his delegation of authority to the secretary of the army on the basis that the only armed forces unit in Korea was the 500-man Korean Military Advisory Group which was part of the army, and the top military commander in the Far East, General Douglas MacArthur, was an army officer.[5] When Johnson tried and failed to learn anything more about what was going on, he finally went to bed and left Pace with decision-making authority.[6]

About the time Pace called Johnson, Rusk contacted Dean Acheson at his country place, Harewood Farm, in Maryland. Acheson immediately called President Truman, who was at his home on North Delaware Street in Independence, Missouri, for the weekend. When the president picked up the telephone, Acheson said, "Mr. President. I have very serious news. The North Koreans have invaded South Korea."[7]

Acheson told the president that on their own initiative he and Rusk had already notified the secretary-general of the United Nations of the invasion and had asked him to call an emergency meeting of the UN Security Council to take place as early as the next day, Sunday. Truman approved these preliminary steps. Acheson, who also thought that Johnson was still not back from Japan, asked, and the president agreed, that he assume responsibility for dealing with the crisis. Furthermore, remembering "the absurd restrictions that Johnson had imposed on communication between the two departments," he asked Truman to make it clear to Secretary Pace that he wanted "fullest cooperation" between the Departments of State and Defense.[8]

Sunday

Throughout the night and into the morning, state department officials, in cooperation with UN Secretary-General Trygve Lie, prepared for a 2 P.M. emergency session of the UN Security Council on Sunday, June 25.[9] From the beginning, President Truman made it clear that the United States would work entirely through the United Nations.[10] Reports coming into Washington from Korea that Sunday morning were sketchy. The decision makers knew little more than the fact that the North Koreans had launched a military operation of considerable scope against their neighbor to the south. Although it was generally assumed that the Soviet Union was in some way behind the action, its involvement remained unclear.[11]

Early Sunday morning, Johnson conferred with General Bradley about whether they should make a previously scheduled trip to Norfolk, Virginia, that afternoon, and they decided there was no reason not to go. After all, there was nothing more they could do and they would only be an hour's flying time from Washington.[12] A joint state department–defense department conference on Korea had been called by the State Department for 11:30 A.M., but Johnson, adhering to his earlier decision that the army was still the service most vitally concerned, decided that Secretary Pace and the JCS could adequately represent the Defense Department; he chose to work on his afternoon speech and not attend.

At the 11:30 A.M. conference, which Acheson joined about 12:30 P.M., the various communiqués were pieced together to reveal that a full-scale invasion was under way and the South Korean defensive position was deteriorating rapidly. Pace reported that a Korean army request for an emergency supply of ammunition had been approved and that some of it was already on its way from Japan via air and more supplies were being shipped to the southern port of Pusan. The need to provide more aid and obtain more information was discussed. A rough draft of possible future actions was also formulated.[13]

About the time this meeting was breaking up, Johnson and Bradley were boarding a military aircraft to Norfolk, where the secretary was to address a group of civilian leaders attending a department of defense orientation session. Before departing, Johnson made it clear that he wished to be kept fully informed of any significant developments that might be reported while he was gone.[14] At 2:45 P.M. the aircraft took off from Washington National Airport.[15]

On the hour-long flight, Johnson and Bradley discussed the Korea situation and the impact it would have on Formosa and its security. The discussion was triggered by a draft memorandum Bradley had written that morning setting forth his view, with which Johnson concurred, that "South Korea will not fall in the present attack unless the Russians actively participate in the operation." Undoubtedly, Bradley's views were heavily influenced by the assurances he had received from his old friend Lynn Roberts at their private meeting in Tokyo just five days before.

It appears that at this very early stage, neither Bradley nor Johnson gave any thought to the notion that South Korea might have to be defended by U.S. ground troops. Since Korea was regarded as having little strategic value, they were far more concerned about the effect the attack might have on the security of Formosa, which they believed was critically important to U.S. strategic interests in the Far East. During their short flight, the secretary and the general became convinced that events in Korea might offer the opportunity to extend to Nationalist China the aid that they had been advocating for the past nine months and that if Korea fell "we may want to recommend even stronger action in the case of Formosa."[16]

When they arrived in Norfolk, Johnson and Bradley were rushed to the deck of the aircraft carrier *Midway*, where the secretary, in shirtsleeves, spoke to about sixty business and professional leaders. Johnson began, in his usual forceful style, by reporting on the progress of unification, defending his economy program, and warning of the threat of war from the Soviet Union. After delivering what for him had become his standard remarks, he departed from his prepared text to address the disturbing reports from Korea. Indicating that he could say very little on the subject until the president had spoken, he expressed confidence in South Korea's ability to repel the attack and said that if it did not, "it will be evidence of [Russian] assistance." He then elaborated on the material and training assistance the United States had provided to the South Korean government over the past year.[17] To the group on the deck of the *Midway* that day, Johnson seemed concerned but not alarmed by events in Korea.

On the quick flight back to Washington, Johnson learned of two significant developments. First, President Truman had decided to return from Independence and had called a dinner conference with top diplomatic and military advisors at Blair House for approximately 7:30 P.M. that evening.[18] Second, the UN Security Council, with Yugoslavia abstaining and the Soviet Union unwilling to exercise its veto power because it had been boycotting the UN, had approved by a 9-to-0 vote a U.S.-sponsored resolution which declared the North Korean action "a breach of the peace," demanded immediate withdrawal, and called upon all members "to render every assistance to the United Nations in the execution of this resolution."[19] These two developments made it clear that the matter was more serious than Johnson and Bradley had originally thought.

Johnson and Bradley landed at 6:15 and hurried over to the Pentagon, where they huddled with the three service secretaries (Pace of army, Finletter of air force, and Matthews of navy) and the JCS (Collins of army, Vandenberg of air force, and Sherman of navy). At this meeting, Johnson told them that when they gathered that evening at Blair House, there would be no omnibus defense department recommendations about action that should be taken; each service secretary and chief would, when called upon, present his individual assessment and viewpoint. This approach, as Johnson later recalled, was followed "so that each member would feel no inhibition on the President having the benefit of whatever he honest to God thought was the situation."[20]

Johnson did not want to present a single defense department recommendation because he felt that no military course of action would be called for since the JCS and the president had said all along that if South Korea was attacked it should be written off due to its lack of strategic importance to the United States. Johnson believed that preserving the security of Formosa was of far greater importance and that is what he and Bradley hoped to discuss that evening.[21]

As the Pentagon session ended, all the attendees except the secretary departed directly for Blair House. Johnson was dropped off at National Airport, where he joined Acheson and Undersecretary Webb to await the arrival of the commander in chief. At 7:20 P.M., the president's plane, the *Independence*, touched down and Truman, in a "grim mood," was greeted by his two ranking cabinet officials and the undersecretary of state. The four men posed briefly for photographs before the normally accommodating president snapped, "That's enough! We've got a job to do!" and they hurried to a waiting limousine.[22]

On the ride to Blair House, the president expressed his determination not to let the North Korean attack succeed and said that if necessary he was going to "hit them hard." In these emotional moments, the president seems to have lost sight of the fact that his administration had written off the defense of South Korea because it had little strategic value. According to Webb, the president angrily exclaimed, "By God, I am going to let them have it."[23] Secretary Johnson, sitting in the jump seat in front of Truman, swung around, shook the president's hand, and in a voice full of emotion said, "I'm with you, Mr. President."[24]

Webb, concerned that Truman had already made up his mind, told the president that Acheson and others had been formulating specific recommendations and that they hoped he would listen to them "before making up your mind as to the actions to be taken." Truman replied, "Well, O.K., of course, but you know how I feel."[25]

When the foursome arrived at Blair House they were welcomed by the military leaders Johnson had been meeting with an hour before and a state department contingent which included Assistant Secretaries Rusk and John D. Hickerson (UN Affairs) and Ambassador-at-Large Philip C. Jessup.[26] Webb and the president went alone into a cloakroom for a few minutes so he could give the president a preview of what Acheson would be recommending during the meeting.[27] When they emerged, the group of fourteen gathered in the garden for drinks and waited for dinner to be served. As they sipped their drinks, Acheson related what had transpired at the UN Security Council meeting. After he finished, the president, speaking in a soft voice and repeating himself said, "We can't let the UN down! We can't let the UN down!"[28]

During the predinner gathering, Secretary Johnson announced that he wanted to share General MacArthur's recently expressed views on the strategic importance of Formosa but that in doing so he did not wish to prejudge the immediate problem in Korea. He then called on General Bradley to read the five-page memorandum which MacArthur had presented to them in Tokyo the week before. Secretary Acheson, whose views on Formosa had continually run counter to those of Johnson, feared that this maneuver might be "an opening gun in a diversionary argument that Johnson wished to start with me." However, when Bradley finished reading the document, Truman announced the serving of dinner and requested that all substantive discussions be postponed until after the meal.[29]

After dessert and coffee had been served by Alonzo Fields, the chief butler, and his hastily gathered staff,[30] and with French doors open to let in the cool evening air, Acheson began talking about the Korean problem. Almost immediately Johnson interrupted him to say that before they broached that subject he wished to discuss Formosa. Johnson characterized what followed as "the only really violent discussion Secretary Acheson and myself ever had." Johnson's position was that "the security of the United States was more affected by Formosa than Korea" and that he would "insist" upon the former issue being discussed.[31] Everyone around the table knew that this had been a touchy subject for many months because of Johnson and MacArthur's desire to provide military aid to Chiang Kai-shek's regime and Acheson's desire not to. Nevertheless, Johnson pushed the matter by urging a reversal of the administration's policy toward the Nationalist government.

Having been baited by Johnson, the secretary of state began criticizing Chiang as a corrupt and incompetent leader who had lost the confidence of his people. Johnson replied, "I can say more bitter things about robber barons than you. But all I'm concerned about is the security of the United States."[32] At that juncture, the president put a stop to the heated argument with the announcement that the issue of Formosa would be taken up later.

When the conferees finished dessert and the long mahogany table was cleared, the president opened the discussion of how to deal with the attack by North Korea, declaring that he approached this crisis with an "open mind," had no intention of making critical decisions at this time, and wanted everyone present to say whatever was on their mind. He then turned the meeting over to Acheson, who ticked off a number of recommendations, most of which had been vetted at the late-morning meeting of state and defense department officials and discussed with the president in the Blair House cloakroom: first, General MacArthur should furnish the South Korean forces with military equipment and supplies; second, U.S. aircraft should cover the evacuation of American personnel and if necessary destroy North Korean tanks and planes in order to accomplish the task; third, consideration should be given to what other assistance should be extended to South Korea; fourth, the Seventh fleet should be sent from the Philippines to Formosa to prevent a Chinese Communist attack against Formosa and a Nationalist attack against the mainland; and fifth, aid to Indochina, including Vietnam, should be increased.[33]

Next, the president called on Johnson to present the views of the Defense Department. Consistent with his pre-meeting game plan, Johnson stated that there would be no departmental recommendations but that each service secretary and each member of the JCS would present individual assessments. Starting with General Bradley, who attended despite a serious intestinal infection, Johnson asked each to present his views. During those presentations the president frequently interrupted, asked questions, and made comments. The chief executive's questions and remarks were reassuring to the Pentagon officials because they revealed a high level of knowledge and awareness of the situation.[34] What the military leaders' assessments had in common was their tentativeness. Their reluctance to make recommendations stemmed from the dearth of information from Korea, the difficulties of undertaking military activities in that na tion, and a tendency to stick with their carefully considered and long-held position that Korea was not of strategic importance to the United States and should not be defended with American forces.[35]

During the course of the presentations of the military leaders, it appeared that while the plight of the South Koreans was serious, there was a sense of confidence that their armed forces were beginning to stabilize the situation and could repel the invasion unless North Korea was backed with considerable outside assistance. Nevertheless, since the military situation was clouded by a lack of information, General Collins suggested, and the president agreed, that General MacArthur should send a survey team to Korea to gather information firsthand.[36]

Although they lacked hard evidence, all those present were convinced that the attack had been orchestrated by the Soviet Union, but no one believed it was the beginning of a major Soviet move that would bring on World War III. They did, however, think there was a strong possibility that the Soviets or Chinese Communists might use the occasion to push their advantage at a number of locations throughout the world.[37] Bradley said that since the Soviets were not yet ready for war, this might be a good occasion "to draw the line," but he questioned the advisability of committing U.S. ground forces to Korea.[38]

Johnson warned that a Chinese Communist attack on Formosa was highly likely in view of the fact that troops on the mainland adjacent to the island had been increased from 40,000 to 156,000 in the past two weeks.[39] He urged that the Seventh fleet immediately begin to head north to the Straits of Formosa and that several islands in the U.S.-held Ryukyus be prepared to service fighter aircraft because "the Formosan situation could be handled" from those positions. He also voiced approval of the recommendation that General MacArthur provide additional supplies to the South Koreans, but he wisely advised that "the instructions to the General should be detailed so as not to give him too much discretion." In an observation which would be remembered later as remarkably prescient, Johnson stated that "there should not be a real delegation of Presidential authority to General MacArthur."[40] Johnson knew General MacArthur well enough to realize that he might go much farther than was intended if clear restrictions were not placed on him.[41]

The president inquired about current military strength and was told that about 123,000 of the 592,000 in the army were in the Far East, as were 375 jet fighters and 62 bombers.[42] When he asked what should be done if the South Koreans did not hold, there was a diversity of opinion. General Vandenburg and Admiral Sherman were confident that air and naval power would he decisive in holding back the attackers, while Generals Bradley and Collins were of the opinion that ground forces would be required. Secretary Johnson declared that he was firmly opposed to using ground forces, and Secretary Pace and General Bradley expressed doubts about the wisdom of such a move.[43]

Having listened intently to the multitude of suggestions and views put forth, the president announced that the following actions should be taken:

- General MacArthur should send additional supplies to South Korea
- MacArthur should send a survey team to Korea
- The fleet should steam north toward Japan, but its actual mission would be decided when it reached the Formosa Straits
- The air force should prepare plans to "wipe out all Soviet air bases in the Far East" (Truman stressed that this was a directive to make plans, not an order to strike)
- The State and Defense Departments should make an assessment of "the next probable place in which Soviet action might take place."[44]

The last two directives were the result of discussions of the likelihood of Soviet air intervention on the side of North Korea or possible action elsewhere.

The president closed the meeting by reiterating his intention to work through the United Nations and announcing that he would deliver a message to congressional leaders on the situation on Tuesday. No one, he admonished, should make statements to the press until after his speech. At that point he was reminded that Secretaries Acheson and Johnson were scheduled to appear before the Senate Appropriations Committee the next morning and that Korea would certainly come up. The president said he wanted his directive of silence adhered to. With that, the meeting ended.[45]

As the meeting was breaking up, two things were evident. First, all were in agreement that the North Korean aggression must not go unchallenged; however, there was no apparent consensus about how that should be done. Second, more information would be required before the next course of action could be decided. As General Bradley testified later, "I don't think you can say that any of us knew, to start, when we went into this thing, what would be involved." He added, "No one believed that the North Koreans were as strong as they turned out to be."[46]

It was nearly 11 P.M. when Johnson, Bradley, and the others from the Pentagon left Blair House through the back door to return to their offices. The president stayed to have a drink with a few of the state department people,[47] but those from the Pentagon had hours of work ahead of them as they began implementing the chief executive's directives.

Back at the Pentagon, Johnson and his advisors began working on the language of the orders to be teletyped to MacArthur. This was an especially onerous task since there were no written directives from the Blair House conference. The officials present had to use their handwritten notes and memories to translate the president's oral decisions into concrete and comprehensive written orders.

Monday

By 2 A.M. on Monday, June 26, the orders were ready, and the JCS and service secretaries conveyed them to MacArthur via a teletype conference. The directives were deliberately written in such a way as to "exclude the use of ground forces in Korea."[48] However, contrary to Johnson's earlier advice, they were still quite general. Johnson did not stay for the telecon but headed home to review the testimony he was to present on Capitol Hill later that morning.

When Secretaries Acheson and Johnson appeared before the Appropriations Committee at 10 A.M. on Monday to urge immediate passage of the second year of the $1.22 billion Mutual Defense Assistance Program, they refused to comment on the situation in Korea. Several senators, especially Republicans, pushed the question of whether the United States had been caught off guard by the invasion, but as tempting as it was to respond to that and similar questions, the two witnesses remained silent.[49]

Johnson returned to his Pentagon office, where he plunged into another of what were to be countless meetings that week with the JCS, service secretaries, Deputy Secretary Early, and Assistant Secretary Burns. These sessions generally consisted of up-to-date situation reports and discussions of possible responses to each new development. Throughout the numerous deliberative sessions of that week, Johnson, long known for his arrogant know-it-all attitude, seemed more willing than ever before to listen to the views of the military experts and to patiently think through options and alternatives.[50]

At about the time Johnson was on the Hill testifying before the Senate Appropriations Committee, President Truman was issuing his first public statement on Korea. He expressed pleasure with the rapidity of the UN Security Council's order to North Korea to withdraw north of the 38th parallel and declared that the United States would "vigorously support the effort of the Council to terminate this serious breach of the peace." He closed with a warning that the North Koreans needed to realize how "seriously" the United States viewed its action and stressed that nations that supported the UN Charter could not tolerate such behavior.[51]

Pressure began to build on Monday for the administration to take action. A *New York Times* editorial, without any evidence, asserted that the attack by North Korea was "obviously Soviet-authorized" and said that "the time for temporizing had run out." "We can lose half a world at this point, if we lose heart," advised the *Times*.[52] When the Senate convened at noon, Republican senators William Knowland, Styles Bridges, and George Malone warned of the dangers of appeasement. Recalling the aftermath of the Munich capitulation, the senators said that unless a line was drawn in Korea, communism would spread throughout Asia.[53]

During a meeting with the president, Truman asked Tom Connally, chairman of the Senate Foreign Relations Committee, for his advice on whether he should seek a declaration of war from Congress or some other form of support if he decided to send American troops into combat. Using a memorable analogy, Connally responded:

If a burglar breaks into your house, you can shoot him without going down
to the police station and getting permission. You might run into a long debate by Congress, which would tie your hands completely. You have the
right to do it as commander in chief under the UN Charter.[54]

As the day wore on, the news reaching Washington from Korea became in-
creasingly dismal. In the morning, Ambassador Muccio cabled from Seoul
characterizing the situation as one of "rapid deterioration and disintegration."[55]
In early afternoon, Johnson received a cable reporting that South Korean
(ROK) forces were disintegrating.[56] In the late afternoon, South Korean ambassador John M. Chang, after receiving an urgent telephone call from President
Rhee, asked for and received an immediate audience with President Truman.
Chang told Truman that the North Korean advance was rolling relentlessly
south, forcing the ROK government to withdraw from Seoul to Suwon, twenty
miles south. It was feared that complete disaster was near unless extensive military aid was forthcoming.

The president informed the South Korean ambassador that orders had been
given for delivery of arms and ammunition and that they were already on their
way. No mention was made, however, of the possibility of a commitment of U.S.
forces.[57] That afternoon the American press carried reports that at least 75,000
North Korean troops were involved in the invasion and that President Rhee had
publicly lamented that the military aid being extended to his government "was
too little too late."[58]

By late Monday, officials at defense and state were stating privately that American military involvement in South Korea was highly unlikely in view of that nation's lack of strategic importance and the military commitments of the United
States to prevent Communist aggression around the world. The dominant view
still seemed to be that if the ROK forces held that would be fine, but if not, South
Korea would just have to be "written off."[59]

In this mood of pessimism, Acheson, after consulting with Johnson on the
gravity of the situation, called the president around 7:30 P.M. and informed him
that the situation had become very serious. Truman directed the same thirteen
advisors who had gathered the evening before to convene again at 9 P.M. at Blair
House.

The president opened the second crucial meeting at Blair House by calling
on the Joint Chiefs to give the latest reports available. On an optimistic note,
General Vandenberg reported that the first Soviet Yak fighter had been shot
down and Truman said that he hoped it would not be the last.[60] However, all of
the other reports were pessimistic, and the most unsettling dispatch was from
General MacArthur, who reported a virtual collapse of the ROK Army and the
movement of the North Koreans into the suburbs of Seoul. MacArthur concluded by saying, "Our estimate is that a complete collapse is imminent."[61] As
they digested this report and many others, the assembled advisors agreed that

the situation had become desperate. If Korea was to be saved, something had to be done quickly.

Truman turned to Acheson as he did the night before and as he would throughout the crisis. Acheson was prepared, as always, with a series of crisp recommendations, as follows:

- U.S. naval and air forces should give full support to South Korean forces south of the 38th parallel
- The Seventh fleet should be positioned in the straits between Formosa and the mainland to prevent either side from attacking the other
- Military assistance must be stepped up to the Philippines and Indochina

Acheson also announced that the United States would sponsor a resolution at Tuesday's UN Security Council meeting calling for additional assistance to the South Korean government. He then handed the president a proposed public statement that could be released if the recommended actions were approved.[62]

The secretary of state's recommendations were momentous because they advocated military intervention on the Korean peninsula and defense of Formosa, the former a reversal of the administration's judgment concerning Korea's limited strategic value and the latter a reversal of its hands-off policy regarding Formosa. Yet without any comment, probably because he and Acheson had already discussed the proposals, the president turned to Johnson and asked what the Defense Department felt should be done.[63]

Johnson played it the same way he had played it on Sunday night—each service secretary and chief would be free to provide individual assessments but the department would have no overall recommendation. As for himself, Johnson said that Acheson's proposals "pleased him very much" and said that if "we hold the line as indicated that was alright."[64]

The Colonel was not only pleased, he was delighted with Acheson's recommendation that Formosa be defended. For months, Johnson had been fighting to convince Acheson and Truman that the United States had to take action to prevent the island from falling into Chinese Communist hands. It gave him great personal satisfaction to hear Acheson, who had disagreed with him so violently on numerous occasions on the matter of supporting Chiang's government, to now be urging action to protect Formosa. To Johnson, the fact that Acheson's recommendation to place the U.S. Navy in the Straits of Formosa was designed to limit the war to Korea was not as important as the fact that the administration would be protecting the Nationalist government.[65]

On the first and perhaps the most important of the proposals—the commitment of U.S. naval and air forces to stop the North Korean advance—neither Johnson nor his military advisors commented. They did not endorse it nor did they oppose it, although the secretary signified his tacit approval by commenting that Acheson's proposed action "suits me."[66] When the military representatives were asked if they had any objections to intervention by U.S. air and naval forces, they had none.[67]

Recalling the Monday-night meeting a year later, Johnson said, "Neither I nor any member of the Military Establishment . . . recommended we go into Korea. The recommendations came from the Secretary of State, but I want to repeat that it was not opposed by the Defense Department, all the members of which had severally pointed out the trouble, the trials, tribulations, and the difficulties."[68]

In presenting their assessments to the president, the Pentagon officials generally were optimistic that U.S. air and sea power could halt the invaders. However, Generals Bradley and Collins, as they had the night before, expressed the view that ground troops might be needed. Johnson said that he hoped that the call for air and naval action would "settle the Korea question" because he did not want to see ground forces committed.[69]

General Bradley was skeptical that air power would be enough to stem the attack of the North Koreans. He warned that if ground troops were committed, general mobilization would be necessary. The president said he did not wish to mobilize immediately but that it was something that should be considered again in a few days. "I don't want to go to war," said Truman.[70]

A discussion of the probable Soviet reaction to events followed, and a consensus emerged that Russia did not want a general war and probably would not intervene directly in Korea.[71] It was agreed, however, that there was, in Johnson's words, a "calculated risk" that the contemplated intervention by the United States in Korea might bring the USSR or China into the conflict, but it was understood that the risk had to be taken.[72] If that happened, Johnson declared, the United States should withdraw since Korea was not the place to get involved in a shooting war with either of these nations.[73]

The impact that the appeasement policies of the 1930s had on the decision makers was apparent in this session and others throughout the crisis. They all remembered what had happened a dozen years before when aggressor nations were permitted to go unchecked, and they did not want to make the same mistakes.[74] Johnson feared for the security of Japan and Formosa should Korea fall. Nearly all the advisors were aware of the importance of this crisis to the future of the United Nations. This would be a major test for the relatively young peace organization, and its success in dealing with the problem would have an enormous impact on its future.[75]

When those present finished their say, the president stepped in and approved all three of Acheson's original proposals. In doing so, Truman effectively declared war on Korea, although neither he nor anyone else at the meeting remembered discussing whether Congress would need to vote on the issue. He also reversed administration policy on Formosa and set the United States on a tortuous path which delayed diplomatic recognition of mainland China for decades, further alienated Mao Tse-tung, and led to an alliance and defense pact with Chiang's Nationalist government in Formosa. Finally, he significantly escalated America's role in Vietnam.

Truman had a sense of the importance and long-lasting effects of the decisions he made that Monday night, although he could not possibly have foreseen the carnage and bloodshed that would result from his rather routine-sounding approval of Acheson's three recommendations. Those who were there remember his saying wistfully, "Everything I have done in the past five years has been to try to avoid making a decision as I had to make tonight."[76]

Before dismissing the group, Truman announced that he wanted Acheson and Johnson to be at the White House in the morning, when he would inform the top congressional leadership of the actions being taken. He also directed Johnson to convey to General MacArthur the order to use U.S. air and naval power to halt the North Korean attack. At around 10 P.M., the second historic meeting at Blair House adjourned.[77]

It is doubtful that those assembled at Blair House that Monday, including Johnson, realized the magnitude of the decisions arrived at, especially the commitment of U.S. military forces against the North Korean army. Once that decision had been made, there was no turning back. In his memoirs, Truman would characterize the decision to defend South Korea as "the toughest decision I had to make as President."[78]

How can Secretary Johnson's actions be characterized at that critical conference? Johnson was certainly not enthusiastic about committing U.S. military forces to Korea. Nevertheless, he supported the president's decision. When asked a year later why he backed the president, Johnson replied, "If you let this one happen others would happen in more rapid order. . . . Moreover, we have joined the United Nations . . . and this . . . was a testing ground for the Charter."[79] In those early days of the conflict, Johnson was still optimistic that naval and air forces would carry the day. He did not envision commitment of ground troops or involvement in a long and costly military conflict.[80]

Before leaving Blair House that night, Johnson delegated to Secretary Pace responsibility for conveying the agreed-upon decisions to General MacArthur. This freed him to concentrate on the draft of the president's statement to congressional leaders the following morning, which Acheson and his advisors had prepared. After going over the draft, the defense secretary expressed dissatisfaction with several sentences and made suggestions for improvement.[81] He then left for home, leaving staff members from the Departments of State and Defense to work out the differences.

Tuesday

Johnson arrived early at his office on Tuesday morning, June 27, for a briefing on the situation in Korea. The Pentagon was beginning to receive fragmentary reports from the survey team MacArthur had dispatched to Seoul. The twelve-man team, headed by Brigadier General John Church, was reporting that the ROK Army had completely collapsed due to "lack of leadership . . . rather than fear."[82] The morning briefings, based on reports from MacArthur's staff, General Church, and Ambassador Muccio, were usually presented by either General Bradley or Deputy Secretary Early, and they were to become a daily occurrence for the remainder of Johnson's days in office.[83]

Johnson next turned to the latest draft statement to congressional leaders, a copy of which had been forwarded to the president. Although generally pleased, he and Bradley still did not care for the wording pertaining to the defense of Formosa. To present their arguments in favor of revisions, they motored across the Potomac to the White House. When they arrived in the Oval Office, they found the president reworking the draft. He readily accepted their suggested changes—changes opposed by Acheson, who arrived a short time later.[84] Johnson assured Truman he would return for the meeting with congressional leaders and then left for a speaking engagement at the Industrial College of the Armed Forces.

By 11:30 A.M. he was back at the West Wing to join the president and Secretary Acheson as they entered the Cabinet Room to meet fourteen top congressional leaders—nine Democrats and five Republicans. Only one, Senator Connally, chairman of the Foreign Relations Committee, had been briefed on the substance of the president's statement. The purpose of the meeting was to inform Congress about what was being done, not to seek its opinion or blessing. Some of the president's advisors, including Acheson, had urged the president to seek passage of a congressional resolution endorsing the actions he had taken, but others, including Johnson, had argued against such a course because they feared it would open the door to a general debate.[85]

As they sat around the long table in the Cabinet Room, Truman called upon Acheson to recapitulate the events of the past two days. Following his concise summary of events, the president emphasized the important test the invasion presented to the United Nations. Truman then read the statement, whose wording Johnson had revised less than two hours before. Concerning the North Korean attack, the statement said, "the attack upon Korea makes it plain beyond all doubt that Communism has passed beyond the use of subversion to conquer independent nations and will now use armed invasion and war." The president went on to point out that the UN Security Council had ordered the North Koreans to withdraw and had called on all member nations to "offer every assistance" to implement the resolution. "In these circumstances," the president's statement read, "I have ordered United States air and sea forces to give the Korean Government troops cover and support."

Although the commitment of the navy and air force to Korea would be the focal point of questions from members of Congress, Johnson was much more interested in the next part of the president's statement, which justified the move by the Seventh fleet to defend Formosa:

> In these circumstances the occupation of Formosa by Communist forces would be a direct threat to the security of the Pacific area and to the United States forces performing their lawful and necessary functions in that area.[86]

When he finished reading his prepared statement, the president asked for the views of the congressional leaders. They responded with requests for clarification.[87] The first question related to what specific forces General MacArthur had dispatched. General Vandenberg began to answer, but was interrupted by Secretary Johnson, who claimed that the information was secret and could not be divulged for security reasons. He did, however, say that sufficient forces had been committed and were already on their way into combat. Secretary Pace pointed out that no ground troops were committed.

A question was asked about whether or not the navy would have to be expanded to meet the additional burden being placed upon it. Again Johnson replied, this time by assuring the legislators that the JCS were studying the question and that should a military buildup become necessary there would be a balanced program. Such a statement coming from a defense secretary who had been regarded as anti-navy since assuming office came as a relief to the friends of the navy.

Acheson was asked whether UN member states, specifically those in Europe, would provide military assistance. He responded that based on diplomatic traffic, most Western European countries would offer some military assistance but that the French, who were tied up in Indochina, would not be able to assist.

Near the end of the conference, the president, reflecting his view that the Korean conflict was part of a global strategy by the Soviets to test America's resolve, said, "If we let Korea down, the Soviets would swallow one piece of Asia after another. We had to take a stand somewhere or let all of Asia go by the board."

Before the meeting adjourned, the question arose again about the possibility of the commitment of U.S. ground forces. The members of Congress were told by the president that "ground troops were not planned to be used"—a view Johnson had advocated from the beginning.[88]

When the hour-long meeting ended, the departing guests were handed copies of the president's statement, which had been distributed to the press a few minutes earlier. As the officials were leaving the White House they were besieged by reporters anxious to get their reactions to the statement. As usual, Johnson was asked for a comment. Walking toward Blair House, where he and the other cabinet members were to join the president for lunch, Johnson told a reporter, "We are doing over there what the UN asked us to do." Then, when asked about the possibility of broader U.S. action, he zeroed in on the matter of ground forces: "None of our ground troops [will] be committed into the Korean conflict."[89]

Referring to the possible insertion of ground troops, Johnson told one reporter that "there is no absolute bar against this being done later if necessary."[90]

At lunch the cabinet members talked of what had transpired since Saturday evening, but no new proposals for action were considered. As soon as he could break away, Johnson hurried back to the Pentagon to study the latest reports from Korea and to catch up on routine work that had stacked up since he had left for his trip to the Far East more than two weeks before. While he was work-ing in his office that Tuesday afternoon, important developments were taking place in Washington and at Lake Success, New York.

On the Hill, members of the Senate and House had started to react publicly to the president's announcement. The overwhelming response of the lawmak-ers was that of support for Truman's actions. A few voices were raised to chal-lenge the president's right to commit the nation's armed forces to the defense of Korea, but no one in the Senate criticized the decision itself. In the House, only American Labor Party representative Vito Marcantonio was critical. Be-fore recessing, the House, encouraged by public support for the president's ac-tion, voted 315 to 4 to extend for one year the Selective Service Act, which was scheduled to expire on June 30.[91]

At 3 P.M. on Tuesday, the UN Security Council was called into session at Lake Success, which is where the UN met until its headquarters building was com-pleted in Manhattan. As he had since January, when the Security Council re-fused to unseat Nationalist China for Communist China, Soviet Ambassador Malik boycotted the meeting, which was fortunate for the South Koreans be-cause he could have vetoed all UN support. U.S. ambassador to the UN Warren R. Austin, claiming the organization was facing the "gravest crisis of its history" because of North Korea's disregard of its resolution of two days before, introduced a second resolution. This resolution was debated for several hours and was finally approved at 11:45 P.M. by a vote of 7 to 1, with Yugoslavia opposing and India and Egypt abstaining.[92] While the first resolution authorized military assistance through the United Nations, the second permitted member nations to make mili-tary commitments to the South Koreans to enable them to repel the aggressor.

Halfway around the world, North Korean troops were driving the remaining defenders from the streets of the South Korean capital city of Seoul. As the ROK Army, or what was left of it, fled southward in disarray, the invaders halted briefly to catch their breath and prepared to resume their offensive.[93]

Wednesday

Wednesday, June 28, dawned clear and warm as Louis Johnson rose at 6 A.M. to meet the challenges of the fourth full day of the Korean crisis. While Dean Acheson later referred to this as "a day of pause in the rush of decision," there was not much time for Secretary Johnson to pause.[94]

When he arrived at the Pentagon, Johnson received his usual morning briefing before turning his attention to a draft policy statement just received from Secretary Acheson. The subject was the U.S. response in the event that Soviet forces intervened in the fighting in Korea. Acheson maintained that "major decisions about the extension of the Korean issue into a major war" must be made in Washington and should "not be merely the result of a series of events in Korea." He advocated that if Soviet forces opposed U.S. forces in Korea, U.S. forces "should defend themselves, should take no action on the spot to aggravate the situation and should report the situation to Washington."[95] Johnson pledged full support for Acheson's proposal, which was to be considered at that afternoon's NSC meeting.

In addition, Johnson directed the JCS to prepare for the NSC and the president a comprehensive document on the Korean situation and the various contingencies which might arise.[96] The JCS immediately went to work, ordering the Joint Strategic Survey Committee to prepare by 8 A.M. on Friday an answer to the question "In the event that the current course of action now being undertaken in Korea is unsuccessful, what course of action, from a military point of view, should be undertaken?" The Joint Chiefs asked the committee to consider air operations north of the 38th parallel as well as other actions that could be pursued "in lieu of committing group troops." The idea behind the latter stipulation was put more succinctly by the director of the committee, Rear Admiral Arthur Davis, who noted that the Joint Chiefs "do *not* want to commit troops."[97]

Johnson next went to the White House to meet the president so they could ride up Connecticut Avenue together to the Mayflower, where they were both scheduled to address the opening session of the Reserve Officers Association convention. Speaking first and before an audience of more than a thousand, Johnson praised the president's handling of the Korean situation and called his Sunday-night decisions at Blair House, "the finest hour in American history."[98] He proceeded to declare that the "national defense is stronger today than ever before in our peacetime history" — a continuation of a theme he had been trumpeting for the past year.

Johnson then introduced President Truman, who made no mention of Korea but spoke about the obligation of Americans to serve their country. When the chief executive concluded his remarks, the Reserve Officers' commander asked the audience rhetorically if they supported the president's decision to commit planes and warships to Korea. The response was a prolonged standing ovation.[99] Undoubtedly, this enthusiastic response served to encourage Truman and Johnson that they were pursuing, if not the correct course, at least a popular one.

While Johnson and Truman were being applauded at the Mayflower, Senator Robert Taft was rising on the Senate floor to deliver a stem-winding speech which would play a central part in Louis Johnson's eventual downfall as secretary of defense. Taft not only accused the president of violating the Constitution by declaring war on North Korea without obtaining the approval of Congress, he launched a direct attack on Dean Acheson for the "loss of China" and for effectively inviting the Communists to invade South Korea when he excluded Korea and Formosa from the American defense perimeter in his January 12 address to the National Press Club. Then, in the part of his speech which resonated with Johnson, Taft called on Acheson to resign because President Truman had repudiated his hands-off policy by sending the Seventh fleet into the Formosa Strait to protect Nationalist China.[100]

As "Mister Republican" was holding forth in the Senate, Dwight Eisenhower, who had come down from New York for a routine physical, stopped at the Pentagon to meet with Army Chief of Staff Joe Collins and his assistants. According to his daily diary, Eisenhower was astonished by their complacency and indecisiveness and urged them to do everything possible to get ready for a ground war in Korea, including all-out mobilization. Omar Bradley, who missed the meeting because of illness, wrote that Eisenhower's visit had a profound effect on Collins and the top army brass. They immediately began to plan for a commitment of ground troops for full-scale war in Korea.[101]

Meanwhile, Johnson returned to the Pentagon, where he joined Steve Early for lunch and a review of the agenda for that afternoon's NSC meeting. At 2:30, the NSC met for the first time since the crisis began. In addition to Truman, Johnson, and Acheson, those present included the three service secretaries, the JCS, Secretary of the Treasury John W. Snyder, CIA Director Hillenkoetter, recently appointed National Security Resources Board chairman Stuart Symington, and, for the first time, Ambassador-at-Large Averell Harriman. Harriman, who would within a few days play a key part in Johnson's downfall, had just been recalled by Truman from his post in Paris, where he had been administering the Marshall Plan, to assume the newly created position of special assistant to the president for national security.[102] Harriman had been aching to get back to Washington and he was to become indispensable to Acheson, even though he was deeply disappointed that Truman had picked Acheson rather than him for secretary of state. According to Acheson, Harriman had actually been called back to Washington to smooth out "Cabinet relations on foreign affairs, especially with Defense."[103]

The meeting of the NSC on the afternoon of June 28 opened with a military briefing about the continuing deterioration of the South Korean position. The president responded with an optimistic observation that full U.S. air power had not yet been brought to bear on the enemy. He also said that there were signs that ROK forces were beginning to offer resistance to the advancing enemy forces.

The president then asked his advisors for their views on possible responses if the Soviet Union intervened in Korea or elsewhere. At that point Acheson introduced the policy statement he and Johnson had agreed on that morning which emphasized that the administration needed to control events rather than letting events control it. The two secretaries stressed that they did not want to commit the nation to all-out war with the Soviet Union if it should intervene. They noted a need to think out the response to such a contingency carefully.

The NSC agreed that Johnson and the JCS should draw up a far-reaching set of contingency plans in the event that the Soviets decided to press for advantage at a number of potential trouble spots. Those plans would then be submitted to the NSC for consideration. For the time being, it was agreed that if the U.S. forces found themselves engaged in combat with Soviet forces, they should extract themselves and seek instructions from Washington.[104]

While the NSC meeting was still in progress, Vice President Barkley, a regular NSC member who had just left the Senate floor, reported that the Senate had passed the extension of the Selective Service Act 70 to 0 and that with the House approval the day before, the president was now free to call military reserves to active duty. Ambassador Harriman reported that the U.S. reaction in Korea had been very well received by the NATO nations. Before the meeting adjourned, Johnson indicated that the Pentagon would provide daily military briefings on Capitol Hill for those legislators selected by the president.[105]

About the time the NSC meeting was breaking up in Washington, General MacArthur, wearing his famous old crushed campaign hat and brandishing his even more famous corncob pipe, was boarding his C-54, the *Bataan*, in Tokyo for a risky and dangerous four-hour flight to Suwon, a city south of Seoul, where he would personally survey the situation before making more recommendations. On the way to his destination, the 70-year-old general authorized B-29 bomber strikes north of the 38th parallel to hit the invaders' supply lines and air bases. MacArthur was advised by his aide, Major General Courtney Whitney, that he was not authorized to bomb the north, but MacArthur said to Whitney, "And now you find something in the orders that will protect me and stand up in a court-martial."[106]

MacArthur had given the order because his advisors told him the situation was bad; however, he had no idea how bad it was until he arrived on the scene. After being told that only 25,000 of the 100,000-man ROK Army could be located or accounted for, he traveled in an ancient American sedan to a hill south of Seoul. As he stood watching the city burn and South Korean soldiers fleeing, he concluded that only the commitment of U.S. ground troops could keep South Korea from falling.[107] On the flight back to Japan, the general announced that he would ask the president for two American divisions to stop the North Korean advance.[108]

Thursday

As MacArthur was heading back to Japan, Louis Johnson was preparing for the start of another busy day—it was Thursday, June 29. No sooner had he arrived at the Pentagon than he was presented the first of many reports he was to receive that morning detailing the deteriorating South Korean situation and the inability of the defenders to slow down the rapidly advancing invaders.

While Johnson pored over the mass of discouraging reports, the JCS was completing their review of a draft of a comprehensive directive for General MacArthur which Johnson had called for the day before. The document proposed a significant expansion of the military role of the United States by calling for CINPAC (Admiral Radford) to provide the "fullest possible support" of U.S. naval and air forces to aid South Korea and to grant authority to General MacArthur to extend operations into North Korea if he felt it necessary to prevent the fall of South Korea. Furthermore, the document advised that if the USSR intervened, guidance must be sought from Washington because of the various policy and political issues that would have to be considered before engaging the Soviets.[109]

The JCS gave tentative approval to the draft and then, about 10 A.M., headed to Johnson's office to discuss it. As the four military advisors pulled up chairs around the big Pershing desk to defend the document they had just approved, Johnson inquired about their reactions to the negative reports being received from Korea. There was a consensus that the situation was deteriorating rapidly and that the prospect that air and sea forces alone could halt the drive was increasingly unlikely. While expressing hope that current action might halt the North Korean advance, they reluctantly came to the conclusion "that the use of U.S. [ground] troops in Korea could no longer be avoided" and that they would need to bomb targets north of the 38th parallel. With an urgency and decisiveness no doubt inspired by Eisenhower's visit the previous day, they agreed that they needed to immediately provide support troops, transportation equipment, and signal personnel to assist the ROK forces and combat troops to protect the airfield at the port at Pusan in southeast Korea so that American civilians could be safely evacuated.

Johnson questioned the Joints Chiefs closely about the necessity of such a commitment. He then approved their increasingly hawkish recommendations and their call for authority to hit targets north of the 38th parallel (at this time they did not yet know that MacArthur had already ordered the bombing of airfields in North Korea).

Johnson picked up the white phone and called the president; it was 11:55 A.M. He told the chief executive of the increasingly negative reports coming in from the Far East and called the situation grave. He advised the president to immediately call another meeting of his policy advisors to consider what response should be made to the situation. He also indicated that he would have some recommendations, which for security reasons he could not mention on the phone. Truman agreed to call an emergency NSC meeting for 5 P.M.[110]

At his press conference that afternoon, the president stated emphatically, "We are not at war." In response to a reporter's question, he agreed that it would be correct to characterize the U.S. response to the North Korean attack as a "police action" under UN auspices. While commenting favorably on the UN response and the public reaction in the United States to the moves to assist South Korea, the president refused to answer questions about the possible use of atomic bombs or ground troops to stop the North Koreans.[111]

Shortly before 5 P.M. the press conference ended, and Truman joined the members of the NSC and Rusk, Harriman, and Dulles (who had just returned from the Far East) in the Cabinet Room.

Since the meeting had been called at Secretary Johnson's request, the president immediately turned the floor over to him. Johnson opened his presentation with a dramatic and unsettling assessment of the problems both South Korean and U.S. military forces were confronting in conducting operations in Korea. To address these problems, Johnson, with JCS backing, proposed that a directive consolidating all previous directives be sent to General MacArthur authorizing him to:

- Extend, if he felt necessary, air and naval operations into North Korea
- Deploy U.S. army service troops (i.e., transportation and signal units)
- Commit combat troops to defend the port and airfield at Pusan on the southeastern tip of the peninsula in order to provide for the successful evacuation of remaining American citizens

Johnson's recommendations carefully avoided any suggestion that U.S. ground troops should be deployed in battle areas.[112]

While there were no challenges to Johnson's proposals, there were several requests for elaboration and clarification. The president was concerned because he felt that the proposed directive implied that the United States was planning for war with the USSR and he did not want to give "even the slightest implication of such a plan." "We must be damned careful," Truman warned. "We must not say that we are anticipating a war with the Soviet Union."[113]

The president also directed that any activity north of the 38th parallel should be "only to destroy military supplies." Furthermore, although most felt that the Soviet Union would not intervene, the president wanted it made clear that if it did, MacArthur's forces should defend themselves but should seek immediate instructions from Washington. Acheson insisted that it should be made clear in the directive that aircraft must not violate Chinese or Soviet air space.

Before the session ended, the president, while fully supporting Johnson's proposals, cautioned against the United States "becom[ing] so deeply committed in Korea that we could not take care of other situations as might develop." The NSC meeting concluded by approving the defense secretary's directive to MacArthur. It was 5:40 P.M.

In retrospect, this meeting, at which the first commitment of ground troops was made, marked a significant step along the path to all-out war. However, the commitment of ground forces did not then elicit much debate, probably because their use was to be limited to rear areas.[114]

As Truman and Acheson headed for dinner speaking engagements, Johnson and his advisors, along with several representatives from the State Department, went to the Pentagon, where they finalized instructions to MacArthur. At 6:45 P.M., after getting final approval from Acheson, the new orders were sent out by the JCS. In addition to the directives approved at the NSC meeting, the orders also reaffirmed the need to "defend Formosa against invasion or attack" and granted MacArthur control of the Seventh fleet. Finally, the general was told to provide South Korea with all the munitions deemed necessary and to submit estimates of more ammunition and supply needs.

With the message to MacArthur on its way, Johnson went off to the Statler Hotel, where he joined the DNC finance Committee for dinner. For the remainder of the evening he socialized with old friends who had helped him pull off the nearly impossible task of financing the president's 1948 campaign just two years before. Although the dinner ended what had been an extremely long and taxing day, it offered a pleasant respite for Johnson as he turned his attention, at least for awhile, to the world of politics.[115]

Friday

At about 1:30 A.M. on Friday, June 30, a top-secret message from General MacArthur arrived at the Pentagon. The message consisted for the most part of a report of MacArthur's trip to Korea but, and this is curious, MacArthur's staff had delayed sending it to Washington for almost twelve hours.[116] The general told of the state of disarray in which he found the ROK forces and concluded that U.S. air and sea forces alone could neither hold the enemy nor retake the lost territory. He therefore called for "the introduction of U.S. ground combat forces into the Korean battle area." Specifically, he requested authority to commit a Regimental Combat Team (RCT) immediately and begin building up an army with the strength of two divisions for "an early counteroffensive."[117]

Since MacArthur was asking for army troops, the Pentagon duty officer immediately contacted General Collins, the army chief of staff, who asked that arrangements be made for a teletype conference with MacArthur and his staff. Collins alerted Secretary Pace and General Bradley.[118] At 3:40 A.M., Collins, with a half-dozen of his top advisors and Assistant Secretary of State Rusk, gathered in the War Room deep in the bowels of the Pentagon and began to communicate with MacArthur and his staff half a world away. As Collins recalled, "There was an eerie quality about this telecon that makes it stand out in my memory. The air was fraught with tension as we assembled in the middle of the night in the army's darkened telecon room in the Pentagon."[119]

Collins initiated the telecon with a statement that MacArthur's request to commit combat troops to battle would require presidential approval but that based on the directive sent him eight hours earlier, he could at least authorize

MacArthur to move an RCT to Pusan without getting Truman's prior approval. MacArthur, expanding the intent of Collins's authorization to move troops to Pusan, replied, "Your authorization, while establishing basic principle that U.S. ground forces may be used in Korea, does not give sufficient latitude for efficient operation in the present situation." Then he impatiently added, "Time is of the essence, and a clear-cut decision without delay is imperative."

Referring to President Truman's preference for careful consideration with advisors before committing the RCT to battle areas, Collins told MacArthur that "we should be able to obtain definite decision on your proposal. Does that meet your requirement for the present?"[120] In the darkened war room, Collins and his associates waited anxiously for the general to respond and confirm. Minutes of unbroken silence went by. It soon became apparent that General MacArthur was not going to favor them with any reply. As one writer so aptly put it, "MacArthur was speaking through the eloquence of scornful silence and he clearly had Washington on the defensive."[121]

Collins understood the meaning of MacArthur's silence. After conferring with his staff and the state department representatives, he responded, "I will proceed immediately through Secretary of the Army to request Presidential approval to move one RCT into forward combat area. Will advise you as soon as possible, perhaps within half hour."

No acknowledgment was received from MacArthur. Collins stepped out of the conference room and decided to quickly forward MacArthur's request through Secretary Pace to the president without consulting General Bradley and the Joint Chiefs. Collins contacted Pace at home, who called Truman at 4:57 A.M. The president, who had been alerted that an important request would be forthcoming, was already up, dressed, shaved, and ready for his morning walk.

Pace informed the commander in chief of MacArthur's request. Truman asked what the secretary of defense and JCS thought and was told that because of the press of time they had not been consulted but that Collins and his staff favored its acceptance. The president approved sending the RCT into combat but decided that the request for the buildup of the two divisions would have to await further consultations with his advisors. An answer would be forthcoming within several hours.

Word of the president's immediate decision to deploy the RCT into battle was flashed to MacArthur, the historic message reading, "Your recommendation to move one Regimental Combat Team to combat area is approved. You will be advised later as to further build-up." "Acknowledged," MacArthur's staff instantly replied.

Thus, American troops were committed to a land war on the Asian mainland, a step that the U.S. military had been warned would have disastrous consequences. Without delay, General MacArthur ordered the airlift of an infantry battalion into Korea.[122]

Shortly after 5 A.M., a Pentagon duty officer called Secretary Johnson and told him what had transpired.[123] When Johnson arrived at the Pentagon to begin the day, he received a personal call from the president, who directed him to attend an 8:30 A.M. meeting to discuss MacArthur's request for the buildup of two divisions and the advisability of accepting the offer Chiang Kai-shek had made the day before to furnish combat troops for use in Korea.[124] Johnson immediately summoned the JCS and service secretaries to his office to discuss the proposal of sending two U.S. divisions, but there was little debate; everyone agreed that MacArthur's request should be approved. According to one participant, Johnson astonished the Joint Chiefs and derailed the discussion by declaring that the deployment of two divisions did not require presidential approval and that he had full authority to authorize deployment. It is not certain that he actually made such a statement, but if he did it was ignored. Apparently, there was no discussion on the matter of using Nationalist Chinese troops.[125]

At the 8:30 meeting with the president, which involved essentially the same group of defense and state department officials that the president had been meeting with for the past five days, Truman began by reviewing the decisions he had recently made. He then informed the group that Chiang Kai-shek had offered to send 33,000 soldiers to fight in Korea. This offer had been received by the State Department the afternoon before, and Acheson and the president had conferred on the matter but had not discussed it with Johnson, probably because the defense secretary's views on Formosan matters always served to arouse considerable heat when Acheson was around.

As soon as the president disclosed Chiang's offer to the group at the Friday-morning meeting, Acheson made it known that he opposed the offer because it could widen the war by increasing the possibility of a Chinese Communist attack on Formosa. The JCS also were opposed because they believed the troops would be no better equipped than the ROK forces and the use of U.S. transportation equipment to deliver them would deny the use of such equipment to U.S. forces. Johnson concurred with his military advisors. The president, although he had previously been inclined to accept the offer, agreed to reject Chiang's invitation.

Attention was then focused on the likelihood of Soviet or Chinese intervention, and the consensus of the group was that intervention was highly unlikely. Next, approval was given to bomb targets in North Korea. Finally, the discussion centered on MacArthur's request to deploy at least two divisions of U.S. combat troops into battle areas. When no opposition was raised to that proposal, the president stunned most of those in the room by quietly announcing that he was going to give MacArthur "full authority to use the ground forces under his command," with *no limit* on the number of divisions to be sent.[126] The president effectively provided MacArthur with a blank check concerning the number of troops he could move into combat areas.

When the 30-minute meeting broke up, Johnson and the JCS remained behind to prepare the appropriate directives to MacArthur. After a few minutes
they had formulated a message which said: "Restrictions on use of Army Forces
imposed by JCS are hereby removed and authority granted to utilize Army
Forces available to you as proposed. . . . subject only to requirements for safety
of Japan in the present situation which is a matter for your judgment."[127]

That message went to MacArthur early that afternoon. The general had received far more than the two divisions he had requested. Secretary Johnson
had not actively pushed for this blank check for troops, but he did not oppose
the move either.

Why the defense chief, who had earlier that week expressed serious misgivings about committing ground forces to Korea, took such a passive position on
Friday is unclear. Perhaps it was the unanimity with which the intervention was
being embraced among the top administration officials or perhaps it was his acceptance of Bradley's view that a stand needed to be made somewhere and that
Korea was as good a place as any.[128] For whatever reason, Johnson went along.

After approving dispatch of the orders to McArthur, Johnson joined the president and Acheson and other top state and defense advisors at an 11 A.M. White
House meeting with fifteen congressional leaders from both parties. What took
place at that time is what one writer later called "a somewhat misleading briefing on . . . recent decisions."[129]

President Truman opened that session by reviewing the decisions he had
made since Sunday but focused on those of the past two days, especially the
decision to bomb targets north of the 38th parallel. He announced that he was
committing ground troops to the defense of South Korea. However, his remarks
coupled this commitment with the need to provide security for the evacuation
of American nationals at Pusan and the need for service troops to assist the ROK
forces.

Put in this way, the move did not seem anywhere near as far-reaching to the
members of Congress as it really was. Neither Truman nor General Bradley,
who also gave a briefing to the lawmakers, disclosed the extent of the authority
which the president had given to MacArthur, and Johnson and Acheson did not
volunteer that information.[130] Johnson later conceded that the congressional
attendees were misled; he indicated that the reason for the deception was a concern that if Congress realized that the executive branch was putting "ground
troops in at the start there would have been a great deal of trouble."[131] Acheson
later justified the misleading briefing on the grounds that "General MacArthur
had a touchy operation to perform and required protection."[132]

Given the watered-down version of what the Truman administration had actually decided to do, the congressional leadership backed President Truman. Only
one congressman, Republican Senator Kenneth Wherry, stood up and said that
the president should have consulted Congress before committing troops to war

in Korea. Truman responded that it had been an emergency. "I just had to act as Commander-in-Chief, and I did. I told MacArthur to go to the relief of the Koreans and carry out the instructions of the United Nations Security Council."[133]

While the June 30 meeting with the congressmen was still going on, the White House issued a press statement describing the meeting and announcing that in support of the UN Security Council request to aid South Korea, President Truman had authorized air attacks on "specific military targets" in North Korea and a naval blockade and that General MacArthur had been given authority "to use certain supporting ground units."[134] This deliberately vague statement was less alarming than the more accurate statement developed by Johnson and his advisors earlier that morning, which said the United States would use "all of its resources, including ground combat troops . . . to execute the United Nations mandate."[135]

Although Johnson did not speak in the session with the members of Congress other than to answer questions, he did not hesitate to comment when approached by the press as he left the White House. Asked by *New York Times* correspondent Harold Hinton what had transpired, Johnson, while noting that for security reasons he could not give detailed information, made no attempt to conceal the fact that the president had authorized "the deployment of ground forces to repel the invaders in South Korea."[136] Despite this remarkable candor, most newsmen, who had interviewed other participants at the White House gathering, reported that U.S. troops would only provide supply and munitions support and protection for air bases and would not engage in direct combat.[137] But at the very time the press was printing such accounts, American troops in Japan were preparing to do battle with North Korean forces.

After the cabinet luncheon ended early that Friday afternoon, the extremely hectic week began to wind down. President Truman left for Valley Forge, where he would address the National Boy Scout Jamboree before taking a weekend cruise on the presidential yacht, the *Williamsburg*. The Senate overwhelmingly approved the second year of the $1.2 billion Mutual Defense Assistance Program, and its members then rushed to trains and airports to get out of the city for two days.[138]

Louis Johnson worked at his office in the Pentagon that afternoon on a number of routine tasks that had accumulated during the busy week. Then he and Mrs. Johnson boarded a military aircraft and headed for Clarksburg. On the flight home, the secretary finally had an opportunity to relive the events of the past six days and reflect on the wisdom of the critical decisions that had been made.

Momentous Decisions

It had been an incredible seven days. As the week began on June 24, the official position of the Truman administration was that Korea was of little or no strategic importance to the United States and that the United States would not intervene in the Chinese civil war to protect Formosa. By week's end on June 30, everything had changed. The United States was committed to combat in Korea, a brutal and costly Asian ground war that would last more than three years. And the administration's hands-off policy toward mainland China and the Nationalist government, a policy Johnson fiercely resisted, had become one of the first casualties of the Korean War.

President Truman was comfortable letting Dean Acheson take the lead in steering the decision makers toward these stunning changes in direction. However, the big decisions were Truman's decisions and it is difficult to avoid concluding that he had made up his mind from the beginning on Sunday, when he had determined to "hit them hard." The president, supported by his top advisors, gave little or no thought to the causes of the populist movements being spearheaded by Kim Il Sung, Mao Tse-tung, and Ho Chi Minh, instead believing that the conflicts in Korea, China, and Vietnam were manifestations of a Soviet master plan to dominate Asia that had to be stopped.

In retrospect, Truman's decisions to enter the Korean War and protect Formosa are evidence that he and his principal advisors, including Acheson and Johnson, had little grasp of the real threats to U.S. national security. By turning the attack by the North Koreans into an issue of U.S. global security and by alienating mainland China for generations to come, Truman doomed the military economy program he had imposed on Secretary Johnson and committed the United States to a Cold War buildup that would drain the nation's economy for the remainder of the century.

Johnson, of course, enthusiastically supported Truman's decision to move the Seventh fleet into the Formosa Strait to protect the island against an attack from the mainland. Until the day he died, Johnson, as did MacArthur, remained convinced that Formosa was the strategic cornerstone to the defense of Asia against relentless Communist aggression orchestrated by the USSR.

Johnson continued to believe that Korea held little strategic value, and he was wary of committing to a ground war in Asia. He did not actively support the initial use of air or naval support, nor did he ultimately push for the use of combat ground troops to halt the advancing forces. He did, however, with the support of the JCS and service secretaries, advocate the use of U.S. supply and transportation units to assist ROK forces and combat troops to protect the southern port of Pusan.

At the beginning of the week, Johnson had expressed serious reservations about the commitment of ground troops. But as the days passed, he and the president, heavily influenced by Secretary Acheson and probably by the domestic political atmosphere, moved in the direction of committing troops. What emerged was a decision by President Truman to make a full-fledged and open-ended commitment to use U.S. troops, under UN auspices, to halt the North

Korean aggression against South Korea. Then, as in the years until his death, Louis Johnson believed that those decisions were correct.[139]

The Congress, the press, and the public were initially misled about the full extent of president's decision to commit ground troops in Korea. Yet as word of the president's decisions spread across the nation, it became evident that the American public felt, as Johnson did, that Truman was probably doing the right thing.[140] As Johnson headed out of Washington that Friday afternoon, the nation seemed to be almost as united as it had been eight and a half years earlier, on December 7, 1941.

Unfortunately, the initial euphoria was not destined to last. Little did an anonymous copywriter for the *New York Times* realize the extent of his ability to foresee the future when he wrote, after noting the unity that prevailed in the country, that "political bitterness is . . . almost certain to arise, for example, if events in Korea go badly for the United States."[141] Within a matter of weeks, this prediction became reality, and its consequences spelled the end of Louis Johnson's public career.

CHAPTER SEVENTEEN

"Give Me Two American Divisions and I Can Hold Korea"

W HEN PRESIDENT TRUMAN made his fateful decision during the last week in June 1950 to commit the United States to the defense of the Republic of Korea he could not possibly have realized the magnitude of what he had done. Events occurred so rapidly during those seven days that there was no time to reflect on consequences. The carefully considered Far East policies developed by the State and Defense Departments and approved by the National Security Council were thrown out and replaced with a hastily prepared response based more on emotion and a knee-jerk reaction to Cold War thinking than on logic and strategic soundness. As one CIA analyst put it: "Given the lack of serious analysis that went into the decision, it was a matter of act now think later."[1]

During the first days of deliberation, Secretary Johnson was uncharacteristically cautious. Known for being blunt and decisive—a man who, according to *Newsweek*, "rarely had let any twinge of doubt keep him from blurting out what he thought"[2]—Johnson warned of "the trouble, the trials, tribulations and difficulties" of military intervention in Korea. While he did not push for involvement, he did not resist the move either.[3]

After the president's decision of June 29 to commit ground troops to combat, Johnson's personal position on involvement was beside the point because the nation was, under UN auspices, militarily committed to the defense of South Korea. As secretary of defense, Johnson was the person responsible to the president to see that the nation's military response was adequate.

Joint Resolution

On Monday, July 3, the first workday after Truman gave MacArthur a blank check on the number of ground troops he could deploy in Korea, Johnson found himself dealing with political rather than military matters. That morning, Acheson called him to seek his views on whether the president should deliver a full report on the Korean situation to a joint session of Congress and whether the president should also ask Congress to pass a resolution approving the president's decision to defend South Korea. Johnson expressed doubts about the wisdom of providing a report and advised against seeking a resolution because most members of Congress supported the president and a small but vocal minority could delay and dilute the effect of such a resolution. Johnson did not have strong feelings on these points and he told Acheson that since they were primarily political rather than military questions, he would defer to the State Department. They agreed, however, that the two departments would work out a presidential message on the developments up to that time in case the president decided to convene a joint session of Congress.

A late-afternoon meeting was scheduled with the president, and Acheson sent a draft report and resolution over to Johnson for advance consideration.[4] At four o'clock Johnson and an entourage of advisors rode to Blair House, where they met with the president, the Cabinet, Acheson and some of his associates, and Senator Scott Lucas (D-Illinois), the majority leader.[5]

Acheson opened the meeting with a proposal that the president appear before a joint session of Congress in the near future to provide a full report on the Korean situation but that he not ask for a resolution of support and instead rest on his authority as commander in chief. Senator Lucas was not enthusiastic about a joint session and suggested that the president deliver the message as a "fireside chat" directly to the people.

The president, noting that Johnson agreed with Lucas, claimed that he had not yet made up his mind about how he should proceed but wanted to get the various views before making that decision. In the exchange that followed, there was an even split about the course to be pursued. Johnson reiterated his view that "things were going very well" and that "this was not the time for a message to the Congress." Both Johnson and General Bradley expressed concern that a trip by the president to the Hill might trigger a prolonged debate in Congress over decisions which had apparently been so well accepted.

When the discussion ended, the president announced that as Congress was scheduled to reconvene on July 10, he would not call it back into session early but would wait a week before deciding whether to take the issue directly to the Hill.[6] Ultimately the Johnson-Lucas view prevailed, because it was not until July 19, twenty-five days after the attack, that the president sent a message to Congress and then it was primarily a request for legislation needed to support the war effort. A joint resolution of support for what became known as the Korean War was never introduced.

In retrospect, Truman's decision to not seek congressional approval for the U.S. role in the Korean War was probably a mistake because it enabled the Republicans to attack "Truman's War" as well as his presidency.[7] Moreover, it provided an important precedent for future presidents who would lead the nation into undeclared wars.

Command and Control

After the decisions of the United Nations and the United States to intervene in Korea had been made, the most immediate problem was one of command. For the first time in its history, the United States was fighting a war under authority of an international body which was supposed to have a major say in the military and political objectives and strategies for conducting the conflict. It was, however, apparent from the beginning of the war that the bulk of the responsibility for UN military activity would fall on the United States.[8]

On July 4, the Defense Department received a draft state department resolution to the UN providing for the control of the international military force. Under the proposal, all UN forces would be placed under a unified command, whose leader would be appointed by the United States. Furthermore, it provided that the United States would submit regular reports on the command's activities to the UN Security Council, which would establish a special committee to receive and pass on to the unified command offers of assistance and inform the council about what actions were being taken.

While Johnson and the JCS had several objections to the plan, it was the establishment of the special committee, whose authority was unclear, that concerned them most. They feared that the committee might attempt to exercise operational control over U.S. forces in Korea. The Defense Department wanted assurances that command decisions would be made in Washington and not at UN headquarters in New York. In addition, Johnson, knowing of MacArthur's propensity to expand the authority granted him, wanted to make sure the general would be under U.S. and not UN jurisdiction. Johnson forwarded changes in the resolution strengthening U.S. control over military operations to Acheson on July 6; the president and the UN Security Council approved the changes on July 7.[9] Two days later, the JCS, with Johnson's pro forma concurrence, recommended General MacArthur as the commander of all UN forces in Korea and President Truman formally made the appointment.[10]

The language of the UN resolution and statements by the UN secretary-general provided sufficient assurances that control of events in Korea ultimately would reside in the White House. Nevertheless, the administration went to great pains to maintain the façade that the Korean operations were an

ongoing UN venture. In informing MacArthur of his command responsibilities, Department of Army officials emphasized that his every action should
make clear that he was acting in support of the UN Security Council, not the
United States, and that his command was to fly the blue-and-white UN flag.[11]

On July 25, just two weeks after President Rhee transferred control of the
ROK forces to MacArthur, the UN special committee was formally established,
and from that time on, General MacArthur submitted a report once every two
weeks to the JCS, who in turn forwarded it through Secretary Johnson to the
UN Security Council and its special committee. Information from the council
to the general traveled the reverse route, giving Johnson and the JCS the opportunity to control the flow of information in that direction. Thus, in reality the
U.S. policymakers called all the shots in Korea and merely informed the United
Nations through the Security Council of the actions it had taken.[12]

Technically, the UN made President Truman responsible for carrying out its
call for help to halt North Korean aggression. At the same time, Truman made
sure he maintained complete control of the situation by making all major decisions and personally approving "all strategic plans dealing with the fighting."[13]
This meant that during the Korean War, Secretary Johnson and the JCS found
themselves involved in two basic activities—providing "advice to the commander in chief" and "implement[ing] his directives."[14] While the president
relied on his military advisors, he made it clear from the beginning that he and
not the Pentagon would be running the war.

Before the Korean conflict, Johnson generally met with the president twice a
week (a regularly scheduled private meeting of between thirty and forty-five
minutes and the weekly cabinet meeting), but after the conflict began he met
with Truman nearly every day and sometimes twice a day. Unfortunately, no
written records of the private sessions were made. Johnson frequently brought
General Bradley or General Burns with him to the White House. In addition to
the face-to-face visits, Johnson usually telephoned Truman once or twice a day.[15]
The president was receiving a great deal of counsel and advice from Johnson,
whether he wanted it or not.

Johnson went to the White House primarily as a messenger who would pack-
age and then convey the views of the JCS. But this role cloaked him with considerable power; he "could alter or short-stop communication from the Joint
Chiefs of Staff to the president and the National Security Council—and could
communicate his own views."[16]

Johnson was not a profound military thinker, and it is fortunate that he knew
it. On military matters related to the war, he tended to defer to JCS views; however, he often weighed in on the political implications of Defense Department
decisions. Although the JCS members may have been concerned about the secretary's sensitivity to political concerns, they had no doubt that he could present
their views forcefully to the president. They were especially impressed with his

ability to listen to and understand their positions, frequently on extremely complex matters, and then masterfully articulate those views to the president a short time later—his legal training of reading a complicated brief and then presenting the key points to a court served him well.[17]

Building a Coalition

Once Johnson and the Joint Chiefs had helped develop the machinery for a unified UN command and a way to get their views before the president in a timely fashion, they turned to the much more difficult task of establishing a UN fighting force. From the time the first UN resolution on Korea was passed on June 25, it was apparent that while the United States would take the lead militarily in Korea, several other nations, either as a show of support for the UN or as a goodwill gesture toward their ally the United States, would be sending military forces into the fray.[18]

The difficulties of welding a disparate array of military units from around the world into an efficient fighting force posed both political and military problems. If the Korean "police action" was to truly be a UN effort, there was a definite need for a broad coalition of nations to contribute support troops and fighting forces. It was important for political reasons that offers of military assistance from member nations be accepted; however, if the aid offered did nothing to enhance the military effort or perhaps even hindered it, there would be every reason to refuse it.[19]

From the beginning, Truman clearly wanted "to see as many of the members of the United Nations as possible" take part in the Korean action.[20] Acheson, the State Department, and the civilian secretaries of the three branches of the armed forces strongly agreed with this view of widespread participation. The JCS, however, did not wholeheartedly endorse this view because they were interested in receiving only assistance that would be of true military value.[21] Secretary Johnson, fully cognizant of the validity of both viewpoints, tended to pursue a middle course.

Aside from Chiang's offer to furnish 33,000 Nationalist troops (which was politely rejected), the first outside offer of assistance came on June 28, when Prime Minister Clement Attlee told the president informally that the British wanted to make naval forces in the Pacific available to the UN. The president told Johnson to accept the British offer the moment it was formally made. Johnson, however, expressed concern about the advisability of placing British ships under UN command because of differences in communication signals and "other difficulties" that had emerged during World War II. The president ended the discussion rather abruptly by telling Johnson, "We do want them now!"[22]

The following day the matter of outside assistance came up again, this time at an NSC meeting, when the State Department revealed that Australia, New

Zealand, and Canada had made offers of naval vessels to support the Security Council resolutions. Acheson announced that the Australian offer had been accepted, a revelation that must have angered Johnson since the Defense Department had not been consulted, and he asked Johnson to have the JCS evaluate the other two offers and make a recommendation.

In formally asking the Joint Chiefs to evaluate the two offers and formulate a recommendation, Johnson clearly signaled that every offer of outside assistance need not be accepted. In fact, he told the Joint Chiefs that while "considerations of national policy make it important that such offers be accepted to the maximum extent practicable from the military point of view," they were to keep in mind that a "minimum standard of military effectiveness [existed] that, if not met, might make it necessary to refuse some proffered forces, in spite of their political desirability." He assigned the Joint Chiefs the responsibility for determining what those standards would be and applying them. In the case of both New Zealand and Canada, the Joint Chiefs agreed that the offers should be accepted, and Johnson passed on their recommendations to Acheson.

Two days later, on July 6, the Netherlands offered a destroyer and the Defense and State Departments immediately agreed to accept it. When the UN unified command was established several weeks later, control of all the volunteered naval vessels was transferred to the command.[23]

After the initial offers of aid from Britain, New Zealand, Canada, the Netherlands, and the Chinese Nationalists, no other offers were forthcoming, and it became evident that other UN nations were not anxious to follow the path of armed resistance that the Security Council had committed them to. Thus, if the United States wanted other nations to share in the fight to defend South Korea, it would have to actively organize a coalition. Johnson and Secretary of the Army Pace had first discussed the question of when the United States should actively solicit support from other nations on June 30. As a result of that meeting, Johnson asked both Pace and the JCS to prepare a formal response to the question "Should the U.S. act further to stimulate military contributions from other members of the U.N.?"[24]

While the JCS set about studying the issue, Secretary Pace pursued the matter with the secretaries of the navy and the air force, and on July 7 they sent a message to Johnson lamenting the lack of response from UN members to the Korean operation. The service secretaries requested that efforts be stepped up to gain commitment of ground troops for "symbolic" if not military value. Johnson and General Bradley agreed with the recommendation and forwarded it to the president on July 7. When the chief executive failed to respond in the week that followed, the secretaries sent another memorandum to Johnson on July 13 expressing considerable irritation over the heavy commitment the United States was making while most other UN members were planning to do little if anything. They called for "the maximum amount of pressure" on member nations to provide ground troops.

The next day, even before Johnson could pursue the issue of support with the president, he received a call from Acheson asking if aid was desired from Pakistan, the Philippines, Italy, Turkey, and Saudi Arabia and if additional aid was desired from England and Australia. Immediately, Johnson asked the JCS to quickly assess the desirability of such aid. But before the new offers could be studied, Johnson learned that the president and Secretary Acheson had already begun a concerted effort to secure widespread military support for the Korean venture.[25] In fact, their efforts began on July 13, when, at state department insistence, UN Secretary-General Lie publicly called on the fifty-three nations that had voted for the June 27 resolution to provide "additional effective assistance," especially ground troops.[26]

The fact that the UN appeal had not been discussed with Johnson and the JCS was a major irritant because they were not being consulted about matters that had great impact upon their responsibilities for conducting military operations. They were especially concerned with President Truman's view, as well as that of a growing number of administration officials and a growing segment of the public, that as many members of the UN as possible should contribute forces. Politically such a move could be understood, but militarily it presented major problems because of the danger that MacArthur's unified command "might be overwhelmed by a flood of military units too small to be effective."[27]

While Johnson and the JCS clearly desired additional military assistance, they wanted assistance of sufficient magnitude and quality to make it an asset rather than a liability. After consulting with MacArthur, they concluded that the minimum effective unit size would be one battalion (approximately 1,000 men). Using that template, the JCS advised Johnson on July 14 to advocate acceptance of aid from Pakistan and additional aid from Britain and Australia while urging rejection of offers from the Philippines, Italy, Turkey, and Saudi Arabia. Johnson championed the JCS recommendation, which Truman and Acheson finally agreed to.[28]

The potential for a flood of offers of assistance in response to Secretary-General Lie's appeal for help caused anxiety among the JCS. They asked for, and on July 21 received, a categorical assurance from Johnson that they would be consulted in every case where a nation made an offer of military assistance. At the same time, he asked the JCS to draw up specific guidelines about what constituted "useful assistance" and to devise procedures by which the offers of assistance would be handled. In late July the Joint Chiefs of Staff submitted guidelines to Johnson that expressed a preference for units of at least 1,000 men, but in response to Johnson's request to consider the advisability of accepting token forces for political reasons, they agreed to accept units as small as 200 men.

By late July, the defense and state departments had hammered out comprehensive guidelines for handling offers of assistance, but frictions persisted.[29] In his dealings with Acheson and the State Department over the assistance issue, Johnson was often inconsistent—a fact which antagonized the secretary of state. Johnson would criticize the State Department for not doing enough to enlist support and in the same breath he would chastise it for its willingness to accept any and all offers of assistance.[30] The chaotic situation was made even worse by the fact that Johnson, Steve Early, and General Burns began an active and direct effort in late July to solicit military assistance from foreign governments, a practice that further upset Acheson because he felt that that function was in his realm of responsibility.[31]

From late July through mid-September the JCS used the approved guidelines to evaluate more than two dozen offers of troop commitments and a slightly greater number of other forms of assistance. In practice, the state viewpoint became the standard, since in every case the Defense Department ultimately concurred and the offers were accepted. In only one instance did the JCS recommend rejection of an offer—involving a Belgian C-54 aircraft—and in that instance Johnson, citing political considerations, overrode their recommendation and the plane and its crew were accepted.[32]

Except for two minor offers of assistance which came after Johnson left office in September, all outside offers of military assistance during the Korean war were worked out and made operational while he was secretary of defense. In all, a coalition of fifteen nations in addition to the United States and South Korea made military commitments to the UN effort.[33] But while that number may seem large, those fifteen nations constituted only 9 percent of the total UN fighting forces. Of the remaining troops, 43 percent were South Koreans while 48 percent were from the United States. Thus, while the conflict was technically a UN action, it was in reality a U.S. effort.[34]

Runaway Train

Within a few weeks after President Truman and his advisors made the June 30 commitment of two divisions of ground troops to South Korea, it became apparent that U.S. involvement would be much greater than originally expected.[35] The demands placed on the defense establishment were staggering.

On June 29 MacArthur had said, "Give me two American divisions and I can hold Korea,"[36] but it quickly became evident that he had underestimated the strength of the North Koreans. Just three days later, he requested the "immediate dispatch of one Marine RCT [Regimental Combat Team] with comparable Marine air unit."[37] At the same time, he endorsed a request from the commander of the Far East Air Force, General George Stratemeyer, for an additional 700 aircraft to bring the units to war strength.

On July 3, the JCS recommended to Johnson that the Marine RCT and air unit be sent to Korea along with 200 aircraft—all that could be spared. That afternoon, Johnson and Bradley went to the White House, where they had little difficulty in gaining the president's approval. They felt that these additional forces would satisfy MacArthur for the time being. But they were wrong.[38]

On the morning of July 5, Johnson returned from an Independence Day trip home to find that MacArthur was requesting another infantry division, an engineer brigade, and a regiment of the 82nd Airborne Division. This latest request was especially alarming to Johnson and the JCS because, if honored, it would seriously weaken the general reserve. At that time there were only ten divisions in the entire army—four in Japan, one in Germany, and five in the United States. The latter five divisions and their support personnel made up the 140,000-man general reserve—the force needed to meet any other worldwide emergency that should arise.[39]

Both state and defense department officials were convinced that the Soviets might well take advantage of the Korean conflict to either start a general war or push for a military advantage in any one of a number of strategic spots, such as West Germany, Iran, Turkey, Greece, India, or Japan. The need to meet any challenge in those areas and to be prepared for general hostilities caused Johnson and his advisors to be protective of the general reserve. They wanted to meet the challenge in Korea, but not to the extent that it would deny them the ability to adequately respond to a need at a more crucial spot.[40]

Because of the impact that MacArthur's July 5 request would have on the general reserve, Johnson and the JCS asked him to provide a more thorough assessment of his needs. Specifically, they asked the general to provide an estimate of the force needed to drive the North Koreans north of the 38th parallel. MacArthur immediately replied that it would require "not less than 4 to 4½ full infantry divisions" plus supporting airborne, artillery, and service groups. Without such a 30,000 man force, he concluded, success would be "extremely doubtful."

The JCS, alarmed by the continuing rapid advances of the North Koreans toward Pusan and not wanting to put a field commander in the position of being asked to do a job but not be given the resources to succeed, agreed that they should fulfill MacArthur's latest request. But since his request would involve tapping a division of the general reserve, the JCS decided that Johnson should go to the White House to secure the president's approval. On July 7, Truman granted his approval and the orders were issued. MacArthur now had at his disposal four and a half divisions—enough to get the job done, supposedly.[41]

Two days later, MacArthur jolted the Pentagon when he sent an urgent message touting the high quality of the North Korean troops and concluding that the situation was "critical." This time he strongly urged that "in addition to those forces already requisitioned, an army of at least four divisions, with all its component services, be dispatched to this area without delay."[42] This request, which called for a doubling of his estimate just two days before, shocked

Johnson and the Joint Chiefs because the Korean commitment was beginning to appear like a runaway train.

What had started out eleven days before as a request for two divisions now stood at eight. This forced the Defense Department to squarely face the question of how much of a military commitment the United States should and could make in Korea and still be prepared to meet its other obligations and possible new challenges. While Johnson, the JCS, and the president pondered those larger questions, they were being forced to deal with immediate manpower needs.[43]

Buildup Begins

The Joint Chiefs' first request for additional personnel came on July 6, when they asked Johnson to authorize an immediate 108,500-person increase in total military strength (army 50,000, navy 33,000, air force 25,500) to meet the serious personnel shortages that existed in many units. Since the president had just removed the budgetary limits which had restricted the size of the military, the secretary of defense was free to act on the manpower request, and he approved it the day it was made.

One week later, on July 13, the JCS sent Johnson another request for increased personnel—this time for an additional 115,000, the bulk of which was for the army. This request would bring to full strength those units headed for Korea and fill the openings in general reserve units. They also noted that if MacArthur's latest request for four more divisions was approved, they would be back with still another request. Johnson, spurred on by his confidence in MacArthur and buoyed by an aura of support from Congress and the public for the Korean venture, approved the request.[44]

How long such piecemeal approaches could be used to meet the nation's military personnel needs was unclear, but it was obvious that guidance was needed from the White House. At the July 14 cabinet meeting, President Truman focused all attention on the impact and possible repercussions of the Korean conflict. At this session, state and defense department officials were at odds about the likely locations of possible Soviet aggression but were in "unanimous agreement . . . that the present world situation is one of extreme danger . . . which . . . could present the United States with new outbreaks of aggression possibly up to and including general hostilities." They also agreed that if there was a need to meet force with force in other parts of the world, particularly a significant act of aggression by the USSR, the United States did not have "the capabilities to face the threat."

In light of these perceived threats to the nation's security, the president and the Cabinet concluded that bold and forceful actions must be taken to meet the nation's worldwide diplomatic and military obligations.[45] This decision marked the

Table 1. Increases in U.S. Military Personnel, June and July 1950

	Actual Strength	Authorized Strength	Authorization	Authorization	Proposal
	June 25, 1950	June 1950	July 6	July 13	July 18
Army	592,000	630,000	680,000	730,500	834,000
Navy	381,000	391,000	424,000	443,000	579,000
Marines	75,000	76,000	75,000	75,000	138,000
Air Force	412,000	416,000	441,500	467,000	569,000
TOTAL	1,460,000	1,513,000	1,620,500	1,715,500	2,120,000

Sources: Schnabel, *United States Army in the Korean War,* 43, 118–120; Condit, *History of the Office of the Secretary of Defense,* vol. II, *The Test of War,* 59–62; Bernardo and Bacon, *American Military Policy,* 485–486; *Facts on File Yearbook,* vol. X (1950), 221, 229, 235–236, 243–244.

beginning of the implementation of NSC 68, which had been developed that spring and reviewed but not officially approved by the president. Following the cabinet meeting the president asked the State and Defense Departments to prepare specific recommendations for his consideration on July 18 regarding the huge troop buildups contemplated by NSC 68.[46]

During the next few days, Johnson met frequently with his military advisors as they hammered out their requests for the military buildup. The plan the secretary finally agreed to submit for approval included a substantial increase in military personnel and equipment for all the services. The magnitude of the personnel increases can be seen in table 1. In addition to the proposed increase of more than 400,000 above the July 13 revised figure and 600,000 above the prewar authorization to a total of 2.12 million, there were also requests for nearly 240 additional naval vessels and 3,000 more aircraft. The president accepted these recommendations in principle in a July 18 meeting with Johnson and Acheson. He also approved a request to begin calling up the reserves.[47]

The following day, July 19, in a nationwide radio-television speech and an address to Congress, President Truman presented the administration's position on Korea, explaining what had to be done, why it had to be done, and what would be necessary to do it. Citing the need for U.S. security and the peace of the world, he announced a 600,000-person increase in the armed forces. That increase, he maintained, was essential if the United States was to successfully meet aggression in Korea, provide adequate defense for Western Europe, and protect against any new emergency. The details of the $10 billion program would be forthcoming in five days.

The president also stated that he had given Secretary Johnson authority to exceed budgeted strengths to increase personnel, call up as many National

Guard and reserve units as necessary, and ask the Selective Service to provide the needed personnel. Finally, he announced his intention to ask Congress to remove the statutory limit of 2,005,882 on personnel in the armed forces.[48]

The speech to the nation was regarded as a success by the press and the American public. However, to Truman and his aides, its delivery provided heart-stopping drama. An important section of the speech was to include supportive comments from General MacArthur. Even though MacArthur was given ample time to furnish his comments, they did not arrive until a few minutes before Truman was scheduled to speak to the nation. Later, MacArthur cabled the president and said the speech was a "great state paper, the turning point of this era's struggle for civilization."[49]

In the days and weeks that followed the president's address, Louis A. Johnson became a name that was recognized and feared by thousands of Americans who had never previously heard of the defense chief. Since the president delegated to Johnson the authority to call up the National Guard and activate reserve units, all of these orders came out under Johnson's name, and he was the target of an outpouring of criticism from those called up and their families.[50]

In the process of calling up troops, it was the responsibility of the JCS to select and recommend specific reserve and National Guard units to be activated. Sometimes, to achieve a broader geographic spread and minimize "political repercussions," the recommendations would be modified by the secretary of the army, who no doubt was guided by the more politically astute secretary of defense.[51] The pace of recalls was hectic as 404 Organized Reserve units and 205 National Guard units with a strength of 104,000 were called to active duty between July 20 and August 28. During the same period, the navy and marines recalled 103,000 and the air force recalled 50,000, primarily as individuals rather than units.[52]

Announcements of Selective Service quotas generally came from its director, General Lewis B. Hersey, but there too the criticism was directed at the "Pentagon call" for personnel, and Johnson was the man in charge. Consequently, when a 20,000-person call-up for August was followed by a quota of 50,000 for both September and October, the wrath of the nation's young men and their families was rekindled, and the fire was aimed at Johnson.[53]

While these announcements obviously upset the lives of those directly affected, Johnson and the Truman administration received general public support for the most part, because at that time most Americans were convinced that the United States was doing the right thing in stopping the expansion of communism into South Korea.[54] In fact, it was probably Johnson's awareness of broad public support that caused him to come out publicly in early August in favor of universal military training. In taking this stand for every able-bodied 18-year-old male, he was not really risking much because he was giving voice to an overwhelming national sentiment.[55]

In mid-August, following congressional lifting of the statutory limits on the strength of the armed forces, Johnson approved still another expansion of the army by 227,000, while upping air force manpower by an additional 10,000 and the navy by 9,000.[56] These approvals were necessitated by an August 10 decision, recommended by Johnson and approved by Truman, to send two more infantry divisions to MacArthur. This decision had not been an easy one because it meant that for the next few months the United States would have virtually no general reserve to use for another trouble spot, but MacArthur's urgent plea was so convincing that the Washington decision makers agreed that they should take the gamble.[57] These mid-August decisions marked the last increment of reinforcements to be sent to Korea in 1950 and Secretary Johnson, who believed the war would end in a U.S. victory in six to eight months, felt that no additional troops would be needed to bring the war to a successful conclusion.[58]

Johnson was optimistic as the end of August approached. He did not anticipate that in a matter of weeks the war would enter a whole new phase with the entrance of Chinese Communist troops into the conflict, nor did he realize that his days as secretary of defense were numbered.

Along with the escalating military commitments of July and August came a need for additional funding. Events in Korea obviously had caused the president and secretary of defense to abandon their goals of defense austerity. Truman, who in May had insisted on adherence to a $13.5 billion defense ceiling, found himself asking Congress on July 19 for $10.5 billion in supplementary defense funds. That was followed on August 4 by a request for another $1.6 billion for defense and $4 billion more for military assistance. By year's end, the president had sought and received another $16.8 billion in defense funds, bringing the appropriations for the year to almost $47 billion, or 250 percent more than originally requested.[59]

Throughout July and August, Johnson was heavily involved in defense appropriation issues, formulating requests to Congress and appearing before various congressional committees to explain and justify the administration's requests. The fiscal metamorphosis that he underwent that summer of 1950 was incredible. In early June he was insisting both publicly and privately that the 1951 defense budget would be the same as last year ($13.5 billion) or possibly even lower. By late July, when explaining to legislators the need for the president's $10.5 billion supplementary request, he stated: "In the light of the actual fighting that is now in progress, we have reached the point where military considerations clearly outweigh the fiscal considerations."[60]

In Johnson's numerous appearances before House and Senate committees, he vigorously defended the administration's requests for supplemental defense funds, but he really did not need to do so because Congress was more than willing to go along. With overwhelming public support, Congress "turned for counsel to the nation's military experts who . . . spoke, albeit temporarily, with a united voice." Without hesitation, the legislators approved the administration's request for a massive buildup of military strength and the billions to pay for it.[61]

It was ironic that in the summer of 1950 President Truman and Secretary Johnson, ex-army officers who had previously pinched every defense dollar, were now spending money like two drunken sailors.

MacArthur's Masterstroke

The major reason that the president, the secretary of defense, and the JCS were so willing to propose more men and money for the war in Korea in July and August was that the conflict was not going well for the United States. The enemy was running rampant and needed to be stopped. Throughout July and early August, the North Korean Army advanced steadily southward, and for a time it appeared as if the ROK Army and American forces might literally be driven into the sea. On July 27, MacArthur flew to Eighth Army headquarters to tell General Walton Walker, commander of all U.S. ground forces in Korea, that there would be no more retreating. Two days later Walker issued what the press called his "stand or die" orders. What he actually said to his subordinates was even more dramatic: "There will be no Dunkirk, there will be no Bataan, a retreat to Pusan would be one of the greatest butcheries in history. We must fight to the end."[62]

By late August, General Walker and the UN forces finally succeeded in stabilizing the situation by establishing an effective defensive perimeter around the southern port city of Pusan. U.S. troops were suffering serious setbacks, brought on largely by shortages of men and equipment, and Pentagon officials were eager to give the troops in the field anything they needed.

But the stabilization achieved by late August was not enough for MacArthur. What he desperately wanted was a masterstroke that could turn the tide of the war, and he had been planning that move for some time. From the day in late June when he stood on a hill outside of Seoul and watched the North Koreans roll relentlessly southward, the general, recalling the success of his amphibious landings during World War II, envisioned a bold and extremely risky surprise landing at Inchon on the Korean west coast near the 38th parallel which would cut off the North Korean forces in the south. He had originally hoped to undertake the operation in late July, but inadequate forces made postponement necessary.[63]

When Generals Collins and Vandenburg visited MacArthur in Japan in mid-July, he told them of the planned invasion at Inchon. Collins was alarmed because he believed that the port's 30-foot tides, narrow channel, extensive mudflats, and high sea walls made the success of such an attack highly doubtful. When Collins returned to Washington, he informed Johnson of MacArthur's plan and expressed serious reservations.[64] Reportedly, Johnson differed with his army chief of staff and voiced wholehearted support for the planned invasion.

According to the official history of the war, from that time on it seemed that "in Secretary of Defense Johnson, MacArthur had in Washington a powerful ally during the Inchon landing controversy, for Johnson supported the Far East Commander."[65]

Collins and the other Joint Chiefs remained skeptical, however, and when MacArthur prepared to proceed with his daring plan the JCS decided that Collins and Admiral Sherman should visit Tokyo again and find out exactly what he had in mind.[66] Before they left, Averell Harriman returned from a trip to the Far East enthused about the pending operation. In a meeting with the president on August 9, Harriman persuaded Truman that MacArthur's plan to land at Inchon would win the war. The president, unable to contain his excitement, said to Harriman, "You better get over to the Pentagon as fast as you can and talk to Johnson and Bradley." Thus, while indicating that the decision to proceed was a Pentagon matter, Truman urged Harriman to tell Johnson and Bradley that he was very supportive.[67]

If Johnson, being the politician he was, had not been completely behind the invasion before, he certainly was now. But the Joint Chiefs were still skeptical and, according to Johnson, Collins's August 19 trip to Tokyo was for the purpose of persuading MacArthur to drop the Inchon site and invade farther south.[68] But the visit had no effect on MacArthur, who stuck to his plan, assuring his visitors that "Inchon will not fail. Inchon will succeed. And it will save 100,000 lives."[69]

Despite their skepticism, Collins and the other Joint Chiefs did not want to overrule what they clearly considered to be a decision for the theater commander. In late August they gave a qualified go-ahead but encouraged consideration of a different landing site. On September 1, the North Koreans launched a major offensive against the Pusan perimeter, endangering that last stronghold. With the outcome of that battle unclear, the JCS were concerned because all reserves for Korea were committed to the Inchon attack, and they asked MacArthur for an updated estimate of the situation. When they heard nothing, they sent a September 7 message warning of the disastrous consequences if the venture failed. MacArthur immediately replied with his customary confidence, and they decided to drop their opposition.

Although the president's approval was not required, Johnson and the JCS decided to inform Truman of their decision to support MacArthur's invasion plan. On September 8, Johnson and General Bradley went to the White House to inform the president. Truman welcomed the decision, and Johnson was pleased to be a key player in what turned out to be an extremely important and successful military decision. The secretary returned to his office and authorized the Joint Chiefs to send the following message to MacArthur: "We approve your plan and the president has been so informed."[70]

Just one week later, on September 15, the Inchon invasion went off without a hitch. In fact, it was a spectacular success which elevated MacArthur to near-hero status. The 70,000-man invasion force quickly recaptured Seoul and cut off the North Korean army's supply lines. As a result, the enemy forces broke and began a hasty retreat north toward the 38th parallel. On the 16th, UN forces began to attack out of the Pusan perimeter and succeeded in driving back the enemy. Before long, the northward advance by UN forces turned into a whole-sale rout of the North Korean invaders.[71]

Decision to Go North

The war that had initially gone so poorly for the United States and UN forces turned around completely in September. By the end of the month, many believed that the war would be over by Christmas. But how and when the war would end was dependent on whether UN forces would be permitted to cross the 38th parallel in order to destroy the North Korean Army.[72]

When the war was less than three weeks old, the president directed Johnson and Acheson to make recommendations about whether MacArthur should be allowed to cross the 38th parallel. In the disastrous setbacks of July and early August, that question seemed rather academic, and defense and state officials agreed that it was premature to answer the question, although they felt that the UN resolution of July 7 calling for a restoration of "peace and security in the area" was sufficient legal justification to do so.[73]

Within the State Department a schism developed between those favoring and those opposing the crossing of the 38th parallel. Those opposed included Paul Nitze, George Kennan, and Chip Bohlen, who, along with the CIA, believed that if UN forces crossed into the north, the Chinese and possibly the Soviets might join the conflict and trigger a world war.[74]

But in the Defense Department there was complete unity. The JCS and MacArthur believed that for tactical reasons the enemy should be pursued across the 38th parallel and destroyed. Johnson advocated that position to the NSC, and the president approved the Pentagon recommendation. It was agreed, however, that "no ground operations were to take place north of the 38th parallel in the event of Soviet or Chinese Communist entry" and that Mac-Arthur was not to cross the parallel until Truman gave his approval. These directives, incorporated in a document known as NSC 81/1, were approved on September 11.[75] U.S. policy had profoundly shifted—from the defense of South Korea to military support for the unification of Korea.

The following day, for reasons made clear in the next chapter, Johnson submitted his resignation at the president's request. Three days later, the Inchon invasion took place and in the astonishingly swift success that followed, American optimism about the war soared and the American defense establishment was soon being praised for the job it had done.

Unfortunately, Johnson was not able to bask in the glory of success and adulation that came in the aftermath of Inchon. Johnson later recalled that if he had been permitted to stay on a little longer he could have survived in his post. "I resigned 2 days before Inchon. That hurt me because I had been carrying along with General MacArthur the responsibility for Inchon. . . . I backed MacArthur, and the President, as always, had backed me on it. . . . The date had been fixed quite some time before, so that was distressing because I felt that Inchon would have closed up much of the criticism."[76] But that was not to be; the president had come to the conclusion that it was time for his secretary of defense to leave.

CHAPTER EIGHTEEN

Means of Descent

L OUIS JOHNSON'S FALL from grace with Harry Truman had nothing to do with his principal responsibility of running the Pentagon. Indeed, as the Korean crisis deepened in the summer of 1950, Johnson, ever the great organizer, did a superb job of orchestrating the buildup and seeing that General MacArthur got everything he needed to win the war.

Johnson's descent instead had everything to do with his growing and deeply held conviction that the president was being ill served by his secretary of state, a conviction that was reinforced by Johnson's personal aversion to Acheson and fueled by his ambition to become president. Johnson was convinced that Acheson's opposition to military assistance to Formosa and declaration that Korea was outside the U.S. defensive perimeter had encouraged "world communism" to advance aggressively into the free world, thereby threatening the security of the United States.

In addition to his profound disagreement with Acheson's foreign policy, Johnson had come to dislike the man intensely and resented the fact that Acheson had such a strong influence over Truman. On his part, Acheson provided Johnson with ample justification for his antipathy. From the beginning of their relationship, Acheson was condescending and patronizing in his dealings with Johnson. As Marx Leva recalled, "You really could never talk with Dean Acheson for long without getting a put-down feeling."[1] Moreover, Acheson let it be known in body language and witty asides that he considered Johnson to be far beneath him intellectually and socially. To his friends and colleagues in the State Department, Acheson confided that he thought that Johnson was "nuttier than a fruitcake."[2] Acheson had no respect for Johnson and did little to hide that fact.

Acheson brought out the very worst in Johnson. The defense chief already had a tendency to blow up when things did not go his way, and in his confrontations with Acheson he had great difficulty controlling his hostile outbursts. By contrast, Acheson possessed remarkable self-control. As the hostility between the two headstrong and ambitious men escalated, they began to undercut one another. Acheson, far more subtle and indirect than Johnson, preferred to let his aides Carlisle Humelsine and Lucius Battle attempt to weaken the secretary of defense by spreading stories about Johnson's erratic behavior and mental health.[3]

Johnson's efforts to undermine Acheson were much more direct. During the summer of 1950, Johnson was privately using every opportunity he could to bad-mouth Acheson, sometimes to officials he barely knew.[4] He also began to feed the press, especially Drew Pearson, information calculated to put the secretary of state in a bad light.[5]

Consorting with the Enemy

If Johnson had confined his sniping at Acheson to staff members, the press, or even to virtual strangers, Truman might have overlooked his attempts to weaken Acheson. But when he began to recklessly feed the same sort of information to prominent Republican critics of the president, he angered Truman, a man who had always placed a high value on loyalty and teamwork.

The most flagrant and damaging instance of Johnson consorting with the enemy—the incident which perhaps more than all the others caused his downfall—occurred on Thursday, June 29, 1950. That morning, Averell Harriman, who had been back in the United States for only a few days, stopped by Johnson's office for a private chat. Johnson, recalling Harriman's visit to his office at Steptoe & Johnson the morning after the 1948 election, knew that Harriman yearned to be secretary of state. What he didn't know was that only a few days before, when Harriman was appointed Truman's national security advisor, the president had given him his first assignment. "Help Dean," said Truman. "He's in trouble."[6]

As Johnson and Harriman were getting reacquainted in Johnson's office, Johnson accepted a telephone call from Senator Robert Taft, one of the president's most outspoken critics, who had delivered a blistering speech on the Senate floor the day before lambasting the president for not seeking congressional approval for his actions in Korea and calling for Acheson's resignation. While Harriman sat in stunned disbelief, Johnson praised Taft's speech, especially the part demanding Acheson's resignation, exclaiming, "That was something that needed to be said." Stupefied by what he had heard, Harriman was even more shocked when Johnson, after hanging up, told him that if they "could get Acheson out" he would personally "see that Harriman was made Secretary of State."[7]

Johnson had made a monumental misjudgment. Because he had gone to bat for Harriman in late 1948, trying to get him appointed secretary of state over

Acheson, Johnson believed that Harriman was his friend and supporter. More-over, he obviously thought that Harriman's ambition to be secretary of state would outweigh his loyalty to Acheson and the president. He was dead wrong. Within a few hours, Harriman was in the Oval Office indignantly recounting to the president what Johnson had said. According to Harriman, he told Tru-man, "I can't be bought that easily."[8]

Two days later, on Saturday, July 1, Harriman and Acheson drove out to Gen-eral Marshall's farm, Dodona Manor, near Leesburg, Virginia, on the site of the Civil War battle of Ball's Bluff. Marshall, the army chief of staff throughout World War II, had served as Truman's secretary of state from early 1947 through the 1948 election before resigning due to a kidney ailment. Harriman and Acheson found that the old general had recovered his health and vitality, and he willingly offered advice about how they could help the president meet the challenge in Korea. On the following Monday, Harriman suggested that Tru-man might consider replacing Johnson with Marshall and that Truman should think about going out to Leesburg to see the general.[9]

In light of Harriman's eyewitness account of Johnson's conversation with Senator Taft, it is not surprising that when the president heard reports later that summer that Johnson had leaked information critical of Acheson to the press and members of Congress, he found them plausible. In addition, the Harriman report fueled suspicions about Johnson's loyalty to the administration.

As the summer of 1950 wore on, Truman heard more and more stories about Johnson's questionable actions. To his press secretary, Charlie Ross, the presi-dent said that he had heard that Johnson had met with some West Virginia Re-publicans and had told them he would be willing to run for president as a con-servative *Republican* candidate.[10] In late August, Marquis Childs's syndicated column reported that Johnson had agreed to feed damaging information about Acheson to Republicans who agreed to spare Johnson from their attacks in order to preserve his political prospects.[11] Truman also told close aides that he had firsthand knowledge that Johnson met with Republican senators who were critics of his administration and had "made terrible statements" about the ad-ministration and some of its leaders.[12]

When Republican congressional leaders and reporters and pundits stepped up their attacks on Truman and Acheson in July and August, the president had good reason to suspect that much of the information they were being fed was coming from Johnson.[13] As the president became more irritated, he began to think seriously about getting rid of Johnson.

Siding with Chiang and MacArthur

Johnson's descent was also hastened because he continued to push for military aid to Chiang's Nationalist government and he was regarded as a supporter of

MacArthur's attempts to undermine the administration's policy with respect to Formosa. Although the administration had tilted toward Chiang during the last week in June when it ordered the Seventh Fleet to defend Formosa, Johnson believed that the president had not gone far enough. To his dismay, Truman announced to Congress and the nation on July 19 that the United States would remain militarily neutral regarding Formosa.[14] Like MacArthur, Johnson felt strongly that this policy should be changed and he set out to change it.

On July 27, the Joint Chiefs, who had been asked by the NSC to reassess U.S. policy toward Formosa in light of events in Korea, recommended to the council that Chiang's armed forces on Formosa be strengthened to deter a Communist attack from the mainland. If accepted, the recommendation would mean a further shift in U.S. policy to permit military aid to the Nationalist government. The Joint Chiefs concluded their report by recommending that General MacArthur undertake a survey of Formosa's defenses and determine what was needed.[15] Johnson was supportive of the JCS recommendation because he was worried about recent intelligence reports that indicated a major buildup of Communist forces on the Chinese mainland adjacent to Formosa.[16] At the NSC meeting, Johnson vigorously pushed the proposal and succeeded in winning the president's acceptance of the idea of a military mission, at least in principle. The president also indicated a willingness to authorize reconnaissance flights along the Chinese coast and seemed inclined toward sending substantial military aid to Chiang.[17]

Following the NSC meeting, the Pentagon informed MacArthur that the president had given tentative approval to the survey mission but advised him to delay his visit to Formosa until final details were worked out with the State Department—a process expected to take about one week.[18] MacArthur chose not to wait. On July 31, he surprised everyone by flying to Formosa to personally meet with Chiang; and he aggravated the situation by refusing to take Ambassador Sebald with him. He justified this obvious affront to the State Department by claiming that only military matters were to be discussed.[19]

The visit to Formosa caused great consternation. The legendary general was welcomed as a conquering hero—the proconsul of Japan and the defender of the free world against communism. After being photographed kissing Madame Chiang's hand, MacArthur issued a statement praising the determination of Chiang to resist Communist domination and referring to Chiang as his "old comrade in arms," although he had never met him. Two days of secret talks followed, after which Chiang publicly lauded the general's understanding of the threat to Formosa and claimed that their discussions had laid the basis for "Sino-American military cooperation."[20] The press immediately jumped on such statements and concluded that they were indications that the United States was headed toward major support of the Nationalist regime.[21]

These reports were upsetting not only to Acheson and his advisors but to the president as well. According to Truman, the unfortunate aspect of the visit and the speculation it caused was "the implication . . . that MacArthur rejected my policy of neutralizing Formosa and that he favored a more aggressive method."[22] MacArthur fomented even more hostility by failing to send a report of his visit to Washington until one week after his return and then reporting only to the Defense Department.

Attempts to persuade General MacArthur to discuss his visit with state department officials were met by disdainful silence. Relations between MacArthur, the president, and the State Department were deteriorating rapidly.[23] At the same time, Johnson's relationship with MacArthur could not have been better.

There is no evidence that Johnson actively encouraged MacArthur to make his surprise trip to Formosa. However, the growing friction over Formosa policy between MacArthur, on one hand, and Truman and Acheson, on the other, tended diminish Johnson's standing with Truman and Acheson because his views on the subject were virtually identical with those of MacArthur, the China Lobby, and many leading Republicans.[24] While neither Truman nor Acheson wanted a yes-man in the Defense Department, they were annoyed by Johnson's tendency to oppose settled administration positions and to advocate policies supported by the political opposition and General MacArthur.[25]

Another action that generated considerable heat with Acheson, and no doubt provoked the president, was Johnson's advocacy of plans authorizing Chiang's forces to make preemptive strikes against the Chinese mainland. In mid-July the JCS received intelligence reports that disclosed a concentration of 200,000 Communist troops and 4,000 surface craft on the mainland adjacent to Formosa. The JCS recognized that the buildup posed a serious threat to Formosa and that the Seventh Fleet probably could not keep such an armada from landing a sufficient number of troops to take the island. In consultation with Johnson and General MacArthur, the JCS recommended on July 28 that the Nationalists be given authority to mine mainland coastal waters and attack troop concentrations that were positioned to launch amphibious operations against Formosa. According to the military advisors, these preventive attacks would be strictly defensive in nature. The following day Johnson sent a memorandum to Acheson supporting the JCS recommendation and requesting his concurrence so the proposal could be taken to the president for approval.[26]

Acheson was shocked and alarmed by the proposal and immediately fired back a reply vigorously protesting the contemplated move because he feared it could have the disastrous consequence of precipitating a war with the Chinese Communists or bringing them into the war in Korea or Indochina. He contended that even if the attacks were carried out by the Nationalists, world opinion would hold America responsible, discrediting the United States in the international community. While Acheson was agreeable to the proposed mining operations, he made it clear that "the launching of preventive bombing attacks by either the U.S. or Chinese Nationalist forces . . . would have most serious results and would be unacceptable from a foreign policy point of view."

Because of the seriousness of the JCS recommendation concerning a preventive attack on Chinese mainland troops, Acheson urged that it be discussed with the president immediately.[27] When the subject was brought up at the NSC meeting on August 3, the president listened intently to both sides and then announced that he would take the matter up with Johnson and Acheson the following morning.

At that August 4 meeting, the president, as he usually did when forced to choose between Acheson and Johnson on issues concerning Formosa and the Chinese Nationalists, sided with his secretary of state. Truman not only rejected the JCS proposal in very strong terms, he also directed Johnson to make it crystal clear to General MacArthur that he, Harry S. Truman, was in charge and that there were to be no attacks or any other action that might widen the war.[28]

While Johnson was not pleased with the president's position, he understood what the president had ordered him to do. He sent a message to MacArthur making it clear that "[n]o one other than the President as Commander-in-Chief has the authority to order or authorize preventive action against . . . the mainland." Johnson did, however, put some distance between the president and himself by closing the communiqué with the notation that "[t]his message has the approval of the President and Secretary of State."[29] The defense secretary clearly signaled the general that they, not he, were behind the order.

Within the hour MacArthur replied, in an almost apologetic tone, that he fully understood the president's policy and the limitations of his own authority and gave assurance that he would not in any way exceed the president's directives. Johnson immediately relayed the message to the White House.[30] In most instances such a reply from a military commander would have satisfied Truman, but not when it came from MacArthur. The president had long distrusted the general and wanted to make absolutely sure that MacArthur clearly understood his policy, especially with regard to the Far East. For that reason, he decided to dispatch Averell Harriman to Japan to personally explain the administration's policy.[31]

Harriman arrived in Tokyo on August 6 and spent two days with General MacArthur, his old duck-hunting companion back in the days when the general was superintendent of West Point.[32] During the visit MacArthur discussed the conduct of the war and predicted a quick victory for the UN forces in Korea but focused his attention on his responsibility for defending Formosa. The latter, he contended, was complicated by the tension that resulted from the State Department's hostility to the Nationalist regime. In words that just as easily could have come from Louis Johnson's lips, MacArthur told Harriman, "[W]e have not improved our position by kicking Chiang around." He then expressed the hope that the president would do something to improve that situation.[33]

Harriman also pressed his point, noting the unfortunate diplomatic consequences that could result from any missteps in dealing with China or Formosa.
Harriman made it clear that the president wanted MacArthur to know that "he
must not permit Chiang to be the cause of starting a war with the Chinese Communists on the mainland, the effect which might be to drag us into a world
war."[34] MacArthur assured his messenger that, "As a soldier, I will obey any orders that I receive from the President."[35]

Harriman, however, was not comforted by this assurance. As he reported to
Truman upon his return, "For reasons which are rather difficult to explain, I did
not feel that we came to a full agreement on the way we believe things should
be handled on Formosa and with the Generalissimo." In spite of such doubt,
Harriman said he felt that MacArthur had accepted Truman's position and
would "act accordingly, but without full conviction."[36] Harriman was not the
only one who was concerned about whether real communication had taken
place, for MacArthur reported that upon his guest's departure he had "a feeling
of concern and uneasiness that the situation in the Far East was little understood and mistakenly downgraded in high circles in Washington."[37]

Even though the president said at his August 10 press conference that he and
MacArthur were "in perfect agreement" on policy regarding Formosa,[38] he privately distrusted MacArthur. Since Johnson was in full agreement with Mac-
Arthur's position on Formosa and made clear his admiration and support of the
general, there is little doubt that some of Truman's distrust of MacArthur
rubbed off on Johnson.

Bombing in the North

Johnson lost more ground in mid-August. Once again, he backed MacArthur,
this time on an issue with a Vietnam-era ring to it—bombing in the north.
Several weeks after the Korean war began, the JCS had prepared a list of targets in North Korea which they "thought suitable for destruction by strategic
bombing."[39] Included on the list, which was supposedly approved orally by the
president, was the port city of Rashin, located on the northeastern coast just
seventeen miles from the Soviet border. On August 12, U.S. planes struck this
target, inflicting serious damage to a petroleum storage plant. When word of
the attack reached Washington, state department officials were alarmed by
the proximity of the target to the USSR. Acheson and the other top state department officials accepted George Kennan's assessment that the Soviets had
a "pathological sensitivity about their borders," and they feared that the action
could aggravate the Soviets and possibly lead to a widening of the war.[40]

Acheson was on vacation, and Undersecretary Webb, as acting secretary,
sent a heated letter to Johnson warning him that the Rashin attack was not in
line with the president's June 29 instruction that bombing operations should

"stay well clear" of the Soviet and Chinese borders.[41] That same day Webb met with the president and told him about his letter to Johnson. At Webb's request, Truman declined to take a stand one way or the other.

The following day, August 15, Johnson, Bradley, and Webb discussed the subject prior to a cabinet meeting. The defense secretary assured Webb that there was no reason for concern, and when Webb reiterated his department's alarm, Johnson bristled and became "adamant in his position and stated that regardless of [State's] view, it was essential to destroy this plant [at Rashin] and that they would go back time after time to destroy it."[42] Refusing to be intimidated, Webb insisted that the matter be taken up with the president at the cabinet meeting. Although Truman usually sided with the State Department in disputes with Johnson, in this case he told Johnson and Bradley to "go after any target" they believed was being used to supply North Korean forces.[43]

Two days later, Webb sent Johnson a formal request that the State Department be consulted in advance of any future attacks on Rashin and other targets in the far north. In a chance meeting of the two men several days later, Johnson acknowledged to Webb that prior consultation was appropriate. However, Johnson would not let the matter die. After Acheson returned from vacation, Johnson sent him a strongly worded letter in which he defended the bombing in the north and maintained that military people, not diplomats, would make such decisions. "[O]nce war operations are undertaken," Johnson wrote, "it seems to me they must be conducted to win. To any extent that external appearances are permitted to conflict with or hamper military judgment in actual combat decision, the effectiveness of our forces will be jeopardized."[44] These words seem to be more like those of General MacArthur than those of Johnson, and they foreshadowed the words to be spoken two decades later by many Americans, both civilian and military, with reference to Vietnam.

The implacable tone of Johnson's reply convinced Acheson and his staff that the matter should be dropped. They were, however, concerned that the defense secretary's comments "showed a lack of understanding of the important issues involved and a lack of willingness to integrate military and political policies,"[45] and it is probable that Acheson found a way to convey these views about Johnson to Truman. In Johnson's defense, he was supporting the judgment of the JCS and the theater commander, General MacArthur, all of whom sincerely believed that bombing Rashin would save the lives of American troops and that the Soviets would not intervene. No general, least of all General MacArthur, wants to conduct a war with one hand tied behind his back.

Two Speeches

In this volatile atmosphere, two events occurred during the last weekend of August that jeopardized the relationship between Truman and Johnson even more seriously. Each of the events revolved around speeches, one delivered and the other not. Both served to drive a major wedge between the president and his secretary of defense.

The first incident involved a speech delivered in Boston by Johnson's good friend Secretary of Navy Francis Matthews, on Friday, August 25. In that address, Matthews maintained that the United States had to be willing to pay the price of "instituting a war to compel cooperation for peace." By being "an initiator of a war of aggression" he claimed, the United States "would become the first aggressors for peace."[46] The press quickly pounced on Matthews, characterizing his message as a call for a "preventive war" against the Soviet Union.

Immediately, the State Department, with the president's blessing, disavowed the words as well as the intent of the speech and criticized Matthews for making it.[47] But while the president and other top administration officials were denouncing the speech, Johnson was privately confiding to friends and reporters that he sympathized with Matthews's position. He indicated that a first strike against the Soviets, at a time when the U.S. atomic bomb arsenal and its bomber fleet still gave it a decisive advantage over the USSR, had a certain appeal to it. The idea of preventive war against the Soviet Union was completely unacceptable to Truman. That Johnson should espouse such a view, even in private, was no more pleasing to the president than Matthews's public pronouncements to that effect.[48]

While Truman never acknowledged that Johnson's views on preventive war were instrumental in his decision to fire the secretary of defense, "it was generally understood in Washington circles to have been a factor in the abrupt dismissal."[49] However, as damaging as Johnson's support of Matthews's speech may have been to the defense secretary's career, it was of much less consequence than General MacArthur's speech to the Veterans of Foreign Wars (VFW)—a speech that was never delivered.

With a membership of more than 1.2 million members, the VFW had become one of the most powerful and influential pressure groups in the United States. The national veterans' organization advocated a tough foreign policy and a strong military force to back it up, and it had long held General MacArthur in the highest esteem. It was not surprising that Clyde Lewis, the organization's national commander, wired MacArthur and asked him to provide a statement which could be read to the delegates at the national convention on August 28. The general gladly consented and three days later telegraphed a statement on Formosa to Lewis with a copy to the department of the army, which apparently went unnoticed until it became controversial.[50] Little did anyone realize the firestorm that message was about to unleash.

At a regularly scheduled meeting in the White House on Saturday, August 26, Johnson expected a routine discussion of how the war was going. However, when he was ushered into the Oval Office, he could tell that that was not the case. It was immediately obvious that the president was in a cold anger. Without his usual opening banter, Truman launched into a reading of General MacArthur's message to the VFW—a copy of which had been brought to him by the ubiquitous Averell Harriman just a short time before.[51]

MacArthur began his statement to the VFW by stressing the strategic importance of Formosa to the United States and the necessity of denying the island to the Communists.[52] These statements were generally consistent with the Truman/Acheson position. However, the passages in the general's statement which truly incensed Truman were as follows:

> Nothing could be more fallacious than the threadbare argument by those who advocate appeasement and defeatism in the Pacific that if we defend Formosa we alienate continental Asia.

> Those who speak [for such appeasement and defeatism] do not understand the Orient. They do not grant that it is in the pattern of Oriental psychology to respect and follow aggressive, resolute and dynamic leadership—to quickly turn on a leadership characterized by timidity or vacillation. . . . Nothing in the last five years has so inspired the Far East as the American determination to preserve the bulwarks of our Pacific Ocean strategic position from future encroachment.[53]

In context with the rest of his remarks, these pronouncements were not only thinly veiled criticisms of Truman's leadership, they also created the impression that the United States would use Formosa as a military base and provide military assistance to Chiang's government—points which the Soviets and Chinese were making in the UN and the U.S. was trying to refute. MacArthur's statements placed him at odds with the public statements of Truman and Acheson, and they called into question the administration's carefully crafted policy regarding Formosa, the Chinese Communists, and the Soviet Union.

The president was furious with the general's message because he believed it "called for a military policy of aggression based on Formosa's position" and because "the whole tenor of the message was critical of the very policy which [MacArthur] had so recently told Harriman he would support." According to Truman's later recollection, "There was no doubt in my mind that the world would read it that way and that it must have been intended that way."[54]

When the president finished reading the statement, he asked if any of those present had known of it. No one replied in the affirmative, even though Harriman and Acheson had been aware of it and had discussed it. Johnson and General Collins denied any knowledge of the speech, even though a copy had been sent to the Department of the Army.[55]

The president noted that the situation was complicated by the fact that the speech had been sent to numerous newspapers for an August 28 release and would be reported in the upcoming issue of the *U.S. News & World Report*, which had already gone to press. Truman indicated that he wanted it made clear that the statement "was not official policy." He then supposedly directed Johnson to order withdrawal of the message, and Johnson supposedly replied he would call MacArthur and ask him to withdraw it—points over which there would later be considerable confusion. The president quickly dispensed with the other items on the agenda and dismissed the group.[56]

Things happened so quickly that Johnson did not have time to clarify exactly what he was being asked to do. Furthermore, none of the participants had taken notes of what had been said; those present carried the essence of the president's directives only in their heads.

As Johnson headed back to the Pentagon, and thought about the substance of MacArthur's statement, he had to admit to himself that he agreed with the part about defending Formosa. Sensing an opportunity to advance his own agenda, Johnson began to conjure up even more uncertainty about what precisely the president had directed him to do and how it should be done. As soon as he arrived at his office, he huddled with the JCS and Undersecretary Early, an old friend of MacArthur's, to discuss what action was to be taken. After discussing the awkwardness of ordering the withdrawal of the statement, the group adjourned so that Johnson could pursue the matter with the secretary of state.

Johnson telephoned Acheson and expressed serious reservations about ordering MacArthur to withdraw the statement on the grounds that it would humiliate and possibly insult the general. He said he was concerned that MacArthur would resign or do something else that might harm the president. He suggested as an alternative that a message be sent to MacArthur saying that if the statement was released, "we," meaning himself and the JCS, would issue a press release saying the general's statement was "one man's opinion and not . . . official policy." Acheson replied that MacArthur had made a public statement contrary to the president's stated position and that Truman had to assert his authority and order its withdrawal. Johnson countered rhetorically with the question, "Dare [they] send [MacArthur] a message that the President directs him to withdraw his statement?" Acheson responded that they had no choice.[57] Johnson then stated that he and the JCS were not certain that the president "had actually agreed to send a direct order to MacArthur." Acheson quickly replied that there was no doubt in his mind about what the president had ordered. However, when Johnson persisted, Acheson agreed to call Ambassador Harriman at the White House and get a clarification.

When Harriman was contacted by Acheson a few minutes later, he indicated that he understood things exactly as Acheson had. He also stated that he understood that Johnson intended to "call up" MacArthur and convey the order to withdraw his statement. This course, Harriman claimed, would not be sufficient—something needed to be in writing to prove that a withdrawal order had actually been given. He closed by saying that if Johnson still had doubts about what was to be done, the three of them should meet with the president and have him clarify his position.[58]

Acheson called Johnson and recounted his conversation with Harriman. When the defense chief again expressed doubts about what the president had ordered, it was agreed that they would visit Truman and seek clarification. But before Johnson could call the White House and make an appointment, he was informed that he had an important call — Truman was on the line.[59]

Without an exchange of pleasantries, the president said, "Lou, I want that damn thing withdrawn immediately and you tell MacArthur that's a direct order from me" and, he added, "Make sure he understands it."[60] Then, so there could be no doubt what he wanted done, Truman dictated the following message to be sent to MacArthur:

> The President of the United States directs that you withdraw your message for National Encampment of Veterans of Foreign Wars because various features with respect to Formosa are in conflict with the policy of the United States and its position in the United Nations.[61]

The president curtly ended the conversation. Undoubtedly, the call from the president was prompted by Harriman, whose office was just down the hall from the Oval Office.[62]

Truman's intent could not have been made any clearer, yet the defense secretary still resisted carrying out the directive. While Johnson's real motive for resistance was probably a desire to tilt the president's foreign policy toward Formosa along the lines suggested in McArthur's statement to the VFW, he also believed that MacArthur would either quit at a time when the war was not going well, which could hurt the president, or that the order requesting MacArthur to withdraw the message would enable Republicans to accuse Truman of muzzling MacArthur. Once more, Johnson called Acheson and expressed doubts about whether it was "wise" to order withdrawal. He then put Steve Early on the phone to explain his reservations about the course of action ordered by the president. Early set forth several alternatives to solve the problem with "less trouble," but Acheson, who probably sensed Johnson's underlying motives, could not be convinced.

Still Johnson persisted. Again, he called Harriman, and he and Early made the same pitch they had just made to Acheson. Although thoroughly disgusted, Harriman agreed to take the latest proposals from Johnson and Early to the chief executive.

Truman, amazed and angered by the secretary of defense's obstinacy, told Harriman that he had already dictated to Johnson the message that "he wanted to go and he still wanted it to go." When Truman's angry and resolute reaction was transmitted to Johnson, the secretary of defense decided at last to capitulate. At noon he sent the message to MacArthur.[63]

Within hours, MacArthur, reporting he was "utterly astonished" by Johnson's message, replied that he did not understand how his statement could be so misunderstood.[64] He requested that the order be reconsidered, but if it was not, he asked Johnson to send a message to the VFW withdrawing it. In this way MacArthur could avoid the embarrassment of having to personally withdraw the statement—he would let the secretary of defense do it.

Johnson did not raise the matter again with the president. As an accommodation to MacArthur, Johnson took it upon himself to inform the VFW that MacArthur's statement was being officially withdrawn, and on August 29, he informed MacArthur that he had done so.[65] That same day the president sent a somewhat conciliatory letter to the general restating his Formosan policy and explaining why he had ordered the statement withdrawn.[66]

With that letter, the VFW incident was over, but it was certainly not forgotten. For MacArthur it marked, according to General Bradley, "the first in the sequence of events that were ultimately to lead to General MacArthur's dismissal."[67] As far as Johnson was concerned, the impact of the incident was crucial in driving a final wedge between himself and the president. Truman could not have been happy with Johnson's defense of MacArthur or his reluctance to carry out a direct presidential order. According to Truman's daughter, the VFW "episode was close to the last straw in my father's efforts to be patient with Louis Johnson. The secretary of defense had become an obstructionist force in the government."[68]

The president had tolerated the fact that Johnson had agreed with MacArthur on Formosa and had not supported the Truman/Acheson policy of disengaging the United States from the Chinese Nationalists. But when the VFW incident occurred and Johnson made an obvious attempt to thwart the president's expressed intentions, he went too far. It was one thing to advance opposing views and discuss alternatives when a matter was under discussion, but once the president had made his final decision, it was Johnson's duty to carry it out or to resign. There may have been some confusion about what was expected after their initial meeting, but when Truman called Johnson and told him to send the withdrawal order, there was no excuse for Johnson's hesitancy. The president clearly perceived Johnson's tactics as obstructionist, and rightfully so.[69] There can be little doubt that this event was a key factor that led the president to conclude that it was time to get rid of his secretary of defense.

Bad News

Additional factors were working against Johnson. Among the most damaging was the discouraging news from Korea throughout July and early August. During that period, the American press carried numerous accounts of poorly led, ill-equipped U.S. ground forces being soundly defeated by advancing North

Korean troops. Stories of undisciplined American troops fleeing in the face of the enemy, abandoning equipment and wounded comrades; of bazooka rounds that would bounce off the enemy's Russian-built M-34 tanks; of radios and other electronic equipment that would not work; of World War II ammunition that would not fire; of understrength units; and of untrained recruits being thrown into combat stunned a nation which just five years before had amassed the finest military machine that the world had ever known.[70]

What had happened? What had gone wrong? Who was to blame? These and similar questions were being asked in Washington and around the country. An angry and frustrated nation wanted answers.

As the bad news continued to flow out of Korea, politicians, newsmen, and the public began speculating about what had gone wrong and who was to blame. Certain groups and individuals were protected from the wrath of the critics. For example, military personnel, regardless of rank, were safe because no politician or member of the press was about to heap criticism on a group whose members were laying down their lives for their country. Congress likewise was able to avoid being faulted because it was such a large and diverse group that it was impossible to pinpoint blame, and members of Congress diverted blame from themselves by pointing the finger elsewhere. Acheson was blamed for getting the country into the war but was not held responsible for military setbacks. The president was not yet a good candidate for criticism because it was too early in the war. While Truman was ultimately to come under fire, the nation, as it always does at the beginning of a national crisis, rallied around the chief executive as he led the nation into war against the forces of "godless" Communism.

Louis Johnson had no shield. Johnson was exposed and vulnerable because he was more closely identified with military downsizing and budget-cutting than anyone in the nation. From the time he entered office, he had eagerly sought publicity by talking openly about the savings he was making by cutting the fat out of the military budget. As long as the nation remained at peace, such rhetoric was music to America's ears, but when war came and American boys in poorly equipped understrength units began to die, the nation began searching for a scapegoat. The Defense Department did come under some attack, but it was too large to pinpoint blame. The symbol of that entity—Secretary of Defense Louis Johnson—began to catch the heat.

American troops had been in Korea only a few days when the first public attacks on Johnson began. On July 5, widely read and respected columnists Joseph and Stewart Alsop launched a new round of harsh attacks on Johnson and his policies in their nationally syndicated column. In each instance they blamed the setbacks in Korea on his economizing, which they claimed left American forces unprepared for war. They said there was no excuse for Johnson's failure to provide an adequate defense when the Soviet menace had been so apparent.[71]

Newspapers began carrying front-page stories from reporters in the combat zones with headlines such as "G.I.'s Curse Lack of Tanks, Planes" and "G.I.'s Demand Where Are the Guns."[72] While such accounts were not directly critical of Johnson and the Defense Department, they implied that the government responsible for providing American fighting men with the necessary weapons of war had fallen down on the job. Hanson Baldwin, the renowned military-affairs analyst for the *New York Times*, did not attack Johnson directly but did so in a backhanded fashion by underscoring the lack of adequate equipment, the undue emphasis that had been put on big bombers, and the folly of cutbacks in the number of aircraft carriers and in the strength of the marine corps.[73]

Critics in Congress likewise began to aim arrows at the defense secretary. Heading the parade was young Senator Lyndon Johnson (D-Texas), a leading member of the Senate Armed Services Committee. On July 12, the lanky Texan took to the floor of the Senate and launched an attack in which he blamed the administration's economy program for the debacle in Korea. "Half-strength units" and "inadequate equipment" had not been the intent of Congress when it approved the cuts, he claimed. While acknowledging that he had supported cutting the fat out of the budget, he went on to say, "I did not intend that the knife which trimmed the fat should also cut the muscle."[74] By using Louis Johnson's well-known reference to "cutting fat," the Texas senator was able to place blame squarely on the secretary without naming him. As the *New York Times* noted, the senator's "indictment was aimed at economies effected by Secretary of Defense Louis Johnson."[75]

A day later, the Republicans got into the act when Senator Henry Cabot Lodge Jr. (R-Massachusetts) expressed serious reservations about the secretary of defense and said that he would call for a congressional investigation of "his fitness for office." Within a few days such prominent congressional leaders as Senator Styles Bridges (R-New Hampshire) and Representative Henderson Lanham (D-Georgia) joined in the attack.[76]

While Johnson was not surprised at such rumblings from the Hill, he was taken aback by criticism from a quarter he had not expected—leaders of veterans' organizations. On July 13, the day after Senator Johnson's speech, Clyde Lewis, the national commander of the VFW, issued a statement criticizing the "bungling and shortsightedness" of Truman's top advisors and called for the resignations of Johnson, Acheson, and others responsible for the nation's lack of preparedness. Two days after that, Justice Matthew J. Troy of New York, a prominent leader in the American Legion, criticized Johnson for his defense failures and demanded that he resign.[77] Detractors soon began to aim sarcastic barbs at the secretary with such statements as "Louis said we could lick the Russians. He didn't say anything about the North Koreans."[78]

As the attacks in the press and from Capitol Hill continued throughout July, Johnson became increasingly defensive as he tried to assure his critics that his cost-cutting measures had not weakened America's defensive strength but had actually improved it. To back up his case, he issued a flood of statistics. As one general privately commented after reading one of Johnson's reports, "There are lies, there are damn lies, and there are statistics."[79] Against a backdrop of continual reports of withdrawals and retreats by U.S. armed forces, Johnson's arguments and statistics were not convincing. In August, American ground troops began to solidify and the Pusan defense perimeter took shape, but while the news from the battlefront improved, the daily casualty lists continued to mount.

Political Liability

By mid-August Johnson was becoming a liability to the Truman administration. This became apparent when the Republican state chairmen of the Midwestern and Rocky Mountain states met in Iowa to determine their strategy for the November midterm elections. Out of that meeting came agreement that the conduct of the Korean War would be the key campaign issue and that Secretaries Johnson and Acheson would be major targets. Before returning home, the chairmen unanimously adopted a resolution calling on the president to fire both men.[80] These attacks, along with increased congressional criticism of Johnson, made it abundantly clear to the president's political advisors and Democratic Party candidates everywhere that the secretary of defense would be a major liability in the fall elections.

If Truman, out of loyalty, was still harboring any thoughts of looking beyond the obvious political liabilities that Johnson was bringing to his presidency, the events of the last week in August would have dispelled them. That was the week that Johnson angered the president by privately endorsing Secretary Matthews's view of preventive war and resisting the president's efforts to withdraw MacArthur's VFW statement. That was also the week that Democratic congressman Anthony F. Tauriello of New York began launching well-publicized political attacks against Johnson.

The charges by Representative Tauriello and a subsequent exchange with Johnson turned out to be the last straw. On August 23, Tauriello, a maverick first-term congressman who was virtually unknown, even in the halls of Congress, wrote a blistering letter to Johnson criticizing his "penny pinching" economy program that had so weakened the nation's defenses. These actions, the congressman concluded, had cost Johnson "the confidence of the American people" and thus his continuance in office was "embarrassing to the President." For that reason, Tauriello claimed, Johnson should resign.[81]

At this point, the always-competitive Johnson, furious over the vehemence of the attack, made a serious tactical error by deciding that instead of ignoring Tauriello, he would take him on. In doing so he focused considerable public attention on the obscure congressman's charges. Johnson set his aides to work writing a detailed reply which started out by claiming that Tauriello's attacks were politically motivated. He proceeded to elaborate on all the fine things he had done to strengthen the nation's defenses since he came to office. Included was a partial quote from Carl Vinson, chairman of the House Armed Services Committee, praising Johnson's efforts. On August 30, Johnson sent the letter and indicated that he had no objection to its being released to the press.[82]

Neither Johnson nor his advisors ever dreamed that his reply and the story behind it would become a page-one story in major newspapers all across the country. When Tauriello realized that Johnson had released his reply to journalists, he turned over all of his supporting information to the press, and both the letters from Tauriello and Johnson's reply were printed verbatim in major newspapers.[83] Johnson's reply had little impact; the accounts of his positive contributions were not convincing to a nation which had been bombarded for the past two months by news accounts detailing military setback after military setback. On August 31, open criticism of Johnson and his policies became national news.[84]

On the same day that Johnson sent his reply to Tauriello, the delegates to the national convention of the VFW, meeting in Chicago, passed a resolution calling for Johnson's dismissal. Earlier criticism by the organization's national commander had been one thing, but official condemnation as expressed in a resolution passed by more than a thousand delegates was something else.

And at about the very hour Johnson was taking it on the chin in Chicago, William R. Alexander, Republican senatorial candidate in Oklahoma, labeled Johnson the "most incompetent man in Washington" in a speech before the National Federation of Women's Republican Clubs and called for his removal. This attack came in response to a Republican National Committee document distributed to candidates a few days earlier urging them to attack the administration's Far Eastern policy and those responsible for it in the upcoming campaign, especially Johnson and Acheson.[85]

The president held a scheduled news conference on August 31. With the morning papers carrying the Tauriello, VFW, and Alexander stories, it was not surprising that Truman was asked whether he had, as Tauriello charged, "been embarrassed by [Johnson]." "No," replied the president. "If I had been embarrassed everyone would have found it out because I would have announced it." Later in the same press conference the president was asked, "You don't contemplate any change in the Defense Department?" The president replied, "No."[86]

However, while Truman was publicly claiming that Johnson was not embarrassing him, privately he was acknowledging that he was. It is highly likely that the uneasiness he experienced while defending Johnson was a factor that led him to the conclusion that he would have to let him go.

If, as Truman later recalled, it was September 1 when he actually made the decision to fire Johnson, it is probable that the events of August 30 and 31 pushed him to the edge. If, on the other hand, there was still any lingering doubt in his mind, the events of the first week of September would have erased them. That week was full of assaults on Johnson by the press, notably Drew Pearson and Stewart Alsop; and in Congress by Charles Plumley (R-Vermont) and a renewed attack by Representative Tauriello.[87] The latest attack by Tauriello was especially embarrassing to Johnson because it pointed out that his quotes from Carl Vinson in his earlier reply had actually been selective quotes from a letter which was generally critical of Johnson's economizing efforts.[88]

As damaging as all this was, it was the president's encounter with the Marine Corps League which showed just how great a political liability Johnson had become. In the first days of September, President Truman became aware that the league, an influential organization of active-duty and retired marines and marine supporters, was about to consider resolutions at its national convention calling for the resignation of Secretaries Johnson and Acheson. Truman decided to head off their efforts. Addressing the conventioneers on September 7, the president urged the delegates to refrain from criticizing the members of his Cabinet, claiming that such attacks would really be attacks against him.

The speech was greeted with a standing ovation, and on the following day, the delegates voted down a resolution calling for Secretary Acheson's resignation. However, the group then turned around and adopted a resolution, with only one dissenting vote, criticizing Johnson and calling for his dismissal.[89] This action was not only an insult to Johnson but to the president as well.

Arthur Krock, writing in the *New York Times*, observed that "a number of Democrats, concerned by the persistence and bitterness of attacks on the Secretary's acts and policies fear the public will attribute all our military deficiencies to what this group calls his 'pinch-penny economy.'"[90] These broad-based criticisms, which were made when critical congressional elections were only two months away, inflicted mortal wounds. Harry Truman had to fire Louis Johnson.

No Clue

It would seem that Secretary Johnson had to have known that he was about to be fired. But it appears that he had no idea during the tumultuous months of July and August that his days in office were numbered.[91] To be sure, there were plenty of rumors at Washington parties and in the press, just as there had been from the day he assumed office, but they had always proven false.[92]

Johnson was certainly aware that he had made enemies of many powerful people within the Truman administration, on Capitol Hill, and in the armed forces. Furthermore, Johnson knew that he had a huge public-relations problem on his hands. Indeed, as the attacks against him intensified during the summer of 1950, he began to lose confidence in Steve Early, whose job was to deflect the attacks on him. With instructions not to tell Early, Johnson sent his aide Marx Leva to New York City to consult with Ben Sonnenberg, whom Johnson regarded as the best PR man in the business. As Leva recalled, Sonnenberg advised, "Your man is a dead duck. Why waste time on him?"[93]

Notwithstanding Sonnenberg's blunt assessment, the person who really counted, the president of the United States, was, as far as Louis Johnson knew, still foursquare behind him. After all, on at least two occasions in August, when the president was publicly asked about Johnson's resignation or whether he was embarrassing the chief executive, Truman replied that Johnson was "not going to resign, as long as I am President" and said that the secretary had not "embarrassed" him.[94]

Equally important, the news coming out of Korea by late August was positive and the prospect that General MacArthur's secret invasion at Inchon would completely change the fortunes of war contributed to Johnson's feeling that the worst was over. As September 1950 dawned, Johnson, the eternal optimist, had no clue that his replacement as secretary had already been recruited and that the axe was about to fall.[95]

CHAPTER NINETEEN

"Lou, I've Got to Ask You to Quit"

I F PRESIDENT TRUMAN IS to be believed, he first gave serious consideration to removing Louis Johnson as early as June 1950, even before war came to Korea. Those thoughts crossed his mind because, as he wrote later, "Louis began to show an inordinate egotistical desire to run the whole government. He offended every member of the cabinet. We never had a cabinet meeting that he did not show plainly that he knew more about the problems of the Treasury, Commerce, Labor, Agriculture than did the Secretaries of those departments." Truman was also upset by Johnson's tendency to use the press "for blowing himself up and everyone else down, particularly the Secretary of State."[1]

With the outbreak of the Korean conflict on June 25, Truman put aside any plans he might have had for immediately removing the secretary of defense; a period of grave crisis is not the time to insert a new player into an administration team. Johnson was actually doing a fine job of running the Pentagon and that, the president concluded, would be extremely helpful until such time as the military situation in Korea stabilized. Furthermore, according to one close presidential aide, Truman feared that dismissal at that time "would arouse a storm and provide further ammunition for the critics and opponents."[2]

Lining Up a Replacement

Nevertheless, the president began laying the groundwork for Johnson's eventual removal only a few days after the Korean War began. On Independence Day, normally a day for celebration and relaxation, Truman decided to follow up on Harriman's suggestion of the day before that he consider replacing Johnson with the revered and legendary General George Marshall. Accompanied by his daughter Margaret, Truman drove to General Marshall's farm in northern Virginia to visit with the General and his wife, Katherine. The president wanted to assess for himself the strength and health of the 69-year-old general and to float the idea of his taking on the defense job at the end of the summer if he seemed up to it.[3]

Marshall, who had been serving as chairman of the American Red Cross, was feeling and looking great, and the two old friends enjoyed a pleasant lunch together. Afterward, in a private talk outside under the tall oaks surrounding the old manor house, the president confided to Marshall that he was having problems with Louis Johnson and he asked Marshall to at least consider a return to government service as secretary of defense. By this time, the president had concluded that he needed to bring in someone with sufficient stature to restore cooperation with the State Department; improve relations with the armed services, Congress, and the press; and establish clear lines of authority between and among MacArthur, the JCS, the White House, and the UN. There was no one better than Marshall for these tasks. Truman got the answer he wanted: Marshall said he would think about it.[4]

In late August, the president telephoned Marshall, who was fishing at the Huron Mountain Club in Michigan's Upper Peninsula, and asked him to visit him in Washington after his vacation to talk seriously about the defense department job. On Wednesday, September 6, Marshall came alone to Blair House. After getting Truman to agree that his term would be limited to six months or a year and that Robert Lovett would be appointed as undersecretary so he would be able to succeed him, Marshall said, "Mr. President, I'll do it."[5]

But Marshall warned Truman to give careful thought to "the fact that my appointment may reflect upon you and your Administration. They are still charging me with the downfall of Chiang's government in China. I want to help, not hurt you." Reporting this statement in a letter to Bess, Truman wrote, "Can you think of anyone else saying that? I can't and he's one of the *great*."[6]

Marshall also reminded Truman that he could not be named to the position unless Congress was willing to change that portion of the National Security Act which prohibited a military man from being named secretary of defense. Truman was well aware of the statutory provision, but he believed that Congress would change the law for Marshall. He told Marshall to sit tight until the Johnson dismissal was taken care of.[7]

Truman knew there was one more hurdle to surmount before he could close the deal with Marshall, and that was Katherine Marshall. On September 7, Harriman was dispatched on a mission to the Marshall farm—lunch with the General and Mrs. Marshall. As Truman recorded in his diary of this visit, "Wonder of wonders, Mrs. Marshall is for it!"[8]

Resignation

According to Truman, he made up his mind and decided to ask for Johnson's resignation on Friday, September 1, almost a week before he got the final go-ahead from General and Mrs. Marshall.[9] What followed, however, was a perfect example of how not to fire someone. Primarily out of a reluctance to hurt a longtime associate, the supposedly tough and decisive Harry Truman bungled the dismissal to the point that it became embarrassing if not messy.

Instead of crisply delivering the bad news on that Friday, as he had originally intended, the president let the day slip away. He allowed himself to get bogged down in preparing a radio/TV address to be given that evening. In doing so, he found a convenient excuse to wait until Monday to carry out the distasteful task.[10]

On Monday, September 4, Truman decided he would wait until the following day when Johnson came for his regularly scheduled weekly meeting at 12:30. When Johnson showed up, he unexpectedly brought with him Secretary of the Navy Matthews to discuss several naval matters.[11] The president did not want to bring up Johnson's dismissal with Matthews present. Rather than call Johnson back later that day, he decided to wait until the next day, when General Marshall, who had returned from his vacation in Michigan, was scheduled to visit him at Blair House.[12]

Following the September 6 session with Marshall, which ended with the general's agreement to accept the secretary of defense position, Truman resolved once again that the time had finally come to deal with Johnson.[13] The next day Truman and Johnson met face to face in a National Security Council meeting, but the president gave no indication that he wished to confer with him.[14] That the chief executive was agonizing over the chore and wished to do it as humanely as possible was evident from a letter to his wife Bess, written on the evening of the 7th. "Tomorrow" the president wrote, "I have to break the bad news to Louis Johnson. I think I have a way to do it that will not be too hard on him. . . . I'm hoping that I can get [him] to say publicly that he thinks because of the attacks on him I should ask General Marshall to take over. He can make himself a hero if he'll do that." But, the president added, "If he doesn't, I shall simply fire him as I did Wallace and Morgenthau."[15]

The strong boast he made to Bess on Thursday evening, however, had mellowed by the next morning and the president again decided to postpone the confrontation until Monday the 11th.[16] Just why the president continued to delay on this matter is not clear. In firing Henry Morgenthau, Francis Biddle, and Henry Wallace, all cabinet members, Truman had shown no hesitation and no reluctance. However, those three men, like most top officials Truman had dismissed, were Roosevelt appointees; he could justify such actions by claiming he was merely putting his own people in these positions.[17] But Louis

Johnson was an entirely different story because he was a Truman appointee. To fire Johnson would be an implicit admission that he had made a mistake in appointing him, and no one, especially a president of the United States, likes to admit he was wrong.

On Friday, September 8, George Dixon of the *Washington Times-Herald* reported that Johnson had submitted his resignation. When reporters contacted Johnson at his Pentagon office he denied that there was anything to the reports, as he had done on dozens of other occasions.[18] Whether Dixon had picked up some inside information on the pending dismissal or was merely reporting the latest version of a rumor that had been circulating in Washington for many months is not certain, but the latter possibility seems more likely.

The actual leak about Johnson's dismissal came from DNC chairman William M. Boyle Jr., who probably got his information from Truman's press secretary, Charlie Ross. On the afternoon of September 8, at about the time Johnson was flying back to Clarksburg for a weekend of golf and orchid-tending, Boyle told Associated Press White House correspondent Ernest B. Vaccaro "without attribution" that Johnson would be gone before the November elections.[19] The following day Vaccaro reported the breaking news in the *Washington Star*, attributing the story to a "close advisor to President Truman."[20]

The Vaccaro story was quite different from the numerous earlier reports that Johnson was on the skids because it came from a first-rate reporter who was known to have many reliable contacts at the White House. Especially alarmed was Steve Early, who, as a former White House press secretary, knew when to take something seriously. Early began checking with his inside sources at the White House to see if there was any truth to the report. When no one at the White House would deny the story, Early became convinced that things did not look good for Johnson. The White House would often plant such stories and then not comment on them, thus showing an official that he was out of favor. There is a strong likelihood that this was done in Johnson's case. Another ominous sign had come on September 5, when the White House announced acceptance of Early's previously tendered resignation, which the president had been holding for five days. This paved the way for a new secretary to name his own deputy.[21]

On Sunday afternoon, Johnson flew back to Washington, unaware that anything was wrong. He and Ruth went straight to their apartment at the Mayflower and spent a quiet evening alone.[22] The next morning, when Johnson arrived at his office, Deputy Secretary Early was waiting with the disquieting news. He showed Johnson the Vaccaro story, told of his inability to secure a denial of the report, and then reluctantly, but bluntly, told his boss, "You're fired."

Johnson concluded that Early's reading of the tea leaves was wrong. "I'll find out," he said as he picked up the phone and called the president.[23] Johnson asked the president about the accuracy of the Vaccaro story. However, he did not get a direct answer. Instead, the two men batted around some small talk, after which they discussed the weekend developments in Korea. With no hint that anything ominous was in the offing, the president asked the secretary to drop by the White House that afternoon around four o'clock for an off-the-record visit. This request did not concern the ever-optimistic Johnson because such visits had become rather commonplace following the outbreak of war. When the "happy conversation," as Johnson characterized it, ended, Johnson felt confident that there was nothing to the published report and that Early had been way off base in his assessment.[24]

At 4 P.M. on Monday, September 11, Johnson's limousine slipped quietly up the driveway to the side entrance of the White House so as to not be noticed by reporters. The secretary bounded into the Oval Office with the same energy and enthusiasm that he had displayed on a hundred other such visits. As Truman put it, "Lou came in full of pep and energy. He didn't know anything was wrong."

The president minced no words as he got right to the point. "Lou, I've got to ask you to quit," Truman said. Johnson was stunned. He simply could not believe what he heard. It was as if he had been struck dumb. After an awkward silence, Johnson sputtered, "Mr. President, I can't talk."

At first, Truman thought Johnson was going to faint. After several seconds, the president stepped in to fill the uncomfortable silence by explaining that political pressures were being placed on him by Democratic members of Congress who had been coming to him and insisting that if Johnson remained in the Cabinet it would cost them and the party dearly in the upcoming elections.

Johnson said nothing. The president then told of his offer to General Marshall and expressed hope that Johnson would support his choice. Johnson at last found his voice, and he tried to get the president to reconsider the decision. But Truman stood firm, saying, "I have made up my mind, Lou, and it has to be this way."

Johnson lamely requested that he be given "a couple of days" to think the matter over and the president agreed but made it clear there was no chance he would change his mind. With that, the ten-minute encounter came to an end and a "dejected" and "beaten" Johnson departed.[25] Fortunately for him, no reporters noticed him leave the White House.

While the session had been devastating for Johnson, it was no picnic for the president. No sooner had the secretary departed than the chief executive told Press Secretary Charlie Ross what had transpired and then added, "I felt pretty bad. . . . This is the toughest job I ever had to do. I feel as if I had just whipped my daughter, Margaret."[26]

The Colonel returned to his office at the Pentagon and canceled his remaining appointments before heading back to the Mayflower to tell Ruth the bad news. Realizing that Johnson was emotionally distraught, his close aide, Paul Renfrow, decided to ride with Johnson to make sure he got home safely. Renfrow recalled later that Johnson didn't say a word on the way home and was "as white as he could be." Renfrow was worried because he thought he might be going through "another Forrestal business."[27]

That evening Louis and Ruth dined alone at the Chevy Chase Club.[28] After they returned to their apartment at the Mayflower, a few of Johnson's closest friends and advisors dropped by to talk, commiserate, and explore options. They left before midnight.[29]

Johnson couldn't sleep. It was a warm mid-September evening, so he decided to go downstairs, take a stroll outside, and think. He knew that the Inchon invasion would take place in two days and that everything could change after that. Should he try to stall? Was there a way to talk the president out of his decision? Was there someone he could turn to for help?

Johnson started walking north up Connecticut Avenue and he kept on going—past DuPont Circle, across the Taft Bridge, beyond the Wardman Park Hotel, and all the way out into Chevy Chase. Sometime after 2 A.M., Johnson was five miles from the Mayflower. He turned around and began the long walk home. On the way back, he decided that he had no choice. He had been through this before with Roosevelt. Truman had made his decision and there was no way he could stall or change his mind. Johnson resolved that he would prepare his resignation letter and try to leave with dignity.[30]

It was after 4 A.M. on Tuesday, September 12, with the invasion at Inchon set to begin in about 48 hours, when Johnson reached the Mayflower. As dawn broke, he wrote out his letter of resignation in longhand.[31] After showering, shaving, and changing, he called his driver and went to the Pentagon.

That morning the secretary held his regularly scheduled meetings and carried on as if nothing had happened. At noon he and Secretary of the Air Force Finletter met with the president on some procurement matters. At that time neither Truman nor Johnson mentioned the resignation, but after the visitors left, the president called Steve Early and urged him to get the secretary moving on the matter. Truman, who had great personal and professional respect for Early, told him that he should use his influence to persuade Johnson to "bring me a letter of resignation, saying he had felt the pressure on me and that he thought he should quit and that he should recommend General Marshall to take his place." Urgent action was necessary, the president claimed, because the press had learned of the resignation request.

When Johnson arrived back at the Pentagon around one o'clock, Early confronted him with the need to submit his letter of resignation immediately to avoid embarrassment to himself and the president. Johnson handed Early the draft he had written early that morning and asked him to review and revise it. The deputy went back to his office to work over the draft. When he was satisfied with the substance and tone of the letter, he called Press Secretary Charlie Ross at the White House and read the revised letter to him to assure it would not in any way embarrass the president.

Upon receiving Ross's approval, Early shared the revised letter with Johnson, who gave his go-ahead and directed that it be typed in final form. A few minutes later, before Johnson left for a four o'clock cabinet meeting, he was handed the letter. He put the unsigned document in his pocket and headed for the White House.[32]

After a brief and uneventful cabinet meeting, Johnson followed the president into the Oval Office. As the president later wrote, Johnson "looked like he had been beaten." Despite his resolve to leave with dignity, Johnson "begged" Truman not to carry through with his plan. But as he had the day before, the president stood firm and demanded the resignation letter. Johnson reluctantly handed the letter to Truman. "Louis," the president said, his jaw tightening, "you haven't signed this — sign it."

Johnson made a final appeal to his old friend, claiming he did not think the president would "make him do it."[33] Weeping openly, Johnson finally signed the letter. As he handed the letter to Truman, he said in a barely audible voice that quivered with despair, "You are ruining me."[34] Truman could only say, "This hurts me more than it does you, Lou."[35] Without another word, Johnson departed.

The president then picked up the phone and called Marshall to inform him that he had received Johnson's signed resignation and that he would announce his new appointee and send to Congress the legislation necessary to permit the general to assume the defense post.[36] After speaking with Marshall, Truman called in Charlie Ross to discuss the release of the secretary's letter, his response to it, and the announcement of his selection of Marshall. The president commented, "I tried to make it as easy on Johnson as circumstances would permit — but I had to force him to work in his own interest." He concluded by observing, "[Johnson] is the worst egomaniac I've ever come in contact with — and I've seen a lot."[37]

Charlie Ross called Early to discuss an effective date for the resignation. Early asked if September 19 was possible so that Johnson could deliver a previously scheduled speech to the American Bar Association national convention as secretary of defense. Ross agreed and wrote a response for the president to sign that incorporated that date.

By this time it was nearly six o'clock and the president had gone to Blair House, so Ross took it to him and got his signature. The reply was then sent by special messenger to Johnson at his Mayflower apartment. At 6:40, after being informed that Johnson had received the letter, Ross released the two letters to the press.[38]

Johnson's letter read as follows:

September 12, 1950

My Dear Mr. President:

I have today presented to you the unanimous recommendations of the Joint Secretaries, the Joint Chiefs of Staff and myself for the rearmament of the United States in concert with the rearmament programs of the other free nations. The completion of these unanimous recommendations marks a milestone in our work for the security of the United States and the peace of the world.

When I undertook to serve as Secretary of Defense, at your request and that of Secretary Forrestal, I remarked to you privately and also remarked publicly that it was inevitable, in the conscientious performance of my duties as Secretary of Defense, that I would make more enemies than friends. Somewhat ruefully, I now admit, I was right.

The unification of the armed forces has been accomplished in great degree. If it had not been accomplished we would not have been able to deploy our forces on a fighting front more than 5000 miles from our homeland as speedily as the three services have accomplished that unexpected task.

I am grateful to you for the support you have always given me, in my attempts to bring about unification of the services and in my work to establish alertness without waste or duplication in the Department of Defense.

Under normal conditions, the fact that I have made so many enemies would not concern me too greatly, for I could take comfort in the thought that I have made them in a good cause. But today, when American boys are laying down their lives in the cause of our national security and world peace, it seems to me that the country should have a Secretary of Defense who does not suffer under the handicap of the enemies I have acquired during the eighteen months I have served as a member of your Cabinet.

Accordingly, it is my recommendation that, at your earliest convenience, you accept the resignation which I tender herewith, and name as my successor a man of such stature that the very act of naming him to be Secretary of Defense will promote national and international unity. Such a man, in my opinion, is General George Marshall—and I recommend his name to your thoughtful attention.

I recognize, of course, that many will argue that one of our great Generals should not be Secretary of Defense. I do not believe that this argument has validity in the case of General Marshall, who has already rendered distinguished service to his country, in a civilian capacity, as Secretary of State. I recognize also that an amendment to the National Security Act will be necessary, in order to make it legally permissible for General Marshall to serve as Secretary of Defense—but I believe that Congress will speedily amend the law in General Marshall's case, if you should so recommend.

General Marshall, more than any other individual I can think of, would be an inspiration to the people of the United States and to our allies. Moreover, he is a man who would assure that we would mobilize our forces speedily and that in doing so we would get a dollar's worth of defense for every dollar we spend. I know that you agree with me as to the continuing importance of this latter consideration. In my judgment, it is more essential today than ever before that the program for eliminating waste in the Defense Department be continued, as we proceed to build up our strength.

I want to express to you once more my deep appreciation for the understanding, cooperation, and support you have always given me. I am and shall always be grateful.

Sincerely yours,
LOUIS JOHNSON[39]

In response, President Truman wrote:

My dear Lou:

I have just read your letter.

It is clear to me that in writing it you have been actuated by motives of the highest patriotism, and I salute you. In the terribly regrettable circumstances which have arisen, I feel that I must concur in your judgment and accept your proffered resignation as Secretary of Defense, effective at the close of business on September 19, 1950.

The manner in which you have carried out the purposes of the National Security Act testifies to your high administrative skill and your devotion to the public welfare. The success of your efforts toward the unification of our armed services should be an abiding satisfaction to you, as it is to me. The country is in debt to you for your pioneering achievement in a field fraught with the greatest difficulties. Thanks in great part to your efforts, we build our national defense of the future on a solid foundation.

Your recommendation of General Marshall as your successor betokens the same spirit of patriotism as the rest of your letter. I shall propose at once the legislation necessary to make it effective.

I shall feel free to continue to call upon you for advice.

With my warm personal regards, my thanks again for your distinguished services, and my best wishes, I am

Very sincerely yours,
HARRY S. TRUMAN[40]

Several reporters who had gotten wind of the resignation had remained at the White House, and when they received copies of the two letters they immediately headed for the Mayflower with the hope of interviewing the deposed secretary. When they arrived at the apartment door they were met by Ruth Johnson, who informed them that the Colonel would not be available for comment.[41] For one of the very few times in his public career, Louis Johnson was unwilling to talk to the press.

Averell Harriman was having drinks at the Metropolitan Club with Stewart Alsop and his wife Tish when news of Johnson's dismissal reached them. As

Alsop wrote, Harriman, normally reserved, "did a fairly lively jig" and gave Tish an emotional hug.[42] He then raced to a telephone to call Dean Acheson, who was in New York with Paul Nitze conferring with the U.S. delegation on its talks with the British and the French on the German disarmament question. Acheson took the call and when he came back into the room he announced with evident glee, "Johnson has just been fired, bring out the champagne." Within minutes the delegation adjourned to an adjoining room and the sound of popping corks was heard.[43]

The morning newspapers carried the Johnson resignation and the Marshall appointment as their top two stories. Somewhat surprisingly, reaction to the Johnson dismissal by the press and members of Congress was relatively mild. Of course, Johnson's most outspoken critics, political columnists Joe and Stewart Alsop and Marquis Childs, were pleased with the Johnson dismissal and the Marshall appointment.[44] Others, such as Arthur Krock and Hanson Baldwin, while not openly supportive of the firing, maintained that Johnson's departure would certainly improve relations between military and diplomatic policymakers and make for a more effective foreign policy.[45] Nearly all writers hailed the likelihood of increased cooperation between the State and Defense Departments.

Editorial opinion in major newspapers was divided. The New York Times suggested that the problems at the Defense Department were the fault of Truman, not Johnson. The Chicago Tribune editorial page said that Johnson had been fired to save Acheson. Other editorial comments praised the president's decision to dismiss Johnson and expressed hope for what it portended for the future.[46] Most news magazines were content to merely report the dismissal and speculate on the factors that led the president to make his decision. However, a few magazines, such as Life and Barron's, while claiming that Johnson was not entirely without fault, contended that it was Acheson who was most responsible for the deplorable state of affairs and that the president had dismissed the wrong man.[47]

No defenders of Johnson stepped forward on Capitol Hill, even from among those who had so frequently praised the secretary. Months later, a few congressmen sent personal letters to Johnson saying he had been an administration scapegoat, but none came forward publicly to voice support for him.[48] In June of 1951, during the MacArthur hearings, Senators Hickenlooper, Morse, and Stennis praised Johnson's performance as secretary of defense and said that they were disappointed that he had to resign.[49] But by then it was too late.

That politicians did not rally to publicly defend Johnson at the time of his forced resignation is not surprising. Any politician who stood up for Johnson would have seemed to be defending the nation's state of military preparedness—a stance that would have been politically devastating in view of the military setbacks suffered in Korea that summer. Furthermore, criticism of the president's actions and defense of Johnson could have been interpreted by some voters as being critical of his successor, General Marshall, and no politician was willing to do that. In the immediate aftermath of dismissal, Johnson stood alone.[50]

In the days that followed the dismissal, Johnson took the action hard; however, the agony was not his alone. The president also found the matter to be an extraordinarily painful experience. If there was one thing Truman was known for it was his loyalty to his political friends and his willingness to stick with them when they came under attack or even if they became a political liability.[51] Confiding to Charlie Ross on September 13, the president said, "You know that I would rather cut my own throat than hurt anyone. I've known Lou for thirty years and I hated to have to do this to him, but the worst part about this job I have is that I can't consider my personal feelings. I have to do what is right and I just could not leave Johnson there any longer."[52] When the president spoke this way it was as if he was trying to convince himself that he had done the right thing and had done it as humanely as possible.

Final Days at the Pentagon

In Johnson's final week in office he continued to carry on as if nothing had happened, meeting daily with his military advisors, holding his regularly scheduled sessions with the service secretaries, and even attending the weekly cabinet meetings. Not only was he present at these meetings, he participated as if he would be in his post for the indefinite future.[53]

On Monday, September 18, the three service secretaries and the members of the JCS came to Johnson's office to request permission to finalize plans for a ceremony to mark his Tuesday departure. Johnson declined the offer, saying he preferred to leave quietly.[54]

In the week between the announcement of Johnson's resignation and his September 18 speech to the American Bar Association, there was speculation in the press and on Capitol Hill that the dismissed and humiliated secretary might use the opportunity to lash out at the president, Acheson, and the administration's Far Eastern policy. But those close to Johnson knew him better than that, and they were proven correct.

When Johnson delivered his speech to the nation's lawyers assembled in Constitution Hall and a nationwide radio audience, he remained loyal to the president, in spite of all the personal hurt. Rather than denounce President Truman, Johnson thanked him for "the very high compliment" he had paid him by making him secretary of defense. He even refrained from attacking his numerous critics, claiming that a "good soldier must be prepared . . . to make the sacrifice . . . for the good of the country. That goes not only for a buck private . . . it goes for a Secretary of Defense as well." Johnson spoke of the "headaches and heartaches" of the job but added that there were many compensations. He made no attempt to defend his service as secretary, nor did he assess his performance. He asked only that when the turmoil over his departure from office and the war in Korea had ended in victory, "I trust the historian will find my record of performance creditable, my services honest and faithful, commensurate with the trust that was placed in me and in the best interest of peace and our national defense."[55]

The following day, his last in office, Johnson drove himself to work. He spent the morning cleaning out the big Pershing desk with his longtime personal assistant, Ruth Nutter. Then, shortly before noon, Louis Johnson said a quiet goodbye to his close advisors and friends and slipped out of the Pentagon for the last time.[56]

After a little less than eighteen unbelievably hectic months as secretary of defense, Louis Johnson was once more a private citizen. A few days later when President Truman was asked to comment on Johnson's dismissal, he replied that the matter was closed, and, except for a few lingering articles by newspaper columnists, it was.

But for Johnson, there would never be closure. He rarely discussed his dismissal, but it weighed heavily on him, and those close to him knew it. In a December 1950 letter to Truman, written shortly after his mother had died at age eighty-nine, Johnson, referring to his forced resignation, noted in great despair that "the blow was hard—harder than you realize and it has been rough, very rough; at times it has seemed too much."[57] He found the firing even more difficult to take because of his conviction that had he been permitted to remain in office just a few more weeks, the improvement in the war situation that followed the successful Inchon invasion would have saved him.[58]

Truman's Reasons

The president can be faulted for dithering so long over how to tell his secretary of defense that he was letting him go. However, his reasons for firing Louis Johnson can hardly be questioned. Only Truman knows for sure, but the evidence strongly suggests that the following were among the president's principal reasons for dismissing Johnson:

- A desire to end the feud between Johnson and Dean Acheson—a feud the president not only found personally disturbing but one which complicated the development, implementation, and integration of foreign and military policy and sent mixed signals to enemy and ally alike
- Johnson's statement to Averell Harriman that if they "could get Acheson out," he would see that Harriman was made secretary of state
- Johnson's support of Senator Robert Taft's call for Acheson's resignation
- Johnson's advocacy of military aid to and support of Chiang's Nationalist government, a position favored by General MacArthur and many

in Congress but one that was at odds with the position of Truman and Acheson

- The belief that Johnson had become a political liability to Democratic candidates in the upcoming elections
- Congressional, media, and public criticism of Johnson because of the nation's lack of preparedness for the Korean War, thus making Johnson a scapegoat for carrying out policies established by Truman
- Johnson's failure to immediately carry out the president's order to instruct General MacArthur to withdraw his VFW speech
- Johnson's political ambitions, especially all the talk, public and private, that he had his eye on the presidency

In the final analysis, any of these factors alone would have provided sufficient justification for the president to dismiss Johnson. Together, they probably form as strong a case for dismissal of a cabinet member as the United States has ever seen.

Johnson made enormous contributions to the Defense Department and to the strengthening of the nation's defenses throughout the world. But all of those accomplishments could not negate the fact that by the late summer of 1950 his continuing presence in office was not in the best interests of the president or the nation.

CHAPTER TWENTY

"Lest Darkness Come"

Louis Johnson was tough and resilient. The blow Harry Truman delivered in September 1950 was devastating, but Johnson had always been a fighter. He would survive.

Johnson returned to preside over the law firm he had built. Like Elihu Root, John W. Davis, and Henry Stimson who preceded him and Dean Acheson, Robert Patterson, Warren Christopher, Lloyd Cutler, James Baker, and others who would follow him, Louis Johnson would emerge again from the revolving door of government service and become a prodigious rainmaker for his law firm with its thriving office in Washington.

Loyal to the End?

Except for those closest to him and clients who were dazzled by a man who had instant access to the White House and most of officialdom in Washington, Johnson's political standing faded quickly. On several occasions in the early and mid-1950s his name appeared in news stories indicating that he was considering a run in West Virginia for the U.S. Senate. But there is no evidence to suggest that he seriously contemplated such a move.[1] And, in sharp contrast to what news magazines and pundits had been saying in 1949, there is no evidence that anyone floated his name as even a dark horse presidential aspirant in 1952.

In spite of the humiliation and pain that Truman's dismissal brought to Johnson, he never turned on the president, nor did he ever directly criticize him. At the congressional hearings on General MacArthur's dismissal in June 1951, Johnson was grilled for two days, and the Republican senators gave him plenty of opportunities to question the president's judgment. Johnson chose not to rise to

the bait, but in a subtle, indirect way he did take issue with the president's decision to fire him. When asked by a senator why he was "ousted" from the Defense
Department, Johnson replied, "My answer is truthfully under oath, I don't know;
I don't know to this day." He went on to explain how he was forced to resign two
days before the successful Inchon landings even though he had backed Mac-
Arthur and the president on the decision to launch the risky attack over the strong
objections of Army Chief of Staff Joe Collins. After extolling, if not bragging,
about his military judgment and support of the president, Johnson concluded his
answer, saying, "No. I do not know why I am out of the Defense Establishment."[2]

By claiming he did not know why he had been fired, Johnson was suggesting
that there was no good reason for his ouster—certainly a criticism of the president's
decision to demand his resignation. And by contending, as he did at the Mac-
Arthur hearings, that the successful Inchon landings "cleared up much of the criticism" about him, Johnson was clearly implying that the president's decision to fire
him just two days before the landings was precipitous and ultimately unwarranted.

Except for this indirect criticism of the president and occasional outbursts
about Acheson and his policies, which of course also constituted indirect criticism of Truman, Johnson remained outwardly loyal and supportive of his old
friend. Major book publishers, magazines, and newspapers begged Johnson to
write, or have written for him, tell-all accounts of his experiences inside the Truman administration. Friends and supporters urged him to write his memoirs.
But he steadfastly refused.[3]

Not until 1963, nearly thirteen years after his dismissal, was Johnson willing to
grant a reporter an interview. Even then, what he said was bland. Johnson surprised the reporter when he opened the interview with the statement that he still
considered Harry Truman a good friend.[4] In fact, the two men did remain on
good terms, occasionally writing to each other and exchanging birthday greet-
ings and get-well cards.[5] On at least one occasion after his ouster, Truman visited
Johnson at his home in Clarksburg, and Johnson paid a visit to the former president when Truman came to Washington in 1955.[6]

From the day Truman fired him until the day of his death, Johnson continued
to maintain, at least publicly, that he did not know why he was asked to step
down. But this had to have been an artifice, a convenient yet self-protective
way to justify his behavior and avoid accepting responsibility for his actions. At
the same time, by continuing to claim he had no idea why Truman got rid of
him, he was trying to persuade others, and perhaps most important himself,
that it was Harry Truman who was in the wrong.

Subdural Hematoma

In the spring of 1952, Johnson returned to the Mayo Clinic in Rochester, Minnesota, where he had been treated in 1942 following his trip to India. Johnson

had been complaining of severe headaches and episodes of confusion and thought it might have something to do with an accidental blow to the head which happened several months before when he was getting out of a taxi in New York City.[7]

The clinic diagnosed Johnson's condition as a subdural hematoma, which, in lay terms, means blood clots near the surface of the brain, a condition often caused by a blow to the head.[8] The doctors at Mayo drilled holes in Johnson's skull and successfully removed the blood clots. The Colonel recovered quickly from the surgery with no aftereffects and he was back at Steptoe & Johnson within a few weeks.[9]

The facts concerning Johnson's brain operation are recounted here because as word of the operation spread to Johnson's detractors in Washington, it became the source of speculation that when Johnson was serving as secretary of defense less than two years before, he was mentally ill and that his condition was due to a brain tumor.[10] This speculation was completely erroneous, however; Mayo Clinic records state that "no tumor or cancer was found."[11] In addition, the chairman of the Department of Neurosurgery at the University of Pennsylvania, Dr. Thomas Langfitt, who had known Johnson for years and was familiar with the details of his operation, has stated that there is no doubt that Johnson was operated on because of subdural hematoma and that it is highly unlikely that this condition could have anything to do with mental illness or the kind of bizarre behavior which Johnson's enemies attributed to him when he was secretary of defense.[12]

Nevertheless, the rumors and speculation persisted. In his widely acclaimed book *Present at the Creation*, Johnson's chief adversary, Dean Acheson, wrote that he was convinced that Johnson was mentally ill and suggested that Johnson's 1952 brain operation was proof of his mental instability.[13] Acheson's opinion gained increasing acceptance among his followers, especially after Johnson's death. Clark Clifford, in his memoir, perpetuated Acheson's campaign of misinformation,[14] and even Truman, writing later about Johnson said, "I am of the opinion that Potomac fever and a pathological condition are to blame for the fiasco at the end."[15]

The fact that Johnson functioned as an extremely articulate, intelligent, and effective lawyer and businessman both before his operation and for more than a decade thereafter completely undermines the speculation by Acheson, Clifford, Truman, and others that Johnson was mentally ill and that his condition was caused by a brain tumor that was operated on in 1952. Law partners and others who were close to Johnson during those years are certain that he was always a highly functioning human being with no trace of mental illness or its hallmark, a departure from reality. All agree that he was intolerant, impatient, and imperious and could fly off the handle. Indeed, he had been this way since he was a young man, he was this way at the Defense Department, and he was this way in his final years at Steptoe & Johnson. But he was never afflicted by a mental illness.[16]

Rainmaker

When Louis Johnson strode confidently into his office at the Shoreham Building that day in late September of 1950, the young lawyers at Steptoe & Johnson were bursting with optimism. The Colonel's cavernous office had been dark for almost two years. Now, having led the Defense Department through a tumultuous eighteen months, the Colonel was back, and he would use his vast network of contacts to bring in cutting-edge legal work from clients who would pay top dollar.

It didn't take long for Johnson to work his magic. Within a few months of his return to private practice, he landed a major new client, the Panhandle Eastern Pipeline Company, through his friend John Bierwirth, who was CEO of National Distillers, yet another client Johnson had brought in. In those days, when Johnson was romancing a new corporate client, he would typically ask for and get an upfront $10,000 retainer and would often persuade the client to designate himself or the firm in general as general counsel. He followed this practice with Panhandle, and within a few years Panhandle's regulatory problems were generating fees that would feed several families at Steptoe & Johnson.[17]

From his huge flag-bedecked office on the tenth floor of the Shoreham Building, which featured a speakerphone (which was rare in those days) and a big 1950 Motorola radio console, Colonel Johnson was the benevolent dictator of the three offices of Steptoe & Johnson from 1950 until the early 1960s. The Colonel brought in all of the new business, he diligently managed and cultivated his stable of blue-chip clients, he hired and fired all of the lawyers and support personnel, and he determined everyone's compensation. At the same time, he kept on top of major issues in Washington so that clients and prospective clients understood they were dealing with an influential Washington insider who knew which lever to pull and which official to call to solve their particular problem.[18]

Jack Corber recalled a day in early 1951 when Johnson's longtime assistant, Ruth Nutter, told him the Colonel needed to see him right away. Corber, fresh out of the University of Michigan Law School and knowing almost nothing about Washington law practice, was quaking in his shoes when he was ushered into Johnson's office. A group of men was seated around Johnson's big desk, and Corber recognized only one of them—handsome, silver-haired Juan Trippe, the well-known CEO of Pan American Airways, Steptoe & Johnson's largest client. While Corber stood there, Johnson, looking not at him but directly at Juan Trippe, said slowly and with considerable emphasis and emotion, "Corber, we are no longer doing any legal work for Pan Am." Then, with a wave of his hand, he dismissed the young lawyer.

Corber was shaken by the experience. It was common knowledge that Pan Am had been paying huge fees to Steptoe & Johnson for years for legal and lobbying work aimed at achieving Trippe's vision of having Pan Am designated as the "chosen instrument" of U.S. policy on foreign aviation, a counterpart to B.O.A.C. in Great Britain and Air France in France.[19] Why did Johnson just fire Pan Am as a client? Was Corber about to lose his job?

Several days later, with Steptoe lawyers continuing their work for Pan Am, Corber heard the real story. Johnson had been at the White House working on an important issue involving international routes for Pan Am and had learned that his client had hired another law firm to work on the same issue. Johnson was furious. To teach Trippe and others at Pan Am a lesson—that they should not use any firm except Steptoe & Johnson for Washington legal matters—Johnson brought Corber in as a prop and "fired" Pan Am. It was a gamble, but the Colonel correctly calculated the odds. Trippe did not call his bluff. Steptoe & Johnson continued to represent Pan Am and the airline did not hire other firms for Washington work without consulting the Colonel.[20]

For smart, aggressive lawyers such as those Johnson assembled at Steptoe & Johnson, the 1950s were great years to be practicing law in Washington. Aside from Steptoe, there were only three other top-tier Washington-based firms—Covington & Burling (Dean Acheson's firm); Hogan & Hartson; and a new upstart, Arnold, Fortas & Porter. And except for Kirkland & Ellis and Pope Ballard of Chicago, Jones Day of Cleveland, and the outposts of a few New York City firms, the great law firms throughout the nation had not yet discovered, as they would in the 1970s, that there was an enormous amount of premium legal work being generated by the federal government and that it was essential to be located in the nation's capital in order to compete for it.

Louis Johnson's West Virginia–based law firm was ahead of the pack. One day in early 1956, Johnson received a telephone call from one of his very wealthy and important friends on the West Coast, Louis B. Mayer, the legendary cofounder of Metro-Goldwyn-Mayer. Like Roosevelt and Truman before him, Louis Mayer wanted to use Louis Johnson as his instrument of confrontation. Due to falling revenues, Mayer had been deposed from MGM's parent company, Loew's Incorporated, and, vowing to get revenge, had hired Johnson and his law firm to orchestrate a proxy fight against those who controlled Loew's and restore Mayer to his rightful place as king of the movie business.[21]

Louis Mayer and the group of insurgents who hired Steptoe & Johnson were not an attractive bunch nor were their motivations—money, power, and access to starlets—particularly appealing. Nevertheless, Johnson and his legal team waged scorched-earth legal warfare against Loew's, which was represented by Louis Nizer, the most famous lawyer of the day.[22] The war was fought in boardrooms, in the media, and in courts in New York, Delaware, Pennsylvania, and the District of Columbia. When the last court had ruled and it was clear that

Johnson and his team had lost the fight, the exhausted Steptoe lawyers drove home to the Maryland suburbs after 2 A.M. John Nolan, one of the young litigators, who had led a marine rifle platoon in Korea, commented on how awful it felt to lose after fighting so long and so hard. The more-senior trial lawyer, Steve Ailes, who would be secretary of the army under President Kennedy, replied, "Just think how much worse it would be if we had won for these guys."[23]

Thanks to Johnson, there would be many more new clients who would bring fascinating legal problems and daunting courtroom challenges to the law firm. As he approached seventy, it was obvious to any observer that Johnson was one of the great legal rainmakers as well as a dynamic and visionary law firm leader. He had survived the blow administered by Harry Truman and there was certainly nothing wrong with his brain.

Darkness Comes

But the rumor that Johnson had a "brain malady" never died. In fact, it was given new life by the medical condition that ultimately led to his death. In 1964, a little more than a year after President John Kennedy and Attorney General Robert Kennedy sent telegrams congratulating Johnson on the fiftieth anniversary of the formation of Steptoe & Johnson, the Colonel began experiencing some difficulty in movement and short periods of mental confusion. He returned to the Mayo Clinic, where his condition was diagnosed as a "degenerative cerebral disease, the result perhaps of arteriosclerosis" or hardening of the arteries.[24]

With no treatment available, his condition gradually deteriorated, and in the next two years he was in and out of several extended-care medical facilities in the District of Columbia.[25] Then, in the spring of 1966, while at the Washington Hospital Center, he suffered a debilitating stroke followed by pneumonia. On April 24, at the age of seventy-five, and with Ruth at his bedside, Louis Johnson died.[26]

As his body was flown back to Clarksburg, expressions of sorrow flowed in from political figures around the country, including a telegram from President Lyndon Johnson, who as a young senator had been one of Johnson's critics. Two days later, more than 300 family members, friends, and public officials crowded into tiny Christ Episcopal Church, in whose manse Johnson had first lived when he had come to "the young man's town" more than fifty years before, to pay final respects to the powerful and controversial man who had risen to national prominence and worked closely with two of the nation's greatest presidents. At 3:30 P.M. on April 26, 1964, the hearse bearing Johnson's remains arrived at the historic pre–Civil War church from the Davis Funeral Home on West Pike Street and the pallbearers carried the heavy coffin inside. The rector began the service with a prayer, the opening line of which was appropriate: "Remember thy servant, O Lord."[27]

After the church service ended, the funeral procession formed for the trip out Main Street, past Louis and Ruth's first house where they had raised their girls, to Elkview Masonic Cemetery on a windy hill overlooking the valley crowded with old factories and warehouses on the fringes of Clarksburg. When the casket was positioned above Johnson's grave, Johnson's longtime friend and colleague, Paul Griffith, stepped forward. Griffith, a brigadier general and former national commander of the American Legion, had served with Johnson when he was assistant secretary of war under Roosevelt, when he was FDR's special envoy to India, and when he was secretary of defense. With the help of other American Legion leaders, Griffith removed the American flag from Johnson's coffin, carefully folded it, and presented it to Ruth Maxwell Johnson.[28]

Witnesses later remembered the smoke and the sound of a powerful old steam locomotive laboring up the valley toward Clarksburg as the big coffin was lowered into the ground.[29]

Johnson was buried under a marker bearing a few lines from one of his speeches delivered on the eve of World War II, words that Louis had told Ruth he wanted to be remembered for.

LET US ARM, LET US ARM SPEEDILY
LEST DARKNESS COME UPON US
WHILE WE ARE ON OUR WAY
AND FIND US UNPREPARED

Conclusion

LOUIS JOHNSON WAS an instrument of confrontation. Playing him with consummate skill, President Roosevelt encouraged Johnson to confront and run roughshod over his isolationist secretary of war. He deployed Johnson to fight against and overcome the army's resistance to sales of the latest warplanes to the Allies. FDR set up his assistant secretary of war to take the heat from the New Dealers and the isolationists while Johnson and selected members of the Roosevelt administration, with the support of their commander in chief, began laying the foundation of the military-industrial complex on the eve of World War II.

As President Truman's secretary of defense, Johnson was not just an instrument of confrontation, he was a battering ram. Lacking Roosevelt's finesse and talent for evasion, deception, and deniability, Truman used Johnson to help him ram through massive and arguably reckless reductions in the defense budget. Once the austere targets were established, Truman left Johnson with the job of fighting the admirals and the generals to implement the draconian cuts. And perhaps most daunting of all, Truman ordered Johnson to finish and win the battle which had driven his predecessor, quite literally, over the edge— unification of the army, the air force, the navy, and the marines under the authority and control of the secretary of defense.

The ways in which Roosevelt and Truman used Johnson as an instrument to confront and carry out extremely unpopular initiatives add to our understanding about how these two very different presidents thought and acted. But the fact that Johnson allowed himself to be used—to help Roosevelt prepare for war and then to help Truman vastly downsize the military—reveals even more about Louis Johnson.

Johnson was driven by politics, power, and personal ambition but rarely by principle. Based on his years as Roosevelt's assistant secretary of war and as the presidents' personal representative to India and his entire background from World War I supply officer to American Legion commander, it can be argued quite persuasively that Johnson's bedrock principle, the place where he would always draw the line, was military preparedness. Yet a decade later, when he was ordered by Truman to slash the defense budget and downsize the military, he went at it with a vengeance. In doing so, he used statistics and his skills as a lawyer and orator to convince himself and the American public that the nation's military preparedness was not being compromised. However, as his generals and admirals had warned him, and as he had to have known in his heart, he sacrificed the principle of military preparedness if indeed it ever was one of his core convictions.

Undoubtedly, in doing Harry Truman's bidding, Johnson was acting out of a sense of loyalty to his commander in chief, just as he remained loyal to FDR even after he was "ousted" from his administration. But loyalty to his president could not have been one of Johnson's unshakeable principles, because there were many occasions during the Truman years when Johnson consorted, if not conspired, with Truman's adversaries, including Senator Taft, General MacArthur, and members of the China Lobby.

With regard to the China Lobby and Johnson's support of the Chinese Nationalist regime, there is considerable evidence suggesting that Johnson felt deeply and sincerely that the United States should defend and support Formosa. Indeed, the fact that he was willing to risk his reputation and standing with the president on that tense Sunday night at Blair House when he insisted on putting Formosa ahead of the defense of South Korea indicates that support of Formosa was a matter of principle to him.

Despite this evidence, however, it would be erroneous to conclude that Louis Johnson would ever allow support of Formosa to take precedence over his political and personal ambitions should they come into conflict. In the spring of 1950, with Senator Joseph McCarthy tapping a wellspring of resentment about the "loss of China" and the spread of communism, it was simply good politics for Johnson to advocate support of Formosa, to criticize Dean Acheson's State Department, and to align himself with General Douglas MacArthur, who regarded Formosa as an unsinkable aircraft carrier. In addition, defense of Formosa would help Johnson achieve his greatest ambition, the presidency, since it would play well to the Red Scare in the United States and would be attractive to moderate Democrats and crossover Republicans.

Looking back at his public career, therefore, it is fair to conclude that Louis Johnson seldom acted on the basis of bedrock principles. He nearly always did what he thought would be politically expedient and what he believed would advance his own personal ambition.

Of course, this fact did not set him apart from many, some would say most, Washington politicians. What did differentiate him, however, was his personality. He was a difficult and complicated man. His arrogance was legendary. He was cocky, self-righteous, and imperious. He rarely raised his voice, but he could silence a room or intimidate a visitor with his icy stare and tight-lipped intensity. At the same time, he had a remarkable ability to befriend not only FDR and Truman but hundreds of powerful people in business and government, individuals on whom he lavished his attention because they would help him succeed in law, government, or the American Legion.

Those who knew Johnson were never neutral. Most who came into contact with him respected his accomplishments but were repelled and alienated by the size of his ego and the way he went about promoting himself, often at the expense of others. Many who worked for him were afraid of him. And his advocates, although relatively few in number, were as outspoken in his defense as his numerous critics were in tearing him down.

One of Johnson's most important and influential supporters was Franklin Roosevelt. He would cut Johnson out of the action when it suited his purposes, and he was certainly not one of Johnson's outspoken defenders, but he was nevertheless a strong believer in Johnson's administrative and organizational skills and his public-speaking abilities. Perhaps because of his own supreme self-confidence, Roosevelt did not seem put off by Johnson's outsize ego and naked ambition, and he more than anyone knew how to extract the best from Johnson's stubborn and prickly persona.

It has been argued that President Roosevelt was a great leader because he had implacable confidence in his vision of how events would unfold and he instinctively knew how to pull American opinion behind him as he moved toward his objective, advancing and then retreating before moving forward again.[1] Johnson's experience as FDR's assistant secretary of war provides solid support for this argument. Whether it was FDR's quiet encouragement of Johnson's efforts to plan for industrial mobilization and procurement reform, his enlistment of Johnson as his public stalking horse for massive air rearmament, or his orders that Johnson facilitate sales of warplanes to the Allies, Roosevelt used Johnson to help him prepare for the war that he knew was inevitable, and he deployed Johnson to help him test and shape public opinion.

Admittedly, Louis Johnson had a subordinate and relatively limited role on the world stage as America lurched toward war in the late 1930s. Nevertheless, his relationship with the leading actor, President Roosevelt, has revealed much about Roosevelt's core convictions and his genius as a leader of his people. He acted as his own secretary of state, and it is quite obvious that by the fall of 1937, when he gave his famous quarantine speech, Roosevelt had a firm grasp of geopolitics and the growing threat to the security of the United States posed by events in Europe and the Far East. With uncanny intuition, Roosevelt knew by 1938 that Adolph Hitler was an insatiable menace.

Instead of relying on oceans to defend the nation, as had his predecessors and as the U.S. Congress and prevailing public opinion would dictate, Roosevelt was convinced that he would have to actively intervene in world affairs to protect the

American people—first through diplomatic means, then as a supplier of arms, and finally, as a last resort, with the military. This strategy was consistent with, and probably emanated from, Roosevelt's fundamental belief, which he had held since his days as assistant secretary of the navy under President Woodrow Wilson, that the United States—using its assets, leverage, and bargaining power—must actively intervene in foreign affairs in order to protect and defend its citizens.

As a steadfast internationalist, and with the knowledge of the growing threats from abroad, FDR began in 1937 to work in an on-again, off-again fashion with Johnson to rearm America, to supply arms to the British and French, and to bring American public opinion in line with his sense of reality as quickly as possible. Through Johnson, Roosevelt's gifts for leadership were revealed.

By contrast, Louis Johnson's relationship with President Truman during the eighteen months he served as secretary of defense exposed the fault lines in Truman's leadership and the limits of his strategic vision. Unlike FDR, whose decisions to rearm America were premised on shrewd and realistic assessments of threats from Europe, Truman's decisions, at least until the outbreak of the Korean War, were based not on strategic considerations but rather on his view of what the nation could afford. He was obsessed with the need to achieve a balanced budget. And he had contempt for the judgment of professional military officers because he was convinced that they were "just like horses with blinders on. They can't see beyond the ends of their noses."[2]

In private meetings with Johnson, the designated secretary of defense, in early 1949, the president secured his commitment to slash the defense budget, cut out all of the "fat" in the military, and bash heads at the Pentagon to make unification of the services work. After he was confirmed as secretary, Johnson successfully carried out the Boss's orders with incredible energy and courage as torrents of criticism cascaded down on him. Although Truman never criticized Johnson publicly, he privately complained to his aides that Johnson was too heavy-handed,[3] and he positioned himself far above the firestorm which was to eventually consume Johnson.

On the question of China policy—the most momentous issue Truman faced and the issue which would eventually erode his presidency—Truman and Johnson stood apart, although both failed to understand the profound and historic consequences of the revolution which took place in China in the late 1940s and early 1950s. Truman preferred to view the world's problems in black-and-white, right-and-wrong terms. China did not fit his worldview. On the one hand, Truman was being told that Mao Tse-tung was leading a popular movement to free the Chinese people from foreign domination and imperialism. On the other hand, he knew that Mao was a Communist and he believed, naively and erroneously, as it turned out, that all Communists were controlled by machinations in the Kremlin and were bent on world conquest. At the same time, while Chiang Kai-shek's defeated Nationalists who had retreated to their redoubt on the island of Formosa were not Communists, Acheson was telling Truman that Chiang's regime was corrupt and had lost the confidence of the Chinese people.

The situation in China was too fluid, too ambiguous for Truman and his advisors. Although Truman prided himself on being decisive, he could not make a decision to support Chiang and he declined to make a decision to open a channel of communications with Mao. Lacking subtlety and unable to visualize alternatives, Truman was trapped into what he believed was his only choice—do nothing until the dust settles.[4] As a result, he alienated Mao and drove his government into closer relations with the Soviets and he gave false hope to Louis Johnson, the China Lobby, and Chiang's corrupt regime holding out on Formosa.

If Truman, as well as Acheson and Johnson, had had a broader, less parochial worldview and a more nuanced understanding of the relationship between communism and nationalism, some sort of rapprochement with mainland China might have been achieved. If that had happened, Truman might not have initiated economic and military assistance to Vietnam with all of the disastrous consequences which followed. And it is even possible that the Korean War could have been avoided, or at least the intervention of Chinese troops there might have been forestalled.

These roseate what-ifs of course did not come to pass, and America faced decades of bloodshed and confrontation in the Far East, ironically forging a close alliance with its defeated enemy, Japan, instead of with its old ally, China. Whether Roosevelt or another president would have made different choices in the Far East will never be known. What is known is that the choices Harry Truman made led to confrontation and conflict.

For a few brief years Louis Johnson occupied a small but significant niche in the story of these two great American presidents. Always controversial, always a fighter, Johnson earned a secure place in history.[5] As Roosevelt's assistant secretary of war, he was both advocate and architect of the arming of America on the eve of World War II. As Truman's embattled secretary of defense, Johnson achieved great success in unifying the armed services and dramatically reducing the defense budget. But like so many shooting stars in the Washington firmament, hubris, presidential ambition, and poor timing led to his descent.

NOTES

Abbreviations

FDRL   Franklin D. Roosevelt Presidential Library and Museum, Hyde Park, New York

FRUS   U.S. Department of State, *Foreign Relations of the United States* (Washington, D.C.: U.S. Government Printing Office, 1974, 1979), cited by year and volume

HSTL   Harry S. Truman Presidential Museum & Library, Independence, Missouri

LC   Library of Congress

NARA   National Archives & Records Administration

NYT   New York Times

OF   Official File, FDRL or Office File, HSTL

PPF   President's Personal File

PP HST   *Public Papers of the Presidents of the United States: Harry S. Truman, 1945–53* (Washington, D.C.: U.S. Government Printing Office, 1961–1966), cited by year

PSF   President's Secretary's File

RG   Record Group (in NARA)

Introduction

1. Margaret Truman, *Harry S. Truman* (New York: William Morrow & Co., 1973), 480.

2. Dean Acheson, *Present at the Creation* (New York: W.W. Norton & Co., 1969), 374.

3. "unsuited," Clark Clifford, *Counsel to the President* (New York: Random House, 1991), 280; "possibly the worst appointment," David McCullough, *Truman* (New York: Simon & Schuster, 1992), 741.

4. Robert Dallek, *Franklin D. Roosevelt and American Foreign Policy, 1932–45* (New York: Oxford University Press, 1979); David Reynolds, *From Munich to Pearl Harbor: Roosevelt's America and the Origins of the Second World War* (Chicago: Ivan R. Dee, 2001).

5. Arnold A. Offner, *Another Such Victory: President Truman and the Cold War, 1945–1953* (Stanford, Calif.: Stanford University Press, 2002), xii (Burns's views paraphrased). See James MacGregor Burns, *Roosevelt: The Lion and the Fox* (New York: Harcourt, Brace and Company, 1956).

6. Clay Blair, *The Forgotten War: America in Korea 1950–1953* (Annapolis, Md.: Naval Institute Press, 1987); Offner, *Another Such Victory*.

7. McCullough, *Truman*; Melvyn P. Leffler, *A Preponderance of Power: National Security, the Truman Administration and the Cold War* (Stanford, Calif.: Stanford University Press, 1992); Alonzo L. Hamby, *Man of the People: A Life of Harry Truman* (New York: Oxford University Press, 1995).

1. Bedford Blood

1. James A. Bell, "Defense Secretary Louis Johnson," *The American Mercury*, June 1950, 647; James M. Callahan, *History of West Virginia, Old and New* (Chicago: American Historical Society, 1923), III: 123.

2. Lula Jeter Parker, *The History of Bedford County, Virginia* (Bedford, Va.: The Bedford Democrat, 1954), 9, 104.

3. Philip A. Bruce, Lyon G. Tyler, and Richard L. Morton, *History of Virginia* (Chicago: American Historical Society, 1924), I: 185; R. H. Early, *Campbell Chronicles and Family Sketches* (Lynchburg, Va.: J. P. Bell Company, 1927), 452; "The Leftwich Historical Association, Inc.," http://www.leftwich.org; Hamilton Eckenrode, *Virginia Soldiers of the American Revolution* (Richmond: State Library and Archives, 1912), I: 265; http://www.leftwich.org/family/I795.html.

4. "The Leftwich Historical Association, Inc."; Walter Lee Hopkins, *Leftwich-Turner Families of Virginia and Their Connections* (Richmond, Va.: J. W. Fergusson, 1931), 66, 89.

5. *Bedford County Families and History*, compiled from Henry Hardesty's *Historical and Geographical Encyclopedia* (1883), edited, indexed, and available from Jim Presgraves, Bookworm & Silverfish, Wytheville, Virginia; Peter Viemiester, ed., *Personal Histories of Bedford County* (1985), Bedford City/County Museum, Genealogy Library, Bedford Library, Bedford, Virginia, 16; Robert J. Driver Jr., *58th Virginia Infantry* (Lynchburg: H. E. Howard, 1990), 17, 22, 24, 27, 31, 33, 36, 62–63, 89; Gordon C. Rhea, *The Battles for Spotsylvania Court House and the Road to Yellow Tavern, May 7–12, 1864* (Baton Rouge: Louisiana State University Press, 1997), 232–252; Eckenrode, *Virginia Soldiers of the American Revolution*, II: 18.

6. Bedford County land records in Bedford County Clerk's Office; "Personal Histories of Bedford County," 16; Early, *Campbell Chronicles*, 96.

7. Jack Alexander, "Stormy New Boss of the Pentagon," *Saturday Evening Post*, July 30, 1949, 67–68; "Louis Johnson Honored," *Norfolk and Western Magazine*, July 1937, 280.

8. William C. Sponaugle, "Biographies of Southwestern Virginians," Vertical File Biography, Virginia Room, Roanoke Public Library; E. B. Jacobs, *History of Roanoke City and Norfolk Western Railroad Company* (Roanoke, Va.: Stone Printers, 1912), 209.

9. Bruce, *History of Virginia*, V: 474; Widow's Service Pension, War of 1812, for Lockey (Leftwich) Johnson of Leesville, Virginia, Surname File Copy, Bedford City/County Museum; Bedford County Clerk's Office Land Records, Book 26, Page 306 of Grantee Records and Book 27, Page 247 of Grantee Records.

10. Marshall Wingfield, *Pioneer Families of Franklin County, Virginia* (Berryville, Va.: Chesapeake Book Company, 1964), 201, 203; Hopkins, *Leftwich-Turner Families and Their Connections*, 88.

11. Interview with Mrs. Virginia Johnson, Roanoke, Virginia, July 16, 1977.

12. Wingfield, *Pioneer Families of Franklin County*, 203.

13. Bruce, *History of Virginia*, V: 474.

14. Virginia Johnson interview.

15. Sponaugle, "Biographies of Southwestern Virginians"; Bruce, *History of Virginia*, V: 474.

16. Raymond P. Barnes, A *History of Roanoke* (Radford, Va.: Commonwealth Press, 1968), 174–197, 230–231, 251, 399; Clare White, *Roanoke, 1740–1982* (Roanoke, Va.: Roanoke Valley Historical Society, 1982), 65, 68–88.

17. White, *Roanoke*, 68–88.

18. Raymond Barnes, "Neighborhood Grocery in Old Days Was Wonderful," *Roanoke World News*, February 27, 1960.

19. Alexander, "Stormy New Boss," 67–68; "Louis Johnson Honored."

20. "Souvenir of Grace Methodist Episcopal Church, South Roanoke, Va., 1926" (n.p., n.d.), see "Historical Sketch" on page 11 (in co-author Roll's possession).

21. Alexander, "Stormy New Boss," 67; Bell, "Defense Secretary Louis Johnson," 647.

22. Interview with Mrs. Ruth Johnson, Clarksburg, West Virginia, June 18, 1976. In 1912, Louis became an Episcopalian; he remained so until his death.

23. Bell, "Defense Secretary Louis Johnson," 647.

24. Ibid.; Alexander, "Stormy New Boss," 68.

25. Coy Barefoot, *The Corner* (Charlottesville, Va.: Howell Press, 2001), 93–108.

26. *University of Virginia Record, 1908–09* (Charlottesville: University of Virginia, February 1902), passim.

27. "Academic Transcript of Louis A. Johnson, University of Virginia," transcript presented to co-author McFarland by Mrs. Ruth Johnson.

28. John Ritchie, *The First Hundred Years: A Short History of the School of Law of the University of Virginia for the Period 1826–1926* (Charlottesville: University Press of Virginia, 1978), 63–118; Bruce Philip Alexander, *History of the University of Virginia, 1819–1919: The Lengthened Shadow of One Man* (New York: Macmillan, 1916), V: 170–177.

29. "Academic Transcript of Louis A. Johnson."

30. Ibid.; Boyd B. Stutler, "A Prominent West Virginian," *The West Virginia Review*, May 1931, 263; Bell, "Defense Secretary Louis Johnson," 648; Alexander, "Stormy New Boss," 68.

31. *Corks and Curls* (yearbook published by the fraternities of the University of Virginia), volumes for 1909, 1910, 1911, and 1912, passim.

32. Robert S. Allen and William V. Shannon, *The Truman Merry-Go-Round* (New York: Vanguard Press, 1950), 446; *College Topics*, March 23, 1912, University of Virginia Library.

33. Barefoot, *The Corner*, 96.

34. *College Topics*, February 7, 21, 24, 1912; *Cavalier Daily*, March 5, 1949, University of Virginia Library; Stutler, "A Prominent West Virginian," 263.

35. Alexander, "Stormy New Boss," 68.

36. Interview with Haymond Maxwell Jr., Clarksburg, West Virginia, June 13, 1976; *College Topics* (University of Virginia), May 16, 1941; *Cavalier Daily*, March 5, 1949.

2. Foot in the Door

1. Phil Conley, "A Young Man of Vision," *West Virginia Review*, July 1932, 410; Dorothy Davis, *History of Harrison County, West Virginia* (Clarksburg, W.Va.: American Association of University Women, 1970), 80; *New York Herald Tribune*, April 11, 1942; Haymond Maxwell interview, June 13, 1976.

2. Callahan, *History of West Virginia*, I: 458, 573–574; Davis, *History of Harrison County*, 80, 278, 335.

3. *Clarksburg Exponent*, August 22, 1912; Davis, *History of Harrison County*, passim.

4. Davis, *History of Harrison County*, 126–156.

5. Conley, "A Young Man of Vision," 411.

6. With two judges dissenting, the case was reported by the Supreme Court of Appeals of West Virginia as *Denham v. Robinson*, 72 W. Va. 243, 77 S.E. 970 (1913).

7. Early, *Campbell Chronicles*, 36–37, 180–181, 207; Parker, *The History of Bedford County*, 15, 27–28, 134; Daughters of the American Revolution, *Bedford Villages — Lost and Found* (Bedford, Va.: DAR, Peaks of Otter Chapter, 1998), II: 112.

8. Anna Rothe, ed., *Current Biography 1949* (New York: H. W. Wilson, 1950), 298; Alexander, "Stormy New Boss," 68; Davis, *History of Harrison County*, 130.

9. Interview with Chesney Carney, Clarksburg, West Virginia, July 12, 1977.

10. Interviews with Ruth Maxwell Johnson, Clarksburg, West Virginia, June 18, 1976, and July 12, 1977; interviews with W. B. "Bill" Maxwell, Clarksburg, West Virginia, June 18, 1976, and July 12, 1977; interview with Haymond Maxwell, Jr., Clarksburg, West Virginia, July 12, 1977.

11. Interview with Jean Kearney, Washington, D.C., March 27, 2002; "everyone in Clarksburg will know my name," interview with Thompson Powers, Washington, D.C., March 12, 2002.

12. *Clarksburg Exponent*, March 17, 19, and April 4, 5, and 8, 1914.

13. Theodore A. Huntley, *John W. Davis* (New York: Duffield and Company, 1924), xii.

14. Ruth Johnson and Haymond Maxwell interviews; interview with Douglas Bailey, Clarksburg, West Virginia, July 12, 1977; Alexander, "Stormy New Boss," 68; C. F. L. Chamberlaine to Louis Johnson, November 30, 1937, Box 7, General Correspondence, Louis A. Johnson Papers, Harrison Institute and Small Library, University of Virginia, Charlottesville, Virginia, hereafter Johnson Papers.

15. Johnson to L. O. Gastineau, December 23, 1935, Box 11, L. O. Gastineau, Johnson Papers.

16. *Clarksburg Exponent*, November 4, 9, 1916; *Clarksburg Daily Telegram*, November 8, 1916.

17. John G. Morgan, "John Jacob Cornwell: Fifteenth Governor," *West Virginia Governors* (Charleston, W.Va.: Newspaper Agency Corp., 1960), 45–47; *Clarksburg Exponent*, January 17, 28, 1917.

18. John T. Harris, comp., *West Virginia Legislative Handbook and Manual and Official Register, 1917* (Charleston, W.Va.: Tribune Printing Co., 1917), 740; *Journal of House of Delegates of the State of West Virginia For the Thirty-Third Regular Session Commencing January 10, 1917 and the Extraordinary Session of 1917* (Charleston, W.Va.: n.p., 1917), 75, 87, 110, 230; *Clarksburg Exponent*, February 23, 1917; *Charleston Mail*, February 19 and March 7, 1917.

19. *Clarksburg Exponent*, January 28, 1917.

20. Rothe, ed., *Current Biography 1949*, 424.

21. John T. Harris, comp., *West Virginia Legislative Handbook and Manual and Official Register, 1918* (Charleston, W.Va.: Tribune Printing Co., 1918), 371; *Clarksburg Exponent*, February 24, 1917; *Charleston Mail*, March 5, 1917.

22. Interview with Stephen Ailes, Washington, D.C., July 27, 1977; Johnson to James Roosevelt, August 12, 1937, Box 85, Confidential File "C," Johnson Papers; John J. Cornwell, *A Mountain Trail: To the School Room, the Editor's Chair, the Lawyer's Office, and the Governorship of West Virginia* (Philadelphia: Dorrance and Co., 1939), 99.

23. Harris, *West Virginia Legislative Handbook*, 1918, 371–372, 771–772; Conley, "Young Man of Vision," 411, *Clarksburg Exponent*, May 16, 20, 22, and 27, 1917.

24. William E. Miller, *You Can't Tell by Looking at 'Em: My Fifty Years with Steptoe & Johnson* (1981), 34.

25. Interview with Herb Underwood, Washington, D.C., March 13, 2003; interview with Philip P. Steptoe Jr., Washington, D.C., October 4, 2002.

26. "Maxwell Family History," a three-page account prepared by Frank J. Maxwell, Jr., Clarksburg, West Virginia, and presented to co-author McFarland; interview with Frank Maxwell Jr., Clarksburg, West Virginia, April 15, 2003; *Clarksburg Telegram*, June 10, 1930; Ruth Johnson interviews; Davis, *History of Harrison County*, 684, 777–779.

27. *Clarksburg Exponent*, August 24, 1917.

28. Ruth Johnson interviews.

29. "Statement of the Military Service of Louis Arthur Johnson" (hereafter Service Record), by E. J. Conley, Adjutant General, Box 148, Biographical Information, Johnson Papers; Officers Training Camp Record—Louis A. Johnson, made available to co-author McFarland by Mrs. Ruth Johnson.

30. Ibid.; *The 80th Division Yearbook, 1920*: Robert D. Burhans, *History and Heraldry of the 80th Division* (Richmond, Va., 1960); *80th Division, Summary of Operations in the World War* (Washington, D.C.: U.S. American Battle Monuments Commission, U.S. Government Printing Office, 1944); letter to co-author Roll dated April 5, 2003, by Bruce and Cecilia Smith writing for The Friends of the 80th Division (hereafter Smith letter).

31. Service Record.

32. *The 80th Division Yearbook 1920* (in co-author Roll's possession); Smith letter; Robert H. Ferrell, *Off the Record: The Private Papers of Harry S. Truman* (New York: Penguin, 1980), 192.

33. Ruth Maxwell to Mrs. W. B. Maxwell (her mother), October 31, 1918, loaned to co-author Roll by Steven Maxwell.

34. *The 80th Division Yearbook, 1920*; Service Record.

35. Johnson to Ruth Maxwell, November [n.d.] 1918, loaned to co-author McFarland by Ruth Johnson; Ruth Johnson interviews.

36. Stutler, "A Prominent West Virginian," 264; Service Record.

37. Lonnie J. White, *The 90th Division in World War I* (Manhattan, Kans.: Sunflower University Press 1996), 176–184.

38. Johnson to Ruth Maxwell, March 14, 1919, loaned to co-author McFarland by Ruth Johnson.

39. Ruth Johnson interviews.

40. Herbert Corey, "The Secret Shake-Up in the U.S. Army," *Liberty*, March 11, 1939, 21; Bell, "Defense Secretary Louis Johnson," 648–649; Alexander, "Stormy New Boss," 27.

41. Service Record.

42. Susan Maxwell (Ruth Maxwell's stepsister) to Mrs. W. B. Maxwell, October 11, 1919, and Ruth Maxwell to Mrs. W. B. Maxwell, January 11, 1920, loaned to co-author Roll by Steven Maxwell.

43. *Clarksburg Exponent*, February 8, 1920; Ruth Johnson interviews; Mrs. Marcellus (Kate) Johnson to Mrs. W. B. Maxwell, February 3, 1920, loaned to co-author Roll by Steven Maxwell; interview with Norma Monroe, Maxwell family housekeeper, Clarksburg, West Virginia, July 16, 1982.

44. Johnson to Mrs. W. B. Maxwell, February 11, 1920; Ruth Johnson to Mrs. W. B. Maxwell, February 15, 1920, loaned to co-author Roll by Steven Maxwell.

45. Douglas Bailey interview.

46. Ruth Johnson to "Margaret" who was taking care of "my babies," December 30,

1923; Ruth Johnson to Mrs. W. B. Maxwell, January 9, March 9, May 4, May 12, May 13, May 26, and July 8, 1924, loaned to co-author Roll by Steven Maxwell.

47. Ruth Johnson to Mrs. W. B. Maxwell, September 18, 1924, loaned to co-author Roll by Steven Maxwell.

48. Ruth Johnson to Mrs. W. B. Maxwell, date illegible but probably written in 1925, loaned to co-author Roll by Steven Maxwell.

49. Chesney Carney interview; interview with Lem Jarvis, Clarksburg, West Virginia, July 13, 1977.

50. The challenged law was reported in Acts W. Va. c 71.

51. *Pennsylvania v. West Virginia*, 262 U.S. 553 (1923).

52. Miller, *You Can't Tell by Looking at 'Em*, 31–37; interview with William E. Miller, Washington, D.C., July 27, 1977; Stephen Ailes interview; Conley, "Young Man of Vision," 410.

53. Ralph Bohannon to co-author McFarland, January 28, 1978.

54. Conley, "Young Man of Vision," 411.

55. William H. Harbaugh, *Lawyer's Lawyer: The Life of John W. Davis* (New York: Oxford University Press, 1973), 207.

56. Ibid., 216.

57. Davis, *History of Harrison County*, 150; *Clarksburg Exponent*, August 11, 1924.

58. Johnson to Ruth Maxwell, March 14, 1919, loaned to co-author McFarland by Ruth Johnson; Roscoe Baker, *The American Legion and American Foreign Policy* (New York: Bookman Associates, 1954), 12–13.

59. Biographical sketch of Louis Johnson from history file, National Publicity Division, American Legion Library and Archives, Indianapolis, Indiana.

60. McCullough, *Truman*, 150.

61. Photographs on battlefield in France, on Champs-Elysées in Paris, and in Venice and signed menu from S.S. *Pennland* loaned to co-author Roll by James Guiher Jr.

62. *Presenting Louis A. Johnson of West Virginia* (Charleston, W.Va.: Woodward Printers, n.d.), 3–7; *West Virginia Legionnaire*, September 15, 1930; Davis, *History of Harrison County*, 265; Conley "Young Man of Vision," 411; *1931 Handbook of the American Legion Department of West Virginia* (Charleston, W.Va.: n.p., 1931).

63. Baker, *The American Legion*, 25.

64. Philip Von Blon, "Keynotes and Drumbeats," *The American Legion Monthly* (October 1932), 16–20; Paul H. Griffith oral history; "Johnson Tribute," NYT, September 16, 1932, 1, 15.

65. "State Pays Johnson Tribute," *Pittsburgh Sun-Telegraph*, September 26, 1932, 1.

66. Speeches of Louis A. Johnson, Box 1, October 1932–October 1933, Johnson Papers; NYT, November 12, 1932, 1, 6.

67. Richard Norton Smith, *An Uncommon Man: The Triumph of Herbert Hoover* (New York: Simon & Schuster, 1984), 140; David Burner, *Herbert Hoover: A Public Life* (New York: Knopf, 1978), 312; David M. Kennedy, *Freedom from Fear: The American People in Depression and War, 1929–1945* (New York: Oxford University Press, 1999), 92.

68. Roger Daniels, *The Bonus March: An Episode of the Great Depression* (Westport, Conn.: Greenwood, 1971), 43–56.

69. Von Blon, "Keynotes and Drumbeats," 16; Daniels, *The Bonus March*, 187.

70. Roger Burlingame, "The Counter Attack," *The Atlantic Monthly* 152 (November 1933), 27.

71. Frank Freidel, *Franklin D. Roosevelt: Launching the New Deal* (Boston: Little, Brown and Co., 1973), 246–247; Richard Seelye Jones, *A History of the American Legion* (Indianapolis: Bobbs-Merrill, 1946), 152–153.

72. Alexander, "Stormy New Boss," 69; *NYT*, April 30, 1933, 33.

73. Franklin D. Roosevelt to Johnson, May 16, 1933, PPF 350, FDRL; *NYT*, April 30, 1933, 33.

74. Burlingame, "The Counter Attack," 529.

75. *NYT*, May 11, 1933, 1; Freidel, *Launching the New Deal*, 448–449; Jones, *History of the American Legion*, 151–153.

76. Freidel, *Launching the New Deal*, 449; Jones, *History of the American Legion*, 153.

77. Memorandum to the President from Stephen Early, September 16, 1935, PPF 2822, FDRL; Stephen Early to Johnson, August 27, 1936, PPF 350, FDRL; Ruth Johnson interviews.

78. Telegram, Johnson to Roosevelt, August 1, 1933, Telegram, Roosevelt to Johnson, August 8, 1933, Johnson to Roosevelt, August 7, 1933, Roosevelt to Johnson, September 11, 1933, all in PPF 350, FDRL; "to offer their loyal cooperation and services," *NYT*, August 4, 1933, 8.

79. Roosevelt to Johnson, September 18, 1933, PPF 350, FDRL.

80. Telegrams: Johnson to Roosevelt, September 19 and October 9, 1933, Roosevelt to Johnson, October 23, 1933, Memorandum to the President from Stephen Early, September 16, 1935, all in PPF 350, FDRL; *NYT*, October 3, 1933, 1.

81. Roosevelt to Johnson, August 26, 1935, Johnson to Roosevelt, September 5, 1935, both in PPF 2822, FDRL; "Arms Before Men," *Time*, August 22, 1938, 24; "Transcript of Radio Address of Col. Louis Johnson, October 20, 1936," Box 1, Speeches by Johnson, Johnson Papers; Johnson to Stephen Early, January 11, 1936, Memorandum for Stephen Early from Johnson, July 24, 1936, and October 15, 1936, Box 8, Johnson, Stephen T. Early Papers (hereafter Early Papers), FDRL.

82. Arthur Koontz to Marvin McIntyre, July 16, 1934, OF 300, Box 73, West Virginia, FDRL.

83. Paul Dickson and Thomas B. Allen, *The Bonus Army* (New York: Walker & Co., 2004), 254; "Two Records: Hoover vs. Roosevelt," Memorandum by Johnson to Colonel J. Monroe Johnson, January 31, 1936, PPF 350, FDRL.

84. Maxine Block, ed., *Current Biography 1942* (New York: H. L. Wilson Co., 1942), 424.

3. *Like Feuding Schoolboys*

1. *NYT*, August 28, 1936, 1.

2. Ibid.; James A. Farley interview, New York City, August 1, 1968.

3. Ruth Johnson interviews.

4. *NYT*, August 28, 1936, 1, 18; *NYT*, September 2, 1936, 12; *Army and Navy Journal*, September 12, 19, 1936.

5. *Army and Navy Journal*, September 19, 1936.

6. *NYT*, June 25, 1936, 16; *NYT*, August 6, 1936, 12; Stephen Early to Louis Johnson, August 27, 1936, PPF 2822, FDRL; "Transcript of Radio Address of Louis Johnson over NBC," October 20, 1936, Box 1, Johnson Papers; James Farley interview.

7. Homer Cummings to Roosevelt, September 24, 1936, OF 62, President's Index (retained in White House), FDRL; Grace Tully, *FDR: My Boss* (New York: Charles Scribner's Sons, 1949), 196–197.

8. Memo of telegram, Marvin H. McIntyre to Stephen Early, September 2, 1936, Box 4, OF 25, War Department and Cross Reference, FDRL; Telegram, Roosevelt to Harry Woodring, September 25, 1936, PPF 663, Harry Woodring, FDRL; *NYT*, September 26, 1936, 1.

9. *NYT*, November 4, 1936, 1; *Washington Evening Star*, July 14, 1937, 1; James Farley

interview; Bell, "Defense Secretary Louis Johnson," 649; Burlingame, "The Counter Attack," 27.

10. Dozens of letters of endorsement of Johnson's appointment as secretary of war,
most of which are dated January and February 1937, are found in OF 25A, War Department Endorsements for Secretary, FDRL.

11. Richard F. Fenno Jr., *The President's Cabinet: An Analysis in the Period from Wilson to Eisenhower* (Cambridge, Mass.: Harvard University Press, 1959), 58.

12. John C. O'Laughlin to General Douglas MacArthur, November 28, 1936, Box 54,
John C. O'Laughlin Papers, LC, hereafter O'Laughlin Papers; Jesse H. Jones, with Edward Angly, *Fifty Billion Dollars: My Thirteen Years with the RFC* (New York: Macmillan, 1951), 256; *NYT*, December 18, 1936, 19.

13. *Army and Navy Journal*, November 28, 1936, and January 30, 1937; *Army and
Navy Register*, September 5, 1936; *Army Ordnance*, November/December 1936, 166; *The
Reserve Officer*, October 1936, 3.

14. Keith D. McFarland, *Harry H. Woodring: A Political Biography of FDR's Controversial Secretary of War* (Lawrence: University Press of Kansas, 1975), 109.

15. *NYT*, May 18, 1937, 1; James A. Farley, *Jim Farley's Story: The Roosevelt Years*
(New York: McGraw-Hill Co., 1948), 80–81; James Farley interview.

16. McFarland, *Harry H. Woodring*, 109–110; interviews with Gerald P. Nye, Washington, D.C., July 25, 1968, and Charles I. Faddis, Waynesburg, Pennsylvania, August 4,
1970; "Arms Before Men," 24.

17. *NYT*, May 18, 1937, 1; *NYT*, September 12, 1937, 1, 8.

18. James Farley interview.

19. Lawrence Houghterling to Roosevelt, June 7, 1937, forwarded to Harry Woodring
for comments, and Woodring to Roosevelt, June 11, 1937, both in PSF, Woodring, Box
38, FDRL; *NYT*, June 4, 1937, 1.

20. Woodring to Roosevelt, June 11, 1937, OF 25A, Endorsements for Assistant Secretary, FDRL; *NYT*, June 15, 1937, 17.

21. James Farley interview.

22. White House Memo for the President from Senator Matthew M. Neely, April 27,
1938, OF 25A, Endorsements for Assistant Secretary, FDRL.

23. James Farley interview; Eugene Gerhart, *America's Advocate: Robert H. Jackson*
(Indianapolis: Bobbs-Merrill, 1958), 163–164.

24. Drew Pearson and Robert S. Allen, "The Merry-Go Round," *Akron Beacon Journal*, December 1, 1938.

25. Diane A. Bailey, *The Mayflower: Washington's Second Best Address* (Washington,
D.C.: The Donning Company, 2001), 15–16, 96–99; Judith R. Cohen, *The Mayflower Hotel: Grande Dame of Washington, D.C.* (New York: Balance House, Ltd., 1987), 30, 42.

26. *NYT*, June 29, 1937, 9.

27. McFarland, *Harry H. Woodring*, 110–115; Forrest Pogue, *George C. Marshall:
Education of a General* (New York: Viking, 1963), 318; Ed Cray, *General of the Army:
George Marshall, Soldier and Statesman* (New York: W.W. Norton & Co., 1990), 127.

28. Pogue, *George C. Marshall: Education of a General*, 318; Thomas Parrish,
Roosevelt and Marshall: The Personal Story (New York: William Morrow and Company,
1989), 81; Conrad Black, *Franklin Delano Roosevelt: Champion of Freedom* (New York:
Public Affairs, 2003), 497.

29. "The Policy and Status of the U.S. Army," *Congressional Digest*, March 1938, 73;
Congressional Directory, December 21, 1937, 429; McFarland, *Harry H. Woodring*, 83.

30. Keith D. McFarland, "F.D.R. and the Great War Department Feud," *Army*,
March 1976, 36–37.

31. Robert Sherwood, *Roosevelt and Hopkins: An Intimate History* (New York: Harper & Brothers, 1948), 135.

32. Fenno, *President's Cabinet*, 45–36, Elting Morrison, *Turmoil and Tradition: A Study of the Life and Times of Henry L. Stimson* (New York: History Book Club, 2003), 488–489; *New York Herald Tribune*, June 21, 1940.

33. McFarland, *Harry H. Woodring*, 145–146; Burns, *Roosevelt: The Lion and the Fox*, 372.

34. Burns, *Roosevelt: The Lion and the Fox*, 372; Cordell Hull, *The Memoirs of Cordell Hull* (New York: Macmillan, 1948), 205–206; Frances Perkins, *The Roosevelt I Knew* (New York: Viking, 1946), 55; John T. Flynn, *The Roosevelt Myth* (Garden City, N.Y.: Garden City Publishing Co., 1949), 55; McFarland, "F.D.R. and the Great War Department Feud," 35–37; Arthur Krock, *Memoirs: Sixty Years on the Firing Line* (London: Cassell, 1970), 202.

35. "Scandalous Spats," *Time*, October 9, 1939, 16.

36. Harry H. Woodring Papers, Spencer Research Library, University of Kansas, Lawrence, Kansas, hereafter Woodring Papers; John C. O'Laughlin to Gen. John Perkins, December 3, 1938, O'Laughlin Papers; William Ritchie to co-author McFarland, June 2, 1969.

37. Harry Woodring to John J. Ewing, November 22, 1938, Woodring Papers, Spencer Research Library; interview with Helen Woodring, Wilmington, Delaware, July 20, 1968; interview with William Ritchie, Washington, D.C., June 13, 1969.

38. *Topeka* (Kansas) *Capital*, November 11, 1947.

39. Marquis W. Childs, *I Write from Washington* (New York: Harper, 1942), 161.

40. "Scandalous Spats"; "The High Cost of Peace," *Fortune*, March 19, 1939, 45.

41. William R. Frye, *Marshall: Citizen Soldier* (Indianapolis: Bobbs-Merrill, 1947), 253–254.

42. Bernard M. Baruch, *The Public Years* (New York: Holt, Rinehart and Winston, 1960), 277.

43. William A. Wieland to Louis Johnson, January 25, 1938, White House Memo for the Files, February 4, 1938, Memorandum for the President from Marvin McIntyre, February 4, 1938, all in OF 25, War Department 1938–39, Box 6, FDRL; Memo regarding Johnson and Latin American Flight, January 25, 1938, OF 25-V, War Department, Chief of Air Corps 1938, FDRL; Drew Pearson and Robert Allen, "The Merry-Go-Round," *Akron Beacon Journal*, February 25, 1938.

44. *NYT*, February 10, 1938, 10; *NYT*, February 16, 1938, 42; *NYT*, February 18, 1938, 1; *NYT*, February 19, 1938, 14; *NYT*, February 21, 1938, 1; *NYT*, February 28, 1938, 3; *NYT*, March 1, 1938, 11; General Curtis E. LeMay with MacKinley Kantor, *Mission with LeMay* (Garden City, N.Y.: Doubleday, 1965), 152–166.

45. *Army and Navy Journal*, November 25, 1939; Edward Jablonski, *Flying Fortress* (Garden City, N.Y.: Doubleday, 1965), 17–19.

46. "Daily Air Corps Record 1938–39," January 14, 1938, Box 56, Official File 1932–46, Henry H. Arnold Papers, LC.

47. Drew Pearson and Robert S. Allen, "The Merry-Go-Round," *Akron Beacon Journal*, December 20, 1939.

48. John C. O'Laughlin to General John J. Pershing, January 15, 1938, Box 58, O'Laughlin Papers; interview with Col. Malin Craig Jr., Washington, January 31, 1975.

49. John C. O'Laughlin to General John Pershing, February 12, 1938, Box 58, O'Laughlin Papers.

50. Katherine T. Marshall, *Together: Annals of an Army Wife* (New York: Tupper and Love, 1946), 41.

51. Pogue, *George C. Marshall: Education of a General*, 314, 315, 319.

52. Frye, *Marshall: Citizen Soldier*, 248.

53. Hugh A. Drum to Malin Craig, May 31, 1938, and Craig to Drum, June 1, 1938, both in Box 85, Johnson Papers; John C. O'Laughlin to General John J. Pershing, April 1, 1939, Box 58, O'Laughlin Papers; Boake Carter, "New Army Head Personal Choice: Why Selected," n.p. n.d., Clippings, Woodring Papers, Spencer Research Library; Frye, *Marshall: Citizen Soldier*, 246; Pogue, *George C. Marshall: Education of a General*, 329.

54. John C. O'Laughlin to General John J. Pershing, January 14, 1939, Box 58, O'Laughlin Papers.

55. Pogue, *George C. Marshall: Education of a General*, 326.

56. Cray, *General of the Army*, 137–138.

57. Pogue, *George C. Marshall: Education of a General*, 325.

58. Cray, *General of the Army*, 139.

59. Pogue, *George C. Marshall: Education of a General*, 330.

60. Doris Fleeson, "Story behind Marshall Blast by Woodring," *St. Louis Post Dispatch*, August 4, 1954.

61. George Marshall to Louis Johnson, March 12, 1949, Box 60, Folder—Louis Johnson, George C. Marshall Papers, George C. Marshall Research Library, Lexington, Virginia.

62. *Army and Navy Journal*, February 19, 1938; *Army and Navy Register*, December 14, 1938; Forest C. Pogue, *George C. Marshall: Ordeal and Hope, 1939–1943* (New York: Viking, 1966), 21–22; "Arms Before Men," 25.

63. General William Ritchie to co-author McFarland, June 2, 1969; William Ritchie interview; Nancy H. Hooker ed., *The Moffat Papers* (Cambridge, Mass.: Harvard University Press, 1956), 327, *Washington Times Herald*, December 27, 1939; Drew Pearson and Robert Allen, "The Merry-Go-Round," *Akron Beacon Journal*, October 21, 1939; Joseph Alsop and Robert Kintner, "The Capital Parade," *San Francisco Chronicle*, September 25, 1939; Jonathan Mitchell, "M-Day Man: Louis Johnson," *The New Republic*, February 22, 1939, 63–65.

64. William Ritchie interview.

65. General George Van Horn Mosely to General Douglas MacArthur, September 26, 1938, and October 21, 1939, Mosely File, Record Group 10, Private Correspondence, 1932–1964, Papers of General Douglas MacArthur, MacArthur Memorial Library and Archives, Norfolk, Virginia; Malin Craig interview; "Arms Before Men," 25.

66. William Ritchie interview; Malin Craig interview.

67. *Army and Navy Journal*, February 19, 1938, and March 12, 1938; Drew Pearson and Robert Allen, "The Merry-Go-Round," *Akron Beacon Journal*, September 2, 1939, October 21, 1939, and February 24, 1942; numerous press clippings, Box 74, Johnson Papers. Johnson's detractors included Boake Carter and Jay Franklin. See Jay Franklin, "We the People: The Liquidation of Louis Johnson," released September 15, 1939, Box 74, Johnson Papers.

68. Alsop and Kintner, "The Capital Parade."

69. "Scandalous Spats," 16.

70. *Washington Daily News*, September 28, 1939.

71. "Johnson v. Woodring," *Newsweek*, September 27, 1937, 42; Walter Winchell, "Winchell on Broadway," *Akron Beacon Journal*, March 8, 1938; John C. O'Laughlin to General Robert Wood, November 1, 1938, Box 71, O'Laughlin to Gen. John J. Pershing, February 25, 1939, Box 58, both in O'Laughlin Papers; Stephen Early to Johnson, July 29, 1940, Box 8, Johnson Papers.

72. Harold L. Ickes, *The Secret Diary of Harold L. Ickes*, vol. II, *The Inside Struggle, 1936–1939* (New York: Simon and Schuster, 1953–1954), 538, 552, 553, 716–718, 720

(hereafter *The Inside Struggle*); and vol. III, *The Lowering Clouds, 1939–1941*, 51, 55 (hereafter *The Lowering Clouds*).

73. Ickes, *The Inside Struggle*, 718, 720.

74. McFarland, *Harry H. Woodring*, 153–154.

75. Ickes, *The Lowering Clouds*, 196.

76. Farley, *Jim Farley's Story*, 114; James Farley interview.

77. *NYT*, October 12, 1939, 1, 10; *Congressional Record*, 76th Congress, 2nd Session, vol. 85, pt. 2, Appendix, 277–278; Charles Faddis interview; L. C. Arends to co-author Mc-Farland, May 2, 1968; interview with Dow W. Harter, Washington, D.C., June 13, 1969.

78. McFarland, *Harry H. Woodring*, 155–158.

4. *"Basic Shift in Mobilization Planning"*

1. Robert A. Divine, *The Reluctant Belligerent: American Entry into World War II*, 2nd ed. (New York: John Wiley & Son, 1979); Robert A. Divine, *The Illusion of Neutrality: Franklin D. Roosevelt and the Struggle over the Arms Embargo* (Chicago: University of Chicago Press, 1962); Arnold A. Offner, *American Appeasement: United States Foreign Policy and Germany, 1933–1938* (Cambridge, Mass.: Belknap Press of Harvard University Press, 1969).

2. Burns, *Roosevelt: The Lion and the Fox*, 400–404.

3. Dallek, *Franklin D. Roosevelt and American Foreign Policy*, 3–19, 529–532.

4. Alexander, "Stormy New Boss"; Jonathan Mitchell, "M-Day Man," 63–64; Block, ed., *Current Biography 1942*, 425; James Farley interview; Haymond Maxwell interview; Ruth Johnson interviews.

5. Burns, *Roosevelt: The Lion and the Fox*, 318–319; Frank Freidel, *Roosevelt: A Rendezvous with Destiny* (Boston: Little, Brown and Company, 1990), 265.

6. Mark S. Watson, *Chief of Staff: Prewar Plans and Preparations* (Washington, D.C.: U.S. Government Printing Office, 1950), 145.

7. Albert A. Blum, "Birth and Death of the M-Day Plan," in *American Civil Military Decisions: A Book of Case Studies*, ed. Harold Stein (Tuscaloosa: University of Alabama Press, 1963), 63–64, 69–70; "M-Day Man," 63.

8. The National Defense Act of 1920 provided that "the Assistant Secretary of War, under the direction of the Secretary of War, shall be charged with supervision of the procurement of all military supplies and other business of the War Department pertaining thereto and the assurance of adequate provision for mobilization of material and industrial organizations essential to war-time needs." 41 Stat. 759 (June 4, 1920), 764–765.

9. Bernard Baruch to Johnson, October 24, 1938, Johnson to Bernard Baruch, October 25, 1938, August 5, 1939, and February 14, 1940, and other Baruch-Johnson correspondence found in Box 2, Johnson Papers; Assistant Secretary of War Louis Johnson to Bernard Baruch, October 5, 1927, Box 117, Mobilization of Personnel, RG 107, Records of the Secretary of War, NARA.

10. James Grant, *Bernard M. Baruch: The Adventures of a Wall Street Legend* (New York: John Wiley & Sons, 1997), 265–268; Baruch, *Public Years*, 277; W. L. White, *Bernard Baruch: Portrait of a Citizen* (New York: Harcourt, Brace and Company, 1950), 87–91; Bernard M. Baruch, *Baruch: My Own Story* (New York: Henry Holt and Company, 1957), 267–268; *Washington Post*, February 14, 1943, B7.

11. R. Ellerton Smith, *The Army and Economic Mobilization* (Washington, D.C.: U.S. Government Printing Office, 1959), 54–57.

12. William Ritchie interview.

13. "Arms Before Men," 25.

14. *NYT,* May 4, 1938, 1; *NYT,* September 4, 1938, III: 7, *NYT,* October 23, 1938, 12; *NYT,* December 2, 1938, 6; *NYT,* December 5, 1938, 16; *Business Week,* October 22, 1938, 27; *Nation's Business,* April 1938, 27; War Department, Office of the Secretary of War, "Assistant Secretary of War Annual Report, 1938," in *Annual Report of the Secretary of War, 1938* (Washington, D.C.: U.S. Government Printing Office, 1938), 19; War Department, Office of the Secretary of War, "Assistant Secretary of War Annual Report, 1939," in *Annual Report of the Secretary of War, 1939* (Washington, D.C.: U.S. Government Printing Office, 1939), 21; Marvin A. Kreidberg and Merton G. Henry, *History of Military Mobilization in the United States Army, 1775–1945* (Washington, D.C.: U.S. Government Printing Office, 1955), 531–532; Louis Johnson, "Educating Industry for an Emergency," *The American Machinist,* February 8, 1938, 49–50.

15. "Arms Before Men," 25; Brig. General Harry K. Rutherford, "Mobilizing Industry for War," in *Industry Goes to War,* ed. Stanley Teele and Cecil Fraser (Freeport, N.Y.: Books for Libraries Press, 1971), 3.

16. Smith, *The Army and Economic Mobilization,* 62–64.

17. "Assistant Secretary of War Annual Report, 1939," 16–17; Memorandum for the President from Assistant Secretary of War Johnson, May 18, 1938, PSF, War Department 1933–41, FDRL.

18. Memorandum for the President from Assistant Secretary of War Louis Johnson, August 12, 1938, OF 25, War Department Education Orders, 1938–41, FDRL.

19. Memorandum for the President from Acting Secretary of War Louis Johnson, November 1, 1938, Box 54, Educational Orders, Johnson Papers; "Annual Report of the Assistant Secretary of War, 1938," 17; Col. Harry Rutherford, "Educational Orders," *Army Ordnance,* November–December 1939, 2–3.

20. Constance Green, Harry Thomson, and Peter Roots, *The Ordnance Department: Planning Munitions for War* (Washington, D.C.: U.S. Government Printing Office, 1955), 57; Smith, *The Army and Economic Mobilization,* 257; "Annual Report of the Assistant Secretary of War, 1939," 17; War Department, Office of the Secretary of War, "Annual Report of the Assistant Secretary of War, 1940," in *Annual Report of the Secretary of War, 1940* (Washington, D.C.: U.S. Government Printing Office, 1940), 6.

21. "Annual Report of the Assistant Secretary of War, 1938," 20; "Annual Report of the Assistant Secretary of War, 1939," 18.

22. Blum, "M-Day Plan," 71.

23. Ibid., 71–72; Memorandum for the President from Assistant Secretary of War Louis Johnson, December 4, 1937, PSF, War Department 1937, Box 102, FDRL; Johnson to President Roosevelt, April [?], 1939, PSF, War Department 1938, Box 103, FDRL.

24. Blum, "M-Day Plan," 73; Byron Fairchild and Jonathan Grossman, *The Army and Industrial Manpower* (Washington, D.C.: U.S. Government Printing Office, 1959), 15–17.

25. Kreidberg and Henry, *History of Military Mobilization,* 532–539.

26. Fairchild and Grossman, *The Army and Industrial Manpower,* 7; *NYT,* April 7, 1938, 15; Joint Army and Navy Selective Service Committee, *American Selective Service* (Washington, D.C.: U.S. Government Printing Office, 1939), 21–24; Louis Johnson, "Whither America?" *Vital Speeches,* April 15, 1938, 404.

27. Memorandum for the President from Assistant Secretary of War Louis Johnson, January 29, 1939, Box 26, Correspondence Roh–Ror, Johnson Papers; Johnson to Secretary of Interior Harold Ickes, March 16, 1939, Box 15, Harold Ickes, Johnson Papers; Johnson to Robert Fechner, December 10, 1938, Box 11, Correspondence Fe–Fi, Johnson Papers; *NYT,* October 20, 1938, 2.

28. Smith, *The Army and Economic Mobilization,* 603; Memorandum for the President from Assistant Secretary of War Louis Johnson, May 18, 1938, PSF, War Department

1933–41, Box 14, FDRL; "Annual Report of the Assistant Secretary of War, 1939"; Faddis to co-author McFarland, April 28, 1968; Watson, *Chief of Staff*, 35.

29. *NYT*, May 11, 1938, 10.

30. Ibid.

31. *NYT*, May 11, 1938, 10; *NYT*, September 4, 1938, 7; *NYT*, November 15, 1938, 1; Mitchell, "M-Day Man," 63; Elliot Janeway, *Struggle for Survival* (New Haven, Conn.: Yale University Press, 1951), 70.

32. Smith, *The Army and Economic Mobilization*, 50–51; *Annual Report of the Secretary of War, 1940*, 4.

33. Interview with Dr. Thomas W. Langfitt Jr., Washington, D.C., March 24, 2003; David A. Remley, *Crooked Road: The Story of the Alaska Highway* (New York: McGraw-Hill, 1976), 120–121.

34. *NYT*, August 22, 1938, 15; *NYT*, August 25, 1938, 13; *NYT*, August 29, 1938, 30; Rothe, ed., *Current Biography 1949*, 299; *Time*, August 22, 1938, 25; Memorandum for the Assistant Secretary of War, October 14, 1938, Box 34, Alaska, Johnson Papers.

35. *NYT*, October 2, 1947, 29; George Marshall to Johnson, March 12, 1949, Box 60, George C. Marshall Papers; Cordell Hull, *The Memoirs of Cordell Hull* (New York: Macmillan, 1948), I: 208; Janeway, *The Struggle for Survival*, 26; Baruch, *The Public Years*, 277.

5. *Understanding FDR*

1. John McVickar Haight Jr., "Roosevelt as Friend of France," *Foreign Affairs Quarterly* 44, no. 3 (April 1966): 519.

2. John McVickar Haight Jr., *American Aid to France, 1938–1940* (New York: Atheneum, 1970), 14–15.

3. Memorandum for the Assistant Secretary of War from Colonel J. H. Burns, June 23, 1938, PSF, War Department, Louis Johnson, Box 105, FDRL.

4. Johnson to Marvin McIntyre, June 23, 1938, PSF, War Department, Louis Johnson, Box 105, FDRL.

5. Haight, *American Aid to France*, 15.

6. Hugh R. Wilson to Roosevelt, July 3, 1938, copy in Woodring Papers.

7. Watson, *Chief of Staff*, 131–132.

8. Haight, *American Aid to France*, 22.

9. Memorandum from Assistant Secretary of War Louis Johnson and Assistant Secretary of Navy Charles Edison to President Roosevelt, September 11, 1938, Box 34, Aircraft Expansion—Requirements and Resources, Johnson Papers.

10. Haight, *American Aid to France*, 16–17.

11. McFarland, *Harry H. Woodring*, 164, 166, 168.

12. Memorandum for the President from Assistant Secretary of War Louis Johnson, October 15, 1938, and Memorandum for the Assistant Secretary of War from Chief of Staff Malin Craig, October 15, 1938, both in Box 34, Aircraft Expansion—Requirements and Resources, Box 34, Johnson Papers; John Morton Blum, *From the Morgenthau Diaries: Years of Crisis, 1928–1938* (Boston: Houghton Mifflin Company, 1959), II: 46. Hereafter *From the Morgenthau Diaries*, II.

13. *Complete Presidential Press Conferences of Franklin D. Roosevelt, 1938*, Number 491, October 14, 1938 (New York: Da Capo Press, 1972), XII: 156–157.

14. Pearson and Allen, "The Merry-Go-Round," *Akron Beacon Journal*, December 1, 1938; "Rearmament or Balderdash, *Newsweek*, December 12, 1938, 11; *Foreign Policy Bul-*

letin, December 16, 1938, 4; *NYT*, October 30, 1938, 1; Minutes of Aircraft Expansion Conference, October 31, 1938, Box 34, Aircraft Expansion Conference, Johnson Papers.

15. Memorandum for the Chief of Staff from Assistant Secretary of War, Louis Johnson, October 14, 1938, PSF, War Department, Louis Johnson, Box 105, FDRL.

16. Memorandum for the Assistant Secretary of War from Chief of Staff Malin Craig, October 15, 1938, PSF, War Department, Louis Johnson, Box 105, FDRL.

17. Excerpt from the Morgenthau diaries, quoted in Haight, *American Aid to France*, 49.

18. Memorandum for the Assistant Secretary of War from Chief of Air Corps General Arnold, October 25 and October 27, 138, Box 34, Aircraft Expansion, Johnson Papers.

19. Letter for the President from Assistant Secretary of War Louis Johnson, Assistant Secretary of Navy Charles Edison and Deputy Administrator of the WPA Aubrey Williams, October 28, 1938, Box 34, Aircraft Expansion, Johnson Papers.

20. *Complete Presidential Press Conferences of Franklin D. Roosevelt*, *1938*, Number 492, October 18, 1938, XII: 165; Irving B. Holley Jr., *Buying Aircraft: Matériel Procurement for the Army Air Force* (Washington, D.C.: U.S. Government Printing Office, 1964), 172–173; *NYT*, October 15, 1938, 1; *NYT*, October 26, 1938, 19; *NYT*, November 6, 1938, 1; *NYT*, December 27, 1938, 1.

21. Watson, *Chief of Staff*, 135–136.

22. Memorandum for the Assistant Secretary of War from Chief of the Air Corps, General Arnold, November 10, 1938 (two separate memos with the same date), AG 580 (10-14-38), "Expansion of the Air Corps," RG 407, Records of the Adjutant General's Office, 1917–, NARA.

23. Blum, *From the Morgenthau Diaries*, II: 47.

24. Ibid., 48–49; quote in Reynolds, *From Munich to Pearl Harbor*, 45–46; emphasis added.

25. Notes taken by General Arnold and sent to General Craig, November 15, 1938, OF 25-T, Army Chief of Staff, Box 6, FDRL.; Henry Harley Arnold, *Global Mission* (New York: Harper, 1949); Blum, *From the Morgenthau Diaries*, II: 48–49; Watson, *Chief of Staff*, 136–138; Reynolds, *From Munich to Pearl Harbor*, 44–47.

26. Quote in Pogue, *George C. Marshall: Education of a General*, 323; Cray, *General of the Army*, 132.

27. Memorandum for the Chief of Staff from Acting Secretary of War Louis Johnson, November 15, 1938, Adjutant General File 580 (10-19-38), "Expansion of the Air Corps," RG 407, Records of the Adjutant General's Office, 1917–, NARA.

28. Memorandum for the President from Louis Johnson, November 19, 1938, PSF, War Department, Box 105, Louis Johnson, FDRL.

29. *Newsweek*, December 12, 1938, 4–10; *Foreign Policy Bulletin* XVIII, no. 8 (December 16, 1938): 4; John C. O'Laughlin to General John J. Pershing, September 24, 1939, Box 58, O'Laughlin Papers; McFarland, *Harry H. Woodring*, 168.

30. Memorandum for the President from Louis Johnson, December 1, 1938, AG 580, 10-19-38, "Expansion of the Air Corps," RG 407, Records of the Adjutant General's Office, 1917–, NARA.

31. Acting Secretary of War Louis Johnson to General Craig, December 10, 1938, AG 580, 10-19-38, "Expansion of the Air Corps," RG 407, Records of the Adjutant General's Office, 1917–, NARA.

32. Memorandum for the Assistant Secretary of War from Chief of Staff Malin Craig, December 17, 1938, AG 580, 10-19-38, "Expansion of the Air Corps," RG 407, Records of the Adjutant General's Office, 1917–, NARA.

33. Watson, *Chief of Staff*, 142–143.

34. *Newsweek*, December 12, 1938, 9–10; Charles Faddis interview.

35. *Cleveland Plain Dealer* (editorial), December 28, 1938; *Portland Oregonian* (editorial), December 10, 1938.

36. Aircraft Expansion Conference, Minutes for October 31 and November 1, 23 Meetings, Box 34, Aircraft Expansion Conference, Johnson Papers; Holley, *Buying Aircraft*, 178; Haight, *American Aid to France*, 65–66.

37. Watson *Chief of Staff*, 138; Frye, *Citizen Soldier*, 259–260; Kreidberg and Henry, *History of Military Mobilization*, 543–545.

38. Frye, *Citizen Soldier*, 252.

39. "Report of the Assistant Secretary of War, 1937," in *Report of the Secretary of War, 1937*, 26; "Annual Report of the Assistant Secretary of War, 1938," 26.

40. John C. O'Laughlin to General John J. Pershing, November 23 and December 17, 1938, both in Box 58, O'Laughlin Papers.

41. Ernest K. Lindley, "A Cabinet Shuffle," *Washington Post*, December 18, 1938; Harlan Miller, "Over the Coffee," *Washington Post*, December 23, 1938; Watson, *Chief of Staff*, 143.

42. John C. O'Laughlin to General John J. Pershing, December 17, 1938, Box 58, O'Laughlin Papers.

43. McFarland, *Harry H. Woodring*, 170–171.

44. Haight, "Roosevelt as Friend of France," 519–520.

45. *Army and Navy Journal*, November 14, 1936; *U.S. Air Service* 22, no. 1 (January 1937): 30.

46. Haight, *American Aid to France*, 10–12; John McVickar Haight Jr., "France's Search for American Military Aircraft Before the Munich Crisis," *Aerospace Historian* 25, no. 3 (Fall 1978): 148.

47. McFarland, *Harry H. Woodring*, 184; Edward R. Stettinius, *Lend-Lease, Weapon for Victory* (New York: Macmillan, 1944), 19.

48. Haight, "Roosevelt as Friend of France," 522–523.

49. The account of the Monnet mission is derived from Senate Committee on Military Affairs, *Hearings on H.R. 3791, An Act to Provide More Effectively for the National Defense*, 76th Cong., 1st Sess., 1939, 91–215; Blum, *From the Morgenthau Diaries*, II, 64–78; Henry Morgenthau, "The Morgenthau Diaries, pt. IV: The Story Behind Lend Lease," *Colliers*, October 18, 1947, 16–17, 71; Memorandum of conversation between John C. O'Laughlin and Secretary of War Harry Woodring, February 19, 1939, Box 71, O'Laughlin Papers; Transcript of conference with the Senate Military Affairs Committee, January 31, 1939, PPF 1-P, Box 262, FDRL; Gerald Nye interview; Arthur Krock, "Behind the Scenes in French Plane Affair," *NYT*, February 21, 1939, 7; Haight, *American Aid to France*, 23–47; McFarland, *Harry H. Woodring*, 184–190.

50. Morgenthau, "The Morgenthau Diaries," 17.

51. Memorandum of conversation between John C. O'Laughlin and Secretary of War Woodring, February 19, 1939, Box 71, O'Laughlin Papers.

52. Morgenthau, "The Morgenthau Diaries," 17.

53. Senate Committee on Military Affairs, *Hearings on H.R. 3791*, 208.

54. Ibid., 94.

55. Arnold, *Global Mission*, 186.

56. *Washington Post*, January 24, 1939, 1; NYT, January 24, 1939, 5.

57. Blum, *From the Morganthau Diaries*, II, 71.

58. *Washington Star*, January 24, 1939.

59. Gerald Nye interview.

60. Senate Committee on Military Affairs, *Hearings on H.R. 3791*, 92.

61. NYT, January 28, 1939, 1; NYT, January 29, 1939, 1; NYT, February 17, 1939, 1;

NYT, February 18, 1939, 1; *NYT*, February 19, 1939, 1; *NYT*, February 21, 1939; *Army and Navy Journal*, February 18, 25, 1939.

62. *Complete Presidential Press Conferences of Franklin D. Roosevelt 1939*, Number 521, January 27, 1939, XIII: 90.

63. Transcript of conference with the Senate Military Affairs Committee, January 31, 1939, PPF 1-P, Box 252, FDRL.

64. Senate Committee on Military Affairs, *Hearings on H.R. 3791*, 181–184.

65. McFarland, *Harry H. Woodring*, 190.

66. Holley, *Buying Aircraft*, 175–176.

67. John C. O'Laughlin to General John J. Pershing, February 18, 1939, Box 58, O'Laughlin Papers.

6. Surviving FDR

1. Louis B. Wehle, *Hidden Threads of History: Wilson through Roosevelt* (New York: Macmillan, 1953), 219–220.

2. As a top official in the War Department, Johnson was careful to avoid making statements that could be interpreted by isolationists as an indication that the administration would take the nation to war. However, he made his fears of war known to people who knew him well. Ruth Johnson interview, July 12, 1977; James Farley interview; Haymond Maxwell interview; Gerald Nye interview; *NYT*, October 12, 1939, 10; Childs, *I Write from Washington*, 161; Baruch, *Public Years*, 276–277; "The High Cost of Peace," *Fortune*, March 1939, 44–45.

3. Memorandum for Assistant Secretary Johnson from the White House, March 15, 1939, Memorandum for the President from Louis Johnson, June 7 and July 10, 1939, and Louis Johnson to President Roosevelt, July 10, 1939, all in OF, War Department, January–May and June–December 1939, FDRL.

4. David Brinkley, *Washington Goes to War* (New York: Alfred A. Knopf, 1988), 61.

5. Baruch, *Public Years*, 272–276, 280.

6. Johnson to Roosevelt, April [n.d.], 1939, PSF, War Department 1938, Box 103, FDRL.

7. *Federal Register*, July 7, 1939, 2786, McFarland, *Harry H. Woodring*, 171; Smith, *The Army and Economic Mobilization*, 42.

8. *NYT*, September 27, 1939, 1; Smith, *The Army and Economic Mobilization*, 99.

9. McFarland, *Harry H. Woodring*, 172.

10. Blum, "M-Day Plan," 74–78.

11. Ibid., 74–75.

12. *NYT*, August 10, 1939, 2.

13. Memorandum for the President from Assistant Secretary of War Louis Johnson, December 14, 1937, Johnson to Bernard Baruch, December 29, 1937, PSF, War Department 1937, both in Box 102, FDRL; Smith, *The Army and Economic Mobilization*, 99.

14. War Resources Board Minutes, August 17, 1939, Box 84, War Resources Board, Johnson Papers; Kreidberg and Henry, *History of Military Mobilization*, 682.

15. Janeway, *Struggle for Survival*, 67; Blum, "M-Day Plan," 75–78.

16. Blum, "M-Day Plan," 82; Fairchild and Grossman, *The Army and Industrial Manpower*, 18–19.

17. Memorandum for the President from Assistant Secretary of War Johnson and Assistant Secretary of Navy Edison, September 6, 1939, Box 84, War Resources Board, Johnson Papers.

18. Ickes, *Secret Diary of Harold L. Ickes*, II: 719–720.

19. Ibid., 720.

20. Blum, "M-Day Plan," 84.

21. Roosevelt to Johnson, September 16, 1939, Box 90, Private Correspondence, Johnson Papers.

22. "economic fascism," Pearson and Allen, "The Merry-Go-Round," *Akron Beacon Journal*, October 6, 1939; Johnson to Stephen Early, October 1, 1939, Box 8, Early Papers, FDRL; Blum, "M-Day Plan," 85; Leo M. Cherne, *Adjusting Your Business to War* (New York: Fox Resource Institute of America, 1939), ix–x.

23. *NYT*, September 27, 1939, 1.

24. *Army and Navy Journal* (editorial), September 30, 1939; *Buffalo Evening News* (editorial), September 29, 1939; "War Board's End," *Newsweek*, October 9, 1939; "Scandalous Spats," *Time*, October 9, 1939, 16; "in the biggest doghouse in Washington," *The Wheeling Intelligencer*, October 2, 1939.

25. Johnson to Early, October 1, 1939, Box 8, Early Papers, FDRL.

26. Blum, "M-Day Plan," 86–87.

27. Ruth Johnson interview, July 12, 1977; Haymond Maxwell interview; Stephen Ailes interview; James Farley interview.

28. Stein, ed., *American Civil Military Decisions*, 96.

29. Gerald Nye interview.

30. Louis Brownlow, *A Passion for Anonymity: The Autobiography of Louis Brownlow* (Chicago: University of Chicago Press, 1958), II: 425.

31. Baruch, *Public Years*, 281.

32. Joseph Alsop and Robert Kintner, *American White Paper: The Story of American Diplomacy and the Second World War* (New York: Simon and Schuster, 1940), 55.

33. McFarland, *Harry H. Woodring*, 196.

34. Beatrice Bishop Berle and Travis Beal Jacobs, eds., *Navigating the Rapids, 1918–1971* (New York: Harcourt Brace Jovanovich, 1973), 244; *NYT*, August 26, 1939, 3; *NYT*, August 29, 1939, 1; "however honorable may have been their intentions," *NYT*, August 30, 1939, 3.

35. *NYT*, August 30, 1939, 3.

36. Joseph P. Kennedy to Johnson, August 31, 1939, Joseph P. Kennedy, Box 16 Johnson Papers; "notably such obsequious courtiers as Mr. Johnson," Arthur Krock, "An Odd Way of Achieving National Unity," *NYT*, August 31, 1939, 40.

37. "remain a neutral nation, but I cannot ask that every American remain neutral in thought as well," "Fireside Chat," September 3, 1939, in *Public Papers and Addresses of Franklin D. Roosevelt, 1939*, ed. Samuel I. Rosenman (New York: Random House, 1939), 460–464. Berle and Jacobs, *Navigating the Rapids*, 250.

38. Johnson to Secretary of State Cordell Hull, October 6, 1939, Box 82, State Department—Correspondence, Johnson Papers.

39. McFarland, *Harry H. Woodring*, 209–210.

40. Memorandum, President Roosevelt to Secretary Woodring, December 6, 1939, Secretary of War General Correspondence 1932–1942, Box 122, International Transfer of Arms, RG 107, Records of the Adjutant General's Office, 1917–, NARA; William L. Langer and S. Everett Gleason, *The Challenge to Isolation, 1937–40* (New York: Harper & Row, 1952), 284; Haight, *American Aid to France*, 164–165; Blum, *From the Morgenthau Diaries*, II, 111–112.

41. Blum, *From the Morgenthau Diaries*, II, 111–112.

42. Ibid., 112–113.

43. For an example of limited production capability, see Haight, *American Aid to France*, 139–141.

44. Blum, *From the Morgenthau Diaries*, II, 115; Memorandum for the Secretary of War from the Chief of the Air Corps, January 12, 1940, Box 223, Aircraft Production, 1939–1941, Henry H. Arnold Papers, LC, hereafter Arnold Papers; *NYT*, March 14, 1940, 12.

45. Blum, *From the Morgenthau Diaries*, II, 113, 116.

46. Ibid.; Howard Mingor, ed., *The Aircraft Yearbook for 1940* (New York: Aeronautical Chamber of Commerce of America, 1940), 27.

47. Blum, *From the Morgenthau Diaries*, II, 117; McFarland, *Harry H. Woodring*, 212–213.

48. *NYT*, March 12, 1940, 6; *NYT*, March 13, 1940, 8; *Washington Post*, March 13, 1940, 1.

49. Whether Johnson fed the information to the press is not certain, but there is considerable evidence that he was feeding inside information to writers such as Joseph Alsop, Robert S. Allen, and Harlan Miller. See correspondence Box 2, Joseph Alsop and Robert Allen, Box 19, Harlan Miller, Johnson Papers.

50. *NYT*, March 12, 1940, 6; *NYT*, March 13, 1940, 8; *NYT*, March 14, 1940, 12.

51. Memorandum of Record by General Henry Arnold, March 13, 1940, Box 223, Aircraft Production 1939–1941, Arnold Papers; John C. O'Laughlin to General John J. Pershing, March 23, 1940, O'Laughlin Papers; Blum, *From the Morgenthau Diaries*, II, 117.

52. Memorandum of Record by General Arnold, March 19, 1940, Box 223, Aircraft Production, 1939–41, Arnold Papers; report of a meeting held in the Chief of Staff's Office 10:30 A.M., March 19, 1940, Chief of Staff Binder, March 1940, RG 165, Records of the War Department General and Special Staffs, NARA; "be considered on trial . . . insofar as any statements were concerned," John C. O'Laughlin to John J. Pershing, March 23, 1940; Pearson and Allen, "The Merry-Go-Round," *Akron Beacon Journal*, April 17, 1940.

53. Government Policy on Aircraft Foreign Sales, March 25, 1940, Box 223, Aircraft Production, 1939–1941, Arnold Papers; *NYT*, March 28, 1940, 4; *NYT*, March 29, 1940, 1; *Army and Navy Register*, March 30, 1940.

54. Press Conference of the Assistant Secretary of War, March 13, 1940, typescript, Box 76, Press Conference, Johnson Papers.

55. Blum, *From the Morgenthau Diaries*, II, 119; Record of Conference held in Chief of Staff's Office, March 22, 1940, and March 23, 1940, "Chief of Staff File, March 1940," Binder, RG 165, Records of the War Department General and Special Staffs, NARA.

56. Blum, *From the Morgenthau Diaries*, II, 119; *NYT*, April 10, 1940, 1; Haight, *American Aid to France*, 224–225.

7. *"But You Promised Me"*

1. Ruth Johnson interviews; Johnson Appointment Calendar, April–June 1940, Boxes 140 and 141, Johnson Papers.

2. Memorandum for the President from Secretary Woodring, August 1939, Box 39, PSF, War Department, 1933–1945, FDRL; Watson, *Chief of Staff*, 157; *Army and Navy Journal*, September 9, 1939; Krock, *Memoirs*, 213–214.

3. Watson, *Chief of Staff*, 161; *NYT*, November 1, 1939, 1.

4. McFarland, *Harry H. Woodring*, 202–204.

5. Senate Appropriations Committee, *Military Establishment Appropriations Bill for 1941, Hearings on HR 9209*, 76th Cong., 3rd Sess., 1941, 126.

6. Watson, *Chief of Staff*, 166–169.

7. Pogue, *George C. Marshall: Ordeal and Hope*, 20, 30; McFarland, *Harry H. Woodring*, 221.

8. Memorandum for the President from Assistant Secretary of War Louis Johnson, May 10, 1940, Box 26, Correspondence Roh–Ror, Johnson Papers.

9. Memorandum for the President from Assistant Secretary of War Louis Johnson, February 17, 1940, Box 34, Aircraft Expansion, Johnson Papers.

10. Memorandum for the President from Assistant Secretary of War Louis Johnson, May 10, 1940, Box 2, Correspondence B. M. Baruch, Johnson Papers.

11. Memorandum for the President from Assistant Secretary of War Louis Johnson, May 15, 1940, Box 26, Correspondence Roh–Ror, Johnson Papers; also in PSF, Louis Johnson, Box 105, FDRL.

12. Ibid.

13. Samuel I. Rosenman, ed., *The Public Papers and Addresses of Franklin D. Roosevelt, 1940* (New York: Macmillan, 1941), 202.

14. Blum, *From the Morgenthau Diaries,* II, 144.

15. Memorandum for Secretary of War Woodring from President Roosevelt, May 24, 1940, Box 2-B, Air Planes, Secretary of War, General Correspondence, 1932–1942, RG 107, Records of the Secretary of War, NARA.

16. Blum, *From the Morgenthau Diaries,* II, 144.

17. NYT, May 29, 1940, 1.

18. Civilian Production Administration, *Industrial Mobilization for War,* vol. I, *Program and Administration* (Washington, D.C.: U.S. Government Printing Office, 1947), 18, Blum, *From the Morgenthau Diaries,* II, 148; Langer and Gleason, *The Challenge to Isolation,* 478.

19. Blum, *From the Morgenthau Diaries,* II, 148, Smith, *The Army and Economic Mobilization,* 266.

20. Smith, *The Army and Economic Mobilization,* 266–267.

21. Civilian Production Board, *Industrial Mobilization for War,* I: 24–25.

22. Smith, *The Army and Economic Mobilization,* 267.

23. *Army and Navy Journal,* June 1, 1940; Ruth Johnson interview, July 12, 1977; John C. O'Laughlin to General John J. Pershing, June 22, 1940, Box 58, Correspondence— Pershing, O'Laughlin Papers; Memorandum for Chief of Staff, May 29, 1940, Chief of Staff Emergency File Binder 2, May 11, 1940–August 16, 1940, Records of the War Department General Staff, Chief of Staff, 1936–1940, RG 165, Records of the War Department General and Special Staffs, NARA.

24. McFarland, *Harry H. Woodring,* 218–219.

25. Langer and Gleason, *Challenge to Isolation,* 338–340, Robert Sobel, *The Origin of Interventionism: The United States and the Russian-Finnish War* (New York: Bookman Association, 1960), 97–100; Memorandum for the Chief of Staff from the Assistant Chief of Staff, G-4, March 9, 1940, and note appended by Secretary Woodring, March 11, 1940, "Chief of Staff of Army," RG 165, Records of the War Department General and Special Staffs, NARA.

26. Winston L. A. Churchill, *Their Finest Hour* (Boston: Houghton Mifflin Company, 1949), 24.

27. Blum, *From the Morgenthau Diaries,* II, 149.

28. Ibid., 150–151.

29. "without endangering the national defense," Watson, *Chief of Staff,* 309; McFarland, *Harry H. Woodring,* 221–224.

30. McFarland, *Harry H. Woodring,* 226–227.

31. *Life,* June 17, 1940, 84; NYT (editorial), June 14, 1940.

32. NYT, June 9, 1940, 6.

33. Morrison, *Turmoil and Tradition,* 479–480.

34. Ibid., 481; Felix Frankfurter to Franklin Roosevelt, June 4 and 5, 1940, Box 98, General Correspondence 1878–1945, Papers of Felix Frankfurter, LC.

35. Norman Moss, *Nineteen Weeks* (New York: Houghton Mifflin Company, 2003), 159.

36. Ibid., 166.

37. Blum, *From the Morgenthau Diaries*, II, 162; Morgenthau Diary, 272, 280–281, FDRL.

38. Roosevelt to Woodring, June 19, 1940, Woodring to Roosevelt, June 20, 1940, Edwin M. Watson to Woodring, June 22, 1940, Roosevelt to Woodring, June 25, 1940, all in Woodring Papers, Spencer Research Library; Farley, *Jim Farley's Story*, 241; McFarland, *Harry H. Woodring*, 228–229.

39. Tully, *FDR: My Boss*, 170.

40. Henry L. Stimson and McGeorge Bundy, *On Active Service in Peace and War* (New York: Harper and Brothers, 1947), 323–324.

41. Farley, *Jim Farley's Story*, 241.

42. Ibid.; John C. O'Laughlin to General John J. Pershing, June 22, 1940, Box 58, Correspondence—Pershing, O'Laughlin Papers; *Army and Navy Journal*, July 27, 1940.

43. Baruch, *Public Years*, 277.

44. Berle and Jacobs, *Navigating the Rapids*, 325; NYT, June 21, 1940, 4.

45. *Charleston Daily Mail*, August 1939; *Parkersburg Sentinel*, August 8, 1939; Lem Jarvis interview; Chesney Carney interview; Douglas Bailey interview.

46. Leonard Wilson to Johnson, December 12, 1938, Box 76, Presidency of Johnson—Correspondence Suggesting, Johnson Papers.

47. Eugene Case to Johnson, November 12, 1938, and January 7, 1939, Johnson to Case, January 11, 1939, Johnson to Leonard Wilson, December 1938, and other letters in Box 76, Presidency of Johnson—Correspondence Suggesting, Johnson Papers.

48. Ibid.

49. Leuchtenburg, *Franklin D. Roosevelt and the New Deal*, 314–316.

50. *Washington Post*, April 10, 1940, 2; *Washington Post*, July 10, 1940, 7; *Star Democrat* (Portland, Oregon), May 13, 1940.

51. *NYT*, April 2, 1940, 7; Telegram: Frank Tierney and Howard Latourette to Johnson, March 31, 1940; Johnson to Frank Tierney and Howard Latourette, April 1, 1940; both in Box 33, Vice Presidency, Johnson Papers.

52. Harlan Miller, "Over the Coffee," *Washington Post*, April 10, 1940.

53. Jerry Owens to Johnson, June 17, 1940, David D. Hill to Johnson, July 1, 1940, both in Box 83, Vice Presidency of Johnson—Correspondence, Oregon Primary, Johnson Papers.

54. Ernest Lindley, "Roosevelt and Who?" *Washington Post*, July 10, 1940; Ray Tucker, "National Whirligig," *Washington Post*, July 13, 1940.

55. Burns, *Roosevelt: The Lion and the Fox*, 428.

56. Ickes, *Secret Diary of Harold L. Ickes*, III: 262; Bernard F. Donahoe, *Private Plans and Public Dangers* (Notre Dame, Ind.: University of Notre Dame Press, 1965), 173–175; *The Knickerbocker News* (Albany, New York), July 18, 1940.

57. John C. O'Laughlin to Herbert Hoover, July 20, 1940, Box 45, General Correspondence—Herbert Hoover, June–July 1940; "would be eminently acceptable as the Vice-Presidential nominee," John C. O'Laughlin to Harry Woodring, July 29, 1940, Box 71, General Correspondence Harry Woodring, both in O'Laughlin Papers.

58. Less than forty-eight hours after Johnson left the president, James Farley reported to Roosevelt that Johnson was telling delegates at the convention that he had the "green light." "Oh, my God," said Roosevelt. "He'll run into a red light at the next block." Farley, *Jim Farley's Story*, 294–295.

59. Hamby, *Man of the People*, 513.

60. "Oh, hell Louis, this convention hall is full of candidates with green lights," Ickes, *Secret Diary of Harold L. Ickes*, III: 262; Burns, *Roosevelt: The Lion and the Fox*, 428–429.

61. Donahoe, *Private Plans and Public Dangers*, 173–175.

62. John C. O'Laughlin to Harry Woodring, July 19, 1940, Box 71, Harry Woodring, O'Laughlin Papers; *Army and Navy Journal*, July 27, 1940.

63. Johnson to Franklin Roosevelt, July 25, 1940, OF 25, War Department, May–June 1940, FDRL, also in Box 95, Correspondence—Franklin Roosevelt, Johnson Papers.

64. Johnson to Clint [no last name], August 17, 1940, Box 95, Correspondence—General, Johnson Papers; O'Laughlin to Harry Woodring, July 29, 1940, Box 71, Harry Woodring, O'Laughlin Papers; Berle and Jacobs, *Navigating the Rapids*, 335; Ruth Johnson interviews.

65. The third paragraph was not inserted until the final copy was typed—almost as if it was an afterthought.

66. Louis Johnson to Franklin Roosevelt, July 24, 1940, OF 25, War Department May–June 1940, FDRL.

67. Johnson to Clint [no last name], August 17, 1940, Box 95, Correspondence—General, Johnson Papers.

68. Ibid.; Telegram, Johnson to Stephen Early, August 2, 1940, Box 8, Louis Johnson, Early Papers, FDRL.

69. Telegram, Roosevelt to Johnson, July 25, 1940, Box 95, Correspondence with Franklin Roosevelt, Johnson Papers.

70. *Washington Times Herald*, July 26, 1940; *Washington Post*, July 26, 1940, 2; *NYT*, July 26, 1940, 1; *Army and Navy Journal*, July 27, 1940; Johnson himself indicated that "the press has been kind and tolerant." Telegram, Johnson to Stephen Early, August 2, 1940, Box 8, Louis Johnson, Early Papers, FDRL.

71. J. Edgar Hoover to Morganthau, January 1, 1942, concluding that Johnson had not revealed confidential War Department information to a group of businessmen (as Laughlin Currie reported to FDR on December 16, 1941) and was not critical of FDR, Morgenthau Diary number 481, page 115 (reel 135), FDRL; "nice line telling him that the whole episode is forgotten," Memorandum, Roosevelt to Early, December 22, 1941, Box 56, Correspondence, Louis Johnson, Early Papers, FDRL.

72. Ickes, *Secret Diary of Harold L. Ickes*, III: 55; Pogue, *George C. Marshall: Ordeal and Hope*, 39–40; Major General Harry H. Arnold to Johnson, August 16, 1940, Box 77, "Resignation as ASW Correspondence A–D," Johnson Papers; Gerald Nye interview; Dow Harter interview; Charles Faddis interview.

73. "childish," "hurt and peeved," "unfairly treated," Johnson to Clint [no last name], August 17, 1940, Box 95, Correspondence—General; Stephen Early to Johnson, July 29, 1940, Box 95, Correspondence with Stephen Early; "without loss of prestige," Stephen Early to Victor Emanuel, July 25, 1940, Box 95, Correspondence with Stephen Early, all in Johnson Papers.

74. Johnson to Palmer Holt, August 19, 1940, Box 95, Correspondence—General, Johnson Papers; *NYT*, August 16, 1940, 9.

75. *NYT*, August 25, 1940, 34; *NYT*, September 5, 1940, 18.

76. Ruth Johnson interviews; Haymond Maxwell interview, W. B. "Bill" Maxwell interview; William Miller interview; Stephen Ailes interview.

77. For a more detailed analysis of this question, see Keith D. McFarland, "F.D.R. and the Great War Department Feud," *Army*, March 1976, 36–42.

78. Ibid., 41–42.

79. Krock, *Sixty Years on the Firing Line*, 254.

80. Citation to Accompany the Award of the Medal for Merit to Louis Johnson, July 16, 1947, Box 96, Citation to Accompany Medal for Merit, Johnson Papers.

8. Personal Representative of the President

1. Haymond Maxwell interview; Chesney Carney interview; *NYT*, April 7, 1938, 15; *NYT*, September 8, 1940, 1; *NYT*, September 15, 1940, 1.

2. Moss, *Nineteen Weeks*, 270, 300–301, 315–316; *NYT*, August 11, 1940, IV: 8.

3. Ruth Johnson interviews; Davis, *History of Harrison County*, 130.

4. Ruth Johnson interviews; Berle and Jacobs, *Navigating the Rapids*, 343–344; George C. Marshall to Johnson, October 30, 1940, and January 3, 1944, Johnson to Marshall, January 1, 1944, all in Box 60, Louis Johnson, George C. Marshall Papers.

5. Johnson to General George Marshall, October 13, 1940; "I want no waiver or exemption," Memorandum for Colonel Desobry [from George Marshall], October 15, 1940, both in Box 60, Louis Johnson, George C. Marshall Papers.

6. Johnson to Steve Early, October 30, 1940, Box 8, Louis Johnson, Early Papers, FDRL; Memorandum of A. A. Berle to President Roosevelt, October 10, 1940, OF 4069, Louis Johnson, FDRL.

7. *NYT*, October 15, 1940, 1; *NYT*, October 17, 1940, 10, 28; "Colonel Lindbergh displays alike his ignorance of the United States," Berle and Jacobs, *Navigating the Rapids*, 343–344, quote on 344.

8. Ruth Johnson interviews; telegram, Roosevelt to Johnson, November 7, 1940, PPF 2822, Louis A. Johnson, FDRL.

9. Telegram, Roosevelt to Johnson, November 17, 1940, PPF 2822, Louis A. Johnson, FDRL.

10. Telegram, Johnson to Roosevelt, December 27, 1940, Roosevelt to Johnson, December 27, 1940, both in PPF 2822, Louis A. Johnson, FDRL.

11. Memorandum for the President from Edwin M. Watson, January 4, 1941, OF 300, West Virginia, FDRL.

12. Sandra G. Boodman, "The Mystery of Chestnut Lodge," *Washington Post Magazine*, October 8, 1989.

13. Marianne Clevinger (Lillian Johnson's careperson) to co-author Roll, March 27, 2003; Frank Maxwell interview; interview with Steven Maxwell, Clarksburg, West Virginia, March 13–14, 2003; "The Mayflower Log," 1937–1940, extant issues loaned to co-author Roll by Mayflower executive offices; interview with Mary Katherine Brown, Clarksburg, West Virginia, April 4, 2003; Jean Kearney interview.

14. Mary Katherine Brown interview.

15. Jean Kearney interview; Steven Maxwell interview; Frank Maxwell interview; "The Mayflower Log"; interview of James Guiher, Jr., Washington, D.C., February 13, 2003.

16. Ruth Johnson interviews.

17. Davis, *History of Harrison County*, 98, 203.

18. Ruth Johnson interview, July 12, 1977; James Guiher interview; Thomas Langfitt interview; Ruth Johnson to co-author McFarland, July 14, 1981.

19. Telegram, Johnson to Early, July 25, 1941, Box 95, Correspondence with Franklin Roosevelt and Steve Early, Johnson Papers.

20. Telegram, Johnson to Stephen Early, October 9, 1941, Box 95, Correspondence with Franklin D. Roosevelt and Stephen Early, Johnson Papers.

21. Johnson to Stephen Early, October 3, 1941, OF 4069, Louis Johnson, FDRL.

22. Ruth Johnson interviews.

23. Telegram, Johnson to Roosevelt, December 7, 1941, PPF 2822, Louis A. Johnson, FDRL; also in Box 95, Correspondence with Franklin D. Roosevelt and Stephen Early, Johnson Papers.

24. Johnson to Roosevelt, December 16, 1941 (emphasis in the original), Box 95, Correspondence with Franklin D. Roosevelt and Stephen Early, Johnson Papers.

25. Telegram, Johnson to Roosevelt, January 30, 1942, PPF 2822, Louis A. Johnson, FDRL.

26. Stanley Wolpert, A New History of India (New York: Oxford University Press, 1977), 294.

27. William Galant, The Long Afternoon: British India, 1601–1947 (New York: St. Martin's Press, 1975), 120–121, 171–174.

28. Ram Gopal, How India Struggled for Freedom (Bombay: Book Centre, 1967), 416–417; Wolpert, A New History of India, 329.

29. Wolpert, A New History of India, 330, 333–334.

30. Gary R. Hess, America Encounters India, 1941–1947 (Baltimore: Johns Hopkins University Press, 1971), 22–23.

31. Memorandum by the Assistant Secretary of State [Berle] to the Secretary of State, December 20, 1941; Memorandum of Conversation by the Assistant Secretary of State [Berle], January 28, 1942; Memorandum by the Assistant Secretary of State Berle to President Roosevelt, January 29, 1941; and Memorandum by President Roosevelt to Assistant Secretary of State Berle, February 4, 1942, all in FRUS 1942, I: 593–595, 597–599.

32. John Morton Blum, ed., The Price of Vision: The Diary of Henry A. Wallace, 1942–1946 (Boston: Houghton Mifflin Company, 1973), 90.

33. Berle and Jacobs, Navigating the Rapids, 341, 343–344, 404, 405; Memorandum by the Assistant Secretary of State [Berle] to the Under Secretary of State [Welles], February 17, 1942, FRUS 1942, I: 602–603.

34. "will go to India to assist in the war effort," NYT, March 10, 1942, 4. For an excellent account of Johnson's mission to India, see chapter entitled "The Louis Johnson Mission: An Attempt to Avert Political Collapse," in Hess, America Encounters India.

35. NYT, March 10, 1942, 4; FRUS 1942, I: 643; Memorandum to the Secretary of the Treasury from Director, Bureau of the Budget, March 16, 1942, OF 4069, Louis Johnson, FDRL.

36. Memorandum by the Assistant Secretary of State [Berle] to the Under Secretary of State [Welles], February 17, 1942, FRUS 1942, I: 603–604.

37. Acting Secretary of State to the Ambassador in the United Kingdom [Winant], February 25, 1942, FRUS 1942, I: 604.

38. James MacGregor Burns, Roosevelt: The Soldier of Freedom (New York: Harcourt Brace Jovanovich, 1970), 219–220; Sherwood, Roosevelt and Hopkins, 511–512; Winston Churchill, The Hinge of Fate (Boston: Houghton Mifflin Company, 1950), 209, 212–214.

39. Sherwood, Roosevelt and Hopkins, 512.

40. Churchill, Hinge of Fate, 214–215.

41. Hess, America Encounters India, 41–42.

42. Memorandum by Assistant Secretary of State [Shaw] of a Conversation with Colonel Louis A. Johnson, March 11, 1942, FRUS 1942, I: 616.

43. Roosevelt to Johnson, March 19, 1942, Box 9, Correspondence—India, Johnson Papers; Department of State Bulletin, March 28, 1942, 260; NYT, March 16, 1942, 6; NYT, March 17, 1942, 6; NYT, March 25, 1942, 3; Washington Post, March 25, 1942, 6.

44. Cable, Roosevelt to Marquess of Linlithgow, March 19, 1942, in Nicholas

Mansergh, ed., *The Transfer of Power 1942–7*, vol. 1: *The Cripps Mission* (London: Her Majesty's Stationery Office, 1970), 445. Hereafter *Cripps Mission*.

45. Memorandum by Assistant Secretary of State [Shaw] of a Conversation with Colonel Louis A. Johnson, March 11, 1942, *FRUS 1942*, I: 616–618.

46. Hess, *America Encounters India*, 42.

47. Ibid., 43–47.

48. Ibid.

49. Effective upon Johnson's arrival the position of commissioner became open and remained vacant throughout his stay. Commissioner Thomas Wilson was instructed by Sumner Welles to return to Washington after Johnson's arrival in India. *FRUS 1942*, I: 617–618.

50. The Personal Representative of the President in India to the Secretary of State, April 4, 1942, *FRUS 1942*, I: 626–627.

51. The Acting Secretary of State [Welles] to the Officer in Charge at New Delhi, April 5, 1942, *FRUS 1942*, I: 627–628.

52. *NYT*, April 5, 1942, 7; *NYT*, April 7, 1942, 1; *NYT*, April 8, 1942, 1; *NYT*, April 9, 1942, 1; *NYT*, April 23, 1942, 9; B. Shiva Rao, "India, 1935–47," in *The Partition of India. Policies and Perspectives, 1935–1947*, ed. C. H. Philips and Mary D. Wainright (London: George Allen and Unwin, 1970), 431–432; Sarvepalli Gopal, *Jawaharlal Nehru: A Biography*, vol. 1, 1889–1947 (London: Jonathan Cape, 1975), 282–283.

53. The Personal Representative of the President in India to the Secretary of State, April 11, 1941, *FRUS 1942*, I: 631; Hess, *America Encounters India*, 47–49; Gopal, *Jawaharlal Nehru*, 283.

54. Burns, *Soldier of Freedom*, 221.

55. Hess, *America Encounters India*, 50.

56. The Personal Representative of the President in India to the Secretary of State, April 11, 1942, *FRUS 1942*, I: 631–632.

57. Ibid.

58. Burns, *Soldier of Freedom*, 221; Sherwood, *Roosevelt and Hopkins*, 524–525.

59. Cable, Churchill to Cripps, April 9, 1942, in *Cripps Mission*, 704.

60. Minutes of British War Cabinet, April 9, 1942, Cable, War Cabinet to Cripps, April 9, 1942, both in *Cripps Mission*, 705–708.

61. Harry Hopkins to President Roosevelt, April 9, 1942, *FRUS 1942*, I: 629.

62. Hess, *America Encounters India*, 50; M. S. Venkataraman and B. K. Shrivostava, "The United States and the Cripps Mission," *India Quarterly*, July 1963, 248–250.

63. President Roosevelt to Prime Minister Churchill, April 11, 1942, *FRUS 1942*, I: 633–634.

64. Burns, *Soldier of Freedom*, 221.

65. Ibid.

66. Churchill, *Hinge of Fate*, 219–220; Burns, *Soldier of Freedom*, 221.

67. Jawaharlal Nehru to President Roosevelt, April 17, 1942, *FRUS 1942*, I: 637–638.

68. Rao, "India, 1935–47," 440–441.

69. *NYT*, April 23, 1942, 9; *NYT*, April 24, 1942, 2; *The Times* (London), April 23, 4; *The Times*, April 24, 1942, 4; Johnson statement to the press, April 22, 1942, OF 48, India— 1942, FDRL; Johnson speech delivered via All-India Radio, April 23, 1942, Box 79, Office Correspondence, 1920–43, Sumner Welles Papers, FDRL.

70. Hess, *America Encounters India*, 56.

71. The Personal Representative of the President in India to the President and Secretary of State, April 21, 1942, and the Secretary of State to the Personal Representative of the President in India, April 27, 1942, both in *FRUS 1942*, I: 638–639, 644–645.

72. Rao, "India, 1935–47," 441.

73. The Personal Representative of the President in India to the President and Secretary of State, May 4, 1942, and the Secretary of State to the Personal Representative of the President in India, May 8, 1942, both in *FRUS 1942*, I: 648–650.

74. While in India Johnson was also involved in certain Indian domestic and military matters, including a request that American military aircraft be given to Britain for the defense of India. *FRUS 1942*, I: 631, 637–638; Acting Secretary of State Sumner Welles to the President, April 24, 1942, OF 48, India—1942, FDRL.

75. The Secretary of State to the Personal Representative of the President in India, May 8 and 13, 1942; The Personal Representative of the President in India to the President and Secretary of State, May 9 and 14, 1942, *FRUS 1942*, I: 650–651, 653–654; *NYT*, May 9, 1942, 3; Paul H. Griffith oral history, 3–4.

76. Major Orrin E. Swenson, Surgeon, to Col. Louis Johnson, May 14, 1942, Box 79, Office Correspondence, 1920–43, Sumner Welles Papers, FDRL; *NYT*, May 14, 1942, 3.

77. *NYT*, May 28, 1942, 8.

78. Ibid.; Mayo Clinic to Sumner Welles, June 24, 1942, Box 79, Office Correspondence, 1920–43, Sumner Welles Papers, FDRL.

79. Cable, L. S. Amery to Churchill, May 29, 1942, in *The Transfer of Power 1942–7*, vol. II, "*Quit India*," ed. Nicholas Mansergh (London: Her Majesty's Stationery Office, 1970), 146. Hereafter "*Quit India*."

80. Ruth Johnson interviews.

81. *FRUS 1942*, I: 647; *NYT*, April 29, 1942, 4; "a great help in clarifying the situation," *The Times* (London), April 29, 1942, 2.

82. *NYT*, April 10, 1942, 1; *Time*, June 1, 1942, 32.

83. For a discussion of various historical interpretations of the failure of the Cripps mission, see Hess, *America Encounters India*, 193–196.

84. The Personal Representative of the President in India to the President and Acting Secretary of State, April 11, 1942, *FRUS 1942*, I: 631; Bell, "Defense Secretary Louis Johnson," 651; Ruth Johnson interviews.

85. Burns, *Soldier of Freedom*, 221.

86. Cable, Churchill to Linlithgow, May 31, 1942, in "*Quit India*," 156.

87. Telegram, Churchill to Hopkins, May 31, 1942, in "*Quit India*," 156.

88. Wolpert, *A New History of India*, 335–336, 344–349.

89. Stuart L. Weiss, *The President's Man: Leo Crowley and Franklin Roosevelt in Peace and War* (Carbondale: Southern Illinois University Press, 1996), 122–131.

90. Ibid.

91. *NYT*, July 11, 1942, 19; *The Roanoke Times*, July 11, 1942; *Roanoke Press*, January 1, 1943.

92. Memorandum to the President from Leo Crowley, July 6, 1942, Memorandum for the President from Adolf Berle, July 2, 1942, both in OF 4069, Louis Johnson, FDRL.

93. James Guiher interview.

94. Weiss, *The President's Man*, 146–147.

95. Interview with Henry Ikenberry, Washington, D.C., January 22, 2003.

96. House Committee on Armed Services, *Investigation of the B-36 Bomber Program*, H.R. Report no. 1470, 81st Cong., 2nd Sess., 1950, 27.

97. "Mr. Odlum Gets the Business," *Fortune*, September 1949, 90.

98. Notations of 1941, 1942, 1944 visits of Johnson and American Legion National Commander found in OF 4069, Louis Johnson, FDRL; *NYT*, September 30, 1944, 7.

99. "Legion Convention Will Get Postwar Program," *NAM News*, September 1944, 3; Roosevelt to Johnson, October 5, 1944, Box 95, Correspondence with Franklin Roosevelt and Stephen Early, Johnson Papers.

100. Interview with Sarah Steptoe, Martinsburg, West Virginia, November 16, 2002; "Memorial Service," held by the Harrison County Bar Association, May 12, 1945; "History of Falling Spring," monograph loaned to co-author Roll by Dr. Phillip P. Steptoe Sr. and his daughter, Mary Lou Steptoe.

101. Johnson to Roosevelt, November 8, 1944, Memorandum for Steve Early from President Roosevelt, November 22, 1944, both in OF 4069, Louis Johnson, FDRL; Johnson to Early, January 19, 1945, Box 8, Correspondence—Johnson 1941–46, Early Papers, FDRL.

102. Upon Roosevelt's death Johnson confided to a friend of the man who had disappointed him so, "He was a great American! I think history will say the greatest of them all!" Johnson to Stephen Early, April 24, 1945, Box 8 Correspondence—Johnson 1941–46, Early Papers, FDRL.

103. Johnson's stature with Truman and others grew rapidly in the fall of 1947 when witnesses testifying before the Senate War Investigating Committee tended to support the view that Johnson's mobilization proposals should have been implemented in 1939 and 1940. NYT, October 21, 1947, 1; NYT, October 24, 1947, 1; NYT, October 25, 1947, 1.

104. William D. Hassett to Sen. Harold H. Burton, September 19, 1945, OF, Louis Johnson, FDRL; Walter A. Millis, ed., The Forrestal Diaries (New York: Viking, 1951), 325.

105. Miller, You Can't Tell by Looking at 'Em, 61–63.

9. Long Shot Pays Off

1. Jean Kearney interview.

2. Hamby, Man of the People, 435–436.

3. Jules Abels, Out of the Jaws of Victory (New York: Henry Holt and Company, 1959), 1–14.

4. Alexander, "Stormy New Boss," 70.

5. Johnson to President Truman, December 5, 1947, PPF 127, Box 176, HSTL.

6. Alexander, "Stormy New Boss," 70.

7. Jack Redding, Inside the Democratic Party (Indianapolis: Bobbs-Merrill, 1958), 169–170.

8. NYT, June 4, 1948, 1; NYT, June 10, 1948, 1.

9. McCullough, Truman, 629.

10. Arthur M. Schlesinger Jr., ed., History of American Presidential Elections, 1789–1968 (New York: Chelsea House, 1972), VI: 3115–3116.

11. President Truman's 1947 Diary Book, July 25, 1947, transcribed by Raymond H. Geselbracht, HSTL.

12. McCullough, Truman, 637.

13. Ibid., 639.

14. Eugene H. Roseboom, A History of Presidential Elections (New York: Macmillan, 1957), 498–501.

15. McCullough, Truman, 642.

16. New York Herald Tribune, September 9, 1948.

17. Truman, Harry S. Truman, 20, Kenneth M. Birkhead oral history, 21.

18. Hamby, Man of the People, 455.

19. Bell, "Defense Secretary Louis Johnson," 652; Matthew J. Connelly oral history, November 30, 1967, 47.

20. Kenneth M. Birkhead oral history, 20–21.

21. Bell, "Defense Secretary Louis Johnson," 652.

22. Ibid.; Alexander, "Stormy New Boss," 70; Redding, Inside the Democratic Party,

167–169. Redding's account has the meeting taking place in June rather than in September. He also claims that the meeting was held at the Mayflower Hotel and that Johnson went to the White House and consulted with Truman before accepting.

23. Irwin Ross, *The Loneliest Campaign: The Truman Victory of 1948* (New York: The New American Library, 1968), 166.

24. Ruth Johnson interviews.

25. *Newsweek*, March 14, 1949, 26; Haymond Maxwell interview; interview with Marx Leva, Washington, D.C., July 29, 1977.

26. Arnold A. Rogow, *James Forrestal: A Study of Personality, Politics and Policy* (New York: Macmillan, 1963), 313.

27. *NYT*, January 20, 1949, 4.

28. Redding, *Inside the Democratic Party*, 170.

29. Truman, *Harry S. Truman*, 20.

30. Abels, *Out of the Jaws of Victory*, 164.

31. Alexander, "Stormy New Boss," 70; Truman, *Harry S. Truman*, 21; Redding, *Inside the Democratic Party*, 110; Walter Waggoner, "Now Louis Johnson Tackles It," *NYT Magazine*, April 3, 1949, 15.

32. Jean Kearney interview; "Master of the Pentagon," *Time*, June 6, 1949, 22–23; Louis H. Renfrow oral history, 35.

33. Louis H. Renfrow oral history, 36.

34. "Master of the Pentagon," *Time*, 22–23; McCullough, *Truman*, 679.

35. "Master of the Pentagon," *Time*, 22–23; McCullough, *Truman*, 679; Robert J. Donovan, *Conflict and Crisis* (New York: Norton and Co., 1977), 419.

36. Alexander, "Stormy New Boss," 70; Abels, *Out of the Jaws of Victory*, 164; *Newsweek*, March 14, 1949, 26.

37. Samuel C. Brightman oral history, 23.

38. Truman, *Harry S. Truman*, 21; Abels, *Out of the Jaws of Victory*, 252; "We'll have to cut him off in a minute," Alfred Steinberg, *The Man from Missouri: The Life and Times of Harry S. Truman* (New York: G. P. Putnam's Sons, 1962), 326.

39. "I got rid of the $30,000," Alexander Heard, *The Costs of Democracy* (Chapel Hill: University of North Carolina Press, 1960), 359; Jules Abels, *The Truman Scandals* (Chicago: Henry Regnery Company, 1956), 128.

40. Steinberg, *Man from Missouri*, 328.

41. Louis H. Renfrow oral history, 95–98.

42. Steinberg, *Man from Missouri*, 326–327.

43. Redding, *Inside the Democratic Party*, 226–227; Steinberg, *Man from Missouri*, 329.

44. McCullough, *Truman*, 684–685.

45. Donovan, *Conflict and Crisis*, 431.

46. Ruth Johnson interviews; Lem Jarvis interview.

47. Jean Kearney interview.

48. Henry Ikenberry interview.

49. Walter Isaacson and Evan Thomas, *The Wise Men: Six Friends and the World They Made* (New York: Touchstone, 1986), 520.

50. Matthew J. Connelly oral history, November 30, 1967, 47.

51. Telegram, President Truman to Johnson, November 11, 1948, PPF 127, Box 176, HSTL.

52. Johnson to President Truman, November 8, 1948, PPF 127, Box 176, HSTL.

53. Truman, *Harry S. Truman*, 42.

54. Ibid.; Abels, *Out of the Jaws of Victory*, 272; *NYT*, January 20, 1949, 4.

55. Redding, *Inside the Democratic Party*, 170.

56. Truman to Carter T. Barron, December 18, 1948, PSF, Political File, Box 57, Louis Johnson, HSTL; PSF, President's Appointment File, Daily Sheets, January 1949, HSTL. Johnson visited the president off the record at least four times between mid-December and mid-January.

57. *Washington Post*, November 8, 1948, 21; *NYT*, January 14, 1949, IV: 3; Ernest Lindley, "Forrestal and Johnson," *Newsweek*, March 14, 1949, 27; "Paid in Full," *Time*, March 14, 1949, 21–22.

58. Ruth Johnson interviews.

59. Remarks, "As Told by Secretary Johnson to the Post Mortem Club, Tuesday, May 17th [1949]," Box 139, Correspondence G–H, Johnson Papers; "Off-the-Record Remarks of Louis Johnson, Secretary of Defense, Waldorf-Astoria Hotel, April 26th, 1951," Box 140, Correspondence R–W, Johnson Papers.

60. Rogow, *James Forrestal*, 313.

61. Johnson to Paul Hammond, April 11, 1957, Box 150, Correspondence re James Forrestal, Johnson Papers.

62. Rogow, *James Forrestal*, 313.

63. Truman, Memorandum on the dismissal of Louis Johnson, September 14, 1950, *PP HST 1950*, PSF, Presidential Appointment File, HSTL, also printed in Ferrell, *Off the Record*, 191–193 (hereafter Truman Memo on Dismissal of Johnson).

64. "Reminiscences of Admiral Robert Lee Dennison," January 17, 1973, U.S. Naval Institute, Annapolis, Maryland, 1975.

65. Dwight D. Eisenhower, *At Ease: Stories I Tell to Friends* (New York: Doubleday and Company, 1967), 332.

66. In 1954, Marshall recalled his experience of working with Woodring and Johnson in the War Department as the "worst experience of my life." That does not sound like someone who would be backing Johnson to become secretary of defense. McFarland, *Harry H. Woodring*, 246–247; Doris Fleeson, "Story behind Marshall Blast by Woodring," *St. Louis Post-Dispatch*, August 4, 1954.

67. Tyler Abell, ed., *Drew Pearson Diaries, 1949–1959* (New York: Holt, Rinehart and Winston, 1974), 9.

68. Ibid.

69. Rogow, *James Forrestal*, 313.

70. Marx Leva interview.

71. *Washington Evening Star*, March 4, 1949; *Washington Post*, March 5, 1949, 9; *Christian Science Monitor*, March 8, 1949.

72. "a promise of a Cabinet post from Truman," Steinberg, *Man from Missouri*, 321; *Washington Post*, November 8, 1949.

73. Millis, *Forrestal Diaries*, 544–545; *NYT*, January 12, 1949, 15; *NYT*, January 14, 1949, 4.

74. Townsend Hoopes and Douglas Brinkley, *Driven Patriot: The Life and Times of James Forrestal* (New York: Random House, 1992), 438.

75. Millis, *Forrestal Diaries*, 549–550; PSF, Presidential Appointment File, Daily Sheet, January 1949, HSTL.

76. Louis H. Renfrow oral history, 51.

77. Millis, *Forrestal Diaries*, 549–550; Transcript of Johnson Press Conference, March 29, 1949, *PP HST*.

78. Ibid.; House Committee on Armed Services, *Hearings on Investigation of the B-36 Bomber Program*, 81st Cong., 1st Sess., 1949, 475–480.

79. Millis, *Forrestal Diaries*, 551–553.

80. Untitled memo by Truman on Johnson Dismissal, September 12, 1950, Box 1, Eben A. Ayers Papers, HSTL.

81. Hoopes and Brinkley, *Driven Patriot*, 133, 443.

82. *NYT*, March 4, 1949, 1.

83. Robert W. Merry, *Taking on the World: Joseph and Stewart Alsop — Guardians of the American Century* (New York: Viking, 1996), 180.

84. *Army and Navy Journal*, March 12, 1949; *NYT* (editorial), March 4, 1949; Marquis Childs, *Washington Post*, March 5, 1949, 9; *New Republic*, March 21, 1949, 6.

85. *NYT*, March 4, 1949, 1–2; *Washington Post*, March 4, 1949, 1; "Stormy New Boss," 67.

86. Truman, *Harry S. Truman*, 407.

87. Fenno, *President's Cabinet*, 49.

88. Louis H. Renfrow oral history, 52.

89. Ibid., 57–59.

90. Millis, *Forrestal Diaries*, 549, Abell, *Drew Pearson Diaries*, 42.

91. *NYT*, March 18, 1949, 3.

92. Steve Neal, *Harry and Ike: The Partnership that Remade the Postwar World* (New York: Touchstone, 2001), 150–151.

93. Louis H. Renfrow oral history, 52; Carl W. Borklund, *Men of the Pentagon* (New York: Frederick A. Praeger, 1966), 66.

94. Waggoner, "Now Louis Johnson Tackles It," 30.

95. Miller, *You Can't Tell by Looking at 'Em*, 73–74.

96. Senate Committee on Armed Services, *Hearings on Nomination of Louis A. Johnson to Be Secretary of Defense*, vol. III (Executive Session), 81st Cong., 1st Sess., 1949.

97. *Congressional Record*, 81st Cong., 1st Sess., 1949, vol. 95, pt. 3, 2973–2975; *Army and Navy Journal*, March 26, 1949.

98. Robert H. Ferrell, ed., *Truman in the White House: The Diary of Eben A. Ayers* (Columbia: University of Missouri Press, 1991), 300.

99. *Newsweek*, July 25, 1949, 19.

100. Waggoner, "Now Louis Johnson Tackles It," 15.

101. *Army and Navy Journal*, April 2, 1949.

102. Hoopes and Brinkley, *Driven Patriot*, 446; Millis, *Forrestal Diaries*, 554.

103. Johnson to Harley M. Kilgore, March 9, 1949, Box 76, Senator Harley Kilgore Collection, West Virginia State Archives, Charleston, West Virginia.

10. *Inside the Pentagon*

1. *NYT*, April 28, 1949, 3.

2. Hoopes and Brinkley, *Driven Patriot*, 464.

3. Carl Vinson to Johnson, May 3, 1950, Box 110, Correspondence — Carl Vinson, Johnson Papers.

4. *Washington Post*, March 4, 1949, 1–2.

5. "Johnson or Truman in '52?" *U.S. News & World Report*, October 28, 1949, 13–15; Alexander, "Stormy New Boss," 67; Bell, "Defense Secretary Louis Johnson," 652.

6. "Off the Record Remarks," Waldorf Astoria Hotel, April 26, 1951, Box 140, Johnson Papers; Ruth Johnson interviews; Haymond Maxwell interview; W. B. Maxwell interview.

7. Brinkley, *Washington Goes to War*, 73.

8. Ibid., 72–75; Borklund, *Men of the Pentagon*, 3–4; Jack Raymond, *Power at the Pentagon* (New York: Harper & Row Publishers, 1964), 1–5.

9. Raymond, *Power at the Pentagon*, 9–10.

10. "gigantic game of musical chairs," "Master of the Pentagon," *Time*, June 6, 1949,

20; Louis H. Renfrow oral history, 59–60; "Mr. Secretary Johnson," *Newsweek*, July 25, 1949, 19.

11. Borklund, *Men of the Pentagon*, 70.

12. Ibid., 66–68.

13. Ibid., 68; Marx Leva interview; interview with J. Lawton Collins, Washington, D.C., July 27, 1977; Johnson to Mary McGrory, May 27, 1949, Box 1, Louis Johnson Correspondence, A. Robert Ginsburgh Papers, HSTL.

14. Memorandum re Secretary's Daily Calendar of Appointments (first 14 months in office), June 8, 1950, Box 119, Johnson Papers; Ruth Johnson interviews.

15. Marx Leva interview; John H. Ohly oral history, 114–120; Hamby, *Man of the People*, 513.

16. Even Johnson's closest friends acknowledged his tendency to be arrogant and overbearing.

17. Borklund, *Men of the Pentagon*, 68.

18. Acheson, *Present at the Creation*, 374.

19. Conversation of co-author McFarland with Paul Nitze, March 25, 1977, Lexington, Virginia (hereafter Nitze conversation).

20. Thomas K. Finletter oral history, 42.

21. Morris J. MacGregor, Jr., *Integration of the Armed Forces 1940–1965* (Washington, D.C.: Center of Military History, U.S. Army, U.S. Government Printing Office, 1981), 322.

22. Steven L. Rearden, *History of the Office of the Secretary of Defense*, vol. 1, *The Formative Years, 1947–1950* (Washington, D.C.: U.S. Government Printing Office, 1984), 49 (hereafter *Formative Years*).

23. Abell, *Drew Pearson Diaries*, 61.

24. "I can't get Calder to take the job," Gordon Gray oral history, 11–12; Omar N. Bradley and Clay Blair, *A General's Life* (New York: Simon and Schuster, 1983), 503.

25. Gordon Gray oral history, 12.

26. Rearden, *Formative Years*, 49.

27. Louis H. Renfrow oral history, 125.

28. Ibid.

29. Merry, *Taking on the World*, 183.

30. Walter J. Boyne, "Stuart Symington," *Air Force Magazine*, February 1999, 71.

31. Thomas K. Finletter oral history, 42.

32. Eisenhower, *At Ease*, 332.

33. J. Lawton Collins interview. Collins's lack of enthusiasm was based on his aversion to Johnson's austerity program, not his personality.

34. Rearden, *Formative Years*, 49–50.

35. John H. Ohly oral history, 114–120; Wilfred J. McNeil oral history, 139; interview with Marx Leva by Alfred Goldberg, Samuel Tucker, and Harry B. Yoshpe, March 8, 1974, Washington, D.C., copy forwarded to co-author McFarland by Leva.

36. Allen and Shannon, *The Truman Merry-Go-Round*, 463; *NYT*, April 8, 1949, 14; *NYT*, April 9, 1949, 16.

37. Pearson, "Washington Merry-Go-Round, Steve Early and Louis Johnson," *San Francisco Chronicle*, April 13, 1949, 18.

38. Abell, *Drew Pearson Diaries*, 62.

39. Eugene M. Zuckert oral history, 24–25.

40. Rearden, *Formative Years*, 48; Allen and Shannon, *Truman-Merry-Go-Round*, 463–465.

41. Paul H. Griffith oral history, 13–15; interview with Paul Griffith, Washington, D.C., March 9, 1977.

42. Louis H. Renfrow oral history, 79.

43. Borklund, *Men of the Pentagon*, 66.

44. Rearden, *Formative Years*, 69, 71, 73.

45. Ibid., 70–71; "Johnson's whipping boy," Nitze conversation.

46. Nitze conversation; J. Lawton Collins interview.

47. Alexander, "Stormy New Boss," 67; Hanson Baldwin, "The War of Unification," *NYT*, October 13, 1949, 4; *Washington Post*, March 27, 1949, 3B; Borklund, *Men of the Pentagon*, 69; Marx Leva interview; J. Lawton Collins interviews.

48. *Army and Navy Journal*, March 26, 1949; Carl Vinson to Johnson, May 3, 1950, Box 110, Correspondence Carl Vinson, Johnson Papers; Senator John Sparkman to co-author McFarland, September 17, 1975; Senator Edwin C. Johnson to co-author McFarland, April 27, 1968.

49. Marx Leva interview; Representative Claude Pepper to co-author McFarland, September 17, 1975.

50. Victor H. Krulak, *First to Fight* (Annapolis, Md.: United States Naval Institute, 1984), 120.

51. Memorandum from Secretary of Defense Johnson to the Secretary of the Army, Navy and Air Force, October 24, 1949, PSF, Military: Army-Navy Unification, Box 125, HSTL.

52. Marx Leva interview by Goldberg, Tucker, and Yoshpe.

53. Marquis Childs, "Johnson's Boner," *Washington Post*, May 3, 1949; Alexander, "Stormy New Boss," 27.

54. Abell, *Drew Pearson Diaries*, 27–28, 61, 86–87; William Ritchie interview.

55. Borklund, *Men of the Pentagon*, 66–68; *Army and Navy Journal*, April 16, 1949; Lawrence Spivak to Johnson, Box 128, Correspondence from March 1949–August 1950, Johnson Papers; Eleanor Roosevelt to Johnson, February 23, March 6, and April 3, 1950, and Johnson to Eleanor Roosevelt, March 10 and April 6, 1950, Box 136, Correspondence re Eleanor Roosevelt, Johnson Papers.

56. Allen and Shannon, *Truman Merry-Go-Round*, 448.

57. Ruth Johnson interviews; Stephen Ailes interview; J. Lawton Collins interview; Hamby, *Man of the People*, 513.

58. MacGregor, *Integration of the Armed Forces*, 346.

59. Ibid., 345–347.

60. Ibid., 366.

61. Ibid., 380. In his memoir, Clark Clifford alleged, unfairly in our judgment, that Johnson "fought the very existence of the Fahy committee" and concluded that Johnson "confined his support of desegregation to empty rhetoric." Clifford, *Counsel to the President*, 212.

62. This assessment of the Truman-Johnson relationship is based on dozens of interviews with family, friends, enemies, and associates of Johnson.

63. Merle Miller, *Plain Speaking: An Oral Biography of Harry S. Truman* (New York: Berkley Publishing Corporation, 1973), 164; Blair, *Forgotten War*, 4, 15.

11. Revolt of the Admirals

1. Johnson to Harley M. Kilgore, March 9, 1949, Box 76, Secretary of Defense File, Kilgore Collection, West Virginia State Archives, Charleston, West Virginia.

2. Paul Y. Hammond, *Organizing for Defense* (Princeton, N.J.: Princeton University Press, 1961), 186–192; Frank N. Trager, "The National Security Act of 1947: Its Thirtieth Anniversary," *Air University Review*, November–December 1977, 5–7.

3. Harry S. Truman, *Memoirs: Years of Trial and Hope* (Garden City, N.Y.: Doubleday and Company, 1956), 46-48; Millis, *Forrestal Diaries*, 46-47, 88. Truman had set forth his views favoring unification in an article entitled "Our Armed Forces Must Be Unified," which appeared in the August 26, 1944, issue of *Collier's*.

4. C. Joseph Bernardo and Eugene H. Bacon, *American Military Policy: Its Development Since 1775* (Harrisburg, Pa.: Stackpole Company, 1961), 452-456.

5. Truman, *Memoirs: Years of Trial and Hope*, 49.

6. *PP HST 1946*, 194, 204; *Washington Post*, April 18, 1946, 1.

7. Millis, *Forrestal Diaries*, 160-161.

8. *NYT*, July 27, 1947, 1, 3.

9. Public Law 253, U.S. Statutes at Large 61 (1947): 495. The act also created the National Security Council, the Central Intelligence Agency, the National Security Resources Board, the Joint Chiefs of Staff, the Munitions Board, and the Research and Development Board.

10. Russell F. Weigley, *History of the United States Army* (New York: Macmillan, 1967), 492-494.

11. R. Gordon Hoxie, *Command Decisions and the Presidency* (New York: Reader's Digest Press, 1977), 141.

12. "seldom had any idea of the value of money," Truman, *Memoirs: Year of Decisions* (Garden City, N.Y.: Doubleday and Company, 1955), 88; "squandered billions of dollars," Richard F. Haynes, *The Awesome Power: Harry S. Truman as Commander in Chief* (Baton Rouge: Louisiana State University Press, 1973), 120, 304; "made excessive demands," Truman, *Memoirs: Years of Trial and Hope*, 31, 34.

13. Herman S. Wolk, "The Defense Unification Battle, 1947-1950: The Air Force," *Prologue* (Spring 1975): 22-23; Haynes, *Awesome Power*, 110-111.

14. Millis, *Forrestal Diaries*, 390-391, 478.

15. Paolo E. Coletta, "The Defense Unification Battle, 1947-1950: The Navy," *Prologue* (Spring 1975): 7.

16. *Survival in the Air Age: A Report by the President's Air Policy Commission* (Finletter Report) (Washington, D.C.: U.S. Government Printing Office, 1948); Congressional Aviation Policy Board, *National Aviation Policy*, S. Rep. 949, 80th Cong., 2nd Sess., 1948.

17. Paul Y. Hammond, "Super Carriers and B-36 Bombers: Appropriations, Strategy and Politics," in Stein, ed., *American Civil Military Decisions*, 486 (Hammond's work on the carrier-bomber controversy is the best account written on the subject); Herman S. Wolk, "Independence and Responsibility: USAF in the Defense Establishment," in *Evaluation of the American Military Establishment Since World War II*, ed. Paul R. Schratz (Lexington, Va.: George C. Marshall Research Foundation, 1978), 60; Truman, *Harry S. Truman*, 407.

18. Jonathan Daniels, *The Man of Independence* (Philadelphia: J. B. Lippincott, 1950), 305.

19. *NYT*, February 12, 1949, 1.

20. *Army and Navy Journal*, April 2, 16, 1949; *Washington Post*, March 29, 1949, 1.

21. Hammond, "Super Carriers and B-36 Bombers," 493; *Washington Post*, April 25, 1949, 1.

22. The capabilities of the giant six-engine bomber were questioned by Air Force pilots and openly challenged by naval aviators.

23. House Committee on Armed Services, *Investigation of the B-36 Bomber Program*, 478-479.

24. Coletta, "Defense Unification: The Navy," 7-9; *NYT*, April 19, 1949, 1.

25. *Army and Navy Journal*, April 16, 1949; *NYT*, April 24, 1949, 1.

26. House Committee on Armed Services, *Hearings on the National Defense Program—Unification and Strategy*, 81st Cong., 1st Sess., 1949, 619–620; Phillip S. Meilinger, "The Admirals' Revolt of 1949: Lessons for Today," *Parameters*, September 1989, 87–88.

27. In his memoirs, Truman makes it clear that it was Johnson's cancellation. Truman, *Memoirs: Years of Trial and Hope*, 53.

28. Secretary Sullivan's letter of resignation, *Washington Post*, April 27, 1949. Years later Sullivan claimed that he had discussed the matter with Johnson on April 20 and that Johnson had given his word that no decision would be made until they talked about it again. John L. Sullivan oral history, 39.

29. House Committee on Armed Services, *Hearings on the National Defense Program—Unification and Strategy*, 619–621; Hammond, "Super Carriers and B-36 Bombers," 493–494; Johnson to Truman, April 23, 1949, Box 156, PSF, Subject File: Secretary of Defense, Truman Papers, HSTL; Johnson to Truman, April 23, 1949, Box 156, PSF, Cabinet, Secretary of Defense, Truman Papers, HSTL. The various memos of the Chiefs of Staff, General Eisenhower, and Secretary Johnson can be found in CCS 561, 5-26-48, RG 330, Records of the Office of the Secretary of Defense, 1921–1995, NARA.

30. John L. Sullivan oral history, 62–63; Ferrell, *Diary of Eben Ayers*, 305–336; Coletta, "Defense Unification Battle, 1947–1950: The Navy," 12.

31. Louis H. Renfrow oral history, 111–112.

32. Sullivan's letter of resignation, *Washington Post*, April 27, 1949.

33. Marquis Childs, "Washington Calling," *Washington Post*, May 3, 1949.

34. Military and congressional sources maintained that the final cost would exceed $800 million. *Washington Post*, April 24, 1949, 1.

35. Marx Leva interview; "The President put me over there at the Pentagon to take charge," Borklund, *Men of the Pentagon*, 71, 75.

36. Louis H. Renfrow oral history, 112–113.

37. *NYT*, April 24, 1949, 1; *Washington Post*, April 26, 1949, 1.

38. "Funny Business," *Washington Post* (editorial), April 28, 1949, 10.

39. *Congressional Record*, 81st Cong., 1st Sess., 1949, vol. 95, pt. 5: 5053.

40. Vincent Davis, *The Admirals Lobby* (Chapel Hill: University of North Carolina Press, 1967), 274.

41. Borklund, *Men of the Pentagon*, 75.

42. House Committee on Armed Services, *Investigation of the B-36 Bomber Program*, 528–555.

43. *Congressional Record*, 81st Cong., 1st Sess., 1949, vol. 95, pt. 5: 6892–6893.

44. *Washington Post*, June 10, 1949, 2.

45. Raymond, *Power at the Pentagon*, 296.

46. Hammond, "Super Carriers and B-36 Bombers," 499–500.

47. Borklund, *Men of the Pentagon*, 80–81.

48. House Committee on Armed Services, *Investigation of the B-36 Bomber Program*, 475–480, 486, 490, 528, 628–629; *Washington Post*, August 24, 1949, 1; *NYT*, August 24, 1949, 1.

49. House Committee on Armed Services, *Investigation of the B-36 Bomber Program*, 655.

50. Robert J. Donovan, *Tumultuous Years: The Presidency of Harry S. Truman, 1949–1953* (New York: W.W. Norton & Company, 1982), 107–108.

51. Ibid; *Time*, May 23, 1949, 18; *NYT*, May 14, 1949, 1, 8. The Johnson-Matthews admiration society lasted for the duration of their tenure in office. Matthews to Johnson, June 1, 1950, Johnson to Matthews, June 9, 1950, both in Box 107, Francis Matthews, Johnson Papers.

52. *Washington Post,* June 29, 1950, 2.

53. *Washington Post,* July 6, 1949, 1; *Washington Post,* July 7, 1949, 12; *Washington Post,* July 8, 1949, 5B; *Washington Post,* July 27, 1949, 4; *Washington Post,* August 11, 1949, 2.

54. *Army and Navy Journal,* June 25, 1949, Rearden, *Formative Years,* 412.

55. Hammond, "Super Carriers and B-36 Bombers," 505; *Washington Post,* August 11, 1949, 1.

56. NYT, June 25, 1949, 2. The article "Admiral Talks Back to the Airman" by Daniel V. Gallery was published in the June 25, 1949, issue of the *Saturday Evening Post.*

57. NYT, June 22, 1949, 1.

58. Memo from Assistant Secretary of Air Force Eugene Zuckert to Secretary of Air Force Symington, August 16, 1949, Box 41, Budget 1949–50, Hoyt Vandenberg Papers, LC; *U.S. News & World Report,* August 12, 1949, 22; NYT, July 28, 1949, 3.

59. House Committee on Armed Services, *Hearings on the National Defense Program—Unification and Strategy,* 624–625.

60. NYT, September 11, 1949, 1; *Washington Post,* September 12, 1949, 6.

61. Donovan, *Tumultuous Years,* 105–106; NYT, September 12, 1949, 3.

62. NYT, September 13, 1949, 1; NYT, September 14, 1949, 20; and NYT, September 16, 1949, 1; Donovan, *Tumultuous Years,* 106.

63. *PP HST 1949,* 480.

64. Hammond, "Super Carriers and B-36 Bombers," 505, 508–512.

65. Donovan, *Tumultuous Years,* 106–107.

66. House Committee on Armed Services, *Hearings on the National Defense Program—Unification and Strategy,* 2.

67. Ibid., 7.

68. Ibid., 39–53.

69. "morally reprehensible," ibid., 51; NYT, October 14, 1949, 1.

70. House Committee on Armed Services, *Hearings on the National Defense Program—Unification and Strategy,* 88.

71. Ibid., 350.

72. Ibid., 349–362; NYT, October 14, 1949, 1; Donovan, *Tumultuous Years,* 111–112.

73. Donovan, *Tumultuous Years,* 111.

74. House Committee on Armed Services, *Hearings on the National Defense Program—Unification and Strategy,* 515–537.

75. Ibid., 536.

76. Blair, *Forgotten War,* 17, 22–23.

77. House Committee on Armed Services, *Hearings on the National Defense Program—Unification and Strategy,* 634.

78. House Committee on Armed Services, *Hearings on the National Defense Program—Unification and Strategy,* 612–613, 619–620, 626–628, 632, 634.

79. *Washington Post,* October 22, 1949, 1.

80. *PP HST 1949,* 531.

81. Admiral Louis E. Denfeld, "Reprisal: Why I Was Fired," *Collier's,* March 18, 1950, 13–15; NYT, October 28, 1; NYT, October 29, 1949, 1.

82. Admiral Louis E. Denfeld, "The Only Carrier the Air Force Ever Sank," *Collier's,* March 25, 1950, 51.

83. NYT, October 28, 1949, 1.

84. *Washington Post,* October 22, 1949, 1.

85. Truman, *Memoirs: Years of Trial and Hope,* 53.

86. NYT, December 15, 1949, 4; NYT, December 25, 1949, 1; NYT, December 30, 1949, 6; Hammond, "Super Carriers and B-36 Bombers," 548.

87. House Committee on Armed Services, *Investigation of the B-36 Bomber Program*, H. R. Report no. 1470, 20–22, 32–33.

88. House Committee on Armed Services, *Unification and Strategy: A Report of Investigation by the Committee on Armed Services of the House of Representatives*, 81st Cong., 2nd Sess., 1950, House Doc. 600, 53, 56.

89. Russell F. Weigley, *The American Way of War: A History of United States Military Strategy and Policy* (New York: Macmillan, 1973), 377–378.

90. Borklund, *Men of the Pentagon*, 75.

91. For an analysis of the political power of the secretary of defense, especially Johnson, see John C. Ries, *The Management of Defense: Organization and Control of the U.S. Armed Services* (Baltimore: Johns Hopkins University Press, 1964), 110–119, 135–145. According to Ries, Johnson "was the first secretary of defense to use his potential power fully" (144).

92. Ferrell, *Diary of Eben Ayers*, 305.

12. *"Like a Meatchopper on Roundsteak"*

1. Carl W. Borklund, *The Department of Defense* (New York: Frederick A. Praeger, 1968), 210.

2. *Army and Navy Journal*, April 2, 1949.

3. House Committee on Armed Services, *Hearings on S. 1843, To Convert the National Military Establishment into an Executive Department of the Government of Defense, to Provide the Secretary of Defense with Appropriate Responsibility and Authority, and with Civilian and Military Assistants Adequate to Fulfill His Enlarged Responsibility*, 81st Cong., 1st Sess., 1949, 2710.

4. Senate Committees on Armed Services and Foreign Relations, *Hearings to Conduct an Inquiry into the Military Situation in the Far East and the Facts Surrounding the Relief of General of the Army Douglas MacArthur from His Assignments in That Area*, 82nd Cong., 1st Sess., 1951, pt. 4, 2626–2627.

5. Warner R. Schilling, "The Politics of National Defense: Fiscal 1950," in Warner R. Schilling, Paul Y. Hammond, and Glenn H. Snyder, *Strategy, Politics, and Defense Budgets* (New York: Columbia University Press, 1962), 101.

6. Acheson, *Present at the Creation*, 345.

7. Ruth Johnson interviews.

8. Bell, "Defense Secretary Louis Johnson," 652; Alexander, "Stormy New Boss," 67; Stephen Ailes interview; Lem Jarvis interview.

9. Truman, *Memoirs: Years of Trial and Hope*, 32.

10. Ibid., 31–33, 37.

11. Ibid., 34.

12. Haynes, *Awesome Power*, 120.

13. J. Lawton Collins interview.

14. Truman, *Memoirs: Years of Trial and Hope*, 32–33; *New York Herald Tribune*, December 3 and 17, 1948, Edwin G. Nourse, *Economies in the Public Service* (New York: Harcourt, Brace and Company, 1953), 223, 228, 230.

15. *NYT*, February 2, 1949, 1.

16. Gordon Gray oral history, 12.

17. "Points for Discussion between the President and Civilian Heads of the Military Establishment," March 4, 1949, PSF, Agencies-Military-President's Program, HSTL.

18. Borklund, *Men of the Pentagon*, 84.

19. Senate Subcommittee of the Committee on Appropriations, *National Military Establishment Appropriations Bill for 1950*, 81st Cong., 1st Sess., 1949, 32.

20. Edward A. Kolodziej, *The Uncommon Defense and Congress, 1945–1963* (Columbus: Ohio State University Press, 1966), 165–166; Schilling, "The Politics of National Defense," 113–114; *Army and Navy Journal*, July 30, 1949.

21. *NYT*, October 19, 1949, 4; *NYT*, October 30, 1949, 1.

22. House Committee on Armed Services, *Hearings on S. 1843 to Convert the National Military Establishment into an Executive Department*, 2701.

23. J. Lawton Collins, *War in Peacetime: The History and Lessons of Korea* (Boston: Houghton Mifflin Company, 1969), 74; J. Lawton Collins interview; House Committee on Armed Services, *Hearings on the National Defense Program—Unification and Strategy*, 625–629.

24. Rearden, *Formative Years*, 371–372; Nourse, *Economies in the Public Service*, 249–250.

25. Wilfred J. McNeil oral history, 51.

26. Rearden, *Formative Years*, 372.

27. Collins interview; Collins, *War in Peacetime*, 74.

28. Memo from Assistant Secretary of Air Force Eugene Zuckert to Secretary of Air Force Symington, August 16, 1949, and Memorandum to Joint Chiefs of Staff from Secretary of Defense Johnson, August 18, 1949, both in Box 41, Budget 1949–50, Hoyt Vandenberg Papers, LC; *U.S. News & World Report*, August 12, 1949, 22–23.

29. J. Lawton Collins interview. The 1949 Amendments to the National Security Act authorized a chairman of the Joint Chiefs of Staff. This made it possible for Eisenhower to exit at that time. General Omar Bradley was named chairman and General Collins replaced him as Army Chief of Staff. *Army & Navy Journal*, August 20, 1949.

30. One who did not go along with the cuts was General Eisenhower, who had returned to Columbia University. Eisenhower, *At Ease*, 355; Krock, *Sixty Years on the Firing Line*, 282; Johnson to General Dwight D. Eisenhower, April 11, 1949, Box 105, Dwight Eisenhower, Johnson Papers.

31. "Statement by Secretary of Defense Louis Johnson," January 10, 1950, Box 146, Press Releases 1950: January 3–August 4, Johnson Papers; *Army and Navy Journal*, January 14, 1950.

32. "maximum of national security at a minimum cost," Department of Defense, *Semiannual Report of the Secretary of Defense and the Semiannual Reports of the Secretary of the Army, Secretary of the Navy, Secretary of the Air Force, July 1 to December 31, 1949* (Washington, D.C.: U.S. Government Printing Office, 1950), 1, 6, 42, 50–55; *Army and Navy Journal*, March 11, 1950.

33. Borkland, *Men of the Pentagon*, 84. Nearly half of the dozens of secondary sources consulted which dealt with Johnson's service as secretary of defense referred to his claim to "transform defense fat into muscle."

34. Kolodziej, *Uncommon Defense*, 113–114.

35. J. Lawton Collins interview.

36. General Omar M. Bradley, "A Soldier's Farewell," *Saturday Evening Post*, August 22, 1953, 63.

37. Bradley and Blair, *A General's Life*, 487.

38. *Congressional Record*, 81st Cong., 2nd Sess., 1950, pt. 4: 4681.

39. Ibid., pt. 5: 6177.

40. Borklund, *Men of the Pentagon*, 84–85.

41. *NYT*, August 25, 1949, 1; *Washington Post*, August 25, 1949, 1.

42. "Conference of the Secretary of Defense With Members of Congress," August

24, 1949, 9: 15 A.M., Room 5E—1070, The Pentagon, Box 140, Correspondence (P), Johnson Papers; *NYT*, August 25, 1949, 1, 3.

43. *Washington Post*, August 25, 1949.

44. *NYT*, August 25, 1949, 1.

45. Senator A. H. Vandenberg to Louis Johnson, August 26, 1949, Box 110, Correspondence—A. H. Vandenberg, Johnson Papers.

46. *NYT*, August 25, 1949, 1; *Washington Post*, August 25, 1949, 1.

47. "News of the World," Wednesday, August 24, 1949, Box 148, News of the World, Johnson Papers.

48. *NYT* (editorial), August 26, 1949.

49. *Washington Post* (editorial), August 26, 1949.

50. Among newspapers supporting his move were the *New York-Journal American*, the *St. Louis Globe-Democrat*, the *Cleveland Plain Dealer*, the *Minneapolis Star*, the *San Francisco Examiner*, and the *New York Daily News*. Johnson's personal papers contain hundreds of letters from citizens praising his reductions in defense costs.

51. *Semiannual Report of the Secretary of Defense, July 1 to December 31, 1949*, 50–57; *Army and Navy Journal*, March 11, 1950.

52. *Army and Navy Journal*, March 25, 1950.

53. *Semiannual Report of the Secretary of Defense, July 1 to December 31, 1949*, 51, 54; *NYT*, August 25, 1949, 1. For a listing of all facilities affected, see *U.S. News & World Report*, September 9, 1949, 22–23.

54. *Semiannual Report of the Secretary of Defense, July 1 to December 31, 1949*, 53–55.

55. Ibid., 42.

56. Memorandum from President Truman to Secretary of Defense, April 20, 1950, PSF, Subject File, Louis Johnson, HSTL. In this confidential letter Truman said, "These military fellows get an idea that they have to act like a pack-rat and store material."

57. *Semiannual Report of the Secretary of Defense, July 1 to December 31, 1949*, 52–54.

58. Louis Johnson to George E. Oyler, September 9, 1949, Box 1, Correspondence File D–J, Johnson, Louis Correspondence, Ginsburgh Papers, HSTL.

59. *Semiannual Report of the Secretary of Defense, July 1 to December 31, 1949*, 53–55; *Army and Navy Journal*, October 29, 1949.

60. "Typescript of Staff Meeting," April 14 and May 12, 1950, Box 147, Typescript of Staff Meetings of the Secretary of Defense and His Staff, Johnson Papers.

61. Paul Y. Hammond, "NSC-68: Prologue to Rearmament" in Schilling, Hammond, and Snyder, *Strategy, Politics, and Defense Budgets*, 13.

62. "Typescript of Staff Meeting," April 14, 1950, Box 147, Typescript of Staff Meetings of the Secretary of Defense and His Staff, Johnson Papers.

63. Directive from Secretary of Defense to Defense Management Committee, May 12, 1950, Box 111, Directives (Folder no. 2), Johnson Papers.

64. Memorandum from Secretary of Defense Johnson to the Secretary of the Army, Navy, Air Force, February 1, 1950, Box 111, Directives (Folder no. 1), Johnson Papers; *Army and Navy Journal*, March 25, 1950; *NYT*, February 2, 1950, 23; *NYT*, March 8, 1950, 1; *NYT*, March 9, 1950, 2; *NYT*, April 11, 1950; and *NYT*, May 4, 1950, 23L; *Semiannual Report of the Secretary of Defense, July 1 to December 31, 1949*, 119.

65. J. Lawton Collins interview; Stephen Ailes interviews.

66. *Army and Navy Journal*, April 9 and October 1 and 15, 1950. For the pre- and post-October pay scales, see *Army and Navy Journal*, May 21 and October 1, 1950.

67. "Legislation Passed When Louis Johnson was Secretary of Defense," September 19, 1950, Box 148, Biographical Information, Johnson Papers.

68. Ibid., *Semiannual Report of the Secretary of Defense, July 1 to December 31, 1949*,

95, 208–209; *Semiannual Report of the Secretary of Defense, January 1 to June 30, 1950,* 28, 50, 61, 99–100; *Army and Navy Journal,* November 19, 1949.

69. *Semiannual Report of the Secretary of Defense, July 1 to December 31, 1949,* 6.

70. "if Joe Stalin starts something," Borklund, *Men of the Pentagon,* 86; "the biggest pop-off in Washington," "Needed: A Big Man for a Big Job" (editorial), *Collier's,* April 15, 1950, 82.

71. *Semiannual Report of the Secretary of Defense, July 1 to December 31, 1949,* 50–52; *Semiannual Report of the Secretary of Defense, January 1 to June 30, 1950,* 49–50; *Army and Navy Journal,* March 11, 25, 1950.

72. *Second Report of the Secretary of Defense, 1949,* 318; *Semiannual Report of the Secretary of Defense, January 1 to January 30, 1950,* 55, 206.

73. *Army and Navy Journal,* March 25, 1950; *Semiannual Report of the Secretary of Defense, July 1 to December 31, 1949,* 44.

74. Weigley, *History of the United States Army,* 502–503; Blair, *Forgotten War,* 28.

75. Matthew B. Ridgway, *Soldier* (New York: Harper & Brothers, 1956), 191.

76. Walter Millis, *Arms and the State* (New York: The Twentieth Century Fund, 1958), 235–236; Nitze conversation.

77. Millis, *Arms and the State,* 235.

78. *Congressional Record,* 81st Cong., 1st Sess., 1949, vol. 95, pt. 4: 4427.

13. "My God, the Russians Have the Bomb"

1. Weigley, *History of the United States Army,* 501–502; Millis, *Forrestal Diaries,* 350; James R. Shepley and Clay Blair Jr., *The Hydrogen Bomb: The Men, the Menace, and the Mechanism* (New York: David McKay Co., 1954), 13; Schilling, "The Politics of National Defense," 33, 250.

2. Haynes, *Awesome Power,* 64–65, 68–69; FRUS 1949, I: 481.

3. Truman, *Memoirs: Years of Trial and Hope,* 2; Haynes, *Awesome Power,* 70–71, 73–74.

4. Ibid., 74; Truman, *Memoirs: Years of Trial and Hope,* 295.

5. David E. Lilienthal, *The Journals of David E. Lilienthal,* vol. II, *The Atomic Energy Years, 1945–1959* (New York: Harper and Row, 1964), 118; Haynes, *Awesome Power,* 74.

6. Harry S. Borowski, "Air Force Atomic Capability from V-J Day to the Berlin Blockade—Potential or Real?" *Military Affairs* (October 1980), 105–110.

7. Lilienthal, *Atomic Energy Years,* 510–511.

8. Richard G. Hewlett and Frances Duncan, *A History of the United States Atomic Energy Commission,* vol. II, *Atomic Shield, 1947–1952* (State College: Pennsylvania State University Press, 1969), 47.

9. Blair, *Forgotten War,* 9–10; Stephen M. Millett, "The Capabilities of the American Nuclear Deterrent 1945–1950," *Aerospace Historian,* March 1980, 28–29.

10. Millett, "The Capabilities of the American Nuclear Deterrent," 30.

11. David Alan Rosenberg, "American Atomic Strategy and the Hydrogen Bomb Decision," *Journal of American History* (June 1979): 71.

12. Millis, *Forrestal Diaries,* 487–488.

13. Truman, *Memoirs: Year of Decisions,* 509; Walter LaFeber, *America, Russia and the Cold War, 1945–1975,* 3rd ed. (New York: John Wiley and Sons, 1975), 50–51.

14. FRUS 1948, I: pt. 2, 625, 628; quote on 628.

15. Typical was the attitude of General Curtis Le May, commander of the Strategic Air Command from October 1948 to 1957, who maintained that during the period from

1949 through mid-1950, the air force "could have destroyed all of Russia (I mean by that, all of Russia's capability to wage war) without losing a man" to the defenders. General Curtis E. LeMay with McKinley Kantor, *Mission with LeMay: My Story* (Garden City, N.Y.: Doubleday, 1965), 481; Rosenberg, "American Atomic Strategy," 68.

16. Senator Brien McMahon to Johnson, July 14, 1949, *FRUS 1949*, I: 482.

17. George H. Gallup, *The Gallup Poll: Public Opinion, 1935–1971* (New York: Random House, 1972), II: 839, 850, 858, 888, 939.

18. J. Lawton Collins interview; Shepley and Blair, *Hydrogen Bomb*, 11.

19. Lilienthal, *Journals of David E. Lilienthal*, II: 496, 509–511, quote on 509.

20. *NYT*, April 7, 1949, 1; Lilienthal, *Journals of David E. Lilienthal*, II: 510.

21. Rosenberg, "American Atomic Strategy," 76.

22. Ibid.; Truman, *Memoirs: Years of Trial and Hope*, 305.

23. Rosenberg, "American Atomic Strategy," 72. For an insider view of this study, see Philip M. Morse, *In at the Beginnings: A Physicist's Life* (Cambridge, Mass.: MIT Press, 1977), 247–259.

24. Rosenberg, "American Atomic Strategy," 72–73.

25. Ibid., 73.

26. Ibid., 76–77.

27. Truman, *Memoirs: Years of Trial and Hope*, 297–298; Hewlett and Duncan, *History of the United States Atomic Energy Commission*, II: 289–293.

28. *FRUS 1949*, I: 419–430.

29. Ibid., 443–461; Truman, *Memoirs: Years of Trial and Hope*, 302–303.

30. Hewlett and Duncan, *History of the United States Atomic Energy Commission*, II: 294.

31. Hewlett and Duncan, *History of the United States Atomic Energy Commission*, II: 300; *FRUS 1949*, I: 471–474.

32. Truman, *Memoirs: Years of Trial and Hope*, 303–304; Acheson, *Present at the Creation*, 316–318; Lilienthal, *Journals of David E. Lilienthal*, II: 543–545; *FRUS 1949*, I: 576–582.

33. Acheson, *Present at the Creation*, 318–319; Lilienthal, *Journals of David E. Lilienthal*, II: 548–552; *FRUS 1949*, I: 490–498.

34. *FRUS 1949*, I: 497.

35. Lilienthal, *Journals of David E. Lilienthal*, II: 552; Acheson, *Present at the Creation*, 319.

36. Lilienthal, *Journals of David E. Lilienthal*, II: 552.

37. Ibid., 565, 574; Hewlett and Duncan, *History of the United States Atomic Energy Commission*, II: 304.

38. Acheson, *Present at the Creation*, 319.

39. Ibid.; Truman, *Memoirs: Years of Trial and Hope*, 304; *NYT*, July 28, 1949, 1.

40. Lilienthal, *Journals of David E. Lilienthal*, II: 565.

41. Acheson, *Present at the Creation*, 321.

42. Hewlett and Duncan, *History of the United States Atomic Energy Commission*, II: 362–363; Shepley and Blair, *Hydrogen Bomb*, 12–14.

43. Lilienthal, *Journals of David E. Lilienthal*, II: 509–510.

44. Hewlett and Duncan, *History of the United States Atomic Energy Commission*, II: 364–365; Shepley and Blair, *Hydrogen Bomb*, 12. Johnson left office in the fall of 1950 still not certain that the Soviets had in fact detonated an atomic bomb and as late as 1953 expressed doubt that they had the weapon. Shepley and Blair, *Hydrogen Bomb*, 18.

45. Neil P. Davis, *Lawrence and Oppenheimer* (New York: Simon and Schuster, 1968), 393; Norman Moss, *Men Who Play God: The Story of the Hydrogen Bomb* (New York:

Harper and Rowe, 1969), 24; Hewlett and Duncan, *History of the United States Atomic Energy Commission*, II: 367. Truman's doubts lingered as late as 1953, even after he had left the presidency. Shepley and Blair, *Hydrogen Bomb*, 18, NYT, January 28, 1953, 1.

46. Hewlett and Duncan, *History of the United States Atomic Energy Commission*, II: 367–368.

47. Ibid., 367; Lilienthal, *Journals of David E. Lilienthal*, II: 571–572.

48. Hewlett and Duncan, *History of the United States Atomic Energy Commission*, II: 367; Truman, *Memoirs: Years of Trial and Hope*, 306–307.

49. *PP HST 1949*, 485.

50. "The Story Explodes around the World," *Newsweek*, October 3, 1949, 17.

51. Ibid., 18–19.

52. *FRUS 1949*, I: 501–503.

53. Lilienthal, *Journals of David E. Lilienthal*, II: 565, 574, 576.

54. Hewlett and Duncan, *History of the United States Atomic Energy Commission*, II: 370.

55. *FRUS 1949*, I: 504.

56. Lilienthal, *Journals of David E. Lilienthal*, II: 580.

57. *FRUS 1949*, I: 481.

58. Rosenberg, "American Atomic Strategy," 78.

59. There was no complete account of the events surrounding the expansion of the U.S. atomic weapons arsenal until 1976, when the U.S. State Department published volume 1 of *Foreign Relations of the United States, 1949*. Three years later, in 1979, the first account based on original sources appeared when David Rosenberg published his in-depth article "American Atomic Strategy."

60. Edward Teller with Allen Brown, *The Legacy of Hiroshima* (Garden City, N.Y.: Doubleday and Company, 1962), 39–40.

61. Ibid., 23, 44; Shepley and Blair, *Hydrogen Bomb*, 53–56.

62. Tris Coffin, "How We Almost Missed the H-Bomb," *Coronet*, September 1953, 108; Lewis L. Strauss, *Men and Decisions* (Garden City, N.Y.: Doubleday and Company Inc., 1962), 215–216.

63. Strauss, *Men and Decisions*, 216–217; Hewlett and Duncan, *History of the United States Atomic Energy Commission*, II: 373–374.

64. Hewlett and Duncan, *History of the United States Atomic Energy Commission*, II: 374.

65. Davis, *Lawrence and Oppenheimer*, 300–307; Stanley A. Blumberg and Gwinn Owens, *Energy and Conflict: The Life and Times of Edward Teller* (New York: G. P. Putnam & Sons, 1976), 200–201, 209; Herbert F. York, *The Advisors—Oppenheimer, Teller, and the Superbomb* (San Francisco: W. H. Freeman and Co., 1976), 63–65, 47, 52–53.

66. Hewlett and Duncan, *History of the United States Atomic Energy Commission*, II: 384–385; York, *The Advisors*, 46–56.

67. Originally the vote was 4 to 1, but Gordon Dean, who had recently come on the commission, changed his vote, which made it 3 to 2 against development. Strauss, *Men and Decisions*, 218–219.

68. Coffin, "How We Almost Missed the H-Bomb," 110; "Mr. Secretary, isn't it an American tradition," Shepley and Blair, *Hydrogen Bomb*, 80–81. The Johnson-Strauss meeting probably took place on October 11, 1949. Since Johnson's engagement calendar for that day shows the meeting to be less than twenty-five minutes, it is highly likely that the story that the Johnson-Strauss conversation went into the evening was an exaggeration. Johnson Appointment Calendar, Box 140, Johnson Papers.

69. Coffin, "How We Almost Missed the H-Bomb," 110; Hewlett and Duncan, *History of the United States Atomic Energy Commission*, II: 382.

70. Coffin, "How We Almost Missed the H-Bomb," 107; Davis, *Lawrence and Oppenheimer*, 303; Rosenberg, "American Atomic Strategy," 80–81.

71. Coffin, "How We Almost Missed the H-Bomb," 105; Shepley and Blair, *Hydrogen Bomb*, 81; Strauss, *Men and Decisions*, 223–224.

72. *FRUS 1949*, I: 587–588.

73. Lilienthal, *Journals of David E. Lilienthal*, II: 613–615; Hewlett and Duncan, *History of the United States Atomic Energy Commission*, II: 395, 398.

74. Acheson, *Present at the Creation*, 348.

75. An excellent account of the public and congressional debate over the H-Bomb can be found in Donna M. Rodriguez, "Maintaining Superiority: The American Decision to Develop the Hydrogen Bomb, 1949–1950" (master's thesis, East Texas State University, 1979).

76. *Washington Post*, November 18, 1949, 1; *NYT*, November 21 (editorial), 1949, 24; *NYT*, November 26, 1949, 1; *NYT*, November 27, 1949, 1.

77. James Reston, "U.S. Hydrogen Bomb Delay Urged," *NYT*, January 17, 1950.

78. Hewlett and Duncan, *History of the United States Atomic Energy Commission*, II: 399–400.

79. Ibid., 400; *FRUS 1950*, I: 503–511.

80. Rosenberg, "American Atomic Strategy," 82.

81. Ibid., 83; *FRUS 1950*, I: 511.

82. Rosenberg, "American Atomic Strategy," 83–84.

83. Hewlett and Duncan, *History of the United States Atomic Energy Commission*, II: 403–405.

84. Acheson, *Present at the Creation*, 348; Lilienthal, *Journals of David E. Lilienthal*, II: 623–625.

85. Acheson, *Present at the Creation*, 348.

86. Lilienthal, *Journals of David E. Lilienthal*, II: 630.

87. Lilienthal, *Journals of David E. Lilienthal*, II: 625–632; Hewlett and Duncan, *History of the United States Atomic Energy Commission*, II: 406–408; Acheson, *Present at the Creation*, 349.

88. Lilienthal, *Journals of David E. Lilienthal*, II: 632–633. For another account of the January 31 meeting by one who was present, see R. Gordon Arnesson, "The H-Bomb Decision," *Foreign Service Journal*, May 1969, 27–28 and June 1969, 26–27.

89. Coffin, "How We Almost Missed the H-Bomb," 107.

90. According to Warner R. Schilling, there really was no other viable alternative; "The H-Bomb Decision: How to Decide Without Actually Choosing," *Political Science Quarterly* 76 (March 1961).

91. Truman, *Memoirs: Years of Trial and Hope*, 309–310.

92. Rosenberg, "American Atomic Strategy," 62.

93. Shepley and Blair, *Hydrogen Bomb*, 150–157; Walter Miller, *Arms and Men: A Study in American Military History* (New York: G. P. Putnam & Sons, 1956), 346–347.

94. *FRUS 1950*, I: 141–142; quote on 142.

95. Hammond, "NSC-68: Prologue to Rearmament," 274–279.

96. J. Lawton Collins interview; Nitze conversation; David S. McLellan, *Dean Acheson: The State Department Years* (New York: Dodd, Mead and Company, 1976), 203.

97. Donovan, *Tumultuous Years*, 62, 86–87; Rearden, *Formative Years*, 128; Blair, *Forgotten War*, 16.

98. Lilienthal, *Journals of David E. Lilienthal*, II: 565.

99. LaFeber, *America, Russia and the Cold War*, 94, 96; Weigley, *The American Way of War*, 378–379.

100. Hammond, "NSC-68: Prologue to Rearmament," 293.

101. Ibid., 292–293; Senate Committees on Armed Services and Foreign Relations, *Hearings to Conduct an Inquiry into the Military Situation in the Far East*, pt. 4, 2595, 2687–88, 2690; Princeton Seminars, 778, Dean Acheson Papers, HSTL; Acheson, *Present at the Creation*, 371; Rearden, *Formative Years*, 71.

102. Isaacson and Thomas, *Wise Men*, 482–484.

103. Hammond, "NSC-68: Prologue to Rearmament," 296–297.

104. Ibid., 298–301.

105. *FRUS 1950*, I: 241.

106. Ibid., 282–284.

107. Memorandum of Conversation at the State Department, Wednesday, March 22, 1950, 3:00 P.M., *FRUS 1950*, I: 204.

108. Ibid., 204–205.

109. Princeton Seminars, 779–780, Dean Acheson Papers, HSTL; "No one . . . is going to make arrangements for [me]," Acheson, *Present at the Creation*, 373; Nitze conversation.

110. Acheson, *Present at the Creation*, 373; Paul Nitze with Ann M. Smith and Stephen L. Rearden, *From Hiroshima to Glasnost: At the Center of Decision* (New York: Grove Weidenfeld, 1989), 95.

111. Acheson, *Present at the Creation*, 373.

112. Ibid., 373–374; Princeton Seminars, 780, Dean Acheson Papers, HSTL.

113. Acheson, *Present at the Creation*, 374.

114. *FRUS 1950*, I: 238.

115. Ibid., 261.

116. Ibid., 282.

117. Hammond, "NSC-68: Prologue to Rearmament," 319–321; Joyce and Gabriel Kolko, *The Limits of Power: The World and United States Foreign Policy, 1945–1954* (New York: Harper and Row, 1972), 508.

118. Isaacson and Thomas, *Wise Men*, 495–498; Nitze, *From Hiroshima to Glasnost*, 98.

119. Hammond, "NSC-68: Prologue to Rearmament," 325–326.

120. J. Lawton Collins interview.

121. *FRUS 1950*, I: 235.

122. Lilienthal, *Journals of David E. Lilienthal*, II: 510.

123. J. Lawton Collins interview. General Collins believed that Johnson's acute political "sense" led him to continually take positions which afforded him the opportunity to take an "I-told-you-so attitude."

124. Hammond, "NSC-68: Prologue to Rearmament," 340–344.

125. Ibid., 340.

126. Ibid., 337.

127. *Washington Post*, April 27, 1950, 1; *NYT*, April 27, 1950, 1.

14. Entangling Alliance

1. Johnson Appointment Calendar, April 4, 1949, Box 141, Johnson Papers; *NYT*, April 5, 1949, 1.

2. Marx Leva interview; Joseph J. Ellis, *Founding Brothers: The Revolutionary Generation* (New York: Alfred A. Knopf, 2000), 128–129.

3. NATO Information Service, *NATO Handbook* (Brussels: NATO Information Service, 1980), 13–14.

4. *PP HST 1949*, 198; Donovan, *Tumultuous Years*, 44.

5. Donovan, *Tumultuous Years*, 46; Isaacson and Thomas, *Wise Men*, 446–551.

6. Isaacson and Thomas, *Wise Men*, 450.

7. Blair, *Forgotten War*, 12.

8. McLellan, *Dean Acheson*, 152.

9. *NYT*, April 22, 1949, 1; *NYT*, April 24, 1949, 1; *NYT*, April 26, 1949, 1.

10. Excerpts from Johnson speech before the St. Louis Post, American Ordnance Association, St. Louis, Missouri, April 19, 1948, Box 96, Speech Excerpts, Johnson Papers.

11. Haymond Maxwell interview; Ruth Johnson interviews.

12. Johnson Speech before Daughters of the American Revolution, Washington, D.C., April 21, 1948, Box 96, Speech Excerpts, Johnson Papers; Louis Johnson, "The World Situation as I See It," *National Defense News*, May–June 1948, 14–17.

13. Johnson Speech before Daughters of the American Revolution; Johnson, "The World Situation as I See It," 14–17.

14. Johnson to President Truman, April 15, 1948, PPF 127, HSTL.

15. *PP HST 1948*, 153, 291, 292, 304, 314. Throughout the spring the president made public statements about the importance and value of the UN and he made a commitment on behalf of the nation to make it work.

16. Isaacson and Thomas, *Wise Men*, 441–442.

17. Among the Johnson papers is an unsigned, undated two-page memo which began, "If you are asked about the position you took in your speech of April 1948, before the Daughters of the American Revolution, the following reply is suggested." Subsequent paragraphs of the document contain the points Johnson made to the Senate Foreign Relations Committee in the April 1949 North Atlantic Treaty hearings. The memo was attached to a copy of the DAR Speech, Box 96, Speech Excerpts, Johnson Papers.

18. *NYT*, April 28, 1949, 1; *NYT*, April 29, 1949, 10; *Washington Post*, April 28 and 29, 1949.

19. Senate Committee on Foreign Relations, *Hearings on the North Atlantic Treaty*, 81st Cong., 1st Sess., 1949, pt. 1, 145–147. For an excellent account of how the Truman administration advocated the North Atlantic Treaty's virtues and blunted its critics, see Lawrence S. Kaplan, "NATO and the Language of Isolationism," *The South Atlantic Quarterly* (Spring 1958): 204–213.

20. Senate Committee on Foreign Relations, *Hearings on the North Atlantic Treaty*, pt. 1, 147–148.

21. Ibid., 148–187.

22. Ibid., 172.

23. Ibid., 64; *Washington Post*, April 28, 1949, 1.

24. Senate Committee on Foreign Relations, *Hearings on the North Atlantic Treaty*, pt. 1, 85.

25. Ibid., 182–187.

26. Ibid., 185.

27. *NYT*, April 29, 1949, 10; *Washington Post*, April 29, 1949, 1.

28. Nearly every Johnson associate interviewed or contacted by the authors acknowledged the extreme degree to which Johnson was a political animal and said that political considerations influenced his actions more than anything else.

29. Donovan, *Tumultuous Years*, 50.

30. Blair, *Forgotten War*, 12; Donovan, *Tumultuous Years*, 51–52.

31. Senate Committee on Foreign Relations, *Hearings on the North Atlantic Treaty*, pt. 1, 147, 166.

32. Senate Committees on Armed Services and Foreign Relations, *Joint Hearings on Military Assistance Program, 1949*, 81st Cong., 1st Sess., 1949, 14.

33. Dulles, a leading Republican foreign affairs expert, had been appointed to the Senate by Governor Thomas Dewey on July 7, 1949, to fill the unexpired term of Robert F. Wagner.

34. *NYT*, July 30, 1949, 1.

35. House Committee on Foreign Affairs, *Hearings on Mutual Defense Assistance Act of 1949*, 81st Cong., 1st Sess., 1949, 45–47.

36. McLellan, *Dean Acheson*, 164–165.

37. House Committee on Foreign Affairs, *Hearings on Mutual Defense Assistance Act of 1949*, 61.

38. Ibid., 71.

39. Arthur Vandenberg Jr., ed., *The Private Papers of Senator Vandenberg* (Boston: Houghton Mifflin Company, 1952), 508.

40. Senate Committees on Armed Services and Foreign Relations, *Joint Hearings on Military Assistance Program, 1949* (Executive Session), 20–25, 33–34.

41. Vandenberg, *Private Papers of Senator Vandenberg*, 508.

42. Acheson, *Present at the Creation*, 310; *NYT*, August 5, 1949, 1.

43. Acheson, *Present at the Creation*, 310; Senate Committees on Armed Services and Foreign Relations, *Joint Hearings on Military Assistance Program, 1949*, 10–12, 16, 36.

44. Senate Committees on Armed Services and Foreign Relations, *Joint Hearings on Military Assistance Program, 1949* (Public Hearing), 51–52.

45. Ibid., 75.

46. Acheson, *Present at the Creation*, 311.

47. Johnson rarely stumbled before congressional committees. Even critics acknowledged he was always prepared and careful in his testimony.

48. Acheson, *Present at the Creation*, 311.

49. *NYT*, August 12, 1949, 1; *NYT*, August 16, 1949, 1; *NYT*, August 19, 1949, 1.

50. Senate Committees on Armed Services and Foreign Relations, *Joint Hearings on Military Assistance Program, 1949* (Executive Session), 69–125, 352–366.

51. *NYT*, September 23, 1949, 1; *Washington Post*, September 23, 1949, 1.

52. *NYT*, September 29, 1949, 1; *Washington Post*, September 29, 1949, 2.

53. Senate Committees on Armed Services and Foreign Relations, *Joint Hearings on Military Assistance Program, 1949* (Executive Session), 44, 61. At various times Senators Vandenberg and Lodge expressed confidence in Johnson and his abilities as secretary of defense.

54. "with all our combined might," *NYT*, October 6, 1949, 1, 6; *Washington Post*, October 6, 1949, 10.

55. *FRUS 1949*, IV: 351–352, 356–358, 362–364.

56. Ibid., 357.

57. Ibid., 358.

58. Ibid., 357. The source of the quote is Najeeb Halaby, director, Office of Foreign Military Affairs, Department of Defense.

59. Ibid., 353–356; *Department of State Bulletin* XXI (December 19, 1949): 948; *NYT*, December 2, 1949, 2, 21; *NYT*, December 3, 1949, 1, 3.

60. *FRUS 1949*, IV: 357–358, 360–362.

61. *PP HST 1950*, 131–132.

62. *First Semiannual Report on the Mutual Defense Assistance Program: Memo from the President*, House Document 613, 81st Cong., 2nd Sess., 1950, 24, 45; Richard P. Stebbins, *The United States in World Affairs, 1950* (New York: Harper and Brothers, 1951), 120.

63. Senate Committees on Foreign Relations and Armed Services, *Joint Hearings on Mutual Defense Assistance Program, 1950*, 81st Cong., 2nd Sess., 1950, 25.

64. *NYT*, April 2, 1950, 1.

65. *First Semiannual Report on the Mutual Defense Assistance Program*, 54; *PP HST*, 1949, 445–449.

66. Senate Committees on Foreign Relations and Armed Services, *Joint Hearings on Mutual Defense Assistance Program*, 1950, 12, 38; *NYT*, June 3, 1950, 1; *NYT*, June 6, 1950, 1.

67. Stebbins, *The United States in World Affairs*, 1950, 132. The measure was passed 66 to 0 in the Senate on June 30 and 361 to 1 in the House on July 19, 1950.

68. *NYT*, November 28, 1949, 1.

69. McLellan, *Dean Acheson*, 146–147.

15. *"Till the Dust Settles"*

1. Interview with Laidler Mackall, Washington, D.C., May 8, 2003.

2. Interview with Richard A. Whiting, Washington, D.C., May 17, 2002.

3. Rearden, *Formative Years*, 236–237.

4. Richard P. Stebbins, *The United States in World Affairs*, 1949 (New York: Harper & Brothers, 1949), 460.

5. The prevalent American attitude seemed to be embodied in a 1949 statement by General Bradley, chairman of the JCS, when he said, "If the whole of Asia came under the influence of the Soviets we would think it a great loss. . . . [H]owever, we believe that Europe is more important . . . than Asia." Stebbins, *The United States in World Affairs*, 1949, 105.

6. Paul Y. Hammond, *Cold War and Détente: The American Foreign Policy Process Since 1945* (New York: Harcourt, Brace Jovanovich, 1975), 57; Foster Rhea Dulles, *America's Rise to World Power, 1898–1954* (New York: Harper, 1955), 249.

7. Robert D. Marcus, *A Brief History of the United States Since 1945* (New York: St. Martin's Press, 1975), 63–64.

8. Kenneth W. Condit, *The History of the Joint Chiefs of Staff: The Joint Chiefs of Staff and National Policy*, vol. II, *1947–1949* (Wilmington, Del.: Michael Glazier, 1976), 516; James F. Schnabel and Robert J. Watson, *The History of the Joint Chiefs of Staff: The Joint Chiefs of Staff and National Policy*, vol. III: *The Korean War*, pt. I (Wilmington, Del.: Michael Glazier, 1979), 36.

9. Ruth Johnson interviews.

10. Acheson, *Present at the Creation*, 306, 334–336; Abell, *Drew Pearson Diaries*, 89.

11. Donovan, *Tumultuous Years*, 71.

12. Thomas G. Patterson, J. Garry Clifford, and Kenneth J. Hagan, *American Foreign Policy: A History* (Lexington, Va.: D. C. Heath and Company, 1977), 460–461; *NYT*, April 4, 1948, 21; *NYT*, September 29, 1949, 1; *NYT*, October 7, 1949, 10.

13. Department of State, *United States Relations with China, with Special Reference to the Period 1944–1949* (Washington, D.C.: Department of State, 1949), 261, 270, 773–774, 808–814.

14. Foster Rhea Dulles, *American Policy toward Communist China* (New York: Thomas Y. Crowell Company, 1972), 28–30; John C. Campbell, *The United States in World Affairs, 1948–49* (New York: Harper & Brothers, 1949), 272; McLellan, *Dean Acheson*, 186.

15. Campbell, *The United States in World Affairs 1948–49*, 276–277; LaFeber, *America, Russia, and the Cold War*, 88. On the congressional China bloc, see James Fetzer, "Congress and China, 1941–1950" (Ph.D. diss., Michigan State University, 1969).

16. Rearden, *Formative Years*, 229; Acheson, *Present at the Creation*, 306.

17. Donovan, *Tumultuous Years*, 76; Acheson, *Present at the Creation*, 306.

18. Donovan, *Tumultuous Years*, 76–77.

19. Steinberg, *Man from Missouri*, 354.

20. Memorandum by Rear Admiral Sidney W. Souers to the National Security Council, April 4, 1949, *FRUS 1949*, IX: 307; "unsinkable aircraft carrier," Message, May 29, 1950, RG 6, Box 8, Folder 4, Formosa File, Papers of General Douglas MacArthur, MacArthur Memorial Library and Archives; *FRUS 1950*, VI: 161–165.

21. "seriously unfavorable from a strategic viewpoint," Condit, *History of the Joint Chiefs of Staff*, II: 482–487, quote at 482.

22. Memorandum by the Secretary of Defense [Johnson] to the Executive Secretary of the National Security Council [Souers], April 2, 1949, *FRUS 1949*, IX: 307–308.

23. Department of State, *United States Relations with China, with Special Reference to the Period 1944–1949* (Washington, D.C.: U.S. Government Printing Office, 1949), xiv–xvii (hereafter China White Paper).

24. The assessment of one scholar was that "[s]ince the documents in the White Paper did not warrant the assertion that the Soviet Union had systematically sought to extend its power and influence to China, Acheson must have come to such a sweeping conclusion through the medium of Cold-War visions." Akira Hriye, *The Cold War in Asia* (Englewood Cliffs, N.J.: Prentice Hall, 1974), 170.

25. China White Paper, vii, xiv–xv.

26. Senate Committees on Armed Services and Foreign Relations, *Hearings to Conduct an Inquiry into the Military Situation in the Far East*, pt. 4, 2679.

27. Ibid.

28. Secretary of Defense to the Secretary of State [Acheson], July 21, 1949, in Senate Committees on Armed Services and Foreign Relations, *Hearings to Conduct an Inquiry into the Military Situation in the Far East*, pt. 4, 1382.

29. Koo oral history, vol. VI, pt. I, sec. 4, 248, V. K. Wellington Koo Papers, Butler Library, Columbia University.

30. Acheson, *Present at the Creation*, 302.

31. Ted Morgan, *Reds: McCarthyism in Twentieth-Century America* (New York: Random House, 2003), 384–385.

32. Walter Lippman, "The White Paper: The Chiang Stranglehold," September 12, 1949, in *Commentaries on American Foreign Policy* (New York: American Institute of Pacific Relations, 1950), 7; McLellan, *Dean Acheson*, 196.

33. Ibid., 194.

34. Memorandum by the Joint Chiefs of Staff to the Secretary of Defense, August 17, 1949, *FRUS 1949*, IX: 376–378.

35. J. Lawton Collins interview.

36. Senate Committees on Armed Services and Foreign Relations, *Hearings to Conduct an Inquiry into the Military Situation in the Far East*, pt. 4, 2594.

37. Ibid., 2594–2595.

38. Ibid., 2678.

39. J. Lawton Collins interview.

40. See, e.g., Dorothy Borg and Waldo Heinrichs, eds., *Uncertain Years: Chinese American Relations, 1947–1950* (New York: Columbia University Press, 1980), 176; Donovan, *Tumultuous Years*, 86.

41. Notes of a Conversation with Mr. Paul Griffith, December 29, 1949, Notes of a Conversation with Mr. Paul Griffith, June 3, 1950, Koo Oral History, vol. VI, pt. I, sec. 4, 244–245, 248–249; pt. J, sec. 2, 94; pt. J, sec. 3, 160, 184; pt. J, sec. 5, 444, 450, V. K. Wellington Koo Papers, Butler Library.

42. Ibid., pt. I, sec. 4, 250; pt. J, sec. 2, 112; pt. J, sec. 3, 224.

43. Ibid., pt. J, sec. 2, 111.

44. Ibid., pt. J, sec. 3, 160.

45. Ibid., pt. I, sec. 6, 301.

46. Senate Committees on Armed Services and Foreign Relations, *Hearings to Conduct an Inquiry into the Military Situation in the Far East*, pt. 4, 2664.

47. Memorandum of Conversation, by the Secretary of State, December 29, 1949, *FRUS 1949*, vol. IX, 464.

48. Wilber W. Hoare Jr., "The Joint Chiefs of Staff and National Policy," vol. IV: "The Korean Conflict," Chapter IV, "The Knotty Problem of Formosa," August 1953, 4–5, in RG 218, Records of the United States Joint Chiefs of Staff, NARA (hereafter "Knotty Problem of Formosa").

49. Acheson, *Present at the Creation*, 350; J. Lawton Collins interview; Memorandum by the Joint Chiefs of Staff to the Secretary of Defense, December 2, 1949, *FRUS 1949*, vol. IX, 461.

50. Memorandum of Conversation, by the Secretary of State, December 29, 1949, *FRUS 1949*, vol. IX, 466.

51. Senate Committees on Armed Services and Foreign Relations, *Hearings to Conduct an Inquiry into the Military Situation in the Far East*, pt. 4, 2577–2578.

52. Memorandum for the President from the Secretary of Defense, December 15, 1949, RG 6, FECOM, Formosa File, Papers of General Douglas MacArthur, MacArthur Memorial Library and Archives.

53. Rearden, *Formative Years*, 236.

54. McLellan, *Dean Acheson*, 205.

55. Ferrell, *Off the Record*, 46–47.

56. Senate Committees on Armed Services and Foreign Relations, *Hearings to Conduct an Inquiry into the Military Situation in the Far East*, pt. 4, 2578.

57. Ibid., 2577–2578.

58. Ibid.

59. Ibid.

60. Memorandum of Conversation, by the Secretary of State, December 29, 1949, *FRUS 1949*, vol. IX, 463–467.

61. J. Lawton Collins interview; Hoare, "Knotty Problem of Formosa," 8.

62. Hoare, "Knotty Problem of Formosa," 6–7.

63. NSC 48/2, December 30, 1949, *FRUS 1949*, VII, pt. 2, 1215–1220.

64. Ibid., 1220; Schnabel and Watson, *History of the Joint Chiefs of Staff*, III: 36.

65. McLellan, *Dean Acheson*, 204–206.

66. Drew Pearson, "Johnson, Acheson Cool Off Tempers," *Washington Post*, December 30, 1949; Rearden, *Formative Years*, 238–239.

67. NYT, January 6, 1950, 1, 3.

68. Rearden, *Formative Years*, 239; Donovan, *Tumultuous Years*, 87; "detach" Formosa, Ferrell, *Diary of Eben Ayers*, 335–336, quote at 336.

69. McLellan, *Dean Acheson*, 207–208.

70. *FRUS 1949*, IX: 464.

71. Tang Tsou, *America's Failure in China, 1941–50* (Chicago: University of Chicago Press, 1963), 34. Acheson's speech, "Crisis in Asia—An Examination of U.S. Policy," is in *Department of State Bulletin* XII (January 23, 1950): 111–118.

72. *Department of State Bulletin* XXII (January 23, 1950): 116.

73. Donovan, *Tumultuous Years*, 137.

74. Hamby, *Man of the People*, 514.

75. *FRUS* 1950, VI: 780.

76. Secretary of Defense Johnson to Secretary of State Acheson, April 14, 1950, *FRUS* 1950, VI: 781–784.

77. *FRUS* 1950, VI: 744–754.

78. Ibid., 783–786.

79. Ibid., 791.

80. Ibid., 787–788, 808, 812–813, 816–817; *NYT*, June 11, 1950; *NYT*, June 21, 1959, 18.

81. Rearden, *Formative Years*, 235; Donovan, *Tumultuous Years*, 89.

82. Frank Freidel, *America in the Twentieth Century*, 3rd ed. (New York: Alfred A. Knopf, 1970), 504–505.

83. Blair, *Forgotten War*, 45–46.

84. Rearden, *Formative Years*, 258–259.

85. Schnabel and Watson, *History of the Joint Chiefs of Staff*, III: 23; Rearden, *Formative Years*, 262.

86. Schnabel and Watson, *History of the Joint Chiefs of Staff*, III: 24–25.

87. Senate Committees on Armed Services and Foreign Relations, *Hearings to Conduct an Inquiry into the Military Situation in the Far East*, pt. 4, 2576, 2596; *FRUS* 1949, VII, pt. 2: 1007, 1022–1023.

88. Senate Committees on Armed Services and Foreign Relations, *Hearings to Conduct an Inquiry into the Military Situation in the Far East*, pt. 4, 2576, 2612.

89. *FRUS* 1949, VII, pt. 2: 1056–1057; Senate Committees on Armed Services and Foreign Relations, *Hearings to Conduct an Inquiry into the Military Situation in the Far East*, pt. 4, 2671.

90. Ibid., 2612.

91. Blair, *Forgotten War*, 53.

92. Ibid., 55–57.

93. Pratt, *A History of United States Foreign Policy* (New York: Prentice Hall, 1955), 426–427.

94. John J. Bly, "The Diplomacy of John Foster Dulles in Negotiating the Japanese Peace Treaty" (master's thesis, East Texas State University, 1979), 1–6.

95. "from the military point of view a peace treaty would, at the present time, be premature," *FRUS* 1949, VII, pt. 2: 774–776; Rearden, *Formative Years*, 249–250.

96. *FRUS* 1949, VII, pt. 2: 860.

97. J. Lawton Collins interview.

98. *FRUS* 1950, VI: 1111.

99. McLellan, *Dean Acheson*, 265–266.

100. *FRUS* 1949, VII, pt. 2: 922.

101. *FRUS* 1950, VI: 1109–1111.

102. Ibid., 1151.

103. Ibid., 1150, 1171; Acheson, *Present at the Creation*, 430.

104. *FRUS* 1950, VI: 1171.

105. Acheson, *Present at the Creation*, 430–431; McLellan, *Dean Acheson*, 266–267.

106. Acheson, *Present at the Creation*, 430.

107. *FRUS* 1950, VI: 1174–1176.

108. Ibid., 1177–1178.

109. Ibid., 1178.

110. Ibid., 1178–1182.

111. Donovan, *Tumultuous Years*, 167; Acheson, *Present at the Creation*, 432.

112. News Conference, May 18, 1950, *PP HST* 1950, 420.

113. William J. Sebald with Russell Brinan, *With MacArthur in Japan: A Personal History of the Occupation* (New York: W.W. Norton and Company, 1965), 246–248.

114. *FRUS 1950*, VI: 1205–1208.

115. Acheson, *Present at the Creation*, 430.

116. Senate Committees on Armed Services and Foreign Relations, *Hearings to Conduct an Inquiry into the Military Situation in the Far East*, pt. 4, 2619.

117. Robert H. Ferrell, ed., *Dear Bess: The Letters from Harry to Bess Truman, 1910–1959* (New York: W.W. Norton & Company, 1983), 561.

118. Department of Defense Press Release, June 9, 1950, Box 138, Johnson's Trip to Japan, Johnson Papers; Bradley and Blair, *A General's Life*, 529.

119. Sebald with Brinan, *With MacArthur in Japan*, 250, 252.

120. Ibid., 253.

121. Ibid.

122. "a normal treaty . . . embodying a security reservation," Memorandum on the Peace Treaty Problem [from Douglas MacArthur for Secretary of Defense Johnson], June 14, 1950, RG5, SCAP, Box 1A, Papers of General Douglas MacArthur, MacArthur Memorial Library and Archives; William Manchester, *American Caesar: Douglas MacArthur, 1880–1964* (Boston: Little, Brown and Company, 1978), 532.

123. Sebald with Brinan, *With MacArthur in Japan*, 253.

124. "worse than the Occupation," ibid., 255–256; Manchester, *American Caesar*, 532; June 18, 1950, Douglas MacArthur Daily Appointments, January–June 1950, RG5, Box 3, Papers of General Douglas MacArthur, MacArthur Memorial Library and Archives.

125. Memorandum on Formosa [from Douglas MacArthur for Secretary of Defense Johnson], June 14, 1950, RG 5, SCAP, Box 1A, Papers of General Douglas MacArthur, MacArthur Memorial Library and Archives.

126. *NYT*, June 20, 1950, 20.

127. *NYT*, June 20, 1950, 1, 20; *NYT*, June 25, 1950, 18.

128. Bradley and Blair, *A General's Life*, 530.

129. Memorandum on Concepts Governing Security in Post-War Japan [from Douglas MacArthur for Secretary of Defense Johnson], June 23, 1950, RG 5, Box 1A; Douglas MacArthur, Daily Appointments, June 23, 1950, January–June 1950, RG5, Box 3, both in Papers of General Douglas MacArthur, MacArthur Memorial Library and Archives.

130. *FRUS 1950*, VII: 97.

131. Ibid.

132. Johnson Appointment Calendar, Saturday, June 24, 1950, Box 141, Johnson Papers.

16. Last Week in June

1. The attack was launched at 4:00 A.M. on Sunday, June 25, Korean time, which would have been 3:00 P.M. on Saturday, June 24, in Washington.

2. Senate Committees on Armed Services and Foreign Relations, *Hearings to Conduct an Inquiry into the Military Situation in the Far East*, pt. 4, 2572.

3. Glenn D. Paige, *The Korean Decision, June 24–30, 1950* (New York: Free Press, 1968), 89.

4. Merry, *Taking on the World*, 193–194.

5. Paige, *The Korean Decision*, 89–90.

6. Senate Committees on Armed Services and Foreign Relations, *Hearings to Conduct an Inquiry into the Military Situation in the Far East*, pt. 4, 2572.

7. McCullough, *Truman*, 775.

8. Acheson, *Present at the Creation*, 404. Throughout this fateful week, the State and Defense Departments shared all communiqués and there was full cooperation between the two departments.

9. Trygve Lie, *In the Cause of Peace* (New York: Macmillan, 1954), 327–328.

10. Truman, *Memoirs: Years of Trial and Hope*, 332, 333; FRUS 1950, VII: 160.

11. J. Lawton Collins interview; Collins, *War in Peacetime*, 44.

12. Senate Committees on Armed Services and Foreign Relations, *Hearings to Conduct an Inquiry into the Military Situation in the Far East*, pt. 4, 2572–2573.

13. Schnabel and Watson, *History of the Joint Chiefs of Staff*, III: 71–72.

14. Paige, *The Korean Decision*, 109.

15. Specific times for Johnson's activities are based on his personal engagements calendar, June 1–September 19, 1950, Box 141, Johnson Papers.

16. Schnabel and Watson, *History of the Joint Chiefs of Staff*, III: 70–71.

17. "it will be evidence of [Russian] assistance," *Washington Post*, June 26, 1950, 2; *NYT*, June 26, 1950, 12.

18. Truman, *Memoirs: Years of Trial and Hope*, 333.

19. U.S. Department of State, *United States Policy in the Korean Crisis* (Washington, D.C.: U.S. Government Printing Office, 1950), 15; "to render every assistance to the United Nations," Paige, *The Korean Decision*, 117–120, quote on 117.

20. J. Lawton Collins interview; "so that each member would feel no inhibition," Senate Committees on Armed Services and Foreign Relations, *Hearings to Conduct an Inquiry into the Military Situation in the Far East*, pt. 4, 2621–2622.

21. Joseph C. Goulden, *Korea: The Untold Story of the War* (New York: Times Books, 1982), 57.

22. Donovan, *Tumultuous Years*, 197.

23. Ibid.

24. Ferrell, *Truman: A Life*, 322.

25. Ibid., 323.

26. An extremely accurate journalistic account of this historic meeting is Beverly Smith's "Why We Went to War in Korea," *Saturday Evening Post*, November 1, 1951. Smith had "eyes only" access to White House documents and interviewed a number of participants in preparing his account. Testimony of Johnson, Acheson, and General Bradley of this and other crucial meetings during the last week in June of 1950 can be found in Senate Committees on Armed Services and Foreign Relations, *Hearings to Conduct an Inquiry into the Military Situation in the Far East*.

27. Ferrell, *Truman: A Life*, 323.

28. "We can't let the UN down!" Phillip C. Jessup, *The Birth of Nations* (New York: Columbia University Press, 1974), 10; Paige, *The Korean Decision*, 125.

29. Acheson, *Present at the Creation*, 405–406.

30. Alonzo Fields, *My 21 Years in the White House* (New York: Coward-McCann, 1960), 154–155.

31. "the only really violent discussion Secretary Acheson and myself ever had," Senate Committees on Armed Services and Foreign Relations, *Hearings to Conduct an Inquiry into the Military Situation in the Far East*, pt. 4, 2580. The account of this episode by Johnson is not referred to by Acheson nor is it confirmed by any of the participants interviewed by Paige. See Paige, *The Korean Decision*, 126 n. 78.

32. Albert L. Warner, "How the Korean Decision Was Made," *Harper's Magazine*, June 1951, 102.

33. Senate Committees on Armed Services and Foreign Relations, *Hearings to Conduct an Inquiry into the Military Situation in the Far East*, pt. 4, 2580; FRUS 1950, VII, pt. 1: 157–158; "open mind," Paige, *The Korean Decision*, 126; Donovan, *Tumultuous Years*, 198. In Truman's *Memoirs: Years of Trial and Hope*, 333, he implies that he was not open-minded on the subject and had already concluded that the North Koreans had to be stopped.

34. Senate Committees on Armed Services and Foreign Relations, *Hearings to Conduct an Inquiry into the Military Situation in the Far East*, pt. 4, 2580.

35. J. Lawton Collins interview; Paige, *The Korean Decision*, 128.

36. Collins, *War in Peacetime*, 14.

37. Paige, *The Korean Decision*, 132–133.

38. *FRUS 1950*, VII, pt. 1: 158; "to draw the line," Bradley and Blair, *A General's Life*, 535–536.

39. Senate Committees on Armed Services and Foreign Relations, *Hearings to Conduct an Inquiry into the Military Situation in the Far East*, pt. 4, 2621.

40. Quotes in *FRUS 1950*, VII: 160; McCullough, *Truman*, 779.

41. Like many people in the Defense Department, both civilian and military, Johnson respected but did not always trust MacArthur. J. Lawton Collins interview; Matthew B. Ridgway, *Soldier: Memoirs of Matthew B. Ridgway* (New York: Harper and Brothers, 1956), 192.

42. Paige, *The Korean Decision*, 134–136. In *Forgotten War*, Blair states that there were only 108,500 ground troops in the Far East out of a total of 591,000 (28).

43. *FRUS 1950*, VII: 158–160.

44. Ibid., 159–160.

45. Ibid., 161.

46. Senate Committees on Armed Services and Foreign Relations, *Hearings to Conduct an Inquiry into the Military Situation in the Far East*, pt. 2, 948.

47. Donovan, *Tumultuous Years*, 199.

48. Matthew B. Ridgway, *Soldier: The Memoirs of Matthew B. Ridgway* (New York: Harper, 1956), 192.

49. *NYT*, June 27, 1950, 1.

50. J. Lawton Collins interview; Paige, *The Korean Decision*, 147.

51. *PP HST 1950*, 491–492.

52. "War in Korea" (editorial), *NYT*, June 26, 1950, 26.

53. *Congressional Record*, 81st Cong., 2nd Sess., 1950, vol. 96, pt. 7, 9154, 9157 ff., 9180, 9184.

54. Ferrell, *Truman: A Life*, 324–325.

55. The Ambassador in Korea to the Secretary of State, June 26, 1950, *FRUS 1950*, vol. VII, 70.

56. Schnabel and Watson, *History of the Joint Chiefs of Staff*, III: 84. The ROK Army was a small, ill-equipped, and poorly trained force. Allen R. Millett, *The Korean War* (Seoul: Korea Institute of Military History, 1997), I: 87–91.

57. Truman, *Memoirs: Years of Trial and Hope*, 336; Paige, *The Korean Decision*, 158.

58. "was too little too late," *NYT*, June 27, 1950, 1.

59. "written off," *New York Herald Tribune*, June 29, 1950, 4; *NYT*, June 27, 1950, 1.

60. Donovan, *Tumultuous Years*, 205.

61. Truman, *Memoirs: Years of Trial and Hope*, 337.

62. Donovan, *Tumultuous Years*, 206–207.

63. *FRUS 1950*, VII: 179–180.

64. Ibid., 180.

65. J. Lawton Collins interview.

66. *FRUS 1950*, VII: 182.

67. Ibid., 182–183.

68. Senate Committees on Armed Services and Foreign Relations, *Hearings to Conduct an Inquiry into the Military Situation in the Far East*, pt. 4, 2584.

69. *FRUS 1950*, VII: 183; Paige, *The Korean Decision*, 165.

70. Donovan, *Tumultuous Years*, 208.

71. *FRUS 1950*, VII: 183; Paige, *The Korean Decision*, 170–171.

72. Senate Committees on Armed Services and Foreign Relations, *Hearings to Conduct an Inquiry into the Military Situation in the Far East*, pt. 4, 2585.

73. Warner, "How the Korean Decision Was Made," 103.

74. Paige, *The Korean Decision*, 174; Truman, *Memoirs: Years of Trial and Hope*, 463.

75. Senate Committees on Armed Services and Foreign Relations, *Hearings to Conduct an Inquiry into the Military Situation in the Far East*, pt. 4, 2585.

76. McCullough, *Truman*, 780.

77. Paige, *The Korean Decision*, 178–179.

78. Truman, *Memoirs: Years of Trial and Hope*, 463.

79. Senate Committees on Armed Services and Foreign Relations, *Hearings to Conduct an Inquiry into the Military Situation in the Far East*, pt. 4, 2585.

80. *FRUS 1950*, VII: 183.

81. Schnabel and Watson, *History of the Joint Chiefs of Staff*, III: 93; Senate Committees on Armed Services and Foreign Relations, *Hearings to Conduct an Inquiry into the Military Situation in the Far East*, pt. 4, 2582.

82. Blair, *Forgotten War*, 82.

83. J. Lawton Collins interview.

84. Paige, *The Korean Decision*, 186; Senate Committees on Armed Services and Foreign Relations, *Hearings to Conduct an Inquiry into the Military Situation in the Far East*, pt. 4, 2710.

85. Acheson, *Present at the Creation*, 414. According to McLellan and Donovan, Truman's failure to seek and obtain a congressional resolution was a major mistake for two reasons: 1) it would have passed, and 2) when support began to fade in subsequent months, the Republicans were able to be more critical of the president than they otherwise would have been. McLellan, *Dean Acheson*, 282; Donovan, *Tumultuous Years*, 219–224.

86. *PP HST 1950*, 492.

87. Truman, *Memoirs: Years of Trial and Hope*, 338–339.

88. *FRUS 1950*, VII: 200–202; "ground troops were not planned to be used," Senate Committees on Armed Services and Foreign Relations, *Hearings to Conduct an Inquiry into the Military Situation in the Far East*, pt. 4, 2609; "If we let Korea down," Truman, *Harry S. Truman*, 463.

89. "We are doing over there what the UN asked us to do," Paige, *The Korean Decision*, 193; "None of our ground troops [will] be committed," *NYT*, June 28, 1950, 1.

90. *Washington Post*, June 28, 1950, 1.

91. Ibid.; *NYT*, June 28, 1950, 3.

92. *FRUS 1950*, VII: 211; "gravest crisis of its history," Paige, *The Korean Decision*, 203.

93. Blair, *Forgotten War*, 75–76; *NYT*, June 29, 1950, 1.

94. Acheson, *Present at the Creation*, 411.

95. *FRUS 1950*, VII: 217.

96. Schnabel and Watson, *History of the Joint Chiefs of Staff*, III: 101.

97. Ibid., 100–101.

98. *Washington Post*, June 29, 1950, 1–2.

99. Ibid.; *NYT*, June 29, 1950, 1.

100. "Speech on the Korean War Situation by Senator Robert Taft (R-Ohio)," *Congressional Record*, vol. 96, pt. 7, 9319–9323.

101. Bradley and Blair, *A General's Life*, 537.

102. Paige, *The Korean Decision*, 221.

103. "Cabinet relations on foreign affairs," Acheson, *Present at the Creation*, 410; Isaacson and Thomas, *Wise Men*, 509–512.

104. Truman, *Memoirs: Years of Trial and Hope*, 340; Paige, *The Korean Decision*, 221–226.

105. Paige, *The Korean Decision*, 224–225.

106. "And now you find something in the orders that will protect me," John Toland, *In Mortal Combat: Korea, 1950–1953* (New York: Quill, William Morrow, 1991), 60; Blair, *Forgotten War*, 76.

107. Douglas MacArthur, *Reminiscences* (New York: McGraw-Hill, 1964), 332–333.

108. Marguerite Higgins, *War in Korea* (Garden City, N.Y.: Doubleday and Company, 1951), 33–34.

109. Schnabel and Watson, *History of the Joint Chiefs of Staff*, III, pt. 1: 103–104.

110. Ibid., 104–106, "the use of U.S. [ground] troops in Korea could no longer be avoided" on 104; Goulden, *Untold Story*, 98–99.

111. *NYT*, June 30, 1950, 1, 3; McCullough, *Truman*, 782.

112. Paige, *The Korean Decision*, 244–250; Smith, "Why We Went to War in Korea," 86, 88.

113. Donovan, *Tumultuous Years*, 112.

114. "so deeply committed in Korea that we could not take care of other situations as might develop," Truman, *Memoirs: Years of Trial and Hope*, 341; Paige, *The Korean Decision*, 244–250; Smith, "Why We Went to War in Korea," 86.

115. Schnabel and Watson, *History of the Joint Chiefs of Staff*, III: 108–109; "defend Formosa against invasion or attack," *FRUS 1950*, VII, 240–241, quote on 240; Johnson's Appointment Calendar, June 24, 1950, Box 141, Johnson Papers.

116. MacArthur's message was not sent until twelve hours after his return to Tokyo. Why it was delayed is the source of considerable controversy and speculation. See Schnabel and Watson, *History of the Joint Chiefs of Staff*, III: 127–129; and Goulden, *Untold Story*, 100, 103–104.

117. *FRUS 1950*, VII: 248–250.

118. Paige, *The Korean Decision*, 253–255.

119. Collins, *War in Peacetime*, 21.

120. Ibid., 21–22.

121. Goulden, *Untold Story*, 102.

122. "I will proceed immediately," "Your recommendation to move one Regimental Combat Team," Collins, *War in Peacetime*, 22–23; Paige, *The Korean Decision*, 256; Goulden, *Untold Story*, 102–103; Blair, *Forgotten War*, 82–84.

123. During these critical hours, Secretary Johnson was not kept informed of developments. According to Collins, this should have been done by Secretary Pace "if he felt it was necessary." Collins to co-author McFarland, June 29, 1982. Why Pace did not contact Johnson is unclear, but it is known that the secretary of the army did not think highly of the secretary of defense. Frank Pace Jr. oral history, 79–80, 85.

124. Truman, *Memoirs: Years of Trial and Hope*, 343.

125. Schnabel and Watson, *History of the Joint Chiefs of Staff*, III: 117; Blair, *Forgotten War*, 84.

126. "full authority to use ground troops," Paige, *The Korean Decision*, 257–260; Truman, *Memoirs: Years of Trial and Hope*, 342–343.

127. Schnabel and Watson, *History of the Joint Chiefs of Staff*, III: 122; "restrictions on use of Army Forces imposed by JCS are hereby removed," *FRUS 1950*, VII: 263.

128. This is what Johnson said a year later when he commented that he believed Russia was behind the North Korean aggression and that it was time to take a stand. Senate

Committees on Armed Services and Foreign Relations, *Hearings to Conduct an Inquiry into the Military Situation in the Far East*, pt. 4, 2585–2586.

129. Goulden, *Untold Story*, 105. A similar assessment from Senator H. Alexander Smith (R-New Jersey) can be found in Senate Committees on Armed Services and Foreign Relations, *Hearings to Conduct an Inquiry into the Military Situation in the Far East*, pt. 4, 2610.

130. Paige, *The Korean Decision*, 262–264.

131. Ibid., 264.

132. Ibid.

133. George Elsey, Summary of June 30 Meeting, George M. Elsey Papers, HSTL; "I just had to act as Commander-in-Chief, and I did," Hamby, *Man of the People*, 538; Donovan, *Tumultuous Years*, 218, 222.

134. *NYT*, July 1, 1950, 3.

135. Schnabel and Watson, *History of the Joint Chiefs of Staff*, III: 120–121.

136. *NYT*, July 1, 1950, 1, 3.

137. *Washington Post*, July 1, 1950, 1; *Dallas Morning News*, July 1, 1950, 2.

138. *Washington Post*, July 1, 1950, 1–2.

139. Senate Committees on Armed Services and Foreign Relations, *Hearings to Conduct an Inquiry into the Military Situation in the Far East*, pt. 4, 2585; Ruth Johnson interviews.

140. *NYT*, July 2, 1950, IV: 2E. A Gallup poll taken in late August of 1950 found that 65 percent of those interviewed thought the United States was correct in defending South Korea while only 20 percent felt it was a mistake. Gallup, *The Gallup Poll*, II: 942.

141. *NYT*, July 2, 1950, IV: 2E.

17. "Give Me Two American Divisions and I Can Hold Korea"

1. Goulden, *Untold Story*, 133.

2. *Newsweek*, March 14, 1949, 25.

3. Senate Committees on Armed Services and Foreign Relations, *Hearings to Conduct an Inquiry into the Military Situation in the Far East*, pt. 4, 2584–2585.

4. *FRUS 1950*, VII: 282–283.

5. Johnson's activities during this period can be found in his daily engagement calendar, which not only recorded where he went and when but includes a listing of every person he talked to on the phone for that day. Johnson Appointment Calendar, June 1–September 19, 1950, Box 141, Johnson Papers.

6. "things were going very well," *FRUS 1950*, VII: 287–291; Acheson, *Present at the Creation*, 414.

7. Ronald J. Caridi, *The Korean War and American Politics: The Republican Party as a Case Study* (Philadelphia: University of Pennsylvania Press, 1969), 54.

8. Schnabel and Watson, *History of the Joint Chiefs of Staff*, III: 131.

9. Ibid., 132–134.

10. James F. Schnabel, *United States Army in the Korean War: Policy and Direction—The First Year* (Washington, D.C.: U.S. Government Printing Office, 1972), 102; *NYT*, July 9, 1950, 5.

11. Ibid.

12. Schnabel and Watson, *History of the Joint Chiefs of Staff*, III: 137–141.

13. Haynes, *Awesome Power*, 184–185.

14. Wilber W. Hoare Jr., "Truman," in *The Ultimate Decision: The President as Commander in Chief*, ed. Ernest R. May (New York: George Braziller, 1960), 199.

15. Johnson Appointment Calendar, June 25–September 19, 1950, Box 141, Johnson Papers.

16. Hoare, "Truman," 187.

17. J. Lawton Collins interview.

18. Truman, *Memoirs: Years of Trial and Hope*, 340, 342; *NYT*, June 29, 1950, 3.

19. Schnabel and Watson, *History of the Joint Chiefs of Staff*, III: 144.

20. Truman, *Memoirs: Years of Trial and Hope*, 342.

21. Schnabel and Watson, *History of the Joint Chiefs of Staff*, III: 144, 154, quotes on 144.

22. Ibid., 142–143.

23. "considerations of national policy make it important," "minimum standard of military effectiveness," Ibid., 143–145, quotes at 144; U.S. Department of State, *U.S. Policy in the Korean Crisis* (Washington, D.C.: U.S. Government Printing Office, 1950), 29–30, 47–48.

24. Schnabel and Watson, *History of the Joint Chiefs of Staff*, III: 147–148.

25. Ibid., 148–151.

26. Lie, *In the Cause of Peace*, 336–339.

27. Schnabel and Watson, *History of the Joint Chiefs of Staff*, III: 152.

28. Ibid., 153, 164.

29. Ibid., 154–156, 166; *FRUS 1950*, VII, 457–458.

30. Senate Committees on Armed Services and Foreign Relations, *Hearings to Conduct an Inquiry into the Military Situation in the Far East*, pt. 4, 2669–2670; Schnabel and Watson, *History of the Joint Chiefs of Staff*, III: 155, 157.

31. Senate Committees on Armed Services and Foreign Relations, *Hearings to Conduct an Inquiry into the Military Situation in the Far East*, pt. 4, 2669–2670; *FRUS 1950*, VII, 473–474, 481–482.

32. Schnabel and Watson, *History of the Joint Chiefs of Staff*, III: 161–168.

33. Australia, Belgium, Canada, Columbia, Ethiopia, France, Greece, Luxembourg, the Netherlands, New Zealand, the Philippines, South Africa, Thailand, Turkey, and the United Kingdom provided military forces. According to Schnabel, "[o]nly a few countries sent forces of real military value." Schnabel and Watson, *History of the Joint Chiefs of Staff*, III: 161.

34. Freidel, *America in the Twentieth Century*, 507–508; Stebbins, *The United States in World Affairs, 1950*, 215.

35. J. Lawton Collins interview.

36. Higgins, *War in Korea*, 33.

37. Schnabel and Watson, *History of the Joint Chiefs of Staff*, III: 178.

38. Ibid., 178–179.

39. Ibid., 179–180; Schnabel, *U.S. Army in the Korean War*, 44–45, 118.

40. Paige, *The Korean Decision*, 170–171; Schnabel and Watson, *History of the Joint Chiefs of Staff*, III: 180; Schnabel, *U.S. Army in the Korean War*, 79.

41. Schnabel and Watson, *History of the Joint Chiefs of Staff*, III: 180–182; Donovan, *Tumultuous Years*, 255.

42. "in addition to those forces already requisitioned," Schnabel, *U.S. Army in the Korean War*, 84; Blair, *Forgotten War*, 120.

43. Schnabel and Watson, *History of the Joint Chiefs of Staff*, III: 183–185; Blair, *Forgotten War*, 120; McCullough, *Truman*, 789.

44. Schnabel and Watson, *History of the Joint Chiefs of Staff*, III: 182, 186–187; *Army and Navy Journal*, July 15, 1950.

45. "unanimous agreement," "capabilities to face the threat," *FRUS 1950*, I: 345.

46. Ibid., 346; Haynes, *Awesome Power*, 188.

47. Schnabel and Watson, *History of the Joint Chiefs of Staff*, III: 187.

48. NYT, July 20, 1950, 3; McCullough, *Truman*, 791–792.

49. Offner, *Another Such Victory*, 378.

50. As the summer of 1950 wore on and Johnson began receiving the brunt of the criticism for the nation's lack of military preparedness, he increasingly became the scapegoat for those who were upset over the calling of "our boys" into the service. Johnson was not helped by Truman's statements that he "told Secretary of Defense Johnson to call up all the men he needed." *Time*, July 31, 1950, 10.

51. Schnabel, *U.S. Army in the Korean War*, 124.

52. Schnabel and Watson, *History of the Joint Chiefs of Staff*, III: 189.

53. Conversations of co-author McFarland with veterans of the Korean War and their families, who recall that Louis Johnson was the man who called them back into the service.

54. John C. Mueller, "Trends in Popular Support for the Wars in Korea and Vietnam," *American Political Science Review* (June 1971): 361.

55. NYT, August 17, 1950, 1; NYT, August 23, 1950, 5; NYT, August 27, 1950, 1.

56. Schnabel and Watson, *History of the Joint Chiefs of Staff*, III: 189–190.

57. Ibid., 199; Truman, *Memoirs: Years of Trial and Hope*, 358.

58. House Subcommittee of the Appropriations Committee, *Hearings on Supplemental Appropriations Bill for FY 1951*, 81st Cong., 2nd Sess., 1950, 20; Schnabel and Watson, *History of the Joint Chiefs of Staff*, III: 199.

59. Kolodziej, *Uncommon Defense*, 133; John L. Gaddis, *Strategies of Containment: A Critical Appraisal of Postwar American National Security Policy* (New York: Oxford University Press, 1982), 113.

60. House Committee, *Supplemental Appropriations Bill for FY 1951*, 4.

61. Kolodziej, *Uncommon Defense*, 138.

62. Blair, *Forgotten War*, 168.

63. MacArthur, *Reminiscences*, 334.

64. Collins, *War in Peacetime*, 115–116.

65. "in Secretary of Defense Johnson, MacArthur had in Washington a powerful ally," R. E. Appleman, *South to the Naktong, North to the Yalu: June–November 1950* (Washington, D.C.: U.S. Government Printing Office, 1961), 495. Appleman was a combat historian on active duty in the army. This comment, like most others suggesting that Johnson was a vigorous supporter of the Inchon invasion, is based on Johnson's statements during the MacArthur dismissal hearings that "I had been carrying along with General MacArthur the responsibility for Inchon." Senate Committees on Armed Services and Foreign Relations, *Hearings to Conduct an Inquiry into the Military Situation in the Far East*, pt. 4, 2618. Years later, General Collins claimed that Johnson was not a proponent of the invasion and that it was only after the fact that Johnson became a vocal supporter. J. Lawton Collins interview; Robert Debs Heinl Jr., *Victory at High Tide: The Inchon-Seoul Campaign* (Philadelphia: J. B. Lippincott Co., 1968), 276.

66. Collins, *War in Peacetime*, 121.

67. Frances H. Heller, ed., *The Korean War, A 25-Year Perspective* (Lawrence: Regents Press of Kansas, 1977), 26; McCullough, *Truman*, 796.

68. Senate Committees on Armed Services and Foreign Relations, *Hearings to Conduct an Inquiry into the Military Situation in the Far East*, pt. 4, 2618.

69. MacArthur, *Reminiscences*, 350.

70. Schnabel and Watson, *History of the Joint Chiefs of Staff*, III: 211–214.

71. McCullough, *Truman*, 798.

72. Schnabel, *U.S. Army in the Korean War*, 173–182.

73. Ibid., 177–178.

74. McCullough, *Truman*, 799; Donovan, *Tumultuous Years*, 271.

75. Truman, *Memoirs: Years of Trial and Hope*, 359; *FRUS 1950*, VII: 712–716.

76. Senate Committees on Armed Services and Foreign Relations, *Hearings to Conduct an Inquiry into the Military Situation in the Far East*, pt. 4, 2618.

18. Means of Descent

1. Rearden, *Formative Years*, 128.

2. Acheson, *Present at the Creation*, 373–374; "nuttier than a fruitcake," Nitze conversation.

3. Donovan, *Tumultuous Years*, 159.

4. Ibid., 266.

5. Ferrell, *Off the Record*, 192.

6. Donovan, *Tumultuous Years*, 261.

7. Interview with Ken Hechler, Washington, D.C., June 5, 2003; "That was something that needed to be said," and "see that Harriman was made Secretary of State," Isaacson and Thomas, *Wise Men*, 520; "could get Acheson out," Ferrell, *Diary of Eben Ayers*, 361; Donovan, *Tumultuous Years*, 265–266.

8. Isaacson and Thomas, *Wise Men*, 520. In his letter of April 18, 1982, to co-author McFarland, Harriman tried to distance himself from this incident, saying that it was a "gross exaggeration."

9. Isaacson and Thomas, *Wise Men*, 525.

10. Ferrell, *Diary of Eben Ayers*, 361.

11. Marquis Childs, "Get Acheson," *Washington Post*, August 25, 1950.

12. Truman Memo on Dismissal of Johnson (see ch. 9, n.63).

13. Ibid.

14. *NYT*, July 20, 1950, 3.

15. *FRUS 1950*, VI: 392–394.

16. Ibid., 401.

17. Hoare, "Knotty Problem of Formosa," 16; *FRUS 1950*, VI: 394; Truman, *Memoirs: Years of Trial and Hope*, 349.

18. Schnabel and Watson, *History of the Joint Chiefs of Staff*, III: 510.

19. Manchester, *American Caesar*, 562.

20. *NYT*, August 2, 1950, 15.

21. Trumbull Higgins, *Korea and the Fall of MacArthur* (New York: Oxford University Press, 1960), 37; Schnabel and Watson, *History of the Joint Chiefs of Staff*, III: 510.

22. Truman, *Memoirs: Years of Trial and Hope*, 354.

23. Manchester, *American Caesar*, 563–565; Schnabel and Watson, *History of the Joint Chiefs of Staff*, III: 513.

24. Senate Committees on Armed Services and Foreign Relations, *Hearings to Conduct an Inquiry into the Military Situation in the Far East*, pt. 4, 2615, 2618–2619, 2651–2652; Dulles, *American Policy toward Communist China*, 95–96.

25. Truman, *Memoirs: Years of Trial and Hope*, 355; Acheson, *Present at the Creation*, 441.

26. *FRUS 1950*, VI: 401.

27. Ibid., 402–404, "the launching of preventive bombing attacks" on 403.

28. Schnabel and Watson, *History of the Joint Chiefs of Staff*, III: 511–512; Schnabel, *U.S. Army in the Korean War*, 369; Hoare, "Knotty Problem of Formosa," 19.

29. Quotes in *FRUS 1950*, VI: 423; Manchester, *American Caesar*, 565.

30. *FRUS 1950*, VI: 423–424.

31. Ferrell, *Off the Record*, 47; Truman, *Memoirs: Years of Trial and Hope*, 349.

32. Isaacson and Thomas, *Wise Men*, 522.

33. "[W]e have not improved our position by kicking Chiang around," *FRUS 1950*, VI: 427–430, quote on 430. Truman, *Memoirs: Years of Trial and Hope*, 349–353; Manchester, *American Caesar*, 565–566.

34. Truman, *Memoirs: Years of Trial and Hope*, 351.

35. Isaacson and Thomas, *Wise Men*, 523.

36. Truman, *Memoirs: Years of Trial and Hope*, 351–352.

37. MacArthur, *Reminiscences*, 341.

38. Truman, *Memoirs: Years of Trial and Hope*, 354; *PP HST 1950*, 580.

39. Schnabel, *U.S. Army in the Korean War*, 345.

40. Acheson, *Present at the Creation*, 425.

41. *FRUS 1950*, VII: 576–577.

42. *FRUS 1950*, VII: 581.

43. Offner, *Another Such Victory*, 384.

44. "[O]nce war operations are undertaken," *FRUS 1950*, VII: 593, 614, quote on 614; Doris M. Condit, *History of the Office of the Secretary of Defense*, vol. II, *The Test of War, 1950–1953* (Washington, D.C.: U.S. Government Printing Office, 1988), 73–74.

45. "showed a lack of understanding of the important issues involved," *FRUS 1950*, VII: 614, n.1; Acheson, *Present at the Creation*, 425.

46. *NYT*, August 26, 1950, 1, 3.

47. *NYT*, August 27, 1950, 2; *NYT*, August 28, 1950, 1.

48. Donovan, *Tumultuous Years*, 251; Manchester, *American Caesar*, 569; Samuel P. Huntington, *The Common Defense: Strategic Programs in National Politics* (New York: Columbia University Press, 1961), 17; Higgins, *Korea*, 40.

49. Stebbins, *The United States in World Affairs, 1950*, 250.

50. MacArthur, *Reminiscences*, 341; Manchester, *American Caesar*, 568.

51. Acheson, *Present at the Creation*, 423; Truman, *Memoirs: Years of Trial and Hope*, 354–356; Manchester, *American Caesar*, 568–569; Senate Committees on Armed Services and Foreign Relations, *Hearings to Conduct an Inquiry into the Military Situation in the Far East*, pt. 4, 2616.

52. *U.S. News & World Report*, September 1, 1950, 32–34.

53. "Those who speak . . . do not understand the Orient," ibid.; *Newsweek*, September 4, 1950, 26.

54. Truman, *Memoirs: Years of Trial and Hope*, 354–355.

55. Donovan, *Tumultuous Years*, 263; Acheson, *Present at the Creation*, 423; Senate Committees on Armed Services and Foreign Relations, *Hearings to Conduct an Inquiry into the Military Situation in the Far East*, pt. 4, 2586–2587; *FRUS 1950*, VI, 454.

56. *FRUS 1950*, VI: 454–455; Truman, *Memoirs: Years of Trial and Hope*, 356; Acheson, *Present at the Creation*, 423–424.

57. James, D. Clayton, *The Years of MacArthur*, Vol. III (Boston: Houghton Mifflin Company, 1985), 461–462; "Dare [they] send [MacArthur] a message," *FRUS 1950*, VI: 454–455, quote on 454; Acheson, *Present at the Creation*, 423–424.

58. *FRUS 1950*, VI: 455–457.

59. Ibid., 457.

60. Miller, *Plain Speaking*, 292.

61. Schnabel and Watson, *History of the Joint Chiefs of Staff*, III: 517; Donovan, *Tumultuous Years*, 264; "The President of the United States directs that you withdraw your message," *FRUS 1950*, VI: 457.

62. Conjecture on this point is based on the fact that only Acheson, Harriman, and Charlie Ross were aware of Johnson's foot-dragging at this time. Since Acheson did not contact the president and since Ross had not been at the conference, this leaves only Harriman as a possibility.

63. "he wanted to go and he still wanted it to go," *FRUS 1950*, VI: 457–460, quote on 460; Donovan, *Tumultuous Years*, 264–265.

64. Manchester, *American Caesar*, 570.

65. Schnabel and Watson, *History of the Joint Chiefs of Staff*, III: 518.

66. Truman, *Memoirs: Years of Trial and Hope*, 356–358.

67. Schnabel and Watson, *History of the Joint Chiefs of Staff*, III: 518.

68. Truman, *Harry S. Truman*, 479.

69. Ibid.

70. Blair, *Forgotten War*, 75–264.

71. Joseph and Stewart Alsop, "Matter of Fact," *New York Herald Tribune*, July 5, 9, and 10, 1950; "Mr. Johnson's Pearl Harbor," *New York Herald Tribune*, July 19, 1950.

72. *NYT*, July 9, 1950, 1; and *NYT*, July 16, 1950, 1.

73. Hanson Baldwin, "The Outlook in Korea," *NYT*, July 9, 1950; "Too Few and Too Weak," *NYT*, July 12, 1950.

74. *Congressional Record*, 81st Cong., 2nd Sess., 1950, vol. 96, pt. 8, 9989.

75. *NYT*, July 13, 1950, 1.

76. *NYT*, July 14, 1950, 3; *Facts on File Yearbook, 1950* (New York: Facts on File, 1950), 230.

77. *NYT*, July 14, 1950, 1; *NYT*, July 16, 1950, 3.

78. Borklund, *Men of the Pentagon*, 86.

79. "There are lies, there are damn lies, and there are statistics," ibid., 87; *Army and Navy Journal*, July 29, 1950.

80. *NYT*, August 20, 1950, 1.

81. Anthony F. Tauriello to Louis Johnson, August 23, 1950, Box 140, Correspondence R–V, Johnson Papers.

82. *NYT*, August 31, 1950, 1.

83. Ibid.; *Washington Post*, August 31, 1950, 1; *Dallas Morning News*, August 31, 1950.

84. The major wire services transmitted the story to most daily newspapers.

85. *NYT*, August 31, 1950, 5.

86. *PP HST 1950*, 606.

87. See Drew Pearson's column of September 4, 1950, in the *Washington Post* and Stewart Alsop's column of September 3, 1950, in the *Washington Post*; *NYT*, September 4, 1950, 1; *NYT*, September 5, 1950, 1.

88. *NYT*, September 4, 1950, 1.

89. *NYT*, September 8, 1950, 1; *NYT*, September 9, 1950, 1, 5.

90. Arthur Krock, "The Secretary of Defense and His Critics," *NYT*, September 5, 1950, 6.

91. Arthur Krock, "The Dismissal of the Secretary of Defense," *NYT*, September 14, 1950.

92. Ruth Johnson interviews.

93. Marx Leva oral history, 77.

94. "not going to resign, as long as I am President," News Conferences, August 3 and 31, 1950, *PP HST 1950*, 570, 606–608, quote on 570; Condit, *History of the Office of the Secretary of Defense*, II: 33.

95. Krock, "The Dismissal of the Secretary of Defense."

19. *"Lou, I've Got to Ask You to Quit"*

1. Truman Memo on Dismissal of Johnson (see ch. 9, n.63).
2. Ferrell, *Diary of Eben Ayers*, 369.
3. McCullough, *Truman*, 793.
4. Cray, *General of the Army*, 684.
5. Forrest C. Pogue, *George C. Marshall: Statesman, 1945–1959* (New York: Viking, 1987), 420–422; "Mr. President, I'll do it," McCullough, *Truman*, 798.
6. Ferrell, *Off the Record*, 189.
7. Pogue, *Statesman*, 422.
8. "Wonder of wonders, Mrs. Marshall is for it," Cray, *General of the Army*, 685; Isaacson and Thomas, *Wise Men*, 525.
9. Truman Memo on Dismissal of Johnson.
10. Ibid.
11. George M. Elsey, "Memorandum for Record"—Charles Ross's account "concerning the circumstances of the resignation of the Secretary of Defense, Louis Johnson," September 13, 1950, PSF, General File, Johnson, Louis, HSTL, hereafter Elsey Memo.
12. Truman to Bess Truman, September 7, 1950, in Ferrell, *Off the Record*, 189.
13. Ibid.
14. Johnson Appointment Calendar, September 7, 1950, Box 141, Johnson Papers.
15. Truman to Bess Truman, September 7, 1950.
16. Elsey Memo.
17. Truman, *Harry S. Truman*, 253, 265, 319.
18. "Boot for Johnson," *Newsweek*, September 25, 1950, 29.
19. Donovan, *Tumultuous Years*, 266.
20. *Washington Star*, September 9, 1950.
21. "Boot for Johnson."
22. Ruth Johnson interviews.
23. Donovan, *Tumultuous Years*, 266.
24. "Boot for Johnson"; Ruth Johnson interviews.
25. Elsey Memo; Truman Memo on Dismissal of Johnson.
26. Elsey Memo.
27. Louis H. Renfrow oral history, 133.
28. Ruth Johnson interviews.
29. William K. Hutchinson, "True Story of Secretary Johnson's Dramatic Resignation," *Julius Klein Newsletter* II, no. 10 (October 1950).
30. Ibid.; Jean Kearney interview.
31. Hutchinson, "True Story"; "Boot for Johnson," 29; First Draft—Secretary of Defense to President, Box 115, Re: Johnson Resignation, Johnson Papers.
32. Elsey Memo; Truman Memo on Dismissal of Johnson.
33. Ibid.
34. Donovan, *Tumultuous Years*, 267.
35. Hutchinson, "True Story."
36. Elsey Memo.
37. Truman Memo on Dismissal of Johnson.
38. Elsey Memo.
39. *NYT*, September 13, 1950, 10.
40. Ibid.
41. Ibid.
42. Merry, *Taking on the World*, 201.

43. Nitze, *From Hiroshima to Glasnost*, 105.

44. Alsop and Childs columns, *Washington Post*, September 15, 1950; Reston column, *NYT*, September 13, 1950.

45. Krock and Baldwin columns, *NYT*, September 14, 1950.

46. Pogue, *George C. Marshall: Statesman*, 423–424.

47. *Life*, September 25, 1950, 34; *Barron's*, September 16, 1950, 3.

48. *NYT*, September 13–25, 1950; *Washington Post*, September 13–25, 1950; Rep. Overton Brooks to Johnson, August 11, 1950, OF 1285, Defense, Department of, Box 1594, HSTL. Rep. John Phillips to Johnson, September 18, 1950, and Rep. Walter Judd to Johnson, December 27, 1950, Box 115, Re: Johnson Resignation, Johnson Papers.

49. *Washington Evening Star*, June 15, 1951; Senate Committees on Armed Services and Foreign Relations, *Hearings to Conduct an Inquiry into the Military Situation in the Far East*, pt. 4, 2626, 2627, 2654.

50. Marx Leva interview.

51. Stewart Alsop, "The Code of Harry Truman," *Washington Post*, September 15, 1950.

52. Truman, *Harry S. Truman*, 480.

53. Johnson Appointment Calendar, September 13–18, 1950, Box 141, Johnson Papers; Marx Leva interview; J. Lawton Collins interview.

54. *Army and Naval Journal*, September 16, 1950.

55. *Washington Post*, September 19, 1950, 1.

56. *NYT*, September 20, 1950, 37.

57. Johnson to Truman, December 7, 1950, PSF, Subject File: Cabinet (Defense), Box 157, HSTL.

58. Senate Committees on Armed Services and Foreign Relations, *Hearings to Conduct an Inquiry into the Military Situation in the Far East*, pt. 4, 2618; Ruth Johnson interviews.

20. *"Lest Darkness Come"*

1. *Parkersburg* (West Virginia) *News*, May 5, 1953; Chesney Carney interview; Haymond Maxwell interview.

2. "No. I do not know why I am out of the Defense Establishment," Senate Committees on Armed Services and Foreign Relations, *Hearings to Conduct an Inquiry into the Military Situation in the Far East*, pt. 4, 2618; Borklund, *Men of the Pentagon*, 88.

3. *Rochester* (Minnesota) *Post Bulletin*, January 11, 1963.

4. Ibid.

5. Numerous letters and telegrams between Truman and Johnson, PSF, Box 124, General File, Johnson, Louis, and PPF 127, HSTL.

6. *Clarksburg News*, September 4, 1952; *NYT*, April 17, 1955, 66.

7. Miller, *You Can't Tell by Looking at 'Em*, 96.

8. *NYT*, April 29, 1952, 19; Thomas Langfitt interview.

9. Miller, *You Can't Tell by Looking at 'Em*, 96.

10. Nitze conversation.

11. Dr. Hugh R. Butt (Mayo Clinic) to Ruth Johnson, October 25, 1977 (in co-author McFarland's possession).

12. Thomas Langfitt interview.

13. Acheson, *Present at the Creation*, 374, 441.

14. Clifford, *Counsel to the President*, 280.

15. Truman Memo on Dismissal of Johnson.

16. Henry Ikenberry interview; Laidler Mackall interview; Thompson Powers interview; Richard Whiting interview; Herb Underwood interview; interviews in Washington, D.C., with Jack Corber, May 17, 2003, Jim Holden, February 20, 2003, John Nolan, April 8, 2003, and Dick Taylor, March 4, 2003.

17. Miller, *You Can't Tell by Looking at 'Em*, 77–79; Henry Ikenberry interview.

18. John Nolan interview.

19. Marylin Bender and Selig Altschul, *The Chosen Instrument* (New York: Simon and Schuster, 1982), 363, 436, 439, 442–445.

20. Jack Corber interview.

21. Bosley Crowther, *Hollywood Rajah: The Life and Times of Louis B. Mayer* (New York: Holt, Rinehart and Winston, 1960), 312–325.

22. Louis Nizer, *My Life in Court* (Garden City, N.Y.: Doubleday & Company, 1961), chapter 6.

23. John Nolan interview.

24. Dr. Butt (Mayo Clinic) to Ruth Johnson, December 6, 1977 (letter in co-author McFarland's possession).

25. Miller, *You Can't Tell by Looking at 'Em*, 96–97; William Miller to co-author McFarland, March 18, 1983.

26. *Washington Post*, April 25, 1966, B: 2.

27. *Clarksburg Exponent*, April 26 and 27, 1966.

28. *Clarksburg Exponent*, April 27, 1966.

29. John Nolan interview.

Conclusion

1. Black, *Champion of Freedom*, 427.

2. Blair, *Forgotten War*, 4, quoting from Miller, *Plain Speaking*, 205.

3. Ferrell, *Diary of Eben H. Ayers*, 305, 307; Hamby, *Man of the People*, 513.

4. Ferrell, *Truman: A Life*, 316.

5. Janeway, *Struggle for Survival*, 26.

SELECT BIBLIOGRAPHY

Authors' Interviews

Stephen Ailes, Washington, D.C., July 27, 1977. Interviewed by Keith McFarland.

Douglas Bailey, Clarksburg, West Virginia, July 12, 1977. Interviewed by Keith McFarland.

Mary Katherine Brown, Clarksburg, West Virginia, April 4, 2003. Interviewed by David Roll.

Chesney Carney, Clarksburg, West Virginia, July 12, 1977. Interviewed by Keith McFarland.

J. Lawton Collins, Washington, D.C., July 27, 1977. Interviewed by Keith McFarland.

Jack Corber, Washington, D.C., May 17, 2003. Interviewed by David Roll.

Malin Craig Jr., Washington, D.C., January 31, 1975. Interviewed by Keith McFarland.

Charles I. Faddis, Waynesburg, Pennsylvania, August 4, 1970. Interviewed by Keith McFarland.

James A. Farley, New York, New York, August 1, 1968. Interviewed by Keith McFarland.

Paul Griffith, Washington, D.C., March 9, 1977. Interviewed by Keith McFarland.

James Guiher, Jr., Washington, D.C., February 13, 2003. Interviewed by David Roll.

Dow W. Harter, Washington, D.C., June 13, 1969. Interviewed by Keith McFarland.

Ken Hechler, Washington, D.C., June 5, 2003. Interviewed by David Roll.

Jim Holden, Washington, D.C., February 20, 2003. Interviewed by David Roll.

Henry Ikenberry, Washington, D.C., January 22, 2003. Interviewed by David Roll.

Lem Jarvis, Clarksburg, West Virginia, July 13, 1977. Interviewed by Keith McFarland.

Ruth Maxwell Johnson, Clarksburg, West Virginia, June 18, 1976, and July 12, 1977. Interviewed by Keith McFarland.

Virginia Johnson, Roanoke, Virginia, July 16, 1977. Interviewed by Keith McFarland.

Jean Kearney, Washington, D.C., March 27, 2002. Interviewed by David Roll.

Dr. Thomas W. Langfitt Jr., Washington, D.C., March 24, 2003. Interviewed by David Roll.

Marx Leva, Washington, D.C., July 29, 1977. Interviewed by Keith McFarland.

Laidler Mackall, Washington, D.C., May 8, 2003. Interviewed by David Roll.

Frank Maxwell, Clarksburg, West Virginia, April 15, 2003. Interviewed by David Roll.

Haymond Maxwell Jr., Clarksburg, West Virginia, June 13, 1976, June 18, 1976, and July 12, 1977. Interviewed by Keith McFarland.

Steven Maxwell, Clarksburg, West Virginia, March 13–14, 2003. Interviewed by David Roll.

W. B. "Bill" Maxwell, Clarksburg, West Virginia, June 18, 1976, and July 12, 1977. Inter-
    viewed by Keith McFarland.
William E. Miller, Washington, D.C., July 27, 1977. Interviewed by Keith McFarland.
Norma Monroe, Clarksburg, West Virginia, July 16, 1982. Interviewed by Keith McFar-
    land.
Paul Nitze, Lexington, Virginia, March 25, 1977. Interviewed by Keith McFarland.
John Nolan, Washington, D.C., April 8, 2003. Interviewed by David Roll.
Gerald P. Nye, Washington, D.C., July 25, 1968. Interviewed by Keith McFarland.
Thompson Powers, Washington, D.C., March 12, 2002. Interviewed by David Roll.
William Ritchie, Washington, D.C., June 13, 1969. Interviewed by Keith McFarland.
Sarah Steptoe, Martinsburg, West Virginia, November 16, 2002. Interviewed by David
    Roll.
Dick Taylor, Washington, D.C., March 4, 2003. Interviewed by David Roll.
Herb Underwood, Washington, D.C., March 13, 2003. Interviewed by David Roll.
Richard A. Whiting, Washington, D.C., May 17, 2002. Interviewed by David Roll.
Helen Coolidge Woodring, Wilmington, Delaware, July 20, 1968. Interviewed by
    Keith McFarland.

Library and Archival Material

Dean Acheson Papers. Harry S. Truman Presidential Museum & Library, Indepen-
    dence, Missouri.
Henry H. Arnold Papers. Library of Congress, Washington, D.C.
Eben A. Ayers Papers. Harry S. Truman Presidential Museum & Library, Indepen-
    dence, Missouri.
Defense Department. Records of the Office of the Secretary of Defense. RG 330,
    Records of the Office of the Secretary of Defense, 1921–1995, NARA, College
    Park, Maryland.
Defense Department. Records of the U.S. Joint Chiefs of Staff. RG 218, Records of the
    U.S. Joint Chiefs of Staff, 1941–1978, NARA, College Park, Maryland.
Stephen T. Early Papers. Franklin D. Roosevelt Presidential Library and Museum,
    Hyde Park, New York.
George M. Elsey Papers. Harry S. Truman Presidential Museum & Library, Indepen-
    dence, Missouri.
Papers of Felix Frankfurter. Library of Congress, Washington, D.C.
A. Robert Ginsburgh Papers. Harry S. Truman Presidential Musuem & Library, Inde-
    pendence, Missouri.
Louis A. Johnson Papers. Harrison Institute and Small Library, University of Virginia,
    Charlottesville, Virginia.
Senator Harley Kilgore Collection. West Virginia State Archives, Charleston, West
    Virginia.
V. K. Wellington Koo Papers. Butler Library, Columbia University, New York, New
    York.
Papers of General Douglas MacArthur. MacArthur Memorial Library and Archives,
    Norfolk, Virginia.
George C. Marshall Papers. George C. Marshall Research Library, Lexington, Vir-
    ginia.
Henry Morgenthau Jr. Diaries. Franklin D. Roosevelt Presidential Library and Mu-
    seum, Hyde Park, New York.
John C. O'Laughlin Papers. Library of Congress, Washington, D.C.

Franklin D. Roosevelt Papers. Official File, President's Personal File, President's Secretary's File. Franklin D. Roosevelt Presidential Library and Museum, Hyde Park, New York.

Harry S. Truman Papers. Office File, President's Personal File, President's Secretary's File. Harry S. Truman Presidential Museum & Library, Independence, Missouri.

Hoyt Vandenberg Papers. Library of Congress, Washington, D.C.

War Department. Records of the Adjutant General, 1936–1940. RG 407, Records of the Adjutant General's Office, 1917–, NARA, Washington, D.C.

———. Records of the War Department General Staff, 1936–1940. RG 165, Records of the War Department General and Special Staffs, NARA, Washington, D.C.

———. Secretary of War, General Correspondence, 1932–1942. RG 107, Records of the Secretary of War, NARA, Washington, D.C.

Sumner Welles Papers. Franklin D. Roosevelt Presidential Library and Museum, Hyde Park, New York.

Harry H. Woodring Papers. Spencer Research Library, University of Kansas, Lawrence, Kansas.

Oral Histories

Harry S. Truman Presidential Museum & Library, Independence, Missouri
Kenneth M. Birkhead
Samuel C. Brightman
Matthew J. Connelly
Thomas K. Finletter
Gordon Gray
Paul H. Griffith
Marx Leva
Wilfred J. McNeil
John H. Ohly
Frank Pace Jr.
Louis H. Renfrow
John L. Sullivan
Eugene M. Zuckert

Official and Semi-Official Publications

"Annual Report of the Assistant Secretary of War, 1940." In *Annual Report of the Secretary of War, 1940.*

"Assistant Secretary of War Annual Report, 1938." In *Annual Report of the Secretary of War, 1938.*

"Assistant Secretary of War Annual Report, 1939." In *Annual Report of the Secretary of War, 1939.*

Complete Presidential Press Conferences of President Franklin D. Roosevelt. New York: Da Capo Press, 1972.

Condit, Doris M. *History of the Office of the Secretary of Defense.* Vol. II, *The Test of War, 1950–1953.* Washington, D.C.: U.S. Government Printing Office, 1988.

Condit, Kenneth W. *The History of the Joint Chiefs of Staff: The Joint Chiefs of Staff and National Policy.* Vol. II, *1947–1949.* Wilmington: Michael Glazier, 1976.

Department of Defense. *Semiannual Report of the Secretary of Defense and the Semiannual Reports of the Secretary of the Army, Secretary of the Navy, Secretary of the*

Air Force. July 1 to December 31, 1949, and January 1 to July 30, 1950. Washington, D.C.: U.S. Government Printing Office, 1950.

Department of State. *Foreign Relations of the United States, 1942.* Washington, D.C.: U.S. Government Printing Office, 1960.

——. *Foreign Relations of the United States, 1948–50.* Washington, D.C.: U.S. Government Printing Office, 1979.

——. *United States Policy in the Korean Crisis.* Washington, D.C.: U.S. Government Printing Office, 1950.

——. *United States Relations with China, with Special Reference to the Period 1944–1949.* Washington, D.C.: U.S. Government Printing Office, 1949.

Department of State Bulletin XXII (January 23, 1950).

Fairchild, Byron, and Jonathan Grossman. *The Army and Industrial Manpower.* Washington, D.C.: U.S. Government Printing Office, 1959.

First Semiannual Report on the Mutual Defense Assistance Program: Memo from the President. House Document 613, 81st Cong., 2d Sess., 1950.

Holley, Irving B., Jr. *Buying Aircraft: Matériel Procurement for the Army Air Force.* Washington, D.C.: U.S. Government Printing Office, 1964.

House Armed Services Committee. *Hearings on Investigation of the B-36 Program.* 81st Cong., 1st Sess., 1949.

——. *Hearings on the National Defense Program—Unification and Strategy.* 81st Cong., 1st Sess., 1949.

——. *Hearings on S. 1843, To Convert the National Military Establishment into an Executive Department of the Government, to be Known as the Department of Defense, to Provide the Secretary of Defense with Appropriate Responsibility and Authority, and with Civilian and Military Assistants Adequate to Fuilfill His Enlarged Responsibility.* 81st Cong., 1st Sess., 1949.

——. *Investigation of the B-36 Bomber Program.* H. R. Report No. 1470. 81st Cong., 2d Sess., 1950.

——. *Report on Unification and Strategy.* House Document 600. 81st Cong., 2d Sess., 1950.

House Committee on Foreign Affairs. *Hearings on Mutual Defense Assistance Act of 1949.* 81st Cong., 1st Sess., 1949.

Kreidberg, Marvin A., and Merton G. Henry. *History of Military Mobilization in the United States Army, 1775–1945.* Washington, D.C.: U.S. Government Printing Office, 1955.

MacGregor, Morris J., Jr. *Integration of the Armed Forces 1940–1965.* Washington, D.C.: Center of Military History, U.S. Army, U.S. Government Printing Office, 1981.

Mansergh, Nicholas, ed. *The Transfer of Power 1942–7.* Vols. I and II. London: Her Majesty's Stationery Office, 1970.

Public Papers of the Presidents of the United States. Harry S. Truman, 1945–1953. Washington, D.C.: U.S. Government Printing Office, 1961–1966.

Rearden, Steven L. *History of the Office of the Secretary of Defense.* Vol. I, *The Formative Years, 1947–1950.* Washington, D.C.: U.S. Government Printing Office, 1984.

Schnabel, James F. *United States Army in the Korean War. Policy and Direction: The First Year.* Washington, D.C.: U.S. Government Printing Office, 1972.

Schnabel, James F., and Watson, Robert J. *The History of the Joint Chiefs of Staff: The Joint Chiefs of Staff and National Policy.* Vol. III, *The Korean War,* Pt. I. Wilmington: Michael Glazier, Inc., 1979.

Senate Committee on Armed Services. *Hearings on Nomination of Louis A. Johnson to Be Secretary of Defense*, Vol. III (Executive Session). 81st Cong., 1st Sess., 1949.

Senate Committees on Armed Services and Foreign Relations. *Hearings to Conduct an Inquiry into the Military Situation in the Far East and the Facts Surrounding the Relief of General of the Army Douglas MacArthur from His Assignments in That Area*. 82d Cong., 1st Sess., 1951.

———. *Joint Hearings on Military Assistance Program, 1949*. 81st Cong., 1st Sess., 1949.

Senate Committee on Foreign Relations. *Hearings on the North Atlantic Treaty*. 81st Cong., 1st Sess., 1949, Pt. 1.

Senate Committee on Military Affairs. *Hearings on H.R. 3791, An Act to Provide More Effectively for the National Defense*. 76th Cong., 1st Sess., 1939.

Smith, R. Ellerton. *The Army and Economic Mobilization*. Washington, D.C.: U.S. Government Printing Office, 1959.

Survival in the Air Age: A Report by the President's Air Policy Commission (Finletter Report). Washington, D.C.: U.S. Government Printing Office, 1948.

War Department. Office of the Secretary of War. *Annual Report of the Secretary of War, 1933–1940*. Washington, D.C.: U.S. Government Printing Office.

Watson, Mark S. *Chief of Staff: Prewar Plans and Preparations*. Washington, D.C.: U.S. Government Printing Office, 1950.

Books and Memoirs

Abell, Tyler, ed. *Drew Pearson Diaries, 1949–1959*. New York: Holt, Rinehart and Winston, 1974.

Abels, Jules. *Out of the Jaws of Victory*. New York: Henry Holt and Company, 1959.

Acheson, Dean. *Present at the Creation*. New York: W.W. Norton & Co., 1969.

Allen, Robert S., and William S. Shannon. *The Truman Merry-Go-Round*. New York: Vanguard Press, 1950.

Baruch, Bernard M. *The Public Years*. New York: Holt, Reinhart and Winston, 1960.

Berle, Beatrice Bishop, and Travis Beal Jacobs, eds. *Navigating the Rapids, 1918–1971*. New York: Harcourt Brace Jovanovich, 1973.

Bernardo, C. Joseph, and Eugene Hayward Bacon. *American Military Policy: Its Development Since 1775*. Harrisburg, Pa.: Military Service Pub. Co., 1955.

Black, Conrad. *Franklin Delano Roosevelt: Champion of Freedom*. New York: Public Affairs, 2003.

Blair, Clay. *The Forgotten War: America in Korea, 1950–1953*. Annapolis: Naval Institute Press, 1987.

Blum, John Morton. *From the Morgenthau Diaries: Years of Crisis, 1928–1938*. Vol. 2. Boston: Houghton Mifflin Company, 1959.

Borg, Dorothy, and Waldo Heinrichs, eds. *Uncertain Years: Chinese American Relations, 1947–1950*. New York: Columbia University Press, 1980.

Borklund, Carl W. *Men of the Pentagon*. New York: Frederick A. Praeger, 1966.

Bradley, Omar N., and Clay Blair. *A General's Life*. New York: Simon and Schuster, 1983.

Burns, James MacGregor. *Roosevelt: The Lion and the Fox*. New York: Harcourt, Brace and Company, 1956.

———. *Roosevelt: The Soldier of Freedom*. New York: Harcourt Brace Jovanovich, 1970.

Collins, J. Lawton. *War in Peacetime: The History and Lessons of Korea*. Boston: Houghton Mifflin Company, 1969.

Cray, Ed. *General of the Army: George Marshall, Soldier and Statesman*. New York: W.W. Norton & Co., 1990.

Dallek, Robert. *Franklin D. Roosevelt and American Foreign Policy, 1932–45*. New York: Oxford University Press, 1979.

Divine, Robert A. *The Illusion of Neutrality: Franklin D. Roosevelt and the Struggle over the Arms Embargo*. Chicago: University of Chicago Press, 1962.

———. *The Reluctant Belligerent: American Entry into World War II*. 2nd ed. New York: John Wiley & Son, 1979.

Donovan, Robert J. *Tumultuous Years: The Presidency of Harry S. Truman, 1949–1953*. New York: W.W. Norton & Company, 1982.

Facts on File Yearbook, Vol. X. New York: Pearson's Index, Facts on File, Inc., 1950.

Farley, James A. *Jim Farley's Story: The Roosevelt Years*. New York: McGraw-Hill Co., 1948.

Fenno, Richard F., Jr. *The President's Cabinet: An Analysis in the Period from Wilson to Eisenhower*. Cambridge, Mass.: Harvard University Press, 1959.

Ferrell, Robert H., ed. *Dear Bess: The Letters from Harry to Bess Truman, 1910–1959*. New York: W.W. Norton & Company, 1983.

———, ed. *Off the Record: The Private Papers of Harry S. Truman*. New York: Harper & Row, 1980.

———, ed. *Harry S. Truman: A Life*. Columbia: University of Missouri Press, 1995.

———, ed. *Truman in the White House: The Diary of Eben A. Ayers*. Columbia: University of Missouri Press, 1991.

Freidel, Frank. *America in the Twentieth Century*. 3rd ed. New York: Alfred A. Knopf, 1970.

———. *Franklin D. Roosevelt: Launching the New Deal*. Boston: Little, Brown and Co., 1973.

Gopal, Ram. *How India Struggled for Freedom*. Bombay: Book Centre Limited, 1967.

Goulden, Joseph C. *Korea: The Untold Story of the War*. New York: Times Books, 1982.

Haight, John McVickar, Jr. *American Aid to France, 1938–1940*. New York: Atheneum, 1970.

Hamby, Alonzo L. *Man of the People: A Life of Harry Truman*. New York: Oxford University Press, 1995.

Hammond, Paul Y. *Organizing for Defense*. Princeton, N.J.: Princeton University Press, 1961.

Haynes, Richard F. *The Awesome Power: Harry S. Truman as Commander in Chief*. Baton Rouge: Louisiana State University Press, 1973.

Hess, Gary R. *America Encounters India, 1941–1947*. Baltimore: John Hopkins University Press, 1971.

Hewlett, Richard G., and Frances Duncan. *A History of the United States Atomic Energy Commission*. Vol. II, *Atomic Shield, 1947–1952*. College Park: Pennsylvania State University Press, 1969.

Hoopes, Townsend, and Douglas Brinkley. *Driven Patriot: The Life and Times of James Forrestal*. New York: Random House, 1992.

Ickes, Harold L. *The Secret Diary of Harold L. Ickes*. Vol. II, *The Inside Struggle, 1936–1939*, and Vol. III, *The Lowering Clouds, 1939–1941*. New York: Simon and Schuster, 1954.

Isaacson, Walter, and Evan Thomas. *The Wise Men: Six Friends and the World They Made*. New York: Touchstone, 1986.

James, D. Clayton. *The Years of MacArthur*, Vol. III, *Triumph and Disaster 1945–1964*. Boston: Houghton Mifflin Company, 1985.

Kolodziej, Edward A. *The Uncommon Defense and Congress, 1945–1963*. Columbus: Ohio State University Press, 1966.

Langer, William L., and S. Everett Gleason. *The Challenge to Isolation, 1937–40*. New York: Harper & Row, 1952.

Leffler, Melvyn P. *A Preponderance of Power: National Security, the Truman Administration and the Cold War.* Stanford, Calif.: Stanford University Press, 1992.

Lie, Trygve. *In the Cause of Peace.* New York: Macmillan, 1954.

Lilienthal, David E. *The Journals of David E. Lilienthal.* Vol. II, *The Atomic Energy Years, 1945–1959.* New York: Harper Row, 1964.

Manchester, William. *American Caesar: Douglas MacArthur, 1880–1964.* Boston: Little, Brown and Company, 1978.

McCullough, David. *Truman.* New York: Simon & Schuster, 1992.

McFarland, Keith D. *Harry H. Woodring: A Political Biography of FDR's Controversial Secretary of War.* Lawrence: University Press of Kansas, 1975.

McLellan, David S. *Dean Acheson: The State Department Years.* New York: Dodd, Mead and Company, 1976.

Merry, Robert W. *Taking on the World: Joseph and Stewart Alsop—Guardians of the American Century.* New York: Viking, 1996.

Miller, William E. *You Can't Tell by Looking at 'Em: My Fifty Years with Steptoe & Johnson.* Washington, D.C., 1981.

Millis, Walter A., ed. *The Forrestal Diaries.* New York: Viking, 1951.

Nitze, Paul, Ann M. Smith, and Stephen L. Rearden. *From Hiroshima to Glasnost: At the Center of Decision.* New York: Grove Weidenfeld, 1989.

Offner, Arnold A. *American Appeasement: United States Foreign Policy and Germany, 1933–1938.* Cambridge, Mass.: Belknap Press of Harvard University Press, 1969.

——. *Another Such Victory: President Truman and the Cold War, 1945–1953.* Stanford, Calif.: Stanford University Press, 2002.

Paige, Glenn D. *The Korean Decision, June 24–30, 1950.* New York: Free Press, 1968.

Pogue, Forrest C. *George C. Marshall: Education of a General, 1889–1939.* New York: Viking, 1963.

——. *George C. Marshall: Ordeal and Hope, 1939–1943.* New York: Viking, 1966.

——. *George C. Marshall: Statesman, 1945–1959.* New York: Viking, 1987.

Rearden, Steven. *History of the Office of the Secretary of Defense.* Vol. 1. *The Formative Years, 1947–1950.* Washington, D.C.: U.S. Government Printing Office, 1984.

Redding, Jack. *Inside the Democratic Party.* Indianapolis: Bobbs-Merrill, 1958.

Reynolds, David. *From Munich to Pearl Harbor: Roosevelt's America and the Origins of the Second World War.* Chicago: Ivan R. Dee, 2001.

Rogow, Arnold A. *James Forrestal: A Study of Personality, Politics and Policy.* New York: Macmillan Company, 1963.

Rosenman, Samuel I., ed. *The Public Papers of Franklin D. Roosevelt, 1940.* New York: MacMillan, 1941.

Rothe, Anna, ed. *Current Biography, 1949.* New York: H.W. Wilson, 1950.

Sebald, William J., and Russell Brinan. *With MacArthur in Japan: A Personal History of the Occupation.* New York: W.W. Norton & Company, 1965.

Shepley, James R., and Clay Blair, Jr. *The Hydrogen Bomb: The Men, the Menace, and the Mechanism.* New York: David McKay Co., 1954.

Sherwood, Robert. *Roosevelt and Hopkins: An Intimate History.* New York: Harper & Brothers, 1948.

Stebbins, Richard P. *The United States in World Affairs, 1949.* New York: Harper & Brothers, 1949.

——. *The United States in World Affairs, 1950.* New York: Harper & Brothers, 1951.

Stein, Harold, ed. *American Civil Military Decisions: A Book of Case Studies.* Tuscaloosa: University of Alabama Press, 1963.

Strauss, Lewis L. *Men and Decisions.* Garden City, N.Y.: Doubleday and Company, 1962.

Truman, Harry S. *Memoirs: Year of Decisions*. Garden City, N.Y.: Doubleday and
    Company, 1955.
———. *Memoirs: Years of Trial and Hope*. Garden City, N.Y.: Doubleday and Com-
    pany, 1956.
Truman, Margaret. *Harry S. Truman*. New York: William Morrow & Co., 1973.
Vandenberg, Arthur, Jr., ed. *The Private Papers of Senator Vandenberg*. Boston: Hough-
    ton Mifflin Company, 1952.
Weigley, Russell F. *History of the United States Army*. New York: Macmillan, 1967.
Weiss, Stuart L. *The President's Man: Leo Crowley and Franklin Roosevelt in Peace and
    War*. Carbondale: Southern Illinois University Press, 1996.
Wolpert, Stanley. *A New History of India*. New York: Oxford University Press, 1977.

Articles

Alexander, Jack. "Stormy New Boss of the Pentagon." *Saturday Evening Post*, July 30,
    1949.
"Arms Before Men." *Time*, August 22, 1938.
Bell, James A. "Defense Secretary Louis Johnson." *The American Mercury*, June 1950.
Blum, Albert A. "Birth and Death of the M-Day Plan." In *American Civil Military De-
    cisions: A Book of Case Studies*, ed. Harold Stein. Tuscaloosa: University of Ala-
    bama Press, 1963.
"Boot for Johnson." *Newsweek*, September 25, 1950.
Burlingame, Roger. "The Counter Attack." *The Atlantic Monthly*, November 1933.
Coffin, Tris. "How We Almost Missed the H-Bomb." *Coronet*, September 1953.
Conley, Phil. "A Young Man of Vision." *West Virginia Review*, July 1932.
Haight, John McVickar, Jr. "Roosevelt as Friend of France." *Foreign Affairs Quarterly*
    44, no. 3 (April 1966).
Hammond, Paul Y. "NSC-68: Prologue to Rearmament." In Warner R. Schilling, Paul
    Y. Hammond, and Glenn H. Snyder, *Strategy, Politics, and Defense Budgets*. New
    York: Columbia University Press, 1962.
———. "Super Carriers and B-36 Bombers: Appropriations, Strategy and Politics." In
    American Civil Military Decisions: A Book of Case Studies, ed. Harold Stein.
    Tuscaloosa: University of Alabama Press, 1963.
Johnson, Louis. "The World Situation as I See It." *National Defense News*, May–June
    1948.
"Johnson or Truman in '52?" *U.S. News & World Report*, October 28, 1949.
"Master of the Pentagon." *Time*, June 6, 1949.
McFarland, Keith D. "F.D.R. and the Great War Department Feud." *Army*, March
    1976.
———. "The 1949 Revolt of the Admirals." *Parameters*, June 1981.
Mitchell, Jonathan. "M-Day Man: Louis Johnson." *The New Republic*, February 22,
    1939.
"Mr. Secretary Johnson." *Newsweek*, July 25, 1949.
Rao, B. Shiva. "India, 1935–47." In *The Partition of India: Policies and Perspectives,
    1935–1947*, ed. C. H. Philips and Mary D. Wainright. London: George Allen and
    Union Ltd., 1970
Rosenberg, David Alan. "American Atomic Strategy and the Hydrogen Bomb Deci-
    sion." *Journal of American History* (June 1979).
"Scandalous Spats." *Time*, October 9, 1939.

Smith, Beverly. "Why We Went to War in Korea." *Saturday Evening Post*, November 1, 1951.

Stutler, Boyd B. "A Prominent West Virginian." *The West Virginia Review*, May 1931.

Waggoner, Walter. "Now Louis Johnson Tackles It." *New York Times Magazine*, April 3, 1949.

Warner, Albert L. "How the Korean Decision Was Made." *Harper's Magazine*, June 1951.

INDEX

Acheson, Dean: and Asia and Far East policy, 251–53, 262–64; and budget cuts, 189, 193; and China policy, 251, 253–57; criticized, 292; and destroyer deal, 112; and electoral politics, 335; feud with LJ, 225, 320–21; and foreign policy, 363; and Formosa issue, 255–57, 257–61, 279–80, 320; and Japan, 267–71, 272–74; and Korean War, 265–67, 276–79, 283–85, 288–93, 295–96, 298, 299, 301, 304, 307, 309–10, 318, 326–27, 333; and LJ's downfall, 320, 323–26, 348, 350, 353; and MacArthur's VFW speech, 329–31; mental illness accusations, 2, 156, 354; and military assistance, 240–44; and NATO, 234, 237, 239, 246–49; and NSC 68, 224–25, 227–29, 231; and nuclear weapons, 211–13, 217, 220–24; and Vietnam, 264

Adjusting Your Business to War (Cherne), 80

Ailes, Steve, 16, 357

air bases, 55

Air Force: and atomic blitz theory, 183, 186, 208–10; base closures, 198; and budget cuts, 176, 180, 194–95; and Korean War, 285–86, 288–89, 313; Long Range Detection System, 214; and military unification, 162; personnel cutbacks, 202; racial integration, 164–65; reserves, 314–15; service secretaries, 156–57; and supercarrier cancellation, 175

air power and aircraft: and atomic blitz theory, 183, 186, 208–10; B-12 bombers, 69–71, 69–73; B-17 bombers, 38–39, 93, 98; B-18 bombers, 68; B-29 bombers, 293; B-36 bombers, 148, 171–73, 176–78, 183, 185–87, 231; C-54 (Belgian aircraft), 310; Germany, 57–58; Hawk 75-A aircraft, 68; and Korean War, 280–82, 285–86, 288–89,

298, 300, 313, 326–27; and military unification, 171; P-36 aircraft, 67; P-40 aircraft, 69; production of, 60, 87, 92–95; rearmament program, 58–67, 73, 76, 85; sales, 67–73, 85–89, 89–90, 96–98; Yak fighters, 284

aircraft carriers, 158, 173–76, 180, 183–87

Alaska, 55, 56

Alcan Highway, 56

Alexander, Albert, 246

Alexander, William R., 336

"alien property," 127–29

Allen, Robert, 44, 163

alliances, 228, 233, 234–49

Allied Expeditionary Force, 24

All-India Congress, 124, 127

All-India Radio, 125

allocations, 50–52

Alsop, Joseph, 44, 158–59, 163, 333, 347–48

Alsop, Stewart, 158–59, 333, 337, 347–48

Alvarez, Luis, 219

ambition of LJ: early career, 14–17; FDR's manipulation of, 106–107; and LJ's downfall, 321–22, 351; presidential ambitions, 154, 258, 320; and social skills, 29; VP bid, 101–103; *vs.* principle, 359–61; and Washington connections, 112

American Bar Association, 345, 349

American Legion: endorsement of LJ candidacy, 101–102; founded, 20; and fundraising efforts, 134; at LJ's funeral, 358; LJ's involvement in, 21, 24–26, 160–61; national convention, 80; postwar issues, 129–30; and Truman campaign, 140–41

Anderson, August, 197

Andrews, Frank Maxwell, 38

Anglo-French Purchasing Committee, 86, 89–90

appeasement, 283, 286, 329
appropriations bills, 92, 95, 191–95, 315
Arends, Leslie, 45, 162
Argentina, 38–39
arms sales, 84. *See also* air power and aircraft
Army: base closures, 198; and budget cuts, 180,
     194–95; combat readiness, 202; expansion
     of, 91, 314–15; force size, 61; and Korean
     War, 312, 313; and military unification,
     169; racial integration, 157, 164–65; ser-
     vice secretaries, 156–57
Army Air Corps, 62, 85, 169
Army and Navy Journal, 66, 148
Army Corps of Engineers, 56
Army-Navy Munitions Board, 54, 86
Arnold, Fortas & Porter, 356
Arnold, Hap: and air rearmament, 60–62; and
     aircraft sales, 69–72, 86–90, 96; LJ's rela-
     tionship with, 112; and LJ's resignation,
     106; and military unification, 169
arrogance of LJ, 82, 101, 360–61
Arthur, America, 5
Arthur, James Lewis, 5, 8, 14, 17
Arthur, Katherine Leftwich, 4, 6, 7, 21
Arthur family, 5
Articles of War, 20
Asia. *See* foreign policy; *specific countries*
assertiveness of LJ, 37, 42
Associated Press, 71
Atlantic Charter, 116–17
Atomic Energy Act, 206, 213
Atomic Energy Commission, 206, 209, 211, 214,
     217–19, 221–23
atomic weapons. *See* nuclear weapons
Attlee, Clement, 307
Austin, Warren R., 238, 290
Australia, 307–308, 309
Axis powers, 127
Ayers, Eben, 187
Azad, Maulana Abul Kalam, 122

B-12 bombers, 69–73
B-17 bombers, 38–39, 93, 98
B-18 bombers, 68
B-29 bombers, 293
B-36 bombers, 148, 171–73, 176–78, 183, 185–87,
     231
Bajpai, Girja Shankar, 117
Baldwin, Hanson, 334, 348
Bankhead, William, 102, 103
Barkley, Alben, 136, 212, 234, 293
Barlow, Lester, 151

Barron's, 348
Baruch, Bernard: fundraising efforts, 137; and
     LJ's resignation, 99–100; and mobiliza-
     tion, 49–50, 52–53, 56; and the War Re-
     sources Board, 76–78, 81–82
Battle, Lucius, 321
Beatty, Morgan, 197
Bedford County, Virginia, 4–6, 13
Belgium, 92, 310
Bell, Lawrence D., 57
Bell Aircraft, 57
Berle, Adolf, Jr., 84, 112, 113, 117–20
Berlin Airlift, 131, 237
Bethesda Naval Hospital, 153
Bevin, Ernest, 235
biased neutrality, 83–84
Biddle, Francis, 341
Bierwirth, John, 355
Biltmore Hotel, 139
Birmingham, Alabama, 11
Blair, Clay, 3
Blair House, 211–12, 214–15, 278–79, 284, 289,
     304, 340
Blake, Ed, 25
Blandy, William Henry Purnell, 185
Blaustein, Jacob, 140
Blue Ridge Division, 19, 28
Bogan, Gerald P., 182, 185
Bohemian Grove, 105, 106, 256
Bohlen, Charles "Chip," 230, 235, 318
Bolling Field, 60, 105
bombers. *See* air power and aircraft
Bonus Army, 26–29
Boone, Joe J., 199–200
Boykins, Frank W., 197
Boyle, William M., Jr., 342
Bradley, Mary, 271
Bradley, Omar: and Asia and Far East policy,
     262–63, 271; and bombing in North Ko-
     rea, 327; and budget cuts, 195; and con-
     gressional hearings, 182–85; and Formosa
     issue, 261, 263, 273, 279; and Harmon Re-
     port, 210; and Inchon invasion, 317; and
     Japan, 269, 270, 273, 274; and Korean
     War, 276–78, 280–82, 286, 288, 292, 296–
     97, 299, 304, 306, 308, 311; and Mac-
     Arthur's VFW speech, 332; and military
     assistance, 242, 244; and NATO, 245–47;
     and NSC 68, 226–27, 228; and nuclear
     weapons, 215, 219; relationship with LJ,
     159; and supercarrier project, 173
brain operation, 354

Bridges, Henry Styles, 45, 254, 283, 334
Brinkley, Douglas, 147
Britain. *See* Great Britain
Brooklyn Naval Yard, 197
Brooks, Overton, 162
Brussels Pact, 236
budget cuts: Air Force, 176, 180, 194–95; Army, 180, 194–95; and the Cold War, 166, 203, 204; Defense Department, 188, 194; and Korean War, 188–205, 315, 333–34; LJ accused of bias, 180; LJ's legacy, 359; LJ's task, 154; and military unification, 170, 193; and National Security Act, 179, 193; Navy, 176, 180, 194–95, 198; and NSC 68, 224–31; and nuclear weapons, 186, 203, 205, 208, 219–20; personnel cutbacks, 196–98, 198–201, 202, 208; speeches on, 201; and supercarrier cancellation, 158, 173–76, 183–87; and Truman, 163, 166, 176, 188–95, 203–204, 362
Buenos Aires, Argentina, 38–39
Bullitt, William C., 58, 59, 67, 68–69, 70
Bureau of the Budget, 93
Burke, Arleigh, 181, 185
Burke-Wadsworth Selective Service Act, 54, 111
Burns, James H.: and air rearmament, 62, 65; and Korean War, 283, 306, 310; on LJ's temper, 156; and NSC 68, 226–32; and nuclear weapons, 219; Pentagon appointed, 161; relationship with LJ, 112; and the War Resources Board, 77; and World War II, 84
Burns, James MacGregor, 3, 47
Bush, Vannevar, 205, 214–15
Business Weekly, 100
Butler, Robert, 139
Byrd, Harry F., 197
Byrnes, James, 102

Cable, John, 71
Cairo Declaration, 265
Calder, Curtis, 157, 160
Cambodia, 264
Camp Lee, 19
campaign finance, 138–44
Canada, 210–14, 308
Career Compensation Act, 200
carriers, 180
Carter, Josiah T., 14, 15, 18, 21
Caufield, Leo, 17
Central Intelligence Agency (CIA), 259, 261, 267, 303, 318

Ceylon (Sri Lanka), 127
Chamber of Commerce, 23
Chang, John M., 284
"change orders," 88
Charleston, West Virginia, 15, 23
Chemidlin, Paul, 71
Cherne, Leo, 80
Chestnut Lodge, 114
Chiang Kai-shek, 253, 263, 297, 307, 322–26, 350, 363
Chicago Tribune, 348
Childs, Marquis, 147, 322, 348
China: China Aid Act, 253, 254; China Lobby, 254, 256–57, 262, 324, 360, 363; China White Paper, 255–57; and communism, 253–55; and Formosa issue, 255–57, 257–61, 324–25, 326; and Japan, 268; and Korean War, 281, 286, 290, 295, 301, 315; in MacArthur's VFW speech, 329; and military assistance, 250–51; and Pacific War, 125; Truman's policy on, 362; and Vietnam, 264
Chinese Nationalists. *See* Chiang Kai-shek; Formosa (Taiwan)
Christ Episcopal Church, 15, 23, 357
Church, John, 288
Churchill, Winston, 96, 116, 119–21, 121–37
civil rights, 133, 135, 136, 164–65
Civilian Conservation Corps, 54
civilian employees of the military, 196–98
Clark, Bennett Champ, 45, 65, 72
Clark, George Rogers, 150
Clark, Grenville, 97–98
Clarksburg, West Virginia, 11–12, 14
Clarksburg Exponent, 14
Clifford, Clark, 144, 354
coal industry, 12
Cohen, Ben, 112
Cold War: and Asia and Far East policy, 251–53; and budget cuts, 166, 203, 204; impact on Truman, 131; and Korean War, 189, 265–67, 301, 303; and military unification, 170; and NATO, 236; and NSC 68, 224–31, 225. *See also* Soviet Union
Cole, Will H., 14
Collins, Harry E., 85, 87, 281
Collins, J. Lawton "Lightning Joe": and Formosa, 259; and Inchon invasion, 316–17, 353; and Japan, 268; and Korean War, 278, 281, 286, 292, 296–97; and MacArthur's VFW speech, 329; relationship with LJ, 159

Commission on Postwar America, 129
communism: and Asia and Far East policy,
      252, 262, 263–64; domination of foreign
      policy, 362–63; and fall of China, 253–55;
      and Japan, 268–69; and Korean War, 284,
      288; spread of, 166, 203, 320; and VFW,
      26. *See also* Cold War; Soviet Union
Compton, Karl T., 77, 220
Cone, Carrol, 139–40
confirmation hearings, 151
Congress: and air rearmament, 63, 65, 67; and
      aircraft sales, 85; appropriations bills, 92,
      95; Aviation Policy Board, 171; and budget
      cuts, 190, 191–95; Committee on Atomic
      Energy, 211, 212–13, 215–16, 219, 222; criti-
      cized, 135; critics of LJ in, 162–63; and
      German aggression, 92; and isolationism,
      48, 65; and Korean War, 286, 287–89, 292,
      299–300, 302, 304, 314–15, 333–34; and LJ's
      downfall, 106, 346–47, 351; MacArthur
      hearings, 352–53; and military assistance,
      240–45; and mobilization, 51, 52; and Na-
      tional Security Act, 179, 340; and NATO,
      235; and Neutrality Act, 83, 84; and nu-
      clear weapons, 208–209, 221–23; and the
      revolt of the admirals, 158, 174–79, 181–87;
      support for LJ in, 162; and surplus weap-
      onry, 202; and Truman campaign, 141. *See
      also* House of Representatives; Senate;
      specific individuals
Conley, Phil, 25
Connally, Richard, 162
Connally, Tom, 212, 240, 283–84, 288
Connelly, Matthew, 143, 145
conservatism, 35
Consolidated Vultee Aircraft Corporation. *See*
      Convair
Consolidation Directive No. 1, 172, 180
contracts with the U.S. government, 39–40, 95,
      244
Convair (Consolidated Vultee Aircraft Corpo-
      ration), 128–29, 139, 148, 150, 172–73, 176–
      78
Coolidge, Calvin, 23
Coolidge, Marcus, 33
Corber, Jack, 355–56
Corcoran, Thomas, 45, 106, 258, 259
Cornwell, John J., 16, 17, 22
Council for National Defense, 17, 79
Covington & Burling, 356
Craig, Malin, 32, 38–42, 60–62, 64–65, 69, 72
Cripps, Stafford, 119–21, 122, 126

critics of LJ, 56, 159, 161–62, 239, 334–35
Crommelin, John G., 181, 185
cronyism charges, 160–61
Crowley, Leo, 127–28
Cummings, Homer S., 31
Curtis P-40 fighters, 69
Curtis-Wright Corporation, 57
Czechoslovakia, 58

Daladier, Edouard, 69
Daniels, Jonathan, 103
Daughters of the American Revolution, 236–
      38
Davies, John, 227
Davis, Arthur, 291
Davis, John W., 14–15, 22, 23, 129, 130
Davis & Davis, 14
Davis Polk & Wardwell, 14, 129
death of LJ, 357–58
Defense Assistance Program, 240
Defense Committee (NATO), 245–48, 249
Defense Department: and Asia policy, 262; and
      budget cuts, 188, 194; and China White
      Paper, 256–57; created, 131; and Formosa
      issue, 256–57, 258–61, 263; and Japan, 268,
      271–72, 274; and Korean War, 266, 275,
      282, 287–90, 305, 313, 318, 333; and LJ's res-
      ignation, 348; and NSC 68, 225–31, 232;
      and nuclear weapons, 208, 218, 222. *See
      also* Pentagon; *specific individuals*
Defense Ministry (India), 121
Dekker, Dirk, 118
"delay orders," 88
Delta Chi fraternity, 10
demobilization, 208
Democratic National Committee (DNC), 113,
      133–34, 138–44
Democratic National Convention, 101–102, 136
Democratic Party: and civil rights, 136; corrup-
      tion in, 127; and electoral politics, 335;
      fundraising efforts, 137–38; LJ as a liabil-
      ity, 337; and LJ's downfall, 343, 351; and
      LJ's House of Delegates campaign, 15–16;
      LJ's involvement in, 21, 23, 130, 134; LJ's
      mayoral campaign, 14–15; LJ's VP candi-
      dacy, 100, 101–103; support for LJ, 32; and
      Truman campaign, 133; Veterans Com-
      mittee, 29, 31
Denfeld, Louis, 159, 173–74, 181–83, 185–87, 210
Denham, Sherman C., 14
Denmark, 246
Dennison, Robert L., 146, 209

Department of Defense, 154, 180
Dern, George H., 30
deterrence, 209, 246
Detroyat, Michael, 68
Dewey, Thomas, 97, 134, 135, 137, 142, 160
Dewey Ballantine, 129
Dillon Read, 227
Dinner Key, 142
diplomacy, 245–48
disability benefits, 26–29
Distinguished Service Medal, 152
Dixiecrats, 136, 142
Dixon, George, 342
Dobie, Armistead, 9
Dodona Manor, 322
Donnell, Forrest, 239
Douglas, William O., 135–36
draft, 54
Drum, Hugh, 41–42
Dubinsky, David, 140
Dulles, John Foster, 241, 270–72, 274, 295
Durham, Carl, 212

Early, Stephen: on Canal Zone bids, 40; considered for secretary of war, 31; and Formosa issue, 261; and isolationism, 113; and
    Korean War, 283, 288, 292, 310; and LJ's
    correspondence, 115; and LJ's resignation, 99–100, 105–107, 337–38, 342–45; at
    LJ's swearing in, 35; and MacArthur's
    VFW speech, 331; and nuclear weapons,
    215, 219; and personnel cutbacks, 196; and
    public relations, 159–60, 163–64; relationship with LJ, 28–29, 112; on South
    American bomber flight, 39; support of
    LJ, 128, 130; and the War Resources
    Board, 81; and Woodring, 32, 44, 97
Eberstadt, Ferdinand, 148, 169
Eccles, Marriner, 133
economization of the military, 168, 172, 179,
    188, 189–91, 232–33. See also budget cuts
economy, 26, 75, 169, 197, 235, 248. See also
    budget cuts
Economy Act, 27
Edison, Charles, 60, 77, 79
education of LJ, 8–10
educational orders, 50–52, 64, 65, 76
ego of LJ, 152, 154, 201, 345, 361
Ehrlich, Henry, 44
80th Division (Blue Ridge Division), 19
82nd Airborne Division, 311
Eisenhower, Dwight D.: and Forrestal, 150;

and Korean War, 294; and LJ's appointment, 172; and military unification, 169;
    and nuclear secrecy, 212; as presidential
    candidate, 135; relationship with LJ, 159;
    and supercarrier cancellation, 173; support of LJ, 145–46
elections: Al Smith campaign, 23; campaign
    finance issues, 138–44; FDR campaigns,
    26, 29, 31, 101–103, 113; fundraising efforts,
    134, 138–44; House of Delegates campaign
    of LJ, 15–16; liability of LJ, 335–37, 343, 351;
    mayoral campaign of LJ, 14–15; midterm
    elections, 59, 73, 337; organizational skills
    of LJ, 20, 25; public opinion, 135; Truman,
    1, 131–32, 133–43, 141; VP bid of LJ, 101–103;
    whistlestop campaign, 139, 141
electric power, 55, 56
Elks, 23
Elkview Masonic Cemetery, 358
Emanuel, Victor, 55, 128, 157
Embrick, Stanley, 41
enemies of LJ, 346. See also critics of LJ
Engel, Albert J., 195, 197
England. See Great Britain
Eniwetok Atoll, 224
Episcopal Church, 15, 23, 357
espionage, 213
Evans, Tom, 140
Executive Order No. 9877, 171
Executive Order No. 9981, 164

factory allocations, 50–52
Faddis, Charles, 45, 65
Fahy Committee, 164–65
Fair Deal, 251
Far East. See specific countries
Farley, James A., 32–35, 45, 103, 109
Farmer, Guy, 131
fascism, 49, 80
Federal Advisory Council, 29
Fields, Alonzo, 279
finances of LJ, 14, 23
Finland, 96
Finletter, Thomas, 156, 159, 171, 278, 344
fitness of LJ, 8, 10, 18, 22
Fleeson, Doris, 147
Ford, Gerald, 98
Foreign Affairs Committee, 241, 244
foreign aid, 224–31, 235, 237
foreign policy: Asia and Far East policy, 251–
    53, 261–64, 271; China, 362; communism's domination of, 362–63; FDR, 46–

47, 62–65, 73, 98, 361–62; Formosa, 257–61; Japan, 267–71; Korea, 265–67; MacArthur's VFW speech, 328–32, 335–36, 351; and military assistance, 240–45; and NSC 68, 224–31; Truman, 142, 363; Vietnam, 264–65

Foreign Relations Committee, 240

Formosa (Taiwan): Acheson on, 255–57, 257–61, 279–80, 320; Chiang regime in, 254; and China White Paper, 255–57; diplomatic sensitivity, 324–26; and Far East policy, 271–74; and fear of communism, 363; and Korean War, 273–74, 277–80, 285–87, 289, 292, 296, 301, 323–26; and LJ's downfall, 323–24, 350–51, 360; LJ's position on, 257–61; MacArthur speech on, 328–32; and military assistance, 250, 259–60, 261, 273; and NATO, 250; and political divisions, 261–64

Forrestal, James: accomplishments, 168; and B-36 purchases, 173, 178; and budget cuts, 191, 193; compared to LJ, 162, 187; funeral, 153; memos to LJ, 155; mental health problems, 145–46, 150; and military unification, 147–48, 169–71; and NATO, 237; resignation, 147–49, 151–52; as secretary of defense, 131; and Truman campaign, 139

Forrestal, Josephine, 148

Fort Harrison, 18

France: and air power, 59; aircraft purchases, 67–68, 73, 85; attacked, 92; and German air power, 58; and NATO, 246; surrender, 98

Frankfurter, Felix, 97

Franklin, John, 160

French Legion of Honor Medal, 24

friendships of LJ, 15

Fuchs, Klaus, 213

fundraising, 134, 137–44

funeral, 357–58

fusion bomb. *See* hydrogen bomb

Gallahan, Daniel, 62

Gallery, Dan, 180

Gandhi, Mohandas K., 116, 124, 125, 127

General Advisory Committee (GAC), 218–19, 220

General Aniline and Film Company (GAF), 127–29, 150

General Dyestuff, 127–29, 150

George VI, 75

German-Soviet Non-Aggression Pact, 78, 83

Germany: aggression, 58, 75–76, 79, 84, 90, 92; air strength, 57–58, 85; preparations for war, 48; rearmament debate, 249; submarine warfare, 16–17

Gibbons, Henry, 40

Gifford, Walter S., 77

Gleason, Everett, 227

Good Neighbor Policy, 38–39

Government of India Act, 116

Grace Church, 8

Grady, Henry F., 118, 125

Gray, Gordon, 157–58, 164–65

Great Britain: and air power, 59; aircraft purchases, 68, 85; British Expeditionary Force, 96; and German air power, 58; and India, 116–17; and Korean War, 307, 309; and nuclear secrets, 210–14; and Pacific War Aims, 125; War Cabinet (Britain), 122

Great Depression, 26, 48, 75, 169

Greenfield, Albert, 140

Griffith, Paul, 25, 118, 160, 258–59, 358

Guiher, Jim, 24, 112, 114

Gurney, Chan, 151, 162

Halaby, Najeeb E., 161, 227

Halsey, William W. "Bull," 181, 182

Hamby, Alonzo, 3

Harmon, Hubert R., 210

Harmon Board, 209–10

Harriman, Averell: and Inchon invasion, 317; and Korean War, 292–93, 295; and LJ-Acheson feud, 321–22; and LJ's downfall, 347–48, 350; and MacArthur, 325–26, 329–32; and Truman campaign, 143

Harrington, Arthur W., 118

Harrison, Davis, Haymond and Maxwell, 12

Harrison, Thomas W., 114

Harrison County, West Virginia, 12–13

Harrison County Bar Association, 23

Harrison House, 114

Harsch, Joseph C., 147

Harter, Dow, 45, 87

Hatfield, Henry Drury, 16

Hawk 75-A aircraft, 68

Haynes, Elizabeth, 5

health issues, 114, 126, 353–55, 357

Helis, William, 140

Hell's Bottom, 155

Hersey, Lewis B., 314

Hickenlooper, Bourke, 212–13, 216, 239, 348

Hickerson, John D., 279
Highland, Virgil L., 14
highway system, 55–56
Hillenkoetter, Roscoe Henry, 292
Hinton, Harold, 300
Hitler, Adolph, 58, 63, 75–76, 83, 361
Ho Chi Minh, 263, 301
hobbies of LJ, 114
Hogan & Hartson, 356
Holland, 92
Hollywood, 142
honeymoon, 21
honors bestowed on LJ, 24, 25, 46, 110
Hoopes, Townsend, 147
Hoover, Herbert, 26, 184
Hoover, J. Edgar, 106
Hope, Victor Alexander John (Lord Linlithgow), 116, 120, 122
Hopkins, Harry: and air rearmament, 62; and aircraft procurement, 58–59; and Indian independence, 122–24, 126–27; and LJ-Woodring feud, 45; on Marshall, 42; resignation, 106–107; on Woodring departure, 32
hospital closings, 199–200
House of Representatives: appropriations bills, 191–95; Appropriations Committee, 92, 194–95, 200, 232–33; Armed Services Committee, 163, 177, 179, 181–87, 193–95, 199–200; and China White Paper, 257; Foreign Affairs Committee, 241, 244; and Korean War, 290, 293; LJ's critics in, 45; Military Affairs Committee, 87–88, 89; and military assistance, 240–45; and military unification, 170
Houser, Robert, 227
housing, 200–201
Hull, Cordell, 56, 84, 96, 103, 117, 125
Humelsine, Carlisle, 321
Humphrey, Hubert, 136
hydrogen bomb, 217–24

I Never Promised You a Rose Garden (Greenberg), 114
Ickes, Harold, 32, 44, 45, 55, 97, 102
ideological divisions, 35
I.G. Farben, 127
Ikenberry, Henry, 128, 143
impatience of LJ, 354–55
Inauguration Day, 145
Inchon invasion, 316–19, 338, 344, 353
independence movements, 116–21

India, 116–21, 121–27
Indian National Congress, 116, 118–22, 124
Indian Press Association, 124–25
Indochina, 264, 280, 285
industrial mobilization, 12, 35, 47, 49, 52–54, 56, 76–82
Industrial Mobilization Board, 76
Industrial Mobilization Plan, 52–53, 56, 76–81, 78, 82
insubordination of LJ, 37, 40, 43
integration of the military, 157, 164–65
international law, 237
internationalism, 362
isolationism: and air power, 63, 71–73; and Congress, 48, 65; and FDR, 2, 47–48, 92, 359; and Lindbergh, 113; LJ's speeches against, 50, 115; and military preparedness, 48, 107; and the Pentagon project, 154; and public opinion, 48, 50, 53, 58; and War Department, 74; and Woodring, 359
Israel, 140
Italy, 48, 98, 309

Jackson, Robert, 62
Jackson, Thomas Jonathan "Stonewall," 5, 14
James, Jack, 275
Janeway, Eliot, 56
Japan: and Asia and Far East policy, 262, 363; and Formosa, 258; and Korean War, 286; and Pacific War, 117, 118, 124–25, 127; peace treaty, 267–71, 271–74; Pearl Harbor attack, 56; preparations for war, 48
Jarvis, Lillian, 18
Jefferson, Thomas, 5, 9, 13, 234
Jessup, Philip C., 269, 279
Jewish community, 140
Jinnah, Mohammad Ali, 116
Johnson, Edwin, 45, 221
Johnson, J. Monroe, 32
Johnson, John Wesley, 5–6
Johnson, Kay (daughter), 151–52
Johnson, Lillian (daughter), 21, 114, 150–52
Johnson, Louis Arthur: ambition, 14–17, 29, 100–103, 106–107, 112, 152, 154, 258, 320, 322, 351, 359–61; arrogance, 82, 101, 360–61; assertiveness, 37, 42; death, 357–58; decision-making style, 162; education, 8–10; ego, 152, 154, 201, 345, 361; finances, 14, 23; fitness, 8, 10, 18, 22; friendships, 15; health issues, 114, 126, 353–55, 357; hobbies, 114; honors bestowed, 24, 25, 46, 110; insubordination, 37, 40, 43; legacy, 107,

358–60, 362; loyalty, 107, 138, 149, 166, 189, 349, 352–53, 360; marriage, 20–21, 114; military service, 17–20, 23; negotiation skills, 121–26; office of, 149–50, 155; oratorical skills, 10, 16, 25–26, 50, 65, 361; organizational skills, 8, 20, 24, 25, 29, 30, 31, 56, 130, 134, 159, 320, 361; pets, 114; resignations, 1, 99–100, 103–107, 105, 320–38, 339–51, 353; social skills, 12–13, 23, 101, 361; spiritual life, 8, 15; work ethic, 7, 91, 155–56

Johnson, Lyndon, 334, 357
Johnson, Marcellus Alexander, 4–7, 21
Johnson, Martin, 6
Johnson, Ruth Maxwell, 21–22, 114, 145, 151, 271, 342, 347, 358
Joint Army and Navy Munitions Board, 77
Joint Chiefs of Staff (JCS): and budget cuts, 194–95; and China White Paper, 256–57; and Formosa, 255, 257–61, 323–25; and Harmon Report, 210; and Inchon invasion, 316–17; and Japan, 267–69, 268–69, 270; and Korean War, 280, 282–84, 289, 291, 293, 295–98, 305–12, 314; and LJ's retirement, 349; and military assistance, 240, 244; and military unification, 170; and NATO, 248; and NSC 68, 226–27, 230–31; and nuclear weapons, 217–21; and supercarrier cancellation, 175; and Vietnam, 264
Joint Congressional Aviation Policy Board, 171
Joint Congressional Committee on Atomic Energy, 211, 212–13, 215–16, 219, 222
Joint Strategic Survey Committee (JSSC), 227, 291
Jones, Jesse, 102
Jones Day, 356
Judd, Walter H., 254
Judiciary Committee, 16

Kannee, Henry, 88
Kearny, Jean, 133, 138, 142–43
Kennan, George, 227, 230, 318
Kennedy, John F., 357
Kennedy, Joseph P., 84, 178
Kennedy, Robert, 357
Key West, 147–48
Kilgore, Harley, 147, 264
Kimball, Dan A., 176, 181
Kim Il Sung, 263, 265–66, 301
King, Ernest J., 169, 183
Kinkaid, Thomas C., 182

Kintner, Robert, 44
Kirkland & Ellis, 356
Knowland, William, 212–13, 254, 260, 283
Knox, Frank, 97
Knudsen, William S., 95
Koo, Wellington, 258
Korean Military Advisory Group, 266, 276
Korean War: and air power, 285–86, 288–89, 313, 326–27; and Asia and Far East policy, 263–64, 363; attacks into North Korea, 318–19; and budget cuts, 188–205, 315, 333–34; and China, 281, 286, 290, 295, 301, 315; and communism, 284, 288; and communist threat, 248, 288; escalation, 286–87; first reports, 276–82; and Formosa, 273–74, 277–80, 285–87, 287–88, 289, 292, 296, 301, 323–26; Inchon invasion, 316–18, 353; initial response, 282–87; and LJ's downfall, 332–35; and LJ's resignation, 1–2; MacArthur's leadership, 293–96, 296–300, 305–307; media coverage, 275, 300, 302, 332–34; and military assistance, 280, 283, 285–90, 307–10; military preparedness, 312–16, 348; North Korean attack, 275–76; and personnel cuts, 196–98; political response to, 290–93; strategic value, 265–67; 38th parallel, 318–19; troop requests, 310–12; Truman's position on, 300–303; and the UN, 265, 276, 278–79, 283, 285–89, 290, 300, 303–10, 304–305
Krock, Arthur, 84, 337, 348
Kronheim, Milton, 140

La Grange, Amaury de, 57, 67–68
LaGuardia, Fiorello, 30–31
Landis, James, 133
Landon, Alf, 31, 97
Landon, Truman H., 227
Langfitt, Frank, 24, 55–56, 114
Langfitt, Thomas, 354
Lanham, Henderson, 334
Laos, 264
LaRowe, John Sterling, 10
Latin America, 96
Lawrence, Earnest O., 219
law school, 9–10
leadership skills of LJ, 9–10, 93
League of Nations, 20
Leahy, William, 169, 172
LeBaron, Robert, 219, 227
Leffler, Melvyn, 3
Leftwich, Sarah, 6

Leftwich, Thomas, 5, 17
Leftwich family, 5
legislation sponsored by LJ, 16
Lemnitzer, Lyman, 161, 237, 264
lend-lease program, 56, 63, 111–12
Leva, Marx, 147, 149, 159, 163, 219, 320, 338
Lewis, Clyde, 328, 334
Lewis, Fulton, 88
Liaison Committee, 85–86, 87, 90
Lichtblau, Nathan, 139, 140
Lie, Trygve, 276, 309
Life, 97, 142, 348
Lilienthal, David E., 207, 209, 211–13, 215, 217–
    18, 220–21, 223–24
Lindbergh, Charles, 113
Lindley, Ernest, 101–102
Lippmann, Walter, 257
Li Tsung-jen, 254
Lodge, Henry Cabot, 92, 334
Loew's Incorporated, 356
Long, Huey, 140
Lord Amery, 126
Lord Linlithgow, 116, 120, 122
Lovett, Robert A., 235, 340
Loy, James, 227
loyalty of LJ, 107, 138, 149, 166, 189, 349, 352–53,
    360
Lucas, Scott, 304
Luce, Clare Booth, 135
Luce Publications, 254
Luftwaffe, 58

MacArthur, Douglas: assessment of Korean sit-
    uation, 280–82, 288–89; authority in Ko-
    rea, 293–96, 305–307; bombing of North
    Korea, 326; and the Bonus Army, 26; and
    Far East policy, 271–74; and Formosa,
    258, 260, 279–80, 323–26, 328–32; hear-
    ings, 2, 352–53; and Inchon invasion, 316–
    18, 318–19, 338, 344, 353; and Japan, 267–
    70, 270–71, 271–74; and LJ's downfall,
    322–26, 350–51, 360; and military
    buildup, 310–12, 312–16; and military
    unification, 169; and North Korean at-
    tack, 276, 282–87; on South Korean readi-
    ness, 266–67; and 38th parallel issue, 318;
    troop requests, 296–300; and UN forces,
    309; VFW speech, 328–32, 335–36, 351
MacGregor, Morris, 165
Mackall, Laidler, 250
Mackay Trophy, 39
Madame Chiang Kai-shek, 258–59, 323

Maddocks, Ray T., 227
Mahon, George, 204
Malik, Jacob Alexsandrovich, 290
Malone, George, 151, 283
Management Committee, 161, 199
Manhattan Project, 218
Mao Tse-tung, 253, 255, 263, 268, 286–87, 301,
    362
Marcantonio, Vito, 290
March, Peyton C., 20
Marine Corps, 174, 202, 313, 314, 337
marriage, 20–21, 114
Marshall, George Catlett: on air power, 38, 62–
    65; and aircraft sales, 86–89, 96, 98; as
    chief of staff, 40–42; and China policy,
    253; and LJ-Acheson feud, 322; LJ's rela-
    tionship with, 112; as LJ's replacement,
    340–41, 343, 345–47, 348–49; and LJ's res-
    ignation, 106; and military unification,
    169; and NATO, 235; and the Neutrality
    Act, 83; and racial integration, 165; and
    rearmament, 93; support of LJ, 42–43, 46,
    56, 145, 146; and Truman campaign, 142;
    and war readiness, 84; and the War Re-
    sources Board, 77
Marshall, Katherine, 40, 340
Marshall Plan, 131, 236, 251
Martin, Glenn L., 57, 151
Martin 166 aircraft, 69
Masons, 23
Matthews, Francis P., 158, 179, 181–83, 278, 328,
    341
Maxwell, Emma, 18
Maxwell, Ruth Frances, 17, 18, 21
Maxwell, Sue, 21
Maxwell, William Brent, 17–18
May, Andrew, 45, 65, 89
Maycock, Wellburn, 141
Mayer, Louis B., 356
Mayflower Hotel, 34
Mayo Clinic, 126, 353–54
McCarran, Pat, 254
McCarthy, Joseph, 257, 263, 360
McClellan, George, 150
McCloy, John J., 129, 160
McCullough, David, 3
McGrath, J. Howard, 134, 138
McIntyre, Marvin, 44
McMahon, Brien, 208, 211–12, 216, 219–21, 238
McNarney, Joseph T., 161, 180, 196, 199
McNary, Charles, 101
McNeil, Wilfred J., 149, 159

McNutt, Paul, 30, 33, 102
Medal for Merit, 46, 110
media. *See* press; radio; television; *specific pub-
    lications*
medical care, 200
Meet the Press, 164
mental health issues, 21, 114, 145–46, 353–55
Mesta, Perle, 144, 148
Meuse-Argonne offensive, 19
Michelson, Charles, 35
militarism, 48, 61
Military Affairs Committees, 33, 72, 87–88, 89
military assistance: and Asia and Far East pol-
    icy, 251; and Formosa, 250, 259–60, 261,
    273; and India, 117; and Korean War, 280,
    283, 285–90, 307–10; legislation support-
    ing, 300; and NATO, 237–38, 240–45,
    247, 248; and rearming Germany, 249;
    and Vietnam, 264–65
Military Assistance Program (MAP), 240, 249
Military Committee (NATO), 245
Military Liaison Committee, 206, 214, 220,
    230–31
Military Production and Supply Board, 245
military secrecy, 207–208
military service of LJ, 17–20, 23
military-industrial complex, 110, 359
Miller, Bill "Smokey," 131
Millis, Walter, 204
ministerial posting of LJ, 117–21
Minor, Raleigh, 9
Mitchell, Billy, 169
mobilization: and Baruch, 49–50, 52–53, 56;
    bottlenecks, 54–56; demobilization, 208;
    and factory allocations, 51; industrial, 12,
    35, 47, 49, 52–54, 56, 76–82; and Korean
    War, 286, 292; and LJ, 35, 47, 52–54, 362;
    and NSC 68, 224–31, 232; and Officer Re-
    serve Corps, 112–13; Protective Mobiliza-
    tion Plan, 60, 64, 91; War Department,
    52–54, 91; and Woodring, 49; World War
    II, 44. *See also* preparedness
Moist, Ronald, 114
Monnet, Jean, 67, 69
Monroe Doctrine, 238
Morgenthau, Henry, Jr.: and air rearmament,
    60, 62, 94; and aircraft sales, 69–70, 72–
    73, 85–87, 89–90, 96, 98; fired, 341; and
    LJ's resignation, 106; and LJ-Woodring
    feud, 45; and Woodring's removal, 97
Morris, Stanley, 112
Morse, Wayne Lyman, 348

Moulton, Harold, 77
Muccio, John, 266–67, 276, 284, 288
Munich crisis, 58, 75
Munitions Board, 77
Munitions Building, 76, 78
Murphy, Frank, 31
Murphy, J. Ray, 33
Muslim League, 116–17
Mutual Defense Assistance Act, 244, 261
Mutual Defense Assistance Program, 264, 283,
    300

National Defense Act, 35
National Defense Advisory Commission
    (NDAC), 94–95
National Defense Management Committee,
    180, 196
National Defense Power Committee, 55
National Distillers, 355
National Guard, 199, 313–14
National Guard Armory, 145
National Military Establishment, 131, 152, 154,
    167, 170, 190
National Press Club, 263, 292
National Recovery Act, 28
National Recovery Administration, 28
National Security Act: amendments, 157, 179;
    and budget cuts, 179, 193; Defense De-
    partment created, 131; and the Korean
    War, 189; and LJ's resignation, 346–47;
    and military unification, 168, 170–71, 179;
    and secretary of defense position, 340
National Security Council (NSC): and Asia
    and Far East policy, 252, 262; and For-
    mosa, 255, 260–61, 323; and Korean War,
    291–95, 306; NSC 8/2, 266; NSC 30, 208;
    NSC 48/2, 258, 263, 265; NSC 68, 204,
    224–32, 247, 313; NSC 81/1, 318; and nu-
    clear weapons, 217, 224–31; and Vietnam,
    264
nationalism, 116
Nationalist Government. *See* Chiang Kai-
    shek; Formosa (Taiwan)
Navy: and air rearmament, 65; aviation, 202; on
    B-12 bomber sales, 70; and budget cuts,
    176, 180, 194–95, 198; force size, 61; and
    Formosa, 258; and Korean War, 281–82,
    285–86, 288–89, 300, 313; and LJ's ap-
    pointment, 172; and military unification,
    162, 169, 186; and NATO, 247; offices, 35;
    personnel cutbacks, 202; procurement
    funds, 95; racial integration, 164–65; re-

serves, 314; "revolt of the admirals," 168–87; service secretaries, 156–57; super-carrier cancellation, 158, 173–76, 183–87
Neely, Matthew, 33–35, 113–14
negotiation skills, 121–26
Nehru, Jawaharlal, 116, 122, 124–27, 252–53
Nelson, Donald, 82, 95
Netherlands, 308
networking skills of LJ, 23
neutrality, 67, 83–84
Neutrality Act, 67, 68, 83, 84
New Deal, 49, 53, 55, 101, 133, 135–36
New York Times: on China policy, 254; criticism of LJ, 84; on destroyer deal, 112; on Korean War, 283, 300, 302, 334; on LJ's appointment, 148; on LJ's resignation, 348; on midterm elections, 337; on personnel cutbacks, 197–98; on supercarrier cancellation, 175; on the War Department, 97
New Zealand, 307–308
newspapers. *See* press
Newsweek, 216, 303
Nimitz, Chester W., 182
90th Division, 19–20
Nitze, Paul, 204, 227–29, 318, 348
Nizer, Louis, 356
Nolan, John, 357
nonintervention, 50
nonviolence, 124, 125
Norris, George, 65
North Atlantic Council, 247
North Atlantic Treaty Organization (NATO), 226, 234, 235, 236–40, 240–45, 245–50
North Korean Democratic People's Republic, 265–67
Norway, 246–47
Nourse, Edwin G., 191
nuclear weapons: atomic blitz theory, 183, 186, 208–10; and budget cuts, 186, 203, 205, 208, 219–20; and the Cold War, 166; espionage, 213; hydrogen bomb, 217–18, 218–24; and Korean War, 295; and military assistance, 242, 244; and military unification, 171; and NATO, 246; and NSC, 217, 224–32; nuclear secrecy, 210–14; size of arsenal, 206–208; and the Soviet Union, 205, 214–17, 221, 223; and Truman, 3, 205, 207–208, 212–15, 217–18, 220, 222–23
Nutter, Ruth, 131, 350, 355
Nye, Gerald P., 65, 115

occupation, 267–68

Odd Fellows, 23
Odlum, Floyd, 139, 148, 157, 176–78
office of LJ, 149–50, 155
Officer Reserve Corps, 112–13
Officer Training School, 17
Offner, Arnold, 3
Ohio, 22
Ohly, John M., 159
oil industry, 18
O'Kelliher, Victor, 258–59
Okinawa, 258, 262, 273, 281
O'Laughlin, C. O., 66
Old Executive Office Building, 35
Olds, Robert C., 39
Oliphant, Herman, 62
Oppenheimer, Robert, 214–15, 218–20
oratorical skills of LJ, 10, 16, 25–26, 50, 65, 361
orchids, 114
Organizational Policy and Research Division (Op 23), 181
organizational skills of LJ, 8, 20, 24, 25, 29, 30, 31, 56, 130, 134, 159, 320, 361
Organized Reserves, 199, 314
Ortiz, Robert M., 38–39

P-36 aircraft, 67
P-40 aircraft, 69, 86–87
Pace, Frank, Jr.: and budget cuts, 191; and Korean War, 275–76, 278, 281, 287, 296–97, 308; and nuclear weapons, 209; proposed cutbacks, 200
"Pacific War Aims," 125
Pakistan, 117, 127, 309
Palestine, 133
Pan Am, 355–56
Panama Canal, 39
Panhandle Eastern Pipeline Company, 355
patronage, 134–35
Patterson, Robert P., 97, 99, 103, 105, 129, 169–70
Pauley, Edwin, 140
Pearl Harbor, 56, 115
Pearson, Drew: on army secretary position, 157; on Asia policy, 262; on Early appointment, 160; on FDR, 109; on Forrestal, 146, 150; on LJ's downfall, 321, 337; LJ's relationship with, 163; on LJ-Woodring feud, 44
Pennsylvania, 22
Pentagon, 153–67, 199. *See also* Defense Department
People's Republic of China, 259. *See also* China
Pepper, Claude, 197

Perkins, Frances, 80
Pershing, John, 66, 78, 150
personnel cutbacks. *See* budget cuts
Personnel Policy Board, 164
pets of LJ, 114
Philippines, 258, 262, 285, 309
physical strength of LJ, 8, 10, 18, 22
Pike, Sumner T., 211, 212
Plumley, Charles, 195, 337
plutonium, 210. *See also* nuclear weapons
Poe, Edgar Allen, 9
Poland, 79
political ambitions of LJ, 14–17, 29, 100–103,
     258, 320, 322, 351
political campaigns. *See* elections
Pope Ballard, 356
Poplar Forest, 5, 13
population growth, 12
postwar plans, 129–30
Potsdam agreement, 260
Pratt, John, 77
preparedness: and the Cold War, 166; in the
     Far East, 281; and isolationism, 48, 107;
     LJ's legacy, 107, 358, 360; and LJ's resig-
     nation, 348; and LJ-Woodring feud, 45;
     and mobilization, 52–54; and NATO,
     245–48; and NSC 68, 224–31; speeches
     on, 66; support for LJ, 197–98. *See also*
     mobilization
Present at the Creation (Acheson), 2, 354
presidential ambitions of LJ, 154, 258, 320, 322
press: on air rearmament, 65; on B-12 crash, 71;
     on Korean War, 275, 300, 302, 332–34; on
     LJ's downfall, 322, 337; LJ's relationship
     with, 163–64; on LJ's resignation, 105,
     342, 347–48; on LJ-Woodring feud, 44;
     and MacArthur's VFW speech, 329–30;
     press corps, 163–64; on selective service,
     111; and Truman campaign, 141–42. *See
     also specific publications*
preventive war, 328, 335
procurement procedures: and air rearmament,
     60–61; B-36, 185–86; and B-12 bomber
     sales, 70; and B-36 purchases, 177; and
     budget cuts, 198–99; factory allocations,
     50–52; and LJ-Woodring feud, 38, 39; and
     military unification, 172; and NATO,
     247; and War Department, 95
Progressive Party, 135
Prospect House, 148
Protective Mobilization Plan, 60, 64, 91
public opinion: Burns on, 47; on FDR, 110; and

isolationism, 48, 50, 53, 58; on Korean
     War, 302; on LJ, 187; and NSC 68, 233; on
     nuclear weapons, 208, 221, 223; and presi-
     dential elections, 135; on rearmament,
     362; on Truman candidacy, 136, 141
public relations, 13, 53–54, 159–60, 163–64
public-speaking skills. *See* oratorical skills of LJ
Pullman Company, 160
Purvis, Arthur, 86–87

quarantine speech, 48, 361

racial integration, 157, 164–65
Radford, Arthur W., 182, 183, 185, 271, 294
radio, 140–41, 164, 201, 313, 349
railroads, 6–7, 80, 139, 141
Rashin, North Korea, 326–27
Rayburn, Sam, 212, 244
rearmament. *See* mobilization; preparedness
Redding, Jack, 138, 144
reformism of LJ, 14
Regimental Combat Team (RCT), 296–300,
     310–11
religious life of LJ, 8, 15
Renfrow, Louis, 147, 149, 150, 160–61, 175, 343–44
reorganization of the military. *See* unification
     of the military
Republic of Korea (ROK), 262, 263, 266–67,
     288. *See also* Korean War
Republican National Committee, 336
Republican Party: on bomber sales, 71–72; and
     China Lobby, 324; and FDR cabinet, 97;
     LJ's supporters in, 162; and MacArthur
     hearings, 352–53; midterm elections, 73;
     national convention, 101; presidential
     elections, 131–32, 135; and Truman ad-
     ministration, 322
Reserve Officers Association, 291
resignations of LJ, 1, 99–100, 103–107, 320–38,
     339–51, 353
Rhee, Syngman, 265–66, 274, 284, 306
Ridgeway, Matthew, 202–203
Rixey, John Strode, 11
Rixey & Johnson, 12
Roanoke, Virginia, 6–8
Roanoke Epworth League, 8
Roanoke Machine Works, 7
Robbins, Thomas H., 227
Roberts, W. Lynn, 266–67, 273, 277
Rooney, John, 197
Roosevelt, Eleanor, 142, 164
Roosevelt, Franklin Delano: and air rearma-

ment, 59, 62–65; and aircraft sales, 67–73, 85–90; biased neutrality, 83–84; and the Bonus Army, 26–29; death, 130, 169; election, 26, 29, 31, 101–103, 113; foreign policy, 46–47, 62–65, 73, 98, 361–62; and Indian independence, 116–26; internationalism, 110, 362; and isolationism, 2, 47–48, 92, 359; LJ's misreading of, 73–74; and LJ's resignation, 105; and LJ-Woodring feud, 36–40, 42–46, 107–10; and Marshall, 40–42; and military preparedness, 51; relationship with LJ, 2–3, 75–76; removal of Woodring and LJ, 97–99; return from illness, 23; secretary of war appointments, 1, 30–31, 99–100; speeches, 47–48, 84, 361; support for LJ, 56, 361–62; at VA meeting, 28; and vice presidency, 101–103; and the War Resources Board, 76–83; and Woodring, 65–67, 96; and World War II, 57–74
Roosevelt, Theodore, Jr., 20
Root, Elihu, Jr., 129
Root Ballantine, 129
Rosenthal, Louis, 143
Rosier, Joseph, 114
Ross, Charlie, 216, 322, 342–45
Rotary Club, 23
Roy E. Parrish Post No. 13, 24
Royall, Kenneth, 149, 156–57
Rusk, Dean, 275–76, 279, 295, 296
Russell, William, 5
Rutherford, Harry, 77
Ryukyus (Okinawa), 258, 262, 273, 281

The Saturday Evening Post, 180
Saudi Arabia, 309
Saunders, Edgar, 6
Saunders, Henry, 6
schizophrenia, 114
Scripps-Howard, 254
Sebald, William J., 270–72, 323
Second Bombardment Wing, 39
Second Officer's Reserve Training School, 18
secrecy, military, 207–208, 210–14
secretary of defense position, 1, 131, 145, 149–52, 168, 187, 340
segregation in the military, 164–65
seizure of assets, 127–29
selective service, 54, 111, 290, 293, 314
Senate: and aircraft sales, 87; appropriations bills, 191–95; Appropriations Committee, 232–33, 282–83; Armed Services Committee, 151, 163, 179, 193, 242, 248, 334; and China White Paper, 257; confirmation hearings, 151; Foreign Relations Committee, 237–40, 242, 248; and German aggression, 92; and Korean War, 290, 293, 300; LJ's critics in, 45; Military Affairs Committee, 33, 72, 89; and military assistance, 240–45; and military unification, 170; and NATO, 237–40; Special Committee to Investigate the National Defense Program, 130; Vandenberg Resolution, 235; and World War II, 92
service secretaries, 156–59
Seventh fleet, 280–82, 285, 292, 296, 301, 324
Sheppard, Harry, 175–76
Sherman, Forrest P., 185, 278, 281, 317
Sherwood, Robert, 36
Shoreham Building, 143, 355
Short, Dewey, 162
Shriver, Sargent, 98
Singapore, 118
Smith, H. Alexander, 23, 238, 254, 260
Smith, Merriman, 216
Smyth, Henry, 224
Snyder, John W., 139, 191, 292
social skills of LJ, 12–13, 23, 101, 361
Sonnenberg, Ben, 338
Souers, Sidney, 220, 222–23, 228–29
South America, 38–39
Southeast Asia, 264–65
Soviet Union: and Asia and Far East policy, 262; attack on Finland, 96; and Cold War, 166, 203; and Japan, 268; and Korean War, 276, 281–83, 286, 289–95, 311–12; MacArthur's VFW speech, 329; and NATO, 235; and the Neutrality Act, 83; and NSC 68, 224–31; and nuclear weapons, 205, 214–17, 221, 223; and preventive war, 328; and Truman campaign, 142; and the UN, 131; and Vietnam, 264
Sparkman, John, 134, 162
specifications for war materials, 55
speeches: on budget cuts, 201; to the Daughters of the American Revolution, 236–37, 237–38; on defense preparedness, 25–26; FDR's quarantine speech, 47–48, 361; frequency of, 156; on isolationism, 50, 115; and LJ's downfall, 327–32; on military preparedness, 66; and military unification, 152; on the Neutrality Act, 83, 84; to Reserve Officers Association, 291; Truman's whistlestop campaign, 139, 141
spiritual life of LJ, 8, 15

Spivak, Lawrence, 164
sports, 8, 10, 15, 20, 22
Spotsylvania Court House battle, 5
Spruance, Raymond, 182
Sri Lanka, 127
Stalin, Joseph, 142, 189, 263
Stassen, Harold, 135
State Council of Defense, 17
State Department: and Asia policy, 262; and
    Formosa issue, 255–60, 263; Good Neigh-
    bor Policy, 38; and Japan, 268–72, 274;
    and Korean War, 266–67, 275, 282, 298,
    304, 307–308, 310, 313, 318; LJ as liaison,
    84; and LJ's resignation, 348; and NATO,
    246; and NSC 68, 225–31; and nuclear
    weapons, 213, 217–18, 222; offices, 35; and
    rearmament, 61; and World War II, 57
States' Rights Party, 136
statutory authority of LJ, 49
Stennis, John Cornelius, 348
Steptoe, James C., Sr., 13
Steptoe, Philip Pendleton, 13, 17, 21–22, 112, 129
Steptoe, Rixey, & Johnson, 13
Steptoe & Johnson: and China Lobby, 262;
    Clarksburg offices, 18; fiftieth anniver-
    sary, 357; founded, 12–14; LJ's departure
    from, 34, 150; LJ's involvement in, 128;
    LJ's return to, 111–12, 355–57; political
    connections, 16; postwar vision, 129–30;
    rise of, 21–23; and Truman campaign,
    139, 143; Washington offices, 131
Steptoe Gas Bill, 22
Stettinius, Edward R., Jr., 77
Stimson, Henry S., 97, 99, 103, 129
stockpiling, 54–55
strategic bombing, 173, 175, 326
strategic materials, 54–55, 76
Strategic War Materials Act, 54
Stratemeyer, George, 310
Strauss, Lewis, 218–19
stroke, 357
submarine warfare, 16–17
Sudeten annexation, 58
Sullivan, John, 156–58, 173–75, 187
supercarrier, 158, 173–76, 183–87
supporters of LJ: and budget cuts, 204; in Con-
    gress, 162; in Democratic Party, 32; Early,
    128, 130; Eisenhower, 145–46; FDR, 56,
    361–62; inner circle, 159–62; Marshall,
    42–43, 46, 56, 145, 146; press, 197–98; in
    Republican Party, 162; Vandenberg, 197;
    Vinson, 162, 336–37

Supreme Court, 22
surplus war materials, 96–97, 202, 241
swearing in ceremony, 151–52
Symington, Stuart, 156–58, 173, 176, 177–78,
    183, 292

Taft, Robert, 135, 263, 291–92, 321, 350, 360
Taft-Hartley Act, 141
Tauriello, Anthony F., 335–36
television, 313
Teller, Edward, 218–19
Temperance Hall, 9
Temporary Commission on Korea, 265
thermonuclear bombs. See nuclear weapons
38th parallel, 318–19
Thurmond, Strom, 136, 142
Time, 44
Tobey, Charles W., 196–97
travels: for Alaska highway, 55–56; Europe, 24–
    25; Far East trip, 271–74; holidays, 261;
    honeymoons, 21, 22; and military pre-
    paredness, 50–51; with Truman, 147–48;
    to Washington, 34
Treasury Department, 67, 69–70, 72, 85
Tribune (Oakland), 254
Trippe, Juan, 355–56
Troy, Matthew J., 334
Truman, Bess, 144, 341
Truman, Harry S.: and the American Legion,
    140–41; appointments, 156–59; Asia and
    Far East policy, 262, 271–74, 303, 362;
    awards for LJ, 110; and bombing North
    Korea, 327; and B-36 purchases, 177; and
    budget cuts, 163, 166, 176, 188–95, 203–
    204, 362; and China policy, 251–57; and
    congressional hearings, 181; and Denfeld
    transfer, 185; electoral campaigns, 1, 133–
    43; expansion of military, 314–16; and
    FDR's death, 130–32; foreign policy, 142,
    363; and Formosa issue, 257–61, 325; on
    Forrestal's mental health, 146; Gray ap-
    pointment, 157–58; and Inchon invasion,
    316–18; integration in the military, 165;
    introduction to LJ, 19; and Japan, 267–71;
    and Korean War, 265–67, 276, 278, 280–
    84, 286–88, 292, 295–98, 300–302, 304–
    305, 309, 311–12, 318–19; and LJ-Acheson
    feud, 321; and LJ's downfall, 319–32, 335–
    37; on LJ's VP bid, 102–103; media broad-
    casts, 313; and military assistance, 240,
    244; and military unification, 147–48, 163,
    166–67, 169–71; and NATO, 234–37, 248;

and NSC 68, 225–26, 229, 231, 233; and nuclear weapons, 3, 205, 207–208, 212–15, 217–18, 220, 222–23; patronage, 134–35; praise for LJ, 46, 56; presidential campaign, 1, 133–38; public opinion on, 136, 141; relationship with LJ, 24, 165, 350, 353, 354, 362; and resignation of LJ, 339–51; and supercarrier project, 173–74; and the UN, 306; vacations, 143–44; and Vietnam, 264; and West Germany, 249
Truman, Margaret, 138, 144
Truman Doctrine, 131, 236
Tucker, Ray, 102
Tufts, Robert, 227
Turkey, 309
Turnip Day, 131, 136, 141
Tydings, Millard, 151, 162, 174, 212

unemployment, 197
unification of the military: and Air Force, 162; and budget cuts, 170, 193; committee report on, 185–86; defended, 182–85; discontent with, 169–72; and Forrestal, 147–48, 169–71; and the Korean War, 188, 189–91; legacy of LJ, 359, 362; LJ's speech on, 152; and National Security Act, 168, 170–71, 179; Navy, 162, 169, 186; and resignation of LJ, 346, 347; and supercarrier project, 175; and Truman, 147–48, 163, 166–67, 169–71
Union Leader (Manchester), 254
Union National Bank, 18, 150
United Nations: and atomic weapons, 205–206; and the Cold War, 131; and Korean War, 265, 276, 278–79, 283, 285–89, 290, 300, 303–10; and military assistance, 241; and NATO, 236, 237–38; and Palestine issue, 133; Security Council, 276, 278–79; UN Charter, 238, 284
United Press International, 275
universal military training, 314
University of Virginia, 8, 9–10, 98
uranium, 210–14
U.S. Army of Occupation, 19–20, 24
U.S. Congress. See Congress
U.S. Employment Service, 29
U.S. House of Representatives. See House of Representatives
U.S. News & World Reports, 329–30
U.S. Senate. See Senate
U.S. Supreme Court. See Supreme Court
USS Midway, 278

USS Roanoke, 234
USS United States, 158, 173
utilities, 55

Vaccaro, Ernest B., 342
Van Zandt, James E., 177, 178, 182
Vandenberg, Arthur: and congressional hearings, 183; and Japan, 270; and Korean War, 278; and military assistance, 241–43; and NATO, 235; and nuclear weapons, 212, 215, 220; and presidential elections, 135; support for LJ, 197
Vandenberg, Hoyt, 158–59, 173, 209–10, 281, 284, 289, 316–17
Vandenberg Resolution, 235
Vaughn, Harry, 134, 160
veterans, 26–28
Veterans Administration, 200
Veterans Advisory Committee, 113
Veterans Committee of the Democratic National Committee, 29, 31
Veterans of Foreign Wars (VFW), 26, 83, 328–32, 334, 335–36, 351
vice presidency, 100, 101–103
Vietnam, 253, 263–65, 280, 287, 327, 363
Vinson, Carl: and B-36 purchases, 177–78; and budget cuts, 195; and congressional hearings, 182; on hospital closings, 200; and National Security Act, 179; proposed diplomatic mission, 142; relationship with LJ, 165; on secretary of defense position, 153–54; and supercarrier project, 174, 176; support for LJ, 162, 336–37
Vinson, Fred, 151
Virginia, 4–6
Vorhees, Tracy, 260

Waldo Hotel, 11
Walker, Walton, 316
Wallace, Henry, 103, 118, 135, 341
War Cabinet (Britain), 122
War Council meetings, 38, 41
War Department: and air rearmament, 64; and aircraft production, 94–95; and aircraft sales, 68, 70–72, 87; allocations and educational orders, 50–52; circumvented, 85; FDR appointments, 1; headquarters moved, 76; ideological divisions, 35; and isolationism, 74; leadership at, 47, 93; LJ's impact on morale, 42; and LJ's resignation, 105; LJ's standing at, 43; and LJ-Woodring feud, 37, 43–46, 56, 107–10; and

mobilization, 52–54, 91; new war plans, 61; procurement funds, 95; and World War II, 84. *See also* Defense Department

War Industries Board, 49, 81–82

war materials, 54–55, 76, 96–97, 127–29, 202, 241

War of 1812, 5

War Plans Division, 41

War Production Board, 82

Warren, Earl, 135

War Resources Administration, 53, 56

War Resources Board, 76–81, 81–83, 94

Washington Daily News, 44

Washington Post, 197–98, 221

Washington press corps, 163–64

Washington Star, 71, 342

Washington Times-Herald, 342

Watson, Edwin M. "Pa," 44, 62, 97, 113–14

Wavell, Archibald, 121, 122

wealth of LJ, 14, 23

Webb, James E., 191, 212, 226, 278–79, 326–27

Webster, William, 214

Wedemeyer, Albert C., 253

Welles, Sumner, 39, 45, 83, 84, 112, 121

Westervelt, William I., 33–34

West Germany, 249

West Virginia, 17, 22

West Virginia House of Delegates, 15, 16

West Virginia Military Area, 112

West Virginia Supreme Court of Appeals, 13

Wherry, Kenneth, 151, 162, 175–76, 299–300

Wherry-Spence Act, 200–201

whistlestop campaign, 139, 141

Whiting, Dick, 250

Whitney, Cornelius Vanderbilt, 139

Whitney, Courtney, 293

Wieland, William A., 39

Wilkie, Wendell, 101, 111

Williams, Aubrey, 45, 60

Wilson, Hugh R., 57

Wilson, Thomas, 117, 119

Wilson, Woodrow, 9, 17, 20, 362

Winant, John G., 119

Winchell, Walter, 44

Wood, Robert E., 77, 84

Woodring, Harry H.: as acting secretary of war, 31; and air rearmament, 59, 64, 65–67; and aircraft production, 94; and aircraft sales, 67, 69–70, 72–73, 85–90, 97; and B-17 bomber dispute, 38–39; contract awards, 39–40; credibility problems, 42–43; and FDR, 65–67, 96, 97–99; feud with LJ, 30–46, 93, 95, 107–10; and George Marshall, 41–42; and isolationism, 359; and mobilization, 49; named secretary of war, 31–34; offered ambassadorship, 46; relationship with LJ, 35; resignation, 1, 98–99, 104–105; and the War Resources Board, 80

Woodring, Helen, 33

work background of LJ, 7, 10

work ethic of LJ, 7, 91, 155–56

Works Progress Administration (WPA), 58–59, 62

World War I, 16–20, 24, 48, 54, 166

World War II, 44–45, 51, 57–74, 84, 110, 127–29, 359

World's Fair, New York City, 75

Worth, Cedric R., 176, 178

Wright, Burdett, 57

Wright, Fielding, 136

Yak fighters, 284

Z Committee, 220–24

Keith D. McFarland is President of Texas A&M University-Commerce and author of *Harry H. Woodring: A Political Biography of FDR's Controversial Secretary of War* and *The Korean War: An Annotated Bibliography*.

David L. Roll is a Steptoe & Johnson partner whose practice focuses on anti-trust and regulatory law and litigation.